10

13⁰⁰
Bio
Pol.

D1005082

PRAISE FOR
Living History

"Engaging . . . compelling . . . Clinton emerges from the book as a complex, three-dimensional figure."

—*Los Angeles Times*

"Affecting . . . often revealing."

—*The New Yorker*

"Clinton is at her best when she is least guarded about herself. . . . [Her] palpable humanity is the pleasant surprise of *Living History*."

—*Time*

"Surprisingly readable . . . A more human view of a well-known yet not well-understood public figure."

—*BusinessWeek*

"Provides insights both naïve and profound. . . . Hillary Clinton has lived the history of her generation of women."

—*The Baltimore Sun*

"A fascinating tale."

—*Chicago Tribune*

"An important book . . . far more than just titillating tidbits . . . Clinton takes on all comers and gives a glimpse of herself and her family that you may not have seen before. . . . A solidly written, personal account from a major player in one of the country's most politically contentious periods . . . riveting."

—*The Denver Post*

"A pleasure to read—an articulate, well-written and detail-rich account of the Clinton's historic time in the White House that will hold up as a solid work of autobiography for years to come."

—*The Washington Monthly*

"Forget the hype and read Hillary's book because it's worth it. . . . A smart, well-crafted memoir . . . *Living History* . . . gives us insight into the thinking processes of a person who remains a prominent figure on the American political stage."

—*The Kansas City Star*

"*Living History* is Hillary Rodham Clinton's frank, vividly written portrait of the Clintons' controversial White House years. . . . Offers a front-row seat into her whirling world of politics, the remarkable people she met and the pride she took in successfully raising a daughter in the limelight. . . . Her crisp writing flows from one crisis to the next with plenty of anecdotes to keep things lively."

—*Rocky Mountain News*

"The story of Hillary Rodham Clinton as a mother, activist, lawyer, First Lady and debate-provoking political icon is interesting and . . . inspiring."

—*Houston Chronicle*

"Hillary's *History* comes alive. . . . Her eye for detail and the courage to be self-deprecating provide humor and a human dimension in her account."

—*Boston Herald*

"It is inspiring. Clinton does write movingly about people she met, places she visited and causes she supported in this country and around the globe in her eight years as first lady."

—*The Courier-Journal* (Louisville, KY)

About

LIVING HISTORY

In *Living History*, Hillary Rodham Clinton writes with candor, humor and passion about coming-of-age during a time of tumultuous social and political change in America and about the White House years. She tells the story of her thirty-year adventure in love and politics with Bill Clinton, during which she survived personal betrayal, relentless partisan investigations and constant public scrutiny. And she provides a clear reflection of her views and opinions on the most current political topics—health care, international relations, human rights, women's rights and much more.

Intimate, powerful and inspiring, *Living History* captures the essence of this remarkable woman and the challenging process through which she came to define herself and find her own voice—as a wife, a mother and as one of the most formidable figures in the history of American politics.

Also by Hillary Rodham Clinton

AN INVITATION TO THE WHITE HOUSE

DEAR SOCKS, DEAR BUDDY

IT TAKES A VILLAGE

LIVING
HISTORY

Hillary Rodham Clinton

Scribner

New York • London • Toronto • Sydney

SCRIBNER
1230 Avenue of the Americas
New York, NY 10020

Copyright © 2003 by Hillary Rodham Clinton

All rights reserved, including the right of
reproduction in whole or in part in any form.

First Scribner trade paperback edition 2004

SCRIBNER and design are trademarks of
Macmillan Library Reference USA, Inc., used under license
by Simon & Schuster, the publisher of this work.

For information about special discounts for bulk purchases,
please contact Simon & Schuster Special Sales:
1-800-456-6798 or business@simonandschuster.com.

Designed by C. Linda Dingler
Text set in Janson Text

Manufactured in the United States of America

10 9 8 7 6 5 4 3 2 1

The Library of Congress has cataloged the Simon & Schuster edition as follows:
Clinton, Hillary Rodham.
Living history/Hillary Rodham Clinton.
p. cm.
1. Clinton, Hillary Rodham. 2. Clinton, Bill, 1946– . 3. United States. Congress.
Senate—Biography. 4. Presidents' spouses—United States—Biography. 5. Women
legislators—United States—Biography. 6. Legislators—United States—Biography.
7. United States—Politics and government—1993–2001. 8. United States—Politics
and government—2001– . I. Title.

E887.C55 A3 2003b
973.929/092 B 22   20033276264

ISBN 0-7432-2224-5
       0-7432-2225-3 (Pbk)

Permissions acknowledgments appear on page 567.

To my parents,
my husband,
my daughter—
and all the good souls around the world
whose inspiration, prayers, support and love
blessed my heart and sustained me in
the years of living history.

CONTENTS

AUTHOR'S NOTE

IN 1959, I WROTE MY AUTOBIOGRAPHY FOR AN AS-
signment in sixth grade. In twenty-nine pages, most half-filled with
earnest scrawl, I described my parents, brothers, pets, house, hobbies,
school, sports and plans for the future. Forty-two years later, I
began writing another memoir, this one about the eight years I spent
in the White House living history with Bill Clinton. I quickly realized
that I couldn't explain my life as First Lady without going back to the
beginning—how I became the woman I was that first day I walked into
the White House on January 20, 1993, to take on a new role and experiences that would test and transform me in unexpected ways.

By the time I crossed the threshold of the White House, I had been
shaped by my family upbringing, education, religious faith and all that
I had learned before—as the daughter of a staunch conservative father
and a more liberal mother, a student activist, an advocate for children, a
lawyer, Bill's wife and Chelsea's mom.

For each chapter, there were more ideas I wanted to discuss than
space allowed; more people to include than could be named; more
places visited than could be described. If I mentioned everybody who
has impressed, inspired, taught, influenced and helped me along the
way, this book would be several volumes long. Although I've had to be
selective, I hope that I've conveyed the push and pull of events and relationships that affected me and continue to shape and enrich my world
today.

Since leaving the White House, I have embarked on a new phase of
my life as a U.S. Senator from New York, a humbling and daunting responsibility. A complete account of my move to New York, campaign
for the Senate and the honor of working for the people who elected me

will have to be told another time, but I hope this memoir illustrates how my success as a candidate for the Senate arose out of my White House experiences.

During my years as First Lady, I became a better student of how government can serve people, how Congress really works, how people perceive politics and policy through the filter of the media and how American values can be translated into economic and social progress. I learned the importance of America's engagement with the rest of the world, and I developed relationships with foreign leaders and an understanding of foreign cultures that come in handy today. I also learned how to keep focused while living in the eye of many storms.

I was raised to love my God and my country, to help others, to protect and defend the democratic ideals that have inspired and guided free people for more than two hundred years. These ideals were nurtured in me as far back as I can remember. Back in 1959, I wanted to become a teacher or a nuclear physicist. Teachers were necessary to "train young citizens" and without them you wouldn't have "much of a country." America needed scientists because the "Russians have about five scientists to our one." Even then, I was fully a product of my country and its times, absorbing my family's lessons and America's needs as I considered my own future. My childhood in the 1950s and the politics of the 1960s awakened my sense of obligation to my country and my commitment to service. College, law school and then marriage took me into the political epicenter of the United States.

A political life, I've often said, is a continuing education in human nature, including one's own. My involvement on the ground floor of two presidential campaigns and my duties as First Lady took me to every state in our union and to seventy-eight nations. In each place, I met someone or saw something that caused me to open my mind and my heart and deepen my understanding of the universal concerns that most of humanity shares.

I always knew that America matters to the rest of the world; my travels taught me how the rest of the world matters to America. Listening to what people in other countries are saying and trying to understand how they perceive their place in the world is essential to a future of peace and security at home and abroad. With this in mind, I have included voices we don't hear often enough—voices of people in every corner of the globe who want the same things we do: freedom from hunger, disease and fear, freedom to have a say in their own destinies, no matter their DNA or station in life. I have devoted considerable space in these pages to my foreign travels because I believe that the people and places are important, and what I learned from them is part of who I am today.

The two Clinton terms covered not only a transforming period in my life but also in America's. My husband assumed the Presidency determined to reverse the nation's economic decline, budget deficits and the growing inequities that undermined opportunities for future generations of Americans.

I supported his agenda and worked hard to translate his vision into actions that improved people's lives, strengthened our sense of community and furthered our democratic values at home and around the world. Throughout Bill's tenure, we encountered political opposition, legal challenges and personal tragedies, and we made our fair share of mistakes. But when he left office in January 2001, America was a stronger, better and more just nation, ready to tackle the challenges of a new century.

Of course, the world we now inhabit is very different from the one described in this book. As I write this in 2003, it seems impossible that my time in the White House ended only two years ago. It feels more like another lifetime because of what happened on September 11, 2001. The lost lives. The human grief. The smoldering crater. The twisted metal. The shattered survivors. The victims' families. The unspeakable tragedy of it all. That September morning changed me and what I had to do as a Senator, a New Yorker and an American. And it changed America in ways we are still discovering. We are all on new ground, and somehow we must make it common ground.

My eight years in the White House tested my faith and political beliefs, my marriage and our nation's Constitution. I became a lightning rod for political and ideological battles waged over America's future and a magnet for feelings, good and bad, about women's choices and roles. This book is the story of how I experienced those eight years as First Lady and as the wife of the President. Some may ask how I could write an accurate account of events, people and places that are so recent and of which I am still a part. I have done my best to convey my observations, thoughts and feelings as I experienced them. This is not meant to be a comprehensive history, but a personal memoir that offers an inside look at an extraordinary time in my life and in the life of America.

LIVING HISTORY

AN AMERICAN STORY

I WASN'T BORN A FIRST LADY OR A SENATOR. I WASN'T born a Democrat. I wasn't born a lawyer or an advocate for women's rights and human rights. I wasn't born a wife or mother. I was born an American in the middle of the twentieth century, a fortunate time and place. I was free to make choices unavailable to past generations of women in my own country and inconceivable to many women in the world today. I came of age on the crest of tumultuous social change and took part in the political battles fought over the meaning of America and its role in the world.

My mother and my grandmothers could never have lived my life; my father and my grandfathers could never have imagined it. But they bestowed on me the promise of America, which made my life and my choices possible.

My story began in the years following World War II, when men like my father who had served their country returned home to settle down, make a living and raise a family. It was the beginning of the Baby Boom, an optimistic time. The United States had saved the world from fascism, and now our nation was working to unite former adversaries in the aftermath of war, reaching out to allies and to former enemies, securing the peace and helping to rebuild a devastated Europe and Japan.

Although the Cold War was beginning with the Soviet Union and Eastern Europe, my parents and their generation felt secure and hopeful. American supremacy was the result not just of military might, but of our values and of the abundant opportunities available to people like my parents who worked hard and took responsibility. Middle-class America was flush with emerging prosperity and all that comes with it—new houses, fine schools, neighborhood parks and safe communities.

Yet our nation also had unfinished business in the post-war era, particularly regarding race. And it was the World War II generation and their children who woke up to the challenges of social injustice and inequality and to the ideal of extending America's promise to all of its citizens.

My parents were typical of a generation who believed in the endless possibilities of America and whose values were rooted in the experience of living through the Great Depression. They believed in hard work, not entitlement; self-reliance not self-indulgence.

That is the world and the family I was born into on October 26, 1947. We were middle-class, Midwestern and very much a product of our place and time. My mother, Dorothy Howell Rodham, was a homemaker whose days revolved around me and my two younger brothers, and my father, Hugh E. Rodham, owned a small business. The challenges of their lives made me appreciate the opportunities of my own life even more.

I'm still amazed at how my mother emerged from her lonely early life as such an affectionate and levelheaded woman. She was born in Chicago in 1919. Her father, Edwin John Howell, Jr., was a Chicago firefighter, and his wife, Della Murray, was one of nine children from a family of French Canadian, Scottish and Native American ancestry. My maternal grandparents were certainly not ready for parenthood. Della essentially abandoned my mother when she was only three or four, leaving her alone all day for days on end with meal tickets to use at a restaurant near their five-story walk-up apartment on Chicago's South Side. Edwin paid sporadic attention to her, better at bringing the occasional gift, like a large doll won at a carnival, than at providing any kind of home life. My mother's sister, Isabelle, was born in 1924. The girls were often shuttled from one relative to another and from school to school, never staying anywhere long enough to make friends. In 1927, my mother's young parents finally got a divorce—rare in those days and a terrible shame. Neither was willing to care for their children, so they sent their daughters from Chicago by train to live with their paternal grandparents in Alhambra, a town near the San Gabriel Mountains east of Los Angeles. On the four-day journey, eight-year-old Dorothy was in charge of her three-year-old sister.

My mother stayed in California for ten years, never seeing her mother and rarely seeing her father. Her grandfather, Edwin Sr., a former British sailor, left the girls to his wife, Emma, a severe woman who wore black Victorian dresses and resented and ignored my mother except when enforcing her rigid house rules. Emma discouraged visitors and rarely allowed my mother to attend parties or other functions. One Halloween, when she caught my mother trick-or-treating with school friends, Emma decided to confine her to her room for an entire year, except for the hours she was in school. She forbade my mother to eat at the kitchen table or linger in the front yard. This cruel punishment went on for months until Emma's sister, Belle Andreson, came for a visit and put a stop to it.

My mother found some relief from the oppressive conditions of Emma's house in the outdoors. She ran through the orange groves that stretched for miles in the San Gabriel Valley, losing herself in the scent of fruit ripening in the sun. At night, she escaped into her books. She was an excellent student whose teachers encouraged her reading and writing.

By the time she turned fourteen, she could no longer bear life in her grandmother's house. She found work as a mother's helper, caring for two young children in return for room, board and three dollars a week. She had little time for the extracurricular athletics and drama that she loved and no money for clothes. She washed the same blouse every day to wear with her only skirt and, in colder weather, her only sweater. But for the first time, she lived in a household where the father and mother gave their children the love, attention and guidance she had never received. My mother often told me that without that sojourn with a strong family, she would not have known how to care for her own home and children.

When she graduated from high school, my mother made plans to go to college in California. But Della contacted her—for the first time in ten years—and asked her to come live with her in Chicago. Della had recently remarried and promised my mother that she and her new husband would pay for her education there. When my mother arrived in Chicago, however, she found that Della wanted her only as a housekeeper and that she would get no financial help for college. Heartsick, she moved into a small apartment and found an office job paying thirteen dollars for a five-and-a-half-day week. Once I asked my mother why she went back to Chicago. "I'd hoped so hard that my mother would love me that I had to take the chance and find out," she told me. "When she didn't, I had nowhere else to go."

My mother's father died in 1947, so I never even met him. But I knew my grandmother, Della, as a weak and self-indulgent woman wrapped up in television soap operas and disengaged from reality. When I was about ten and Della was baby-sitting my brothers and me, I was hit in the eye by a chain-link gate while at the school playground. I ran home three blocks, crying and holding my head as blood streamed down my face. When Della saw me, she fainted. I had to ask our next-door neighbor for help in treating my wound. When Della revived, she complained that I had scared her and that she could have gotten hurt when she fell over. I had to wait for my mom to return, and she took me to the hospital to get stitches.

On the rare occasions when Della would let you into her narrow world, she could be enchanting. She loved to sing and play cards. When we visited her in Chicago, she often took us to the local Kiddieland or movie theater. She died in 1960, an unhappy woman and a mystery, still. But she did bring my mother to Chicago, and that's where Dorothy met Hugh Rodham.

My father was born in Scranton, Pennsylvania, the middle son of Hugh Rodham, Sr., and Hannah Jones. He got his looks from a line of black-haired Welsh coal miners on his mother's side. Like Hannah, he was hardheaded and often gruff, but when he laughed the sound came from deep inside and seemed to engage every part of his body. I inherited his laugh, the same big rolling guffaw that can turn heads in a restaurant and send cats running from the room.

The Scranton of my father's youth was a rough industrial city of brick factories, textile mills, coal mines, rail yards and wooden duplex houses. The Rodhams and Joneses were hard workers and strict Methodists.

My father's father, Hugh Sr., was the sixth of eleven children. He started work at the Scranton Lace Company when he was still a boy and ended up as supervisor five decades later. He was a gentle, soft-spoken man, quite the opposite of his formidable wife, Hannah Jones Rodham, who insisted on using all three of her names. Hannah collected rent from the houses she owned and ruled her family and anyone else within her reach. My father worshipped her and often told me and my brothers the story of how she had saved his feet.

Around 1920, he and a friend had hitched a ride on the back of a horse-drawn ice wagon. As the horses were struggling up a hill, a motorized truck plowed into the back of the wagon, crushing my dad's legs. He was carried to the nearest hospital, where the doctors deemed his lower legs and feet irreparably damaged and prepared him for surgery to amputate both. When Hannah, who had rushed to the hospital, was told what the doctors intended, she barricaded herself in the operating room with her son, saying no one could touch his legs unless they planned to save them. She demanded that her brother-in-law, Dr. Thomas Rodham, be called in immediately from another hospital where he worked. Dr. Rodham examined my dad and announced that "nobody is going to cut that boy's legs off!" My father had passed out from pain; he awoke to find his mother standing guard, assuring him that his legs were saved and that he'd be whipped hard when he finally got home. That was a family story we heard over and over again, a lesson in confronting authority and never giving up.

Hannah strikes me as a determined woman whose energies and intelligence had little outlet, which led to her meddling in everyone else's business. Her eldest son, my uncle Willard, worked as an engineer for the city of Scranton, but he never left home or married and died shortly after my grandfather in 1965. Her youngest, Russell, was her golden boy. He excelled in academics and athletics, became a doctor, served in the Army, married, had a daughter and came back to Scranton to practice medicine. In early 1948, he fell into a debilitating depression. My grandparents asked my father to come home to help Russell. Shortly after my dad arrived, Russell tried to kill himself. My father found him hanging in the attic and cut him down. He brought Russell back to Chicago to live with us.

I was eight or nine months old when Russell came to stay. He slept on the couch in the living room of our one-bedroom apartment while seeking psychiatric treatment at the Veterans Administration Hospital. He was a handsome man, with fairer hair and complexion than my dad's. One day, when I was about two, I drank from a Coke bottle filled with turpentine left by a workman. Russell immediately induced vomiting and rushed me to the emergency room. He gave up medicine shortly thereafter, and jokingly called me his last patient. He stayed in the Chicago area, where he was a frequent visitor to our home. He died in 1962 in a fire caused by a burning cigarette. I felt so sorry for my father, who had tried for years to keep Russell alive. Modern antidepressants might have helped him, and I wish they'd been available back then. Dad wanted to tell his father about Russell's death in person, and waited until my grandfather came for a visit. When he finally learned about Russell's death, my grandfather sat at our kitchen table and sobbed. He died brokenhearted three years later.

Despite his financial success later in life, my dad was perceived growing up—by himself and by his parents—as neither as dutiful and reliable as his older brother, Willard, nor as smart and successful as his younger brother, Russell. He was always in trouble for joyriding in a neighbor's brand-new car or roller-skating up the aisle of the Court Street Methodist Church during an evening prayer service. When he graduated from Central High School in 1931, he thought he would go to work in the lace mill beside his father. Instead, his best friend, who had been recruited by Penn State for the football team, told the coach he would not come unless his favorite teammate came too. Dad was a solid athlete, and the coach agreed, so Dad went to State College and played for the Nittany Lions. He also boxed and joined the Delta Upsilon fraternity, where, I'm told, he became an expert at making bathtub gin. He graduated in 1935 and at the height of the Depression returned to Scranton with a degree in physical education.

Without alerting his parents, he hopped a freight train to Chicago to look for work and found a job selling drapery fabrics around the Midwest. When he came back to tell his parents and pack his bags, Hannah was furious and forbade him to go. But my grandfather pointed out that jobs were hard to come by, and the family could use the money for Russell's college and medical education. So my father moved to Chicago. All week, he traveled around the upper Midwest from Des Moines to Duluth, then drove to Scranton most weekends to turn over his paycheck to his mother. Though he always suggested that his reasons for leaving Scranton were economic, I believe my father knew that he had to make a break from Hannah if he was ever to live his own life.

Dorothy Howell was applying for a job as a clerk typist at a textile company when she caught the eye of a traveling salesman, Hugh Rodham. She was attracted to his energy and self-assurance and gruff sense of humor.

After a lengthy courtship, my parents were married in early 1942, shortly after the Japanese bombed Pearl Harbor. They moved into a small apartment in the Lincoln Park section of Chicago near Lake Michigan. My dad enlisted in a special Navy program named for the heavyweight boxing champion Gene Tunney and was assigned to the Great Lakes Naval Station, an hour north of Chicago. He became a chief petty officer responsible for training thousands of young sailors before they were shipped out to sea, mostly to the Pacific Theater. He told me how sad he felt when he accompanied his trainees to the West

Coast, where they joined their ships, knowing some would not survive. After he died, I received letters from men who had served under him. Often they enclosed a photo of a particular class of sailors, my proud father front and center. My favorite photograph shows him in his uniform smiling broadly, as handsome, to my eyes, as any 1940s movie star.

My father kept close ties with his family in Scranton and drove each of his children from Chicago to Scranton to be christened in the Court Street Methodist Church, where he had worshipped as a child. Grandma Rodham died when I was five and she was going blind when I knew her, but I remember she would try to dress me and braid my hair every morning. I was much closer to my grandfather, who had already retired with a gold watch after fifty years of employment when I was born. He was a kind and proper man, who proudly carried his gold watch on a chain and wore a suit with suspenders every day. When he came to visit us in Illinois, he would take off his suit coat and roll up his shirtsleeves to help my mother around the house.

My father was always strict with his kids, but he was much harder on the boys than on me. Grandpa Rodham often intervened on their behalf, endearing him even more to us. As children, my brothers and I spent a lot of time at his duplex on Diamond Avenue in Scranton, and each summer we spent most of August at the cottage he had built in 1921 about twenty miles northwest of Scranton in the Pocono Mountains overlooking Lake Winola.

The rustic cabin had no heat except for the cast-iron cook stove in the kitchen, and no indoor bath or shower. To stay clean, we swam in the lake or stood below the back porch while someone poured a tub of water onto our heads. The big front porch was our favorite place to play and where our grandfather shared hands of cards with my brothers and me. He taught us pinochle, the greatest card game in the world, in his opinion. He read us stories and told us the legend of the lake, which he claimed was named after an Indian princess, Winola, who drowned herself when her father would not let her marry a handsome warrior from a neighboring tribe.

The cabin is still in our family and so are many of our summer traditions. Bill and I took Chelsea to Lake Winola for the first time when she was not yet two. My brothers spend part of every summer there. Thankfully they have made some improvements. A couple of years ago they even put in a shower.

In the early fifties, few people lived off the two-lane highway that ran in front of the cottage, and there were bears and bobcats in the woods up the mountain behind us. As children we explored the surrounding countryside, hiking and driving the back roads and fishing and boating on the Susquehanna River. My father taught me to shoot a gun behind the cottage, and we practiced aiming at cans or rocks. But the center of our activities was the lake, across the road and down the path past Foster's store. I made summer friends who took me waterskiing or to the movies that were projected onto sheets in an open field on the lake shore. Along the way, I met people I never would have encountered in Park Ridge, such as a family my grandfather called "mountain people," who lived without electricity or a car. A boy from that family, about my age, once showed up at the cottage on horseback to ask me if I wanted to go for a ride.

When I was as young as ten or eleven, I played pinochle with the men—my grandfather, my father, Uncle Willard and assorted others, including such memorable characters as "Old Pete" and Hank, who were notorious sore losers. Pete lived at the end of a dirt road and showed up to play every day, invariably cursing and stomping off if he started losing. Hank came only when my father was there. He would totter up to the front porch with his cane and climb the steep stairs yelling, "Is that black-haired bastard home? I want to play cards." He'd known my dad since he was born and had taught him to fish. He didn't like losing any better than Pete did and occasionally upended the table after a particularly irksome defeat.

After the war, my dad started a small drapery fabric business, Rodrik Fabrics, in the Merchandise Mart in Chicago's Loop. His first office overlooked the Chicago River, and I can remember going there when I was only three or four. To keep me away from the windows, which he left open for the fresh air, he told me a big bad wolf lived down below and would eat me up if I fell out. Later, he started his own print plant in a building on the North Side. He employed day laborers, as well as enlisting my mother, my brothers and me when we were old enough to help with the printing. We carefully poured the paint onto the edge of the silk screen and pulled the squeegee across to print the pattern on the fabric underneath. Then we lifted up the screen and moved down the table, over and over again, creating beautiful patterns, some of which my father designed. My favorite was "Staircase to the Stars."

In 1950, when I was three years old and my brother Hugh was still an infant, my father had done well enough to move the family to suburban Park Ridge. There were fancier and more fashionable suburbs north of Chicago, along Lake Michigan, but my parents felt comfortable in Park Ridge among all the other veterans who chose it for its excellent public schools, parks, tree-lined streets, wide sidewalks and comfortable family homes. The town was white and middle-class, a place where women stayed home to raise children while men commuted to work in the Loop, eighteen miles away. Many of the fathers took the train, but my dad had to make sales calls on potential customers, so he drove the family car to work every day.

My father paid cash for our two-story brick house on the corner lot of Elm and Wisner Streets. We had two sundecks, a screened-in porch and a fenced-in backyard where the neighborhood kids would come to play or to sneak cherries from our tree. The post-war population explosion was booming, and there were swarms of children everywhere. My mother once counted forty-seven kids living on our square block.

Next door were the four Williams children, and across the street were the six O'Callaghans. Mr. Williams flooded his backyard in the winter to create an ice rink where we skated and played hockey for hours after school and on weekends. Mr. O'Callaghan put up a basketball hoop on his garage that drew kids from all over to play pickup games and the old standbys, HORSE and the shorter version, PIG. The games I most enjoyed were the ones we made up, like the elaborate team contest called "chase and run," a complex form of hide-and-seek, and the near daily softball and kickball marathons played on our corner with sewer covers as bases.

My mother was a classic homemaker. When I think of her in those days, I see a woman in perpetual motion, making the beds, washing the dishes and putting dinner on the table precisely at six o'clock. I came home from Field School for lunch every day—tomato or chicken noodle soup and grilled cheese or peanut butter or bologna sandwiches. While we ate, Mom and I listened to radio programs like *Ma Perkins* or *Favorite Story*.

"Tell me a story," it began.

"What kind of story?"

"Any kind."

My mother also found lots of what people now call "quality time" for my brothers and me. She didn't learn to drive until the early 1960s, so we walked everywhere. In the winter, she bundled us up on a sled and pulled us to the store. Then we held and balanced the groceries for the trip home. In the middle of hanging the wash on a clothesline in the backyard, she might help me practice my pitching or lie down on the grass with me to describe the cloud shapes overhead.

One summer, she helped me create a fantasy world in a large cardboard box. We used mirrors for lakes and twigs for trees, and I made up fairy-tale stories for my dolls to act out. Another summer, she encouraged my younger brother Tony to pursue his dream of digging a hole all the way to China. She started reading to him about China and every day he spent time digging his hole next to our house. Occasionally, he found a chopstick or fortune cookie my mother had hidden there.

My brother Hugh was even more adventurous. As a toddler he pushed open the door to our sundeck and happily tunneled through three feet of snow until my mother rescued him. More than once he and his friends went off to play in the construction sites that had sprung up all around our neighborhood and had to be escorted home by the police. The other boys got in the patrol car, but Hugh insisted on walking home beside it, telling the police and my parents that he was heeding the warning never to get in a stranger's car.

My mother wanted us to learn about the world by reading books. She was more successful with me than with my brothers, who preferred the school of hard knocks. She took me to the library every week, and I loved working my way through the books in the children's section. We got a television set when I was five, but she didn't let us watch it much. We played card games—War, Concentration, Slapjack—and board games like Monopoly and Clue. I am as much of a believer as she is that board games and card playing teach children math skills and strategy. During the school year, I could count on my mother's help with my homework, except for math, which she left to my father. She typed my papers and salvaged my disastrous attempt to make a skirt in my junior high home economics class.

My mother loved her home and her family, but she felt limited by the narrow choices of her life. It is easy to forget now, when women's choices can seem overwhelming, how few there were for my mother's generation. She started taking college courses when we were older. She never graduated, but she amassed mountains of credits in subjects ranging from logic to child development.

My mother was offended by the mistreatment of any human being, especially children. She understood from personal experience that many children—through no fault of their own—were disadvantaged and discriminated against from birth. She hated self-righteousness and pretensions of moral superiority and impressed on my brothers and me that we were no better or worse than anyone else. As a child in California, she had watched the Japanese Americans in her school endure blatant discrimination and daily taunts from the Anglo students. After she returned to Chicago, she often wondered what had happened to one particular boy she liked. The kids called him "Tosh," short for Toshihishi. She saw him again when she returned to Alhambra to serve as Grand Marshal at their sixtieth high school reunion. As she had suspected, Tosh and his family had been interned during World War II, and their farm had been taken from them. But she was heartened to learn that, after years of struggling, Tosh had become a successful vegetable farmer himself.

I grew up between the push and tug of my parents' values, and my own political beliefs reflect both. The gender gap started in families like mine. My mother was basically a Democrat, although she kept it quiet in Republican Park Ridge. My dad was a rock-ribbed, up-by-your-bootstraps, conservative Republican and proud of it. He was also tightfisted with money. He did not believe in credit and he ran his business on a strict pay-as-you-go policy. His ideology was based on self-reliance and personal initiative, but, unlike many people who call themselves conservatives today, he understood the importance of fiscal responsibility and supported taxpayer investments in highways, schools, parks and other important public goods.

My father could not stand personal waste. Like so many who grew up in the Depression, his fear of poverty colored his life. My mother rarely bought new clothes, and she and I negotiated with him for weeks for special purchases, like a new dress for the prom. If one of my brothers or I forgot to screw the cap back on the toothpaste tube, my father threw it out the bathroom window. We would have to go outside, even in the snow, to search for it in the evergreen bushes in front of the house. That was his way of reminding us not to waste anything. To this day, I put uneaten olives back in the jar, wrap up the tiniest pieces of cheese and feel guilty when I throw anything away.

He was a tough taskmaster, but we knew he cared about us. When I worried about being too slow to solve math problems in Miss Metzger's fourth-grade weekly math contests, he woke me up early to drill me on my multiplication tables and teach me long division. In the winter, he would turn off the heat at night to save money, then get up before dawn to turn it back on. I often woke up to the sound of my father bellowing his favorite Mitch Miller songs.

My brothers and I were required to do household chores without any expectation of an allowance. "I feed you, don't I?" Dad would say. I got my first summer job when I was thirteen, working for the Park Ridge Park District three mornings a week supervising a small park a few miles from my house. Since my dad left for work early in our only car, I pulled a wagon filled with balls, bats, jump ropes and other supplies back and forth. From that year on, I always had a summer job and often worked during the year.

My dad was highly opinionated, to put it mildly. We all accommodated his pronouncements, mostly about Communists, shady businessmen or crooked politicians, the three lowest forms of life in his eyes. In our family's spirited, sometimes heated, discussions around the kitchen table, usually about politics or sports, I learned that more than one opinion could live under the same roof. By the time I was twelve, I had my own positions on many issues. I also learned that a person was not necessarily bad just because you did not agree with him, and that if you believed in something, you had better be prepared to defend it.

Both my parents conditioned us to be tough in order to survive whatever life might throw at us. They expected us to stand up for ourselves, me as much as my brothers. Shortly after we moved to Park Ridge, my mother noticed that I was reluctant to go outside to play. Sometimes I came in crying, complaining that the girl across the street was always pushing me around. Suzy O'Callaghan had older brothers, and she was used to playing rough. I was only four years old, but my mother was afraid that if I gave in to my fears, it would set a pattern for the rest of my life. One day, I came running into the house. She stopped me.

"Go back out there," she ordered, "and if Suzy hits you, you have my permission to hit her back. You have to stand up for yourself. There's no room in this house for cowards." She later told me she watched from behind the dining room curtain as I squared my shoulders and marched across the street.

I returned a few minutes later, glowing with victory. "I can play with the boys now," I said. "And Suzy will be my friend!"

She was and she still is.

As a Brownie and then a Girl Scout, I participated in Fourth of July parades, food drives, cookie sales and every other activity that would earn a merit badge or adult approval. I began organizing neighborhood kids in games, sporting events and backyard carnivals both for fun and to raise nickels and dimes for charities. There is an old photograph from our local newspaper, the *Park Ridge Advocate*, that shows me and a bunch of my friends handing over a paper bag of money for the United Way. We raised it from the mock Olympics our neighborhood staged when I was twelve.

Surrounded by a father and brothers who were sports fanatics, I became a serious fan and occasional competitor. I supported our school's teams and went to as many games as possible. I rooted for the Cubs, as did my family and most folks on our side of town. My favorite was Mr. Cub himself, Ernie Banks. In our neighborhood, it was nearly sacrilegious to cheer for the rival White Sox of the American League, so I adopted the Yankees as my AL team, in part because I loved Mickey Mantle. My explanations of Chicago sports rivalries fell on deaf ears during my Senate campaign years later, when skeptical New Yorkers were incredulous that a Chicago native could claim youthful allegiance to a team from the Bronx.

I played in a girls' summer softball league through high school, and the last team I played for was sponsored by a local candy distributor. We wore white knee socks, black shorts and pink shirts in honor of our namesake confection, Good & Plenty. The Park Ridge kids traveled in packs to and from Hinckley Park, swimming in summer in the cold pool waters and skating in winter on the big outdoor rink. We walked or rode our bikes everywhere—sometimes trailing the slow-moving town trucks that sprayed a fog of DDT at dusk in the summer months. Nobody thought about pesticides as toxic then. We just thought it was fun to pedal through the haze, breathing in the sweet and acrid smells of cut grass and hot asphalt as we squeezed a few more minutes of play out of the dwindling light.

We sometimes ice-skated on the Des Plaines River while our fathers warmed themselves over a fire and talked about how the spread of communism was threatening our way of life, and how the Russians had the bomb and, because of Sputnik, we were losing the space race. But the Cold War was an abstraction to me, and my immediate world seemed safe and stable. I didn't know a child whose parents were di-

vorced, and until I went to high school, I didn't know anybody who died
of anything except old age. I recognize that this benign cocoon was an
illusion, but it is one I would wish for every child.

I grew up in a cautious, conformist era in American history. But in
the midst of our *Father Knows Best* upbringing, I was taught to resist
peer pressure. My mother never wanted to hear about what my friends
were wearing or what they thought about me or anything else. "You're
unique," she would say. "You can think for yourself. I don't care if
everybody's doing it. We're not everybody. You're not everybody."

This was fine with me, because I usually felt the same way. Of
course, I did make some effort to fit in. I had enough adolescent vanity
that I sometimes refused to wear the thick glasses I had needed since I
was nine to correct my terrible eyesight. My friend starting in sixth
grade, Betsy Johnson, led me around town like a Seeing Eye dog.
Sometimes I encountered classmates and failed to acknowledge
them—not because I was stuck-up, but because I didn't recognize anyone. I was in my thirties before I learned to wear soft contact lenses
strong enough to correct my vision.

Betsy and I were allowed to go to the Pickwick Theater by ourselves on Saturday afternoons. One day, we watched *Lover Come Back*
with Doris Day and Rock Hudson twice. Afterwards, we went to a
restaurant for a Coke and fries. We thought we had invented dipping
the french fries into ketchup when the waitress at Robin Hood's told us
she never saw anybody do that before. I didn't know what a fast-food
meal was until my family started going to McDonald's around 1960.
The first McDonald's opened in the nearby town of Des Plaines in
1955, but my family didn't discover the chain until one opened closer to
us in Niles. Even then, we went only for special occasions. I still remember seeing the number of burgers sold change on the Golden
Arches sign from thousands to millions.

I loved school, and I was lucky enough to have some great teachers
at Eugene Field School, Ralph Waldo Emerson Junior High and Maine
Township High Schools East and South. Years later, when I chaired the
Arkansas Education Standards Committee, I realized how fortunate I
had been to attend fully equipped schools with highly trained teachers
and a full range of academic and extracurricular offerings. It's funny
what I remember now: Miss Taylor reading to my first-grade class from
Winnie-the-Pooh every morning. Miss Cappuccio, my second-grade
teacher, challenging us to write from one to one thousand, a task that

little hands holding fat pencils took forever to finish. The exercise helped teach me what it meant to start and finish a big project. Miss Cappuccio later invited our class to her wedding, where she became Mrs. O'Laughlin. That was such a kind gesture, and for seven-year-old girls, seeing their teacher as a beautiful bride was a highlight of the year.

I was considered a tomboy all through elementary school. My fifth-grade class had the school's most incorrigible boys, and when Mrs. Krause left the room, she would ask me or one of the other girls to "be in charge." As soon as the door closed behind her, the boys would start acting up and causing trouble, mostly because they wanted to aggravate the girls. I got a reputation for being able to stand up to them, which may be why I was elected co-captain of the safety patrol for the next year. This was a big deal in our school. My new status provided me my first lesson in the strange ways some people respond to electoral politics. One of the girls in my class, Barbara, invited me home for lunch. When we got there, her mother was vacuuming and casually told her daughter and me to go fix ourselves peanut butter sandwiches, which we did. I did not think anything of it until we got ready to go back to school and were saying good-bye to her mother.

She asked her daughter why we were leaving so early, and Barbara told her, "Because Hillary's a patrol captain and has to be there before the other kids."

"Oh, if I'd known that," she said, "I'd have fixed you a nice lunch."

My sixth-grade teacher, Elisabeth King, drilled us in grammar, but she also encouraged us to think and write creatively, and challenged us to try new forms of expression. If we were sluggish in responding to her questions, she said, "You're slower than molasses running uphill in winter." She often paraphrased the verse from Matthew: "Don't put your lamp under a bushel basket, but use it to light up the world." She pushed me, Betsy Johnson, Gayle Elliot, Carol Farley and Joan Throop to write and produce a play about five girls taking an imaginary trip to Europe. It was an assignment from Mrs. King that led me to write my first autobiography. I rediscovered it in a box of old papers after I left the White House, and reading it pulled me back to those tentative years on the brink of adolescence. I was still very much a child at that age, and mostly concerned with family, school and sports. But grade school was ending, and it was time to enter a more complicated world than the one I had known.

UNIVERSITY OF LIFE

"WHAT YOU DON'T LEARN FROM YOUR MOTHER, YOU learn from the world" is a saying I once heard from the Masai tribe in Kenya. By the fall of 1960, my world was expanding and so were my political sensibilities. John F. Kennedy won the presidential election, to my father's consternation. He supported Vice President Richard M. Nixon, and my eighth-grade social studies teacher, Mr. Kenvin, did too. Mr. Kenvin came to school the day after the election and showed us bruises he claimed he had gotten when he tried to question the activities of the Democratic machine's poll watchers at his voting precinct in Chicago on Election Day. Betsy Johnson and I were outraged by his stories, which reinforced my father's belief that Mayor Richard J. Daley's creative vote counting had won the election for President-Elect Kennedy. During our lunch period, we went to the pay phone outside the cafeteria and tried calling Mayor Daley's office to complain. We reached a very nice woman who told us she would be sure to pass on the message to the Mayor.

A few days later, Betsy heard about a group of Republicans asking for volunteers to check voter lists against addresses to uncover vote fraud. The ad called for volunteers to gather at a downtown hotel at 9 A.M. on a Saturday morning. Betsy and I decided to participate. We knew our parents would never give us permission, so we didn't ask. We took the bus downtown, walked to the hotel and were directed into a small ballroom. We went up to an information table and told the people we were there to help. The turnout must have been less than expected. We were each handed a stack of voter registration lists and assigned to different teams who, we were told, would drive us to our destinations, drop us off and pick us up a few hours later.

Betsy and I separated and went off with total strangers. I ended up with a couple who drove me to the South Side, dropped me off in a poor neighborhood and told me to knock on doors and ask people their names so I could compare them with registration lists to find evidence to overturn the election. Off I went, fearless and stupid. I did find a vacant lot that was listed as the address for about a dozen alleged voters. I woke up a lot of people who stumbled to the door or yelled at me to go away. And I walked into a bar where men were drinking to ask if certain people on my list actually lived there. The men were so shocked to see me they stood silent while I asked my few questions, until the bartender told me I would have to come back later because the owner wasn't there.

When I finished, I stood on the corner waiting to be picked up, happy that I'd ferreted out proof of my father's contention that "Daley stole the election for Kennedy."

Of course, when I returned home and told my father where I had been, he went nuts. It was bad enough to go downtown without an adult, but to go to the South Side alone sent him into a yelling fit. And besides, he said, Kennedy was going to be President whether we liked it or not.

My freshman year at Maine East was a culture shock. The baby boomers pushed enrollment near five thousand white kids from different ethnic and economic groups. I remember walking out of my homeroom the first day of class and hugging the walls to avoid the crush of students, all of whom looked bigger and more mature than me. It didn't help that I had decided the week before to get a more "grown-up" hairdo to begin my high school years. Thus began my lifelong hair struggles.

I wore my long straight hair in a ponytail or held back by a headband, and whenever my mother or I needed a permanent or trim we visited her dear friend Amalia Toland, who had once been a beautician. Amalia would take care of us in her kitchen while she and my mother talked. But I wanted to show up at high school with a shoulder-length pageboy or flip like those of the older girls I admired, and I begged my mother to take me to a real beauty parlor. A neighbor recommended a man who had his shop in a small windowless room in the back of a nearby grocery store. When I got there, I handed him a photo of what I wanted and waited to be transformed. Wielding scissors, he began to cut, all the time talking to my mother, often turning around to make a point. I watched in horror as he cut a huge hunk of hair out of the right side of my head. I shrieked. When he finally looked at where I was pointing, he said, "Oh, my scissors must have slipped, I'll have to even up the other side." Shocked, I watched the rest of my hair disappear, leaving me—in my eyes, at least—looking like an artichoke. My poor mother tried to reassure me, but I knew better: My life was ruined.

I refused to leave the house for days, until I decided that if I bought a ponytail of fake hair at Ben Franklin's Five and Dime Store, I could pin it to the top of my head, put a ribbon around it and pretend the slipped scissors disaster never happened. So that's what I did, which saved me from feeling self-conscious and embarrassed that first day— until I was walking down the grand central staircase in between classes. Coming up the stairs was Ernest Ricketts, known as "Ricky," who had been my friend since the day we first walked to kindergarten together. He said hello, waited until he passed me, and then, as he had done dozens of times before, reached back to pull my ponytail—but this time it came off in his hand. The reason we are still friends today is that he did not add to my mortification; instead, he handed my "hair" back to me, said he was sorry he scalped me and went on without drawing any more attention to the worst moment—until then, at least—of my life.

It's a cliché now, but my high school in the early 1960s resembled the movie *Grease* or the television show *Happy Days*. I became President of the local fan club for Fabian, a teen idol, which consisted of me and two other girls. We watched *The Ed Sullivan Show* every Sunday night with our families, except the night he showcased the Beatles on February 9, 1964, which had to be a group experience. Paul McCartney was my favorite Beatle, which led to debates about each one's respective merits, especially with Betsy, who always championed George Harrison. I got tickets to the Rolling Stones concert in Chicago's McCormick Place in 1965. "(I Can't Get No) Satisfaction" became a catchall anthem for adolescent angst of all varieties. Years later, when I met icons from my youth, like Paul McCartney, George Harrison and Mick Jagger, I didn't know whether to shake hands or jump up and down squealing.

Despite the developing "youth culture," defined mostly by television and music, there were distinct groups in our school that determined one's social position: athletes and cheerleaders; student council types and brains; greasers and hoods. There were hallways I didn't dare walk down because, I was told, the "shop" guys would confront people. Cafeteria seating was dictated by invisible borders we all recognized. In my junior year, the underlying tensions broke out with fights between groups in the parking lot after school and at football and basketball games.

The administration moved quickly to intervene and established a student group called the Cultural Values Committee consisting of representative students from different groups. The principal, Dr. Clyde Watson, asked me to be on the committee, giving me the chance to meet and talk with kids whom I did not know and previously would have avoided. Our committee came up with specific recommendations to promote tolerance and decrease tension. Several of us were asked to appear on a local television show to discuss what our committee had done. This was both my first appearance on television and my first experience with an organized effort to stress American values of pluralism, mutual respect and understanding. Those values needed tending, even in my suburban Chicago high school. Although the student body was predominantly white and Christian, we still found ways to isolate and demonize one another. The committee gave me the opportunity to make new and different friends. A few years later, when I was at a dance at a local YMCA and some guys started hassling me, one of the former committee members, a so-called greaser, intervened, telling the others to leave me alone because I was "okay."

All, however, was not okay during my high school years. I was sitting in geometry class on November 22, 1963, puzzling over one of Mr. Craddock's problems, when another teacher came to tell us President Kennedy had been shot in Dallas. Mr. Craddock, one of my favorite teachers and our class sponsor, cried, "What? That can't be," and ran out into the hall. When he returned, he confirmed that someone had shot the President and that it was probably some "John Bircher," a reference to a right-wing organization bitterly opposed to President Kennedy. He told us to go to the auditorium to await further information. The halls were silent as thousands of students walked in disbelief and denial to the school auditorium. Finally, our principal came in and said we would be dismissed early.

When I got home, I found my mother in front of the television set watching Walter Cronkite. Cronkite announced that President Kennedy had died at 1 P.M. CST. She confessed that she had voted for Kennedy and felt so sorry for his wife and children. So did I. I also felt sorry for our country and I wanted to help in some way, although I had no idea how.

I clearly expected to work for a living, and I did not feel limited in my choices. I was lucky to have parents who never tried to mold me into any category or career. They simply encouraged me to excel and be happy. In fact, I don't remember a friend's parent or a teacher ever telling me or my friends that "girls can't do this" or "girls shouldn't do that." Sometimes, though, the message got through in other ways.

The author Jane O'Reilly, who came of age in the 1950s, wrote a famous essay for *Ms.* magazine in 1972 recounting the moments in her life when she realized she was being devalued because she was female. She described the instant of revelation as a *click!*—like the mechanism that triggers a flashbulb. It could be as blatant as the help-wanted ads that, until the mid-sixties, were divided into separate columns for men and women, or as subtle as an impulse to surrender the front section of the newspaper to any man in the vicinity—*click!*—contenting yourself with the women's pages until he finishes reading the serious news.

There were a few moments when I felt that *click!* I had always been fascinated by exploration and space travel, maybe in part because my dad was so concerned about America lagging behind Russia. President Kennedy's vow to put men on the moon excited me, and I wrote to NASA to volunteer for astronaut training. I received a letter back informing me that they were not accepting girls in the program. It was the first time I had hit an obstacle I couldn't overcome with hard work and determination, and I was outraged. Of course, my poor eyesight and mediocre physical abilities would have disqualified me anyway, regardless of gender. Still, the blanket rejection hurt and made me more sympathetic later to anyone confronted with discrimination of any kind.

In high school, one of my smartest girlfriends dropped out of the accelerated courses because her boyfriend wasn't in them. Another didn't want to have her grades posted because she knew she would get higher marks than the boy she was dating. These girls had picked up the subtle and not-so-subtle cultural signals urging them to conform to sexist stereotypes, to diminish their own accomplishments in order not to outperform the boys around them. I was interested in boys in high school, but I never dated anyone seriously. I simply could not imagine giving up a college education or a career to get married, as some of my girlfriends were planning to do.

I was interested in politics from an early age, and I loved to hone my debating skills with my friends. I would press poor Ricky Ricketts into daily debates about world peace, baseball scores, whatever topic came to mind. I successfully ran for student council and junior class Vice President. I was also an active Young Republican and, later, a Goldwater girl, right down to my cowgirl outfit and straw cowboy hat emblazoned with the slogan "AuH$_2$O."

My ninth-grade history teacher, Paul Carlson, was, and still is, a dedicated educator and a very conservative Republican. Mr. Carlson encouraged me to read Senator Barry Goldwater's recently published book, *The Conscience of a Conservative*. That inspired me to write my term paper on the American conservative movement, which I dedicated "To my parents, who have always taught me to be an individual." I liked Senator Goldwater because he was a rugged individualist who swam against the political tide. Years later, I admired his outspoken support of individual rights, which he considered consistent with his old-fashioned conservative principles: "Don't raise hell about the gays, the blacks and the Mexicans. Free people have a right to do as they damn please." When Goldwater learned I had supported him in 1964, he sent the White House a case of barbecue fixings and hot sauces and invited me to come see him. I went to his home in Phoenix in 1996 and spent a wonderful hour talking to him and his dynamic wife, Susan.

Mr. Carlson also adored General Douglas MacArthur, so we listened to tapes of his farewell address to Congress over and over again. At the conclusion of one such session, Mr. Carlson passionately exclaimed, "And remember, above all else, 'Better dead than red!' " Ricky Ricketts, sitting in front of me, started laughing, and I caught the contagion. Mr. Carlson sternly asked, "What do you think is so funny?" And Ricky replied, "Gee, Mr. Carlson, I'm only fourteen years old, and I'd rather be alive than anything."

My active involvement in the First United Methodist Church of Park Ridge opened my eyes and heart to the needs of others and helped instill a sense of social responsibility rooted in my faith. My father's parents claimed they became Methodists because their great-grandparents were converted in the small coal-mining villages around Newcastle in the north of England and in South Wales by John Wesley, who founded the Methodist Church in the eighteenth century. Wesley taught that God's love is expressed through good works, which he explained with a simple rule: "Do all the good you can, by all the means you can, in all the ways you can, in all the places you can, at all the times you can, to all the people you can, as long as ever you can." There will always be worthy debates about whose definition of "good" one follows, but as a young girl, I took Wesley's admonition to heart. My father prayed by his bed every night, and prayer became a source of solace and guidance for me even as a child.

I spent a lot of time at our church, where I was confirmed in the sixth grade along with some of my lifelong buddies, like Ricky Ricketts and Sherry Heiden, who attended church with me all the way through high school. My mother taught Sunday school, largely, she says, to keep an eye on my brothers. I attended Bible school, Sunday school, and youth group and was active in service work and in the altar guild, which cleaned and prepared the altar on Saturdays for Sunday's services. My quest to reconcile my father's insistence on self-reliance and my mother's concerns about social justice was helped along by the arrival in 1961 of a Methodist youth minister named Donald Jones.

Rev. Jones was fresh out of Drew University Seminary and four years in the Navy. He was filled with the teachings of Dietrich Bonhoeffer and Reinhold Niebuhr. Bonhoeffer stressed that the role of a Christian was a moral one of total engagement in the world with the promotion of human development. Niebuhr struck a persuasive balance between a clear-eyed realism about human nature and an unrelenting passion for justice and social reform. Rev. Jones stressed that a Christian life was "faith in action." I had never met anyone like him. Don called his Sunday and Thursday night Methodist Youth Fellowship sessions "the University of Life." He was eager to work with us because he hoped we would become more aware of life outside of Park Ridge. He sure met his goals with me. Because of Don's "University," I first read e. e. cummings and T. S. Eliot; experienced Picasso's paintings, especially *Guernica*, and debated the meaning of the "Grand Inquisitor" in Dostoyevsky's *Brothers Karamazov*. I came home bursting with excitement and shared what I had learned with my mother, who quickly came to find in Don a kindred spirit. But the University of Life was not just about art and literature. We visited black and Hispanic churches in Chicago's inner city for exchanges with their youth groups.

In the discussions we had sitting around church basements, I learned that, despite the obvious differences in our environments, these kids were more like me than I ever could have imagined. They also knew more about what was happening in the civil rights movement in the South. I had only vaguely heard of Rosa Parks and Dr. Martin Luther King, but these discussions sparked my interest.

So, when Don announced one week that he would take us to hear Dr. King speak at Orchestra Hall, I was excited. My parents gave me permission, but some of my friends' parents refused to let them go hear such a "rabble-rouser."

Dr. King's speech was entitled, "Remaining Awake Through a Revolution." Until then, I had been dimly aware of the social revolution occurring in our country, but Dr. King's words illuminated the struggle taking place and challenged our indifference: "We now stand on the border of the Promised Land of integration. The old order is passing away and a new one is coming in. We should all accept this order and learn to live together as brothers in a world society, or we will all perish together."

Though my eyes were opening, I still mostly parroted the conventional wisdom of Park Ridge's and my father's politics. While Don Jones threw me into "liberalizing" experiences, Paul Carlson introduced me to refugees from the Soviet Union who told haunting tales of cruelty under the Communists, which reinforced my already strong anti-Communist views. Don once remarked that he and Mr. Carlson were locked in a battle for my mind and soul. Their conflict was broader than that, however, and came to a head in our church, where Paul was also a member. Paul disagreed with Don's priorities, including the University of Life curriculum, and pushed for Don's removal from the church. After numerous confrontations, Don decided to leave First Methodist after only two years for a teaching position at Drew University, where he recently retired as Professor Emeritus of Social Ethics. We stayed in close touch over the years, and Don and his wife, Karen, were frequent visitors at the White House. He assisted at my brother Tony's wedding in the Rose Garden on May 28, 1994.

I now see the conflict between Don Jones and Paul Carlson as an early indication of the cultural, political, and religious fault lines that developed across America in the last forty years. I liked them both personally and did not see their beliefs as diametrically opposed then or now.

At the end of my junior year at Maine East, our class was split in two, and half of us became the first senior class at Maine Township High School South, built to keep up with the baby boomers. I ran for student government President against several boys and lost, which did not surprise me but still hurt, especially because one of my opponents told me I was "really stupid if I thought a girl could be elected President." As soon as the election was over, the winner asked me to head the Organizations Committee, which as far as I could tell was expected to do most of the work. I agreed.

That actually turned out to be fun because, as the first graduating class, we were starting all the high school traditions like homecoming parades and dances, student council elections, pep rallies and proms. We staged a mock presidential debate for the 1964 election. A young government teacher, Jerry Baker, was in charge. He knew I was actively supporting Goldwater. I had even persuaded my dad to drive Betsy and me to hear Goldwater speak when he came on a campaign swing by train through the Chicago suburbs.

One of my friends, Ellen Press, was the only Democrat I knew in my class, and she was a vocal supporter of President Johnson. Mr. Baker, in an act of counterintuitive brilliance—or perversity—assigned me to play President Johnson and Ellen to represent Senator Goldwater. We were both insulted and protested, but Mr. Baker said this would force each of us to learn about issues from the other side. So I immersed myself—for the first time—in President Johnson's Democratic positions on civil rights, health care, poverty and foreign policy. I resented every hour spent in the library reading the Democrats' platform and White House statements. But as I prepared for the debate, I found myself arguing with more than dramatic fervor. Ellen must have had the same experience. By the time we graduated from college, each of us had changed our political affiliations. Mr. Baker later left teaching for Washington, D.C., where he has served for many years as Legislative Counsel for the Air Line Pilots Association, a position that puts to good use his ability to understand both Democratic and Republican perspectives.

Being a high school senior also meant thinking about college. I knew I was going but did not have a clue about where. I went to see our overburdened and unprepared college counselor, who gave me a few brochures about Midwestern colleges but offered neither help nor advice. I got needed guidance from two recent college graduates who were studying for their master's in teaching at Northwestern University and had been assigned to teach government classes at Maine South: Karin Fahlstrom, a graduate of Smith, and Janet Altman, a graduate of Wellesley. I remember Miss Fahlstrom telling our class she wanted us to read a daily newspaper other than Colonel McCormick's *Chicago Tribune*. When I asked which one, she suggested *The New York Times.* "But that's a tool of the Eastern Establishment!" I responded. Miss Fahlstrom, clearly surprised, said, "Well, then, read *The Washington Post!*" Up until then, I had never even seen either of those newspapers and didn't know the *Tribune* wasn't the gospel.

In mid-October, both Misses Fahlstrom and Altman asked if I knew where I wanted to go to college; I didn't, and they recommended I apply to Smith and Wellesley, two of the Seven Sisters women's colleges. They told me that if I went to a women's college, I could concentrate on my studies during the week and have fun on the weekends. I had not even considered leaving the Midwest for college and had only visited Michigan State because its honors program invited Merit Scholar finalists to its campus. But once the idea was presented, I became interested. They invited me to attend events to meet alumnae and current students. The gathering for Smith was at a beautiful, large home in one of the wealthy suburbs along Lake Michigan, while Wellesley's was in a penthouse apartment on Lake Shore Drive in Chicago. I felt out of place at both. All the girls seemed not only richer but more worldly than I. One girl at the Wellesley event was smoking pastel-colored cigarettes and talking about her summer in Europe. That seemed a long way from Lake Winola and my life.

I told my two teacher mentors that I didn't know about "going East" to school, but they insisted that I talk with my parents about applying. My mother thought I should go wherever I wanted. My father said I was free to do that, but he wouldn't pay if I went west of the Mississippi or to Radcliffe, which he heard was full of beatniks. Smith and Wellesley, which he had never heard of, were acceptable. I never visited either campus, so when I was accepted, I decided on Wellesley based on the photographs of the campus, especially its small Lake Waban, which reminded me of Lake Winola. I have always been grateful to those two teachers.

I didn't know anyone else going to Wellesley. Most of my friends were attending Midwestern colleges to be close to home. My parents drove me to college, and for some reason we got lost in Boston, ending up in Harvard Square, which only confirmed my father's views about beatniks. However, there weren't any in sight at Wellesley, and he seemed reassured. My mother has said that she cried the entire thousand-mile drive back from Massachusetts to Illinois. Now that I have had the experience of leaving my daughter at a distant university, I understand exactly how she felt. But back then, I was only looking ahead to my own future.

CLASS OF '69

IN 1994, *FRONTLINE*, THE PBS TELEVISION SERIES, PRO-
duced a documentary about the Wellesley class of 1969, "Hillary's
Class." It was mine, to be sure, but it was much more than that. The producer, Rachel Dretzin, explained why *Frontline* decided to scrutinize our
class twenty-five years after we graduated: "They've made a journey unlike any other generation, through a time of profound change and upheaval for women."

Classmates of mine have said that Wellesley was a girls' school
when we started and a women's college when we left. That sentiment
probably said as much about us as it did the college.

I arrived at Wellesley carrying my father's political beliefs and my
mother's dreams and left with the beginnings of my own. But on that
first day, as my parents drove away, I felt lonely, overwhelmed and out
of place. I met girls who had gone to private boarding schools, lived
abroad, spoke other languages fluently and placed out of freshman
courses because of their Advanced Placement test scores. I had been out
of the country only once—to see the Canadian side of Niagara Falls.
My only exposure to foreign languages was high school Latin.

I didn't hit my stride as a Wellesley student right away. I was enrolled in courses that proved very challenging. My struggles with math
and geology convinced me once and for all to give up on any idea of becoming a doctor or a scientist. My French professor gently told me,
"Mademoiselle, your talents lie elsewhere." A month after school
started, I called home collect and told my parents I didn't think I was
smart enough to be there. My father told me to come on home and my
mother told me she didn't want me to be a quitter. After a shaky start,

the doubts faded, and I realized that I really couldn't go home again, so I might as well make a go of it.

One snowy night during my freshman year, Margaret Clapp, then President of the college, arrived unexpectedly at my dorm, Stone-Davis, which perched on the shores above Lake Waban. She came into the dining room and asked for volunteers to help her gently shake the snow off the branches of the surrounding trees so that they wouldn't break under the weight. We walked from tree to tree through knee-high snow under a clear sky filled with stars, led by a strong, intelligent woman alert to the surprises and vulnerabilities of nature. She guided and challenged both her students and her faculty with the same care. I decided that night that I had found the place where I belonged.

Madeleine Albright, who served as Ambassador to the United Nations and Secretary of State in the Clinton Administration, started Wellesley ten years before me. I have talked with her often about the differences between her time and mine. She and her friends in the late fifties were more overtly committed to finding a husband and less buffeted by changes in the outside world. Yet they too benefited from Wellesley's example and its high expectations of what women could accomplish if given the chance. In Madeleine's day and in mine, Wellesley emphasized service. Its Latin motto is *Non Ministrari sed Ministrare*— "Not to be ministered unto, but to minister"—a phrase in line with my own Methodist upbringing. By the time I arrived, in the midst of an activist student era, many students viewed the motto as a call for women to become more engaged in shaping our lives and influencing the world around us.

What I valued most about Wellesley were the lifelong friends I made and the opportunity that a women's college offered us to stretch our wings and minds in the ongoing journey toward self-definition and identity. We learned from the stories we told one another, sitting around in our dorm rooms or over long lunches in the all-glass dining room. I stayed in the same dorm, Stone-Davis, all four years and ended up living on a corridor with five students who became lifelong friends. Johanna Branson, a tall dancer from Lawrence, Kansas, became an art history major and shared with me her love of paintings and film. Johanna explained on *Frontline* that from the first day at Wellesley, we were told we were ". . . the cream of the cream. That sounds really bratty and elitist now. But at the time, it was a wonderful thing to hear if you were a girl . . . you didn't have to take second seat to anybody."

Jinnet Fowles, from Connecticut and another art history student, posed hard-to-answer questions about what I thought could really be accomplished through student action. Jan Krigbaum, a free spirit from California, brought unflagging enthusiasm to every venture and helped establish a Latin American student exchange program. Connie Hoenk, a long-haired blonde from South Bend, Indiana, was a practical, down-to-earth girl whose opinions frequently reflected our common Midwestern roots. Suzy Salomon, a smart, hardworking girl from another Chicago suburb who laughed often and easily, was always ready to help anyone.

Two older students, Shelley Parry and Laura Grosch, became mentors. A junior in my dorm when I arrived as a freshman, Shelley had an unusual grace and bearing for a young person. She would look at me calmly with huge, intelligent eyes while I carried on about some real or perceived injustice in the world, and then she would gently probe for the source of my passion or the factual basis for my position. After graduation, she taught school in Ghana and elsewhere in Africa, where she met her Australian husband, and finally settled in Australia. Shelley's roommate was the indomitable Laura Grosch, a young woman of large emotions and artistic talent. When I saw "Fooly Scare," one of Laura's paintings in her dorm room, I liked it so much that I bought it over a course of years of tiny payments. It hangs in our Chappaqua home today. All of these girls matured into women whose friendships have sustained and supported me over the years.

Our all-female college guaranteed a focus on academic achievement and extracurricular leadership we might have missed at a coed college. Women not only ran all the student activities—from student government to newspaper to clubs—but we also felt freer to take risks, make mistakes and even fail in front of one another. It was a given that the President of the class, the editor of the paper and top student in every field would be a woman. And it could be any of us. Unlike some of the smart girls in my high school, who felt pressure to forsake their own ambitions for more traditional lives, my Wellesley classmates wanted to be recognized for their ability, hard work and achievements. This may explain why there is a disproportionate number of women's college graduates in professions in which women tend to be underrepresented.

The absence of male students cleared out a lot of psychic space and created a safe zone for us to eschew appearances—in every sense of the word—Monday through Friday afternoon. We focused on our studies without distraction and didn't have to worry about how we looked when we went to class. But without men on campus, our social lives were channeled into road trips and dating rituals called "mixers." When I arrived in the fall of 1965, the college still assumed the role of surrogate parent to the students. We couldn't have boys in our rooms except from 2 to 5:30 P.M. on Sunday afternoons, when we had to leave the door partly open and follow what we called the "two feet" rule: two (out of four) feet had to be on the floor at all times. We had curfews of I A.M. on weekends, and Route 9 from Boston to Wellesley was like a Grand Prix racetrack Friday and Saturday nights as our dates raced madly back to campus so we wouldn't get in trouble. We had reception desks in the entrance halls of each dorm where guests had to check in and be identified through a system of bells and announcements that notified us if the person wanting to see us was male or female. A "visitor" was female, a "caller" male. Notice of an unexpected caller gave you time to either get fixed up or call down to tell the student on duty you weren't available.

My friends and I studied hard and dated boys our own age, mostly from Harvard and other Ivy League schools, whom we met through friends or at mixers. The music was usually so loud at those dances you couldn't understand anything being said unless you stepped outside, which you only did with someone who caught your interest. I danced for hours one night at the Alumni Hall on our campus with a young man whose name I thought was Farce, only to learn later it was Forrest. I had two boyfriends serious enough to meet my parents, which, given my father's attitudes toward anyone I dated, was more like a hazing than a social encounter. Both young men survived, but our relationships didn't.

Given the tenor of the times, we soon chafed at Wellesley's archaic rules and demanded to be treated like adults. We pressured the college administration to remove the *in loco parentis* regulations, which they finally did when I was college government President. That change coincided with the elimination of a required curriculum that students also deemed oppressive.

Looking back on those years, I have few regrets, but I'm not so sure that eliminating both course requirements and quasi-parental supervision represented unmitigated progress. Two of the courses I got the most out of were required, and I now better appreciate the value of core courses in a range of subjects. Walking into my daughter's coed dorm at

Stanford, seeing boys and girls lying and sitting in the hallways, I wondered how anyone nowadays gets any studying done.

By the mid-1960s, the sedate and sheltered Wellesley campus had begun to absorb the shock from events in the outside world. Although I had been elected President of our college's Young Republicans during my freshman year, my doubts about the party and its policies were growing, particularly when it came to civil rights and the Vietnam War. My church had given graduating high school students a subscription to *motive* magazine, which was published by the Methodist Church. Every month I read articles expressing views that sharply contrasted with my usual sources of information. I also had begun reading *The New York Times*, much to my father's consternation and Miss Fahlstrom's delight. I read speeches and essays by hawks, doves and every other brand of commentator. My ideas, new and old, were tested daily by political science professors who pushed me to expand my understanding of the world and examine my own preconceptions just when current events provided more than enough material. Before long, I realized that my political beliefs were no longer in sync with the Republican Party. It was time to step down as President of the Young Republicans.

My Vice President and friend, Betsy Griffith, not only became the new President, but stayed in the Republican Party, along with her husband, the political consultant John Deardourff. She fought hard to keep her party from taking a hard right turn and was a staunch supporter of the Equal Rights Amendment. She obtained her Ph.D. in history and wrote a well-received biography of Elizabeth Cady Stanton before putting her feminism and women's education credentials to work as headmistress of the Madeira School for Girls in northern Virginia. All that, however, was far in the future when I officially left the Wellesley College Young Republicans and submerged myself in learning everything I could about Vietnam.

It's hard to explain to young Americans today, especially with an all-volunteer military, how obsessed many in my generation were with the Vietnam War. Our parents had lived through World War II and had told us stories about America's spirit of sacrifice during that time and the consensus among people after the bombing of Pearl Harbor that America needed to fight. With Vietnam, the country was divided, leaving us confused about our own feelings. My friends and I constantly discussed and debated it. We knew boys in ROTC programs who looked forward to serving when they graduated, as well as boys who intended to resist the draft. We had long conversations about what we would do if we were men, knowing full well we didn't have to face the same choices. It was agonizing for everyone. A friend from Princeton finally dropped out and enlisted in the Navy, because, he told me, he was sick of the controversy and uncertainty.

The debate over Vietnam articulated attitudes not only about the war, but about duty and love of country. Were you honoring your country by fighting a war you considered unjust and contrary to America's self-interest? Were you being unpatriotic if you used the system of deferments or the lottery to avoid fighting? Many students I knew who debated and protested the merits and morality of that war loved America just as much as the brave men and women who served without question or those who served first and raised questions later. For many thoughtful, self-aware young men and women there were no easy answers, and there were different ways to express one's patriotism.

Some contemporary writers and politicians have tried to dismiss the anguish of those years as an embodiment of 1960s self-indulgence. In fact, there are some people who would like to rewrite history to erase the legacy of the war and the social upheaval it spawned. They would have us believe that the debate was frivolous, but that's not how I remember it.

Vietnam mattered, and it changed the country forever. This nation still holds a reservoir of guilt and second-guessing for those who served and those who didn't. Even though as a woman I knew I couldn't be drafted, I spent countless hours wrestling with my own contradictory feelings.

In hindsight, 1968 was a watershed year for the country, and for my own personal and political evolution. National and international events unfolded in quick succession: the Tet Offensive, the withdrawal of Lyndon Johnson from the presidential race, the assassination of Martin Luther King, Jr., the assassination of Robert Kennedy and the relentless escalation of the Vietnam War.

By the time I was a college junior, I had gone from being a Goldwater Girl to supporting the anti-war campaign of Eugene McCarthy, a Democratic Senator from Minnesota, who was challenging President Johnson in the presidential primary. Although I admired President Johnson's domestic accomplishments, I thought his dogged support for a war he'd inherited was a tragic mistake. Along with some of my friends, I would drive up from Wellesley to Manchester, New Hamp-

shire, on Friday or Saturday to stuff envelopes and walk precincts. I had
the chance to meet Senator McCarthy when he stopped into his headquarters to thank the student volunteers who had rallied around his opposition to the war. He nearly defeated Johnson in the New Hampshire
primary, and on March 16, 1968, Senator Robert F. Kennedy of New
York entered the race.

Dr. King's assassination on April 4, 1968, near the end of my junior
year, filled me with grief and rage. Riots broke out in some cities. The
next day I joined in a massive march of protest and mourning at Post
Office Square in Boston. I returned to campus wearing a black armband
and agonizing about the kind of future America faced.

Before I arrived at Wellesley, the only African Americans I knew
were the people my parents employed in my father's business and in our
home. I had heard Dr. King speak and participated in exchanges with
black and Hispanic teenagers through my church. But I had not had a
black friend, neighbor or classmate until I went to college. Karen
Williamson, a lively, independent-minded student, became one of my
first friends there. One Sunday morning, she and I went off campus to
attend church services. Even though I liked Karen and wanted to get to
know her better, I was self-conscious about my motives and hyperaware
that I was moving away from my past. As I got to know my black classmates better, I learned that they too felt self-conscious. Just as I had
come to Wellesley from a predominantly white environment, they had
come from predominantly black ones. Janet McDonald, an elegant,
self-possessed girl from New Orleans, related a conversation she had
with her parents shortly after she arrived. When she told them, "I hate
it here, everyone's white," her father agreed to let her leave, but her
mother insisted, "You can do it and you are going to stay." This was
similar to the conversation I had with my own parents. Our fathers
were willing—even anxious—for us to come home; our mothers were
telling us to hang in there. And we did.

Karen, Fran Rusan, Alvia Wardlaw and other black students started
Ethos, the first African American organization on campus, to serve as a
social network for black students at Wellesley and as a lobbying group
in dealing with the college administration. After Dr. King's assassination, Ethos urged the college to become more racially sensitive and to
recruit more black faculty and students and threatened to call a hunger
strike if the college did not meet their demands. This was Wellesley's
only overt student protest in the late 1960s. The college addressed it by

convening an all-campus meeting in the Houghton Memorial Chapel so Ethos members could explain their concerns. The meeting began to disintegrate into a chaotic shouting match. Kris Olson, who along with Nancy Gist and Susan Graber would go on with me to Yale Law School, worried that the students might shut down the campus and go on strike. I had just been elected college government President, so Kris and the Ethos members asked me to try to make the debate more productive and to translate the legitimate grievances many of us felt toward institutions of authority. To Wellesley's credit, it made an effort to recruit minority faculty and students that began bearing fruit in the 1970s.

Senator Robert F. Kennedy's assassination two months later on June 5, 1968, deepened my despair about events in America. I was already home from college when the news came from Los Angeles. My mother woke me up because "something very terrible has happened again." I stayed on the phone nearly the whole day with my friend Kevin O'Keefe, an Irish-Polish Chicagoan who loves the Kennedys, the Daleys and the thrill of high-stakes politics. We always liked talking about politics, and that day he raged against losing John and Robert Kennedy when our country so badly needed their strong and graceful leadership. We talked a lot then, and in the years since, about whether political action is worth the pain and struggle. Then, as now, we decided that it was, if only, in Kevin's words, to keep "the other guys away from power over us."

I had applied for the Wellesley Internship Program in Washington, D.C., and though dismayed and unnerved by the assassinations, I was still committed to going to Washington. The nine-week summer program placed students in agencies and congressional offices for a first-hand look at "how government works." I was surprised when Professor Alan Schechter, the program's Director and a great political science teacher, as well as my thesis adviser, assigned me to intern at the House Republican Conference. He knew I had come to college as a Republican and was moving away from my father's opinions. He thought this internship would help me continue charting my own course—no matter what I eventually decided. I objected to no avail and ended up reporting for duty to a group headed by then Minority Leader Gerald Ford and including Congressmen Melvin Laird of Wisconsin and Charles Goodell of New York, who befriended and advised me.

The interns posed for their obligatory photographs with the members of Congress, and years later, when I was First Lady, I told former President Ford I had been one of the thousands of interns whom he'd given an introductory look inside the Capitol. The photo of me with him and the Republican leaders made my father very happy; he had it hanging in his bedroom when he died. I also signed a copy of that photo for President Ford and presented it to him with thanks and apologies for having strayed from the fold.

I think about that first experience in Washington every time I meet with the interns in my Senate office. I particularly remember a session Mel Laird held with a large group of us to discuss the Vietnam War. Although he may have harbored concerns about how the Johnson Administration had financed the war and whether the escalation went beyond the congressional authority granted by the Gulf of Tonkin resolution, he remained publicly supportive as a Congressman. In the meeting with interns, he justified American involvement and advocated vigorously for greater military force. When he stopped for questions, I echoed President Eisenhower's caution about American involvement in land wars in Asia and asked him why he thought this strategy could ever succeed. Although we didn't agree, as our heated exchange demonstrated, I came away with a high regard for him and an appreciation for his willingness to explain and defend his views to young people. He took our concerns seriously and respectfully. Later, he served as President Nixon's Secretary of Defense.

Congressman Charles Goodell, who represented western New York, was later appointed to the Senate by Governor Nelson Rockefeller to replace Robert Kennedy until an election could be held. Goodell was a progressive Republican who was defeated in 1970 in a three-way election by the much more conservative James Buckley. Buckley lost in 1976 to Daniel Patrick Moynihan, my predecessor, who held the seat for twenty-four years. When I ran for that Senate seat in 2000, I delighted in telling people from Jamestown, Goodell's hometown, that I had once worked for the Congressman. Toward the end of my internship, Goodell asked me and a few other interns to go with him to the Republican Convention in Miami to work on behalf of Governor Rockefeller's last-ditch effort to wrest his party's nomination away from Richard Nixon. I jumped at the chance and headed for Florida.

The Republican Convention was my first inside look at big-time politics, and I found the week unreal and unsettling. The Fontainebleau Hotel on Miami Beach was the first real hotel I had ever stayed in, since my family favored either sleeping in the car on the way to Lake Winola or staying in small roadside motels. Its size, opulence and service were a surprise. It was there that I placed my first-ever room service order. I can still see the giant fresh peach that came wrapped in a napkin on a plate when I asked for peaches with cereal one morning. I had a roll-away bed shoehorned into a room with four other women, but I don't think any of us slept much. We staffed the Rockefeller for President suite, taking phone calls and delivering messages to and from Rockefeller's political emissaries and delegates. Late one night, a Rockefeller campaign staffer asked everybody in the office if we wanted to meet Frank Sinatra and got back the predictably enthusiastic screams of delight at the prospect. I went with the group to a penthouse to shake hands with Sinatra, who courteously feigned interest in meeting us. I took the elevator down with John Wayne, who appeared under the weather and complained all the way down about the lousy food upstairs.

Although I enjoyed all my new experiences, from room service to celebrities, I knew Rockefeller would not be nominated. The nomination of Richard Nixon cemented the ascendance of a conservative over a moderate ideology within the Republican Party, a dominance that has only grown more pronounced over the years as the party has continued its move to the right and moderates have dwindled in numbers and influence. I sometimes think that I didn't leave the Republican Party as much as it left me.

I came home to Park Ridge after the Republican Convention with no plans for the remaining weeks of summer except to visit with family and friends and get ready for my senior year. My family was on the annual pilgrimage to Lake Winola so I had the house to myself, which was just as well since I'm sure I would have spent hours arguing with my father over Nixon and the Vietnam War. My dad really liked Nixon and believed he would make an excellent President. About Vietnam, he was ambivalent. His questions about the wisdom of U.S. involvement in the war were usually trumped by his disgust with the long-haired hippies who protested it.

My close friend Betsy Johnson had just returned from a year of study in Franco's Spain. Although much had changed since our high school days—the neat flips and sweater sets we used to wear had been displaced by lanky hair and frayed blue jeans—one constant remained: I could always count on Betsy's friendship and shared interest in politics. Neither of us had planned to go into Chicago while the Democratic Convention was in town. But when massive protests broke out downtown, we knew it was an opportunity to witness history. Betsy called and said, "We've got to see this for ourselves," and I agreed.

Just like the time we had gone downtown to check voting lists in junior high school, we knew there was no way our parents would let us go if they knew what we were planning. My mother was in Pennsylvania, and Betsy's mom, Roslyn, thought of going downtown as a visit to Marshall Field's to shop and Stouffer's for lunch, wearing white gloves and a dress. So Betsy told her mother, "Hillary and I are going to the movies."

She picked me up in the family station wagon, and off we went to Grant Park, the epicenter of the demonstrations. It was the last night of the convention, and all hell broke loose in Grant Park. You could smell the tear gas before you saw the lines of police. In the crowd behind us, someone screamed profanities and threw a rock, which just missed us. Betsy and I scrambled to get away as the police charged the crowd with nightsticks.

The first person we ran into was a high school friend whom we hadn't seen in a while. A nursing student, she was volunteering in the first-aid tent, patching up injured protesters. She told us that what she had been seeing and doing had radicalized her, and she seriously thought there might be a revolution.

Betsy and I were shocked by the police brutality we saw in Grant Park, images also captured on national television. As Betsy later told *The Washington Post*, "We had had a wonderful childhood in Park Ridge, but we obviously hadn't gotten the whole story."

Kevin O'Keefe and I spent hours that summer arguing about the meaning of revolution and whether our country would face one. Despite the events of the last year, we both concluded there would not be one, and, even if there was, we could never participate. I knew that despite my disillusionment with politics, it was the only route in a democracy for peaceful and lasting change. I did not imagine then that I would ever run for office, but I knew I wanted to participate as both a citizen and an activist. In my mind, Dr. King and Mahatma Gandhi had done more to bring about real change through civil disobedience and nonviolence than a million demonstrators throwing rocks ever could.

My senior year at Wellesley would further test and articulate my beliefs. For my thesis, I analyzed the work of a Chicago native and community organizer named Saul Alinsky, whom I had met the previous summer. Alinsky was a colorful and controversial figure who managed to offend almost everyone during his long career. His prescription for social change required grassroots organizing that taught people to help themselves by confronting government and corporations to obtain the resources and power to improve their lives. I agreed with some of Alinsky's ideas, particularly the value of empowering people to help themselves. But we had a fundamental disagreement. He believed you could change the system only from the outside. I didn't. Later, he offered me the chance to work with him when I graduated from college, and he was disappointed that I decided instead to go to law school. Alinsky said I would be wasting my time, but my decision was an expression of my belief that the system could be changed from within. I took the law school admissions test and applied to several schools.

After I was accepted by Harvard and Yale, I couldn't make up my mind where to go until I was invited to a cocktail party at Harvard Law School. A male law student friend introduced me to a famous Harvard law professor straight out of *The Paper Chase*, saying, "This is Hillary Rodham. She's trying to decide whether to come here next year or sign up with our closest competitor." The great man gave me a cool, dismissive look and said, "Well, first of all, we don't have any close competitors. Secondly, we don't need any more women at Harvard." I was leaning toward Yale anyway, but this encounter removed any doubts about my choice.

All that remained was graduation from Wellesley, and I thought it would be uneventful, until my classmate and friend Eleanor "Eldie" Acheson decided our class needed its own speaker at graduation. I had met Eldie, the granddaughter of President Truman's Secretary of State, Dean Acheson, in a freshman political science class where we had to describe our political backgrounds. Eldie later told *The Boston Globe* that she was "shocked to find out that not just Hillary, but other very smart people, were Republican." The discovery "depressed" her, but "it did explain why they won presidential elections from time to time."

Wellesley had never had a student speaker, and President Ruth Adams was opposed to opening that door now. She was uncomfortable with the student milieu of the 1960s. I had weekly meetings with her in my capacity as President of college government, and her usual question to me was a variant of Freud's: "What do you girls want?" To be fair to her, most of us had no idea. We were trapped between an outdated past and an uncharted future. We were often irreverent, cynical and self-righteous in our assessments of adults and authority. So, when Eldie announced to President Adams that she represented a group of students who wanted a student speaker, the initial negative response was expected. Then Eldie upped the pressure by declaring that if the request was denied, she would personally lead an effort to stage a countercommencement. And, she added, she was confident her grandfather would attend. When Eldie reported that both sides were dug in, I went to see President Adams in her little house down on the shore of Lake Waban.

When I asked her, "What is the real objection?" she said, "It's never been done." I said, "Well, we could give it a try." She said, "We don't know whom they are going to ask to speak." I said, "Well, they asked me to speak." She said, "I'll think about it." President Adams finally approved.

My friends' enthusiasm about my speaking worried me because I didn't have a clue about what I could say that could fit our tumultuous four years at Wellesley and be a proper send-off into our unknown futures.

During my junior and senior years, Johanna Branson and I lived in a large suite overlooking Lake Waban, on the third floor of Davis. I spent many hours sitting on my bed looking out the window at the still lake waters, worrying about everything from relationships to faith to antiwar protests. Now, as I thought about all that my friends and I had experienced since our parents dropped off such different girls four years before, I wondered how I could ever do justice to this time we shared. Luckily, my classmates started coming by the suite to leave favorite poems and sayings; wry takes on our shared journey; suggestions for dramatic gestures. Nancy "Anne" Scheibner, a serious religion major, wrote a long poem that captured the zeitgeist. I spent hours talking to people about what they wanted me to say and hours more making sense of the disparate and conflicting advice I received.

I went out to dinner the night before graduation with a group of friends and their families and ran into Eldie Acheson and her family. When she introduced me to her grandfather, she told Dean Acheson, "This is the girl who's going to speak tomorrow," and he said, "I'm looking forward to hearing what you have to say." I felt nauseated. I still wasn't sure what I was going to say, and I hurried back to my dorm to pull an all-nighter—my last one in college.

My parents were excited about seeing their daughter graduate, but my mother had been experiencing health problems. A doctor had prescribed blood thinners, and he advised her not to travel for a while. So, regrettably, she couldn't come to my graduation, and my father wasn't keen on coming alone.

When I told my parents that I would be speaking, however, he decided he had to be there. And, in typical Hugh Rodham fashion, he flew to Boston late the night before, stayed out by the airport, took the MTA to campus, attended graduation, came to the Wellesley Inn for lunch with some of my friends and their families and then went right back home. All that mattered to me was that he made it to my graduation, which helped diminish the disappointment I felt over my mother's absence. In many ways, this moment was as much hers as mine.

The morning of our graduation, May 31, 1969, was a perfect New England day. We gathered in the Academic Quadrangle for the commencement ceremony on the lawn between the library and the chapel. President Adams asked me what I was going to say, and I told her it was still percolating. She introduced me to Senator Edward Brooke, our official commencement speaker and the Senate's only African American member, for whom I had campaigned in 1966 when I was still a Young Republican. After staying up all night trying to piece a speech together from a communally written text, I was having a particularly bad hair day, made worse by the mortarboard perching on top. The pictures of me that day are truly scary.

Senator Brooke's speech acknowledged that our "country has profound and pressing social problems on its agenda" and that "it needs the best energies of all its citizens, especially its gifted young people to remedy these ills." He also argued against what he called "coercive protest." At the time, the speech sounded like a defense of President Nixon's policies, notable more for what it didn't say than what it did. I listened in vain for an acknowledgment of the legitimate grievances and painful questions so many young Americans had about our country's direction. I waited for some mention of Vietnam or civil rights or of Dr. King or Senator Kennedy, two of our generation's fallen heroes. The Senator seemed out of touch with his audience: four hundred smart, aware, questioning young women. His words were aimed at a different Wellesley, one that predated the upheavals of the 1960s.

I thought how prescient Eldie had been to know that a predictable speech like this one would be such a letdown after the four years we, and America, had experienced. So I took a deep breath and began by defending the "indispensable task of criticizing and constructive protest." Paraphrasing Anne Scheibner's poem, which I quoted at the end, I stated that "the challenge now is to practice politics as the art of making what appears to be impossible, possible."

I spoke about the awareness of the gap between the expectations my class brought to college and the reality we experienced. Most of us had come from sheltered backgrounds, and the personal and public events we encountered caused us to question the authenticity, even the reality, of our pre-college lives. Our four years had been a rite of passage different from the experiences of our parents' generation, which had faced greater external challenges like the Depression and World War II. So we started asking questions, first about Wellesley's policies, then about the meaning of a liberal arts education, then about civil rights, women's roles, Vietnam. I defended protest as "an attempt to forge an identity in this particular age" and as a way of "coming to terms with our humanness." It was part of the "unique American experience" and "if the experiment in human living doesn't work in this country, in this age, it's not going to work anywhere."

When I had asked the class at our graduation rehearsal what they wanted me to say for them, everyone answered, "Talk about trust, talk about the lack of trust both for us and the way we feel about others. Talk about the trust bust." I acknowledged how hard it was to convey a feeling that permeates a generation.

And, finally, I spoke of the struggle to establish a "mutuality of respect between people." Running throughout my words, however, was an acknowledgment of the fears many of us felt about the future. I referred to a conversation from the previous day with a classmate's mother "who said that she wouldn't want to be me for anything in the world. She wouldn't want to live today and look ahead to what it is she sees because she's afraid." I said, "Fear is always with us, but we just don't have time for it. Not now."

The speech was, as I admitted, an attempt to "come to grasp with some of the inarticulate, maybe even inarticulable things that we're feeling" as we are "exploring a world that none of us understands and attempting to create within that uncertainty." This speech may not have been the most coherent one I have ever delivered, but it struck a chord with my class, which gave me an enthusiastic standing ovation, partly, I believe, because my efforts to make sense of our time and place—played out on a stage in front of two thousand spectators—

reflected the countless conversations, questions, doubts and hopes each of us brought to that moment, not just as Wellesley graduates, but also as women and Americans whose lives would exemplify the changes and choices facing our generation at the end of the twentieth century.

Later that afternoon, I took one last swim in Lake Waban. Instead of going to the little beach by the boathouse, I decided to wade in near my dorm, an area officially off-limits to swimming. I stripped down to my bathing suit and left my cut-off jeans and T-shirt in a pile on the shore with my aviator-like eyeglasses on top. I didn't have a care in the world as I swam out toward the middle, and because of my nearsightedness, my surroundings looked like an Impressionist painting. I had loved being at Wellesley and had taken great solace in all seasons from its natural beauty. The swim was a final good-bye. When I got back to shore, I couldn't find my clothes or my glasses.

I finally had to ask a campus security officer if he had seen my belongings. He told me that President Adams had seen me swimming from her house and directed him to confiscate them. Apparently, she was sorry she had ever let me speak. Dripping wet, I followed him, somewhat blindly, to retrieve my possessions.

I had no idea that my speech would generate interest far beyond Wellesley. I had only hoped that my friends thought I had been true to their hopes, and their positive reaction heartened me. When I called home, however, my mother told me that she had been fielding phone calls from reporters and television shows asking me for interviews and appearances. I appeared on Irv Kupcinet's interview show on a local Chicago channel, and *Life* magazine featured me and a student activist named Ira Magaziner, who addressed his graduating class at Brown University. My mother reported that opinion about my speech seemed to be divided between the overly effusive—"she spoke for a generation"—to the exceedingly negative—"who does she think she is?" The accolades and attacks turned out to be a preview of things to come: I have never been as good as or as bad as my most fervid supporters and opponents claimed.

With a big sigh of relief, I took off for a summer of working my way across Alaska, washing dishes in Mt. McKinley National Park (now known as Denali National Park and Preserve) and sliming fish in Valdez in a temporary salmon factory on a pier. My job required me to wear knee-high boots and stand in bloody water while removing guts from the salmon with a spoon. When I didn't slime fast enough, the supervisors yelled at me to speed up. Then I was moved to the assembly packing line, where I helped pack the salmon in boxes for shipping to the large floating processing plant offshore. I noticed that some of the fish looked bad. When I told the manager, he fired me and told me to come back the next afternoon to pick up my last check. When I showed up, the entire operation was gone. During a visit to Alaska when I was First Lady, I joked to an audience that of all the jobs I've had, sliming fish was pretty good preparation for life in Washington.

YALE

WHEN I ENTERED YALE LAW SCHOOL IN THE FALL of 1969, I was one of twenty-seven women out of 235 students to matriculate. This seems like a paltry number now, but it was a breakthrough at the time and meant that women would no longer be token students at Yale. While women's rights appeared to be gaining some traction as the 1960s skittered to an end, everything else seemed out of kilter and uncertain. Unless you lived through those times, it is hard to imagine how polarized America's political landscape had become.

Professor Charles Reich, who became best known to the general public for his book *The Greening of America*, was camping out with some students in a shantytown in the middle of the law school's courtyard, to protest the "establishment," which, of course, included Yale Law School. The shantytown lasted a few weeks before being peacefully disassembled. Other protests, however, were not so peaceful. The decade of the 1960s that had begun with so much hope ended in a convulsion of protest and violence. White, middle-class anti-war activists were found plotting to build bombs in their basements. The non-violent, largely black civil rights movement splintered into factions, and new voices emerged among urban blacks belonging to the Black Muslims and Black Panther Party. J. Edgar Hoover's FBI infiltrated dissident groups and, in some cases, broke the law in order to disrupt them. Law enforcement sometimes failed to distinguish between constitutionally protected, legitimate opposition and criminal behavior. As domestic spying and counterintelligence operations expanded under the Nixon Administration, it seemed, at times, that our government was at war with its own people.

Yale Law School historically attracted students interested in public service and our conversations inside and outside the classroom reflected a deep concern about the events enveloping the country. Yale also encouraged its students to get out in the world and apply the theories they learned in the classroom. That world and its realities came crashing down on Yale in April 1970, when eight Black Panthers, including party leader Bobby Seale, were put on trial for murder in New Haven. Thousands of angry protesters, convinced the Panthers had been set up by the FBI and government prosecutors, swarmed into the city. Demonstrations broke out in and around campus. The campus was bracing for a huge May Day rally to support the Panthers when I learned, late on the night of April 27, that the International Law Library, which was in the basement of the law school, was on fire. Horrified, I rushed to join a bucket brigade of faculty, staff and students to put out the fire and to rescue books damaged by flames and water. After the fire was out, the law school's Dean, Louis Pollak, asked everyone to gather in the largest classroom. Dean Pollak, a gentleman scholar with a ready smile and an open door, asked us to organize round-the-clock security patrols for the remainder of the school year.

On April 30, President Nixon announced that he was sending U.S. troops into Cambodia, expanding the Vietnam War. The May Day protests became a larger demonstration, not only to support a fair trial for the Panthers, but also to oppose Nixon's actions in the war. Throughout the era of student protests, Yale's President, Kingman Brewster, and the university chaplain, William Sloane Coffin, had taken a conciliatory approach, which helped Yale avoid the problems occurring elsewhere. Rev. Coffin became a national leader of the anti-war movement through his articulate moral critique of American involvement. President Brewster addressed student concerns and appreciated the anguish felt by many. He had even said he was "skeptical of the ability of black revolutionaries" to achieve a fair trial anywhere in the United States. Faced with the prospect of violent demonstrators, Brewster suspended classes and announced that the dorms would be open to serve meals to anyone who came. His actions and statements inflamed alumni, as well as President Nixon and Vice President Spiro Agnew.

Then, on May 4, National Guard troops opened fire on students protesting at Kent State University in Ohio. Four students were killed. The photograph of a young woman kneeling over the body of a dead student represented all that I and many others feared and hated about what was happening in our country. I remember rushing out the door of the law school in tears and running into Professor Fritz Kessler, a refugee who fled Hitler's Germany. He asked me what the matter was and I told him I couldn't believe what was happening; he chilled me by saying that, for him, it was all too familiar.

True to my upbringing, I advocated engagement, not disruption or "revolution." On May 7, I kept a previously planned obligation to speak at the convention banquet of the fiftieth anniversary of the League of Women Voters in Washington, D.C., an invitation stemming from my college commencement address. I wore a black armband in memory of the students who had been killed. My emotions, once again, were close to the surface as I argued that the extension of America's Vietnam War into Cambodia was illegal and unconstitutional. I tried to explain the context in which protests occurred and the impact that the Kent State shootings had on Yale law students, who had voted 239–12 to join more than three hundred schools in a national strike to protest "the unconscionable expansion of a war that should never have been waged." I had moderated the mass meeting where the vote took place, and I knew how seriously my fellow students took both the law and their responsibilities as citizens. The law students, who had not previously joined other parts of the university in protest actions, debated the issues in a thoughtful, albeit lawyerly, fashion. They were not the "bums" that Nixon labeled all student protesters.

The keynote speaker at the League convention was Marian Wright Edelman, whose example helped direct me into my lifelong advocacy for children. Marian had graduated from Yale Law School in 1963 and became the first black woman admitted to the bar in Mississippi. She spent the mid-sixties running the NAACP Legal Defense and Educational Fund office in Jackson, traveling throughout the state setting up Head Start programs and risking her neck to advance civil rights in the South. I had first heard about Marian from her husband, Peter Edelman, a Harvard Law School graduate who had clerked on the Supreme Court for Arthur J. Goldberg and had worked for Bobby Kennedy. Peter had accompanied Senator Kennedy to Mississippi in 1967 on a fact-finding trip to expose the extent of poverty and hunger in the Deep South. Marian was one of the Senator's guides for his travels around Mississippi. After that trip, Marian continued working with Peter, and after Senator Kennedy's assassination, they married.

I first met Peter Edelman at a national conference on youth and community development held in October of 1969 at Colorado State

University in Fort Collins, Colorado, and sponsored by the League. The League had invited a cross section of activists from around the country to discuss ways in which young people could become more positively involved in government and politics. I was invited to serve on the Steering Committee along with Peter, who was then the Associate Director of the Robert F. Kennedy Memorial; David Mixner, of the Vietnam Moratorium Committee; and Martin Slate, a fellow Yale law student who had been a friend of mine from the days he was at Harvard and I was at Wellesley. One of the issues that united us was our belief that the Constitution should be amended to lower the voting age from twenty-one to eighteen. If young people were old enough to fight, they were entitled to vote. The 26th Amendment finally passed in 1971, but young people between the ages of eighteen and twenty-four did not choose to vote in the numbers many of us then anticipated, and that group today still has the lowest registration and voter turnout of any age group. Their apathy makes it less likely that our national politics will reflect their concerns and safeguard their future.

During a break in the conference, I was sitting on a bench talking with Peter Edelman when our conversation was interrupted by a tall, elegantly dressed man.

"Well, Peter, aren't you going to introduce me to this earnest young lady?" he asked. That was my first encounter with Vernon Jordan, then the Director of the Voter Education Project of the Southern Regional Council in Atlanta and an advocate of the lower voting age. Vernon, a smart and charismatic veteran lawyer of the civil rights movement, became my friend that day, and later, my husband's. He and his accomplished wife, Ann, can always be counted on for good company and wise counsel.

Peter told me about Marian's plans to start an anti-poverty advocacy organization and urged me to meet her as soon as I could. A few months later, Marian spoke at Yale. I introduced myself to her afterwards and asked for a summer job. She told me I could have a job, but she couldn't pay me. That was a problem since I had to earn enough money to supplement the scholarship Wellesley had awarded me for law school and the loans I had taken out. The Law Student Civil Rights Research Council gave me a grant, which I used to support my work during the summer of 1970 at the Washington Research Project Marian had started in Washington, D.C.

Senator Walter "Fritz" Mondale of Minnesota, later Vice President under Jimmy Carter, decided to hold Senate hearings to investigate the living and working conditions of migrant farmworkers. The 1970 hearings coincided with the ten-year anniversary of Edward R. Murrow's famous television documentary *Harvest of Shame*, which had shocked Americans in 1960 with its exposé of the deplorable treatment migrants endured. Marian assigned me to do research on the education and health of migrant children. I had some limited experience with migrant children who had attended my elementary school for a few months each year and with others my church had arranged for me to baby-sit when I was about fourteen years old. Every Saturday morning during harvest season, I went with several of my Sunday school friends to the migrant camp, where we took care of the children under ten while their older brothers and sisters worked in the fields with their parents.

I got to know one seven-year-old girl, Maria, who was preparing to receive her First Communion when her family returned to Mexico at the end of the harvest. But she wouldn't be able to mark that passage unless her family saved enough money to buy her a proper white dress. I told my mother about Maria, and she took me to buy a beautiful dress. When we presented it to Maria's mother, she started crying and dropped to her knees to kiss my mother's hands. My embarrassed mother kept saying she knew how important it was for a little girl to feel special on such an occasion. Years later, I realized that my mother must have identified with Maria.

Although these children lived harsh lives, they were bright, hopeful and loved by their parents. The children dropped whatever they were doing to run down the road when their families came home from the fields. Fathers would scoop up excited kids, and mothers would bend over to hug toddlers. It was just like my neighborhood when fathers came home from the city after work.

But as I conducted my research, I learned how often farmworkers and their children were—and still too often are—deprived of basics like decent housing and sanitation. Cesar Chavez started the National Farm Workers Association in 1962, organizing workers in the California fields, but conditions in most of the rest of the country hadn't changed much since 1960.

The hearings I attended in July 1970 were part of a series the Senate Committee had been holding to take testimony and evidence from farmworkers, advocates and employers. Witnesses presented evidence that some corporations owned large farms in Florida where migrants were treated as badly as they had been a decade before. Several students I knew from Yale attended on behalf of the corporate clients of the law firms they were working for as summer associates. The students told me they were learning how to rehabilitate a corporate client's tarnished image. I suggested that the best way to do that would be to improve the treatment of their farmworkers.

When I returned to Yale for my second year in the fall of 1970, I decided to concentrate on how the law affected children. Historically, children's rights and needs were covered in family law and usually defined by whatever their parents decided, with some notable exceptions, like the right of a child to receive necessary medical treatment even over the religious objections of his or her parents. But starting in the 1960s, courts began finding other circumstances in which children had, to a limited extent, rights separate from their parents.

Two of my law school professors, Jay Katz and Joe Goldstein, encouraged my interest in this new area and suggested that I learn more about child development through a course of study at the Yale Child Study Center. They sent me to meet the Center's Director, Dr. Al Solnit, and its chief clinician, Dr. Sally Provence. I persuaded them to let me spend a year at the Center attending case discussions and observing clinical sessions. Dr. Solnit and Professor Goldstein asked me to serve as their research assistant for *Beyond the Best Interests of the Child*, a book they were writing with Anna Freud, Sigmund's daughter. I also began consulting with the medical staff at Yale-New Haven Hospital about the newly acknowledged problem of child abuse and helping to draft the legal procedures for the hospital to use when dealing with suspected child abuse cases.

These activities went hand-in-hand with my assignments at the New Haven Legal Services office. A young legal aid lawyer, Penn Rhodeen, taught me how important it was for children to have their own advocates in situations involving abuse and neglect. Penn asked me to assist him in representing an African American woman in her fifties who had served as a foster mother for a two-year-old mixed-race girl since the child's birth. This woman had already raised her own children and wanted to adopt the little girl. The Connecticut Department of Social Services, however, followed its policy that foster parents were not eligible to adopt and removed the girl from the woman's care and placed her with a more "suitable" family. Penn sued the bureaucracy, arguing that the foster mother was the only mother the little girl had ever known and that removing her would inflict lasting damage. Despite our best efforts, we lost the case, but it spurred me to look for ways that children's developmental needs and rights could be recognized within the legal system. I realized that what I wanted to do with the law was to give voice to children who were not being heard.

My first scholarly article, titled "Children Under the Law," was published in 1974 in the *Harvard Educational Review*. It explores the difficult decisions the judiciary and society face when children are abused or neglected by their families or when parental decisions have potentially irreparable consequences, such as denying a child medical care or the right to continue school. My views were shaped by what I had observed as a volunteer for Legal Services representing children in foster care and by my experiences at the Child Study Center in Yale-New Haven Hospital; I advised doctors on their rounds as they tried to ascertain whether a child's injuries were the result of abuse and, if so, whether a child should be removed from his or her family and put into the uncertain care of the child welfare system. These were terrible decisions to make. I come from a strong family and believe in a parent's natural presumptive right to raise his or her child as he or she sees fit. But my experiences in Yale-New Haven Hospital were a long way from my sheltered suburban upbringing.

There may have been child abuse and domestic violence in Park Ridge, but I didn't see it. In New Haven, by contrast, I saw children whose parents beat and burned them; who left them alone for days in squalid apartments; who failed and refused to seek necessary medical care. The sad truth, I learned, was that certain parents abdicated their rights as parents, and someone—preferably another family member, but ultimately the state—had to step in to give a child the chance for a permanent and loving home.

I thought often of my own mother's neglect and mistreatment at the hands of her parents and grandparents, and how other caring adults filled the emotional void to help her. My mother tried to repay the favor by taking in girls from a local group home to assist her around our house. She wanted to give them the same chance she had been given to see an intact supportive family in action.

Who would have predicted that during the 1992 presidential campaign, nearly two decades after I wrote the article, conservative Republicans like Marilyn Quayle and Pat Buchanan would twist my words to portray me as "anti-family"? Some commentators actually claimed that

I wanted children to be able to sue their parents if they were told to take out the garbage. I couldn't foresee the later misinterpretation of my paper; nor could I have predicted the circumstances that would motivate the Republicans to denounce me. And I certainly didn't know that I was about to meet the person who would cause my life to spin in directions that I could never have imagined.

BILL CLINTON

BILL CLINTON WAS HARD TO MISS IN THE AUTUMN OF 1970. He arrived at Yale Law School looking more like a Viking than a Rhodes Scholar returning from two years at Oxford. He was tall and handsome somewhere beneath that reddish brown beard and curly mane of hair. He also had a vitality that seemed to shoot out of his pores. When I first saw him in the law school's student lounge, he was holding forth before a rapt audience of fellow students. As I walked by, I heard him say: ". . . and not only that, we grow the biggest watermelons in the world!" I asked a friend, "Who *is* that?"

"Oh, that's Bill Clinton," he said. "He's from Arkansas, and that's all he ever talks about."

We would run into each other around campus, but we never actually met until one night at the Yale law library the following spring. I was studying in the library, and Bill was standing out in the hall talking to another student, Jeff Gleckel, who was trying to persuade Bill to write for the *Yale Law Journal*. I noticed that he kept looking over at me. He had been doing a lot of that. So I stood up from the desk, walked over to him and said, "If you're going to keep looking at me, and I'm going to keep looking back, we might as well be introduced. I'm Hillary Rodham." That was it. The way Bill tells the story, he couldn't remember his own name.

We didn't talk to each other again until the last day of classes in the spring of 1971. We happened to walk out of Professor Thomas Emerson's Political and Civil Rights course at the same time. Bill asked me where I was going. I was on the way to the registrar's office to sign up for the next semester's classes. He told me he was heading there too. As we walked, he complimented my long flower-patterned skirt. When

I told him that my mother had made it, he asked about my family and where I had grown up. We waited in line until we got to the registrar. She looked up and said, "Bill, what are you doing here? You've already registered." I laughed when he confessed that he just wanted to spend time with me, and we went for a long walk that turned into our first date.

We both had wanted to see a Mark Rothko exhibit at the Yale Art Gallery but, because of a labor dispute, some of the university's buildings, including the museum, were closed. As Bill and I walked by, he decided he could get us in if we offered to pick up the litter that had accumulated in the gallery's courtyard. Watching him talk our way in was the first time I saw his persuasiveness in action. We had the entire museum to ourselves. We wandered through the galleries talking about Rothko and twentieth-century art. I admit to being surprised at his interest in and knowledge of subjects that seemed, at first, unusual for a Viking from Arkansas. We ended up in the museum's courtyard, where I sat in the large lap of Henry Moore's sculpture *Draped Seated Woman* while we talked until dark. I invited Bill to the party my roommate, Kwan Kwan Tan, and I were throwing in our dorm room that night to celebrate the end of classes. Kwan Kwan, an ethnic Chinese who had come from Burma to Yale to pursue graduate legal studies, was a delightful living companion and a graceful performer of Burmese dance. She and her husband, Bill Wang, another student, remain friends.

Bill came to our party but hardly said a word. Since I didn't know him that well, I thought he must be shy, perhaps not very socially adept or just uncomfortable. I didn't have much hope for us as a couple. Besides, I had a boyfriend at the time, and we had weekend plans out of town. When I came back to Yale late Sunday, Bill called and heard me coughing and hacking from the bad cold I had picked up.

"You sound terrible," he said. About thirty minutes later, he knocked on my door, bearing chicken soup and orange juice. He came in, and he started talking. He could converse about anything—from African politics to country and western music. I asked him why he had been so quiet at my party.

"Because I was interested in learning more about you and your friends," he replied.

I was starting to realize that this young man from Arkansas was much more complex than first impressions might suggest. To this day, he can astonish me with the connections he weaves between ideas and words and how he makes it all sound like music. I still love the way he thinks and the way he looks. One of the first things I noticed about Bill was the shape of his hands. His wrists are narrow and his fingers tapered and deft, like those of a pianist or a surgeon. When we first met as students, I loved watching him turn the pages of a book. Now his hands are showing signs of age after thousands of handshakes and golf swings and miles of signatures. They are, like their owner, weathered but still expressive, attractive and resilient.

Soon after Bill came to my rescue with chicken soup and orange juice, we became inseparable. In between cramming for finals and finishing up my first year of concentration on children, we spent long hours driving around in his 1970 burnt-orange Opel station wagon—truly one of the ugliest cars ever manufactured—or hanging out at the beach house on Long Island Sound near Milford, Connecticut, where he lived with his roommates, Doug Eakeley, Don Pogue and Bill Coleman. At a party there one night, Bill and I ended up in the kitchen talking about what each of us wanted to do after graduation. I still didn't know where I would live and what I would do because my interests in child advocacy and civil rights didn't dictate a particular path. Bill was absolutely certain: He would go home to Arkansas and run for public office. A lot of my classmates said they intended to pursue public service, but Bill was the only one who you knew for certain would actually do it.

I told Bill about my summer plans to clerk at Treuhaft, Walker and Burnstein, a small law firm in Oakland, California, and he announced that he would like to go to California with me. I was astonished. I knew he had signed on to work in Senator George McGovern's presidential campaign and that the campaign manager, Gary Hart, had asked Bill to organize the South for McGovern. The prospect of driving from one Southern state to another convincing Democrats both to support McGovern and to oppose Nixon's policy in Vietnam excited him. Although Bill had worked in Arkansas on campaigns for Senator J. William Fulbright and others, and in Connecticut for Joe Duffey and Joe Lieberman, he'd never had the chance to be in on the ground floor of a presidential campaign.

I tried to let the news sink in. I was thrilled.

"Why," I asked, "do you want to give up the opportunity to do something you love to follow me to California?"

"For someone I love, that's why," he said.

He had decided, he told me, that we were destined for each other, and he didn't want to let me go just after he'd found me.

Bill and I shared a small apartment near a big park not far from the University of California at Berkeley campus where the Free Speech Movement started in 1964. I spent most of my time working for Mal Burnstein researching, writing legal motions and briefs for a child custody case. Meanwhile, Bill explored Berkeley, Oakland and San Francisco. On weekends, he took me to the places he had scouted, like a restaurant in North Beach or a vintage clothing store on Telegraph Avenue. I tried teaching him tennis, and we both experimented with cooking. I baked him a peach pie, something I associated with Arkansas, although I had yet to visit the state, and together we produced a palatable chicken curry for any and all occasions we hosted. Bill spent most of his time reading and then sharing with me his thoughts about books like *To the Finland Station* by Edmund Wilson. During our long walks, he often broke into song, frequently crooning one of his Elvis Presley favorites.

People have said that I knew Bill would be President one day and went around telling anyone who would listen. I don't remember thinking that until years later, but I had one strange encounter at a small restaurant in Berkeley. I was supposed to meet Bill, but I was held up at work and arrived late. There was no sign of him, and I asked the waiter if he had seen a man of his description. A customer sitting nearby spoke up, saying, "He was here for a long time reading, and I started talking to him about books. I don't know his name, but he's going to be President someday." "Yeah, right," I said, "but do you know where he went?"

At the end of the summer, we returned to New Haven and rented the ground floor of 21 Edgewood Avenue for seventy-five dollars a month. That bought us a living room with a fireplace, one small bedroom, a third room that served as both study and dining area, a tiny bathroom and a primitive kitchen. The floors were so uneven that plates would slide off the dining table if we didn't keep little wooden blocks under the table legs to level them. The wind howled through cracks in the walls that we stuffed with newspapers. But despite it all, I loved our first house. We shopped for furniture at the Goodwill and Salvation Army stores and were quite proud of our student decor.

Our apartment was a block away from the Elm Street Diner, which we frequented because it was open all night. The local Y down the street had a yoga class that I joined, and Bill agreed to take with me—as long as I didn't tell anybody else. He also came along to the Cathedral of Sweat, Yale's gothic sports center, to run mindlessly around the mezzanine track. Once he started running, he kept going. I didn't.

We ate often at Basel's, a favorite Greek restaurant, and loved going to the movies at the Lincoln, a small theater set back on a residential street. One evening after a blizzard finally stopped, we decided to go to the movies. The roads were not yet cleared, so we walked there and back through the foot-high snowdrifts, feeling very much alive and in love.

We both had to work to pay our way through law school, on top of the student loans we had taken out. But we still found time for politics. Bill decided to open a McGovern for President headquarters in New Haven, using his own money to rent a storefront. Most of the volunteers were Yale students and faculty because the boss of the local Democratic Party, Arthur Barbieri, was not supporting McGovern. Bill arranged for us to meet Mr. Barbieri at an Italian restaurant. At a long lunch, Bill claimed he had eight hundred volunteers ready to hit the streets to out-organize the regular party apparatus. Barbieri eventually decided to endorse McGovern. He invited us to attend the party meeting at a local Italian club, Melebus Club, where he would announce his endorsement.

The next week, we drove to a nondescript building and entered a door leading to a set of stairs that went down to a series of underground rooms. When Barbieri stood up to speak in the big dining room, he commanded the attention of the local county committee members—mostly men—who were there. He started by talking about the war in Vietnam and naming the boys from the New Haven area who were serving in the military and those who had died. Then he said, "This war isn't worth losing one more boy for. That's why we should support George McGovern, who wants to bring our boys home." This was not an immediately popular position, but as the night wore on, he pressed his case until he got a unanimous vote of support. And he delivered on his commitment, first at the state convention and then in the election, when New Haven was one of the few places in America that voted for McGovern over Nixon.

After Christmas, Bill drove up from Hot Springs to Park Ridge to spend a few days with my family. Both my parents had met him the previous summer, but I was nervous because my dad was so uninhibited in his criticism of my boyfriends. I wondered what he would say to a

Southern Democrat with Elvis sideburns. My mother had told me that in my father's eyes, no man would be good enough for me. She appreciated Bill's good manners and willingness to help with the dishes. But Bill really won her over when he found her reading a philosophy book from one of her college courses and spent the next hour or so discussing it with her. It was slow going at first with my father, but he warmed up over games of cards, and in front of the television watching football bowl games. My brothers basked in Bill's attention. My friends liked him too. After I introduced him to Betsy Johnson, her mother, Roslyn, cornered me on the way out of their house and said, "I don't care what you do, but don't let this one go. He's the only one I've ever seen make you laugh!"

After school ended in the spring of 1972, I returned to Washington to work again for Marian Wright Edelman. Bill took a full-time job with the McGovern campaign.

My primary assignment in the summer of 1972 was to gather information about the Nixon Administration's failure to enforce the legal ban on granting tax-exempt status to the private segregated academies that had sprung up in the South to avoid integrated public schools. The academies claimed they were created simply in response to parents deciding to form private schools; it had nothing to do with court-ordered integration of the public schools. I went to Atlanta to meet with the lawyers and civil rights workers who were compiling evidence that, on the contrary, proved the academies were created solely for the purpose of avoiding the constitutional mandate of the Supreme Court's decisions, starting with *Brown* v. *Board of Education*.

As part of my investigation, I drove to Dothan, Alabama, for the purpose of posing as a young mother moving to the area, interested in enrolling my child in the local all-white academy. I stopped first in the "black" section of Dothan to have lunch with our local contacts. Over burgers and sweetened iced tea, they told me that many of the school districts in the area were draining local public schools of books and equipment to send to the so-called academies, which they viewed as the alternatives for white students. At a local private school, I had an appointment to meet an administrator to discuss enrolling my imaginary child. I went through my role-playing, asking questions about the curriculum and makeup of the student body. I was assured that no black students would be enrolled.

While I was challenging discrimination practices, Bill was in Miami working to ensure McGovern's nomination at the Democratic Convention on July 13, 1972. After the convention, Gary Hart asked Bill to go to Texas, along with Taylor Branch, then a young writer, to join a local Houston lawyer, Julius Glickman, in a triumvirate to run the McGovern campaign in that state. Bill asked me if I wanted to go too. I did, but only if I had a specific job. Anne Wexler, a veteran campaigner I knew from Connecticut, then working on behalf of McGovern, offered me a job heading up the voter registration drive in Texas. I jumped at the chance. Although Bill was the only person I knew when I got to Austin, Texas, in August, I quickly made some of the best friends I've ever had.

In 1972, Austin was still a sleepy town compared to Dallas or Houston. It was, to be sure, the state capital and the home of the University of Texas, but it seemed more typical of the past than of the future of Texas. It would have been hard to predict the explosive growth of high-technology companies that transformed the little city in the Texas hill country into a Sunbelt boomtown.

The McGovern campaign set up shop in an empty storefront on West Sixth Street. I had a small cubicle that I rarely occupied because I spent most of my time in the field, trying to register the newly enfranchised eighteen- to twenty-one-year-olds and driving around South Texas working to register black and Hispanic voters. Roy Spence, Garry Mauro and Judy Trabulsi, all of whom stayed active in Texas politics and played a part in the 1992 presidential campaign, became the backbone of our young voter outreach efforts. They thought they could register every eighteen-year-old in Texas, which would, in their minds, turn the electoral tide McGovern's way. They also liked to have fun and introduced me to Scholz's Beer Garden, where we would sit outside at the end of eighteen- or twenty-hour days trying to figure out what else we could do in the face of ever-worsening poll numbers.

Hispanics in South Texas were, understandably, wary of a blond girl from Chicago who didn't speak a word of Spanish. I found allies at the universities, among organized labor, and lawyers with the South Texas Rural Legal Aid Association. One of my guides along the border was Franklin Garcia, a battle-hardened union organizer, who took me places I could never have gone alone and vouched for me to Mexican Americans who worried I might be from the immigration service or some other government agency. One night when Bill was in Brownsville meeting with Democratic Party leaders, Franklin and I picked him up and drove over the border to Matamoros, where Franklin promised a meal we'd never forget. We found ourselves in a local dive that had a decent mariachi band and served the best—the only—barbecued *cabrito*, or goat head, I had ever eaten. Bill fell asleep at the table while I ate as fast as digestion and politeness permitted.

Betsey Wright, who had previously been active in the Texas State Democratic Party and had been working for Common Cause, came over to work in the campaign. Betsey grew up in West Texas and graduated from the university in Austin. A superb political organizer, she had been all over the state, and she didn't disguise what we'd pretty much figured out—that the McGovern campaign was doomed. Even Senator McGovern's stellar war record as an Air Force bomber pilot, later commemorated in Stephen Ambrose's book *The Wild Blue*, which should have given his anti-war position credibility in Texas, was buried under the incoming attacks from Republicans and missteps by his own campaign. When McGovern picked Sargent Shriver to succeed Senator Thomas Eagleton as his Vice Presidential nominee, we hoped both Shriver's work under President Kennedy and his Kennedy family connection through Jack and Bobby Kennedy's sister Eunice might revive interest.

When the period for voter registration ended thirty days before the election, Betsey asked me to help run the campaign in San Antonio for the last month. I stayed with a college friend and dove into the sights, sounds, smells and food of that beautiful city. I ate Mexican food three times a day, usually at Mario's out on the highway or at Mi Tierra downtown.

When you run a presidential campaign in a state or city, you're always trying to persuade national headquarters to send in the candidates or other top-level surrogates. Shirley MacLaine was the best-known supporter we had coaxed to San Antonio until the campaign announced that McGovern would fly in for a rally in front of the Alamo, a symbolic backdrop. For more than a week, all our efforts were focused on turning out as big a crowd as possible. That experience made me realize how important it is for the staff from campaign headquarters to respect the local people. Campaigns send in advance staff to plan the logistics of a candidate's visit. This was my first time to see an advance team in action. I learned that they operated under tremendous stress, wanted all the essentials—phones, copiers, a stage, chairs, sound system—to appear yesterday, and that in a tight or a losing race, somebody has to be responsible for paying the bills. Every time the advance team ordered something, they'd tell me the money to pay for it would be wired down immediately. But the money never appeared. On the night of the big event, McGovern did a great job. We raised just enough money to pay the local vendors, which turned out to be the only successful venture during my month-long sojourn.

My partner in all this was Sara Ehrman, a member of Senator Mc-Govern's legislative staff who had taken a leave to work on the campaign and later moved to Texas to organize field operations. A political veteran with an effervescent wit, Sara was the embodiment of both maternal warmth and bare-knuckled activism. She never minced words or parsed her opinions, no matter her audience. And she had the energy and spunk of a woman half her age—and still does. She had been running the San Antonio campaign when I walked in one October day and told her I was there to help. We sized each other up and decided we would enjoy the ride together, and it was the start of a friendship that endures today.

It was obvious to all of us that Nixon was going to trounce McGovern in the November election. But, as we soon would learn, this didn't deter Nixon and his operatives from illegally using campaign funds (not to mention official government agencies) to spy on the opposition and finance dirty tricks to help ensure a Republican victory. A botched break-in at Democratic Committee offices at the Watergate complex on June 17, 1972, would lead to the downfall of Richard Nixon. It would also figure in my future plans.

Before returning to our classes at Yale, for which we were enrolled but had not yet attended, Bill and I took our first vacation together to Zihuatanejo, Mexico, then a sleepy little charmer of a town on the Pacific Coast. Between swims in the surf, we spent our time rehashing the election and the failings of the McGovern campaign, a critique that continued for months. So much had gone wrong, including the flawed Democratic National Convention. Among other tactical errors, Mc-Govern arrived at the podium for his acceptance speech in the middle of the night, when no one in the country was awake, let alone watching a political convention on television. Looking back on our McGovern experience, Bill and I realized we still had much to learn about the art of political campaigning and the power of television. That 1972 race was our first rite of political passage.

After completing law school in the spring of 1973, Bill took me on my first trip to Europe to revisit his haunts as a Rhodes Scholar. We landed in London, and Bill proved himself to be a great guide. We spent hours touring Westminster Abbey, the Tate Gallery and Parliament. We walked around Stonehenge and marveled at the greener-than-green hills of Wales. We set out to visit as many cathedrals as we could, aided by a book of meticulously charted walking maps covering a square mile of countryside per page. We meandered from Salisbury to Lincoln to Durham to York, pausing to explore the ruins of a monastery laid waste by Cromwell's troops or wandering through the gardens of a great country estate.

Then at twilight in the beautiful Lake District of England, we found ourselves on the shores of Lake Ennerdale, where Bill asked me to marry him.

I was desperately in love with him but utterly confused about my life and future. So I said, "No, not now." What I meant was, "Give me time."

My mother had suffered from her parents' divorce, and her sad and lonely childhood was imprinted on my heart. I knew that when I decided to marry, I wanted it to be for life. Looking back to that time and to the person I was, I realize how scared I was of commitment in general and of Bill's intensity in particular. I thought of him as a force of nature and wondered whether I'd be up to the task of living through his seasons.

Bill Clinton is nothing if not persistent. He sets goals, and I was one of them. He asked me to marry him again, and again, and I always said no. Eventually he said, "Well, I'm not going to ask you to marry me any more, and if you ever decide you want to marry me then you have to tell me." He would wait me out.

ARKANSAS TRAVELER

Soon after we returned from Europe, Bill offered to take me on another journey—this time to the place he called home.

Bill picked me up at the airport in Little Rock on a bright summer morning in late June. He drove me down streets lined with Victorian houses, past the Governor's Mansion and the State Capitol, built to resemble the Capitol building in Washington. We made our way through the Arkansas River Valley with its low-slung magnolia trees, and into the Ouachita Mountains, stopping at overlooks and dropping by country stores so Bill could introduce me to the people and places he loved. As dusk fell, we arrived, at last, in Hot Springs, Arkansas.

When Bill and I first met, he spent hours telling me about Hot Springs, founded around the hot sulfur springs that Indians had bathed in for centuries and that Hernando de Soto had "discovered" in 1541, believing them to be the fountain of youth. The thoroughbred racetrack and illegal gambling had attracted visitors like Babe Ruth, Al Capone and Minnesota Fats. When Bill was growing up, a lot of the restaurants in town had slot machines, and the nightclubs featured the famous entertainers of the 1950s—Peggy Lee, Tony Bennett, Liberace and Patti Page. Attorney General Robert Kennedy shut down the illegal gambling operations, which slowed business for the big hotels, restaurants and bathhouses on Central Avenue. But the city rebounded, as more and more retirees discovered the area's mild weather, its lakes and natural beauty—and the generous spirit of so many people who lived there.

Hot Springs was Virginia Cassidy Blythe Clinton Dwire Kelley's natural element. Bill's mother was born in Bodcaw, Arkansas, and raised in nearby Hope, eighty miles to the southwest. During World War II, she attended nursing school in Louisiana, and that's where she met her first husband, William Jefferson Blythe. After the war, they moved to Chicago and lived on the North Side, not far from where my parents were living. When Virginia became pregnant with Bill, she went home to Hope to wait for the baby. Her husband was driving down to see her when he had a fatal accident in Missouri in May of 1946. Virginia was a twenty-three-year-old widow when Bill was born on August 19, 1946. She decided to go to New Orleans to train to become a nurse anesthetist because she knew she could make more money that way to support herself and her new son. She left Bill in the care of her mother and father, and when she got her degree, she returned to Hope to practice.

In 1950, she married Roger Clinton, a hard-drinking car dealer, and moved with him to Hot Springs in 1953. Roger's drinking got worse over the years, and he was violent. At the age of fifteen, Bill was finally big enough to make his stepfather stop beating his mother, at least when he was around. He also tried to look out for his little brother, Roger, ten years younger. Virginia was widowed again in 1967 when Roger Clinton died after a long battle with cancer.

We first met in New Haven during a visit she made to see Bill in the spring of 1972. We were each bewildered by the other. Before Virginia arrived, I had trimmed my own hair (badly) to save money. I didn't use makeup and wore jeans and work shirts most of the time. I was no Miss Arkansas and certainly not the kind of girl Virginia expected her son to fall in love with. No matter what else was going on in her life, Virginia got up early, glued on her false eyelashes and put on bright red lipstick, and sashayed out the door. My style baffled her, and she didn't like my strange Yankee ideas either.

I had a much easier time relating to Virginia's third husband, Jeff Dwire, who became a supportive ally. He owned a beauty parlor and treated Virginia like a queen. He was kind to me from the first day we met and encouraging of my continuing efforts to build a relationship with Bill's mother. Jeff told me to give it time, she would come around.

"Oh, don't worry about Virginia," he would tell me. "She just has to get used to the idea. It's hard for two strong women to get along."

Eventually Virginia and I grew to respect each other's differences and developed a deep bond. We figured out that what we shared was more significant than what we didn't: We both loved the same man.

Bill was coming home to Arkansas and taking a teaching job in

Fayetteville, at the University of Arkansas School of Law. I was moving to Cambridge, Massachusetts, to work for Marian Wright Edelman at the newly created Children's Defense Fund (CDF). I rented the top floor of an old house, where I lived alone for the first time. I loved the work, which involved a lot of travel and exposure to problems affecting children and teenagers around the country. In South Carolina, I helped investigate the conditions under which juveniles were incarcerated in adult jails. Some of the fourteen- and fifteen-year-olds I interviewed were in jail for minor transgressions. Others were already serious offenders. Either way, none of them should have been sharing cells with hard-core adult criminals, who could prey on them or further educate them in criminality. CDF led an effort to separate out juveniles and provide them with more protection and faster adjudication.

In New Bedford, Massachusetts, I went door to door trying to identify the source of a troubling statistic. At CDF, we took census figures of school-age children and compared those numbers to school enrollments. We often found significant discrepancies, and we wanted to determine where these unaccounted-for children were. Knocking on doors was revelatory and heartbreaking. I found children who weren't in school because of physical disabilities like blindness and deafness. I also found school-age siblings at home, baby-sitting their younger brothers and sisters while their parents worked. On the small back porch off her family's home in a neighborhood of Portuguese-American fishermen, I met a girl in a wheelchair, who told me how much she wanted to go to school. She knew she couldn't go because she couldn't walk.

We submitted the results of our survey to Congress. Two years later, at the urging of CDF and other strong advocates, Congress passed the Education for All Handicapped Children Act, mandating that children with physical, emotional and learning disabilities be educated in the public school system.

Despite the satisfaction of my work, I was lonely and missed Bill more than I could stand. I had taken both the Arkansas and Washington, D.C., bar exams during the summer, but my heart was pulling me toward Arkansas. When I learned that I had passed in Arkansas but failed in D.C., I thought that maybe my test scores were telling me something. I spent a lot of my salary on my telephone bills and was so happy when Bill came to see me over Thanksgiving. We spent our time exploring Boston and talking about our future.

Bill told me he enjoyed teaching and loved living in a rented house on the outskirts of Fayetteville, a friendly, slow-paced college town. But the political world called, and he was trying to recruit a candidate to run against Arkansas's only Republican Congressman, John Paul Hammerschmidt. He hadn't found another Democrat in northwest Arkansas willing to run against the popular four-term incumbent, and I could tell that he had begun to consider entering the race himself. If he decided to do it, I wasn't sure what it would mean for us. We agreed that I would come down to Arkansas after Christmas 1973 so we could try to figure out where we were heading. By the time I arrived for New Year's, Bill had decided to run for Congress. He believed that the Republican Party would be hurt by the Watergate scandal and that even well-entrenched incumbents could be vulnerable. He was excited by the challenge and had started to put together his campaign.

I was aware of the announcement from Washington that John Doar had been selected by the House Judiciary Committee to head up the impeachment inquiry to investigate President Nixon. We had met Doar at Yale, when he served as a "judge" during a mock trial, in the spring of 1973. As Directors of the Barristers Union, Bill and I were responsible for supervising a simulated case for course credit. Doar, recruited as the trial judge, was a Gary Cooper type: a quiet, lanky lawyer from Wisconsin who had worked in the Kennedy Justice Department to help end segregation in the South. He had argued some of the government's most important voting rights cases in federal court, and he had worked on the ground in Mississippi and Alabama during the most violent episodes of the sixties. In Jackson, Mississippi, he had stepped between angry protesters and armed police to prevent a potential massacre. I admired his courage and his relentless, organized application of the law.

One day early in January, while I was having coffee with Bill in his kitchen, the phone rang. It was Doar asking him to join the impeachment staff he was organizing. He told Bill that he had asked Burke Marshall, his old friend and colleague from the Kennedy Justice Department's Civil Rights Division, to recommend a few young lawyers to work on the inquiry. Bill's name was at the top of the list, along with three other Yale classmates: Michael Conway, Rufus Cormier and Hillary Rodham. Bill told Doar he had decided to run for Congress, but he thought the others on the list might be available. Doar said he would call me next. He offered me a staff position, explaining that the job would pay very little, the hours would be long and most of the work would be painstaking and monotonous. It was, as they say, an offer I couldn't refuse. I couldn't imagine a more important mission at this juncture in American history. Bill was excited for me, and we were both relieved to put our personal discussion on hold for a while longer. With Marian's blessing, I packed my bags and moved from Cambridge into a spare room in Sara Ehrman's Washington apartment. I was on my way to one of the most intense and significant experiences of my life.

The forty-four attorneys involved in the impeachment inquiry worked seven days a week, barricaded in the old Congressional Hotel on Capitol Hill across from the House office buildings in southeast Washington. I was twenty-six years old, awed by the company I was keeping and the historic responsibility we had assumed.

Although Doar headed the staff, there were two teams of lawyers: one selected by Doar and appointed by the Democratic Chairman of the committee, Congressman Peter Rodino of New Jersey; the other, appointed by the Republican ranking member, Congressman Edward Hutchinson of Michigan, and selected by Albert Jenner, the legendary litigator from the Chicago-based firm of Jenner & Block. Seasoned lawyers under Doar directed each area of the investigation. One of them was Bernard Nussbaum, an experienced and pugnacious Assistant U.S. Attorney from New York. Another was Joe Woods, a corporate lawyer from California with a dry wit and meticulous standards, who supervised my work on procedural and constitutional issues. Bob Sack, a lawyer with an elegant writing style who frequently leavened our serious moments with puns and asides, was later appointed to the federal bench by Bill. But most of us were young, eager law school graduates who were willing to work twenty-hour days in makeshift offices, reviewing documents, researching and transcribing tapes.

Bill Weld, later the Republican Governor of Massachusetts, worked with me on the constitutional task force. Fred Altschuler, a superb legal draftsman from California, asked me to help him analyze the reporting structure of the White House staff in order to determine what decisions the President likely made. I shared an office with Tom Bell, a lawyer from Doar's family firm in New Richmond, Wisconsin. Tom and I spent late nights together wrestling over fine points of legal interpretation, but we also laughed a lot. He didn't take himself too seriously and wouldn't let me either.

Andrew Johnson was the only previous President to be impeached, and historians generally agreed that the Congress had misused its solemn constitutional responsibility for partisan political purposes. Dagmar Hamilton, a lawyer and professor of government at the University of Texas, researched English impeachment cases; I took on the American cases. Doar was committed to running a process that the public and history would judge as nonpartisan and fair, no matter what the outcome. Joe Woods and I drafted procedural rules to present to the House Judiciary Committee. I accompanied Doar and Woods to a public meeting of the committee and sat with them at the counsel's table while Doar presented the procedures he wanted the members to accept.

There were never leaks from our investigation, so the media were grasping for any nugget of human interest to report. Since women were rare in this environment, their mere presence was considered newsworthy. The only problem I encountered was when a reporter asked me how it felt "being the Jill Wine Volner of the Impeachment inquiry." We had seen the media focus on Jill Wine Volner, the young lawyer who had served in the office of Special Prosecutor Leon Jaworski. Volner conducted the memorable cross-examination of Rose Mary Woods, Nixon's private secretary, about the missing 18½-minute section of a particularly significant tape. Volner's legal skills and attractiveness were the subject of many stories.

John Doar was allergic to publicity. He enforced a strict policy of total confidentiality, even anonymity. He warned us not to keep diaries, to place sensitive trash in designated bins, never to talk about work outside the building, never to draw attention to ourselves and to avoid social activities of all kinds (as if we had time). He knew that discretion was the only way to achieve a fair and dignified process. When he heard the reporter ask the question comparing me to Volner, I knew I would never be let out in public again.

After working on procedures, I moved on to research the legal grounds for a presidential impeachment and wrote a long memo summarizing my conclusions about what did—and did not—constitute an impeachable offense. Years later, I reread the memo. I still agreed with its assessment of the kinds of "high Crimes and Misdemeanors" the framers of the Constitution intended to be impeachable.

Slowly and surely, Doar's team of lawyers put together evidence that made a compelling case for the impeachment of Richard Nixon. One of the most meticulous, inspirational and demanding lawyers with whom I have ever worked, Doar insisted that no one draw conclusions until all the facts were evaluated. In those days before personal computers, he directed us to use index cards to keep track of the facts, the same method he had applied in the civil rights cases he tried. We typed one fact per card—the date of a memo, the topic of a meeting—and cross-referenced it with other facts. Then we looked for patterns. By the end of the inquiry, we had compiled more than five hundred thousand index cards.

Our work accelerated after we received the subpoenaed tapes from the Watergate Grand Jury. Doar asked some of us to listen to the tapes to further our understanding of them. It was hard work sitting alone in a windowless room trying to make sense of the words and to glean their context and meaning. And then there was what I called the "tape of tapes." Richard Nixon taped himself listening to earlier tapes he had made of himself and discussing what he heard on them with his staff. He justified and rationalized what he had previously said in order to deny or minimize his involvement in ongoing White House efforts to defy the laws and the Constitution. I would hear the President saying things like, "What I meant when I said that was . . ." or, "Here's what I was really trying to say . . ." It was extraordinary to listen to Nixon's rehearsal for his own cover-up.

On July 19, 1974, Doar presented proposed articles of impeachment that specified the charges against the President. The House Judiciary Committee approved three articles of impeachment citing abuse of power, obstruction of justice and contempt of Congress. The charges against President Nixon included paying off witnesses to silence them or influence their testimony, misusing the Internal Revenue Service to obtain the tax records of private citizens, directing the FBI and the Secret Service to spy on Americans and maintaining a secret investigative unit within the Office of the President. The votes were bipartisan, earning the confidence of both the Congress and the American public. Then, on August 5, the White House released transcripts of the June 23, 1972, tape often called the "smoking gun," on which Nixon approved a cover-up of the money used by his reelection committee for illegal purposes.

Nixon resigned the Presidency on August 9, 1974, sparing the nation an agonizing and divisive vote in the House and trial in the Senate. The Nixon impeachment process of 1974 forced a corrupt President from office and was a victory for the Constitution and our system of laws. Even so, some of us on the committee staff came away from the experience sobered by the gravity of the process. The tremendous powers of congressional committees and special prosecutors were only as fair and just and constitutional as the men and women who wielded them.

Suddenly I was out of work. Our close-knit group of lawyers met for one last dinner together before we scattered to the four winds. Everyone talked excitedly about plans for the future. I was undecided, and when Bert Jenner asked me what I wanted to do, I said I wanted to be a trial lawyer, like him. He told me that would be impossible.

"Why?" I asked.

"Because you won't have a wife."

"What on earth does that mean?"

Bert explained that without a wife at home to take care of all my personal needs, I would never be able to manage the demands of everyday life, like making sure I had clean socks for court. I've since wondered whether Jenner was pulling my leg or making a serious point about how tough the law still could be for women. Ultimately it didn't matter; I chose to follow my heart instead of my head. I was moving to Arkansas.

"Are you out of your mind?" said Sara Ehrman when I broke the news. "Why on earth would you throw away your future?"

That spring, I had asked Doar for permission to visit Bill in Fayetteville. He didn't like the idea but grudgingly gave me a weekend off. While there, I went with Bill to a dinner party where I met some of his law school colleagues, including Wylie Davis, then the Dean. As I was leaving, Dean Davis told me to let him know if I ever wanted to teach. Now I decided to take him up on the idea. I called to ask if the offer was still open, and he said it was. I asked him what I'd be teaching, and he said he would tell me when I got there in about ten days to start classes.

My decision to move did not come out of the blue. Bill and I had been pondering our predicament since we started dating. If we were to be together, one of us had to give ground. With the unexpected end of my work in Washington, I had the time and space to give our relationship—and Arkansas—a chance. Despite her misgivings, Sara offered to drive me down. Every few miles, she asked me if I knew what I was doing, and I gave her the same answer every time: "No, but I'm going anyway."

I've sometimes had to listen hard to my own feelings to decide what was right for me, and that can make for some lonely decisions if your friends and family—let alone the public and the press—question your choices and speculate on your motives. I had fallen in love with Bill in law school and wanted to be with him. I knew I was always happier with Bill than without him, and I'd always assumed that I could live a fulfilling life anywhere. If I was going to grow as a person, I knew it was time for me—to paraphrase Eleanor Roosevelt—to do what I was most afraid to do. So I was driving toward a place where I'd never lived and had no friends or family. But my heart told me I was going in the right direction.

On a hot August evening, the day I arrived, I saw Bill give a campaign speech before a good-size crowd in the town square in Bentonville. I was impressed. Maybe, despite the tough odds, he had a chance. The next day, I attended the reception for new law school faculty held by the Washington County Bar Association at the local Holiday Inn. I had been in Arkansas less than forty-eight hours, but I'd been given my assignments. I would be teaching criminal law and trial advocacy and running the legal aid clinic and the prison projects, both of which required that I supervise the students providing legal assistance to the poor and incarcerated. And I'd be doing what I could to help Bill in his campaign.

Bill Bassett, President of the bar association, took me around to meet the local lawyers and judges. He introduced me to Tom Butt, the chancery court judge, saying, "Judge, this is the new lady law professor. She's going to teach criminal law and run the legal aid programs."

"Well," said Judge Butt, peering down at me, "we're glad to have you, but you should know I have no use for legal aid, and I'm a pretty tough S.O.B."

I managed to smile and say, "Well, it's nice meeting you too, Judge." But I wondered what on earth I had gotten myself into.

Classes started the next morning. I had never taught law school before and was barely older than most of my students, younger than some. The only other woman on the faculty, Elizabeth "Bess" Osenbaugh, became a close friend. We talked about problems in the law and in life, usually over turkey sandwiches on kaiser rolls from Fayetteville's closest thing to a real deli. Though in his seventies, Robert Leflar was still teaching his legendary conflicts of law course in Fayetteville, and an equally renowned course in appellate judging at New York University Law School. He and his wife, Helen, befriended me, and during the first summer I was there, let me stay in their native stone and wood house designed by the prize-winning Arkansas architect Fay Jones. I had good-natured debates with Al Witte, who claimed the title of toughest law professor but was really a softie underneath. I appreciated the kindness of Milt Copeland, with whom I shared an office. And I admired the activism and scholarship of Mort Gitelman, who championed civil rights.

Just as the semester was beginning, Virginia's husband, Jeff Dwire, died suddenly from heart failure. It was devastating for Virginia, who was widowed for the third time, and for Bill's brother, Roger, who was ten years younger and had developed a close relationship with Jeff. Losing Jeff was painful for all of us. Virginia had endured so much over the years. I was amazed at her resilience and saw the same trait in Bill, who had emerged from his difficult childhood without a shred of bitterness. If anything, his experiences have made him more empathetic and optimistic. His energy and disposition drew people to him, and, until stories emerged during his presidential campaign, very few knew about the painful circumstances he had endured.

Bill returned to the campaign trail after Jeff's funeral, and I explored life in a small college town. After the intensity of New Haven and Washington, the friendliness, slower pace and beauty of Fayetteville were a welcome tonic.

One day when I was standing in line at the A&P, the cashier looked up and asked me, "Are you the new lady law professor?" I said I was, and she told me I was teaching one of her nephews, who had said I was "not bad." Another time, I dialed information looking for a student who hadn't shown up for a class conference. When I told the operator the student's name, she said, "He's not home."

"Excuse me?"

"He's gone camping," she informed me. I had never before lived in a place so small, friendly and Southern, and I loved it. I went to Arkansas Razorbacks football games and learned to "call the hogs." When Bill was in town, we spent evenings with friends eating barbecue and weekends playing volleyball at the home of Richard Richards, another of our colleagues on the law school faculty. Or we got together for a round of Charades organized by Bess Osenbaugh.

Carl Whillock, then an administrator at the university, and his delightful wife, Margaret, lived in a big yellow house across the street from the law school. They were the first people to invite me over, and we became fast friends. Margaret had been left by her first husband when her six children were under ten. Conventional wisdom decreed that no man would assume the burden of marriage to a divorcée with six kids, no matter how vivacious and attractive she was. But Carl didn't follow convention, and he signed on for the whole load. I once introduced Margaret to Eppie Lederer, otherwise known as Ann Landers, at the White House. "Honey, your husband deserves sainthood!" Eppie exclaimed after she heard Margaret's story. She was right.

Ann and Morriss Henry also became close friends. Ann, a lawyer, was active in politics and community affairs on her own and on behalf of Morriss, who served in the State Senate. She also had three children and was deeply involved in their schools and sports programs. Ann, who freely expressed her well-informed opinions, was superb company.

Diane Blair became my closest friend. Like me, she was a transplant from Washington, D.C., who had moved to Fayetteville with her first husband. She taught political science at the university and was considered one of the best professors on campus. We played tennis and traded favorite books. She wrote extensively about Arkansas and Southern politics, and her book about the first woman to be elected to the Senate on her own, Hattie Caraway, Democrat from Arkansas, was sparked by her strong convictions about women's rights and roles.

During the national debate about whether or not the country should ratify the Equal Rights Amendment to the Constitution, Diane debated ultraconservative activist Phyllis Schlafly in front of the Arkansas General Assembly. I helped prepare her for the Valentine's Day confrontation in 1975. Diane won the debate hands down, but both of us knew that the combination of religious and political opposition to the ERA in Arkansas wouldn't yield to compelling arguments, logic or evidence.

Diane and I regularly met for lunch in the Student Union. We always chose a table by the big windows that looked out toward the Ozark Hills and share stories and gossip. She and I also spent long hours with Ann at the Henrys' backyard pool. They loved hearing about the cases I handled at the legal aid clinic, and I often sought their opinions about some of the attitudes I encountered. One day, the Washington County prosecuting attorney, Mahlon Gibson, called to tell me an indigent prisoner accused of raping a twelve-year-old girl wanted a woman lawyer. Gibson had recommended that the criminal court judge, Maupin Cummings, appoint me. I told Mahlon I really didn't feel comfortable taking on such a client, but Mahlon gently reminded me that I couldn't very well refuse the judge's request. When I visited the alleged rapist in the county jail, I learned that he was an uneducated "chicken catcher." His job was to collect chickens from the large warehouse farms for one of the local processing plants. He denied the charges against him and insisted that the girl, a distant relative, had made up her story. I conducted a thorough investigation and obtained expert testimony from an eminent scientist from New York, who cast doubt on the evidentiary value of the blood and semen the prosecutor claimed proved the defendant's guilt in the rape. Because of that testimony, I negotiated with the prosecutor for the defendant to plead guilty to sexual abuse. When I appeared with my client before Judge Cummings to present that plea, he asked me to leave the courtroom while he conducted the necessary examination to determine the factual basis for the plea. I said, "Judge, I can't leave. I'm his lawyer."

"Well," said the judge, "I can't talk about these things in front of a lady."

"Judge," I reassured him, "don't think of me as anything but a lawyer."

The judge walked the defendant through his plea and then sentenced him. It was shortly after this experience that Ann Henry and I discussed setting up Arkansas's first rape hot line.

A few months into my new life, I received a call from a female jailer in the Benton County jail, north of Fayetteville. She told me about a woman who had been arrested for disturbing the peace by preaching the gospel on the streets of Bentonville; she was scheduled to appear before a judge who intended to send her down to the state mental hospital because nobody knew what else to do with her. The jailer asked me to come as soon as I could because she didn't think the lady was crazy, just "possessed by the Lord's spirit."

When I got to the courthouse, I met the jailer and the inmate, a gentle-looking soul wearing an ankle-length dress and clutching her well-worn Bible. She explained that Jesus had sent her to preach in Bentonville and that, if released, she would go right back out to continue her mission. When I learned that she was from California, I persuaded the judge to buy her a bus ticket home instead of ordering her to be committed to the state hospital, and I convinced her that California needed her more than Arkansas.

Bill had won the primary for Congress and the Democratic runoff in June, with a little help from my father and my brother Tony, who spent a few weeks in May doing campaign grunt work, putting up posters and answering phones. It still amazes me that my diehard Republican father worked for Bill's election, a testament to how much he had come to love and respect him.

By Labor Day, Bill's campaign was picking up momentum, and the Republicans began a barrage of personal attacks and dirty tricks. It was my first up-close exposure to the efficacy of lies and manipulation in a campaign.

When President Nixon was in Fayetteville for the 1969 Texas vs. Arkansas football game, a young man climbed into a tree to protest the Vietnam War—and Nixon's presence on campus. Five years later, Bill's political opponents claimed that Bill was the guy in the tree. It didn't matter that Bill was studying in Oxford, England, at the time, four thousand miles away. For years after, I ran into people who believed the charge.

One of Bill's mailings to voters was not delivered, and the bales of postcards were later found stashed behind a post office. Other incidents of sabotage were reported, but no foul play could be proved. When election night came that November, Bill lost by 6,000 votes out of more than 170,000 cast—52 to 48 percent. Long after midnight, as Bill, Virginia, Roger and I were leaving the little house that had served as Bill's campaign headquarters, the phone rang. I picked it up, sure that it would be some friend or supporter calling to commiserate. Someone shouted into the phone, "I'm so glad that nigger-loving Commie fag Bill Clinton lost," and then hung up. What could inspire such bile? I thought. It was a question I would ask many times in the years ahead.

At the end of the school year, I decided to take a long trip back to Chicago and the East Coast to visit friends and people who had offered me jobs. I still wasn't sure what to do with my life. On the way to the airport, Bill and I passed a red brick house near the university with a "For Sale" sign out front. I casually mentioned that it was a sweet-looking little house and never gave it a second thought. After a few weeks of traveling and thinking, I decided I wanted to return to my life in Arkansas and to Bill. When Bill picked me up, he asked, "Do you remember that house you liked? Well, I bought it, so now you'd better marry me because I can't live in it by myself."

Bill proudly drove up the driveway and ushered me inside. The house had a screened-in porch, a living room with a beamed cathedral ceiling, a fireplace, a big bay window, a good-sized bedroom and bathroom and a kitchen that needed a lot of work. Bill had already bought an old wrought-iron bed at a local antiques store and had been to Wal-Mart for sheets and towels.

This time I said "yes."

We were married in the living room on October 11, 1975, by the Reverend Vic Nixon. Vic, a local Methodist minister, and his wife, Freddie, had worked on Bill's campaign. There for the ceremony were my parents and brothers; Virginia and Roger; Johanna Branson; Betsy Johnson Ebeling, now married to our high school classmate Tom; F. H. Martin, who had served as treasurer of Bill's 1974 campaign, and his wife, Myrna; Marie Clinton, Bill's cousin; Dick Atkinson, a friend from Yale Law School, who had joined us on the law school faculty; Bess Osenbaugh and Patty Howe, a close friend who had grown up with Bill in Hot Springs. I wore a lace-and-muslin Victorian dress I had found shopping with my mother the night before. I walked into the room on my father's arm, and the minister said, "Who will give away this woman?" We all looked at my father expectantly. But he didn't let go. Finally Rev. Nixon said, "You can step back now, Mr. Rodham."

After the ceremony, Ann and Morriss Henry hosted a reception in their big backyard, where a few hundred friends gathered to celebrate with us.

After all that has happened since, I'm often asked why Bill and I have stayed together. It's not a question I welcome, but given the public nature of our lives, it's one I know will be asked again and again. What can I say to explain a love that has persisted for decades and has grown through our shared experiences of parenting a daughter, burying our parents and tending our extended families, a lifetime's worth of friends, a common faith and an abiding commitment to our country? All I know is that no one understands me better and no one can make me laugh the way Bill does. Even after all these years, he is still the most interesting, energizing and fully alive person I have ever met. Bill Clinton and I started a conversation in the spring of 1971, and more than thirty years later we're still talking.

LITTLE ROCK

BILL CLINTON'S FIRST ELECTION VICTORY AS ATTORNEY General of Arkansas in 1976 was anticlimactic. He had won the primary in May and had no Republican opponent. The big show that year was the presidential contest between Jimmy Carter and Gerald Ford.

Bill and I had met Carter the year before when he gave a speech at the University of Arkansas. He had sent two of his top lieutenants, Jody Powell and Frank Moore, to Fayetteville to help in Bill's 1974 campaign, a sure sign he was surveying the political landscape with an eye toward a national run.

Carter introduced himself to me by saying, "Hi, I'm Jimmy Carter and I'm going to be President." That caught my attention, so I watched and listened closely. He understood the mood of the country and bet that post-Watergate politics would create an opening for a newcomer from outside Washington who could appeal to Southern voters. Carter correctly concluded he had as good a chance as any, and as his introduction implied, he certainly had the confidence necessary to undertake the ego-mangling of a presidential campaign.

He also guessed that President Ford's pardon of Richard Nixon would be a good issue for the Democrats. Although I believed Ford's pardon was the right decision for the country, I agreed with Carter's analysis that it would remind voters that Gerald Ford had been Richard Nixon's choice to succeed the disgraced Spiro Agnew as Vice President.

At the end of our meeting, Carter asked me if I had any advice for him.

"Well, Governor," I said, "I wouldn't go around telling people you're going to be President. That could be a little off-putting to some."

"But," he replied with that trademark smile, "I am going to be."

With Bill's election assured, we both felt free to get involved in Carter's campaign when he became the Democratic nominee. We went to the July convention in New York City to talk to his staff about working for him in the election. Then we left for a glorious two-week vacation in Europe that included a pilgrimage to the Basque town of Guernica. I had wanted to visit the site that inspired Picasso's masterpiece since Don Jones showed my Methodist youth group a reproduction of the painting. Twentieth-century warfare started in Guernica in 1937 when Francisco Franco, Spain's fascist dictator, called in the Luftwaffe, Hitler's air force, to annihilate the town. Picasso captured the horror and panic of the massacre in a painting that became an anti-war emblem. When Bill and I walked Guernica's streets and drank coffee in the central plaza in 1976, the rebuilt town looked like any other mountain village. But the painting had branded Franco's crime into my memory.

Upon our return to Fayetteville, Carter's staff asked Bill to head the campaign in Arkansas and me to be the field coordinator in Indiana. Indiana was a heavily Republican state, but Carter thought his Southern roots and farming background might appeal even to Republican voters. I thought it was a long shot, but I was game to try. My job was to set up a campaign in every county, which meant finding local people to work under the direction of regional coordinators, mostly brought in from around the country. The Indianapolis campaign office was in a building that had housed an appliance store and a bail-bonding firm. We were right across the street from the city jail, and the neon sign flashing "Bail Bondsman" still hung above the Carter-Mondale posters in the front windows.

I learned a lot in Indiana. One night, I had dinner with a group of older men who were in charge of the Democratic Party's get-out-the-vote efforts for Election Day. I was the only woman at the table. They wouldn't give me any specifics, and I kept pressing for details about how many phone calls, cars and door hangers they planned to put out on Election Day. All of a sudden, one of the men reached across the table and grabbed me by my turtleneck. "Just shut up, will you. We said we'd do it, we will, and we don't have to tell you how!" I was scared. I knew he had been drinking, and I also knew that all eyes were on me. My heart was beating fast as I looked him in the eye, removed his hands from my neck and said, "First, don't ever touch me again. Second, if you were as fast with the answers to my questions as you are with your hands, I'd have the information I need to do my job. Then I could leave you alone—which is what I'm going to do now." My knees were shaking, but I got up and walked out.

Even though Carter did not carry Indiana, I was thrilled that he won the national election, and I looked forward to the new administration. But Bill and I had more immediate concerns. We had to move to Little Rock, which meant leaving the house we had been married in. We bought a 980-square-foot house on a quaint street in the Hillcrest section not far from the Capitol. Fayetteville was too far to commute, so I couldn't continue teaching at the university, which saddened me because I enjoyed my colleagues and students. I had to decide what to do next, and I didn't think it was a good idea to work for any state-funded institution or in any other public job such as prosecutor, defender or legal aid lawyer where my work might overlap or conflict with that of the Attorney General. I began to seriously consider joining a private firm, a career choice I had resisted before. Representing private clients, I thought, would be an important experience and would help us financially since Bill's salary as Attorney General would be $26,500.

The Rose Law Firm was the most venerable firm in Arkansas and reputed to be the oldest firm west of the Mississippi River. I had gotten to know one of the partners, Vince Foster, while I was running the legal aid clinic at the law school. When I tried to send law students into Judge Butt's court to represent indigent clients, the judge required the students to qualify their clients under a nineteenth-century statute that permitted free legal assistance only when a person's assets were worth no more than ten dollars and the clothes on his or her back. It was an impossible standard to meet for anyone who owned an old clunker car or a television or anything else worth more than ten dollars. I wanted to change the law, and I needed the help of the Arkansas Bar Association to do it. I also wanted the bar to provide financial assistance to the legal aid clinic at the law school to help pay for a full-time administrator and legal secretary since it provided real-world experience to future lawyers. Vince was the head of the bar committee that oversaw legal aid, so I went to visit him. He enlisted several other leading lawyers to help me, including Henry Woods, the state's premier trial lawyer, and William R. Wilson, Jr., a self-proclaimed mule-skinner's assistant—a "swamper"—who was also one of the best lawyers around. Judge Butt and I appeared before the state bar's executive committee and presented our opposing arguments. The committee voted to support the clinic and endorsed repealing the statute, thanks to the support Vince recruited.

After the 1976 election, Vince and another Rose Firm partner, Herbert C. Rule III, came to see me with a job offer. In keeping with the firm's steadfast efforts to follow proper procedures, Herb, an erudite Yale College alum, had already obtained an opinion from the American Bar Association that approved the employment by a law firm of a lawyer married to a state's Attorney General and set forth the steps to be taken to avoid conflicts of interest.

Not all the Rose Firm lawyers were as enthusiastic as Vince and Herb about having a woman join them. There had never been a woman associate, although the firm had hired a female law clerk in the 1940s, Elsijane Roy, who stayed only a few years before leaving to become the permanent clerk for a federal judge. Later appointed to succeed that judge by President Carter, she became the first woman appointed to the federal bench in Arkansas. Two of the senior partners, William Nash and J. Gaston Williamson, were Rhodes Scholars, and Gaston had served on the committee that had selected Bill for his Rhodes Scholarship. Herb and Vince took me around to meet them and the other lawyers, fifteen in all. When the partners voted to hire me, Vince and Herb gave me a copy of *Hard Times* by Charles Dickens. But who could have known what an appropriate gift that would be?

I joined the litigation section, headed by Phil Carroll, a thoroughly decent man, former prisoner of war in Germany and first-class lawyer who became President of the Arkansas Bar Association. The two lawyers with whom I worked most were Vince and Webster Hubbell.

Vince was one of the best lawyers I've ever known and one of the best friends I've ever had. If you remember Gregory Peck's performance as Atticus Finch in *To Kill a Mockingbird*, you can picture Vince. He actually looked the part, and his manner was similar: steady, courtly, sharp but understated, the sort of person you would want around in times of trouble.

Vince and I had adjacent offices at the firm, and we shared a secretary. He was born and raised in Hope, Arkansas. The backyard of his boyhood home bordered the backyard of Bill's grandparents, with whom Bill lived until he was four. Bill and Vince played together as little boys, although they lost touch when Bill moved to Hot Springs in 1953. When Bill ran for Attorney General, Vince became a strong supporter.

Webb Hubbell was a big, burly, likable man, a former University of Arkansas football star and an avid golfer, which endeared him to Bill from the outset. He was also a great raconteur in a state where story-telling is a way of life. Webb had a wealth of experience in all sorts of fields; he would eventually become Mayor of Little Rock, and he served for a time as Chief Justice of the Arkansas Supreme Court. He was great fun to work with and a loyal, supportive friend.

Hubbell looked like a good ol' boy, but he was a creative litigator, and I loved to listen to him talk about arcane Arkansas law. His memory was phenomenal. He also had a tricky back that would sometimes go out on him. Once Webb and I stayed at the office all night working on a brief that was due the next day. Webb lay on the floor on his hurting back spouting citations of cases back to the nineteenth century; my job was to run around the law library hunting them down.

In the first jury trial I handled on my own, I defended a canning company against a plaintiff who found the rear end of a rat in the can of pork and beans he opened for dinner one night. He didn't actually eat it but claimed that the mere sight was so disgusting that he couldn't stop spitting, which in turn interfered with his ability to kiss his fiancée. He sat through the trial spitting into a handkerchief and looking miserable. There was no doubt that something had gone wrong in the processing plant, but the company refused to pay the plaintiff since it argued that he hadn't really been damaged; and besides, the rodent parts which had been sterilized might be considered edible in certain parts of the world. Although I was nervous in front of the jury, I warmed to the task of con-vincing them that my client was in the right and was relieved when they awarded the plaintiff only nominal damages. For years after, Bill used to kid me about the "rat's ass" case and mimic the plaintiff's claim he could no longer kiss his fiancée because he was so busy spitting.

I also continued my work in child advocacy through my law prac-tice. Beryl Anthony, an attorney in El Dorado, asked me to help him represent a couple who wanted to adopt the foster child who had lived with them for two and a half years. The Arkansas Department of Human Services refused, citing a policy against permitting foster par-ents to adopt. I'd encountered the same policy in Connecticut when I was working as a law student at legal services. Beryl, married to Vince's older sister, Sheila, had heard from Vince about my interest in such is-sues. I jumped at the chance to work on the case. Our clients, a local stockbroker and his wife, had the means to fund an effective challenge to the policy. The Arkansas Department of Human Services had its own lawyers, so I didn't have to worry about going up against the Attorney General.

Beryl and I presented expert testimony about the stages of a child's development and the degree to which a child's emotional well-being depends on the presence of a consistent caregiver in early life. We persuaded the judge that the contract the foster parents had signed—agreeing not to adopt—should not be enforceable if its terms were contrary to the child's best interests. We won the case but our victory didn't change the state's formal policy about foster children's placement because the state didn't appeal the decision. Thankfully our victory did serve as a precedent that the state eventually adopted. Beryl was elected to Congress in 1978, where he served for fourteen years, and Sheila Foster Anthony became a lawyer herself.

My experience on this case and others convinced me that Arkansas needed a statewide organization devoted to advocating for children's rights and interests. I was not alone in thinking that. Dr. Bettye Caldwell, an internationally recognized professor of child development at the University of Arkansas at Little Rock, knew of my work and asked me to form one with her and other Arkansans concerned about the status of children in the state. We founded the Arkansas Advocates for Children and Families, which spearheaded reforms in the child welfare system and continues to advocate for children today.

While I was working on lawsuits at Rose and taking on child advocacy cases pro bono, I was also learning about the expectations and unspoken mores of life in the South. Wives of elected officials were constantly scrutinized. In 1974, Barbara Pryor, wife of the Governor-elect, David Pryor, had drawn withering criticism for her newly permed short hairdo. I liked Barbara and thought the public attention to her hair was ridiculous. (Little did I know.) I assumed that as a busy mother of three sons she was looking for an easy style. In a show of solidarity, I decided to subject my stubbornly straight hair to a tight permanent that would, I thought, replicate Barbara's. I had to have the permanent applied twice in order to get the desired effect. When I showed up with my frizzed hair, Bill just shook his head, wondering why I had cut off and "messed up" my long hair.

One of the reasons Vince and Webb became such good friends is that they accepted me for who I was, often poking fun at my intensity or explaining patiently why some idea of mine would never fly. We made it a habit to escape from the office for regular lunches, often going to an Italian restaurant called the Villa. It was a checkered-cloth-and-candle-in-the-Chianti-bottle sort of place near the university, where we could avoid the usual business crowds. It was fun to exchange war stories about our battles in the Arkansas court system or just to talk about our families. Of course, this too raised some eyebrows. In Little Rock at that time, women did not usually have meals with men who were not their husbands.

While being a politician's wife as well as a trial lawyer occasionally got people talking when I stepped out in public, I was not usually recognized. Once, another attorney and I chartered a small plane to fly to Harrison, Arkansas, for a court appearance, only to land at the airstrip and find there were no taxis. I walked over to a group of men standing around the hangar. "Is anybody driving into Harrison?" I asked. "We need to go to the courthouse."

Without turning around, one man offered, "I am. I'll take you."

The man drove an old junker stuffed with tools, so we all crammed into the front seat and headed for Harrison. We barreled along with the radio blaring until the news came on and the announcer said, "Today, Attorney General Bill Clinton said that he would be investigating Judge So-and-so for misbehavior on the bench . . ." All of a sudden our driver shouted, "Bill Clinton! You know that son of a bitch Bill Clinton?"

I braced myself and said, "Yeah, I do know him. In fact, I'm married to him."

That got the man's attention, and he turned to look at me for the first time. "You're married to Bill Clinton? Well, he's my favorite son of a bitch, and I'm his pilot!"

This was when I noticed that our Samaritan had a black disk over one eye. He was called One-Eyed Jay, and sure enough, had been flying Bill in little airplanes all over. Now I just hoped old One-Eyed Jay's driving was as good as his flying, and I was grateful when he delivered us to the courthouse safe and sound, if a bit rumpled.

The years 1978 through 1980 were among the most difficult, exhilarating, glorious and heartbreaking in my life. After so many years of talking about the ways Bill could improve conditions in Arkansas, he finally had a chance to act when he was elected Governor in 1978. Bill started his two-year term with the energy of a racehorse exploding from the gate. He had made dozens of campaign promises, and he started fulfilling them in his first days in office. Before long, he had delivered a thick, detailed budget book to every legislator and presented sweeping initiatives to create a new economic development department, reform rural health care, overhaul the state's inadequate education system and fix the state highways. Since new revenue would be needed to support these measures, particularly road improvement, taxes had to be raised. Bill and his advisers thought the people would accept an increase in car tag fees for the promise of better highways. But that proved to be woefully wrong.

In 1979, I was made a partner at the Rose Law Firm, and I devoted as much energy as possible to my job. Often, I hosted social events at the Governor's Mansion or presided over meetings of the Rural Health Advisory Committee, which Bill had asked me to chair as part of his effort to improve access to quality health care in rural Arkansas. I continued my involvement with Marian Wright Edelman and the Children's Defense Fund and commuted to Washington, D.C., every few months to chair board meetings. And based on my experience and my work on his campaign, President Carter had appointed me to the board of the Legal Services Corporation, a position for which I had to be confirmed by the U.S. Senate. The Corporation was the nonprofit federal program created by Congress and President Nixon that funded legal assistance for the poor. I served with Mickey Kantor, a former legal services lawyer who had represented migrant workers in Florida. He later became a successful lawyer in Los Angeles and served as Chairman of Bill's 1992 presidential campaign.

As if that weren't enough, Bill and I were also trying to have a baby. We both love children, and anyone with kids knows there is never a "convenient" time to start a family. Bill's first term as Governor seemed as inconvenient a time as any. We weren't having any luck until we decided to take a vacation in Bermuda, proving once again the importance of regular time off.

I persuaded Bill to attend Lamaze classes with me, a new enough phenomenon that it prompted many people to wonder why their Governor was planning to deliver our baby. When I was about seven months' pregnant, I was in court, trying a lawsuit with Gaston Williamson and chatting with the judge, when I mentioned that Bill and I were attending "birthing" classes every Saturday morning.

"What?" the judge exploded. "I've always supported your husband, but I don't believe a husband has any business being there when the baby is born!" And he wasn't kidding.

Around this same time, in January 1980, the Arkansas Children's Hospital was planning to build a big expansion and needed a good bond rating. Dr. Betty Lowe, the hospital's Medical Director and later Chelsea's pediatrician, asked if I would go with a group of trustees and doctors to help make the case before the rating agencies in New York City. I had gotten so big that I made some people nervous, but I went, and for years Betty told people that the rating agencies agreed with their plans as a way of getting a very pregnant Governor's wife out of their offices before she delivered.

As my March due date drew near, my doctor said I couldn't travel, which meant that I missed the annual White House dinner for the Governors. Bill got back to Little Rock on Wednesday, February 27, in time for my water to break. That threw him and the state troopers into a panic. Bill ran around with the Lamaze list of what to take to the hospital. It recommended bringing a small plastic bag filled with ice to suck on during labor. As I hobbled to the car, I saw a state trooper loading a thirty-nine-gallon black garbage bag filled with ice into the trunk.

After we arrived at the hospital, it became clear that I would have to have a cesarean, not something we had anticipated. Bill requested that the hospital permit him to accompany me into the operating room, which was unprecedented. He told the administrators that he had gone with his mother to see operations and knew he'd be fine. That he was the Governor certainly helped convince Baptist Hospital to let him in. Soon thereafter, the policy was changed to permit fathers in the delivery room during cesarean operations.

Our daughter's birth was the most miraculous and awe-inspiring event in my life. Chelsea Victoria Clinton arrived three weeks early on February 27, 1980, at 11:24 P.M., to the great joy of Bill and our families. While I was recovering, Bill took Chelsea in his arms for father-daughter "bonding" laps around the hospital. He would sing to her, rock her, show her off and generally suggest that he had invented fatherhood.

Chelsea has heard us tell stories about her childhood many times: She knows she was named after Judy Collins's version of Joni Mitchell's song "Chelsea Morning," which her father and I heard as we strolled around Chelsea in London, during the wonderful vacation we took over Christmas in 1978. Bill said, "If we ever have a daughter, we should name her Chelsea." And he started singing along.

Chelsea knows how mystified I was by her arrival and how inconsolable she could be when she cried, no matter how much I rocked her. She knows the words I said to her in my effort to calm us both: "Chelsea, this is new for both of us. I've never been a mother before, and you've never been a baby. We're just going to have to help each other do the best we can."

Early on the morning after Chelsea's birth, my law partner Joe Giroir called and asked me if I wanted a ride to work. He was kidding, of course, but up until then, I had not succeeded in persuading my partners to formally adopt a parental leave plan. In fact, as I grew bigger and bigger, they just averted their eyes and talked about anything else besides my plans for when the baby came. Once Chelsea arrived, however, they told me to take whatever time I needed.

I was able to take four months off from full-time work to stay home with our new daughter, though with less income. As a partner, I continued to receive a base salary, but my income depended on the fees I generated, which naturally decreased during the time I wasn't working. I never forgot how much more fortunate I was than many women to be given this time with my child. Bill and I both recognized the need for parental leave, preferably paid. We emerged from our experience committed to ensuring that all parents have the option to stay home with their newborn children and to have reliable child care when they return to work. That's why I was so thrilled when the first bill he signed as President was the Family and Medical Leave Act.

We were living in the Governor's Mansion, which had a built-in support system to help with Chelsea. Eliza Ashley, the invaluable cook who had worked in the mansion for decades, loved having a child in the house. Carolyn Huber, whom we had coaxed away from the Rose Law Firm to manage the mansion during Bill's first term, was like a member of the family. Chelsea came to think of her as a surrogate aunt, and her help was priceless. But I never took any of our blessings for granted. As soon as Bill and I decided to start a family, I had begun to plan for a more stable financial future.

Money means almost nothing to Bill Clinton. He is not opposed to making money or owning property; it has simply never been a priority. He's happy when he has enough to buy books, watch movies, go out to dinner and travel. Which is just as well, because as Governor of Arkansas he never made more than $35,000 a year, before taxes. That was a good income in Arkansas, and we lived in the Governor's Mansion and had an official expense account that covered meals, which made it a better one. But I worried that because politics is an inherently unstable profession, we needed to build up a nest egg.

I'm sure I inherited my concerns from my notoriously frugal father, who made smart investments, put his kids through college and retired comfortably. My dad taught me how to follow the stock market when I was still in grade school and frequently reminded me that "money doesn't grow on trees." Only through hard work, savings and prudent investing could you become financially independent. Still, I had never given much thought to savings or investments until I realized that if our growing family were going to have any financial cushion, it would be mostly my responsibility. I started looking for opportunities I could afford. My friend Diane Blair was married to someone who knew the intricacies of the commodities market, and he was willing to share his expertise.

With his gravelly drawl, large frame and silver hair, Jim Blair was an imposing figure and an exceptional lawyer whose clients included the poultry giant Tyson Foods. Jim also held strong political opinions. He championed civil rights, opposed the Vietnam War and supported Senators Fulbright and McGovern against the political tides. He was blessed with a great personal warmth and a mischievous sense of humor. When he married Diane, he found a soul mate, as did she. Bill performed their wedding ceremony in 1979, and I served as their "best person."

The commodities markets were booming in the late 1970s, and Jim had developed a system of trading that was making him a fortune. By 1978, he was doing so well that he encouraged his family and best friends to jump into the market. I was willing to risk $1,000 and let Jim guide my trades through the colorfully named broker Robert "Red" Bone. Red was a former poker player, which made perfect sense, given his calling.

The commodities market is nothing like the stock exchange—in fact, it has more in common with Las Vegas than Wall Street. What investors buy and sell are promises (known as "futures") to purchase or sell certain goods—wheat, coffee, cattle—at a fixed price. If the price is higher when those commodities are brought to market, the investor makes money. Sometimes it's a great deal of money, because each dollar invested can control many times its value in futures. Price fluctuations of a few cents are amplified by huge volumes. On the other hand, if the market in hogbellies or corn is glutted, then the price drops and the investor loses big.

I did my best to educate myself about cattle futures and margin calls to make it less frightening. I won and lost money over the months and followed the markets closely. For a while, I opened a smaller, broker-controlled account with another investment firm in Little Rock. But soon after I got pregnant with Chelsea in 1979, I lost my nerve for gambling. The gains I had made suddenly seemed like real money we could use for our child's higher education. I walked away from the table $100,000 ahead. Jim Blair and his compatriots stayed in the market longer and lost a good deal of the money they had made.

The large return on my investment was examined ad infinitum after Bill became President, although it never became the focus of a serious investigation. The conclusion was that, like many investors at the time, I'd been fortunate. Bill and I weren't so lucky with another investment we made during the same period. Not only did we lose money on a piece of property called Whitewater Estates, the investment would spawn an investigation fifteen years later that endured throughout Bill's Presidency.

It all started one day in the spring of 1978 when a businessman and longtime politico named Jim McDougal approached us with a sure-thing deal: Bill and I entered a partnership with Jim and his young wife, Susan, to buy 230 undeveloped acres on the south bank of the White River in North Arkansas. The plan was to subdivide the site for vacation homes, then sell the lots at a profit. The price was $202,611.20.

Bill had met McDougal in 1968 when Jim was working on Senator J. William Fulbright's reelection campaign and Bill was a twenty-one-year-old summer volunteer. Jim McDougal was a character: charming, witty and eccentric as the day is long. With his white suits and baby blue Bentley, McDougal looked as if he'd just stepped out of a Tennessee Williams play. Despite his colorful habits, he had a solid reputation. He seemed to do business with everybody in the state, including the impeccable Bill Fulbright, for whom he helped make a lot of money in real estate. His credentials were reassuring to both of us. Bill had also made a small real estate investment with McDougal the year before that had turned a reasonable profit, so when Jim suggested Whitewater, it seemed like a good idea.

The North Arkansas Ozarks were booming with second homes for people flocking down south from Chicago and Detroit. The attraction was obvious: forested land with low property taxes in gently rolling countryside bordered by mountains and laced with lakes and rivers that offered some of the best fishing and rafting in the country. If all had gone according to plan, we would have turned over the investment after a few years and that would have been the end of it. We took out bank loans to buy the property, eventually transferring ownership to the Whitewater Development Company, Inc., a separate entity in which we and the McDougals had equal shares. Bill and I considered ourselves passive investors; Jim and Susan managed the project, which was expected to finance itself once the lots started to sell. But by the time the development was surveyed and lots were ready for sale, interest rates had gone through the roof, climbing close to 20 percent by the end of the decade. People could no longer afford to finance second homes. Rather than take a huge loss, we held on to Whitewater, making some improvements and building a model home while hoping for an economic turnaround. From time to time, over the next several years, Jim asked us to write checks to help make interest payments or other contributions, and we never questioned his judgment. We didn't realize that Jim McDougal's behavior was turning the corner from "eccentric" to "mentally unstable" and that he was becoming involved in a raft of dubious business schemes. It would be years before we learned anything about his double life.

Nineteen eighty was a big year for us. We were new parents, and Bill was running for reelection. His opponent in the primary election was a seventy-eight-year-old retired turkey farmer, Monroe Schwarzlose, who spoke for a lot of rural Democrats when he criticized the increase in the cost of car tags and capitalized on the impression of some that Bill was "out of touch" with Arkansas. Schwarzlose ended up getting one-third of the vote. It didn't help that Jimmy Carter's Presidency was beset by problems. The economy was slowly sinking as interest rates continued to climb. The administration was sidetracked by a series of international crises, culminating in the taking of American hostages in Iran. Some of those troubles spilled over into Arkansas in the spring and summer of 1980, when hundreds of detained Cuban refugees—mostly inmates from prisons and mental hospitals whom Castro released to the United States in the infamous Mariel boat lift—were sent to a "resettlement camp" at Fort Chaffee, Arkansas. In late May, the refugees rioted and hundreds broke out of the fort, heading toward the nearby community of Fort Smith. County deputies and local citizens loaded their shotguns and waited for the expected onslaught. The situation was made worse because the Army, under a doctrine known as *posse comitatus*, had no police authority off the base and were not even empowered to forcefully keep the detainees—who were not technically prisoners—on the grounds. Bill sent state troopers and National Guardsmen to round up the Cubans and control the situation. Then he flew up to oversee the operation.

Bill's actions saved lives and prevented widespread violence. When Bill went back a few days later to follow up, I joined him. There were still signs on gas stations: "All out of ammo, come back tomorrow," and in front of homes: "We shoot to kill." I also attended some tense meetings Bill held with James "Bulldog" Drummond, the frustrated general in command of Fort Chaffee, and representatives from the White House. Bill wanted federal assistance to contain the detainees, but General Drummond said his hands were tied because of orders from above. The White House message seemed to be: "Don't complain, just handle the mess we gave you." Bill had done just that, but there was a big political price to pay for supporting his President.

After the June riots, President Carter had promised Bill that no more Cubans would be sent to Arkansas. In August, the White House broke that promise, closing sites in Wisconsin and Pennsylvania and sending more refugees to Fort Chaffee. That reversal further undermined support for Bill Clinton and Jimmy Carter in Arkansas.

Southerners have an expression to describe something or someone whose luck turns all bad. By now it was clear that Jimmy Carter's Presidency was snakebit. It was harder to admit that Bill Clinton's Governorship was suffering the same fate.

Bill's Republican opponent, Frank White, began running negative ads. Against footage of dark-skinned Cuban rioters, a voice-over announced that "Bill Clinton cares more about Jimmy Carter than he does about Arkansas." I initially dismissed the ads, thinking that everyone in Arkansas knew what a good job Bill had done containing the violence. Then I started fielding questions at school assemblies and civic clubs: "Why did the Governor let the Cubans riot?" "Why didn't the Governor care about us more than about President Carter?" Ads like this one, which demonstrated the power of a negative message, became all too common in 1980, largely because of a strategy employed by the National Conservative Political Action Committee (NCPAC), formed by the Republicans to design and run negative ads all over the country. By October, I thought the polls showing Bill ahead were wrong and that Bill might actually lose. Bill had used a young, abrasive New York pollster, Dick Morris, for his successful 1978 race, but no one on his staff or in his office could stand working with Morris, so they persuaded Bill to use a different team in 1980. I called Morris to ask what he thought was happening. He told me Bill was in real trouble and probably would lose unless he made some kind of dramatic gesture, like repealing the car tag tax or repudiating Carter. I couldn't persuade anyone else to ignore the polls that showed Bill winning. Bill himself was uncertain. He didn't want to break publicly with the President or call a special session to repeal the car tag hike. So he just upped his campaigning and kept on explaining himself to voters.

Right before the election, we had a disturbing conversation with an officer in the National Guard who had been in charge of some of the troops called up to quell riots at the base. He told Bill that his elderly aunt had informed him that she intended to vote for Frank White because Bill had let the Cubans riot. When this officer explained to his aunt that he had been there and knew for a fact that Governor Clinton had stopped the rioting, his aunt said that wasn't true because she had seen what happened on television. The ads trumped not just the news, but personal witness. That 1980 campaign, where truth was turned on its head, convinced me of the piercing power of negative ads to convert voters through distortion.

Exit polls showed Bill winning by a wide margin, but he lost, 52 to 48 percent. He was devastated. The big hotel room his campaign had rented was filled with shocked friends and supporters. He decided he would wait until the next day to make any public comments and asked me to go and thank everyone for their help and invite them to come over to the Governor's Mansion the following morning. The gathering on the back lawn was like a wake. Bill had now lost two elections—one for Congress, one as an incumbent Governor—and many wondered whether this defeat would break him.

Before the week was out, we found an old home to buy in the Hillcrest section of Little Rock, near where we had lived before. On two lots, it had a converted attic that we used for Chelsea's nursery. Bill and

I are partial to older homes and traditional furniture, so we haunted thrift stores and antique shops. When Virginia visited, she asked us why we liked old things. As she explained, "I've spent my whole life trying to get away from old homes and furniture." When she figured out our taste, though, she cheerfully sent over a Victorian "courting couch" she had in her garage.

Chelsea was the only bright spot in the painful months following the election. She was the first grandchild in our families, so Bill's mother was more than happy to do a lot of baby-sitting, as were my parents when they came to visit. It was in our new house that Chelsea celebrated her first birthday, learned to walk and talk and taught her father a lesson in the perils of multitasking. One day Bill was holding her while watching a basketball game on television, talking on the phone and doing a crossword puzzle. When she couldn't get his attention, she bit him on the nose!

Bill took a job at Wright, Lindsey and Jennings, a Little Rock law firm. One of his new colleagues, Bruce Lindsey, became one of Bill's closest confidants. But before Frank White had moved into the mansion, Bill was unofficially campaigning to get his job back.

The pressures on me to conform had increased dramatically when Bill was elected Governor in 1978. I could get away with being considered a little unconventional as the wife of the Attorney General, but as First Lady of Arkansas, I was thrown into an unblinking spotlight. And for the first time, I came to realize how my personal choices could impact my husband's political future.

My parents raised me to focus on the inner qualities of people, not the way they dressed or the titles they held. That sometimes made it hard for me to understand the importance of certain conventions to others. I learned the hard way that some voters in Arkansas were seriously offended by the fact that I kept my maiden name.

Because I knew I had my own professional interests and did not want to create any confusion or conflict of interest with my husband's public career, it made perfect sense to me to continue using my own name. Bill didn't mind, but our mothers did. Virginia cried when Bill told her, and my mother addressed her letters to "Mr. and Mrs. Bill Clinton." Brides who kept their maiden names were becoming more common in some places in the mid-1970s, but they were still rare in most of the country. And that included Arkansas. It was a personal decision, a small (I thought) gesture to acknowledge that while I was com-

mitted to our union, I was still me. I was also being practical. By the
time we married, I was teaching, trying cases, publishing and speaking
as Hillary Rodham. I kept my name after Bill was elected to state office
partly because I thought it would help avoid the appearance of conflict
of interest. And there's one case I think I would have lost had I taken
Bill's name.

I was helping Phil Carroll defend a company that sold and shipped
creosote-treated logs by railroad. As a shipment was unloaded at its
destination, the logs came loose from their supports on one of the
flatbed cars and injured some employees of the company that had purchased the logs. The ensuing lawsuit was tried before a judge who had
been accused of misconduct on the bench, mostly due to his excessive
acquaintance with alcohol. Under Arkansas law, judicial investigations
were conducted by the Attorney General, namely my husband. The
judge, who knew me only as "Ms. Rodham," paid close attention to me,
often making comments like, "How pretty you look today," or, "Come
up here so I can get a good look at you."

At the end of the plaintiff's case, Phil moved for a directed verdict in
favor of our client, since there was no evidence connecting our client to
the alleged negligence that had caused the accident. The judge agreed
and granted the motion. Phil and I packed up and went back to Little
Rock. A few days later, an attorney for one of the other defendants
called to tell me what had happened while the jury was out. The judge
had started ranting to the lawyers about Bill Clinton's investigation and
how mistreated he felt. Finally, one of them interrupted him and asked,
"Judge, you know that lady lawyer, Hillary Rodham, who was here with
Phil Carroll? That's Bill Clinton's wife."

"Well, goddammit, if I'd known that," the judge exclaimed, "they'd
never have gotten that directed verdict!"

The winter after Bill's defeat, a few of our friends and supporters
came to talk to me about using "Clinton" as my last name. Ann Henry
told me some people were upset when they received invitations to
events at the Governor's Mansion from "Governor Bill Clinton and
Hillary Rodham." Chelsea's birth announcement, also featuring our
two names, was apparently a hot subject of conversation around the
state. People in Arkansas reacted to me much as my mother-in-law had
when she first met me: I was an oddity because of my dress, my Northern ways and the use of my maiden name.

Jim Blair joked about staging an elaborate scenario on the steps of the Capitol. Bill would put his foot on my throat, yank me by my hair and say something like, "Woman, you're going to take my last name and that's that!" Flags would wave, hymns would be sung and the name would change.

Vernon Jordan came to town to give a speech and asked me if I would make him breakfast, including grits, at our house the next morning. In our little kitchen, perched on a too small chair, he ate my instant grits and urged me to do the right thing: start using Bill's last name. The only person who didn't ask me or even talk to me about my name was my husband. He said my name was my business, and he didn't think his political future depended on it one way or another.

I decided it was more important for Bill to be Governor again than for me to keep my maiden name. So when Bill announced his run for another term on Chelsea's second birthday, I began calling myself Hillary Rodham Clinton.

The 1982 campaign was a family endeavor. We loaded Chelsea, diaper bag and all, into a big car driven by a true friend, Jimmy Red Jones, and we drove around the state. We started in the South, where spring had snuck in under the pine trees, and ended in Fayetteville in a snowstorm. I've always liked campaigning and traveling through Arkansas, stopping at country stores, sale barns and barbecue joints. It's a continuing education in human nature, including your own. I had been surprised when I had gone door-to-door for Bill in his 1978 campaign and encountered women who told me their husbands did the voting for them or met African Americans who thought there was still a poll tax to be paid.

In 1982, with Chelsea on my hip or holding my hand, I walked up and down streets meeting voters. I remember meeting some young mothers in the small town of Bald Knob. When I said I bet they were having a good time talking to their babies, one of them asked, "Why would I talk to her? She can't talk back." I knew from my Yale Child Study days—and from my mother—how important it was to talk and read to babies to build their vocabularies. Yet when I tried to explain this, the women were polite but dubious.

After Bill's election in 1982, a humbler, more seasoned Governor returned to the State House, though no less determined to get as much done as possible in two years. And there was so much to be done. Arkansas was a poor state, last or close to last by many measures, from percentage of college graduates to per capita personal income. I had helped Bill tackle health care reform in his first term, successfully setting up a network of health clinics, recruiting more doctors, nurses and midwives into rural areas—over the opposition of the state's medical society. When Governor White tried to make good on his 1980 campaign promise to dismantle the network, people flooded into the Capitol to protest, and White had to retreat. Bill and I agreed that Arkansas would never prosper without an overhaul of its education system. Bill announced that he was forming an Education Standards Committee to recommend sweeping educational reforms, and he wanted me to be its Chair.

I had chaired the Rural Health Committee, and Bill asked me to tackle education because he wanted to send a signal about how serious he was. Nobody, including me, thought it was a good idea. But Bill wouldn't take no for an answer. "Look on the bright side," he said. "If you're successful, our friends will complain that you could have done even more. And our enemies will complain that you did too much. If you accomplish nothing, our friends will say, 'She should never have tried this.' And our enemies will say, 'See, she couldn't get anything done!'" Bill was convinced he was right to appoint me, and eventually I relented.

Again, this was a politically risky move. Improving the schools would require an increase in taxes—never a popular idea. The fifteen-member committee also recommended that students be subjected to standardized tests, including one before they could graduate from eighth grade. But the cornerstone of the proposed reform plan was mandatory teacher testing. Though this enraged the teachers union, civil rights groups and others who were vital to the Democratic Party in Arkansas, we felt there was no way around the issue. How could we expect children to perform at national levels when their teachers sometimes fell short? The debate was so bitter that one school librarian said I was "lower than a snake's belly." I tried to remember that I was being called names not because of who I was but what I represented.

Getting the legislature to approve and fund the reform package turned into a knock-down-drag-out fight among interest groups. Teachers worried about their jobs. Legislators representing rural areas fretted that the plan would consolidate their small school districts. In the midst of this contention, I stepped before a joint session of the Arkansas legislature's House and Senate to plead our case for improving all schools, big and small. For whatever reason—probably a combination of skill and lots of practice—public speaking has always been one of my strong suits. I laughed when Representative Lloyd George, a legislator from rural Yell County, later announced to the assembly: "Well, fellas, it looks like we might have elected the wrong Clinton!" It was another example of a phenomenon I call "the talking dog syndrome." Some people are still amazed that any woman (this includes Governors' wives, corporate CEOs, sports stars and rock singers) can hold her own under pressure and be articulate and knowledgeable. The dog can talk! In fact, it's often an advantage if people you hope to persuade underestimate you at first. I would have been willing to bark my whole speech in order to guarantee education reform!

We won some votes and lost some, and we had to fight the teachers union in court. But by the end of Bill's term in office, Arkansas had a plan in place to raise school standards, tens of thousands of children had a better chance to realize their learning potentials and teachers got a desperately needed raise in pay. I was particularly pleased when Terrel Bell, President Reagan's Secretary of Education, praised the Arkansas reform plan, commenting that Bill had been "a prime leader in education."

The public success of education reform legislation was followed by a devastating personal challenge. In July 1984, I received a call in the middle of the week from Betsey Wright, who had become Bill's Chief of Staff in 1983 after his reelection. She told me Bill was on his way to see me. I had just finished lunch with some friends, so I excused myself and stood outside the restaurant until Bill pulled up. We sat in the car while he told me that the head of the state police had just informed him that his brother, Roger, was under police surveillance. The police had videotaped him selling drugs to an informer. The state police director then told Bill they could arrest Roger right then or continue to run up the charges and increase the pressure on him to identify his supplier, the real target. Roger was selling, he said, to finance a serious cocaine habit. The director then asked Bill what he wanted him to do. Bill replied there was no choice. The operation against Roger had to run its course. As a big brother, however, it was excruciatingly painful to know that, at best, his brother would be going to jail and, at worst, he might kill himself with drug abuse.

Bill and I berated ourselves for not seeing signs of Roger's abuse and taking some kind of action to help him. We worried that this news, and Bill's knowledge beforehand, would deeply hurt his mother. Finally, the wait was over. Roger was arrested and charged with possessing and selling cocaine. Bill explained to both Roger and Virginia that he had learned about the investigation but felt duty-bound not to tell his mother or warn his brother. Virginia was shocked by the accusations and the realization that Bill and I had known that Roger was headed for prison. Although I understood their pain and anger, I believed Bill had taken the only course open to him by keeping the information from his family. Roger agreed to counseling before he left to serve his prison sentence. In the course of those sessions, Roger admitted how much he hated his father, and Virginia and Bill learned for the first time how profoundly Roger had been affected by his father's alcoholism and violence. Bill realized that living with alcoholism and the denial and secrecy that it spawned had also created consequences and problems for him that would take years to sort out. This was one of many family crises we would face. Even strong marriages can be strained when trouble comes. In the years ahead, we would have rough patches, but we were determined to get through them.

Starting in 1987, more than a few Democratic Party leaders were urging Bill to consider a run for the Presidency in 1988 when Ronald Reagan's second term would end. Both Bill and I hoped Senator Dale Bumpers would decide to run, and we thought he would. He had been a first-rate Governor and Senator and could have been a formidable national candidate. In late March, though, he decided not to run. The interest in Bill increased, and he asked me what I thought. I did not think he should run and told him so. It looked as if Vice President Bush would be nominated as the successor to President Reagan, running for Reagan's surrogate third term. I thought that Bush would be hard to beat. But there were other reasons too. Bill had been elected in 1986 to a fourth term as Governor and the first four-year term since Reconstruction. He had not yet served as Chairman of the Democratic Leadership Council and had just begun his chairmanship of the National Governors Association. He was only forty years old. His mother was dealing with problems in her nursing practice, and his brother was readjusting to life after prison. If that weren't enough, my father had just suffered a stroke and my parents were moving to Little Rock so that Bill and I could help them out. I thought it was the wrong time in our lives and told him I just was not convinced.

One day he thought he would run, the next day, he was ready to say he would not. Finally, I persuaded him to set a date by which he would make a decision. Anyone who knows Bill understands he has to have a deadline or he will continue to explore every possible pro and con. He picked July 14 and reserved a room in a hotel to make his announcement—whatever it might be. A number of his friends from around the country came down to be with him the day before. Some were pushing him to run; others thought it was premature and he should wait. Bill analyzed every point anyone raised. I thought it was significant that he was still debating less than twenty-four hours before he had to comment publicly. That meant to me that he was leaning against running but not quite ready to slam the door.

Much has been written about the reasons for his decision not to run, but it finally came down to one word: Chelsea. Carl Wagner, a longtime Democratic activist and father of an only daughter, told Bill he would effectively be turning his daughter into an orphan. Mickey Kantor delivered the same message while he and Bill sat on the back porch of the Governor's Mansion. Chelsea came out and asked Bill about our upcoming vacation plans. When Bill said he might not have one if he ran for President, Chelsea looked at him and said, "Then Mom and I will go without you." That sealed the decision for Bill.

Chelsea was beginning to understand what it meant to have a father in the public eye. When she was little and Bill was Governor, she had no idea what he did. Once when she was about four and someone asked her, she replied, "My daddy talks on the telephone, drinks coffee and makes 'peeches."

The 1986 Governor's campaign was the first one she had been old enough to follow. She could read and watch the news and be exposed to some of the mean-spiritedness that politics seems to generate. One of Bill's opponents was Orval Faubus, the infamous former Governor who defied court orders to integrate Little Rock's Central High School in 1957. President Eisenhower sent troops to enforce the law. Because of my concerns about what Faubus and his supporters would say and do, Bill and I tried to prepare Chelsea for what she might hear about her father or, for that matter, about her mother. We sat around our dinner table in the Governor's Mansion role-playing with her, pretending we were in debates where one of us acted like a political opponent who criticized Bill for not being a good Governor. Chelsea's eyes grew big at the idea that anyone would say such bad things about her daddy.

I loved Chelsea's growing assertiveness, though it wasn't always convenient. Around Christmas, 1988, I went duck hunting with Dr.

Frank Kumpuris, a distinguished surgeon and good friend of mine, who invited me to join him, his two doctor sons, Drew and Dean, and a few other buddies at their hunting cabin. I hadn't shot much since my days at Lake Winola with my dad, but I thought it would be fun. That's how I found myself standing hip deep in freezing water, waiting for dawn in eastern Arkansas. When the sun rose, the ducks flew overhead and I made a lucky shot, hitting a banded duck. When I got home, Chelsea was waiting for me, outraged to wake up and learn that I had left home before dawn to go "kill some poor little duck's mommy or daddy." My efforts at explaining were futile. She didn't speak to me for a whole day.

Although Bill decided not to run in 1988, the nominee, Governor Michael Dukakis of Massachusetts, asked him to give the nominating speech at the Democratic Convention in Atlanta. It turned into a fiasco. Dukakis and his staff had reviewed and approved every word of Bill's text ahead of time, but the speech was longer than the delegates or the television networks expected. Some delegates on the floor began yelling at Bill to finish. This was a humiliating introduction to the nation, and many observers assumed Bill's political future was over. Eight days later, though, he was on Johnny Carson's *Tonight Show*, making fun of himself and playing his saxophone. Yet another comeback.

After Bill was reelected Governor in 1990, Democrats across the country approached him once again about running for President. That encouragement reflected the assessment that George H. W. Bush was out of touch with most Americans. Although Bush's popularity remained astronomical in the aftermath of the Gulf War, I thought his performance on domestic issues—particularly the economy—made him vulnerable. I had realized how unfamiliar President Bush was with many of the problems facing America when I spoke with him at an Education Summit he had convened of all the Governors in Charlottesville, Virginia, in September 1989. As the wife of the Democratic co-chair of the Summit for the National Governors Association, I was seated next to President Bush at a grand dinner held at Monticello. We enjoyed a cordial relationship and had been around each other many times at the White House or the annual Governors meetings. We talked about the American health care system. I said we had the best system in the world if you wanted a heart transplant but not if you wanted a baby to survive his or her first birthday. Our rate of infant mortality at that time placed us behind eighteen other industrialized nations, including Japan, Canada and France. President Bush was incredulous and said, "You can't be right about that."

I told him, "I'll get you the statistics to prove it."

He replied, "I'll get my own."

The next day, during a meeting with the Governors, he slipped Bill a note: "Tell Hillary she was right."

This time I believed Bill should carefully consider whether to run. In June of 1991, he attended the annual Bilderberg Conference in Europe, which brought together leaders from all over the world. After listening to Bush Administration officials defend their policies, he called to tell me how frustrated he was with their prescriptions for economic growth and nearly everything else. "This is crazy," he said. "We're not doing anything to get the country ready for the future." I could tell as much from the tone of his voice as his words that he was seriously thinking through the arguments he would make if he decided to run. He had enhanced his national standing through his work in the National Governors Association, and his record in Arkansas on education, welfare reform and economic development was considered a success. When we attended the annual Governors Conference in Seattle in August, I was not surprised that a number of his Democratic colleagues told him they would support him if he was serious about running.

After the conference, Bill, Chelsea and I took a short vacation to Victoria and Vancouver, Canada, to talk over what he should do. Chelsea, now eleven, was significantly more mature than she had been four years earlier and ready to offer her opinions. She and I agreed: Bill could be a good President. Luckily, the primary campaign would be shorter and more focused than usual because Senator Tom Harkin of Iowa was running, which meant Bill could bypass the Iowa caucus and go straight to New Hampshire. He already had spent time there setting up a DLC chapter, and he thought he could compete against Senator Paul Tsongas of Massachusetts for the "new Democrat" vote. As Bill discussed the pros and cons with us, he assured Chelsea that his schedule would include all of her important dates, like the annual Arkansas Ballet performance of *The Nutcracker*, and that we would still go to Renaissance Weekend over New Year's like we always did. I could not have predicted all that would happen, but I believed Bill was prepared on the substance of what needed to be done for the country and how to run a winning political campaign. We figured: What did we have to lose? Even if Bill's run failed, he would have the satisfaction of knowing he had tried, not just to win, but to make a difference for America. That seemed to be a risk worth taking.

CAMPAIGN ODYSSEY

I GOT A HINT OF WHAT IT TOOK TO SURVIVE A PRESI-dential campaign in September 1991, when I bumped into Hal Bruno in a hallway of the Biltmore Hotel in Los Angeles. Bruno, a veteran television producer and a casual acquaintance, was in town to check out potential presidential candidates during the fall meeting of the Democratic National Committee.

He asked me how it was going.

I must have looked bewildered. "I don't know. This is all new to me. Do you have any suggestions?"

"Just this," he said. "Be very careful who you trust. This is different from anything you have been through before. Other than that, try to enjoy the experience!"

It was sage advice, though it would be impossible to run an undertaking as complex and pressured as a presidential campaign without trusting an awful lot of people. We started with the array of friends and campaign professionals we knew we could rely on.

As soon as he decided in September to enter the race, Bill contacted a skeletal crew of advisers to help him launch his candidacy. Craig Smith, a longtime aide, left the Governor's payroll to work on operations until a full-fledged campaign could be assembled, and he then became its Director of State Operations. On October 2, 1991, many of Bill's advisers were in Little Rock to help him shape his announcement speech scheduled for the following day. The scene of creative chaos in the mansion that night would be typical of the entire campaign. Stan Greenberg, the pollster, and Frank Greer, the media adviser, along with Al From, the President of the Democratic Leadership Council (DLC), and Bruce Reed, the DLC's Policy Director, huddled around Bill all day and into the night, trying to get him to finish his crucial speech. Bill made phone calls, read through his previous speeches and dove into trays of food laid out on the table. Chelsea, eleven years old and a budding ballerina, jetéd between rooms and pirouetted around her father and our guests until her bedtime. At four in the morning, the speech was done.

At noon the next day, in front of the Old State House in Little Rock, a reenergized Bill Clinton stood with Chelsea and me before a bank of microphones and TV cameras and declared his intention to run for President. His speech laid out his emerging critique of the Bush Administration. "Middle-class people are spending more time on the job, less time with their children and bringing home less money to pay more for health care and housing and education. The poverty rates are up, the streets are meaner and ever more children are growing up in broken families. Our country is headed in the wrong direction, fast. It's falling behind, it's losing its way, and all we've gotten out of Washington is status quo paralysis, neglect and selfishness . . . not leadership and vision."

The campaign he wanted to run would be "about ideas, not slogans" and would offer "leadership that will restore the American dream, fight for the forgotten middle class, provide more opportunity, demand more responsibility from each of us and create a stronger community in this great country of ours." Behind his rhetoric were the specific plans that Bill would present during the course of the primary campaign to persuade Democratic voters that he had the best chance to defeat President Bush.

The mainstream media didn't give Bill much hope of making it through the primaries, let alone being elected President. He was initially dismissed as an obscure if colorful outsider, handsome and articulate but, at age forty-six, too young and inexperienced for the job. As his message of change caught on with potential voters, the press—and President Bush's backers—started to take a closer look at Bill Clinton. And at me.

If the first forty-four years of my life were an education, the thirteen-month presidential campaign was a revelation. Despite all the good advice we had received and all the time Bill and I had spent in the political arena, we were unprepared for the hardball politics and relentless scrutiny that comes with a run for the Presidency. Bill had to make the case nationwide for his political beliefs, and we had to endure exhaustive inspection of every aspect of our lives. We had to get acquainted with a national press corps that knew little about us and even less about where we came from. And we had to manage our own emotions in the glare of the public spotlight, through the course of an increasingly mean-spirited and personal campaign.

I relied on my friends and staff to help us through the rough patches. Bill put together a terrific team, including James Carville and Paul Begala, who had masterminded Harris Wofford's election to the Senate from Pennsylvania in 1991. James, a Louisiana Cajun and ex-Marine, bonded with Bill immediately; they both relished their Southern roots, adored their mamas and understood that presidential politics was a contact sport. Paul, a talented Texan who occasionally had to serve as a translator for Carville's rapid-fire patois, embodied a passion for populism and commitment to civility, no easy feat. David Wilhelm, who became campaign manager, was from Chicago and intuitively understood how to win the contest for delegates on the ground, person by person. Another Chicagoan, Rahm Emanuel, had sharp political skills and a genius for fund-raising, and became the finance manager. George Stephanopoulos, a Rhodes Scholar and aide to Congressman Richard Gephardt, figured out how to respond instantly and effectively to the political attacks and to seize the offensive with the press. Bruce Reed, also a Rhodes Scholar, who came to the campaign from the Democratic Leadership Council, had a gift for expressing complex policy ideas in simple and compelling language and was instrumental in articulating Bill's campaign message. The DLC and its founder Al From were essential to the development of Bill's policies and message in the campaign.

Bill and I also relied on a dedicated team from Arkansas, including Rodney Slater, Carol Willis, Diane Blair, Ann Henry, Maurice Smith, Patty Howe Criner, Carl and Margaret Whillock, Betsey Wright, Sheila Bronfman, Mack and Donna McLarty and so many others who put their lives on hold to elect the first President from Arkansas.

I had begun to assemble my own staff as soon as Bill announced his candidacy. This was a departure from protocol, in which the candidate's staff controls his wife's schedule and message. I was different—something that would become increasingly apparent in the months ahead.

The first person I called for help was Maggie Williams, then in a Ph.D. program at the University of Pennsylvania. Maggie and I had worked together at the Children's Defense Fund during the 1980s. I admired her skills as a leader and communicator and thought she would be able to handle with aplomb whatever happened. Although she couldn't come on full-time until late 1992, she offered advice and support throughout the campaign.

Three young women who started working for me in the campaign became invaluable and stayed with me through the eight White House years. Patti Solis, a politically active daughter of Mexican immigrants, had grown up in Chicago and worked for Mayor Richard M. Daley. She had never done scheduling in a presidential campaign, and I had never had anyone tell me what I had to do and where and when to do it, but Patti turned out to be a natural as my scheduler, juggling the challenges of politics, people and preparation with intelligence, decisiveness and laughter. She ran my life hour by hour for nine years, becoming a close friend and valued adviser on whom I still rely today.

Capricia Penavic Marshall, a dynamic young lawyer from Cleveland, was also the daughter of immigrants—her mother from Mexico and her father a Croatian refugee from Tito's Yugoslavia. When she saw Bill on television giving a speech in 1991, she decided she wanted to be involved in his campaign and worked for months rounding up convention delegates in Ohio. Finally, she was hired onto my staff to do advance work, primarily a young person's game and a premier educational experience in politics and in life. Capricia took to advance like a pro, and despite an unfortunate first trip where she was waiting for me at the wrong airport in Shreveport, we hit it off. Her good-humored grace under pressure served her—and me—well when she became the White House social secretary in Bill's second term.

Kelly Craighead, a beautiful former competitive diver from California, was already an experienced events planner when she became my trip director, which meant she oversaw my life on the road. Everywhere I went over the next eight years—around the block or around the world—Kelly was by my side. Her slogan, "Fail to plan, plan to fail," became one of our campaign mantras. No one worked harder or longer hours to iron out every last detail of any trip I took. Hers was a demanding and exhausting job, requiring the combined talents of a general and a diplomat. She also had a lot of insight, dedication and spunk. Knowing that she was looking out for me gave me comfort and confidence on even the hardest days throughout the White House years.

In addition to all the young people who signed on to help, Brooke Shearer volunteered to travel with me. Brooke, her husband, Strobe Talbott, and her entire family had been friends of Bill's since he and

Strobe were Rhodes Scholars together. As soon as Bill and I became a couple, they became friends of mine. And their sons became close to Chelsea. Brooke, who had lived in Washington and worked in journalism, brought a wealth of experience about the national media and a wry take on the absurdities of campaigns.

I learned quickly that, in a race for the Presidency, nothing is off-limits. Innocent comments or jests erupt into controversies within seconds of being reported on the news wires. Rumors become the story *du jour.* And while our past experiences may have seemed like ancient history to us, every detail of our lives was being sifted and combed as if we were some sort of archaeological dig. I had seen this before in other people's campaigns: Senator Ed Muskie defending his wife in 1972 and Senator Bob Kerrey telling a risqué joke in 1992 without realizing that a boom microphone was nearby. But until you are the focus of the klieg lights, you simply cannot imagine their heat.

One evening, when Bill and I were stumping in New Hampshire, he introduced me to a crowd of supporters. Recounting my two decades of work on children's issues, he joked that we had a new campaign slogan: "Buy one, get one free." He said it as a way of explaining that I would be an active partner in his administration and would continue to champion the causes I had worked on in the past. It was a good line, and my campaign staff adopted it. Widely reported in the press, it then took on a life of its own, disseminated everywhere as evidence of my alleged secret aspirations to become "co-President" with my husband.

I hadn't had enough exposure to the national press corps to fully appreciate the extent to which the news media was a conduit for everything that happened on a campaign. Information, policy positions and quotes were filtered through a journalistic lens before they reached the public. A candidate can't get his or her ideas across without media coverage, and a journalist can't report effectively without access to the candidate. Thus, candidates and reporters are at once adversarial and mutually dependent. It's a tricky, delicate and important relationship, and I didn't fully understand it.

The "buy one, get one free" comment was a reminder to Bill and me that our remarks might be taken out of context because news reporters didn't have time or space to provide the text of an entire conversation. Simplicity and brevity were essential to reporters. So were snappy lines and catchphrases. One of the masters of political innuendo weighed in early.

Former President Nixon's political instincts remained finely tuned, and he commented on our campaign in an interview during a visit to Washington in early February. "If the wife comes through as being too strong and too intelligent," he remarked, "it makes the husband look like a wimp." He then went on to note that voters tended to agree with Cardinal de Richelieu's assessment: "Intellect in a woman is unbecoming."

"This man never does anything without a purpose," I remember thinking when I saw Nixon's comment reported in *The New York Times*. My service on the 1974 impeachment staff aside, I suspected that Nixon understood better than many the threat Bill posed to the Republican hold on the Presidency. He probably believed that denigrating Bill because he put up with an outspoken wife, and vilifying me as "unbecoming," might scare voters anxious for a change but uncertain about us.

By then Bill's entire life was under a media microscope. He already had been asked more questions about personal matters than any presidential candidate in American history. While the mainstream press still avoided printing unsubstantiated rumors, the supermarket tabloids were offering cash for shocking stories from Arkansas. Eventually one of these fishing expeditions hooked a whale of a tale.

I was in Atlanta campaigning on January 23 when Bill called to warn me about an upcoming tabloid story in which a woman named Gennifer Flowers claimed she had a twelve-year affair with him. He told me it wasn't true.

The campaign staff went into a tailspin over the story, and I knew that some of them thought the race was over. I asked David Wilhelm to set up a conference call for me to talk to everyone. I said that all of us were in this campaign because we believed Bill could make a difference for our country and that it was up to the voters to decide whether or not we'd be successful.

"So," I ended, "let's get back to work."

Like a rampant virus, the Flowers story hopped between species of media, from the *Star*, a supermarket tabloid, to *Nightline*, a respected network news show. Despite our efforts to keep going, the wall-to-wall press coverage made it impossible for the campaign to focus attention on substantive issues. And the New Hampshire primary was just weeks away. Something had to be done. Our friend Harry Thomason, along with Mickey Kantor, James Carville, Paul Begala and George Stephanopoulos, consulted with Bill and me about what we could do. They recommended that we appear on the Sunday night television show *60 Minutes* right after the Super Bowl, when we would be seen by the largest possible audience. I took a lot of convincing that such exposure was worth the risks, loss of privacy and potential impact on our families, especially on Chelsea. Finally, I was persuaded that if we didn't deal with the situation publicly, Bill's campaign would be over before a single vote was cast.

The *60 Minutes* interview took place on January 26 in a suite at a Boston hotel starting at 11 A.M. The room had been transformed into a set, with banks of temporary lights on poles surrounding the couch where Bill and I were sitting. Partway through the interview, a heavy pole loaded with lights fell toward me. Bill saw it falling and pulled me out of the way just as the tower crashed where I'd been sitting. I was shaken up, and Bill held me tight, whispering over and over, "I've got you. Don't worry. You're okay. I love you."

The interviewer, Steve Kroft, started with a series of questions about our relationship and the state of our marriage. He asked whether Bill had committed adultery and whether we had been separated or had contemplated divorce. We declined to answer such personal questions about our private lives. But Bill acknowledged that he had caused pain in our marriage and said he would leave it to voters to decide whether that disqualified him from the Presidency.

Kroft: I think most Americans would agree that it's very admirable that you have stayed together, that you've worked your problems out, that you seem to have reached some sort of an understanding and an arrangement.

An arrangement? An understanding? Kroft may have been trying to pay us a compliment, but his categorization of our marriage was so off target that Bill was incredulous. So was I.

Bill Clinton: Wait a minute. You're looking at two people who love each other. This is not an arrangement or an understanding. This is a marriage. That's a very different thing.

I wish I had let him have the last word, but now it was my turn to add my two cents, and I did.

Hillary Clinton: You know, I'm not sitting here, some little woman standing by my man like Tammy Wynette. I'm sitting here because I love him and I respect him and I honor what he's been through and what we've been through together. And you know, if that's not enough for people, then heck, don't vote for him.

Although the interview lasted fifty-six minutes, CBS broadcast about ten minutes, leaving out much of what was important—at least as far as I was concerned. We hadn't known how drastically they would cut our words. Still, I was relieved that it was over. Bill and I felt good about how we had responded and so did everyone with us. Apparently, most Americans agreed with our basic point: that the election was about them, not our marriage. Twenty-three days later, Bill became known as the "Comeback Kid" for his strong second-place finish in the New Hampshire primary.

I didn't fare as well. The fallout from my reference to Tammy Wynette was instant—as it deserved to be—and brutal. Of course, I meant to refer to Tammy Wynette's famous song, "Stand by Your Man," not to her as a person. But I wasn't careful in my choice of words, and my comment unleashed a torrent of angry reactions. I regretted the way I had come across, and I apologized to Tammy personally and later publicly in another television interview. But the damage was done. And more was on the way.

In early March, with the Democratic primary season in high gear, former California Governor and Democratic presidential candidate Jerry Brown went on the offensive against Bill, focusing on my law practice and on the Rose Law Firm, where I had been a partner since 1979. After Bill became Governor again in 1983, I asked my law partners to calculate my share of profits, without including fees earned by other lawyers for work done for the state or any state agency. The Rose Firm had provided these services to the Arkansas State government for decades. There was no conflict of interest, but I wanted to avoid every appearance of one. The firm agreed to wall me off from the work and any fees derived from it. When Frank White tried to make this an issue in the 1986 Arkansas gubernatorial campaign, he was embarrassed when the facts established that other Arkansas law firms had received significantly more business from the state while Bill was Governor.

Spoon-fed false information by Bill's political adversaries in the state, Jerry Brown recycled the charges for the debate in Chicago two days before the March 17 primaries in Illinois and Michigan. Brown accused Bill of steering state business to the Rose Firm to increase my income. It was a spurious and opportunistic charge that had no basis in fact. And it's what led to the infamous "cookies and tea" incident.

Bill and I were at the Busy Bee Coffee Shop in Chicago, trailed by a gaggle of cameras and microphones. With the Illinois primary looming, reporters were throwing questions at Bill about Brown's charges. Then a reporter asked me what I thought of Brown's accusations against us. My answer was long and rambling:

"I thought, number one, [the remark] was pathetic and desperate, and also thought it was interesting because this is the sort of thing that happens to . . . women who have their own careers and their own lives. And I think it's a shame, but I guess it's something that we're going to have to live with. Those of us who have tried and have a career—tried to have an independent life and to make a difference—and certainly like myself who has children . . . you know I've done the best I can to lead my life, but I suppose it'll be subject to attack. But it's not true and I don't [know] what else to say except it's sad to me."

Then came the reporter's follow-up—about whether I could have avoided an appearance of conflict of interest when my husband was Governor.

"I wish that were true," I replied. "You know, I suppose I could have stayed home and baked cookies and had teas, but what I decided to do was fulfill my profession, which I entered before my husband was in public life. And I've worked very, very hard to be as careful as possible, and that's all I can tell you."

It wasn't my most eloquent moment. I could have said, "Look, short of abandoning my law firm partnership and staying home, there was nothing more I could have done to avoid the appearance of a conflict of interest." Besides, I've done quite a lot of cookie-baking in my day, and tea-pouring too!

My aides, aware that the press had picked up on the "cookies and tea" comment, suggested that I talk to reporters a second time to explain in greater detail—and more articulately—what I meant. On the spot, I had an impromptu mini–press conference. But it had little effect. Thirteen minutes after I answered the question, a story ran on the AP wire. CNN quickly aired one too, and followed with an afternoon segment that made little reference to the initial question—about conflicts of interest and the Rose Law Firm—but reduced everything I said to, "I could have stayed home and baked cookies and had teas." The theme for most news organizations that day was that I had made a serious political error.

I had made an awkward attempt to explain my situation and to suggest that many women who juggle careers and lives are penalized for the choices they make. It turned into a story about my alleged callousness toward stay-at-home mothers. Some reporters merged "tea and cookies" and "standing by my man like Tammy Wynette" into one quote, as if I had uttered both phrases in the same breath—not fifty-one days apart. The controversy was a boon to GOP strategists. Republican Party leaders labeled me a "radical feminist," a "militant feminist lawyer" and even "the ideological leader of a Clinton-Clinton Administration that would push a radical-feminist agenda."

I got hundreds of letters about "cookies and tea." Supporters offered their encouragement and praised me for defending a broad array of choices for women. Critics were venomous. One letter referred to me as the Antichrist, and another said I was an insult to American motherhood. I often worried about how much attention Chelsea paid and how much sank in. She wasn't six anymore.

Some of the attacks, whether demonizing me as a woman, mother and wife or distorting my words and positions on issues, were politically motivated and designed to rein me in. Others may have reflected the extent to which our society was still adjusting to the changing roles of women. I adopted my own mantra: Take criticism seriously, but not personally. If there is truth or merit in the criticism, try to learn from it. Otherwise, let it roll right off you. Easier said than done.

While Bill talked about social change, I embodied it. I had my own opinions, interests and profession. For better or worse, I was outspoken. I represented a fundamental change in the way women functioned in our society. And if my husband won, I would be filling a position in which the duties were not spelled out, but the performance was judged by everybody. I soon realized how many people had a fixed notion of the proper role of a President's wife. I was called a "Rorschach test" for the American public, and it was an apt way of conveying the varied and extreme reactions that I provoked.

Neither the fawning admiration nor the virulent rage seemed close to the truth. I was being labeled and categorized because of my positions and mistakes, and also because I had been turned into a symbol for women of my generation. That's why everything I said or did—and even what I wore—became a hot button for debate.

Hair and fashion were my first clues. For most of my life, I had paid little attention to my clothes. I liked headbands. They were easy, and I couldn't imagine that they suggested anything good, bad or indifferent about me to the American public. But during the campaign, some of my friends began a mission to spruce up my appearance. They brought me racks of clothes to try on, and they told me the headband had to go.

What they understood, and I didn't, was that a First Lady's appearance matters. I was no longer representing only myself. I was asking the American people to let me represent them in a role that has conveyed everything from glamour to motherly comfort.

My good friend Linda Bloodworth-Thomason suggested that a friend of hers in Los Angeles, the hairstylist Christophe Schatteman, cut my hair. She was convinced it would improve my appearance. I thought the whole notion was a stretch. But soon, I was like a kid in a candy store, trying out every style I could. Long hair, short hair, bangs, flips, braids and buns. This was a new universe and it turned out to be fun. But my eclectic experimentation spawned stories about how I could never stick with any hairstyle and what that revealed about my psyche.

Early in the campaign, I also got a glimpse of the difficulties of serving in what is, by definition, a derivative position. I was Bill's principal surrogate on the campaign trail. I wanted to support his campaign and to advance his ideas, but as we had already learned from Bill's "buy one, get one free" remark, I had to be careful where I stepped. I had taken leave from my law firm and resigned from all of the charitable and corporate boards on which I served. That meant leaving the board of Wal-Mart, on which I had sat for six years at the invitation of Sam Walton, who taught me a great deal about corporate integrity and success. While on the board, I chaired a committee that looked into ways that Wal-Mart could become more environmentally sensitive in its practices, and I worked to promote a "Buy America" program that helped put people to work and saved jobs around the country. Resigning from the Wal-Mart board and others like the Children's Defense Fund left me feeling vulnerable and unsettled. I had worked full-time during my marriage to Bill and valued the independence and identity that work provided. Now I was solely "the wife of," an odd experience for me.

My new status hit home over something mundane: I had ordered new stationery to answer all the campaign mail I was receiving. I had chosen cream paper with my name, *Hillary Rodham Clinton*, printed neatly across the top in navy blue. When I opened the box I saw that the order had been changed so that the name on it was *Hillary Clinton*. Evidently, someone on Bill's staff decided that it was more politically expedient to drop "Rodham," as if it were no longer part of my identity. I returned the stationery and ordered another batch.

After Bill won the California, Ohio and New Jersey primaries on June 2, his nomination was assured, but his election was not. After all the negative publicity in the campaign, he was running third in the polls behind Ross Perot and President Bush. He decided to reintroduce himself to America and began appearing on popular television shows. Thanks to a suggestion from Mandy Grunwald, a consultant who had joined the campaign, he played the saxophone on *The Arsenio Hall Show*. His staff also persuaded me to give more interviews and to agree to a *People* magazine story, complete with a cover photo that included Chelsea. I was not enthusiastic but finally was persuaded by the argument that most Americans didn't even know we had a child. On the one hand, I was pleased that we had sheltered Chelsea from the media and protected her during the brutal primary season. On the other hand, I believed that being a mother was the most important job I had ever had. If people didn't know that, they certainly couldn't understand us. The article was fine, but it prompted me to restate my position that Chelsea deserved her privacy, which, I believe, is essential for any child to develop and explore her own choices in life. So Bill and I established guidelines: When Chelsea was with us as part of our family—attending an event with Bill or me—the press would naturally cover her. But I would not agree to more articles or interviews that included her. This was one of the best decisions Bill and I made, and we stuck with it through the next eight years. I'm also grateful that, with few exceptions, the press respected her privacy and her right to be left alone. As long as Chelsea did not seek out their attention or do something that was of public interest, she would be off-limits.

In July 1992, the Democratic Party held its convention in New York City to formally nominate Bill and his running mate, Senator Al Gore from Tennessee. New York was a great choice. Although we had nothing to do with its selection as the host city, New York was one of Bill's and my favorite cities in the world, and we were delighted that it would be the place where Bill was nominated for President. Bill had chosen Al after an exhaustive process led by Warren Christopher, a former Deputy Secretary of State and distinguished lawyer from California. I had met Al and his wife, Tipper, at political events during the 1980s, but neither Bill nor I knew them well. Some political observers were surprised that Bill would select a running mate who seemed so like him. Southerners from neighboring states, they were close in age, of the same religion and considered to be serious students of public policy. But Bill respected Al's record of public service and believed he would add strengths to Bill's own background.

Many people have told me that the picture of Al, Tipper, their children, Bill, Chelsea and me—all standing on the porch of the Governor's Mansion on the day Bill publicly announced his selection—perfectly captured the energy of the campaign and its potential for change. I think what I felt that day reflected the emotions of many Americans. It was a new generation's turn to lead, and people conveyed an optimism about the prospects for a new direction for our country. On the final night of the convention, we were giddy and elated as we all hugged and danced on the stage.

The next morning, July 17, we started on our magical bus tours or, as I called them, "Bill, Al, Hillary and Tipper's Excellent Adventures."

The bus trips were the joint brainchild of David Wilhelm, the campaign manager, and Susan Thomases, whom Bill and I had known for more than twenty years. She was a warmhearted friend and a hard-driving lawyer, and she understood that good campaign scheduling had to tell a story about a candidate, had to illustrate his concerns and plans so that voters understood what made him tick and what positions he'd champion. Susan moved with her husband and son to Little Rock to supervise campaign scheduling for the general election. She and David wanted to build on the convention's excitement and drama and thought that a bus trip through battleground states would visually convey the partnership and generational change Bill and Al represented, as well as their message: "Putting People First."

Traveling on the buses gave us all a chance to get to know one another better. Bill, Al, Tipper and I spent hours talking, eating, waving out the window and stopping the bus convoy to conduct impromptu rallies. Loose and relaxed, Al was quick with one-liners and deadpan comments. He quickly learned that a small crowd up ahead on the side of the road, no matter where we were or what time it was, would tempt Bill to yell, "Stop the bus." Al would peer out the window ahead, see one lone soul waving or watching, and shout out, "I feel a sojourn coming on." When we were met by hundreds of patient supporters as we pulled into Erie, Pennsylvania, at 2 A.M., Al delivered a rousing version of his standard appeal stump speech: "What's up—health care costs and interest rates—should be down, and what's down—employment and hope—should be up. We have to change direction." Then he announced to the three of us—who were barely keeping our eyes open— "I think there are two people drinking coffee in the all-night diner around the corner. Let's go see them." Even Bill passed on that offer.

Tipper and I talked for hours about our experiences as political spouses, our children and what we hoped Bill and Al could do to help solve the country's problems. Tipper had become controversial when she spoke out against violent and pornographic music lyrics in 1985. I admired her willingness to take a stand and empathized with the criticism she had encountered. I also admired the work she had done on behalf of the homeless and mentally ill. An accomplished photographer, she helped chronicle the campaign with her ever-present camera.

One evening in the rural Ohio River Valley, we stopped at the farm of Gene Branstool for a barbecue and a meeting with local farmers. As we were getting ready to leave, Branstool said some folks had gathered at a crossroads a few miles away and we should stop. It was a lovely summer night, and people were sitting on their tractors waving flags while children stood at the edge of fields holding signs and welcoming us. My favorite said, "Give us eight minutes and we'll give you eight years!" In the waning light, we were astonished to see thousands of people filling the large field.

From Vandalia, Illinois to St. Louis, Missouri to Corsicana, Texas to Valdosta, Georgia, we were met by similarly huge crowds radiating a joyous intensity that I have never seen anywhere else in politics.

Back in Little Rock, the vast third floor of the old Arkansas Gazette Building served as Clinton campaign headquarters. James Carville insisted that people from each part of the campaign—including press, political and research—work together in the same large space. It was a brilliant and effective way to diminish the hierarchy and encourage the free flow of information and ideas. Every day at 7 A.M. and 7 P.M., Carville and Stephanopoulos held meetings in what was dubbed the "war room" to assess the news of the day and formulate a response to news stories and attacks from the Bush campaign. The idea was that no attack on Bill would go unanswered. The physical setup of the war room allowed Carville, Stephanopoulos and the "rapid response" team to react immediately to correct distortions put out by the opposition and to work aggressively to get out our message throughout the day.

One night, Patti Solis's phone rang in the back of the headquarters in Little Rock. Another campaign aide, Steve Rabinowitz, rushed to pick up the receiver and, for no particular reason, blurted out: "Hillary-land!" He was embarrassed to hear my voice on the line, but I thought he had come up with a great nickname. Patti loved it too, and tacked a sign on the wall behind her desk that said "Hillaryland." The name stuck.

Over time, my confidence that Bill would win the election grew. Americans wanted new leadership. Twelve years of Republicans in the White House had quadrupled the national debt, produced large and growing budget deficits and led to a stagnant economy in which too many people couldn't find or keep a decent job, or afford health care insurance for themselves and their children. President Bush had vetoed the Family and Medical Leave Act twice and had backed off women's rights. Though a supporter of family planning when he was Ambassador to the United Nations and as a Texas Congressman, Bush became an anti-choice Vice President and President. With rates of crime, unemployment, welfare dependency and homelessness climbing, the Bush Administration seemed increasingly out of touch.

To Bill and me, no issue was more distressing than the health care crisis in America. Everywhere we went, we heard story after story about the inequities of the health care system. Growing numbers of citizens were being deprived of necessary health care because they were uninsured and didn't have the means to pay their own medical bills.

In New Hampshire, Bill and I met Ronnie and Rhonda Machos, whose son, Ronnie Jr., had been born with a serious heart condition. When Ronnie lost his job and his health insurance, he faced crushing medical bills to provide the care his son needed. The Gores told us about the Philpott family from Georgia, whose seven-year-old son, Brett, had shared a hospital room with young Albert Gore after his devastating car accident. Al and Tipper spoke often about the tremendous financial burden the Philpott family had faced because of Brett's illness.

As moving as each story was, we knew that for every tragic case we heard about or witnessed, thousands more went untold.

I don't think Bill expected that health care reform would become a cornerstone of his campaign. After all, James Carville's famous war room slogan was "It's the economy, stupid." But the more Bill studied the problem, the clearer it became that reforming health care insurance and reining in skyrocketing costs were integral to fixing the economy, as well as taking care of people's urgent medical needs. "Don't forget about health care," Bill told his staff over and over again. They began to collect data, including a study by Ira Magaziner, the mover and shaker I had first heard of in 1969 when we were featured in *Life* magazine after delivering our college commencement speeches. Bill had met Ira the same year, when Ira arrived at Oxford University as a Rhodes Scholar.

Bill, Ira and a growing team of expert advisers began developing ideas about how to tackle health care after the election. Bill previewed those plans in a campaign book entitled *Putting People First* and in a speech he delivered in September setting forth his goals to address the health care crisis. The reforms he outlined included controlling spiraling health care costs, reducing paperwork and insurance industry red tape, making prescription drugs more affordable and, most important, guaranteeing that all Americans had health insurance. We knew that trying to fix the health care system would be a huge political challenge. But we believed that if voters chose Bill Clinton on November 3, it meant that change was what they wanted.

INAUGURATION

BILL AND I SPENT THE LAST TWENTY-FOUR HOURS of the 1992 campaign crisscrossing the country, making final stops in Philadelphia, Pennsylvania; Cleveland, Ohio; Detroit, Michigan; St. Louis, Missouri; Paducah, Kentucky; McAllen and Ft. Worth, Texas; and Albuquerque, New Mexico. We saw the sun rise in Denver, Colorado, and landed back in Little Rock, where Chelsea met us at the airport at around 10:30 A.M. After a quick stop to change clothes, the three of us went to our polling site, where I proudly cast my vote for Bill to be my President. We spent the day at the Governor's Mansion with family and friends, making calls to supporters around the country. At 10:47 P.M., the television networks declared that Bill had won.

Though I had expected a victory, I was overwhelmed. After President Bush called Bill to concede, Bill and I went into our bedroom, closed the door and prayed together for God's help as he took on this awesome honor and responsibility. Then we gathered everyone up for the drive to the Old State House, where the campaign had begun thirteen months before. We joined the Gores in front of a huge crowd of ecstatic Arkansans and ardent supporters from every corner of America.

Within hours, the kitchen table in the Governor's Mansion became the nerve center of the Clinton transition. In the next few weeks, potential cabinet nominees came in and out, phones rang around the clock, piles of food were consumed. Bill asked Warren Christopher to head his transition and to work with Mickey Kantor and Vernon Jordan to vet candidates for major positions. They first concentrated on the economic team, because that was Bill's highest priority. Senator Lloyd Bentsen of Texas agreed to become Secretary of the Treasury; Robert

Rubin, the co-Chairman of the investment bank Goldman Sachs, accepted Bill's offer to become the first head of a soon-to-be-created National Economic Council; Laura D'Andrea Tyson, a professor of economics at the University of California at Berkeley, became Chair of the Council of Economic Advisers; Gene Sperling, a former aide to Governor Mario Cuomo of New York, became Rubin's deputy and later succeeded him; and Congressman Leon Panetta, the Democratic Chairman of the House of Representatives Budget Committee, became the Director of the Office of Management and Budget. They worked with Bill to forge the economic policy that put our nation on the path to fiscal responsibility in government and unprecedented growth in the private sector.

We were also facing the more mundane challenges of any family changing jobs and residences. In the midst of forming a new Administration, we had to pack up the Governor's Mansion, the only home Chelsea remembered. And since we didn't own a house of our own, everything would come with us to the White House. Friends pitched in to organize and sort, piling boxes in every room. Loretta Avent, a friend from Arizona who had joined me on the campaign after the convention, took charge of the thousands of gifts that arrived from all over the world, filling a huge section of the large basement. Periodically, Loretta would shriek up the stairs: "Wait till you see what just came." And I'd go down to find her clutching a portrait of Bill made out of seashells and mounted on a red velvet background or a collection of stuffed dogs dressed in baby clothes sent to our now famous black-and-white cat, Socks.

We had to find a new school in Washington for Chelsea, who was almost a teenager and not happy with the prospect of dismantling her life. Bill and I wondered how we could give her a normal childhood in the White House, where her new reality would include twenty-four-hour Secret Service protection. We had already decided to bring Socks to Washington, although we had been warned that he could no longer roam free, collecting dead birds and mice as trophies. Because the White House fence was wide enough for him to slip through into traffic, we reluctantly decided he would have to be on a leash whenever he was outside.

I had taken a leave of absence to campaign, but now I resigned my law practice and started putting together a staff for the office of First Lady, while helping Bill in any way I could. We were both grappling with what my role should be. I would have a "position" but not a real "job." How could I use this platform to help my husband and serve my country without losing my own voice?

There is no training manual for First Ladies. You get the job because the man you married becomes President. Each of my predecessors brought to the White House her own attitudes and expectations, likes and dislikes, dreams and doubts. Each carved out a role that reflected her own interests and style and that balanced the needs of her husband, family and country. So would I. Like all First Ladies before me, I had to decide what I wanted to do with the opportunities and responsibilities I had inherited.

Over the years, the role of First Lady has been perceived as largely symbolic. She is expected to represent an ideal—and largely mythical—concept of American womanhood. Many former First Ladies were highly accomplished, but true stories of what they had done in their lives were overlooked, forgotten or suppressed. By the time I was preparing to take on the role, history was finally catching up to reality. In March 1992, the Smithsonian's National Museum of American History revised its popular First Ladies Exhibit to acknowledge the varied political roles and public images of these women. In addition to gowns and china, the museum displayed the camouflage jacket Barbara Bush wore when she visited the troops of Desert Storm with her husband and featured a quote from Martha Washington: "I am more like a state prisoner than anything else." The exhibit's chief curator, Edith Mayo, and the Smithsonian were criticized for rewriting history and demeaning the "family values" of the First Ladies.

As I studied the marriages of previous Presidents, I recognized that Bill and I were not the first couple who relied on each other as partners in life and politics. Because of research done by the Smithsonian and historians such as Carl Sferrazza Anthony and David McCullough, we now know about the political advice Abigail Adams provided her husband, which earned her the derogatory nickname "Mrs. President"; the behind-the-scenes role Helen Taft played in pushing Theodore Roosevelt to choose her husband as his successor; the "unofficial Presidency" run by Edith Wilson after her husband's stroke; the political firestorms ignited by Eleanor Roosevelt; and the painstaking review by Bess of Harry Truman's speeches and letters.

Like those of many previous White House inhabitants, the relationship that Bill Clinton and I had built was rooted in love and respect, shared aspirations and accomplishments, victories and defeats. That wasn't about to change with an election. After seventeen years of marriage, we were each other's biggest cheerleaders, toughest critics and best friends.

Yet it wasn't clear to either of us how this partnership would fit into the new Clinton Administration. Bill couldn't appoint me to an official position, even if he had wanted to. Anti-nepotism laws had been on the books since President John F. Kennedy appointed his brother Bobby to be Attorney General. But there were no laws to prevent me from continuing my role as Bill Clinton's unpaid adviser and, in some cases, representative. We had worked together for so long, and Bill knew he could trust me. We always understood that I would contribute to my husband's administration. But we didn't know precisely what my role would be until late in the transition, when Bill asked me to oversee his health care initiative.

He was in the process of centralizing economic policy in the White House and wanted a similar structure for health care. With so many government agencies claiming a stake in reform, he worried that turf wars could stifle creativity and new approaches. Bill decided that Ira Magaziner should coordinate the process inside the White House to develop the legislation, and he wanted me to head up the initiative to make it law. Bill intended to announce our appointments right after the inauguration. Because of our experience in Arkansas, where Bill had appointed me to lead committees on rural health care and public education, neither of us spent much time worrying about reactions my involvement might provoke. When it came to political spouses, we certainly didn't expect the nation's capital to be more conservative than Arkansas.

We were running late when we left Little Rock on the evening of January 16, 1993. Thousands of our friends and supporters jammed into a huge hangar at Little Rock Airport for an emotional farewell ceremony. I was excited about what lay ahead of us, but my enthusiasm was tinged with melancholy. Bill was on the verge of tears as he recited the lyrics of a song to the crowd of well-wishers, "Arkansas runs deep in me, and it always will." What seemed like a thousand hugs and waves later, we boarded our chartered plane. Once we were airborne, the lights of Little Rock disappeared beneath the clouds, and there was nothing to do but look ahead.

We flew to Charlottesville, Virginia, to continue the journey to

Washington by bus, following the 121-mile route Thomas Jefferson had taken to his inauguration in 1801. I thought it was an appropriate way to initiate the Presidency of William Jefferson Clinton.

The next morning, we met up with Al and Tipper and toured Monticello, the great house Jefferson designed. Then we boarded another bus together, just as we had during the campaign, and headed north to Washington. Route 29 was lined with thousands of people cheering us on, waving flags, holding balloons and banners. Some held homemade signs to encourage us, congratulate us or chastise us: "Bubbas for Bill." "We are counting on you." "Keep your promises—AIDS won't wait." "You're socialists, stupid." My favorite was a plain, hand-lettered sign with two words: "Grace, Compassion."

The sky was still clear, but the temperature was dropping as we pulled into Washington, D.C. By some act of providence, the punctuality-impaired President-elect was running on time, and we arrived at the Lincoln Memorial five minutes early for the first official event—a concert on the steps in front of an enormous crowd that stretched down the Mall. Harry Thomason, Rahm Emanuel and Mel French, another friend from Arkansas, were the impresarios of the inaugural festivities. Harry and Rahm were so relieved to see us that they hugged each other.

I had never sat in an enclosure of bulletproof glass—a strange sensation and somewhat alienating. I was grateful, though, for the little heaters by our feet because the temperature had dropped precipitously. Pop diva Diana Ross sang a spectacular rendition of "God Bless America." Bob Dylan played to the packed Mall, just as he had on that August day in 1963 when Martin Luther King, Jr., delivered his "I Have a Dream" speech from the same steps. I felt extremely fortunate to have seen Reverend King speak when I was a teenager in Chicago, and now here I was listening to my husband honor the man who helped this nation overcome its painful history:

"Let us build an American home for the twenty-first century, where everyone has a place at the table and not a single child is left behind," Bill said. "In this world and the world of tomorrow, we must go forward together or not at all."

The sun was setting when Bill, Chelsea and I led thousands of swaying, singing celebrants in a march across Memorial Bridge.

We stopped on the other side of the Potomac River to ring a replica of the Liberty Bell, touching off a celebration in which thousands of "Bells of Hope" were rung simultaneously across the country and even aboard the space shuttle *Endeavor* as it circled the planet. We lingered a while as fireworks lit up the night sky over the capital. Then it was off to another event, and still another. By then, all the celebrations were blending together in a kaleidoscope of faces and stages and voices.

During inaugural week, our families and personal staff stayed with us in Blair House, the traditional guest residence for visiting heads of state and Presidents-elect. Blair House and its professional staff run by Benedicte Valentiner, known to all as Mrs. V., and her deputy, Randy Baumgardner, made us feel welcome in the quietly elegant mansion that became an oasis during a hectic week. Blair House is famous for being able to accommodate any special need. Our crew was tame compared to certain visiting heads of state who demanded that their guards be nude to ensure they carried no weapons, or imported their own cooks to prepare everything from goat to snake.

Bill gave a lot of speeches that week, but he still hadn't finished writing the biggest one of his life: the inaugural address. Bill is a wonderful writer and gifted speechmaker who makes it look easy, but his constant revisions and last-minute changes are nerve-racking. He's never met a sentence he couldn't fool with. I was used to his constant tinkering, but even I could feel my anxiety rise as the day grew nearer. Bill worked on the draft whenever there was a moment between events.

My husband likes to pull everybody around him into his creative tumult. David Kusnet, his main speechwriter; Bruce Reed, his Deputy Domestic Policy Adviser; George Stephanopoulos, his Communications Director; Al Gore and I all put our two cents in. Bill also called in two longtime friends: Tommy Caplan, a marvelous wordsmith and novelist who had been one of his roommates at Georgetown University, and the Pulitzer Prize–winning author Taylor Branch, who had worked with us in Texas for the McGovern campaign. In the midst of the process, Bill received a letter from Father Tim Healy, the former President of Georgetown and head of the New York Public Library. He and Bill shared a Georgetown connection, and Father Healy had been writing the letter to Bill when he died suddenly of a heart attack as he returned home from a trip. The letter was found in Father Healy's typewriter and sent on to Bill, who found in this posthumous message a wonderful phrase. Father had written that Bill's election would "force the spring" and lead to a flowering of new ideas, hope and energy that would reinvigorate the country. I loved his words and his apt metaphor for Bill's ambitions for his Presidency.

It was fascinating to watch my husband that week as he literally became President before my eyes. Throughout the inaugural festivities, Bill received security briefings to prepare him for the historic responsibilities he was about to assume. With remarkable agility, he was already shifting his attention from a major speech to news of U.S. planes that were bombing Iraq in response to Saddam Hussein's contempt for U.N. demands to briefings about the worsening conflict in Bosnia.

He was still writing his speech the day before inauguration. To give him time to work, I agreed to fill in for him at his afternoon events, although I had to keep my own schedule too. That afternoon, I also squeezed in an appearance at events sponsored by my alma maters, Wellesley College and Yale Law School. On the way back from the Mayflower Hotel, my car got stuck in a gridlock of inaugural crowds and out-of-state vehicles on Pennsylvania Avenue, within sight of Blair House. I was so late and frustrated that I jumped out and took off running through the traffic. Capricia Marshall, who was watching from a window in Blair House, still laughs when she describes the sight of me darting between cars, wearing heels and a snug gray flannel dress, with my alarmed Secret Service detail scrambling behind.

Bill finally finished writing and rehearsing the big speech an hour or two before dawn on the morning of his inauguration.

We slept very briefly and then started our extraordinary day with an emotional interfaith service at the Metropolitan A.M.E. Church. Then we went to the White House, where the Bushes greeted us at the North Portico with their spaniels, Millie and Ranger, darting around their legs. They were very welcoming and put us at ease. Although the campaign had been bruising for both our families, Barbara Bush had been gracious to me when we had met in the past and had given me a walking tour of the family quarters of the White House after the election. George Bush had always been friendly when we had seen him at the annual National Governors Association conferences, and I had sat next to him at NGA dinners at the White House and at the Education Summit in Charlottesville at Monticello in 1989. When the summer Governors Conference was held in Maine in 1983, the Bushes opened their property at Kennebunkport for a big clambake. Chelsea, only three at the time, came along, and when she had to go to the bathroom, then Vice President Bush took her by the hand and showed her the way.

The Gores joined us at the White House, along with Alma and Ron Brown, who was Chairman of the DNC and soon to be sworn in as

Commerce Secretary, and Linda and Harry Thomason, who had co-chaired the inauguration.

President and Mrs. Bush guided our party to the Blue Room, where we had coffee and made small talk for twenty minutes or so until it was time to leave for the Capitol. Bill rode in the presidential limousine with George Bush, while Barbara Bush and I followed in another car. The crowds lining Pennsylvania Avenue cheered and waved as we passed. I admired Mrs. Bush's élan as we prepared to watch one President, her husband, make way for another.

At the Capitol we stood on the West Front with its breathtaking view down the Mall to the Washington Monument and the Lincoln Memorial. The huge crowd spilled out beyond the Monument.

Following custom, the United States Marine Band struck up "Hail to the Chief" one final time for George Bush just before noon, and again to the new President a few minutes later. I had always been stirred by those chords, and now I felt moved beyond words to hear them play for my husband. Chelsea and I reverently held the Bible as Bill took the oath of office. Then he gathered Chelsea and me in his arms and, kissing each of us, whispered, "I love you both so much."

Bill's speech stressed the themes of sacrifice and service for America and called for the changes he had featured in his campaign. "There is nothing wrong with America that cannot be cured by what is right with America," he said, calling Americans to "a season of service" on behalf of those in need at home and those around the world whom we must help to build democracy and freedom.

After the swearing-in ceremony, while some of our new staffers hurried to the White House to start unpacking and organizing our things, Bill and I lunched in the Capitol with members of Congress. Just as the mantle of power passes from one President to the next at noon on Inauguration Day, so does possession of the White House. The belongings of a new President and his family cannot be moved into the White House until after he is sworn in. At 12:01 P.M., George and Barbara Bush's moving vans pulled away from the delivery entrance as ours came in. Our luggage, furniture and hundreds of boxes were unloaded in a mad dash in the few hours between the ceremony at the Capitol and the end of the inaugural parade. Aides scrambled to locate what we would need immediately and stuffed the rest of our possessions into closets and spare rooms to deal with later.

White House security procedures require that essential employees be cleared with the uniformed Secret Service guards, a process known by its acronym, WAVES, which stands for "Workers and Visitors Entry System." A list of prescreened guests or staff is then WAVE-d into the White House. Unfortunately, my personal assistant, Capricia Marshall, hadn't quite mastered the system. She thought being "waved in" involved a welcoming hand gesture. Capricia, who would not let my inaugural gown out of her sight that day, carried it from Blair House, waving at guards as she went from gate to gate trying to find someone to WAVE her in. It's a testament to her persuasiveness—and her eventual inclusion in the WAVES system—that my violet blue lace–covered ball gown made it past White House security on Inauguration Day.

After lunch, Bill, Chelsea and I drove from the Capitol down the parade route to the Treasury Building; there, with the Secret Service's reluctant blessing, we got out and walked along Pennsylvania Avenue to the reviewing stand in front of the White House, where I sat down in front of a space heater to watch the parade. Because Democrats hadn't had a winner in sixteen years, everyone wanted to participate. We couldn't say no and didn't want to. There were six marching bands from Arkansas alone, in a parade that lasted three hours.

We first walked into the White House as its new residents in the early evening after the last float passed by. I remember looking around in wonder at this house I had visited as a guest. Now, it would be my home. It was during my walk up the path toward the White House and up the stairs of the North Portico and into the Grand Foyer that the reality hit me: I was actually the First Lady, married to the President of the United States. It was the first of many times I would be reminded of the history I was now joining.

Members of the permanent White House staff, numbering about one hundred, were waiting to greet us in the Grand Foyer. These are the men and women who run the house and tend to the special needs of its residents. The White House has its own engineers, carpenters, plumbers, gardeners, florists, curators, cooks, butlers and housekeepers who continue from one administration to the next. The entire operation is overseen by the "ushers," a quaint term from the nineteenth century still used to describe the administrative staff. In 2000, I published my third book, *An Invitation to the White House*, which was both a tribute to the permanent White House staff and a behind-the-scenes look at the extraordinary job they do every day.

We were escorted upstairs to the private residence on the second floor, which looked barren as our belongings had not been unpacked. But we had no time to worry about any of that. We had to get ready to go out.

One of the most convenient features of the residence is the beauty salon, put in by Pat Nixon on the second floor. Chelsea, her friends, my mother, my mother-in-law and my sister-in-law, Maria, crowded in and jockeyed to be transformed, like Cinderellas, for the balls.

Bill wanted to attend each of the eleven inaugural balls that evening, and not just for the customary five-minute drop-by and wave. We were going to celebrate. Chelsea and four of her girlfriends from Arkansas accompanied us to several events, including the MTV Ball, before returning to the White House for a sleepover. The Arkansas Ball, held in the Washington Convention Center, was the biggest and most fun for us because that's where our families and twelve thousand of our friends and supporters had gathered. Ben E. King handed Bill a saxophone, and the crowd erupted in cheers and Razorback hog calls of "Soooooo-ey!"

No one had more fun than Bill's mother, Virginia. She was the belle of at least three balls. She probably already knew half the revelers, and she was quickly meeting the rest. She also made a special friend that night: Barbra Streisand. She and Barbra struck up a friendship at the Arkansas Ball that continued with weekly phone calls for the next year.

Bill and I carried on at the balls, and by the end of the evening, we had danced to so many renditions of "Don't Stop Thinking About To-morrow," the unofficial campaign theme song, that I had to kick off my shoes to give my feet a rest. Neither of us wanted the night to end, but I finally coaxed Bill out of the Midwestern Ball at the Sheraton Hotel when the musicians started packing away their instruments. We headed back to the White House well after two in the morning.

When we stepped out of the elevator into the second floor residence, we looked at each other in disbelief: this was now our home. Too tired to explore these grand new surroundings, we crashed into bed.

We had been asleep for only a few hours when we heard a brisk knock on the bedroom door.

Tap, tap, tap.

"Whuh?"

TAP, TAP, TAP.

Bill bolted up in bed, and I groped for my glasses in the dark, thinking there must be some sort of emergency on our very first morning.

Suddenly the door swung open and a man in a tuxedo stepped into the bedroom carrying a silver breakfast tray. This is how the Bushes began their day, with a bedroom breakfast at 5:30 A.M., and it's what the butlers were accustomed to. But the first words this poor man heard from the forty-second President of the United States were, "Hey! What are you doing here?"

You never saw anyone back out of a room so quickly.

Bill and I just laughed and settled back under the covers to try to steal another hour of sleep. It struck me that both the White House and we, its new occupants, were in for some major adjustments, publicly and privately.

The Clinton Presidency represented generational and political change that would affect every institution in Washington. For twenty of the previous twenty-four years, the White House had been a Republican domain. Its occupants had been members of our parents' generation. The Reagans often ate dinner in front of the television on TV trays and the Bushes reportedly awoke at dawn to walk the dogs, and then read newspapers and watch the morning news shows on the five television sets in their bedroom. After twelve years, the dedicated permanent staff was used to a predictable routine and regular hours. Children hadn't lived there full-time since Jimmy Carter left office in 1981. I suspected that our family's casual lifestyle and round-the-clock work habits were bound to be as unfamiliar to the staff as the formality of the White House was to us.

Bill's campaign had emphasized *Putting People First*, so on our first full day in the White House we wanted to make good on that promise by inviting thousands of people for an open house, many selected by lottery. They all held tickets and many had lined up in the dark before sunrise to meet us and the Gores. But we hadn't anticipated how long it would take to greet everyone and hadn't scheduled enough time. The lines stretched across the grounds from the East Gate to the South Portico, and I felt terrible when I realized many of the people waiting outside in the cold wouldn't make it inside to the Diplomatic Reception Room before we had to leave. The four of us went outside to tell the hardy souls remaining how sorry we were that we could not stay to greet them, but that they were still welcome to visit their house.

After our other obligations ended late that afternoon, Bill and I were finally free to change into casual clothes and have a look around our new home. We wanted to share these first days and nights in the

White House with our closest friends and family. There were two guest rooms on the second floor, referred to as the Queen's Room and the Lincoln Bedroom, and seven other guest rooms on the third floor. In addition to Chelsea and her friends from Little Rock, our parents, Hugh and Dorothy Rodham and Virginia and Dick Kelley, and our brothers, Hugh Rodham (and his wife, Maria), Tony Rodham and Roger Clinton, were staying with us. And we had also invited four of our best friends, Diane and Jim Blair and Harry and Linda Thomason, to spend the night.

Harry and Linda produced and wrote several television shows, including the hugely successful *Designing Women* and *Evening Shade*, but their hearts never left the Ozarks. Harry had grown up in Hampton, Arkansas, and started out as a high school football coach in Little Rock. Linda came from a family of lawyers and activists in Poplar Bluff, Missouri, just across the Arkansas State line. The only other famous person born in that patch of Missouri, Linda told us with a laugh, was Rush Limbaugh, the right-wing radio host who was one of George Bush's biggest cheerleaders. Linda's and Rush's families knew each other and had a long-standing, amiable rivalry.

After a whirlwind week of inaugural festivities, it felt good to relax with people we had known for years and trusted completely. At the end of the evening, we decided to raid the small family kitchen off the West Sitting Hall. Harry and Bill checked the cabinets while Linda and I opened the refrigerator. It was empty except for one item: a half-full bottle of vodka. We used the contents to toast the new President, the country and our future.

Our parents had already gone to bed, and Chelsea and her guests were finally quiet. The night before, the girls had come back early from the inaugural balls and had a great time going on a scavenger hunt staged for them by the curators and ushers. I thought it would be a good way for her to have fun and get familiar with her new environment. The curators came up with all sorts of historical clues, such as find "the painting with the yellow bird" (*Still Life with Fruit, Goblet and Canary* by Severin Roesen, in the Red Room) and find "the room where it is sometimes said a ghost has been seen." (The Lincoln Bedroom, where guests have reported cold breezes and spectral figures.)

I don't believe in ghosts, but we did sometimes feel that the White House was haunted by more temporal entities. Spirits of administrations past were everywhere. Sometimes they even left notes. Harry and

Linda were given the Lincoln Bedroom that night. When they climbed into the long rosewood bed, they found a folded piece of paper under a pillow.

"Dear Linda, I was here first, and I'll be back," the note said.

It was signed "Rush Limbaugh."

EAST WING, WEST WING

THE WHITE HOUSE IS THE PRESIDENT'S OFFICE AND home, and it is also a national museum. Its organizational culture, I quickly learned, is like a military unit. For years, things had been done a certain way, often by staff who had worked there for decades, perfecting the way the house was run and preserved. The head gardener, Irv Williams, started under President Truman. The permanent staff knew that they provided the continuity from one First Family to the next. In many ways, they were the keepers of the institutional Presidency from one administration to the next. We were merely temporary residents. When the senior President Bush came to unveil his official portrait during Bill's first term, he saw George Washington Hannie, Jr., a butler who had worked at the House for more than twenty-five years. "George, you're still here?"

The veteran butler replied: "Yes, sir. Presidents come and go. But George is *always* here."

Like many venerable institutions, change came slowly to the White House. The phone system was a throwback to another era. To dial out from the residence, we had to pick up the receiver and wait for a White House operator to dial for us. Eventually, I got used to it and came to appreciate the kind and patient operators who worked at the switchboard. When the entire phone system was eventually upgraded with newer technology, I continued to place calls through them.

I knew I would never get used to the Secret Service agent posted outside our bedroom door. This was standard operating procedure for past Presidents, and the Secret Service was adamant, at first, about keeping it that way.

"What if the President has a heart attack in the middle of the night?" one agent asked me when I suggested that he station himself downstairs instead of with us on the second floor.

"He's forty-six years old and in great health," I said. "He's not going to have a heart attack!"

The Secret Service adapted to our needs, and we to theirs. After all, they were the experts when it came to our safety. We just had to find a way to let them do their job and let us be ourselves. For twelve years, they had been used to a predictable routine where spontaneity was the exception, not the rule. Our campaign, with its breakneck pace, frequent stops and rope lines, made our agents scramble. I had many long conversations with the agents assigned to protect us. One of my lead agents, Don Flynn, said: "Now I get it. It's like if one of us was President. We like to go places and do things and stay up late too." That one comment helped set the tone of cooperation and flexibility that came to characterize our relationships with the agents sworn to protect us. Bill, Chelsea and I have nothing but praise for their courage, integrity and professionalism, and we feel lucky to remain friends with many agents who protected us.

Maggie Williams had agreed to help me at the end of the 1992 presidential campaign, but only if I understood that she would return to Philadelphia after the election to finish her Ph.D. at Penn. With the election over, I realized I needed her more than ever. I begged, pleaded, implored and hounded her to stay on through the transition, then to join the administration as my Chief of Staff.

Our first job was to recruit other staffers, pick office space and learn the intricacies of the traditional First Lady duties. Since the Truman Administration, First Ladies and their staffs had operated entirely out of the East Wing, which houses two floors of office space, a large reception room for visitors, the White House movie theater and a long glass colonnade that runs along the edge of the East Garden that Lady Bird Johnson dedicated to Jackie Kennedy. Over the years, as First Ladies expanded their duties, their staffs grew bigger and more specialized. Jackie Kennedy was the first to have her own press secretary. Lady Bird Johnson organized her staff structure to reflect that of the West Wing. Rosalynn Carter's Staff Director operated as a Chief of Staff and attended daily meetings with the President's staff. Nancy Reagan increased the size and prominence of her staff within the White House.

The West Wing is where the Oval Office is located, along with the Roosevelt Room, the Cabinet Room, the Situation Room (where top-secret meetings are held and communications are sent and received), the White House Mess (where meals are served) and offices housing the President's senior staff. The rest of the White House staff work across a driveway in the Old Executive Office Building, or OEOB. No First Lady or her staff had ever had offices in the West Wing or the OEOB (which has since been renamed the Eisenhower Executive Office Building).

Although the visitors office, personal correspondence and the social secretary would remain headquartered in the East Wing, some of my staff would be part of the West Wing team. I thought they should be integrated physically as well. Maggie made her case to Bill's transition staff for the space we wanted in the West Wing, and the Office of the First Lady moved into a suite of rooms at the end of a long corridor on the first floor of the OEOB. I was assigned an office on the second floor of the West Wing just down the hall from the domestic policy staff. This was another unprecedented event in White House history and quickly became fodder for late night comedians and political pundits. One cartoon depicted the White House with an Oval Office rising from the roof of the second floor.

Maggie assumed the title of Assistant to the President—her predecessors had been *Deputy* Assistants to the President—and each morning she attended the 7:30 A.M. senior staff meeting with the President's top advisers. I also had a domestic policy staffer assigned to my office full-time, as well as a presidential speechwriter designated to work on my speeches, especially those relating to health care reform. My staff of twenty included a Deputy Chief of Staff, press secretary, scheduler, travel director and compiler of my daily briefing book. Two of the original staff are still with me today: Pam Cicetti, an experienced executive assistant who became my all-purpose person, and Alice Pushkar, Director of the First Lady's Correspondence, who assumed one of the most daunting of all jobs with poise and imagination.

These physical and staff changes were important if I was going to be involved in working on Bill's agenda, particularly as it related to issues affecting women, children and families. The people I hired were committed to the issues and to the idea that government could—and should—be a partner in creating opportunities for people who were willing to work hard and take responsibility. Most of them came out of the public sector or from organizations committed to improving economic, political and social conditions for the underrepresented and the underprivileged.

Before long, my staff was recognized within the administration and by the press as active and influential, due in large part to the leadership of Maggie and Melanne Verveer, my Deputy Chief of Staff. Melanne and her husband, Phil, had been friends of Bill's since their days at Georgetown University, and she was a longtime Democratic activist and experienced Washington hand. A true policy wonk who loves the complexities and nuances of issues, Melanne had worked for years on Capitol Hill and in the advocacy world. I used to joke that there wasn't a single person in Washington she didn't know. Not only was Melanne a legend in the nation's capital; so was her Rolodex. At last count, it contained six thousand names. There is no way to catalog the many projects that Melanne masterminded, first as Deputy and then, in the second term, as my Chief of Staff. She also became a key player on the President's team, advocating for policies affecting women, human rights, legal services and the arts.

Soon, my staff became known around the White House as "Hillaryland." We were fully immersed in the daily operations of the West Wing, but we were also our own little subculture within the White House. My staff prided themselves on discretion, loyalty and camaraderie, and we had our own special ethos. While the West Wing had a tendency to leak, Hillaryland never did. While the President's senior advisers jockeyed for big offices with proximity to the Oval Office, my senior staff happily shared offices with their young assistants. We had toys and crayons for children in our main conference room and every child who ever visited knew exactly where we stashed the cookies. One Christmas, Melanne ordered lapel buttons that read, in very small letters, HILLARYLAND, and she and I began handing out honorary memberships, usually to long-suffering spouses and children of my overworked staffers. Membership entitled them to visit anytime—and to come to all of our parties.

The West Wing operation was up and running, but my East Wing duties were still giving me the jitters. Just ten days after the inauguration, Bill and I would be hosting our first big event, the National Governors Association annual dinner. Bill had been Chairman of the NGA, and many of those attending were colleagues and friends we had known for years. We wanted the dinner to come off well, and I was eager to dispel the notion, percolating in the news media, that I had little interest in the customary functions of the First Lady's office, which included overseeing White House social events. I had enjoyed those responsibilities, carried out on a far less grand scale, as First Lady of Arkansas and looked forward to them now. But my staff and I needed guidance. I had been to White House dinners since 1977, when President and Mrs. Carter invited then Arkansas Attorney General Bill Clinton and his spouse to a dinner honoring Prime Minister Pierre Trudeau of Canada and his wife, Margaret. We had been back every year Bill was Governor for the very dinner I was now charged with planning. Attending the event as guests was a far cry from hosting it ourselves.

I had the help of our new social secretary, Ann Stock, an energetic woman of impeccable taste and style who had worked in the Carter White House and then as a top executive at Bloomingdale's. Ann and I tried different combinations of linens and place settings before settling on the gold-and-red-rimmed china acquired by Mrs. Reagan. We worked on the seating arrangements, eager to ensure that our guests would be comfortable with their tablemates. We knew almost everyone and decided to mix them up on the basis of interests and personalities. I consulted with the White House florist, Nancy Clarke, as she arranged the tulips I had selected for each table. From that day on, Nancy's cheerful stamina never ceased to amaze me.

Every hour of life in the White House brought some new and unanticipated hurdle. Yet there were few people I could talk to who genuinely understood my experience. My close friends were supportive and always available for conversations by phone, but none of them had lived in the White House. Fortunately, though, someone I knew had, and she understood what I was going through. She became a valued source of wisdom, advice and support.

On January 26, a bitterly cold morning just a few days after the inauguration, I flew to New York City on the regular shuttle. It was my only flight on a commercial airline during my eight years at the White House. Because of the security required and the inconvenience to other passengers, I agreed with the Secret Service to forgo that link to my previous life. Officially, I was going to New York to receive the Lewis Hine Award for my work on children's issues and to visit P.S. 115, a local public school, to promote voluntary tutoring. But I was also making a private stop to have lunch with Jacqueline Kennedy Onassis at her beautiful apartment on Fifth Avenue.

I had met Jackie a few times before and had visited her once during the 1992 campaign. She had been an early supporter of Bill's, contributing financially and attending the convention. She was a transcendent public figure, someone I had admired and respected for as long as I could remember. Not only had Jackie Kennedy been a superb First Lady, bringing style, grace and intelligence to the White House, she also had done an extraordinary job raising her children. Months before, I had asked her advice about bringing up children in the public eye, and on this visit I hoped to hear more from her about how she dealt with the established culture at the White House. It had been thirty years since she lived there, but I sensed that not much had changed.

The Secret Service dropped me off at her apartment shortly before noon, and Jackie greeted me at the elevator door on the fifteenth floor. She was impeccably dressed, wearing silk pants in one of her signature colors—a combination of beige and gray—and a matching blouse with subtle peach stripes. At sixty-three, she remained as beautiful and dignified as she was when she first entered the national consciousness as the glamorous thirty-one-year-old wife of the second-youngest President in American history.

After President Kennedy's death in 1963, she had receded from public view for many years, married Greek shipping tycoon Aristotle Onassis and later launched a successful career as a literary editor for one of the finest publishing houses in New York City. The first thing I noticed about her apartment was that it was overflowing with books. They were stacked everywhere—on and under tables, beside couches and chairs. Books were piled so high in her study that she could rest her plate on them if she was eating at her desk. She is the only person I've met who literally decorated her apartment with books—and pulled it off. I've tried to duplicate the effect I saw in Jackie's apartment and her Martha's Vineyard home with all the books Bill and I own. Predictably, ours never look quite as elegant.

We sat at a table in the corner of her living room overlooking Central Park and the Metropolitan Museum of Art and continued the conversation we had begun at our lunch the summer before. Jackie gave me invaluable advice about how to deal with my loss of privacy, and she told me what she had done to protect her children, Caroline and John. Providing Chelsea with a normal life would be one of the biggest challenges Bill and I faced, she told me. We had to allow Chelsea to grow up and even make mistakes, while shielding her from the constant scrutiny she would endure as the daughter of a President. Her own children, she said, had been lucky to have so many cousins, natural playmates and friends, many of them with fathers in the public eye too. She felt it would be much harder for an only child.

"You've got to protect Chelsea at all costs," Jackie said. "Surround her with friends and family, but don't spoil her. Don't let her think she's someone special or entitled. Keep the press away from her if you can, and don't let anyone use her."

Already, Bill and I had taken a measure of the public's interest in Chelsea and the national fascination with a child growing up in the White House. Our decision about where to send Chelsea to school had inspired passionate debate inside and outside the Beltway, largely because of its symbolic significance. I understood the disappointment felt by advocates of public education when we chose Sidwell Friends, a private Quaker school, particularly after Chelsea had attended public schools in Arkansas. But the decision for Bill and me rested on one fact: Private schools were private property, hence off-limits to the news media. Public schools were not. The last thing we wanted was television cameras and news reporters following our daughter throughout the school day, as they had when President Carter's daughter, Amy, attended public school.

So far, our instincts and Jackie's prescriptions had served Chelsea well. She was adjusting to her new school as comfortably as could be expected, although she missed her friends from Arkansas. She was settling into her two rooms on the second floor. They had been Caroline's and John's and then Lynda and Luci Johnson's, so Jackie knew exactly where they were. One was now Chelsea's bedroom with twin beds so she could have sleepovers, and the other was a den where she could do homework, watch television, listen to music and entertain friends.

I told Jackie how grateful I was that she had created a dining room upstairs and that we were converting the butler's pantry into a small kitchen where we could eat our family meals in a more relaxed and informal atmosphere. One night, I sparked a culinary crisis. Chelsea was not feeling well, and I wanted to make her soft scrambled eggs and applesauce, the comfort foods I had always provided in our pre–White House years. I looked in the small kitchen for utensils and then called downstairs and asked the chef if he could provide me with what I needed. He and the kitchen staff were completely undone at the thought of a First Lady wielding a frying pan with no supervision! They even called my staff to ask if I was cooking myself because I was unhappy with their food. This incident reminded me of Eleanor Roosevelt's similar experiences of adjusting to living in the White House. "Unconsciously, I did many things that shocked the ushers," she wrote in her autobiography. "My first act was to insist on running the elevator myself without waiting for one of the doormen to run it for me. That just wasn't done by the President's wife."

Jackie and I also discussed the Secret Service and the unusual security challenges that the children of Presidents presented. She confirmed my instincts that even though security was necessary, it was important to stress to Chelsea, as she had to her own children, that she owed respect to the agents sworn to protect her. I had seen children of Governors boss around and even defy the middle-aged state troopers assigned to guard them. Jackie told me about the time an older kid had taken John's bicycle and he had asked his security detail to get it back for him. When Jackie found out, she told John he would have to stand up for himself. The successive teams of agents assigned to protect Chelsea understood that, as much as possible, she needed to live the life of a normal teenage girl.

The Service uses code names for its protectees, and each member of a family has a name beginning with the same letter. Bill became "Eagle," I was "Evergreen" and Chelsea, appropriately, was called "Energy." The code names sound whimsical, but they mask a harsh reality: Ongoing threats require the vigilance and intrusiveness of protective security.

Jackie spoke frankly about the peculiar and dangerous attractions evoked by charismatic politicians. She cautioned me that Bill, like President Kennedy, had a personal magnetism that inspired strong feelings in people. She never came out and said it, but she meant that he might also be a target. "He has to be very careful," she told me. "Very careful."

I was still having a hard time understanding how we could salvage any semblance of normality in our lives if we had to keep looking over our shoulders everywhere we went. Jackie knew that, unlike previous presidential couples, we didn't have our own house or vacation getaway to escape to. She urged me to use Camp David and to stay with friends who had homes in secluded places where we could avoid the curiosity seekers and paparazzi.

Not all our conversation was so serious. We gossiped about mutual friends and even fashion. Jackie was one of the twentieth century's iconic trendsetters. My friends and some in the press had kibbitzed about my clothes, my hair and my makeup since the day Bill announced he would run. When I asked her if I should just turn myself over to a team of famous consultants as some in the media had recommended, she looked horrified. "You have to be you," she said. "You'll end up wearing someone else's idea of who you are and how you should look. Concentrate instead on what's important to you." Her words were a relief. With Jackie's tacit permission, I determined to continue having fun while not taking any of it too seriously.

After lingering for two hours, it was finally time for me to leave. Jackie urged me to call or be in touch if I ever had questions or needed to chat. Until her untimely death from cancer sixteen months later, she remained a source of inspiration and advice for me.

I was reassured after my visit with Jackie, but the respite didn't last long. I had agreed to grant my first newspaper interview as First Lady to Marian Burros of *The New York Times*, who typically covered the first big black-tie dinner of each new administration. Her stories usually focused on the choice of food, flowers and entertainment for the evening. I thought the interview offered me a chance to share my ideas about how I intended to make the White House a showcase for American food and culture.

Burros and I met in the Red Room, one of three sitting rooms on the State Floor of the Executive Mansion. We sat on a nineteenth-century American Empire sofa next to the fireplace. Gilbert Stuart's famous 1804 portrait of Dolley Madison, President Madison's wife and one of my feisty predecessors, hung on one wall. As Burros and I talked, I occasionally caught a glimpse of Dolley out of the corner of my eye. She was an extraordinary woman, well ahead of her time, famous for her sociability, trendsetting personal style (she favored turbans), political skills and great courage. During the War of 1812, as invading British troops advanced on Washington, she spent the day preparing what would be her last White House dinner party for President Madison and his military advisers, who were expected to return from the front. Although she finally realized that she had to evacuate, she refused to leave until the British were practically at the door. She fled with the clothes on her back, important state documents and a few treasured items from the Mansion. Her last act was to request that the full-length portrait of George Washington by Gilbert Stuart be cut out from its frame, rolled up and removed to a safe house. Shortly after her escape, Admiral Cockburn and his men sacked the White House, ate the meal she had prepared and burned the Mansion.

I wanted my first White House dinner party to be memorable, but not *that* memorable.

I told Burros that I wanted to put our personal stamp on the White House, as previous First Couples had done. I began by introducing American cuisine to the menu. Ever since the Kennedy Administration, the White House kitchen had been ruled by the French. I understood why Jackie had wanted to improve much about the White House, from decor to cuisine, but that was then. In the three decades since she had occupied the White House, American chefs had revolutionized cooking, starting with the incomparable duo Julia Child and Alice Waters. Child had written Bill and me at the end of 1992, urging us to showcase American culinary arts, and Waters wrote to encourage us to appoint an American chef. I agreed with them. The White House, after all, was one of our nation's most visible symbols of American culture. I hired Walter Scheib, an experienced chef who specialized in American cuisine featuring lighter, fresher ingredients and introduced more food and wine supplied by American purveyors.

The dinner turned out to be a grand success, with the few flaws visible hopefully only to us. The mostly American-grown feast included smoked marinated shrimp, roast tenderloin of beef, baby vegetables in a zucchini basket and Yukon Gold potatoes with Vidalia onions. We ate goat cheese from Massachusetts and drank American wines. Our guests seemed genuinely pleased, particularly with the after-dinner Broadway-style revue put together at the last minute by our Tony Award–winning friend James Naughton and featuring Lauren Bacall and Carol Channing. I heaved a big sigh of relief.

The Burros story ran on the front page of *The New York Times* on February 2, and it broke some minor news. I announced that we were banning smoking in the Executive Mansion as well as the East and West Wings, that broccoli would return to the White House kitchen (having been exiled by the Bushes) and that we hoped to make the White House more accessible to the public. Accompanying the text was a photo of me wearing a bare-shoulder, black Donna Karan evening dress.

To me, the story and the photo seemed harmless enough, but they inspired a lot of commentary. The White House press corps was not happy that I had granted an exclusive interview to a reporter whose beat was not White House politics. In their view, my choice signaled my determination to avoid challenging questions about my role in the policy arena. Some critics suggested that the story was contrived to "soften" my image and portray me as a traditional woman in a traditional role. Some of my most ardent defenders also took exception to the interview and the picture because neither reflected their conception of me as First Lady. If I was serious about substantive policy issues, they reasoned, why was I talking to a reporter about food and entertainment? Conversely, if I was really worrying about floral centerpieces and the color of table linens, how could I be substantive enough to head a major policy effort? What kind of message was I sending, anyway?

It seemed that people could perceive me only as one thing or the other—*either* a hardworking professional woman *or* a conscientious and caring hostess. I was beginning to catch on to what Kathleen Hall Jamieson, a distinguished professor of communications and Dean of the Annenberg School of Communications at the University of Pennsylvania, would later term "the double bind." Gender stereotypes, says Jamieson, trap women by categorizing them in ways that don't reflect the true complexities of their lives. It was becoming clear to me that people who wanted me to fit into a certain box, traditionalist or feminist, would never be entirely satisfied with me as me—which is to say, with my many different, and sometimes paradoxical, roles.

My friends lived the same way. On any given day, Diane Blair might be teaching a political science class hours before preparing dinner for a huge crowd at the Blairs' lakefront home. Melanne Verveer might be running a White House meeting one minute and talking on the phone with her granddaughter the next. Lissa Muscatine, a Rhodes Scholar from Harvard who gave birth to three children while working for me at the White House, might be on an airplane revising speeches or changing diapers at home. So who was the "real" woman? In fact, most of us took on all those roles and more every day of our lives.

I know how hard it is to integrate the many disparate demands, choices and activities women pursue and face every day. Most of us live with nagging voices questioning the choices we make and with loads of guilt, whatever our choice. In my own life I have been a wife, mother, daughter, sister, in-law, student, lawyer, children's rights activist, law professor, Methodist, political adviser, citizen and so much else. Now I was a symbol—and that was a new experience.

Bill and I had worried about the problems we would face when we moved into the White House, but I never expected that the way I defined my role as First Lady would generate so much controversy and confusion. In my own mind, I was traditional in some ways and not in others. I cared about the food I served our guests, and I also wanted to improve the delivery of health care for all Americans. To me, there was nothing incongruous about my interests and activities.

I was navigating uncharted terrain—and through my own inexperience, I contributed to some of the conflicting perceptions about me. It took me awhile to figure out that what might not be important to me might seem very important to many men and women across America. We were living in an era in which some people still felt deep ambivalence about women in positions of public leadership and power. In this era of changing gender roles, I was America's Exhibit A.

The scrutiny was overwhelming. Ever since I had become a Secret Service protectee at the Democratic Convention in New York in July 1992, I had been trying to adjust to my loss of anonymity. Occasionally, I snuck out of the White House wearing sweats, sunglasses and a baseball cap. I loved walking through the Mall, looking at the monuments, or riding my bike along the C&O Canal in Georgetown. I bargained the Secret Service down to only one agent, dressed in casual clothes, walking or biking behind me. I soon learned, though, that they had one of those big black fully loaded vans trailing somewhere nearby just in case. If I moved fast, even people who thought they recognized me weren't sure. One morning, a touring family asked me to take their picture as they posed in front of the Washington Monument. I quickly agreed, and as they stood together smiling, I snapped a photo. As I was leaving, I heard one of the children saying, "Mom, that lady looks familiar." I was out of earshot before I heard whether they guessed who their photographer was.

These moments of quiet anonymity were fleeting, and so was time with close friends. Several from Arkansas had come to work in Bill's administration, but ironically, they were among the people I missed the most those early weeks. We simply hadn't had time to see them.

In early February, Bill and I invited Vince Foster, now Deputy White House Counsel; Bruce Lindsey, also in the Counsel's office and still one of Bill's closest advisers and traveling companions; and Webb Hubbell, Associate Attorney General, to a small, informal dinner in the second-floor dining room of the residence to celebrate our friend Mary

Steenburgen's fortieth birthday. Mary, a fellow Arkansan, had done well in Hollywood, winning an Academy Award for acting, but she had never lost touch with her roots. She, Bruce, Vince and Webb were among our closest friends, and I remember that meal as one of the last carefree times we had together. For a few hours, we screened out the worries of the day and talked about adjusting to Washington and time-less issues—kids, schools, movies, politics. I can still close my eyes and see Vince at that table, looking tired but happy, leaning back and listen-ing with a smile on his face. At that moment, it was impossible to guess the strain he was under as a newcomer to Washington's political world.

1. My mother, Dorothy Howell, married my father, Hugh Rodham, Jr., in 1942 when he was in the Navy. Her childhood experiences opened her heart to those less fortunate and instilled in her a sense of social justice, which she passed on to me and my brothers. I inherited his laugh, the same big guffaw that can turn heads in a restaurant and send cats running from the room.

2. My grandmother, Hannah Jones Rodham, insisted on using all three of her names. She was a formidable personality, but she died when I was five, and I have fewer memories of her than of my grandfather, Hugh, Sr., a kind, patient man. My father worshiped Hannah and told me often how she saved his feet from amputation.

3

3. I was around eight or nine months old when my uncle, Russell Rodham, came to stay. After he gave up medicine, my father's younger brother joked that I was his last patient.

4. My step-grandfather, Max Rosenberg, was Jewish. As a ten-year-old growing up in the Midwest, I was horrified to learn that millions of innocent people had been put to death because of their religion. When I visited Auschwitz as First Lady, I remembered my father's attempt to explain to me the kind of evil that human beings are capable of and why the United States had to fight the Nazis.

5

5. After the war, my father started a small drapery fabric business. He enlisted all of his children when we were old enough to help with the printing. His success brought us to Park Ridge, Illinois, an American town right out of a Norman Rockwell illustration Here we pose in our 1959 Easter finery with our cat, Isis

6

6. Every summer, we spent mo of August at Grandfather Rod ham's cottage overlooking Lal Winola, northwest of Scranto in the Pocono Mountains. We played a lot of cards and board games on the big front porch.

7. In Park Ridge, I organized the kids in games, sporting events and backyard carnivals, for fun and to raise nickels and dimes for charities. When I was twelve, the local paper photographed me and my friends as we handed over a paper bag of money raised for the United Way.

8 and 9. Don Jones, a Methodist youth minister, introduced me to the "University of Life" when he arrived in Park Ridge in 1961 and encouraged our youth group to practice faith through social action. Here I am, standing with a bunch of friends from the group, on one of our more frivolous outings.

9

10. I was interested in politics from an early age. I was an active Young Republican and, later, a Goldwater girl, right down to my cowgirl outfit. During mock election debates in high school, however, I began to have doubts.

11. The Cultural Values Committee was my first experience with an organized effort to stress American values of pluralism, mutual respect and understanding. Our meeting of representatives from different student groups was broadcast on a local TV station. I wore my hair up for my first television appearance.

12. Alan Schechter was my political science professor and thesis adviser at Wellesley. He selected me for my internship in Washington, setting me on my way.

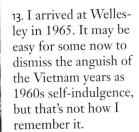

13. I arrived at Wellesley in 1965. It may be easy for some now to dismiss the anguish of the Vietnam years as 1960s self-indulgence, but that's not how I remember it.

15

15. At Wellesley, we—the class of 1969—were trapped between an outdated past and an uncharted future. There had never before been a student speaker at graduation. The accolades and attacks in response to my speech turned out to be a preview of things to come.

16. Patty Howe Criner (left) and my college roommate, Johanna Branson, remain lifelong friends. In 1975, they were in Arkansas for my wedding, along with my father, a man with strong views but the capacity to change.

14. In 1968, I interned at the House Republican Conference in Washington, D.C., working for a group headed by Gerald Ford (on my left), and including Melvin Laird and Charles Goodell (far right), both of whom befriended and advised me. This photo of me with leading Republicans was hanging in my father's bedroom when he died.

17. True to my nature and upbringing, I advocated changing the system from within and decided to go to law school, where I participated with Bill in mock trials.

18. Bill Clinton was hard to miss in 1970 at Yale. He looked more like a Viking than a Rhodes scholar newly returned from Oxford. We started a conversation on our first date in the Spring of 1971, and more than thirty years later, he's still the best company I know.

19. John Doar (left), selected by the House Judiciary Committee to head up the inquiry to impeach President Nixon, offered me a staff position to research the legal grounds for a presidential impeachment. I worked under Joe Woods, next to Doar. What I learned would serve me well.

21. Bill was asked to organize the South for McGovern in 1971. He would have been on the ground floor of a presidential campaign, but he chose to spend most of the summer with me in California.

20. Marian Wright Edelman's example helped direct me into my lifelong advocacy for children and civil rights.

22 and 23. I followed my heart to Arkansas when Bill ran for public office. We loved our life there, including our regular volleyball games. We were married on October 11, 1975, in the living room of our house in Fayetteville.

24

25

24. The 1976 Carter campaign asked me to be the field coordinator for the state of Indiana. Carter lost the state, but I learned a lot, and the job put me to another test.

27

25, 26 and 27. In 1979, Bill was sworn in as the Governor of Arkansas. He later formed an Education Standards Committee and named me Chair. When we proposed mandatory teacher testing, the debate was so bitter that one school librarian said I was "lower than a snake's belly."

28

29

Announcing
Arrival of

my name *Chelsea Victoria Clinton*
born on *Feb. 27th, 1980 11:24pm*
weighed *6* pounds *1¾* ounces
proud parents *Hillary Rodham*
Bill Clinton

28 and 29. Chelsea's birth was the most miraculous event in our lives. She was named after the song "Chelsea Morning," sung by her father as he and I strolled around London's Chelsea district while on vacation in 1978.

30. Bill, Carolyn Huber and I were serenaded by the Arkansas Boys Choir, a lovely respite during the difficult Christmas of 1980. Bill had just lost his reelection campaign, and we were packing up the Governor's Mansion. We wouldn't be gone long.

31. The only time I wasn't employed since I was thirteen was the eight years I spent in the White House. I became the first woman partner at Little Rock's Rose Law Firm and found myself charting new ground.

32. The two Rose Law Firm lawyers with whom I worked most were Vince Foster (left) and Webb Hubbell, shown at one of Chelsea's birthday parties. I had thought of Webb as a loyal, supportive friend. Vince was one of the smartest lawyers I've ever known and one of the best friends I've ever had. I will always wish I had read the signs of his despair and could have helped him.

33. I could get away with "eccentricities" as wife of the Attorney General, but as First Lady of Arkansas, I was thrown into the spotlight. For the first time, I came to realize the impact of my personal choices on my husband's political future. Many Arkansas voters were offended when I kept my maiden name, Rodham. I later added Clinton.

34. My faith has always been a crucial, though deeply personal, part of my life and my family's life. When I was confirmed in the Methodist Church, I took to heart John Wesley's words: "Do all the good you can, by all the means you can . . . as long as ever you can."

35. Tipper and Al Gore traveled around the country with us on our bus in the 1992 presidential campaign. Any time we saw a gathering of two or more people, Bill wanted to stop and talk to them.

37 and 38. My brothers, Hugh and Tony, and my father joined us on the campaign trail. If the first forty-four years of my life were an education, the thirteen-month-long presidential campaign was a revelation.

36. During the 1992 campaign, I had better luck with broccoli than I did with cookies. Everything I said or did, and even how I wore my hair, became a hot button for debate.

LET'S PUT BROCCOLI IN THE WHITE HOUSE AGAIN!

39. Election night at the Old State House in Little Rock, November 3, 1992. Our relationship, rooted in shared dreams, accomplishments, victories, defeats and mutual love and support, would sustain and challenge us when Bill became President.

40. After the election, we celebrated Harry Thomason's birthday with his wife Linda Bloodworth-Thomason in California. Dear friends, Harry and Linda produced and wrote some of the most successful shows on television, but their hearts never left the Ozarks. In 1992 I'm wearing the hat of my lifelong favorite American League team.

40

41. I've always believed that women should be able to make the choices that are right for them, and I thought the same should be true of First Ladies. I could never have predicted that Washington would be more conservative in some respects than Arkansas.

42. Bill wanted to go to the eleven inaugural balls, and not just for the customary five-minute drop-by and wave. We were going to celebrate. We practiced our dancing backstage at one of the warm-up balls earlier in the week.

42

43. January 20, 1993, was the beginning of a new Presidency for America and a new life for our family. As First Lady, I became a symbol—and that was a new experience.

44 and 45. I found someone who understood what I was going through better than anyone. Jackie Kennedy Onassis became a quiet source of inspiration and advice for me. "You've got to protect Chelsea at all costs," Jackie warned me. She confirmed my instincts that we had to do everything possible to allow her to grow up in private and to make her own mistakes.

HILLARYLAND

46, 47, 48 and 49. No First Lady ever had offices in the West Wing, but we knew my staff would be an integral part of the White House team, and we needed a seat at the table—literally and figuratively. Soon my staff became known as "Hillaryland," complete with pin. An extraordinary young staffer, Huma Abedin (left), worked her way up to become my personal assistant. Maggie Williams (right), my Chief of Staff during the first term, is one of the smartest, most creative and most decent people I've ever known.

49

50. My prayer group at a cookout on November 14, 1993. Over the years, these women quietly reached out to me when times were hard—even though many were Republicans. I appreciated their willingness to cross the political divide to help someone in need of support. We prayed with and for one another.

51. Hillaryland was our own little subculture within the White House, and we had our own special ethos. My staff prided themselves on discretion, loyalty and extraordinary camaraderie—and every child who ever visited knew exactly where we stashed the cookies.

52. The people I missed the most those early weeks were old pals from Arkansas who were now working in Bill's administration. We invited them to a small informal dinner to celebrate fellow Arkansan Mary Steenburgen's fortieth birthday. I remember that night as one of the last good times we all had together before Vince Foster's suicide left a gaping hole in our lives.

53. My father had prepared me for whatever life threw my way, except the pain of losing him. The time my mother and I spent at his hospital bedside strengthened my commitment to health care reform and deepened my understanding of the things in life that matter most.

54. Bill announced I would lead a newly formed President's Task Force on National Health Care Reform, with Ira Magaziner as Senior Adviser for Policy Development. His private sector experience, as well as his creative energy and tenacity, made him one of Bill's most valuable advisers. The announcement of my role brought heat from both inside and outside the White House.

54

55

55. After Bill unveiled his economic package on February 17, 1993, before a joint session of Congress, the plan was in place that would help set the country back on its feet. He balanced the budget three years earlier than promised.

56

56. In September 1993, after Bill presented his health care plan to Congress, we had a staff party to celebrate in the Old Executive Office Building, where the office was christened "The Delivery Room." We had started the trek up what one journalist called "the Mount Everest of social policy."

HEALTH CARE

O N JANUARY 25, BILL INVITED ME AND TWO GUESTS to lunch in the President's small study near the Oval Office: Carol Rasco, the newly named White House domestic policy adviser who had served in Bill's administration in Arkansas, and our old friend Ira Magaziner, a successful business consultant who had produced a groundbreaking study on health care costs.

Tall, angular and intense, Ira was prone to worry in the best of times, and on this day he seemed particularly anxious. In a few hours, Bill planned to unveil a health care task force and announce that it would produce reform legislation during his first one hundred days in office. Few on the White House staff knew that Bill had asked me to chair the task force or that Ira would manage the day-to-day operations as a senior adviser to the President for policy and planning. Ira had learned about his new job only ten days before the inauguration.

Bill wanted to approach health care reform from a new angle, and Ira, with his brilliant and creative mind, had a knack for coming up with inventive ways of looking at issues. He also had private sector experience as the owner of a consulting business in Rhode Island that advised multinational companies on how to become more productive and profitable.

After the Navy stewards brought us our food from the White House Mess, Ira delivered troubling news: Some Capitol Hill veterans were warning him that our timetable for delivering a health care reform bill in one hundred days was unrealistic. We had been encouraged by the electoral success of Harris Wofford, the new Democratic Senator from Pennsylvania who had campaigned on a health care platform and often told crowds: "If criminals have the right to a lawyer, working

Americans have the right to a doctor." But Ira was getting a different message.

"They think we're gonna get killed," said Ira, who hadn't touched his sandwich. "We'll need at least four to five years to put together a package that will pass Congress."

"That's what some of my friends are saying too," I said. I had cared about this issue for a long time, well before Bill and I got into politics, and I believed that access to quality affordable health care was a right American citizens should be guaranteed. I knew that Ira felt the same way. That might explain why I didn't run screaming from the room when Bill first broached the idea of my leading the task force and working with Ira on this signature initiative of his Administration. On this day, it was Bill's boundless optimism and his determination that kept me in my chair.

"I'm hearing the same thing," Bill said. "But we have to try. We just have to make it work."

There were compelling reasons to push ahead. By the time Bill became President, thirty-seven million Americans, most of them working people and their children, were uninsured. They weren't getting access to care until they were in a medical crisis. Even for common medical concerns they wound up in an emergency room, where care was most expensive, or they went broke trying to pay for medical emergencies on their own. In the early 1990s, one hundred thousand Americans were losing coverage each month, and two million were without coverage temporarily as they changed jobs. Small businesses were unable to offer coverage for their employees because of the exploding cost of health care premiums. And the quality of medical care was suffering too: In an effort to control costs, insurance companies often denied or delayed treatment prescribed by doctors in deference to their corporate bottom lines.

Rising health care costs were sapping the nation's economy, undermining American competitiveness, eroding workers' wages, increasing personal bankruptcies and inflating the national budget deficit. As a nation, we were spending more on health care—14 percent of our GDP—than any other industrialized country. In 1992, as much as $45 billion in health care costs was spent on administrative costs, rather than going to doctors, nurses, hospitals, nursing homes or other health care providers for direct care.

This terrible cycle of escalating costs and declining coverage was largely the result of a growing number of uninsured Americans. Patients without insurance seldom could afford to pay for their medical expenses out-of-pocket, so their costs were absorbed by the doctors and hospitals that treated them. Doctors and hospitals, in turn, raised their rates to cover the expense of caring for patients who weren't covered or couldn't pay, which is why $2 aspirin tablets and $2,400 crutches sometimes appear on hospital bills. Insurers, confronted with having to cover higher doctor and hospital rates, began trimming coverage and raising the price of premiums, deductibles and co-payments for people with insurance. As the price of premiums went up, fewer employers were willing or able to provide coverage for their workers, so more people lost their insurance. And the vicious cycle continued.

Solving these problems was critical to the well-being of tens of millions of Americans and to our nation as a whole. But even so, we knew it was going to be an uphill battle. For most of the twentieth century, Presidents had tried to reform our nation's health care system, with mixed success. President Theodore Roosevelt and other Progressive leaders were among the first to propose universal health care coverage nearly a century ago. In 1935, President Franklin D. Roosevelt envisioned a national health insurance system as a complement to Social Security, the cornerstone of his New Deal. The idea went nowhere, owing in large measure to opposition from the American Medical Association, the lobbying group representing the nation's doctors, who feared governmental control over their practices.

President Truman took up the cause of universal health care coverage as part of his Fair Deal and included it in his campaign platform in the 1948 election. He, too, was thwarted by well-financed and well-organized opposition from the AMA, the U.S. Chamber of Commerce and others who opposed national health insurance on ideological grounds, suggesting it was linked to socialism and communism. Opponents also believed then, as now, that the existing system worked well enough as is, despite the paradox that the United States spends more on health care than any other nation yet doesn't provide health insurance for everyone. After failing to overcome the opposition, Truman proposed the more modest—and practical—idea of providing health insurance for Social Security recipients.

During the 1940s and 1950s, labor unions bargained for health care benefits in the contracts they negotiated for workers. Other employers began offering these benefits to nonunion employees. This led to an extensive employer-based health care system in which insurance coverage increasingly was linked to one's employment.

In 1965, President Johnson's Great Society initiative led to the creation of Medicaid and Medicare, which provide federally funded health insurance for two underserved groups—the poor and the elderly. The programs serve seventy-six million individuals today. Johnson's effort, made possible by his landslide victory in 1964 and a huge Democratic majority in Congress, still represents the biggest health care success of the twentieth century and the realization of President Truman's goal.

Funded by payroll contributions from workers, Medicare removed the worry for people over sixty-five by making them eligible for physician and hospital services. Although Medicare doesn't cover prescription drugs—and should—it remains a popular and crucial service for older Americans, and its administrative costs are far lower than those of private health insurance companies providing coverage. Medicaid, the program that pays for care for the poorest Americans and those with disabilities, is funded jointly by the states and the federal government and is administered by the states according to federal rules. More politically vulnerable than Medicare because the poor are less politically powerful than the elderly, it has been a godsend for many Americans, especially children and pregnant women.

President Nixon recognized the draining effects of health care costs on the economy and proposed a system of universal health care based on what's known as an "employer mandate": all employers would be required to pay for limited benefits for their employees. Although as many as twenty different health care proposals were introduced in Congress during the Nixon Administration, no proposal for universal coverage got a majority vote from a congressional committee until nearly twenty years later, in 1994.

Presidents Ford and Carter—Republican and Democrat—also pursued reform in the 1970s, but they ran into the same political obstacles that had blocked change for most of the twentieth century. Over several decades, the health insurance industry had grown increasingly powerful. Many insurance companies opposed universal coverage because they feared it could restrict the amount they could charge and limit their ability to turn down high-risk patients. Some thought that universal coverage might sound the death knell for private insurance.

The historical odds were against Bill because attitudes about health care reform were diverse, even among Democrats. As one expert put it, opinions are "theologically held"—thus impervious to reason, evidence or argument. But Bill felt he had to show the public and the Congress that he had the political will to move forward and make good on his campaign promise to take immediate action on health care. Reform was not only good public policy that would help millions of Americans, it also was inextricably tied to reducing the deficit.

I shared Bill's profound concerns about the economy and the fiscal irresponsibility of the prior twelve years, under the Reagan and Bush Administrations. Recent deficit projections by the Bush Administration camouflaged the real deficit by underestimating the effects of a stagnant economy, the impact of health care costs and federal spending on the savings and loan bailout. These costs had helped swell the projected deficit to $387 billion over four years—considerably higher than the estimate the departing Bush White House had released. But beyond budgetary concerns, I believed health care reform could relieve the anguish of working people throughout our wealthy country. As the wife of a Governor and now a President, I didn't have to worry about my family's access to health care. And I didn't think anyone else should have to, either.

My experiences serving on the board of Arkansas Children's Hospital and chairing a state task force on rural health care introduced me to problems embedded in our health care system, including the tricky politics of reform and the financial quandaries faced by families who were too "rich" to qualify for Medicaid but too "poor" to pay for their own care. Traveling around Arkansas in the 1980s, and then around the United States during the presidential campaign, I met Americans who reinforced my belief that we had to fix what was wrong with the system. Bill's commitment to reform represented our greatest hope of guaranteeing millions of hardworking men and women the health care they deserved.

Bill, Ira, Carol and I walked out of the Oval Office, past the bust of Abraham Lincoln by Augustus Saint-Gaudens and across the narrow hall to the Roosevelt Room, where a crowd of cabinet secretaries, senior White House staff and journalists was waiting for what the official schedule listed as a "task force meeting."

Stepping into the Roosevelt Room is stepping back into American history. You are surrounded by banners from every U.S. military campaign and flags from each division of the U.S. Armed Forces, portraits of Theodore and Franklin Roosevelt and the Nobel Peace Prize medal that Theodore Roosevelt won in 1906 for mediating a settlement of the Russo-Japanese War. During our time in the White House, I added a small bronze bust of Eleanor Roosevelt, so that her contributions as a "Roosevelt" would also be acknowledged in the room named for her uncle and husband.

In this historic room, Bill declared that his administration would present a health care reform plan to Congress within one hundred days—a plan that "would take strong action to control health care costs in America and to begin to provide for the health care needs of all Americans."

Then he announced that I would chair a newly formed President's Task Force on National Health Care Reform, which would include the Secretaries of Health and Human Services, Treasury, Defense, Commerce and Labor, as well as the Directors of Veterans Affairs and of the Office of Management and Budget and senior White House staff. Bill explained that I would work with Ira, the cabinet and others to build on what he had sketched out in the campaign and in his inaugural address. "We're going to have to make some tough choices in order to control health care costs . . . and to provide health care for all," he said. "I am grateful that Hillary has agreed to chair the task force, and not only because it means she'll be sharing some of the heat I expect to generate."

Heat came from all directions. The announcement was a surprise inside the White House and federal agencies. A few on Bill's staff had assumed I would be named domestic policy adviser (which Bill and I had never discussed). Others thought I would work on education or children's health, largely because of my past experiences on these issues. Maybe we should have told more staff members, but sensitive internal information was already flowing out of the White House, and Bill wanted to break the story himself and answer the first questions raised.

Many White House aides thought it was a great idea. Several of Bill's key lieutenants heartily endorsed the idea, including Robert Rubin, Chairman of the National Economic Council and later Secretary of the Treasury. One of my favorite people in the administration, Bob is fabulously smart and successful, yet thoroughly self-effacing. He later joked about his extraordinary political acumen: He didn't think my appointment would generate such intense political fallout. I was surprised by the reaction too.

Some of our friends gave us lighthearted warnings about what lay ahead. "What did you do to make your husband so mad at you?" Mario Cuomo, then Governor of New York, asked me during a White House visit.

"What do you mean?"

"Well," Mario replied, "he'd have to be awfully upset about something to put you in charge of such a thankless task."

I heard the warnings, but I didn't fully realize the magnitude of what we were undertaking. My work in Arkansas running the rural health care task force and the Arkansas Education Standards Committee didn't rival the scale of health care reform. But both efforts were considered successful and made me excited and hopeful as I took on this new challenge. The biggest problem seemed to be the deadline that Bill announced. He had won the election in a three-way race with less than a majority of the popular vote—43 percent—and he couldn't afford to lose whatever political momentum he had at the beginning of the new administration. James Carville, our friend, adviser and one of the most brilliant tactical minds in American politics, had given Bill this warning: "The more time we allow for the defenders of the status quo to organize, the more they will be able to marshal opposition to your plan, and the better their chances of killing it."

Democrats in Congress were also urging us to move quickly. A few days after Bill's announcement, House Majority Leader Dick Gephardt asked to meet with me. He was known on Capitol Hill for his Midwestern roots and sensibilities, as well as his command of budget issues. His compassion for people in need reflected his upbringing, and his commitment to health care reform was heightened by his son's bout with cancer years earlier. Through position and experience, Gephardt would be a leading voice in any health care deliberations in the House. On February 3, Gephardt and his top health care aide came to my West Wing office to discuss strategy. For the next hour, we listened as Gephardt outlined his concerns about health care reform. It was an intense meeting.

One of Gephardt's chief worries was that we would be unable to unify Democrats, who were seldom united under the best of circumstances. Health care reform widened existing divisions. I thought of the old Will Rogers joke:

"Are you a member of any organized political party?"

"No, I'm a Democrat."

I knew of the potential divisiveness but hoped that a Democratic Congress would rally around a Democratic President to show what the party could accomplish for America.

Democratic members had already begun to outline their own models for reform in order to influence the President's plans. Some proposed a "single payer" approach, modeled on the European and Canadian health care systems, which would replace the current employer-based system. The federal government, through tax payments, would become the sole financier—or single payer—of most medical care. A few favored a gradual expansion of Medicare that would eventually cover all uninsured Americans, starting first with those aged fifty-five to sixty-five.

Bill and other Democrats rejected the single-payer and Medicare models, preferring a quasi-private system called "managed competition" that relied on private market forces to drive down costs through competition. The government would have a smaller role, including setting standards for benefit packages and helping to organize purchasing cooperatives. The cooperatives were groups of individuals and businesses forged for the purpose of purchasing insurance. Together, they could bargain with insurance companies for better benefits and prices and use their leverage to assure high-quality care. The best model was the Federal Employees Health Benefit Plan, which covered nine million federal employees and offered an array of insurance options to its members. Prices and quality were monitored by the plan's administrators.

Under managed competition, hospitals and doctors would no longer bear the expense of treating patients who weren't covered because everyone would be insured through Medicare, Medicaid, the veterans and military health care plans or one of the purchasing groups.

Perhaps most important, the system would allow patients to choose their own doctors, a non-negotiable item in Bill's view.

Given the multitude of approaches to health care reform, feelings in Congress ran deep, Gephardt told us. Just a week earlier, he had held a health care meeting in his House office in which two members of Congress disagreed so violently that they nearly came to blows. Gephardt was emphatic that our best hope for passage was to attach health care reform to a budget bill known as the Budget Reconciliation Act, which Congress usually voted on in late spring. "Reconciliation" combines a variety of congressional budget and tax decisions into one bill that can be approved or disapproved by a simple majority vote in the Senate without the threat of a filibuster, a delaying tactic often used to kill controversial legislation, which requires sixty votes to break. Many budget items, particularly those relating to tax policy, are so complicated that debate can endlessly tie up proceedings in the full House and Senate. Reconciliation is a procedural tool designed to move controversial tax and spending bills through Congress. Gephardt was suggesting that it be used in an unprecedented way: to legislate a major transformation in American social policy.

Gephardt was sure that Republicans in the Senate would filibuster any health care package we put forward. He also knew that the Senate Democrats would have trouble mustering sixty votes to stop it, given that Democrats held only a fifty-six to forty-four advantage. Gephardt's strategy, therefore, was to circumvent a filibuster by putting health care reform into the budget reconciliation package. A simple majority would be required to pass the bill, and Vice President Gore could cast the tie-breaking fifty-first vote, if needed.

Ira and I knew that Bill's economic team inside the White House would likely reject a budget reconciliation strategy that included health care because it could complicate the administration's efforts on the deficit reduction and economic plan. We broke up our meeting, and I took Gephardt straight to the Oval Office to make his case directly to Bill. Bill was convinced by Gephardt's argument and asked Ira and me to explore the idea with the Senate leadership.

Armed with Gephardt's suggestions and Bill's encouragement, Ira and I trooped up to Capitol Hill the following day to meet with Majority Leader George Mitchell in his office in the Capitol. This was the first of hundreds of visits I made to members of Congress over the course of health care reform. Mitchell's soft-spoken demeanor belied his tough-minded leadership of the Senate Democrats. I respected his opinion, and he agreed with Gephardt. Health care would be impossible to pass unless it was part of reconciliation. Mitchell was also nervous about the Senate Finance Committee, which would otherwise have jurisdiction over many aspects of health care legislation. He was particularly worried that committee Chairman Daniel Patrick Moynihan of New York, a veteran Democrat and a skeptic about health care reform, would react badly to the plan. Moynihan was an intellectual giant and an academic by training—he had taught sociology at Harvard before running for the Senate—as well as an expert on poverty and family is-

sues. He had wanted the President and Congress to take up welfare reform first. He wasn't happy when Bill announced his one-hundred-day
target for health care legislation—and he let everyone know it.

At first I found his position frustrating, but I began to understand.
Bill and I shared Senator Moynihan's commitment to welfare reform,
but Bill and his economic team believed that the government would
never get control of the federal budget deficit unless health care costs
went down. They had concluded that health care reform was essential
to his economic policy and that welfare could wait. Senator Moynihan
anticipated how hard it would be to get health care through his committee. He knew he was going to be responsible for shepherding Bill's
economic stimulus package through the Finance Committee and onto
the Senate floor. That in itself would require extraordinary political
skill and leverage. Some Republicans were already publicizing plans to
vote against it, no matter what it contained. And some Democrats
might need convincing, particularly if the package involved a tax increase.

We left Mitchell's office with a clearer sense of what needed to be
done, particularly on reconciliation. Now we had to convince the economic team—notably Leon Panetta, Director of the Office of Management and Budget—that including health care reform in reconciliation
would serve the overall economic strategy the President was pursuing,
not divert attention from the deficit reduction plan. Bill only had so
much political capital to work with, and he had to use it to get the
deficit down, one of his central campaign promises. The thinking in
some quarters of the West Wing was that Bill's focus on health care
would divert Americans from his economic message and muddy the political waters.

We also had to convince Senator Robert C. Byrd of West Virginia
that health care reform belonged in reconciliation. The Democratic
Chairman of the Senate Appropriations Committee, Byrd had served
in the Senate by then for thirty-four years. Stately and silver-haired, he
was the unofficial historian of the Senate and a parliamentary genius,
famous for standing in the well of the chamber and dazzling his colleagues with quotations from the classics. He was also a stickler for procedural rules and decorum and had invented a procedural hurdle called
the "Byrd rule" to ensure that items placed in the Budget Reconciliation Act were germane to budget and tax law. Democracy was undermined, in his view, if reconciliation was cluttered with bills that had

little to do with passing the nation's budget. Health care, arguably, was a budget bill, as it affected spending, taxes and entitlement programs. But if Senator Byrd thought differently, we would need a waiver of his rule to allow the measure into reconciliation.

Slowly, I was learning what a steep mountain we were climbing. In the absence of an overwhelming crisis like a depression, passing either the economic or the health care plan was going to be difficult; passing both seemed almost insurmountable. Health care reform might be essential to our long-term economic growth, but I didn't know how much change the body politic could digest at one time.

Our goals were simple enough: We wanted a plan that dealt with all aspects of the health care system rather than one that tinkered on the margins. We wanted a process that considered a variety of ideas and allowed for healthy discussion and debate. And we wanted to adhere to congressional wishes as much as we could.

Almost immediately, we hit turbulence.

Bill had assigned Ira the task of setting up the process for health care reform, which turned out to be an unfair burden for someone who was not a Washington insider. In addition to the President's Task Force, which consisted of me, the cabinet secretaries and other White House officials, Ira organized a giant working group of experts divided into teams that would consider every aspect of health care. This group, comprising as many as six hundred people from different government agencies, Congress and health care groups, and including physicians, nurses, hospital administrators, economists and others, met regularly with Ira to debate and review specific parts of the plan in detail. The group was so large that some members concluded they were not at the center of the action where the real work was getting done. Some got frustrated and stopped coming to meetings. Others became narrowly interested in their own piece of the agenda, rather than invested in the outcome of the overall plan. In short, the attempt to include as many people and viewpoints as possible—a good idea in principle—ended up weakening rather than strengthening our position.

On February 24, we were dealt a blow that none of us anticipated. Three groups affiliated with the health care industry sued the task force over its composition, claiming that because I was not technically a government employee (First Ladies derive no salary), I was not legally allowed to chair or even attend closed task force meetings. These groups had seized on an obscure federal law designed to prevent private interests from surreptitiously influencing government decision making and usurping the public's right to know. There was certainly nothing secret about hundreds of people participating in this process, but the press, which was not invited to meetings, jumped on the issue. If I was allowed in the meetings, the lawsuit claimed, government sunshine laws required that the closed meetings be opened to outsiders, including the press. It was a deft political move, designed to disrupt our work on health care and to foster an impression with the public and the news media that we were conducting "secret" meetings.

Soon thereafter, we got more bad news, this time from Senator Byrd. Every Democratic emissary we could think of, including the President, had asked him to allow health care reform into reconciliation. But on March 11, in a phone call with the President, the Senator said he objected on procedural grounds and that the "Byrd rule" would not be waived. The Senate was permitted to debate reconciliation bills for only twenty hours, which he viewed as insufficient time on a health care reform package of such magnitude. It was just too complicated an issue for reconciliation, he told Bill. In retrospect and based on my service in the Senate, I agree with his assessment. At the time, it was a political setback that forced us to refocus our strategy and figure out how to get health care reform through the normal legislative process. Hastily, we held meetings with members of the House and Senate to nail down elements of the plan we would deliver to Congress. We didn't see that Byrd's opinion on reconciliation was a giant red flag. We were trying to move too quickly on a bill that would fundamentally alter American social and economic policy for years to come. And we were already losing the race.

In this climate, and with Bill weathering controversies over gays in the military and his nominations for Attorney General, we savored any successes that came our way. In the middle of March, the House passed Bill's economic stimulus package, and my staff and I decided to have our own small celebration. On March 19, about twenty of us gathered for lunch in the White House Mess. The room, with its oak-paneled walls, Navy memorabilia and leather-cushioned chairs, was a perfect setting for private conversation and as much laughter as we could muster. The gathering offered me a rare opportunity to let my hair down with trusted aides and speak my mind about whatever topic was under discussion. From the moment I set foot in the room, I could feel my mood lighten and my mind relax for the first time in days.

Lunch arrived and we began sharing stories of our first few weeks in the White House. Then I saw Carolyn Huber enter the room. One of my longtime assistants from Arkansas who had come with us to Washington, Carolyn walked over to my chair and bent down to whisper in my ear. "Your father has had a stroke," she said. "He's in the hospital."

THE END OF SOMETHING

I LEFT THE WHITE HOUSE MESS AND WENT UP-stairs to call Drew Kumpuris, my father's doctor in Little Rock. He confirmed that my father had suffered a massive stroke and been taken by ambulance to St. Vincent's Hospital, where he lay unconscious in the intensive care unit. "You've got to come right now," Drew said. I rushed to tell Bill and pack some clothes. Within hours, Chelsea, my brother Tony and I were on a plane to Arkansas for a long, sad trip home.

I can't remember landing in Little Rock that night or driving to the hospital. My mother met me outside the intensive care unit, looking drawn and worried but thankful to see us.

Dr. Kumpuris explained that my dad had slipped into a deep, irreversible coma. We could visit him, but it was doubtful he would know we were there. At first, I was concerned about taking Chelsea to see her grandfather, but she insisted and I relented because I knew how close she felt to him. When we went in, I was relieved that he looked almost peaceful. Since it would have been useless for the doctors to operate on his injured brain, he was not hooked up to the tentacles of tubes, drains and monitors he had needed after his heart bypass operation a decade earlier. Although a mechanical respirator was breathing for him, there were only a few unobtrusive drips and monitors at his bedside. Chelsea and I held his hands. I smoothed his hair and spoke to him, still clinging to a small hope that he might open his eyes again or squeeze my hand.

Chelsea sat by his side and talked to him for hours. His condition didn't seem to upset her. I was amazed at how calmly she dealt with the situation.

Hugh arrived later that night from Miami and joined us in Dad's room. Hugh started telling family stories and singing songs, especially the ones that used to get such a rise out of my father. One of his frequent tirades concerned my brothers' taste—or lack thereof—in television shows. He particularly despised the theme song to *The Flintstones*. So Hugh and Tony stood on either side of his bed and sang that inane song, hoping to provoke some sort of reaction—"Shut that noise up!"—as it had when we were kids. If he heard us that night, he never showed it. But I want to believe that somehow he knew we were there for him just as he had been for us when we were kids.

Mostly, we took turns sitting next to Dad's bed, watching the mysterious green blips on the monitors rise and fall, succumbing to the hypnotic whir and click of the respirator. The center of my turbulent universe of obligations and meetings contracted to that small hospital room in Little Rock until it became a world unto itself, removed from all concerns except the things that matter most.

Bill arrived Sunday, March 21. I was so happy to see him and could feel myself relax for the first time in two days as he took charge of talking to the doctors, helping me think about the decision we would soon have to make about my father's medical options.

Carolyn Huber and Lisa Caputo had come from Washington with me and Chelsea. Carolyn was especially close to my parents. I had met her when I joined the Rose Law Firm, where she had worked for years as an office administrator. She had managed the Arkansas Governor's Mansion during Bill's first term, and we had asked her to come with us to the White House to handle personal correspondence.

Lisa Caputo had been my press secretary since the convention. She and my father hit it off the first time they met when they found out they were both from the Scranton–Wilkes-Barre area of Pennsylvania. "Hillary, you did real good," my dad told me. "You hired someone from God's country!"

Harry Thomason flew in from the West Coast, and he also made travel arrangements for Virginia and Dick Kelley, who had been out of town and who arrived at the hospital Sunday night. Bill and I thought they had been in Las Vegas, their favorite destination. But Harry pulled Bill and me aside to deliver more tragic news. He told us, as gently as he could, that Virginia and Dick had not been in Nevada for a vacation. They had been in Denver, where Virginia was exploring experimental treatments for the cancer that had returned and spread after her mastectomy two years before. She did not want us to know how sick she was, and Harry said she would deny it if we confronted her. Harry had tracked them down, and he felt it was something we needed to know. Bill and I thanked him for his good sense and his good heart and rejoined Virginia and Dick, who were talking to my mother and brothers. We decided to respect Virginia's wishes for now; it was best to deal with one family crisis at a time.

The day after he arrived, Bill had to fly back to Washington. Luckily, Chelsea didn't have to miss school because it was spring break. She stayed with me in Little Rock, and I was profoundly grateful to have her calm and loving companionship. As the hours dragged into days, Dad's condition remained critical. Friends and family members began showing up from all over to lend their emotional support. To pass the time, we played word games or cards. Tony taught me how to play Tetris on his little handheld computer, and I sat for hours, mindlessly fitting together the geometric pieces as they floated down the screen.

I simply couldn't focus on my duties as First Lady. I cleared my schedule, and I asked Lisa Caputo to explain to Ira Magaziner and everyone else that they should go ahead without me. Tipper graciously stepped in on several occasions to attend previously scheduled forums on health care, and Al spoke in my place to leaders of the American Medical Association in Washington and presided over the first public meeting of the Task Force on National Health Care Reform. I just couldn't leave my parents. Normally I am able to handle a great many things at once, but I couldn't pretend that this was a normal time. I knew that our family would soon face the decision to remove my dad from life support.

Perhaps to divert my feelings, in the long hours I spent in the hospital, I talked with doctors, nurses, pharmacists, hospital administrators and family members of other patients about the present health care system. One of the doctors told me how frustrating it was for him to write prescriptions for some of his Medicare patients, knowing that they could not afford to fill them. Other patients paid for their drugs but took smaller doses than prescribed, to make them last longer. Often, these patients ended up right back in the hospital. The health care policy problems we were tackling in Washington were now a part of my daily reality. These personal encounters reinforced my sense of both the difficulty of the assignment Bill had given me and the importance of improving our system.

Bill returned to Little Rock on Sunday, March 28, and we gathered our immediate family together and met with the doctors, who spelled out our options: Hugh Rodham was essentially brain-dead, kept alive by machines. None of us could imagine that the fiercely independent man we had known would want us to keep his body going under such circumstances. I remembered how angry and depressed he had been after his quadruple bypass surgery in 1983. He had enjoyed good health for most of his life and valued his self-reliance. He told me then that he would rather die than be sick and helpless. This was so much worse, although at least he seemed to be unaware of his condition. Each member of the family agreed that we should remove him from the respirator that night after our final good-byes and let God take him home. Dr. Kumpuris told us he would probably die within twenty-four hours.

However, the soul of the former Nittany Lions football player and boxer wasn't quite ready to leave. After the life support was removed, Dad began to breathe on his own, and his heart kept on beating. Bill stayed with us until Tuesday, when he had to resume his schedule. Chelsea and I decided to stay until the end.

While I had canceled every public appearance, including the chance to throw out the first pitch for the Cubs' opening game at Wrigley Field in Chicago, there was one engagement I could not seem to break. Liz Carpenter had been Lady Bird Johnson's press secretary, and now, among her many activities, she hosted a lecture series at the University of Texas in Austin. Many months earlier, I had accepted her invitation to speak on April 6. With my father hovering between life and death, I called her to cancel or reschedule. Liz is a spunky, outgoing woman, and in her inimitable manner, she wouldn't take no for an answer. It would be only a few hours of my time, she told me, and it would take my mind off my father's condition. She even had Lady Bird call to persuade me to come. Liz knew how much I admired Lady Bird Johnson, a gracious woman and one of our most effective and influential First Ladies. Finally, it seemed easier to agree to make the speech than to keep saying no.

On Sunday, April 4, my father was still hanging on to life. He had survived a week without artificial support or food. The hospital had to move him out of intensive care to make room for another patient. He was now in a regular hospital room, lying on the bed, looking as if he had just fallen asleep and would soon wake up. He looked rested and younger than his eighty-two years. The hospital administration had told my mother and me that they would soon require that a feeding tube be surgically inserted so he could be moved to a nursing home.

Both of us were praying that we could avoid that nightmare. I thought of how a feeding tube would horrify my father while—even worse in his value system—his life savings would be siphoned off for nursing care. But if his vegetative state persisted, there was no alternative.

Chelsea needed to get back to school, and we returned to the White House late on April 4. Two days later, I flew to Austin. Since I hadn't planned on making that speech, I had to write one, and when I climbed aboard the plane I didn't have a clue about what I would say.

I believe that when our hearts are raw with grief, we are more vulnerable to hurt, but also more open to new perceptions. I don't know how much I was changed by my father's imminent death, but many of the issues that I had been thrashing around for years came flooding into my mind. The speech I sketched out in longhand was not seamless, or even particularly articulate, but it was an unfiltered reflection of what I was thinking at the time.

Years before, I had begun carrying around a small book that I stuffed with notations, inspirational quotes, sayings and favorite Scripture. On the plane to Austin, I leafed through it and stopped at a magazine clipping of an article written by Lee Atwater before he died of brain cancer at age forty. Atwater was a political wunderkind on the campaigns of Presidents Reagan and George H. W. Bush and a principal architect of the Republican ascendancy in the 1980s. He was a political street fighter and famous for his ruthless tactics. Winning, Atwater proclaimed, was all that mattered—until he got sick. Shortly before he died, he wrote about a "spiritual vacuum at the heart of American society." His message had moved me when I first read it, and it seemed even more important now, so I decided to quote him in my address before the fourteen thousand people gathered for the Liz Carpenter lecture.

"Long before I was struck with cancer, I felt something stirring in American society," Atwater wrote. "It was a sense among the people of the country—Republicans and Democrats alike—that something was missing from their lives—something crucial. . . . I wasn't exactly sure what 'it' was. My illness helped me to see that what was missing in society is what was missing in me: a little heart, a lot of brotherhood.

"The 80s were about acquiring—acquiring wealth, power, prestige. I know. I acquired more wealth, power and prestige than most. But you can acquire all you want and still feel empty. What power wouldn't I trade for a little more time with my family? What price wouldn't I pay for an evening with friends? It took a deadly illness to put me eye to eye with that truth, but it is a truth that the country, caught up in its ruthless ambitions and moral decay, can learn on my dime. . . ."

I drew on different sources to put together a statement about the need to "remold society by redefining what it means to be a human being in the twentieth century, moving into a new millennium. . . .

"We need a new politics of meaning. We need a new ethos of individual responsibility and caring. We need a new definition of civil society which answers the unanswerable questions posed by both the market forces and the governmental ones, as to how we can have a society that fills us up again and make us feel that we are part of something bigger than ourselves."

I suggested a response to Lee Atwater's poignant question: "Who will lead us out of this 'spiritual vacuum?'" The answer, I said, is: "All of us."

When I finished the speech, I hugged Liz Carpenter, Governor Ann Richards and Lady Bird Johnson. Then I headed to the airport to return to the White House, check on my daughter and see my husband before leaving again to help my mother face the reality of moving my dad into a nursing home.

It was a relief to have given the speech, and I thought that would be the end of it. But within weeks, my words were derided in a *New York Times Magazine* cover story facetiously titled "Saint Hillary." The article dismissed my discussion of spirituality as "easy, moralistic preaching" couched in the "gauzy and gushy wrappings of New Age jargon." I was grateful when many people called to thank me for raising questions about meaning in our lives and in society.

The day after my speech in Austin, my father died.

I couldn't help but think how my relationship with my father had evolved over time. I adored him when I was a little girl. I would eagerly watch for him from a window and run down the street to meet him on his way home after work. With his encouragement and coaching, I played baseball, football and basketball. I tried to bring home good grades to win his approval. But as I grew older, my relationship with him inevitably changed, both because of my experiences growing up, which occurred in such a different time and place from his, and because he changed. He gradually lost the energy that got him outside throwing football pass patterns to me and Hugh as we ran around the elm trees in front of our house. Just as those magnificent elms succumbed to disease and had to be cut down in neighborhoods like ours throughout the country, his energy and spirit seemed to wane over time.

More and more, his immediate world seemed to shrink as he lost his father and both brothers in a few short years in the mid-sixties. Then he decided in the early seventies that he had made and saved enough money, so he quit working and dismantled his small company. During my high school and college years, our relationship increasingly was defined either by silence, as I searched for something to say to him, or by arguments, which I often provoked, because I knew he would always engage with me over politics and culture—Vietnam, hippies, bra-burning feminists, Nixon. I also understood that even when he erupted at me, he admired my independence and accomplishments and loved me with all his heart.

I recently reread letters he wrote me when I was at Wellesley and Yale, usually in response to a despondent collect call home in which I expressed doubts about my abilities or confusion about where my life was heading. I doubt anyone meeting my father or being on the receiving end of his caustic criticism would ever have imagined the tender love and advice he offered to buck me up, straighten me out and keep me going.

I also respected my father's willingness to change his views, although he would rarely admit he had. He started out in life inheriting every prejudice imaginable in his working-class, Protestant family—against Democrats, Catholics, Jews and blacks—and anyone else considered outside the tribe. When I got exasperated by these attitudes during our summer visits to Lake Winola, I would announce to all the Rodhams that I intended to grow up and marry a Catholic Democrat—a fate they considered the worst I could meet. Over time, my father softened and changed, largely because of personal experiences with all kinds of people. He owned a building in downtown Chicago with a black man whom he came to respect and admire, causing him to change his views on race. When I grew up and fell in love with a Southern Baptist Democrat, my father was bewildered, but he rallied and became one of Bill's strongest supporters.

When my parents moved to Little Rock in 1987, they bought a condo next door to the one owned by Larry Curbo, a nurse, and Dr. Dillard Denson, a neurologist. They were among my mother's closest friends and began checking in on my parents, visiting with my dad, talking about the stock market or politics and helping out my mother around the house. When Bill and I came to visit, the military and Secret Service used their house as the command center. One night, my parents were watching a television show that featured gay characters. When my father expressed his disapproval of homosexuals, my mother said, "What about Dillard and Larry?"

"What do you mean?" he asked.

So my mother explained to my father that his dear friends and neighbors were a gay couple in a long-lasting committed relationship. One of my father's last stereotypes fell. Larry and Dillard visited my father in the hospital as he lay in a coma. One night, Larry relieved my mother for a few hours so she could go home and get some rest. And it was Larry who held my father's hand and said good-bye as he died. Perhaps fittingly, my father spent his last days at St. Vincent's, a wonderful Catholic hospital, a sign that another of his prejudices had disappeared.

Early the next morning, Bill, Chelsea and I, joined by an intimate group of family and friends, flew back to Little Rock for a memorial service at the First United Methodist Church. With us were my brother Tony, his future wife, Nicole Boxer, my dear friend Diane Blair, who had been staying with us, Bruce Lindsey, Vince Foster and Webb Hubbell. I was touched that Al and Tipper flew down with Mack McLarty, one of Bill's best friends from growing up and now White House Chief of Staff, along with Mack's wife, Donna. The church on that Good Friday was filled for "A Service of Death and Resurrection," led by the church's senior minister, the Rev. Ed Matthews, and the minister who had married Bill and me, the Rev. Vic Nixon. After the service, our family, joined by Dillard and Larry, Carolyn and Dr. John Holden, one of my brothers' best friends from Park Ridge, took my father home to Scranton. In character, my father had chosen and paid for his gravesite years before.

We had a second funeral service at the Court Street Methodist Church, down the street from the house where my dad had grown up. Bill delivered a loving eulogy that conveyed Hugh Rodham's brusqueness and devotion:

"In 1974, when I made my first political race, I ran in a congressional district where there were a lot of Republicans from the Middle West. And my future father-in-law came down in a Cadillac with an Illinois license plate; never told a living soul I was in love with his daughter, just went up to people and said, 'I know that you're a Republican and so am I. I think Democrats are just one step short of communism, but this kid's all right.' "

We laid him to rest in the Washburn Street Cemetery. It was a cold, rain-drenched April day, and my thoughts were as gloomy as the leaden sky. I stood listening to the Military Honor Guard's bugler playing taps. After the burial, we went with some of my father's old friends to a local restaurant, where we reminisced.

We were supposed to be celebrating my father's life, but I was overwhelmed with sadness for what he would now be missing. I thought about how much he enjoyed seeing his son-in-law serve as President and how much he wanted to watch Chelsea grow up. When Bill was preparing his eulogy on the plane from Little Rock, we were all telling stories. Chelsea reminded us that her PopPop had always said that when she graduated from college, he would rent a big limousine and pick her up wearing a white suit. He had many dreams that wouldn't be realized. But I was thankful for the life, opportunities and dreams he passed along to me.

VINCE FOSTER

BILL, CHELSEA AND I WANTED TO SPEND EASTER AT Camp David, and we invited our immediate family and the friends who had come to Scranton. We all needed time to unwind after the funeral and the long weeks of worry, and Camp David was the only haven where we would have the peace and privacy we craved. Jackie Kennedy Onassis had encouraged me to shelter my intimate family life in this protected retreat, surrounded by a forest preserve in Maryland's Catoctin Mountains. Her simple, pragmatic advice, as always, had proved invaluable. I was also pleased that my father had visited the retreat after the inauguration. We could remember his presence in its rustic cabins and his delight in seeing the place that President Eisenhower had renamed for his grandson, David. Now we were with my father's grandchild, Chelsea, to mourn his passing.

That Easter weekend was cold and rainy, and it fit my mood perfectly. I went for a long walk in the drizzle with my mother, and I asked her if she wanted to live with us in the White House. In her characteristically independent manner, she said that she would stay awhile, but that she wanted to go home to attend to all the issues accompanying my father's death. She thanked me for inviting Dillard Denson and Larry Curbo to Camp David. She knew they would continue to be valuable friends as she faced her life alone.

We attended Easter service in the recently built Evergreen Chapel, an A-frame of wood and stained glass that fits beautifully into its wooded setting. I sat in my pew and thought of how my father used to embarrass my brothers and me with his loud, off-key hymn singing. I share his tone deafness, but that morning I sang out, hoping the discordant notes might reach the heavens.

Physically and emotionally drained, I probably should have taken more time to rest and to let myself grieve. But I couldn't ignore the call back to work. Ira had been sending me SOS signals, warning that the health care initiative was being sidelined by budgetary battles. And there was Chelsea, who needed to return to school and to her life. After sharing Easter dinner together with our guests, Bill, Chelsea and I returned to Washington.

The moment I walked into our bedroom on Sunday evening, I sensed something was wrong. I began to unpack our suitcases and realized that a few pieces of furniture were out of place. Items on our bedside tables had been moved around, and there was a gash in the wooden television cabinet that stood between the large windows on the South Wall. I went back into the West Sitting Hall and family den and noticed that other furniture was not where it had been. I called Gary Walters, the chief usher, and asked him what had happened while we were gone. He told me that a security team had searched all of our possessions to check for bugging devices and other breaches of security. He had forgotten to tell me about it, he said.

Nobody on my staff or on the President's staff had been informed about the operation. Helen Dickey, a friend from Little Rock who was staying up on the third floor, heard noises Saturday night and went downstairs to see what was happening. She was confronted by armed men dressed in black, who ordered her out of the area.

I suddenly remembered the Rush Limbaugh note placed in the Lincoln bed for Harry and Linda. I wondered, too, about the source of some bizarre stories that had appeared in the press, one citing an anonymous Secret Service employee who claimed that I had thrown a lamp at my husband. Under other circumstances, it would have been laughable that a major periodical chose to run such a ridiculous story based on nothing more than malicious rumor.

As with many of the good and bad things that have been said about me over the years, reports about my "legendary temper" are exaggerated. But in this case, I admit that I was ready to explode. I called Mack McLarty, Bill's Chief of Staff, and David Watkins, the White House Director of Management and Administration, to let them know exactly what I had discovered and what I thought about it. I wanted to make sure this sort of thing never happened again without our knowledge.

Mack and David let me vent for a while. After looking into it, they reported that arrangements for the search had been made through the usher's office. Mack issued orders that it was not to happen again unless he was informed, and the President approved.

I was grieving my father's death, and I was undone by the invasion of privacy. Yes, we were living in a house that belongs to our nation. But there's an understanding that the individuals who occupy it are allowed some rooms of their own. Ours had been violated, and it made me feel that there was no place where my family and I could go to work through our sadness alone and in peace.

I didn't get much sleep that night, and it was a particularly short one. Starting at about 5 A.M., parents and children were lining up outside the gates for the annual Easter Egg Roll that takes place on the South Lawn Easter Monday. When I looked out the window at around 8 A.M., I saw thousands of children gathered, spoons in hand, waiting to push brightly colored Easter eggs across the grass. They were thrilled to be there, and there was no way I would let my personal concerns ruin their day. So I got dressed and stepped out into the sun. At first, I was going through the motions. Then the children's excitement and laughter, rippling across the wide green lawn, touched my heart and lifted my spirits.

The last few months had been a difficult beginning to a pitiless season in Washington. Looking back, I realize that what sustained me most through this time was what sustained me throughout our White House tenure: my family, friends and faith. My religious faith has always been a crucial part of my life. Until he had his fatal stroke, my father knelt by his bed to say his prayers every night. And I shared his belief in the power and importance of prayer. I've often told audiences that if I hadn't believed in prayer before 1992, life in the White House would have persuaded me.

Before my father's stroke, I received an invitation from my good friend Linda Lader, who, with her husband, Phil, launched the Renaissance Weekends Bill, Chelsea and I had attended since 1983 over New Years'. These gatherings were always stimulating and led to many important friendships in our lives.

Linda invited Tipper and me to a luncheon sponsored by a women's prayer group that included Democrats and Republicans, among them Susan Baker, the wife of the first President Bush's Secretary of State, James Baker; Joanne Kemp, the wife of former Republican Congressman (and future Vice Presidential candidate) Jack Kemp; and Grace Nelson, married to my now Senate colleague Bill Nelson, Democrat from Florida. Holly Leachman was the spiritual spark plug who kept it all going for me and became a dear friend. Throughout my time at the White House, Holly faxed me a daily Scripture reading or faith message and came often to visit just to cheer me up or pray with me.

The lunch on February 24, 1993, was held at the Cedars, an estate on the Potomac that serves as headquarters for the National Prayer Breakfast and the prayer groups it has spawned around the world. Doug Coe, the longtime National Prayer Breakfast organizer, is a unique presence in Washington: a genuinely loving spiritual mentor and guide to anyone, regardless of party or faith, who wants to deepen his or her relationship with God and offer the gift of service to others in need. Doug became a source of strength and friendship, and he, too, often sent me notes of support. All of these relationships began at that extraordinary lunch.

Each of my "prayer partners" told me she would pray for me weekly. In addition, they presented me with a handmade book filled with messages, quotes and Scripture that they hoped would sustain me during my time in Washington. Of all the thousands of gifts I received in my eight years in the White House, few were more welcome and needed than these twelve intangible gifts of discernment, peace, compassion, faith, fellowship, vision, forgiveness, grace, wisdom, love, joy and courage. Over the coming months and years, these women faithfully prayed for and with me. I appreciated their concern and their willingness to ignore Washington's political divide to reach out to someone in need of support. I often pulled out their little book. Susan Baker visited and wrote me, offering encouragement and empathy about events ranging from the loss of my father to the political storms surrounding Bill's Presidency.

As the administration neared its one-hundred-day mark at the end of April, it was obvious that we would not meet our self-imposed deadline for a health care package, and it wasn't because I had spent two weeks in Little Rock. Information about every proposal under consideration to pay for universal health care coverage ended up in the press, agitating members of Congress about strategies before any decisions had been made. We were already on the defensive before we had a plan. I was surprised how readily people leaked information to journalists. Some believed they were influencing events; others seemed to crave the feeling of self-importance, even if they were only quoted as anonymous sources.

The nation was still reeling from the ghastly outcome of the standoff in Waco, Texas, when the Branch Davidians shot and killed four Alcohol, Tobacco and Firearms agents and wounded twenty others as they tried to serve warrants. In the confrontation that followed on April 19, members of the group set the compound on fire, and at least eighty Branch Davidians were killed, including children. It was a devastating loss of life, and though an independent investigation concluded that the Branch Davidian leadership was responsible for the fires and gunshots that resulted in so many deaths, it could do nothing to mitigate the regret we all felt over the violence and death caused by a perversion of religion.

In the former Yugoslavia, Bosnian Serbs were besieging the Muslim town of Srebrenica in a frenzy of "ethnic cleansing." Another example of the misuse of religious differences for purposes of political power. The news media were sending back horrific pictures of civilian massacres and emaciated prisoners, reminiscent of the Nazi atrocities in Europe. The situation became more agonizing as the death toll mounted, and I was disgusted by the failure of the United Nations to intervene or even to protect the Muslim population.

In the shadow of these events, Bill and I hosted twelve Presidents and Prime Ministers at the White House who had come to Washington for the dedication of the Holocaust Museum on April 22. Some of the visiting leaders were pressuring the United States to get more involved in the U.N. effort to stop the slaughter in Bosnia. The most eloquent messenger of this viewpoint was Elie Wiesel, who delivered an impassioned speech about Bosnia at the museum dedication. Wiesel, a Nazi death camp survivor and winner of the Nobel Peace Prize, turned to Bill and said: "Mr. President . . . I have been in the former Yugoslavia. . . . I cannot sleep since what I have seen. As a Jew, I am saying that. We must do something to stop the bloodshed in that country." I had read *Night*, Wiesel's chilling account of his experiences in Auschwitz and Buchenwald, the death camps in Poland and Germany. I admired his writing and dedication to human rights, and since that day, he and his wife, Marion, have been friends.

Sitting in the gray drizzle, I agreed with Elie's words, because I was convinced that the only way to stop the genocide in Bosnia was through selective air strikes against Serbian targets. I knew that Bill was frustrated by Europe's failure to act after it had insisted that Bosnia was in its own backyard and was its own problem to solve. Bill met with his advisers to consider American involvement in the peacekeeping effort and other options to end the conflict. The situation became more agonizing as the death toll mounted.

We were adjusting to the roller-coaster ride of good and bad news at home and around the world. On the Hill, Republicans had mounted a filibuster in the Senate and defeated the President's economic stimulus package after the House had passed it. With so much going on, some of the administration's best moments were eclipsed. To commemorate Earth Day, April 22, Bill pledged to sign an important international biodiversity treaty that President Bush had rejected. The following week, he announced a national service program, AmeriCorps, that would revive the idealism of the Peace Corps and VISTA and direct the energy of young volunteers to tackle the needs of our own country.

Whatever our public demands, Bill and I tried never to lose sight of our obligations as Chelsea's parents. We went to every school event and stayed up with her while she finished her homework. Bill could still help with her eighth-grade algebra, and if he was traveling out of town, she would fax him her problems and then they would talk over solutions. We also continued to insist on her privacy, to the dismay of some in the media and on Bill's staff. The White House Press Office had convinced Bill to let NBC follow him around to film *A Day in the Life* of the President, which would air in early May. I agreed to participate but said Chelsea was off-limits. Bill's staff tried to persuade me that it would be good for our image to be seen with Chelsea at breakfast or talking over homework. When that didn't work, the show's producer tried to persuade me. Finally, anchorman Tom Brokaw called. To Tom's credit, when I said, "Absolutely not," he told me he respected my decision.

We were also in the middle of making the private quarters a real home. This meant painting and wallpapering and installing bookshelves wherever we could. In the midst of the dust, paint and other chemicals used in redecorating, Chelsea developed a frightening respiratory reaction shortly after Easter, and I was more eager than ever to be near her all the time. We tried to keep her condition private, and few people knew how worried I was.

Chelsea recovered as we got the allergies under control. To cheer us both up, I took her to New York to see the American Ballet Theatre perform *Sleeping Beauty.* That was when my hair got me into more trouble. Susan Thomases told me I just had to try this wonderful stylist Frederic Fekkai. I was game and asked if he could stop by our room at the Waldorf-Astoria hotel before we went out that night. I liked him right away, so I agreed to try something new, a "carefree" cut similar to broadcast journalist Diane Sawyer's. It certainly was shorter, and a dramatic change. International headlines ensued.

Lisa Caputo, my press secretary, learned about the haircut in a late night phone call from Capricia Marshall, who was with me in New York.

"Don't be mad at me," said Capricia. "She cut her hair off."

"What!"

"Susan just brought this guy into her hotel room, and when she came out, her hair was gone."

"Oh, my God."

The problem for Lisa was not a momentary public relations gaffe—she was used to handling hair stories—but a more complicated media concern. Since my staff once thought that there would be a health care package to present by May, I had agreed to let Katie Couric and her *Today* show crew trail me around the White House in advance of a major sit-down interview. NBC had spent hours taping me the prior week as a First Lady with a shoulder-length flip. The First Lady about to be interviewed live by Katie Couric had a new look. And there was no way to reshoot the earlier footage so I would look the same throughout the program.

Katie never blinked when she arrived at the White House and found me in my new 'do. Nor did she complain that my pink suit did not exactly complement her salmon-colored outfit. I had always liked watching her on TV, and I was happy to find that she was as down-to-earth in real life as she seemed on the screen—and a good sport too.

I was still learning the ropes and still discovering what it meant to be America's First Lady. The difference between being a Governor's wife and a President's is immeasurable. Suddenly, the people around you spend a lot of time anticipating what will make you happy. Sometimes those people don't know you well or misread you. Everything you say is amplified. And you have to be very careful what you wish for, or you'll get it by the caseload.

I was taking one of my first solo trips as First Lady when a young aide asked me, "What would you like to drink in your suite?"

"You know, I really feel like a Diet Dr Pepper," I said.

For years afterward, every time I opened a fridge in a hotel suite, it was loaded with Diet Dr Pepper. People would come up to me with frosty glasses of it. I felt like the sorcerer's apprentice, the Mickey Mouse character in the classic animated film *Fantasia:* I couldn't turn off the Dr Pepper machine.

This is a benign story, but the implications were sobering. I had to recognize how many people wanted to do whatever they could to please me and how seriously they might misinterpret what I wanted. I simply could not say, "Well, look into it," when presented with a problem. Maybe I should have figured that out earlier. But I didn't, until I was stuck with the consequences of an offhand comment I made after hearing about concerns of financial mismanagement and waste in the White House Travel Office. I said to Chief of Staff Mack McLarty that if there were such problems, I hoped he would "look into it."

"Travelgate," as it came to be known in the media, was perhaps worthy of a two- or three-week life span; instead, in a partisan political climate, it became the first manifestation of an obsession for investigation that persisted into the next millennium.

Before we moved into the White House, neither Bill nor I nor our immediate staff had known that there was a White House Travel Office. The travel office charters planes, books hotel rooms, orders meals and generally takes care of the press when they travel with the President. The costs are billed to the news organizations. Although we didn't know much about what the office did, we certainly didn't want to ignore or appear to condone allegations of misuse of funds anywhere in the White House. An audit by KPMG Peat Marwick had discovered that the Director of the Travel Office kept an off-book ledger, that a minimum of $18,000 of checks had not been properly accounted for and that the office's records were in "shambles." Based on these findings, Mack and the White House Counsel's Office decided to fire the travel office staff and reorganize the department.

These actions, which seemed like no-brainers to the decision makers involved, ignited a firestorm. When Dee Dee Myers, the President's press secretary—and the first woman to hold that position—announced the dismissals in her morning briefing on May 19, 1993, we were surprised by the reaction in the press room. The administration was trying to look out for the media's financial interests, as well as the country's, while some members of the press were focused on the fact that their friends in the travel office, who serve at the pleasure of the President, had been fired. The Administration was charged with amateurism and cronyism due to the fact that a White House employee, who was one of Bill's distant relatives and had experience making travel arrangements, was temporarily put in charge of the revamped travel office. Bill Kennedy, my former law partner who also worked in the counsel's office, had called on the FBI to investigate the case, further inflaming some of the press. I have the highest regard for Bill Kennedy's honesty and legal skills. Like most of us, however, he was a newcomer to Washington and its ways. He didn't know that his direct contact with the FBI, asking them to investigate the alleged misuse of funds, would be considered a serious breach of Washington protocol.

After an internal review, released in full to the media, Mack McLarty publicly reprimanded four Administration officials, including Watkins and Kennedy, for their poor judgment in the way they handled the matter. But at least seven separate investigations—including those conducted by the White House, the General Accounting Office, the FBI and Kenneth Starr's Office of the Independent Counsel—failed to turn up any illegality, wrongdoing or conflicts of interest by anyone in the Administration and confirmed that the initial concerns about the travel office were justified. The Independent Counsel, for example, concluded that the decision to fire the Travel Office political employees was lawful and that there was evidence of financial mismanagement and irregularities. The Justice Department found enough evidence to indict and try the former head of the travel office for embezzlement. According to press reports, he offered to plead guilty to a criminal charge and to serve a brief prison sentence, but the prosecutor insisted on going to trial on a felony charge. After several famous journalists testified as character witnesses at his trial, he was ultimately acquitted.

Despite the unanimous conclusion that there was no illegality in the White House's handling of the affair, it was a disastrously inauspicious first date with the White House press. I'm not sure I've ever learned so much so fast about the consequences of saying or doing anything before knowing exactly what's going on. And for a long time after, I would wake up in the middle of the night worrying that the actions and reactions concerning the travel office helped drive Vince Foster to take his own life. Vince Foster was stung by the travel office affair. A meticulous, decent and honorable man, he felt that he had let down the President, Bill Kennedy, Mack McLarty and me by failing to understand and contain the drama. Apparently, the final blow came in a series of spiteful editorials published in *The Wall Street Journal*, which attacked the integrity and competence of all the Arkansas lawyers in the Clinton Administration. On June 17, 1993, an editorial titled "Who Is Vince Foster?" proclaimed that the most "disturbing" thing about the Administration was "its carelessness about following the law." For the next month, the *Journal* continued its editorial campaign to paint the Clinton White House and my colleagues from the Rose Firm as some sort of corrupt cabal.

Bill and I may have been inexperienced in our White House roles, but we were seasoned enough in the rough world of politics. We knew we had to isolate the attacks and focus on the reality of our lives. Vince Foster had no such defenses. He was new to this culture, and he took the criticism to heart. Although we will never know what went through his mind in those last weeks of his life, I believe that as he absorbed each accusation, he was driven deeper into pain and distress. I will go to my own grave wishing I had spent more time with him and had somehow seen the signs of his despair. But he was a very private person, and nobody—not his wife, Lisa, or his closest colleagues, or his sister Sheila, with whom he had always been close—had any idea of the depth of his depression.

The last time I remember speaking to Vince was in mid-June, on the Saturday night before Father's Day. Bill was out of town giving a commencement address, so I made plans to go out to dinner with Webb Hubbell; his wife, Suzy; the Fosters and a few other couples from Arkansas. We arranged to meet between seven and eight o'clock at the Hubbells' house.

Just as I was getting ready to leave the White House, Lisa Caputo called to tell me that the lead story in the "Style" section of the next day's *Washington Post* would be about Bill's birth father, William Blythe. The story would reveal that he had been married at least twice before he met Bill's mother—something nobody in the family had known—and it would name a man who claimed to be Bill's half-brother. Happy Father's Day.

Bill's press office asked me to call and tell him about the article so that he wouldn't get blindsided by reporters' questions about his father. Then Bill and I had to find Virginia, who also had no idea about her husband's past. I was particularly worried because her cancer was getting worse and she didn't need any more stress.

When I called Webb's house to cancel my dinner plans, Vince picked up the phone. I told him why I couldn't make it that night.

"I've got to find Bill, and then we have to find his mother," I said. "He has to be the one to tell her that this story is coming out."

"Oh, I'm so sorry," Vince said.

"So am I. You know, I'm just so sick of this."

That's the last time I remember talking to Vince.

For the rest of the month and into July, Vince was busy with Bernie Nussbaum, the White House counsel, in vetting candidates to replace both retiring Justice Byron "Whizzer" White on the Supreme Court and William Sessions, who had been asked to step down as head of the FBI. I was still working to keep health care reform on the congressional agenda. And I was preoccupied with preparing for my first trip out of the country as First Lady. Bill was set to attend the G-7 summit, an annual meeting of the seven leading industrial countries, in Tokyo in early July, and I was going with him.

I was looking forward to visiting Japan again. I had been there during Bill's governorship, and I remember standing outside the gates and gazing at the beautiful Imperial Palace grounds. This time we would attend a formal dinner on the inside, hosted by the Emperor and Empress. Gentle, artistic and intelligent, this engaging couple embody the grace of their nation's art as well as the serenity of the peaceful gardens I finally visited while at the Palace. During this trip, I also met with a group of prominent Japanese women—the first of dozens of such meetings that I held around the world—to learn about the issues women were facing everywhere.

I was especially pleased that my mother could come with us on the trip. I thought she could use a radical change of scenery to help her deal with my father's death. She had a great time with us in Japan and Korea, and then she and I met Chelsea in Hawaii where I attended a meeting about Hawaii's statewide health care system. On July 20, Chelsea and I flew to Arkansas to drop off my mother and to visit some friends. That night, sometime between eight and nine o'clock, Mack McLarty called me at my mother's house and told me he had terrible news: Vince Foster was dead; it looked like a suicide.

I was so staggered that I still can't sort out the sequence of events that night. I remember crying and questioning Mack. I just couldn't believe it. Was he sure there wasn't a mistake? Mack gave me some sketchy details about the body discovered in a park, the handgun at the scene, a gunshot wound in the head. He wanted my advice about when to tell the President. At that moment, Bill was appearing on CNN's *Larry King Live* from the White House and had just agreed to go into an extra half hour. Mack asked me if I thought Bill should finish the show. I thought Mack should cut the interview short so he could tell Bill as soon as possible. I couldn't bear the idea of Bill being told on live TV about the tragic death of one of his closest friends.

As soon as Mack got off the line, I told my mother and Chelsea. Then I started dialing everyone I could think of who knew Vince, hoping someone could shed light on how and why this could have happened.

I craved information like oxygen. I was frantic because I felt so far away, and I couldn't figure out what was going on. As soon as Bill finished the show, I called him. He sounded shell-shocked and kept saying, "How could this have happened?" and "I should have stopped it somehow." Immediately after I talked to Bill, he went to the town house Vince and Lisa had rented in Georgetown. In one of our numerous calls, he told me how Webb was a pillar of strength and efficiency, taking charge of the funeral that would be held in Little Rock, making the travel arrangements, doing everything that needed to be done for the family. I'll always be grateful to Webb for that, and when I spoke to him, I offered to help in any way I could. I also talked with Lisa and with Vince's sister Sheila. None of us could believe what we were being told. We were all still clinging to an irrational hope that this awful nightmare stemmed from a misunderstanding, a case of mistaken identity.

I called Maggie Williams, who was devoted to Vince and saw him daily. All she could do was sob, so both of us tried to talk through our tears. I called Susan Thomases, who had known Vince since the 1980s. I called Tipper Gore and asked her if she thought we should bring in counselors to educate the staff about depression. Tipper was both comforting and informative, explaining that many suicides come as a surprise because we don't know how to read the warning signs.

I stayed up all night crying and talking to friends. I wondered ceaselessly whether this tragedy could have been prevented if I or anyone had noticed something amiss in Vince's behavior. When *The Wall Street Journal* editorial page had started pillorying him, I told him to ignore the stories—advice that was easy for me to give but, it seems, impossible for Vince to take. He told mutual friends that he and his friends and clients had always read the *Journal* in Arkansas and he couldn't imagine facing those people after they saw the stories about him.

Vince's funeral service was held in Little Rock's St. Andrew's Cathedral. Vince wasn't Catholic, but Lisa and the children were, and holding it there meant a great deal to them. Bill spoke eloquently of the special man whom he had known all his life, and he ended by quoting a Leon Russell song, "I love you in a place that has no space or time. / I love you for my life. / You are a friend of mine."

After the service, we drove in a long, mournful caravan to Hope, where Vince was born and raised. It was a blazing summer day, and heat rose in waves over the dusty fields. Vince was buried just outside of town. By then, I was beyond words. Numb. All I could feel was a vague notion that Vince was finally safe now, back home where he belonged.

The days that followed seemed to pass in slow motion as we tried to resume a normal routine. But all of us who were close to Vince were still obsessed with the question Why? Maggie was especially heartbroken. Bernie Nussbaum was beside himself that he had been with Vince the morning of his death and never had a clue. It had been the best week for the counsel's office since the inauguration. Ruth Bader Ginsburg was on her way to a seat on the Supreme Court, and just that morning the President had named Judge Louis Freeh as the new FBI Director. Bernie thought Vince seemed relaxed, even lighthearted.

As I learned more about clinical depression, however, I began to understand that Vince may have appeared happy because the idea of dying gave him a sense of peace. As always, Vince had a plan. His father's Colt revolver was already in his car. It is hard to imagine the sort of pain that would make death seem like a welcome relief, but Vince was feeling it. We found out later that he had reached out for psychiatric help a few days before his suicide, but it was too late to save him. He drove out to a secluded park along the Potomac, put the gun's barrel in his mouth and pulled the trigger.

Two days after Vince's death, Bernie Nussbaum went to Vince's office and, with representatives from the Justice Department and the FBI, reviewed every document there for anything that might shed light on his suicide.

Bernie had already conducted a cursory search for a suicide note on the night of Vince's death but had found nothing. According to volumes of subsequent testimony, in the course of this first search, Bernie discovered that Vince had stored in his office some personal files containing work he had done for Bill and me when he was our attorney in Little Rock, including files that had to do with the land deal called Whitewater. Bernie gave these files to Maggie Williams, who delivered them to the residence, and, soon after, they were transferred to the office of Bob Barnett, our private attorney in Washington. Since Vince's office was never a crime scene, these actions were understandable, legal and justifiable. But they would soon spawn a cottage industry of conspiracy theorists and investigators trying to prove that Vince was murdered to cover up what he "knew about Whitewater."

Those rumors should have ended with the official report ruling his death a suicide and with the sheet of notepaper Bernie found torn into twenty-seven pieces at the bottom of Vince's briefcase. It was not so much a suicide note as a cry from the heart, an accounting of the things that were tearing at his soul.

"I was not meant for the job in the spotlight of public life in Washington. Here ruining people is considered sport," he wrote.

". . . The public will never believe the innocence of the Clintons and their loyal staff. . . ."

"The *WSJ* [*Wall Street Journal*] editors lie without consequence."

Those words left me grief-stricken. Vince Foster was a good man who wanted to make a contribution to his country. He could have continued to practice law in Little Rock, to serve someday as President of the Arkansas Bar Association and to never hear a bad word breathed about him. Instead, he came to Washington to work for his friend from Hope. His short time in public service destroyed his self-image and, in his mind, irreparably stained his reputation. Shortly after his death, a columnist for *Time* magazine summed up the sad transformation of his life in Vince's own words: "Before we came here," he had said, "we thought of ourselves as good people." He was speaking not just for himself, but for all of us who had made the journey from Arkansas.

The six months since the exuberance of Inauguration Day had been brutal. My father and close friend dead; Vince's wife, children, family and friends devastated; my mother-in-law dying; the faltering missteps of a new Administration being literally turned into federal cases. I didn't know where to turn, so I did what I often do when faced with adversity: I threw myself into a schedule so hectic that there was no time for brooding. I can see now that I was on automatic pilot, pushing myself to attend health care meetings on the Hill and deliver speeches, often on the verge of weeping. If I met someone who reminded me of my father, or I ran across a nasty comment about Vince, I would feel the tears well up in my eyes. I'm sure that I sometimes appeared brittle, sad and even angry—because I was. I knew that I had to carry on and bear the pain I felt in private. This was one of the times when I kept going on sheer willpower.

The great budget battle finally ended in August, with the passage of Bill's economic plan. Before the vote, I had spoken with wavering Democrats who worried not only about the tough budget vote, but also about how they would explain equally difficult votes that might follow on health care, guns and trade. One Republican Congresswoman called me to explain that she agreed with the President's goal to tame the deficit but had been ordered by her leadership to vote no regardless of her convictions. In the end, not a single Republican voted for the balanced budget package. It squeaked through the House by one vote, and Vice President Gore in his official role as President of the Senate had to vote to break a 50–50 tie. Several courageous Democrats, exemplified by Representative Marjorie Margolis Mezvinsky, who did what they believed to be in America's long-term interests, lost in the next election.

The plan wasn't everything the Administration had wanted, but it signaled the return of fiscal responsibility for the government and the beginning of an economic turnaround for the country, unprecedented in American history. The plan slashed the deficit in half; extended the life of the Medicare Trust Fund; expanded a tax cut called the Earned Income Tax Credit, which benefited fifteen million lower-income working Americans; reformed the student loan program, saving taxpayers billions of dollars; and created empowerment zones and enterprise communities that provided tax incentives for investing in distressed communities. To pay for these reforms, the plan raised taxes on gasoline and on the highest-income Americans, who in return got lower interest rates and a soaring stock market as the economy boomed. Bill signed the legislation on August 10, 1993.

By the middle of August, we were so wrapped up in work that Bill and I both nearly had to be bound, gagged and tossed onto the plane for our vacation on Martha's Vineyard. It turned out to be a wonderful and healing time for me.

It was Ann and Vernon Jordan who persuaded us to come to the Vineyard, where they had been vacationing for years. They found us the perfect spot, a small, secluded house that belonged to Robert

McNamara, the Secretary of Defense under Kennedy and Johnson. The two-bedroom Cape Cod cottage sat on the edge of Oyster Pond, one of the large saltwater ponds off the southern coast of the island. I slept and swam and felt the months of tension beginning to melt away.

The Jordans' party to celebrate Bill's forty-seventh birthday on August 19 was filled with old friends and new people who made me laugh and relax. It was one of the best times I'd had since the inauguration. Jackie Kennedy Onassis was there with her longtime companion, Maurice Templesman. The always gracious Katharine Graham, publisher of *The Washington Post*, came, as did Bill and Rose Styron, who became trusted friends.

Styron, a wry, deeply intelligent Southerner with a wonderful weathered face and piercing eyes, had recently published *Darkness Visible: A Memoir of Madness*, recounting his struggles with clinical depression. I talked to him about Vince at dinner, and we continued the conversation the next day during a long walk on one of the Vineyard's beautiful beaches. He described the overwhelming sense of loss and desperation that can grip a person until the desire for release from the daily pain and disorientation makes death seem a preferable, even rational, choice.

I also spent time with Jackie. Her house, surrounded by several hundred of the most beautiful acres on Martha's Vineyard, had books and flowers everywhere and windows looking out over the gentle dunes leading to the ocean in the distance. The house had the same unpretentious elegance that characterized everything Jackie did.

I loved seeing her and Maurice together. Charming, smart and well read, he radiated love, respect and concern for her, as well as delight in her company. They made each other laugh, one of my criteria for any relationship.

Jackie and Maurice invited us to go sailing on Maurice's yacht with Caroline Kennedy Schlossberg and her husband, Ed Schlossberg, Ted and Vicky Kennedy and Ann and Vernon Jordan. Caroline is one of the few people in the world who can understand Chelsea's unique experiences, and from that visit onward, she became a perceptive friend and role model for my daughter. Ted Kennedy, Caroline's uncle and the paterfamilias of the Kennedy clan, is one of the most effective Senators who has ever served our country and is also an expert sailor. He kept up a running commentary about pirates and naval battles, while his intelligent, effervescent wife, Vicky, provided additional color.

We motored out of Menemsha Harbor on a glorious, sunny day and anchored next to a small island to go swimming before lunch. I went below to put on my bathing suit, and by the time I came back up on deck, Jackie, Ted and Bill were already in the water. Caroline and Chelsea had climbed up to a platform about forty feet above the water. As I looked up, they jumped together and landed in the ocean with a splash.

They came up laughing and swam back to the boat for another jump.

Chelsea said, "Come on, Mom, try it!"

Of course, Ted and Bill started yelling, "Yeah, give it a try—give it a try!" For reasons that escape me to this day, I said okay. I am not all that athletic anymore, but the next thing I knew I was following Caroline and Chelsea up a narrow little ladder to get to the top. By now I was thinking, "How did I get myself into this?" As soon as Caroline and Chelsea reached the platform—boom! Off they went again. Now perched up there alone, looking down at the tiny figures below me treading water, I listened to their shouts, "Come on, come on! Jump!"

Then I heard Jackie's voice rising above the rest: "Don't do it, Hillary! Don't let them talk you into it. Don't do it!"

I thought to myself, "Now there is the voice of reason and experience." I'm sure that there were countless times when Jackie said, "No, I just won't do that." She knew exactly what was going through my mind, and she came to my rescue.

"You know, you're right!" I shouted back.

Slowly I climbed down with as much dignity as I could summon. Then I got into the water and went for a swim with my friend Jackie.

THE DELIVERY ROOM

WHEN WE RETURNED TO WASHINGTON A WEEK BE-
fore Labor Day with an important budget victory under the Administration's belt, it was time for the White House to focus full-time on the health care initiative. Or so I hoped. Bill's one-hundred-day target had long since passed, the task force had disbanded at the end of May, and health care had been relegated to the sidelines for months so that the President and his economic and legislative teams could focus on the deficit reduction package. During the summer, I had phoned members of Congress, working hard to help Bill pass his economic program, the key to everything he hoped to achieve for the country.

But even with the crucial budget victory behind us, health care still had to compete with other legislative priorities. Since the beginning of the Administration, Treasury Secretary Lloyd Bentsen had warned about the timetable for health care, skeptical that it could be passed in less than two years. By late August, Bentsen, Secretary of State Warren Christopher and economic adviser Bob Rubin were adamant about postponing health care reform and moving forward with the North American Free Trade Agreement, known as NAFTA. They believed that free trade was also critical to the nation's economic recovery and NAFTA warranted immediate action. Creating a free trade zone in North America—the largest free trade zone in the world—would expand U.S. exports, create jobs and ensure that our economy was reaping the benefits, not the burdens, of globalization. Although unpopular with labor unions, expanding trade opportunities was an important administration goal. The question was whether the White House could focus its energies on two legislative campaigns at once. I argued that we could and that postponing health care would further weaken its chances. But it was Bill's decision, and because NAFTA faced a legislative deadline, he concluded that it had to be addressed first.

He was also particularly committed to strengthening relations with our closest neighbor to the south. Not only was Mexico the ancestral home of millions of Mexican Americans, it was undergoing profound political and economic changes that had the potential to ripple across Latin America. Bill wanted to support President Ernesto Zedillo, an economist by training, who was transforming the national government from a one-party political system to a multiparty democracy that would tackle long-time problems of poverty and corruption as well as cross-border concerns like immigration, drugs and trade.

Once again, health care would have to wait. Nonetheless, Ira and I and a cadre of health care staffers continued to lay the groundwork for a bill that would deliver quality, affordable health care to all Americans. Bill's dramatic legislative victories over the summer made us optimistic about our chances. We kept reminding ourselves that reform was not just about complex public policies, but about people's lives, and in my quest for solutions, many of those lives touched my own.

While Bill and his advisers were hammering out a policy to jump-start the economy, I had been traveling around the country listening to Americans talk about the hardships of coping with the rising medical costs, inequitable treatment and bureaucratic quagmires they encountered every day. From Louisiana to Montana, and from Florida to Vermont, my travels reinforced my belief that the existing health system could be more efficient and less costly while ensuring that every American who needed medical attention received it.

I spoke to people who temporarily lost their coverage because they switched jobs—which was happening to an average of two million workers each month. I met men and women who discovered they couldn't get insurance if they had "a preexisting condition" like cancer or diabetes that was already diagnosed and part of their medical history. Some elderly Americans living on fixed incomes told me they were forced to choose between paying the rent or buying prescription drugs. My father's hospitalization taught me that even with the best care and support, losing someone you love is indescribably painful. I couldn't bear thinking how much harder it would be if the loss were avoidable.

I also met Americans who made my heart soar with hope. One day when I went to speak to health care reformers on Capitol Hill, I noticed a little boy in the front row sitting in a wheelchair. He had the most beautiful smile on his sweet face, and I couldn't keep my eyes off him. Just before I spoke, I went over to him. When I bent down to say hello, he threw his arms around my neck. I picked him up and discovered that he wore a full body brace that must have weighed forty pounds. I addressed the audience holding him in my arms. That was my introduction to Ryan Moore, a seven-year-old from South Sioux City, Nebraska, who had been born with a rare form of dwarfism. His family constantly battled with their insurance company to pay for the multiple surgeries and treatments he needed. Ryan's condition stunted his body's growth, but it didn't interfere with his positive attitude. He so endeared himself to me and my staff that Melanne hung a giant photo of him on the wall in the Hillaryland offices. Stories like Ryan's kept our eyes on the prize throughout our struggle to bring health care coverage to all Americans, and his courage and hope continue to inspire me today. Ryan is now in high school and dreams of becoming a sportscaster.

By early September, Bill was also focused on preparations for the upcoming visit of Israeli Prime Minister Yitzhak Rabin and Palestinian leader Yasir Arafat and the signing of a new Middle East peace accord. The historic meeting that took place on the White House South Lawn on September 13, 1993, was the result of months of negotiations in Oslo, Norway, and the agreement was known as the Oslo Accords. It was important to establish our government's support for the agreement because the United States is the only country that could push both sides to actually implement the agreement's terms and be trusted by Israel to protect its security. The people of the Middle East and the world would also see Prime Minister Rabin and Chairman Arafat personally commit to what their representatives had negotiated.

I had first met Yitzhak and Leah Rabin earlier that spring when they paid a courtesy call at the White House. The Prime Minister, a man of medium height, did nothing to demand attention, but his quiet dignity and intensity drew me—and so many others—to him. He created an aura of strength; this was a man who made me feel safe. Leah, a striking, dark-haired woman with piercing blue eyes, exuded energy and intelligence. She was also well read, observant and knowledgeable about the arts. Now, on this second visit with me at the White House, she noticed where I had rehung some paintings from the White House art collection. Leah was outspoken, sharing her opinions about personalities and events with blunt remarks that quickly endeared her to me. Both Rabins were realistic about the challenges that lay ahead for

Israel. They believed they had no choice but to try to achieve a secure future for their nation through negotiations with their sworn enemies. Their attitude called to mind the old saying "Hope for the best, plan for the worst." That was also Bill's and my assessment.

On that auspicious day, Bill persuaded Yitzhak to shake hands with Arafat as a tangible sign of their commitment to the peace plan. Rabin agreed, as long as there would be no kissing, a common Arab custom. Before the ceremony, Bill and Yitzhak engaged in a hilarious rehearsal of the handshake, with Bill pretending to be Arafat as they practiced a complicated maneuver that would prevent the Palestinian leader from drawing too close.

The handshake and the agreement, which seemed to offer such hope, were seen by some Israelis and Arabs as a rebuke to their political interests and religious beliefs, which later led to violence and Rabin's tragic assassination. But on that perfect afternoon—under bright warm sunlight that seemed to bestow God's blessing—I hoped only for the best and determined to help in any way I could to support Israel's courageous decision to take this risk for a lasting and secure peace.

Even as he worked on these varied and pressing issues, Bill scheduled a televised prime-time address to Congress on September 22 to outline the health care plan. Following that, I was slated to testify before the five congressional committees that would consider health care legislation, which we hoped would be introduced in early October.

It was an ambitious September schedule, and we couldn't afford more roadblocks. Although the bill itself was not finished, Bill, Ira and I wanted to acquaint Democratic members with it before Bill's big speech so that they would understand the reasoning behind our decisions. But the raw numbers in the bill needed to be calculated and confirmed by budget experts, and that took several weeks longer than anticipated. Instead of circulating an unfinished document, we set up a "reading room" where Democratic staffers could look at the proposal with the understanding that the figures were likely to change. The content of the document was leaked to news organizations, and the ensuing stories left many in Congress thinking that this draft was the final bill. Already wary of health care reform, Senator Moynihan decried the whole enterprise, saying it was based on "fantasy" numbers.

Proponents and opponents of reform had begun organizing their own campaigns to influence the outcome. Groups representing consumers, families, workers, the elderly, children's hospitals and pediatricians were, for the most part, lining up in favor of reform. But business groups, particularly small business, pharmaceuticals and the insurance giants had long viewed reform as a threat. Doctors, too, objected to specific elements of the plan.

It didn't take long to see how well organized and well financed the opposition was. In early September, the Health Insurance Association of America, a powerful interest group representing the nation's insurance companies, launched television advertisements designed to discredit reform. The ads featured a couple at a kitchen table, reviewing their medical bills, worrying aloud that the government was going to force them to sign up for a new health care plan they didn't want. "Things are changing and not all for the better. The government may force us to pick from a few health care plans designed by government bureaucrats," the announcer intoned. It was false and misleading advertising, but it was a clever scare tactic that had the desired effect.

On September 20, two days before Bill was to unveil his health care plan to Congress and the nation, he asked me to look at the speech draft he had just received from the speechwriting team. Over the years, Bill and I have always relied on each other as sounding boards. We also recruit each other as editors whenever we are working on a big speech or any important writing. It was a Sunday afternoon, and I settled into an oversize chair in one of my favorite rooms on the top floor of the White House—the Solarium—where we often retreated to relax, play cards, watch television and feel like a regular family. Quickly thumbing through the pages of the speech, I could see that it wasn't ready—and Bill was supposed to deliver it in just over forty-eight hours. Panic set in. I picked up the phone and asked the White House operator to call Maggie. Always calm in a storm, she glanced at the speech and quickly called a meeting of top health care advisers and speechwriters for that evening. Over bowls of nachos and guacamole, Bill and I and about a dozen staffers sat in the Solarium and tossed around themes for the speech. I suggested that health care reform was part of the American journey, an apt metaphor because in Bill's view, this was our generation's chance to answer a call on behalf of future generations. We settled on the journey theme, and with a combined sense of urgency and relief, we handed a rough draft back to the speechwriters. With constant editing and rewriting from Bill, they wrestled the text into shape for Tuesday night's appearance.

Presidents deliver special addresses to Congress from a podium in the ornate chamber of the House of Representatives. It's a ritual-filled evening. As the President enters the hall, the sergeant-at-arms announces in a somber tone: "The President of the United States." The audience rises, and the President greets members of both parties who, by tradition, sit on opposite sides of the aisle. He then climbs to the lectern and faces the audience. The Vice President and the Speaker of the House sit directly behind him.

The First Lady, along with White House guests and other dignitaries, sits in a special area of the balcony, and it was a favorite Washington parlor game to guess who would be seated with her. On my right that evening was one of the nation's leading pediatricians and one of my favorite people, Dr. T. Berry Brazelton, with whom I had worked on behalf of children's issues for about ten years. More surprising was the guest on my left, Dr. C. Everett Koop. Dr. Koop, a pediatric surgeon by training, had been President Reagan's Surgeon General, in charge of overseeing the nation's Public Health Service. Bearded and bespectacled, he was a Republican and an adamant foe of abortion who had endured a vitriolic confirmation battle. Bill and I had come to admire Dr. Koop for the courageous stands he took as Surgeon General, warning Americans about the dangers of tobacco use and the spread of AIDS and crusading for immunizations, condom use, environmental health and better nutrition. Having witnessed the failings of the system as both a clinician and a policy maker, Koop had become a vocal advocate for health care reform and was an invaluable adviser and ally.

After motioning the audience to sit down, Bill began the speech. To his immense credit, not even I realized that something was wrong. We learned later that an aide had placed the wrong speech in the TelePrompTer—the economic address Bill had given months before. Bill is legendary for extemporizing and ad-libbing, but this speech was too long and too important to do entirely off-the-cuff. For a nerve-racking seven minutes, as his staffers rushed to correct the mistake, he delivered his remarks from memory.

It was a great speech, with just the right mix of passion, wisdom and substance. I was so proud of him that night. It was a courageous path for a new President. Franklin D. Roosevelt had boldly found a way to give older Americans economic security through the Social Security program; Bill wanted, through health care reform, to vastly improve the quality of life for tens of millions of Americans. He held up a red, white and blue "health security card" that he hoped would be issued to every

American, vowing to deliver a plan that would guarantee every citizen health insurance coverage and access to affordable, quality medical care.

"Tonight we come together to write a new chapter in the American story," Bill told the nation. ". . . At long last, after decades of false starts, we must make this our most urgent priority: giving every American health security, health care that can never be taken away, health care that is always there."

When he finished the fifty-two-minute speech, the audience gave him a standing ovation. Although a few Republican lawmakers immediately took issue with some details of the plan, many in both parties said they admired Bill's willingness to tackle an issue that had vexed so many of his predecessors. As one journalist put it, the reform effort was like "scaling the Mount Everest of social policy." We had started the trek. I felt excited yet apprehensive, well aware that a rousing speech was one thing while designing and passing legislation was another. But I was grateful for Bill's commitment and eloquence, and I believed we would reach a compromise because our nation's long-term economic and social well-being depended on it.

After the speech we loaded up the motorcade and headed back to the White House. We had planned a post-speech party on the State Floor, but we decided to go first to the Old Executive Office Building, where the health care staff worked in crowded, makeshift cubicles in room 160. Bill and I thanked them for spending days and nights working for reform. I stood on a chair and declared to laughter and applause that with the impending birth of the health care bill, the room would now be renamed "the Delivery Room."

We had every reason to be optimistic about the reform plan as reviews of Bill's speech and the outlines of the plan were generally positive. The public overwhelmingly supported action on health care reform. News reports praised the plan and our efforts at reaching bipartisan consensus with headlines that read, HEALTH CARE REFORM; WHAT WENT RIGHT?

Although the bill wouldn't be "delivered" for another month, I was eager to proceed with my testimony before the committees reviewing reform. Six days after Bill's speech, on September 28, I had my opportunity. My appearance before the House Ways and Means Committee marked the first time a First Lady was the lead witness on a major administration legislative initiative. Other First Ladies had also testified before Congress, including Eleanor Roosevelt and Rosalynn Carter, who appeared before a Senate subcommittee in 1979 to argue for increased funding of programs that aid mental health patients and support treatment facilities.

The hearing room was packed when I arrived, and I was unusually nervous. Every seat was taken, and there wasn't an inch of empty space left along the side and back walls. Several dozen photographers were sitting or lying on the floor in front of the witness table, clicking furiously as I took my seat. All of the networks had sent camera crews to record the event.

I had worked hard preparing my testimony. In one of our prep sessions, Mandy Grunwald, the savvy media consultant who had worked with James Carville on our 1992 campaign and continued working for the Democratic National Committee, asked me what I really wanted to convey.

I knew I couldn't afford to make any factual mistakes, but I also didn't want the human stories of anxiety and suffering to get lost in the arcana of public policy. I wanted my words to convey the real-life dimension of the health care problem. I decided to start with the personal: why I cared so deeply about improving health care. At 10 A.M., Chairman Dan Rostenkowski, that gruff and gritty old-school pol from Chicago, gaveled the House Ways and Means Committee to order and introduced me.

"During the past months, as I have worked to educate myself about the problems facing our nation and facing American citizens about health care, I have learned a great deal," I said. "The official reason I am here today is because I have had that responsibility. But more importantly for me, I'm here as a mother, a wife, a daughter, a sister, a woman. I'm here as an American citizen concerned about the health of her family and the health of her nation."

For the next two hours, I answered questions from committee members. Later that day, I testified before the House Energy and Commerce Committee, chaired by one of the longest-serving House members and a longtime champion of health care reform, Democratic Congressman John Dingell of Michigan. Over the next two days, I appeared before one other House committee and two Senate committees. The experience was fascinating, challenging and exhausting. I was happy to have had the chance to speak publicly about our plan and pleased that the reviews were generally positive. Members of Congress applauded the testimony and, according to news reports, were impressed that I knew the intricacies of the health care system. This gave me hope. Maybe my testimony had helped people understand why reform was so vital to American citizens and their families, as well as to the nation's economy. I was also just plain relieved that I had gotten it behind me and hadn't embarrassed myself or my husband, who was on the line for choosing me to represent him on such a big undertaking.

While many members genuinely appreciated the finer points of the health care debate, I realized that some of the laudatory responses to my testimony were just the latest example of "the talking dog syndrome," which I had learned about as First Lady of Arkansas. There's a similar thought attributed to Dr. Samuel Johnson by Boswell: "Sir, a woman preaching is like a dog's walking on its hind legs. It is not done well; but you are surprised to find it done at all."

Much of the praise centered on the fact that I hadn't used notes or consulted my aides and that I generally knew my stuff. In short, even many complimentary committee members who appreciated my appearing were not necessarily sold on the substance of the plan.

I also learned that my popularity beyond the Beltway, my positive reception on the Hill and the apparent willingness of Congress to consider health care reform set off alarms among Republicans. If Bill Clinton passed a bill that provided every American with health insurance, he would be a shoo-in for a second term as President. That was an outcome Republican Party planners were determined to prevent. Our own political experts sensed a scorched-earth strategy emerging on the Right. Steve Ricchetti, the chief White House liaison with the Senate, was concerned. "They are going to come after you," he told me one afternoon in my office. "You're too strong in this process. They have to take a pound of flesh out of you, one way or another."

I assured Steve that I had taken heat before, and at least I'd be taking it now for something I believed in.

After my testimony, it was time for what the White House called the health care "roll-out"—a series of speeches and events in which the President generates attention and support for the policy. Bill was scheduled to do the roll-out for much of the first half of October, starting with a trip to California on October 3, where he would hold town meetings to discuss reform and win as many converts as possible. But any presidential agenda is subject to outside events. Bill was en route to California on October 3 when his aides received an urgent call from the

White House Situation Room. Two Black Hawk helicopters had been shot down in Somalia. Details were vague, but it was clear that American soldiers had been killed and that there might be ongoing violence. Troops had originally been sent to the famine-ravaged country by President Bush on a humanitarian aid mission, but it had evolved into a more aggressive peacekeeping effort.

Every President must quickly adopt a strategy when troubling events unfold: He can stop everything else and focus very publicly on the crisis or handle the situation while trying to stick to his official schedule. Bill remained in California but stayed in constant touch with his national security team. Then the news got worse: The body of an American serviceman had been dragged through the streets of Mogadishu, an appalling act of barbarity orchestrated by the Somali warlord General Mohamed Aideed.

Bill was given terrible news about Russia too. There had been an attempted military coup against President Boris Yeltsin. On October 5, in Culver City, California, Bill cut short a town hall meeting about health care and returned to Washington. Over the next few weeks, Bill, the news media and the nation were consumed by Somalia and the unrest in Russia, and health care reform took a backseat.

We had originally envisioned presenting Congress with an outline of principles that would shape the health care reform legislation. But we subsequently learned that Congressman Dan Rostenkowski expected us to produce a detailed bill, complete with legislative language. Giving Congress a comprehensive bill at the outset turned out to be a tremendous challenge and a tactical mistake for us. We thought it would be 250 pages at most, but as drafting continued, it became clear that the bill needed to be much longer, in part because the plan was complex and in part because we acquiesced to some specific requests from interested groups. The American Academy of Pediatrics, for example, insisted that the bill guarantee nine childhood vaccinations in the benefits package as well as six well-child visits. These demands may have been legitimate, but this level of detail should have been negotiated after the bill was introduced, not in the drafting process. The Health Security Act delivered by the White House to Congress on October 27 was 1,342 pages long. A few weeks later, on the last day of the congressional session and with little fanfare, Senate Majority Leader George Mitchell introduced the measure. Though many other bills dealing with complex issues like energy or the budget have more than one thousand pages, opponents used the length of our bill against us. We were proposing to streamline and simplify a major social policy, but it looked like we couldn't streamline and simplify our own bill. It was a smart tactic, and it effectively obscured the fact that our health care legislation would have eliminated thousands of pages of health-related legislation and regulations already on the books.

With so much happening, I could have easily forgotten my own birthday on October 26. But my staff never missed an occasion for a party. The Hillaryland gang invited more than a hundred of my family members and friends to come from around the country for a surprise forty-sixth birthday party at the White House. I knew something was up when I returned to the residence in the evening from meetings with Senator Moynihan and Senator Barbara Mikulski of Maryland, a Capitol Hill veteran known as the "dean" of the women Senators.

All the lights inside the residence were off. A power blackout, I was told. That was my first clue; the power never goes off in the White House. I was ushered upstairs and told to put on a black wig and hoopskirt—the Colonial look, to be sure, and an attempt to replicate the fashions worn by Dolley Madison. Then I was led down to the State Floor, where I was greeted by a dozen staffers in blond wigs representing "a dozen different Hillarys"—headband Hillary, cookie-baking Hillary, health care Hillary. Bill was disguised as President James Madison (with white wig and tights). I loved him for it, but I was glad we were living in the late twentieth century. He looks better in a suit.

WHITEWATER

O
N HALLOWEEN 1993, I PICKED UP A COPY OF THE
Sunday *Washington Post* and learned that our old, money-losing real
estate venture in Arkansas had come back to haunt us. According to unnamed "government sources," the Resolution Trust Corporation (RTC),
a federal agency examining failed savings and loans, had recommended
the criminal investigation of Madison Guaranty Savings and Loan,
owned by Jim McDougal. McDougal and his wife, Susan, had been
our partners in the Whitewater Development Company, Inc., a completely separate entity created to hold land purchased four years before
McDougal bought Madison Guaranty. Because of our past connection
with McDougal, however, we were wrongly implicated in his subsequent
misadventures. During the 1992 presidential race, allegations surfaced in
the press—and were quickly dismissed—that McDougal had received
special favors from the state when Bill was Governor because of his business relationship with us. The story faded when Bill and I proved that
we had lost money on the Whitewater investment and that, while he
was Governor, the Arkansas Securities Department had actually urged
the federal regulators to remove McDougal and shut down Madison
Guaranty.

Now *The Washington Post* was reporting that RTC investigators
were looking into allegations that McDougal had used his S&L to fun-
nel money illegally to political campaigns in Arkansas, including Bill's
gubernatorial reelection campaign in 1986. I was confident nothing
would come of it. Bill and I never deposited money in Madison Guaranty or borrowed from it. As to the campaign contributions, Bill had
supported the law in Arkansas imposing a strict limit of $1,500 per con-
tribution per election. McDougal had already been indicted, tried and

acquitted by the federal government on charges arising from his operation of Madison Guaranty before Bill ran for President.

Bill and I failed to recognize the political significance of Whitewater's sudden reappearance, which may have contributed to some
public relations mistakes in how we handled the growing controversy.
But I could never have predicted how far our adversaries would take it.

The name Whitewater came to represent a limitless investigation of
our lives that cost the taxpayers more than $70 million for the Indepen-
dent Counsel investigation alone and never turned up any wrongdoing
on our part. Bill and I voluntarily cooperated with investigators. Every
time they leaked or leveled a new charge, we bent over backwards to
make sure we hadn't missed or overlooked anything substantive. But as
one allegation followed another, we realized we were chasing ghosts in a
house of mirrors: we would run in one direction only to have the appari-
tion pop up behind us. Whitewater never seemed real because it wasn't.

The purpose of the investigations was to discredit the President
and the Administration and slow down its momentum. It didn't matter
what the investigations were about; it only mattered that there were investigations. It didn't matter that we had done nothing wrong; it only
mattered that the public was given the impression that we had. It didn't
matter that the investigations cost taxpayers tens of millions of dollars;
it only mattered that our lives and the work of the President were
disrupted over and over again. Whitewater signaled a new tactic in political warfare: investigation as a weapon for political destruction.
"Whitewater" became a convenient catchall for any and all attacks that
our political adversaries could design. Whitewater was a political war
from the start, and it raged throughout Bill Clinton's Presidency.

At the time, however, Whitewater seemed to me like a new twist on
an old story with a familiar cast of characters—more of a nuisance than
a threat.

However, in light of the *Post*'s Halloween article and a similar *New
York Times* piece that soon followed, we thought we should take the precaution of hiring a private attorney. Our personal lawyer, Bob Barnett,
recused himself from Whitewater because his wife, Rita Braver, was a
CBS correspondent assigned to cover the White House. Bob is a longtime Democrat, and the favorite debating partner of Democratic presidential and vice presidential nominees. In mock debates staged to
prepare candidates for the rhetorical styles and political arguments of
their opponents, he plays the perfect Republican foil—taking the part of

Vice President and then President George Bush against Congress-woman Geraldine Ferraro in 1984, Governor Michael Dukakis in 1988 and Governor Bill Clinton in 1992; playing former Secretary of Defense Dick Cheney against Senator Joe Lieberman in the 2000 vice presidential debate; and even performing as Congressman Rick Lazio in preparation for my own debate during the 2000 Senate race. Bob became my counsel and adviser in 1992, and I could not have asked for a better friend in the years that followed.

Bob recommended David Kendall, his colleague at Williams and Connolly, to represent us in the Whitewater matter. We had known David for years. Although he was a few years older than Bill and me, we had overlapped at Yale Law School. Like Bill, David was a Rhodes Scholar. As a fellow Midwesterner—David was born and raised in rural Indiana on a farm—he and I had a natural rapport. Soon he became an anchor in our lives.

David was perfect for the job. He had clerked on the Supreme Court for Justice Byron White and had experience in corporate law and in cases involving the media. He had represented clients in several S&L investigations in the 1980s, so he was familiar with S&L issues. At the same time, he had an unwavering social conscience. On his office wall hangs a copy of his arrest record in Mississippi, where he had been jailed briefly as a civil rights activist during the voting rights drive in Freedom Summer in 1964. In one of his first jobs as an attorney, he defended death penalty cases for the NAACP Legal Defense Fund.

Like all really good lawyers, David has the talent to transform seemingly random and disconnected facts into a persuasive narrative. But reconstructing the story of Whitewater would test his skills. First, David took over the files from Vince Foster's office, which had been turned over to Bob Barnett after Vince's death. Then he tracked down other documents from Washington to Flippin, Arkansas, near the Whitewater property.

David met with us in the White House every week or so for the next three months. As I listened with fascination, he filled us in on what he had learned while piecing together gaps in the Whitewater record and tracing Jim McDougal's increasingly bizarre investments. Trying to re-create McDougal's paper trail, he said, was like shoveling smoke.

Neither Bill nor I had ever visited the Whitewater property; we had only seen photographs. David decided that he needed to see the place "in three dimensions and in real time" in order to understand the case.

He flew to southern Missouri (which was closer to the property than Little Rock) and rented a car. Hours after losing his way down back roads, he finally followed a rough track bulldozed through the woods that ended up at the benighted Whitewater development. There were "For Sale" signs here and there, but nobody home. Had he returned a few months later, after the media swarmed in looking to photograph and interview anyone connected to Whitewater, David would have seen a large sign posted on one of the few occupied dwellings on the site: "Go Home, Idiots."

Eventually, David traced the current ownership of certain Whitewater lots to a local Flippin realtor named Chris Wade. We had not known that back in May 1985, McDougal had sold the company's remaining twenty-four lots to Wade. Despite the fact that we were still partners then, McDougal had not informed us, asked us to sign off on the deal or offered to split the $35,000 proceeds. We were also unaware that McDougal acquired in this transaction a small used Piper Seminole plane that became his "corporate aircraft."

By the mid-1980s, McDougal presided over a small corporate empire, at least on paper. In 1982, he had bought a small thrift called Madison Guaranty and quickly opened the cash spigot. McDougal aspired to be a populist banker, and he had grandiose ideas. From what David Kendall could deduce, many of McDougal's deals were questionable. In David's understated terminology, McDougal made "overly optimistic investments." Unfortunately, when he couldn't cover the payments, McDougal shifted money around, borrowing from Peter to pay Paul. Unbeknownst to us, once he even used the Whitewater Development Company to buy property near a trailer park south of Little Rock that he confidently named Castle Grande Estates. His web of business partners and failed schemes would take years to untangle.

Madison Guaranty started out like thousands of other S&Ls that made small home mortgage loans. Then, in 1982, the Reagan Administration deregulated the savings and loan industry. Suddenly, owners like McDougal could make large, reckless loans outside of their traditional businesses, and they eventually drove the whole industry, including Madison Guaranty, into serious financial trouble. One of the ways S&L executives and their lawyers attempted to salvage their failing businesses was by raising capital through preferred stock offerings, which they were permitted to do under federal law, if they had state regulatory approval.

In 1985, Rick Massey, a young lawyer at the Rose Law Firm, along with a friend of his who worked for McDougal, proposed just such a remedy for Madison Guaranty. Because McDougal had been negligent in paying a previous bill from Rose for legal services, the firm insisted that he pay a $2,000 monthly retainer before Massey undertook the work. My partners asked me to request the retainer from McDougal and to become the "billing partner" for Massey because, as a junior associate, he couldn't bill a client himself. After I arranged the retainer, my own involvement in the account was minimal. The stock offering was never approved by Arkansas regulators, and the federal S&L regulators took over Madison Guaranty, removed McDougal as president and initiated an examination of the S&L's transactions because of allegations that McDougal had engaged in a pattern of self-dealing.

The federal investigation and the criminal prosecution it later spawned against McDougal consumed him for years. In 1986, he approached us and asked if we would sign over our 50 percent share in the Whitewater Development Company. I thought it was a great idea. We had made our investment eight years earlier, and it had only cost us money. But before we signed over our stock, I asked McDougal to take our names off the mortgage, and in return for obtaining 100 percent of the remaining equity of the company, assume the remaining debt and release us from any remaining and future liabilities. When he balked at that, alarms started going off in my head. For the first time since we became partners in 1978, I demanded to see the books. I've been asked why I had never done that before and how I could have been so ignorant of McDougal's actions. I've asked myself that too. I just thought we had made a bad investment and had to pay the price for buying real estate for second homes just as interest rates skyrocketed. We were stuck with a loser and had to wait for the market to turn around or until we could sell it. I had no reason to question McDougal, whose investment track record had been impressive in the 1970s and who, I figured, couldn't be expected to make a silk purse out of every sow's ear. I kept paying whatever McDougal said we owed and tended to the more imminent demands in my life, including having a baby, participating in my husband's elections every two years and trying to practice law. Once my accountant analyzed the Whitewater documents I had rounded up with Susan McDougal's help over many months, I realized that the records were in disarray and that Whitewater was a fiasco. I decided that Bill and I had to get everything in order, then extract ourselves from McDougal's mess. Given McDougal's problems, that took years.

First, I wanted to take care of any conceivable obligation the corporation had to the IRS, to the Arkansas Department of Revenue and for local property taxes. Whitewater had never made money, but it was still obligated to submit corporate tax returns, which, I learned in 1989, McDougal had not done in recent years. He had failed to pay property taxes, despite assurances to us to the contrary. To file tax returns now, I needed the signature of an officer of the Whitewater Development Company, Inc., and only the McDougals held titles. I tried for a year to get power of attorney from McDougal so I could file the returns, pay the taxes and sell the property to cover the debt.

Meanwhile, McDougal's life was falling apart. His wife, Susan, had left him in 1985 and later moved to California. The following year he suffered a debilitating stroke, which heightened the manic depression he'd apparently been fighting for some time. I was not eager to contact McDougal, so in 1990, I called Susan in California, explained what I wanted to do, and asked her if she, as corporate secretary, would sign. She agreed, and I overnighted her the forms, which she signed and returned to me. When McDougal found out, he screamed at Susan over the phone and called my office to threaten me. I had turned him into an enemy.

McDougal grew even more embittered after he was indicted and tried for eight federal felony counts for conspiracy, fraud, false statements and fiscal misdealing. He checked himself into a psychiatric hospital before his trial in 1990. He also asked Bill to be a character witness for him, but I talked Bill out of doing it. Bill is always willing to give anyone, especially old friends, the benefit of the doubt, but I just didn't feel he could vouch for McDougal. Both of us realized we had no idea who he really was or what he'd been up to all these years. After the jury acquitted him, McDougal threatened me again, this time implying that he would pay me back for filing the Whitewater tax returns.

And so he did, with considerable help from Bill's political adversaries. Sheffield Nelson, a self-made former CEO of the Arkansas Louisiana Gas Company (Arkla) had switched to the Republican Party to run against Bill for Governor in 1990. Used to getting what he wanted, Nelson became deeply vengeful and antagonistic over his defeat. As soon as Bill announced his run for the Presidency in 1991, Nelson let the Bush White House know he would be willing to offer whatever help he could to defeat Bill. To that end, he persuaded

McDougal to voice any complaints he could about Bill and me, no matter how outlandish.

The result was the first "Whitewater" story, an article that appeared on the front page of the Sunday *New York Times* in March 1992, in the middle of the Democratic primaries.

Jim McDougal was quoted throughout the piece, liberally planting false information about our partnership. The writer made much of our "complicated relationship" with McDougal and erroneously implied that he had made us money in the Whitewater deal and received favors in return. While the article's headline trumpeted that "Clintons Joined S&L Operator in Ozark Real Estate Venture," we had made our investment with the McDougals four years before Jim bought the S&L. The Clinton campaign immediately hired Jim Lyons, a respected corporate attorney from Denver, who, in turn, retained a firm of forensic accountants to assemble and explain the records of the Whitewater investment.

The Lyons report, which cost $25,000 and took a mere three weeks to complete, proved that Bill and I were equally liable with the McDougals for the original loan that we took out to purchase the Whitewater land and that we had lost tens of thousands of dollars on the investment—the final figure was more than $46,000. Ten years and tens of millions of dollars later, the independent counsel's final Whitewater report released in 2002 supported Lyons's findings, as did a separate investigation commissioned by the Resolution Trust Corporation. After the campaign released the Lyons report in March 1992, the press dropped the story. Some Republicans and their allies did not give up so easily. In August 1992, a low-level RTC investigator, L. Jean Lewis, filed a criminal referral concerning Madison that attempted to implicate Bill and me. Chuck Banks, the Republican U.S. Attorney in Little Rock who had been nominated by President Bush to be a federal judge, came under pressure from the Bush Justice Department to take action on this referral and issue grand jury subpoenas that would inevitably become public and signify that we were somehow involved in a criminal investigation. Banks refused, expressing surprise that the RTC had not sent him this information three years earlier when he had been investigating Jim McDougal. Banks said that this referral gave him no basis to suspect us of criminal conduct or to investigate us, and that he was afraid any last-minute investigative activity by him would leak and prejudice the presidential election. Somewhat surprisingly, the final Whitewater report actually documents the involvement of the Bush Administration in trying to create an "October Surprise" just weeks before the election. Not only was Attorney General William Barr involved, but White House Counsel C. Boyden Gray tried to find out about a potential criminal referral from the RTC involving us. When the rumblings of Whitewater resurfaced in the fall of 1993, none of us in the White House could have imagined the array of forces about to converge in what would become—for our adversaries—a perfect political storm.

In mid-November, while David Kendall was immersed in his fact-finding mission, *The Washington Post* submitted a long list of questions about Whitewater and McDougal to the White House. For the next several weeks, an internal debate simmered within the administration about how to handle media requests. Should we answer questions? Show them documents? And if so, which ones? Our political advisers, including George Stephanopoulos and Maggie Williams, favored dumping the documents on the media. So did David Gergen, who had served in the Nixon, Ford and Reagan White Houses and had joined Bill's staff. Gergen contended that the press wouldn't rest until they got information, but once they did, they would move on to something else. There was nothing to hide, so why not? The story would mushroom for a while and then die.

But David Kendall, Bernie Nussbaum and Bruce Lindsey, all lawyers, argued that releasing documents to the press was a "slippery slope." Since the record was still partial and might never be complete, we didn't know the answers to lots of questions about McDougal and his business dealings. The press would not be satisfied, always thinking we were holding something back when we didn't have anything left to tell them. As a lawyer, I tended to agree with this view. Bill didn't pay much attention to the issue, since he knew he hadn't done anything as Governor to favor McDougal, and besides, we had lost money. Consumed with the demands of the Presidency, he told me to decide with David how to handle our response.

Because of our experience with the Nixon impeachment in 1974, Bernie and I believed that we should cooperate fully with the government investigation so that no one could fairly claim that we were stonewalling or claiming executive privilege. So I instructed David to advise the government investigators that we would voluntarily provide them with all documents and cooperate with a grand jury investigation. I did not believe—wrongly, it turned out—that the media would continue to blast us because we hadn't turned over the same documents to them, so long as we had provided them to the Department of Justice.

Even before the Justice Department issued a subpoena, we agreed through David to cooperate fully and without delay, offering to produce all the documents we could find relating to Whitewater and waiving all privileges with respect to the documents we were producing—including any work Vince Foster had done for us as our personal lawyer.

Still confident that this nonscandal would blow over as it had during the campaign, we headed off to Camp David for Thanksgiving. This was a bittersweet time for us. My father would not be at the table vying with Hugh and Tony for one of the drumsticks or asking for more cranberries and watermelon pickle, two of his favorites from childhood. And we knew that Virginia's health was failing. This might be our last Thanksgiving with her, and we were determined to give her a good time, taking care of her without fussing over her, which was just not her style. Virginia required a blood transfusion every few days, so we arranged for her to be transfused at Camp David, which is fully equipped to provide medical care for the President, his family and guests and the sailors and Marines stationed there.

Virginia's husband, Dick, who had served in the Navy in the Pacific Theater during World War II, loved coming to Camp David. He spent a lot of time visiting with the young off-duty Marines, relaxing in the small restaurant and bar in Hickory Lodge on the base. Virginia liked to sit with him, nursing a drink, listening to a twenty-year-old corporal tell her about his family and the girl he planned to marry. In my mind's eye, I can see Virginia wearing red boots, white pants and sweater and a red leather jacket, kidding and laughing with Dick and the young men. Anyone who ever had the pleasure of spending time with Virginia knew her to be an American original—bighearted, good-humored, fun loving and totally without prejudice or pretense.

In early November, the press reported that her cancer had returned, but most people didn't know how serious her condition was, given her positive attitude and how good she continued to look. The makeup and false eyelashes went on no matter how she felt. Cristophe Schatteman, our hairstylist friend from Los Angeles, had flown to Arkansas to fix up Virginia's post-chemo wigs to look exactly like her hair, an act of kindness that speaks volumes about him.

My brother Tony had recently become engaged to Nicole Boxer, the daughter of Senator Barbara Boxer of California and her husband, Stewart. We were planning a spring wedding for Tony and Nicole at the White House, so I invited Nicole, her parents and her brother, Doug, to join us for Thanksgiving dinner at Camp David.

Camp David was a perennial work-in-progress as each new President and First Lady added their personal touches to the compound. It had been built by the CCC and WPA as a work camp during the Depression in the 1930s. President Franklin Roosevelt first decided to use it for a presidential retreat, naming it "Shangri-la" and upgrading its facilities. By the time we arrived, it was both a military installation and a retreat. There were ten rustic lodges for guests, all named for trees. The largest guest lodge, Aspen, reserved for the President, sits atop a hill that slopes down to the putting green installed by President Eisenhower and the pool added by President Nixon. The living room windows overlook the forest preserve that surrounds the camp. The perimeter's security fences, cameras and Marine patrols are out of sight, allowing one to forget that this peaceful setting is a military base, made even more secure because of the special protections afforded the President.

The center of Camp activity is the largest lodge, Laurel, where we gathered to watch football, play games, sit in front of the two-story brick fireplace and eat our meals together. After spending time there, I thought that the central room in Laurel could be more functional and take better advantage of the view. There were few windows on the long back wall facing the woods, and a large pillar blocked the flow of traffic through the room. I worked with the Navy and my friend Kaki Hockersmith, an interior decorator from Arkansas, to develop plans for a renovation that got rid of the pillar and added windows to bring in more light, opening the room to the changing seasons outside.

The Navy cooks and stewards prepared and served the classic Thanksgiving dinner both sides of our family expected. Melding the traditions of my family and Bill's meant we had both bread and cornbread stuffing, pumpkin and mincemeat pies. The buffet tables were groaning under the weight of all the food while everyone observed one tradition that transcends all regions: overindulging.

Over the weekend, two old friends, Strobe Talbott, then serving as Ambassador-at-Large to the New Independent States of the former Soviet Union, later to become Deputy Secretary of State, and Brooke Shearer, Director of the White House Fellows Program and my campaign companion, came to visit with their sons. We didn't talk much about Whitewater, which we saw as a momentary blip on the radar screen. Instead, we discussed the events of the past year. We were more hopeful than ever about the future of the country. We had been through a personally difficult year, but in terms of Bill's agenda, it had been productive. To use a horse-racing metaphor Virginia would have enjoyed: We might have been slow out of the gate, but we were gaining speed. The country was showing signs of economic recovery and increasing consumer confidence. The unemployment rate was down to 6.4 percent, the lowest since early 1991. New home purchases were up, while interest rates and inflation were dropping. In addition to the economic plan, which was essential to the unprecedented expansion, Bill had signed into law the National Service Act, creating AmeriCorps; the Family and Medical Leave Act, which President Bush had vetoed twice; the motor voter legislation, making it easier for working people to register to vote when they went into their local motor vehicle offices; direct student financial aid, cutting the cost of going to college; and one of Strobe's priorities, economic aid for Russia, which was intended to shore up that fledgling democracy.

We came back from the holidays a few pounds heavier but refreshed. I was particularly pleased that Bill signed the Brady bill on November 30, 1993. Like the Family and Medical Leave Act, this bill had been opposed by President Bush. Long overdue, it was commonsense legislation to require a five-day waiting period to check the background of any purchaser of a handgun. The bill wouldn't have been possible without the tireless efforts of James and Sarah Brady. Jim, a former White House press secretary, had suffered brain damage when he was shot in the head in 1981 by a deranged man attempting to assassinate President Ronald Reagan. He and his indomitable wife, Sarah, had dedicated their lives to keeping guns out of the hands of criminals and the mentally ill. Their perseverance resulted in the immensely moving scene in the East Room when Bill, flanked by the Bradys, signed into law the most important gun control bill in twenty-five years. In the years since, no lawful gun owner has lost his guns, but six hundred thousand fugitives, stalkers and felons have been stopped from buying them.

NAFTA was ratified on December 8, 1993, which meant the administration could finally turn its full attention to supporting health care reform. To keep up the momentum, Dr. Koop and I hit the road again. On December 2, we addressed eight hundred doctors and health care professionals attending the Tri State Rural Health Care Forum in Hanover, New Hampshire.

Dr. Koop had become an increasingly enthusiastic advocate of our health care plan. When he spoke, it was like listening to an Old Testament prophet. He could deliver the hard truth and get away with it. He could say, "We have too many specialists in medicine and not enough generalists," and an audience filled with specialists would nod in agreement.

The New Hampshire forum was televised, so it was a particularly important event for our advocacy and a great opportunity to explain the virtues of the Clinton plan. I became engrossed in the discussion. At some point, I looked toward the audience and saw my aide-de-camp Kelly Craighead crawling down the center aisle of the auditorium. She was gesturing frantically, slapping the top of her head and pointing at me. I kept on talking and listening, unable to figure out what she was doing.

It was another hair crisis. Capricia Marshall, who was in Washington watching her television, noticed that a stray piece of hair was sticking straight up from the center of my head. She suspected that the audience would be staring at my hair instead of listening to what I was saying, so she got Kelly on her cell phone: "Get her hair down!"

"I can't, she's sitting in front of hundreds of people."

"I don't care, send her a signal!"

When Kelly told me the story after the event, we all laughed. Just shy of a year into my new life, I was finally catching on to the significance of the insignificant. From then on, we worked out a system of hand gestures, like those of a coach and a pitcher, so that I would know when to smooth my hair down or wipe the lipstick off my teeth.

Back in Washington, the White House Christmas season rituals were in full swing. I could now appreciate the surreal planning I had been urged to begin on a warm day back in May, when Gary Walters, the chief usher, said to me, "You know, Mrs. Clinton, it's getting late to start preparing for Christmas." He told me I had to settle on a design for the White House Christmas card, pick a theme for the decorations and plan the parties we would hold in December. I love Christmas, but

Thanksgiving had always been a fine time to start thinking about it, so this represented a big change in my planning style. I dutifully adjusted and soon began sorting through pictures of snowdrifts on the White House lawn as the scent of magnolias wafted through the windows.

All those months of preparation paid off. I decided to make American crafts my theme and invited artisans from around the country to send in handmade ornaments, which we hung on the more than twenty trees placed throughout the residence. We hosted, on average, one reception or party every day for three solid weeks. I liked planning menus and activities and overseeing the dozens of volunteers who flock to the White House to help hang ornaments. One sad result of the attacks of September 11, 2001, is that the White House is no longer as open as it was during our time there. That first Christmas season, some 150,000 visitors came through the public rooms to view the decorations and sample a cookie or two. Because we wanted to include people of all faiths in the holiday season, we lit the menorah I had commissioned for the White House that December to celebrate Chanukah. Three years later, we held the first Eid al-Fitr event in the White House to honor the end of Ramadan, the Muslim month of fasting.

Christmas is always a big event in the Clinton family. Bill and Chelsea are enthusiastic shoppers, gift wrappers and tree decorators. I love watching them trim our tree together, pausing to reminisce about the origin of each ornament. This year was no different, although it took a while to find the family Christmas decorations. Many of our possessions remained in unlabeled boxes stuffed in rooms on the third floor of the White House or in the presidential warehouse in Maryland. Finally, though, our treasured Christmas stockings hung from the mantel of the fireplace in the Yellow Oval Room, in a house that was starting to feel like home.

This would be the last Christmas for Virginia, who was getting weaker and now required regular transfusions. The indomitable Mrs. Kelley was determined to live every last moment of her life to the hilt, and Bill and I wanted her to spend as much time as possible with us, so we convinced her to stay for a week. She agreed but insisted that she couldn't remain through New Year's because she and Dick were going to Barbra Streisand's concert in Las Vegas. Virginia had formed a deep friendship with Barbra, who had invited them to be her guests at her long-awaited return to the concert stage. I think Virginia willed herself to live long enough to make the trip, because there was nothing she enjoyed more than a swing through the casinos and a chance to see Barbra Streisand perform.

The media fixation with Whitewater continued throughout the holiday season as *The New York Times*, *The Washington Post* and *Newsweek* competed for scoops. Republicans in the House and Senate—particularly Bob Dole—called for an "independent review" of Whitewater. Editorial writers hectored Attorney General Janet Reno to appoint a special counsel. The Independent Counsel Act, which had been voted into law after the Watergate scandal, had recently expired, and investigations now had to be authorized by the Attorney General. The pressure was mounting every day, though there were no facts that came close to meeting the only criterion for appointing a special counsel: credible evidence of wrongdoing.

Vince Foster was being hounded beyond the grave. A week before Christmas, the press reported that some of his files, including Whitewater documents, had been "spirited" out of his office by Bernie Nussbaum. The Justice Department was well aware, of course, that the personal files had been retrieved from his office in the presence of lawyers from the Justice Department and FBI agents, handed over to our lawyers and were being turned over to the Justice Department for examination. But the leak of this "news" tossed fuel on a smoldering fire.

Then we were confronted with an outrageous partisan attack. On Saturday, December 18, I was hosting a holiday reception when David Kendall reached me by telephone.

"Hillary," he said, "I've got to tell you about something very, very ugly. . . ."

I sat down and listened as David summarized a long, detailed article that would appear in the *American Spectator*, a right-wing monthly that regularly attacked the administration. The article, written by David Brock, was filled with the most vile stories I had ever heard, worse than the salacious garbage in supermarket tabloids. Brock's main sources were four Arkansas troopers from Bill's former bodyguard detail. They claimed—among other things—that they had procured women for Bill when he was Governor. Years later, Brock would recant, writing a stunning confession of his political motives and directives at the time.

"Look, it's just a lot of sleaze, but it's going to be out there," said David. "You've got to be prepared."

My first thoughts were for Chelsea and for my mother and Virginia, who had already been through too much.

"What can we do about it?" I asked David. "Is there anything anyone *can* do?"

His advice was to stay calm and say nothing. Comments from us would only help publicize the article. The troopers were doing a reasonable job of discrediting themselves, shamelessly boasting that they expected to cash in on their stories. Two of the four agreed to be identified, and they were shopping around for a book deal. Even more telling, they were being represented by Cliff Jackson, another of Bill's most vehement political enemies in Arkansas. Most of Brock's tales were too vague to be checked on, but certain specifics were easily refuted. The article claimed, for example, that I had ordered the gate logs to the Governor's Mansion destroyed to cover up Bill's supposed liaisons; the mansion, however, never kept such logs. Unfortunately, the fact that Brock's sources were state troopers who had worked for Bill gave their stories a veneer of credibility.

I don't think the full effect of the article hit me until the next evening, at a Christmas party for our friends and family at the White House. Lisa Caputo told me that two of the troopers were touting their stories on CNN that night and that the *Los Angeles Times* was about to publish its own version of the troopers' allegations. It was too much. I wondered if what Bill was trying to do for the country was worth the pain and humiliation our families and friends were about to suffer. I must have looked as devastated as I felt, because Bob Barnett came over to ask if he could help. I told him we had to decide how to respond by the next day. I suggested we go upstairs with Bill for a few minutes to talk it over. Bill paced in the center hall. Bob knelt in front of me as I sank into a small chair against the wall. With his oversize glasses and mild features, Bob looks like everybody's favorite uncle. Now he was talking in a soothing voice, clearly trying to see whether after all that had happened this year, we had the strength for yet another struggle.

I looked at him and said, "I am just so tired of all of this."

He shook his head. "The President was elected, and you've got to stay with this for the country, for your family. However bad this seems, you've got to stick it out," he said. He wasn't telling me anything I didn't know, and it wasn't the first time I had been advised that my actions and words could either strengthen or undermine Bill's Presidency.

I wanted to say, "Bill's been elected, not me!" Intellectually, I understood Bob was right and that I would have to summon whatever energy I had left. I was willing to try. But I just felt so tired. And at the moment, very much alone.

I realized that attacks on our reputations could jeopardize the work Bill was doing to set the country on a different track. Ever since the campaign, I had seen how ferociously the Republicans wanted to hold on to the White House. Bill's political adversaries understood how high the stakes were, which made me want to fight back. I went back downstairs to rejoin the party.

I had scheduled several media interviews that I couldn't cancel. On December 21, I met for a year-end wrap-up with Helen Thomas, the dean of the White House press corps and a legendary journalist, and other wire service reporters. Naturally, they asked me about the *Spectator* article, and I decided to give them an answer. I didn't believe it was a coincidence that these attacks should surface just when Bill's standing in the polls was at the highest level since his inauguration, and I told them so. I also believed the stories were planted for partisan political and ideological reasons.

"I think my husband has proven that he's a man who really cares about this country deeply and respects the Presidency. . . . And when it's all said and done, that's how most fair-minded Americans will judge my husband. And all the rest of this stuff will end up in the garbage can where it deserves to be."

It was not exactly the calm, quiet response David had recommended.

Although the initial damage had been done, the media finally started examining the troopers' motives. It turned out that two were angry because they felt that Bill had been ungrateful to them. They had also been subjects of an investigation into an alleged insurance fraud scheme involving a state vehicle in which they were riding, which had been wrecked in 1990. Another trooper, who reportedly claimed that Bill had offered him a federal job for his silence, later signed an affidavit swearing it never happened. But nearly a decade would pass before we learned the full, chilling story behind what became known as "Troopergate."

David Brock, the author of the *Spectator* article, was seized by an attack of conscience in 1998 and publicly apologized to Bill and me for the lies he had spread about us. He was so consumed with building his right-wing credentials that he allowed himself to be used politically even when he had doubts about his sources. His memoir, *Blinded by the Right*, published in 2002, chronicles his years as a self-described "right-wing hit man." He claims he was not only on the *Spectator*'s legitimate payroll, but was receiving money under the table to dig up and publish whatever dirt anyone would say about us. Among his secret patrons was the Chicago financier Peter Smith, a key supporter of Newt Gingrich. Smith paid Brock to travel to Arkansas to interview the troopers, an arrangement facilitated by Cliff Jackson. According to Brock, the success of the trooper article inspired Richard Mellon Scaife, an ultraconservative billionaire from Pittsburgh, to fund similar stories through a clandestine enterprise called "the Arkansas Project." Through an educational foundation, Scaife also pumped hundreds of thousands of dollars into the *Spectator* to support its anti-Clinton vendetta.

The plot described by Brock and others is convoluted and the cast of characters preposterous. But it is important for Americans to know what was taking place behind the scenes to understand fully the meaning of Troopergate, the tabloid scandals that preceded it and those that would follow. This was all-out political war.

"[I]n pursuit of my budding career as a right-wing muckraker," writes Brock, "I let myself get mixed up in a bizarre and at times ludicrous attempt by well-financed right-wing operatives to tar Clinton with sleazy personal allegations. Operating in conjunction with, but outside of, official GOP or movement organizations and well below the radar of the American public and the press corps as the election campaign unfolded, the effort went far beyond the opposition research typically conducted by political campaigns—not only in its secretiveness and its single-mindedness, but also in its lack of fidelity to any standard of proof, principle or propriety. These activities . . . were a very early hint of how far the political right would go in the coming decade to try to destroy the Clintons."

Along with other members of Scaife's secret Arkansas Project, Brock took on the task of planting and nourishing seeds of doubt about Bill Clinton's character and his fitness to govern. According to Brock's memoir, the "country was being conditioned to see an invention made up entirely by the Republican right . . . from virtually the first moment that they stepped out of Arkansas and onto the national stage, the country never again saw the Clintons."

One frosty morning between Christmas and New Year's, Maggie

Williams and I were having coffee in our favorite spot in the residence: the West Sitting Hall in front of a large fan-shaped window. We were talking and leafing through the newspapers. Most front pages were wall-to-wall Whitewater.

"Hey, look at this!" said Maggie as she handed me a copy of *USA Today*. "It says you and the President are the most admired people in the world." I didn't know whether to laugh or cry. All I could do was hope that the American people would maintain their reserves of fairness and goodwill, as I struggled to maintain my own.

INDEPENDENT COUNSEL

THE SOUND OF A TELEPHONE RINGING IN THE MID-
dle of the night is one of the most jarring in the world. When our
bedroom phone rang long after midnight on January 6, 1994, it was Dick
Kelley calling to tell Bill that his mother had just died in her sleep at her
home in Hot Springs.

We were up for the rest of the night, making and taking phone calls.
Bill spoke twice with his brother, Roger. We reached out to one of our
closest friends, Patty Howe Criner, who had grown up with Bill, and we
asked her to work with Dick on the funeral arrangements. Al Gore
called at about three in the morning. I woke Chelsea and brought her
into our bedroom so Bill and I could tell her. She had been very close to
her grandmother, whom she called Ginger. Now, she had lost two of
her grandparents in less than a year.

Before dawn, the White House Press Office put out the news of
Virginia's death, and when we turned on the television set in our bedroom, we saw the first news item flash on the screen: "The President's
mother died early this morning after a long battle with cancer." It made
her death seem terribly final. We almost never watched the morning
news, but the background noise was a relief from our own thoughts.
Then Bob Dole and Newt Gingrich appeared on the *Today* show for a
previously scheduled appearance. They began talking about Whitewater: "It to me cries out for the appointment of a regulatory, independent counsel," Dole said. I looked over at Bill's face. He was utterly
stricken. Bill was raised by his mother to believe that you don't hit people when they're down, that you treat even your adversaries in life or
politics with decency. A few years later, someone told Bob Dole how

much his words had hurt Bill that day, and to his credit, he wrote Bill a letter of apology.

Bill asked the Vice President to deliver a speech scheduled for Milwaukee that afternoon so he could go to Arkansas right away. I stayed behind to contact family and friends and help with their travel arrangements. Chelsea and I flew to Hot Springs the next day and went straight to Virginia and Dick's lakeside home, where we found friends and family members squeezed into the modest rooms. Barbra Streisand had flown in from California, and her presence added a touch of excitement and glamour that Virginia would have loved. We stood around drinking coffee and eating the mountains of food that show up after any death in Arkansas. We swapped stories about Virginia's amazing life and her appropriately titled autobiography that was moving toward publication, *Leading with My Heart.* She would never see it published, but what a remarkable and honest story it tells. I am convinced that if she had lived to promote it, not only would it have been a best-seller, but it might have helped some people understand Bill a little better. Hours later, the house was still as packed as a church on Easter Sunday, but without Virginia's presence, it felt as though the whole choir were missing.

There wasn't a church in Hot Springs big enough to accommodate a lifetime's worth of Virginia's friends. The memorial service would have to be held at the Convention Center in downtown Hot Springs. Bill told me, "If the weather were better, we could have used Oaklawn racetrack. Mother would have loved that!" I smiled at the thought of the track filled with thousands of racing fans cheering one of their own.

As the funeral procession drove through Hot Springs the next morning, the roads were lined with people who silently paid their respects. The service celebrated Virginia's life with stories and hymns, but nothing could capture the essence of this unique woman who had shared her love of life with anyone who crossed her path.

After the service, we drove to the cemetery in Hope where Virginia would be laid to rest with her parents and first husband, Bill Blythe. Virginia had come home to Hope.

Air Force One picked us up at the airport in Hope for the sad flight back to Washington. The plane was filled with family and friends who tried to lift Bill's spirits. But even on the day he buried his mother, Bill couldn't escape being hounded about Whitewater.

White House staff members and lawyers huddled with the President. Everyone was concerned that the drumbeat for appointing a special prosecutor was drowning out Bill's message, but nobody could predict whether asking for a special prosecutor would quiet the drums. By the time we had landed at Andrews Air Force Base and helicoptered to the White House, Bill was obviously tired of the debate. He had to go back to Andrews to fly to Europe that night for long-scheduled meetings in Brussels and Prague about the expansion of NATO, followed by a state visit to Russia to address President Boris Yeltsin's concern about NATO's plans to move eastward. Before Bill left, he made it clear to me that he wanted the Whitewater issue resolved one way or another, and soon.

I had planned to join Bill in Moscow for the state visit on January 13. At Virginia's funeral, we decided that I should bring Chelsea because we didn't want to leave her in the White House at such a sad time. I knew a decision about the special prosecutor had to be made before we left. That Sunday, a number of leading Democrats appeared on the political talk shows to voice their support for a special prosecutor. None of them could explain exactly why this step was appropriate or necessary. They seemed to be caught up in the moment and wary of pressure from the press. The momentum kept building, and my own determination was wearing down.

My gut instinct, as a lawyer and a veteran of the Watergate impeachment inquiry staff, was to cooperate fully with any legitimate criminal inquiry but to resist giving someone free rein to probe indiscriminately and indefinitely. A "special" investigation should be triggered only by credible evidence of wrongdoing, and there was no such evidence. Without credible evidence, a call for a special prosecutor would set a terrible precedent: From then on, every unsubstantiated charge against a President concerning events during any period of his life could require a special prosecutor.

The President's political advisers predicted that a special prosecutor would eventually be forced on us and argued that it was better to appoint one and get it over with. George Stephanopoulos researched previous independent counsels and cited the case of President Carter and his brother, Billy, who were investigated for a disputed loan to a peanut warehouse in the mid-1970s. The special prosecutor requested by Carter completed his investigation in seven months and exonerated the Carters. That was encouraging. By contrast, the investigation into what was known as "the Iran-Contra affair," begun in the Reagan-Bush Administration, had continued on for seven years. In that case, though, there was illegal activity by White House and other governmental personnel in the conduct of our nation's foreign policy. Several Administration officials were indicted, including Defense Secretary Caspar Weinberger and Lt. Col. Oliver North, who worked on the National Security Council.

Only David Kendall, Bernie Nussbaum and David Gergen agreed with me that we should resist a special prosecutor. Gergen considered a special prosecutor a "dangerous proposition." Bill's staff trooped in to lobby me, one after another, each delivering the same familiar message: I would destroy my husband's Presidency if I didn't support their strategy. Whitewater had to be pushed off the front pages so we could get on with the business of the administration, including health care reform.

I believed that we needed to distinguish between holding our ground when we were in the right and giving in to political expediency and pressure from the press. "Requesting a special prosecutor is wrong," I said. But I couldn't change their minds.

On January 3, Harold Ickes, an old friend and adviser from the 1992 campaign, had joined the administration as Deputy Chief of Staff. Bill had asked Harold, a sandy-haired, hyperkinetic lawyer, to coordinate the upcoming health care campaign. Within days, he was diverted to organize a "Whitewater Response Team" composed of several senior advisers and members of the communications staff and counsel's office. Harold was the best advocate to have in your corner during a fight. Like Kendall, he was a veteran of the civil rights movement in the South—in fact, Harold had been so badly beaten while organizing black voters in the Mississippi Delta that he had lost a kidney. Although he had spent most of his early life avoiding his legacy—at one point he worked breaking horses on a cattle ranch—he was the son of Harold Ickes, Sr., one of the most significant players in Franklin D. Roosevelt's cabinet. Politics pumped through Harold's veins, and the White House seemed to be his natural habitat.

Harold did his best to keep the Whitewater debate under control, but the turmoil continued in the West Wing. Each news story brought us closer to a fateful decision. The day after I returned to the White House from Hot Springs, Harold told me that he had reluctantly concluded we should request a special prosecutor.

On Tuesday evening, January 11, I arranged a conference call with Bill in Prague. David Kendall and I met in the Oval Office with a handful of Bill's top aides for a final debate on the issue. The scene reminded me of a cartoon I had seen: A man stood in front of two doors, obviously trying to decide which one to enter. A sign above the first door said, "Damned if you do." The other said, "Damned if you don't."

It was the middle of the night in Europe. Bill was worn out and exasperated after days of hearing nothing but Whitewater questions from the media. He was also heartbroken about losing his mother, the one steady presence throughout his life and his chief cheerleader, offering unconditional love and support. I felt sorry for him and wished that he didn't have to deal with such a crucial decision under these circumstances. He was terribly hoarse, and we had to lean in close to the black, batwing-shaped conference phone to hear his voice.

"I don't know how much longer I can take this," he said, frustrated that the press didn't want to talk about the historic expansion of NATO that would soon open the door to the former Warsaw Pact nations. "All they want to know is why we're ducking an independent investigation."

George Stephanopoulos opened, calmly making the political arguments for the appointment of a special prosecutor. He said that a special prosecutor would get the media off Bill's back, that it was inevitable and that any further delay would kill our legislative agenda.

Then Bernie Nussbaum made a forceful last-ditch plea for his position. Like me, Bernie knew that the prosecutors would be under enormous pressure to come up with indictments to justify their efforts. As Bernie kept stressing, we were already turning over documents to the Justice Department, and, because there was no credible evidence of wrongdoing, a special prosecutor could not, under the law, be ordered. We could only request one, which seemed truly absurd. A political circus would be welcome compared to a potentially endless legal process.

After several heated rounds back and forth, Bill, exhausted, had heard enough. I wrapped up the meeting, asking only David Kendall to remain for a few more words with the President.

The room was quiet for a moment, and then Bill spoke.

"Look, I think we've just got to do it," he said. "We've got nothing to hide, and if this keeps up, it's going to drown out our agenda."

It was time to fold my cards. "I know that we've got to move past this," I said. "But it's up to you."

David Kendall strongly agreed with Bernie. They were both experienced criminal lawyers who understood that the innocent could be persecuted. But they were outnumbered by the political advisers who just wanted the press to change the subject. David left the room, and I picked up the phone to talk to Bill alone.

"Why don't you sleep on the decision," I said. "If you're still willing to do it, we'll send a request to the Attorney General in the morning."

"No," he said, "let's get this over with." Though he feared, as much as I did, that we were underestimating the consequences of this decision, he told me to go ahead with the request. I felt terrible. He had been pushed into a decision that he didn't feel comfortable about. But given the pressures confronting us, we didn't know what else to do.

I walked into Bernie Nussbaum's office to deliver the bad news in person and hugged my old friend. Though it was late, Bernie began to compose a letter to Janet Reno, relaying the President's formal request that the Attorney General appoint a special prosecutor to conduct an independent investigation of Whitewater.

We will never know if Congress would eventually have forced an independent counsel on us. And we will never know whether releasing an inevitably incomplete set of personal documents to *The Washington Post* would have averted a special prosecutor. With the wisdom of hindsight, I wish I had fought harder and not let myself be persuaded to take the path of least resistance. Bernie and David were right. We were being swept up in what legal analyst Jeffrey Toobin later described as the politicization of the criminal justice system and the criminalization of the political system. What had been promoted as a quick fix to our political problems sapped the administration's energy for the next seven years, unfairly invaded the lives of innocent people and diverted America's attention from the challenges we faced at home and abroad.

It was Bill's innate optimism and resilience that kept him going, inspired me and made it possible to implement most of his agenda for America by the end of his two terms. All that, however, was in the future as Chelsea and I boarded the plane to join Bill in Russia.

The descent into Moscow was turbulent, and I felt queasy when I walked off the plane. Chelsea got into a car with Capricia Marshall and I got into the official limousine with Alice Stover Pickering, wife of our Ambassador to Russia, Thomas Pickering. Both had been in numerous Foreign Service postings around the world. Tom Pickering later served with distinction as Undersecretary of State for Political Affairs under Madeleine Albright. While driving into town for my meeting with

Naina Yeltsin, I felt sick to my stomach. The speeding motorcade, preceded and followed by Russian police cars, could not stop. The backseat of the limousine was totally clean, without a cup, towel or napkin in sight. I bent my head over and threw up on the floor. Alice Pickering appeared totally unfazed and—to diminish my embarrassment—continued pointing out the sights. She never said a word to anyone, which I deeply appreciated. By the time we arrived at Spaso House, the Ambassador's official residence, I was feeling a little better. After a quick shower, a change of clothes and a crucial encounter with a toothbrush, I was ready to start my schedule.

I was looking forward to seeing Mrs. Yeltsin, whom I had enjoyed meeting in Tokyo the previous summer. Naina had worked as a civil engineer in Yekaterinburg, where her husband had been the regional Communist Party head. She had a hearty sense of humor, and we laughed our way through a day of public appearances and private meals with local dignitaries.

This first visit to Russia was intended to strengthen relations between Bill and President Yeltsin so that they could constructively address issues such as the dismantling of the former Soviet Union's nuclear arsenal and the expansion eastward of NATO. While our husbands held their summit talks, Naina and I visited a hospital, newly painted in honor of our visit, to discuss the health care systems in our countries. Russia's was deteriorating in the absence of the government support it had once received. The doctors we met were curious about our health care reform plan. They acknowledged the high quality of American medicine yet criticized our failure to guarantee health care to everyone. They shared our goal of universal coverage but were facing difficulties in achieving it.

I finally caught up with Bill that evening. The Yeltsins hosted a state dinner that began with a receiving line in the newly refurbished St. Vladimir Hall and continued with dinner in the Hall of Facets, a many-mirrored room and one of the most beautiful I've seen anywhere in the world. I sat next to President Yeltsin, with whom I'd never had an extended visit, and he kept up a running commentary about the food and wine, informing me in all seriousness that red wine protected Russian sailors on nuclear-powered submarines from the ill effects of strontium 90. I always did like red wine.

Chelsea joined us after dinner for the entertainment in St. George's

Hall, and then Boris and Naina took us on an extensive tour of the private quarters in the Kremlin, where we spent the night. We enjoyed the Yeltsins immensely, and I hoped we would see more of them.

The next morning, as our long motorcade left the Kremlin, Chelsea and Capricia were somehow left behind, standing on the steps with Chelsea's lone Secret Service agent and one of Bill's valets. They realized what was happening as they watched the last car pull out and two men roll up the red carpet. The agent and Capricia spotted a beat-up white van and raced over to it, determined to commandeer it. The driver, who was delivering sheets, spoke English. Once he understood their story, he loaded the four of them into the back of his van for a mad dash through the barricades to the airport. They made it, only to be refused entrance. The Russian security recognized Chelsea, but they couldn't figure out why she was not with us inside. While they were trying to sort out the confusion, Chelsea and her party picked up their bags and ran toward the terminal. I didn't discover that Chelsea was missing until we were ready to board the plane, and they came panting into the terminal. It seems funny now, but at the time I was beside myself worrying. I resolved not to let Chelsea or Capricia out of my sight for the rest of the trip.

Our next stop, Minsk, Belarus, was hands down one of the most depressed-looking places I've visited, its architecture evoking Soviet-style bleakness and the lingering aura of authoritarian communism; the weather, rainy and gray. Despite Belarusian efforts to build an independent and democratic country, they faced high odds against success. The intellectuals and academics I met who found themselves trying to run the government after the collapse of the Soviet Union seemed no match for the leftover Communists. Our itinerary was filled with reminders of the disasters of the Belarusian past. At Kuropaty Memorial, we laid flowers in memory of the almost three hundred thousand people who had been murdered by the Stalinist secret police. My visit to a hospital treating children who suffered from Chernobyl-related cancers painfully drove home the Soviet Union's cover-up of the accident at the nuclear plant and the potential dangers of nuclear power, including the proliferation of nuclear weapons. The one bright spot was a magnificent performance of the ballet adaptation of *Carmina Burana* in the State Academic Great Opera and Ballet Theatre. Chelsea and I sat on the edge of our seats in sheer delight. The years since our visit have not been kind to Belarus, which is governed again by an authoritarian regime of former Soviet Communists who have cracked down on press freedom and human rights.

On January 20, 1994, the administration's one-year anniversary, Janet Reno announced the appointment of Robert Fiske as special prosecutor. A Republican, Fiske was highly regarded as a thorough and fair-minded lawyer with prosecutorial experience. President Ford had appointed him U.S. Attorney for the Southern District of New York, and he had stayed on through the Carter Administration. He now worked for a Wall Street law firm. Fiske promised a quick and impartial investigation, and he took a leave of absence from his law firm so he could devote all of his time and energies to finishing the investigation. If he had been left to do his job, my concerns, and those of Bernie, David and Bill, would have proved unfounded.

A few days later, the President delivered the State of the Union Address. The speech was forceful and hopeful. Over an objection by David Gergen, Bill added a few theatrics to his remarks on health care: He held up a pen over the podium, promising to veto any health care bill that didn't include universal coverage. Gergen, a veteran of the Nixon, Ford and Reagan Administrations, worried that the gesture was too confrontational. I sided with the speechwriters and political advisers who thought it would be an effective visual signal that Bill would stand strong for his beliefs. Gergen's concerns turned out to have merit as we struggled for any ground on which to compromise.

After weeks of tension, I jumped at the chance to lead the American delegation to Lillehammer, Norway, for the 1994 Winter Olympics. Bill asked me to go, and I decided to take Chelsea. Despite the mishap at the end, she had enjoyed our visit to Russia, and I was happy to see her relax and smile more. Since moving to Washington, she had suffered so many losses: two grandparents; a school friend from Little Rock who died in a jet ski accident and Vince Foster, whose wife, Lisa, had taught her to swim in the Fosters' backyard pool and whose children were her friends. Moving to Washington and being part of the First Family had not been any easier for her than for the rest of us.

A charming village, Lillehammer provided a picture-perfect Olympics venue. Our traveling entourage was assigned rooms in a small hotel outside of town with its own ski run. For the opening ceremonies, where we were supposed to represent our nation, Chelsea and I looked like we were from the North Pole, so layered were we in warm ski clothes. In comparison, the European delegation, mostly royals like

Princess Anne from England, walked about in elegant cashmere coats, bareheaded. We also saw hardy Norwegians camping in the snowy woods so they could claim good observation points along the trails for the cross-country events. A highlight of the trip was my meeting with Gro Brundtland, a medical doctor, who was then Prime Minister of Norway.

Prime Minister Brundtland invited me to breakfast at the Maihaugen Folk Museum, in a rustic lodge with a big roaring fireplace. The first thing she said to me as we sat down to eat was, "I've read the health care plan, and I have several questions."

From that moment, she was a friend for life. I was so happy to find somebody who had read the plan, let alone wanted to talk about it. Of course, it helped that she was a physician, but I was impressed and delighted. Over a feast of fish, bread, cheese and strong coffee, we compared the relative merits of the European health care models and then delved into other related topics. Brundtland later left Norwegian politics to head the World Health Organization, where she championed initiatives I supported on tuberculosis, HIV/AIDS and anti-smoking.

This was my first official overseas trip without the President. I enjoyed representing him and my country, and took advantage of a relaxed schedule. I did a little skiing, cheered our athletes like downhill and slalom medalist Tommy Moe and stood in the snow, watching very fit people rocket past me in a blur. I also had a chance to talk to Chelsea away from the fray. She is bright and inquisitive, and I knew she was following the Whitewater saga in the news. I could tell she was torn between wanting to ask me about it and wanting to let me forget it. I was torn between wanting to share with her my frustrations about what was happening and wanting to shield her as much as possible, not only from the political attacks, but also from my own outrage and disillusionment. This was a constant emotional tug-of-war, and both of us had to work hard to keep our equilibrium.

As expected, the appointment of a special prosecutor quieted the Whitewater uproar for a few days. But just as predictably, a spate of new accusations and rumors filled the scandal vacuum. Newt Gingrich and Republican Senator Al D'Amato of New York clamored for Banking Committee hearings in both the House and the Senate to probe Whitewater allegations.

Robert Fiske managed to forestall the hearings, warning the combative Republicans that they risked interfering with his investigation.

He was moving quickly, as promised, slapping subpoenas on witnesses and hauling them before grand juries in Washington and Little Rock.

Fiske questioned several White House aides about the criminal referrals against Madison Guaranty by the Resolution Trust Corporation, which was a Treasury agency. He was interested in any West Wing contacts with Deputy Secretary of the Treasury Roger Altman about the referral and about Altman's decision to remove himself from his duties as temporary head of the RTC. As I understand the sequence of events, the White House and Treasury Department discussed this matter only when press inquiries—which were the product of improper leaks from the RTC's supposedly confidential investigation—started in the fall of 1993 and required them to respond; otherwise, it never would have come to their attention. Although Fiske and subsequent investigators judged the contacts to be legal, as with so many other aspects of the Whitewater imbroglio, the Republicans kept up a steady stream of accusations against Altman and others. When the final Whitewater report was published in 2002, confirming the contacts the Bush White House had made with RTC officials in the fall of 1992, I did not hear any similar outcry. Eventually, Roger Altman, an honest and extremely able man who served the President and the country well, resigned to return to private life, as did my old friend Bernie Nussbaum, another dedicated public servant.

There were mornings in the spring of 1994 when I woke up aching for all the close friends, associates and relatives who had passed out of our lives or had been unfairly attacked: my father, Virginia, Vince, Bernie, Roger. And some mornings, the press coverage was so wild that it even appeared to affect the stock market. On March 11, 1994, *The Washington Post* ran a story headlined WHITEWATER RUMORS PUSH DOW DOWN 23—PERCEPTION, NOT SPECIFICS, SPOOK MARKETS. On that same day, Roger Ailes, then President of CNBC and now running Fox, accused the Administration of "a cover-up with regard to Whitewater that includes . . . land fraud, illegal contributions, abuse of power . . . suicide cover-up—possible murder."

Then in mid-March, Webb Hubbell suddenly resigned from the Justice Department. Newspaper articles reported that the Rose Firm planned to file a complaint against him with the Arkansas Bar Association for questionable billing practices, including overcharging clients and padding his expenses. The allegations were serious enough for him to step down. By this time, however, I was used to fielding untrue charges, so I assumed that Webb was also being falsely accused. I met with him in the Solarium on the third floor of the White House to ask what was happening. Webb told me that he had gotten into a dispute with some of our former partners over the costs of a patent infringement case he had handled on a contingency basis for his father-in-law, Seth Ward. Webb had lost the case, and Seth refused to pay the costs. Knowing Seth, I had to admit that seemed plausible. Webb told me he was working on a settlement with the Rose partners and assured me that the dispute would be resolved. I believed him and asked what I could do to help him and his family during this period. He said he had put feelers out for business and was confident he would be fine "until this misunderstanding blows over."

The Whitewater investigations and press inquiries were now being handled by the Whitewater Response Team that Mack, Maggie and other senior staff had recommended that we set up to centralize all discussion of the issue.

There were four reasons for creating the team, nicknamed "the Masters of Disaster" and led by Harold Ickes. First, we wanted the staff to focus on the important work of the Administration. Second, if an issue is everyone's business, it becomes no one's responsibility. Third, Fiske's team was sending so many subpoenas that we had to have an organized system for searching files and providing responses. And finally, if staff members talked about Whitewater with Bill or me or among themselves, they would become more vulnerable to lengthy depositions, legal fees and general anxieties.

I was particularly worried about members of my own staff—Maggie Williams, Lisa Caputo, Capricia Marshall and others who had worked so hard and were being rewarded with subpoenas and frightening legal bills. Once Maggie was caught up in the investigation, I couldn't seek her advice about it or offer her any comfort. It's a tribute to her personal strength and the fortitude of everyone working for me that nobody complained or walked away from the challenges we faced.

David Kendall was becoming my main link to the outside world, and he was a godsend. From the very beginning, he advised me not to read newspaper articles and not to watch television reports about the investigation or any of the related "scandals." My press staff summarized what I needed to know in case I was questioned by the media. David urged me not to dwell on the rest of it.

"That's my job," he said. "One of the reasons you hire lawyers is to have them worry for you." David, of course, read everything and worried obsessively about what would happen next. I'm something of an obsessive personality myself, and these were hard instructions to follow. But I learned to let David take over the watch.

Every few days, Maggie would poke her head in my office and say, "David Kendall wants to talk to you." When he came in, she would leave the room. At each meeting, David continued to unravel the story of Jim McDougal and his personal and financial dealings, and I learned something every time.

I tried to deal with the new information by myself. I talked to Bill only when something critical came up. I tried to spare him so that he could concentrate on the duties of his office. It's often said that the President has the loneliest job in the world. Harry Truman once referred to the White House as "the crown jewel in the American penal system." Bill loved his work, but I could see the political war taking its toll, and I tried to protect him from whatever I could.

David was able to fill in most of the gaps in the record, which supported our contention that we had lost money on the Whitewater deal and were never involved in McDougal's wheelings and dealings with his S&L. David also brought us some uncomfortable news about errors he had found in our old financial documents. He had sifted through every piece of paper we could find like a miner panning for gold, and he had come up with a few lead nuggets. One was a mistake in the Lyons report that calculated our Whitewater losses at more than $68,000. We had to reduce that figure by $22,000 after David found that a check Bill had written to help his mother buy her house in Hot Springs had been incorrectly identified as a Whitewater loan payment. David also discovered that our certified public accountant in Little Rock had made an error on our 1980 tax return. An incomplete statement from a brokerage firm led him to claim a loss of $1,000 for us when, in fact, we had made almost $6,500 on trades. The statute of limitations had expired, but we voluntarily decided to make things right with the state of Arkansas and the IRS by writing a check for $14,615 for back taxes and interest.

As more of our financial records were released or found their way into the press, they generated additional stories. In mid-March, The New York Times ran a front-page article headlined TOP ARKANSAS LAWYER HELPED HILLARY CLINTON TURN BIG PROFIT. The story accurately reported the profits I had made in the commodities market in 1979. But it falsely implied that our close friend Jim Blair had somehow engineered my windfall in order to gain influence with Bill Clinton on behalf of his client Tyson Foods. The story was filled with inaccuracies about Blair's and Don Tyson's relationship with Bill when he was Governor. Yet again, I wondered why such stories were printed before they were verified. If Tyson had Bill in his pocket, as the *Times* alleged, why did Tyson back Bill's opponent Frank White in the 1980 and 1982 Governor's races?

Jim was generous enough to share his expertise in trading commodities with his family and friends. With his help, I got into this volatile market and turned $1,000 into $100,000 in a short time. I was lucky enough to lose my nerve and get out before the market dropped. Could I have done it without Jim? No. Did I have to pay my broker more than $18,000 in brokerage fees on my trading? Yes. Did my commodity trading influence Bill's decisions as Governor? Absolutely not.

Once the story about my commodity trading broke, the White House enlisted experts to review records of my trading. Leo Melamed, the former head of the Chicago Mercantile Exchange and a Republican, warned that if we asked for his opinion, he would give it, regardless of the impact. After a thorough review of my trades, he concluded that I had done nothing wrong. The controversy, in his opinion, was "a tempest in a teapot." I wasn't surprised by his conclusions. Our tax returns from 1979, which had reported the significant increase in our income from the commodity trades, had been audited by the IRS, and our records were all in order. In fact, the IRS also audited every return we filed for every year Bill was in the White House.

I now realize that the constant accusations had taken their toll on my relations with the press. I had kept the White House press corps at arm's length for too long. Because I wanted the media to report on health care reform, I offered interviews to correspondents who covered events and speeches around the country. The White House press corps, however, had little access to me. It took me a while to understand that their resentment was justified.

By the end of April 1994, I felt confident enough in David Kendall's research and in my understanding of Whitewater and the surrounding issues that I was ready to offer the media what they wanted: me.

I called my Chief of Staff and said, "Maggie, I want to do it. Let's call a press conference."

"You know you'll have to answer *all* questions, no matter what they throw at you."

"I know. I'm ready."

I discussed my plan beforehand only with the President, David Kendall and Maggie. In order to prepare, I confided in Lisa, White House Counsel Lloyd Cutler, Harold Ickes and Mandy Grunwald. I didn't want a parade of advisers from the West Wing pounding on my door with advice about how to handle this question or that. I wanted to speak as directly as possible.

On the morning of April 22, the White House announced that the First Lady would take questions that afternoon in the State Dining Room. We hoped that a change of scenery would encourage a fresh approach from the media.

I didn't calculate what I would wear to this event—my choice of clothes is almost always a last-minute decision. I felt like wearing a black skirt and a pink sweater set. A few reporters immediately interpreted it as an attempt to "soften" my image, and my sixty-eight-minute encounter with the fourth estate would go down in history as the "Pink Press Conference."

I sat in front of a crowd of reporters and camera operators who filled the dining room.

"Let me thank all of you for coming," I began. "I have wanted to do this in part because I realized that despite my traveling around the country and answering questions, I did not really satisfy a lot of you in having your questions asked and answered. And last week, Helen said, 'I can't travel with her, so how can I ask her questions?' For that reason we are here, and, Helen, you get the first question."

Helen Thomas got right to the point:

"Do you know of any money that could have gone from Madison to the Whitewater project or to any of your husband's political campaigns?" she asked.

"Absolutely not. I do not."

"Actually, on the same theme with your commodities profits—it is difficult for a layman, and probably for a lot of experts, to look at the amount of the investment and the size of the profit. Is there any way you can explain . . ."

And so I began to explain it. And explain it. And explain it again. One after another, the reporters asked me everything they could think

of about Whitewater, and I answered them until they ran out of different ways to ask the same questions.

I was grateful for the questions, which gave me a chance to lay out
everything I knew at that point. I was also able to address a problem
that had plagued me from the beginning. I was asked if I felt that my reluctance to provide information to the press "helped to create any impression that you were trying to hide something?"

"Yes, I do," I said. "And I think that is probably one of the things
that I regret most, and one of the reasons why I wanted to do this. . . . I
think if my father or mother said anything to me more than a million
times, it was: 'Don't listen to what other people say. Don't be guided by
other people's opinions. You know, you have to live with yourself.' And
I think that's good advice.

"But I do think that that advice and my belief in it, combined with
my sense of privacy . . . led me to perhaps be less understanding than I
needed to [be] of both the press and the public's interest, as well as
[their] right to know things about my husband and me.

"So, you're right. I've always believed in a zone of privacy. And I
told a friend the other day that I feel after resisting for a long time I've
been rezoned."

That line made everyone laugh.

After the press conference, David and I had a drink together in the
West Sitting Hall as the sun set beyond the window. Though everyone
thought I had done well, I felt somber about the situation, and as we assessed the day's events, I commented to David: "You know, they're not
going to let up. They're just going to keep on coming at us, no matter
what we do. We really don't have any good choices here."

That night, Richard Nixon, who had suffered a stroke four days
earlier, died at the age of eighty-one. In the early spring of 1993, Nixon
had sent Bill a letter full of insightful observations about Russia, and
Bill had read it to me, announcing that he thought Nixon was a brilliant, tragic figure. Bill invited the former President to the White
House to discuss Russia, and Chelsea and I greeted him as he stepped
off the elevator on the second floor. He told Chelsea that his daughters
had gone to her school, Sidwell Friends. Then he turned to me:

"You know, I tried to fix the health care system more than twenty
years ago. It has to be done sometime."

"I know," I replied, "and we'd be better off today if your proposal
had succeeded."

• • •

One of the women in the *American Spectator* article had taken issue with her portrayal by the Arkansas troopers. Although she was identified in the story only as "Paula," she claimed her friends and family recognized her as the woman who supposedly met with Bill in a Little Rock hotel suite during a convention and later told a trooper she wanted to be the Governor's "regular girlfriend."

At a February convention of the Conservative Political Action Committee, Paula Corbin Jones held a press conference and appeared to identify herself as the Paula in the article. Cliff Jackson, who was trying to raise money for a "Troopergate Whistleblower's Fund," introduced her to the press. She said she wanted to clear her name. But instead of announcing a libel suit against the *Spectator*, she accused Bill Clinton of sexually harassing her by making unwanted advances. Initially, the mainstream press disregarded Jones's claim because her credibility was tainted by her association with Jackson and the disgruntled troopers. We expected this story to die like the other phony scandals.

But on May 6, 1994, two days before the statute of limitations ran out, Paula Jones filed a civil suit against the President of the United States, asking for $700,000 in damages. Someone was raising the stakes in this game. It had moved from the tabloids to the courts.

D-DAY

WASHINGTON IS A CITY OF RITUALS, AND ONE OF the most faithfully observed is the annual Gridiron Dinner, a white-tie affair in which leading Washington journalists dress up in costumes, perform zany skits and sing songs that make fun of the current administration, including the President and First Lady. Guests at the dinner include the club's sixty members as well as their colleagues and dignitaries from the political, business and journalistic worlds. The Gridiron Club was slow to change with the times. Women were not admitted until 1975. (Eleanor Roosevelt used to throw "Gridiron Widows" parties for excluded spouses and female journalists.) In 1992, White House reporter Helen Thomas was elected the first female President. Membership in the club remains highly selective, and invitations to the spring event are among the most coveted in town. The First Couple almost always attend, seated on the ballroom dais, being good sports no matter what is said about them. Sometimes they come up with spoofs of their own.

When the 109th Gridiron Dinner rolled around in March 1994, Bill and I knew we had not sold the administration's health care plan with enough clarity and simplicity to rouse public support or to motivate Congress to act in the face of well-financed, well-organized opponents. The Health Insurance Association of America was concerned that the Administration's plan would curtail insurance companies' prerogatives and profits. To raise doubts about reform, the group launched a second round of advertisements, featuring a couple named Harry and Louise. Sitting at a kitchen table, Harry and Louise asked each other cleverly contrived questions about the plan and wondered aloud what it might cost them. As intended, the ads exploited the fears—pinpointed by focus groups—of the 85 percent of Americans who already had health insurance and worried it might be taken away.

For the Gridiron Dinner, Bill and I decided to stage a parody of the insurance lobby's TV spot, with Bill playing "Harry" and me playing "Louise." It would give us a chance to expose the scare tactics employed by our opponents and have some fun. Mandy Grunwald and comedian Al Franken wrote a script, Bill and I memorized our lines and, after a few rehearsals, recorded our version of "Harry and Louise" on video-tape.

It went like this: Bill and I were seated on a sofa—he in a plaid shirt, drinking coffee, and me in a navy blue sweater and skirt—examining a massive sheaf of papers, meant to be the Health Security Act.

Bill: *Hi, Louise, how was your day?*

Me: *Well, fine, Harry—until now.*

Bill: *Gee, Louise, you look like you've seen a ghost.*

Me: *Well, it's worse than that. I've just read the Clinton health security plan.*

Bill: *Health care reform sounds like a great idea to me.*

Me: *Well, I know, but some of these details sure scare the heck out of me.*

Bill: *Like what?*

Me: *Like for example, it says here on page 3,764 that under the Clinton health security plan, we could get sick.*

Bill: *That's terrible.*

Me: *Well, I know. And look at this, it gets worse. On page 12,743—no, I got that wrong—on page 27,655, it says that eventually we're all going to die.*

Bill: *Under the Clinton health plan? You mean after Bill and Hillary put all those bureaucrats and taxes on us, we're still all going to die?*

Me: *Even Leon Panetta.*

Bill: *Wow, that is scary. I've never been so frightened in all my life.*

Me: *Me neither, Harry.*

Together: *There's got to be a better way.*

Announcer: *"Paid for by the Coalition to Scare Your Pants Off."*

It was an atypical performance for a First Couple, and the audience loved it. The Gridiron Dinner is supposedly off-the-record, and journalists who attend are not supposed to write about it. But full-blown stories about the songs and skits routinely appear the next day. Our videotaped performance was widely covered, even replayed on several Sunday morning news shows. Although some pundits speculated that the spoof would simply attract more attention to the real Harry and

Louise ads, I was glad we raised questions about the tone of the insurance lobby's campaign and the absurdity of its claims. Moreover, it just felt good to inject some levity into an otherwise humorless situation.

While our little skit gave Washington politicos and journalists a good laugh, we knew we were still losing the public relations war on health care reform. Even a popular President armed with a bully pulpit could not match the hundreds of millions of dollars spent to distort an issue through negative and misleading advertisements and other means. We also were confronting the power of the pharmaceutical companies, who feared that controlling the prices of prescription drugs would diminish their profits, and the insurance industry, which spared no expense in its campaign against universal coverage. And some of our supporters were losing enthusiasm for the plan because it didn't fulfill all of their wishes. Finally, our proposal for reform was inherently complex—just like the health care problem itself—which made it a public relations nightmare. Virtually every interest group could find something objectionable in the plan.

We were discovering that some opposition to health care reform, like Whitewater, was part of a political war that was bigger than Bill or the issues we championed. We were on the front lines of an increasingly hostile ideological conflict between centrist Democrats and a Republican Party that was swinging further and further to the right. At stake were American notions of government and democracy and the direction our country would take for years to come. We soon learned that nothing was off-limits in this war and that the other side was far better armed with the tools of political battle: money, media and organization.

Four months earlier, in December 1993, Republican strategist and writer William Kristol, a Chief of Staff to former Vice President Dan Quayle and Chairman of the Project for the Republican Future, had sent a memorandum to Republican congressional leaders urging them to kill health care reform. The plan, he wrote in the memo, is a "serious political threat to the Republican party," and its demise would be "a monumental setback for the President." He wasn't objecting to the plan on its merits; he was applying partisan political logic. He instructed Republicans not to negotiate on the bill or to compromise. The only good strategy, according to Kristol, was to kill the plan outright. The memo didn't mention the millions of Americans without insurance.

In line with the Kristol memo, Jack Kemp and former Reagan Cabinet member William Bennett helped the GOP with targeted radio and television advertising against health care reform. In cities or towns I visited to promote the plan, the airwaves in the region would be flooded with ads critical of reform.

Kristol's memo to the Republican congressional leaders had the desired effect. With the 1994 midterm elections looming in November, moderate Republicans in Congress who were committed to reform began to distance themselves from the administration's plan. Senator Dole was genuinely interested in health care reform but wanted to run for President in 1996. He couldn't hand incumbent Bill Clinton any more legislative victories, particularly after Bill's successes on the budget, the Brady bill and NAFTA. We had offered to work with Senator Dole on a joint bill and, by extension, to jointly share the credit if it passed. The Senator had suggested that we present our bill first and then work out a compromise. It never happened. Kristol's strategy was taking hold.

With every step forward, we seemed to take two steps back. Two important business groups—the Chamber of Commerce and the National Association of Manufacturers—had told Ira in mid-1993 they could live with one key component of the bill, the employer mandate, which would require businesses with more than fifty employees to offer health insurance to their workforces. These business groups knew that most large employers already provided health insurance and concluded that the mandate would eliminate free riders who did not. By the end of March 1994, however, when a subcommittee of the House Ways and Means Committee voted 6–5 for the employer mandate, these two groups, pressured by Republicans and reform opponents, had flipped their positions. The mandate was clearly controversial, and Bill began making concessions and compromises with Congress. Although he had threatened to veto any legislation that didn't include universal coverage, he indicated that he could support something less. This was part of the natural give-and-take expected during legislative bargaining, and it opened the way for the Senate to consider a proposal, sponsored by members of the Finance Committee under Senator Moynihan, to cover 95 percent of all Americans instead of 100 percent. Even that concession didn't produce significantly more allies. In fact, we lost support among some hard-liners who felt that by agreeing to anything less than 100 percent, we were deserting the cause.

In the spring, Dan Rostenkowski was indicted on seventeen counts of conspiring to defraud the government. We lost a key ally in the House as he eventually resigned and was convicted. This followed the disappointing news that Senate Majority Leader George Mitchell had decided not to run for reelection, which meant that the most powerful Democrat in the Senate and the champion of our bill was now, in effect, a lame duck.

We also found out that health care reform represented a steep learning curve for more than a few members of Congress. Given the volume of bills they are expected to vote on, most members focus on legislation related to their committee assignments and don't have time to learn the intricacies of every issue before the House or Senate. But I was surprised to encounter more than one Congressman who didn't know the difference between Medicare and Medicaid, both federally funded health insurance programs. Others had no idea what kind of health insurance coverage they received from the government. Newt Gingrich, who in 1995 would become Republican Speaker of the House, contended during an appearance on *Meet the Press* in 1994 that he didn't have government health insurance but bought it from Blue Cross–Blue Shield. In fact, his policy was one of many offered to federal employees through the Federal Employees Health Benefits Plan. And the government covered 75 percent of the $400 monthly bill for Gingrich and other members of Congress.

This knowledge gap became apparent to me at a meeting I had in the Capitol one day with a group of Senators. Invited to answer questions about the Administration's plan, I had distributed a briefing book summarizing what we proposed. Senator Ted Kennedy, one of the true experts on health care and many other issues in the Senate, was leaning back on two legs of his chair as he listened to question after question posed by his colleagues. Finally, the front legs of his chair struck the floor and he barked out: "If you would just look on page thirty-four of the briefing material you'll find the answer to that question." He knew every detail—including page numbers—off the top of his head.

Even some of our allies in the advocacy community created problems. One of the most important organizations in the reform campaign was the American Association of Retired Persons, or AARP. The powerful senior citizens' lobby group began running its own ads in March 1994, insisting that Congress pass a health care reform bill that would require prescription coverage. The AARP was adamant about prescription drugs and so was I. Although the AARP intended to help us, the ad had a corrosive effect because it made people think that our plan did not contain a prescription drug provision—which, of course, it did.

I worked hard to keep the pro-reform forces together, under the umbrella of the Health Care Reform Project. But we could raise only about $15 million to run a public information campaign and to recruit speakers to fan out across the country. We were thoroughly outspent by our heavyweight corporate opponents who, according to estimates, infused at least $300 million into their campaign to defeat reform.

The insurance industry's distortions were so effective that many Americans didn't understand that key elements of reform—which they supported—were actually in the Clinton plan. One news story in *The Wall Street Journal* on March 10, 1994, summed up our dilemma under the headline MANY DON'T REALIZE IT'S THE CLINTON PLAN THEY LIKE. The writer explained that while Americans strongly supported specific elements in the Clinton plan, "Mr. Clinton is losing the battle to define his own health care bill. In the cacophony of negative television ads and sniping by critics, foes are raising doubts about the Clinton plan faster than the President and Hillary Rodham Clinton can explain it. Unless the Clintons can cut through the confusion, the outlook for passage of major elements of their bill is in doubt."

While Washington was caught up in health care reform and Whitewater, the rest of the world was not. In early May, the U.N. tightened sanctions on the military junta in Haiti, and a new wave of Haitian refugees headed to American shores. A crisis was building, and Bill felt he had to ask Al Gore to fill in for him on a trip to South Africa for Nelson Mandela's presidential inauguration. Tipper and I joined Al as members of the U.S. delegation. I was thrilled at the prospect of taking part in this momentous event. During the 1980s, I had supported the boycott of South Africa, hoping that the apartheid regime would bow to international pressure. On the day Mandela walked out of prison in February 1990, Bill woke Chelsea before dawn so together they could watch the drama unfold.

I traveled in a packed plane for the sixteen-hour flight to Johannesburg. My companions stayed up all night playing cards, listening to music and talking ecstatically about the historic change we were about to witness. After serving twenty-seven years in prison for plotting against South Africa's apartheid government, Nelson Mandela had won that country's first interracial election to become its first black President. The liberation struggle in South Africa was deeply linked with the

American civil rights movement and supported by African American leaders, many of whom were coming with us to honor Mandela.

We landed on the outskirts of Johannesburg, a sprawling modern city in South Africa's dry central highlands. That night we attended a performance at the famous Market Theatre, where for years Athol Fugard and other playwrights had defied government censors and depicted the agony of apartheid. Afterwards, we were treated to a buffet dinner featuring assorted African specialties along with the usual carved meats and salads. I wasn't as adventurous as Maggie and the rest of my staff who dared one another to sample the fried grasshoppers and grubs.

Our delegation drove north to the capital, Pretoria. Because the official transition of power didn't occur until the new President was sworn in, the President's stately residence was still occupied by F. W. de Klerk. The next morning, while Al Gore met with de Klerk and his ministers, Tipper and I had breakfast with Mrs. Marike de Klerk and the wives of other outgoing National Party officials. We sat in a wood-paneled breakfast room thickly decorated with ruffled fabrics and porcelain knickknacks. A lazy Susan in the middle of a big round table was heaped with the jams, breads, biscuits and eggs of a classic Dutch farm breakfast. Although we made light conversation about food, children and the weather, the moment was subsumed in the unspoken subtext: in a few hours, the world these women inhabited would disappear forever.

Fifty thousand people attended the inauguration, a spectacle of celebration, release and vindication. Everyone marveled at the orderly transfer of power in a country that had been so ravaged by racist fear and hatred. Colin Powell, a member of our delegation, was moved to tears during the flyover of jets from the South African Defense Force. Their contrails streaked across the sky, tinted with the red, black, green, blue, white and gold colors of the new national flag. A few years earlier, the same jets were a powerful symbol of apartheid's military power; now they were dipping their wings to honor their new black commander in chief.

Mandela's speech denounced discrimination on the basis of race and gender, two profoundly embedded prejudices in Africa and most of the rest of the world. As we were leaving the ceremony, I saw the Rev. Jesse Jackson weeping with joy. He leaned over and said to me, "Did you ever think any of us would live to see this day?"

We returned by motorcade to the President's residence to find it transformed. The long winding drive through green lawns, which just hours before had been lined with armed military men, was now arrayed with brightly costumed drummers and dancers from throughout South Africa. The mood was light and joyous, as if the air itself had changed in an afternoon. We were ushered into the house for cocktails and to mix and mingle with the dozens of visiting heads of state and their delegations. One of my challenges that afternoon was Fidel Castro. The State Department briefers had warned me that Castro wanted to meet me. They told me to avoid him at all costs, since we had no diplomatic relations with Cuba, not to mention a trade embargo.

"You can't shake hands with him," they told me. "You can't talk to him." Even if I accidentally bumped into him, the anti-Castro factions in Florida would go wild.

I frequently looked over my shoulder during the reception, watching for his bushy gray beard in the crowd of faces. In the middle of a fascinating conversation with somebody like King Mswati III of Swaziland, I'd suddenly spot Castro moving toward me, and I'd hightail it to a far corner of the room. It was ridiculous, but I knew that a single photograph, stray sentence or chance encounter could become news.

Lunch was served on the grounds under an enormous white canvas tent. Mandela rose to address his guests. I love listening to him speak in that slow, dignified manner that manages to be both formal and alive with good humor. He made the expected remarks to welcome us. Then he said something that left me in awe: While he was pleased to host so many dignitaries, he was most pleased to have in attendance three of his former jailers from Robben Island who had treated him with respect during his imprisonment. He asked them to stand so he could introduce them to the crowd.

His generosity of spirit was inspiring and humbling. For months I had been preoccupied with the hostility in Washington and the mean-spirited attacks connected to Whitewater, Vince Foster and the travel office. But here was Mandela, honoring three men who had held him prisoner.

When I got to know Mandela better, he explained that as a young man he had a quick temper. In prison, he learned to control his emotions in order to survive. His years in jail had given him the time and motivation to look deeply into his own heart and to deal with the pain he found. He reminded me that gratitude and forgiveness, which often result from pain and suffering, require tremendous discipline. The day his imprisonment ended, he told me, "as I walked out the door toward the gate that would lead to my freedom, I knew if I didn't leave my bitterness and hatred behind, I'd still be in prison."

Still pondering Mandela's example the night I returned from South Africa, I joined five former First Ladies at the National Garden Gala. I was the honorary Chair of the event at the U.S. Botanic Garden to help raise funds to construct a new garden that would be a living landmark on the Mall, dedicated to eight contemporary First Ladies and honoring our contributions to the nation.

I was delighted that Lady Bird Johnson was able to attend. She and I wrote each other during my years in the White House, and she was a comforting and affirming correspondent. I admired the quiet strength and grace she had brought to her position as First Lady. She began a beautification program that spread wildflowers along thousands of miles of U.S. highways and enhanced our appreciation of the natural landscape. Through Lady Bird's advocacy, a generation of Americans learned new respect for the environment and were inspired to preserve it. She also championed Head Start, the early learning program for disadvantaged children. And when it came to campaigning, she barnstormed the South for her husband in his 1964 race against Barry Goldwater. Throughout a difficult time in the White House, she understood that presidential politics required commitment and sacrifice. With her intelligence and compassion, she held her own in a world dominated by Lyndon Johnson's oversize personality. Disheartened by Washington, I valued her hard-won sense of perspective.

The photos from that gala evening were keepers: Lady Bird, Barbara Bush, Nancy Reagan, Rosalynn Carter, Betty Ford and me. It was quite a sight: all the living First Ladies standing together onstage—except for one.

Some months earlier, Jackie Kennedy Onassis had been diagnosed with non-Hodgkin's lymphoma, an often deadly but sometimes slow-moving cancer. As a result, she was unable to be with us. We'd been told that she had gone through surgery, but not how quickly she had weakened. True to character, she tried to keep her dying as private as she'd kept her life.

On May 19, 1994, Jackie died in her New York apartment, with Caroline, John and Maurice at her side. Early the following morning, Bill and I went to the Jacqueline Kennedy Garden off the east colonnade of the White House to share our thoughts with a gathering of press, staff and friends. Bill recognized her contributions to our country, while I talked about her selfless devotion to her children and grand-children: "She once explained the importance of spending time with family and said: 'If you bungle raising your children, I don't think whatever else you do matters very much.' " I could not have agreed more. I attended her funeral Mass in New York City at St. Ignatius Loyola Roman Catholic Church and then flew to Washington with her family and close friends. Bill met the plane at the airport and went with us to the grave where Jackie was buried beside President John F. Kennedy, their infant son, Patrick, and an unnamed stillborn daughter. After the graveside ceremony, we joined the extended Kennedy clan at Ethel Kennedy's nearby home, Hickory Hill.

Two weeks later, John F. Kennedy, Jr., sent Bill and me a handwritten letter that I cherish. "I wanted you both to understand how much your burgeoning friendship with my mother meant to her," he wrote. "Since she left Washington I believe she resisted ever connecting with it emotionally—or the institutional demands of being a former First Lady. It had much to do with the memories stirred and her desires to resist being cast in a lifelong role that didn't quite fit. However, she seemed profoundly happy and relieved to allow herself to reconnect with it through you. It helped her in a profound way—whether it was discussing the perils of raising children in those circumstances (perilous indeed) or perhaps it was the many similarities between your presidency and my father's."

In early June 1994, Bill and I traveled to England for the commemoration of the fiftieth anniversary of the Normandy invasion that set in motion the end of World War II in Europe. Her Majesty Queen Elizabeth II had invited us to spend the night on the royal yacht HMS *Britannia*, and I was excited by the prospect of getting to know the royal family. I had met Prince Charles the previous year at a small dinner party hosted by the Gores. He was delightful, with a quick wit and a self-deprecating humor. When Bill and I boarded the *Britannia*, we were taken to the Queen, Prince Philip and the Queen Mother, who greeted us with an offer of a drink. When I introduced my trip director, Kelly Craighead, the Queen Mother surprised us all by asking Kelly if she'd like to stay on the yacht to dine with her and a few of the Queen's young military aides.

Kelly said she would be delighted but would have to see if she could be released from her duties. Kelly followed me to my cabin and asked what she should do. I told her she should absolutely stay. Someone else could fill in for her at the formal dinner that night with the Queen and Prince Philip. She ran off to tell one of the military aides, only to return in a panic because she'd learned she was supposed to dress formally for dinner. Her black pantsuit wouldn't do. I pulled out all my dressy clothes and helped Kelly piece together a suitable outfit for dining with the Queen Mother.

At the grand dinner, I sat between Prince Philip and Prime Minister John Major at a head table long enough to accommodate all the Kings, Queens, Prime Ministers and Presidents in attendance. From the raised platform, I looked across the large, crowded room. More than five hundred guests were assembled to commemorate the Anglo-American alliance that proved victorious on D-Day. Among them were former Prime Minister Margaret Thatcher, whose career I had followed with great interest; Churchill's surviving daughter, Mary Soames; and his grandson, Pamela Harriman's son, Winston. Major was easy to talk to. I enjoyed chatting about personalities in the crowd and listened as he described the terrible automobile accident he'd had while working in Nigeria as a young man. He'd been immobilized for months and went through a long, painful recovery.

Prince Philip, a polished conversationalist, carefully divided his time between me and the woman on his other side, Her Majesty Queen Paola of Belgium. Literally pausing in "midchop," he turned his head from her to me and back again as he talked about sailing and the history of the *Britannia*.

The Queen, seated next to Bill, wore a sparkling diamond tiara that caught the light as she nodded and laughed at Bill's stories. She reminded me of my own mother in her appearance, politeness and reserve. I have great admiration and sympathy for the way she has discharged the duties she assumed as a young woman upon her father's death. Holding a demanding, high-profile role for decades through difficult and fast-changing times was hard for me to imagine in light of my more limited experience. When Chelsea was nine, Bill and I took her with us on a short vacation to London. All she wanted to do was to meet the Queen and Princess Diana, which in those days we couldn't arrange. I took her, however, to an exhibit documenting the history of all of England's Kings and Queens. She studied the display carefully, spending nearly one hour reading the description of each monarch and then going back through again. When she finished, she said, "Mommy, I think being a King or Queen is a very hard job."

The morning after our grand dinner, I met Princess Diana for the first time at the Drumhead Service, a traditional religious ceremony for "the Forces Committed," the point at which troops cannot be pulled back from battle. The ceremony was held on the grounds of a Royal Navy base, on a field surrounded by gardens that extended along an oceanfront esplanade. Among the veterans and spectators was Diana, estranged, though not yet divorced, from Prince Charles. She attended the ceremony alone. I watched as she greeted the crowd of supporters, who clearly doted on her. She had a presence that was captivating. Uncommonly beautiful, she used her eyes to draw people in, dropping her head forward to greet you while lifting her eyes upward. She radiated life and a sense of vulnerability that I found heartbreaking. Although there was little time to talk during this visit, I came to know and like her. Diana was a woman torn between competing needs and interests, but she genuinely wanted to make a contribution, to have her life count for something. She became an effective advocate for AIDS awareness and land mine eradication. She was also a devoted mother, and whenever we met, we discussed the challenge of raising children in the public spotlight.

Later that afternoon, we boarded the *Britannia* and sailed out into the English Channel, where we joined a long line of ships, including the *Jeremiah O'Brien*, one of the ships used by the U.S. government to ferry supplies to England during the war. We transferred to the USS *George Washington*, an aircraft carrier anchored off the French coast. This was my first visit to a carrier, a floating city with a population of six thousand sailors and Marines. While Bill worked on the speech he would deliver the next day, I took a tour that included the flight deck, one of the most dangerous workstations in the Armed Forces. Imagine the courage and training it requires to take off and land a fighter jet on that bobbing patch of American real estate in the middle of the ocean. From the captain's bridge high above the deck, I looked out over the enormous carrier and felt the power it represented. I ate dinner in the cafeteria-size galley with some of the crew members, most of whom looked about eighteen or nineteen years old. Fifty years earlier, young men their age had stormed the beaches of Normandy on D-Day.

Although I had read Stephen Ambrose's book *D-Day*, I was not prepared for the height of the cliffs that had to be scaled by Allied forces after they fought their way across the beaches on June 6, 1944. Pointe-du-Hoc looked impenetrable, and I listened with reverence to the veterans who had made that climb.

Bill's relationship with the military had gotten off to a rocky start, so a lot was riding on his speech about D-Day. Like me, he had opposed the Vietnam War, believing that it was misconceived and unwinnable. Because of his work during college for Senator Fulbright with the Senate Foreign Relations Committee in the late 1960s, he knew then what we all know now: The United States government had misled the public about the depth of our involvement, the strength of our Vietnamese allies, the Gulf of Tonkin incident, the success of our military strategy, casualty figures and other data that prolonged the conflict and cost more lives. Bill had tried to explain his deep misgivings about the war in a letter to the head of the University of Arkansas ROTC program in 1969. In deciding to withdraw from the program and submit to the draft lottery, he articulated the inner struggle so many young men felt about a country they loved and a war they couldn't support.

When I first met Bill, we talked incessantly about the Vietnam War, the draft and the contradictory obligations we felt as young Americans who loved our country but opposed that particular war. Both of us knew the anguish of those times—and each of us had friends who had enlisted, were drafted, resisted or became conscientious objectors. Four of Bill's classmates from high school in Hot Springs were killed in Vietnam. I knew that Bill respected military service, that he would have served if he had been called and that he would also have gladly enlisted in World War II, a war whose purpose was crystal clear. But Vietnam tested the intellect and conscience of many in my generation because it seemed contrary to America's national interests and values, not in furtherance of them. As the first modern President to have come of age during Vietnam, Bill carried with him into the White House the unresolved feelings of our country about that war. And he believed it was time to reconcile our differences as Americans and begin a new chapter of cooperation with our former enemy.

With the support of many Vietnam veterans serving in Congress, Bill lifted a U.S. trade embargo on Vietnam in 1994 and a year later normalized diplomatic relations between our countries. The Vietnamese government continued to make good faith efforts to help locate American servicemen missing in action or held as prisoners of war, and, in 2000, Bill would become the first American president to set foot on

Vietnamese soil since U.S. troops left in 1975. His courageous diplomatic actions paid tribute to more than 58,000 Americans who sacrificed their lives in the jungles of Southeast Asia and enabled our country
to heal an old wound and find common ground among ourselves and
with the Vietnamese people.

One of his first challenges as commander in chief became the
promise he made during the campaign to let gays and lesbians serve in
the military as long as their sexual orientation did not in any way compromise their performance or unit cohesion. I agreed with the commonsense position that the code of military conduct should be enforced
strictly against behavior, not sexual orientation. The issue surfaced in
early 1993 and became a battleground between strongly held opposing
convictions. Those who maintained that homosexuals had served with
distinction in every war in our history and should be permitted to continue serving were in a clear minority in the military and the Congress.
Public opinion was more closely divided, but as is often the case, those
who opposed change were more adamant and vocal than those in favor.
What I found disturbing was the hypocrisy. Just three years earlier during the Gulf War, soldiers known to be homosexual—both men and
women—were sent into harm's way because their country needed them
to fulfill its mission. After the war ended, when they were no longer
needed, they were discharged on the basis of their sexual orientation.
That seemed indefensible to me.

Bill knew the issue was a political loser, but it galled him that he
couldn't persuade the Joint Chiefs of Staff to align the reality—that
gays and lesbians have served, are serving and will always serve—with
an appropriate change in policy that enforced common behavior standards for all. After both the House and Senate expressed their opposition by veto-proof margins, Bill agreed to a compromise: the "Don't
Ask, Don't Tell" policy. Under the policy, a superior is forbidden to ask
a service member if he or she is homosexual. If a question is asked, there
is no obligation to answer. But the policy has not worked well. There
are still instances of beatings and harassment of suspected homosexuals,
and the number of homosexual discharges has actually increased. In
2000, our closest ally, Great Britain, changed its policy to permit homosexuals to serve, and there has been no reported difficulty; Canada
ended its ban on gays in 1992. We have a long way to go as a society before this issue is resolved. I just wish the opposition would listen to
Barry Goldwater, an icon of the American Right and an outspoken sup-

porter of gay rights, which he considered consistent with his conservative principles. On the issue of homosexuals in the military, he said, "You don't need to be straight to fight and die for your country. You just need to shoot straight."

Bill addressed the American veterans of our parents' generation in the speech he delivered at the World War II Normandy American Cemetery and Memorial in Colleville-sur-Mer: "We are the children of your sacrifice," he said. These brave Americans joined the armies and resistance fighters of Great Britain, Norway, France, Belgium, Holland, Denmark and others in standing up to Nazism and strengthening a historic alliance that continues to bind the United States and Europe half a century later. The "greatest generation" understood that Americans and Europeans were united in a shared enterprise, one that led to victory in the Cold War and inspired the spread of freedom and democracy across several continents. Given the uncertainties of today's world, America's historic ties to Europe, so evident on those Normandy beaches, remain a key to global security, prosperity and hopes for peace.

Bill's D-Day speech was particularly emotional for him because he had recently received a copy of his father's military record and the history of his unit, which participated in the invasion of Italy. Following the story of his father's service in several newspapers, Bill received a letter from a man living in New Jersey who had emigrated from Nettuno, Italy. As a young boy, he had been befriended by an American soldier who served in the motor pool of the invading army. The soldier, who had taught the youngster how to fix cars and trucks, was Bill's father, William Blythe. Bill was thrilled to hear about his father and felt that he was connecting with that young soldier—and the father he never knew—as he tried to express our generation's gratitude for all that he and millions of others had done for our nation and the world.

That trip had been emotional for me as well. I wanted Bill's Presidency to succeed not simply because he was my husband and I loved him, but because I loved my country and believed he was the right man to lead it at the end of the twentieth century.

MIDTERM BREAK

ARETHA FRANKLIN ROCKED THE ROSE GARDEN ONE unforgettable night in June as part of the In Performance concert series that we held at the White House and that were later televised. She strolled like a queen between tables of guests, who sat in rapt appreciation as Aretha soared through a repertoire of gospel and soul with the singer Lou Rawls. Then she moved on to show tunes and leaned in close to Bill, who swayed in his seat as she sang, "Smile, what's the use of crying . . ."

Ten days later Robert Fiske released the preliminary finding in his fast-moving Whitewater investigation: First, no one in the Clinton White House or Department of the Treasury had tried to influence the RTC inquiry. Second, Fiske concurred with the opinions of the FBI and Park Police that Vince Foster's death was a suicide. He further concluded that there was no evidence his suicide had anything to do with Whitewater.

To the dismay of many on the Republican Right, who had openly fueled speculation about Vince's death, Fiske issued no indictments. A few conservative commentators and members of Congress, such as North Carolina Republican Senator Lauch Faircloth, called for Fiske's head. Ironically, on the day Fiske's findings were made public, my husband inadvertently paved the way for his replacement by signing the renewal of the Independent Counsel Act sent to him by Congress. It was something he had promised to do, and he kept his word.

Because of the growing Republican criticism of Fiske, I had argued against signing the legislation unless the appointment of Fiske was grandfathered into the bill. I feared that the Republicans and their allies in the judiciary, led by Chief Justice William Rehnquist, would figure

out some way to remove Fiske because he was impartial and expedi-
tious. I shared my fears with Lloyd Cutler, who had replaced Bernie
Nussbaum as White House counsel. Lloyd is one of the great men of
Washington, counsel to President Carter and adviser to many other
political leaders. A first-rate lawyer, he helped build one of the most
prestigious law firms in America. When I told him what I feared, he
told me not to worry. Lloyd, a true gentleman, assumed he was dealing
with men of similar manners and even told me he would "eat his hat" if
Fiske was replaced.

According to the newly enacted law, the independent counsel had
to be chosen by a "Special Division," a panel of three federal judges appointed by the Chief Justice of the Supreme Court. Rehnquist had
handpicked David Sentelle, an ultraconservative Republican from
North Carolina, to head the Special Division.

According to news accounts, Judge Sentelle was seen in mid-July
having lunch with Faircloth and Senator Jesse Helms, another of my
husband's outspoken critics. It may have been a coincidence, and Sentelle later claimed that the three were merely old friends discussing
prostate problems. But on August 5, a few weeks after that lunch, the
Special Division announced the appointment of a new independent
counsel. Robert Fiske was out, replaced by Kenneth Starr.

Starr was a forty-eight-year-old Republican insider, a former appeals court judge who had stepped down to become Solicitor General
in the first Bush Administration, a traditional path to the Supreme
Court. He was a partner in Kirkland & Ellis, a law firm with a lucrative
business defending tobacco companies. Starr was a staunch conservative; unlike Fiske, he had never been a prosecutor. He had been outspoken about the Paula Jones lawsuit, appearing on TV that spring to
argue for the right of Jones to sue a sitting President, urging that the
case proceed quickly. He had also offered to write a friend of the court
brief on her behalf. Based on the evidence of these conflicts of interest,
five former Presidents of the American Bar Association called on Starr
to forgo serving as independent counsel. They also issued a statement
questioning the three-judge panel that selected him.

Starr's appointment greatly slowed the progress of the investigation. Most of Fiske's staff resigned rather than work for him; Starr did
not take a leave of absence from his law practice, as Fiske had, and thus
was a part-timer; Starr had zero criminal law experience, so he was
learning on the job. Despite the mandate of the statute that an indepen-

dent counsel conduct an investigation "in a prompt, responsible, and cost-effective manner," Starr never set a timetable or showed any sense of urgency, in contrast to Fiske, who intended to wrap up the investigation by the end of 1994. It appeared from the beginning that Starr's goal was to keep the issue alive at least through the 1996 election.

Given these troubling conflicts of interest and early warning signs, it was clear that Starr was replacing Fiske not to continue an independent investigation, but for partisan purposes. I knew immediately what we were facing, but I also knew there was nothing I could do about it. I had to trust our justice system and hope for the best. I did, however, remind Lloyd Cutler of his hat-eating offer and suggest he might choose a small one made of natural fibers.

Partisan politicking was nothing new in Washington; it came with the territory. But it was the politics of personal destruction—visceral, mean-spirited campaigns to ruin the lives of public figures—that I found disheartening and bad for the country.

All spring and summer, right-wing radio hosts with national audiences stirred up their listeners with terrifying tales from Washington. Rush Limbaugh routinely told his 20 million radio listeners that "Whitewater is about health care." And I finally understood that, yes, it was. The ongoing Whitewater investigation, despite Fiske's findings, was about undermining the progressive agenda by any means. Limbaugh and others rarely criticized the contents of the Health Security Act or any other policy the Democrats introduced. If you believed everything you heard on the airwaves in 1994, you would conclude that your President was a Communist, that the First Lady was a murderess and that together they had hatched a plot to take away your guns and force you to give up your family doctor (if you had one) for a Socialist health care system.

One afternoon in Seattle at the end of July, I pulled into town as part of the Health Security Express. Inspired by the Freedom Riders who traveled by bus across the South in the early sixties to spread the message of desegregation, health reform advocates organized this nationwide bus tour in the summer of 1994. The idea was to spread the word about the health care plan at the grassroots level and generate crowds from the West Coast to Washington, showing Congress that there was support for the bill.

We started in Portland, Oregon, where I sent off the first troop of riders. It was a lively event, despite the record-breaking heat and the vocal protesters who surrounded the site. As the buses pulled out, a small plane dragged a banner across the sky that read: "Beware the Phony Express." Not an inexpensive stunt.

Local and national radio hosts had been inciting protesters all week. One of them had urged listeners to come down and "show Hillary" what they thought of me. The call to arms attracted hundreds of hard-core right-wingers: militia supporters, tax protesters, clinic blockaders. At least half of the 4,500 people who came to my speech in Seattle were protesters.

The Secret Service warned me that we might run into trouble. For once, I agreed to wear a bulletproof vest. By then I had become accustomed to the constant presence of security, to having intimate conversations within earshot of Secret Service men and women who I sometimes thought knew more about me and my family than did my closest friends. They had urged me before to avoid certain places or to wear protective clothing; now, for the first time, I heeded their warning. It was one of the few times I felt in real physical danger. During the rally, I could hardly hear my own voice over the booing and heckling. After the speech ended and we were driving away from the stage, hundreds of protesters swarmed around the limousine. What I could see from the car was a crowd of men who seemed to be in their twenties and thirties. I'll never forget the look in their eyes and their twisted mouths as they screamed at me while the agents pushed them away. The Secret Service made several arrests that day, and they confiscated two guns and a knife hidden in the crowd.

Neither random nor spontaneous, this protest was part of a well-organized campaign to disrupt the health care reform bus caravan and neutralize its message, according to journalists David Broder and Haynes Johnson. Everywhere the buses stopped, they were met with demonstrators. The protests were openly sponsored by a benign-sounding political interest group called Citizens for a Sound Economy (CSE). Reporters eventually discovered and disclosed the fact that CSE worked in concert with Newt Gingrich's Washington office. And, as Broder and Johnson wrote in their book, *The System*, the generous sponsor behind the group was none other than the reclusive but increasingly active Richard Mellon Scaife, the right-wing billionaire who was also financing the Arkansas Project.

When we returned to Washington after the bus trip, we continued to try to work for a compromise with Republicans in Congress on various aspects of reform. I admired Senator John Chafee of Rhode Island for his principled stands and decent manner; he had been an early supporter of reform and an advocate for universal coverage. Senator Chafee had worked with his Republican colleagues to develop his own thoughtful proposal and hoped that, by melding his plan with ours, he would garner enough bipartisan support to pass a bill. Chafee made heroic efforts to bridge the gap between Republicans and Democrats, keeping up his effort until he was the lone Republican still fighting for reform. Finally, he, too, abandoned his cause. Without a single Republican supporter, health care reform was like a patient on life support being given last rites.

Even so, we made a last-ditch effort to bring the Republicans to some sort of compromise. Senator Kennedy pressed Chafee one more time, to no avail. At a heated meeting in the White House, some of Bill's advisers argued that he should publicly address the nation and explain how the Republican leadership had tried to derail reform. He could talk about his attempts to build a consensus and ask why Dole, Gingrich and others were so unwilling to come to the bargaining table. His message would be a presidential challenge to Congress to get the job done. Another group argued vehemently that it was more prudent to let the bill die without fanfare. In advance of the elections, they believed we didn't need another controversy and worried that a presidential statement would draw greater attention to a political failure.

I thought that the country needed to see the President fighting, even if he lost, and that we should try for a vote in the Senate. The Finance Committee's compromise had been voted out of the committee, and Senator Mitchell, as Majority Leader, could bring it directly to the floor. Even if that strategy resulted in a Republican filibuster, as some in our camp predicted, I thought it could work in our favor. Members of Congress would be more accountable to their constituents come the November elections. And Democrats would not be left in the worst of both worlds: the Republicans never having to vote against reform, and the Democratic majority failing to pass new legislation. The more cautious strategy won out, and health care faded with barely a whimper. I still think that was the wrong call. Giving up without one last public fight demoralized Democrats and let the opposition rewrite history.

After twenty months, we conceded defeat. We knew we had alienated a wide assortment of health care industry experts and professionals, as well as some of our own legislative allies. Ultimately, we could never convince the vast majority of Americans who have health insurance that they wouldn't have to give up benefits and medical choices to help the minority of Americans without coverage. Nor could we persuade them that reform would protect them from losing insurance and would make their medical care more affordable in the future.

Bill and I were disappointed and discouraged. I knew I had contributed to our failure, both because of my own missteps and because I underestimated the resistance I would meet as a First Lady with a policy mission. I also felt bad for Ira, who had taken a lot of criticism that was unfair and unwarranted. Bill appreciated his hard work and asked him to head up the Administration's Working Group on Electronic Commerce. Ira did a great job establishing the government's approach for encouraging electronic commerce. He was soon praised in the business community for his insight and became known as the "Internet Czar." But our most critical mistake was trying to do too much, too fast.

That said, I still believe we were right to try. Our work in 1993 and 1994 paved the way for what several economists dubbed the "Hillary Factor," the purposeful restraint on price increases by medical providers and pharmaceutical companies during the 1990s. It also helped to create the ideas and political will that led to important smaller reforms in the years following. Thanks to the leadership of Senator Kennedy and Senator Nancy Kassebaum, a Kansas Republican, the nation now has a law guaranteeing that workers will not lose their insurance when they change jobs. I worked behind the scenes with Senator Kennedy to help create the Children's Health Insurance Program (CHIP), which by 2003 provided coverage to more than 5 million children of working parents too well off for Medicaid but unable to afford private insurance. CHIP represented the largest expansion of public health insurance coverage since the passage of Medicaid in 1965, and it helped reduce the number of Americans without health insurance for the first time in twelve years.

Bill signed a series of bills that I had worked for, including laws ensuring that women be allowed to stay in the hospital for more than twenty-four hours after childbirth, promoting mammography and prostate screening, increasing research into diabetes and improving childhood vaccination rates so that 90 percent of all two-year-olds were immunized against the most serious childhood illnesses for the first time ever. Bill also took on the tobacco lobby and began seriously addressing HIV/AIDS here at home and around the world. He used his presidential prerogative to extend patients' rights to more than eighty-five million Americans and their dependents enrolled in federal health plans and to those covered by Medicare, Medicaid and the Veterans Health System. None of these actions represented a seismic shift on the order of the Health Security Act. But collectively, these reforms of health care policy improved conditions for tens of millions of Americans.

On balance, I think we made the right decision to try to reform the whole system. By 2002, with the economy in trouble again and the financial savings of managed care in the nineties having leveled out, health insurance costs were again rising much faster than inflation, the number of people without insurance was going up and seniors on Medicare still didn't have prescription drug coverage. The people who financed the Harry and Louise ads may be better off, but the American people aren't. Someday we will fix the system. When we do, it will be the result of more than fifty years of efforts by Harry Truman, Richard Nixon, Jimmy Carter and Bill and me. Yes, I'm still glad we tried.

Bill's name wouldn't appear on a ballot in the 1994 midterm congressional election, but we both knew that his Presidency would be part of the electoral calculus—and that the health care setback would likely affect the outcome. There were other factors, including one of the few predictable trends in U.S. politics: Conventional wisdom says that the party in control of the White House usually loses congressional seats in the midterm elections. This may reflect a deep-rooted desire among voters to maintain a balance of power in Washington—never let the President have so much authority that he believes he can act like a King. One way to keep him in line is to reduce his support in Congress. When the economy is down, or other factors diminish the President's popularity, the midterm losses can be greater.

Newt Gingrich and his cohort of self-described Republican "revolutionaries" appeared eager to capitalize on the trend. In September, Gingrich stood on the steps of the Capitol, surrounded by like-minded members, to unveil his game plan for midterm victory: a "Contract with America." The Contract, which provided the basis for Republican proposals to abolish the Department of Education, make deep spending cuts in Medicare, Medicaid, education and the environment and slash tax credits for the working poor, came to be known around the White House as the "Contract *on* America" because of the damage it would cause our country. The numbers behind its contradictory agenda didn't add up. You can't increase military spending, decrease taxes and balance the federal budget unless you cut much of what the government does. Gingrich counted on voters to skip the arithmetic. The Contract was a strategy to nationalize local elections and turn congressional races into a referendum on Republican terms: negative on the Clinton Administration and positive on their Contract.

In American politics, candidates and public officials rely on polls to gauge opinion, but few want to admit it, because they fear that the media and the public will accuse them of pandering to voters. But polls are not supposed to tell politicians what to believe or which policies to pursue; they are diagnostic tools to help politicians make the most effective case for a certain course of action based on an understanding of voter response. Doctors listen to your heart with a stethoscope; politicians listen to voters with a poll. In campaigns, polling helps candidates identify their strengths and weaknesses. Once elected officials are in office, judicious poll-taking can help them communicate effectively to achieve their goals. The best political polling is part statistical science, part psychology and part alchemy. The key is this: To get helpful answers, you must ask the right questions of a representative number of likely voters.

As we moved toward the midterm elections in November, Bill's political advisers assured us that the Democrats were in relatively good shape. But I was worried. After weeks of flying all over the country campaigning for Democratic candidates, I couldn't shake the feeling that the public polls commissioned by outside groups, as well as those taken by Democratic pollsters, were off base. I suspected that pollsters were not measuring, beneath the surface of American politics, the currents of vehement opposition on the Right and the demoralized indifference among our supporters. One of the secrets of understanding polls is to identify the intensity of voters' feelings. A majority of voters may say they care about sensible gun safety measures, but they are not as adamant as the minority of voters who oppose any kind of gun control. The intense voters show up to vote for or against a candidate based on that one position, sometimes known as a wedge issue. The majority vote on a host of other issues or don't vote at all. I knew that many of the Administration's accomplishments could be framed as wedge issues. Most Republican voters were intensely opposed to the upper-income tax increase for deficit reduction, the Brady bill and the assault weapons ban, which had passed in 1994 and made it illegal to manufacture, sell or possess nineteen of the most dangerous semi-automatic weapons. The National Rifle Association, the religious Right and anti-tax interest groups were more motivated than ever.

I also knew that some core Democratic supporters felt disillusioned by our failure to reform health care or betrayed by the Administration's successful push for NAFTA, and I feared that their disappointment might overshadow all the positive accomplishments of the Administration and the Democratic leadership. There seemed little urgency among Democrats to get out the vote. And it was too early for many independent or swing voters to feel the improvement in the economy or see the salutary effects of a reduced deficit on interest rates and job growth.

In October, I called Dick Morris for an outside opinion about our prospects. Bill and I considered Morris a creative pollster and a brilliant strategist, but he came with serious baggage. First of all, he had no compunction about working both sides of the aisle and all sides of an issue. Although he had helped Bill win five gubernatorial races, he also worked for conservative Republican Senators Trent Lott of Mississippi and Jesse Helms of North Carolina. Morris's specialty was identifying the swing voters who seesawed between the two parties. His advice was sometimes off-the-wall; you had to sift through it to extract the useful insights and ideas. And he had the people skills of a porcupine. Nonetheless, I thought Morris's analysis might be instructive, if we could involve him carefully and quietly. With his skeptical views about politics and people, Morris served as a counterweight to the ever optimistic Bill Clinton. Where Bill saw a silver lining in every cloud, Morris saw thunderstorms.

Starting in 1978, Morris worked for Bill on all his gubernatorial campaigns except the one he lost in 1980. But by 1991, Morris had picked up more Republican candidates, and nobody in the Democratic power structure liked or trusted him. Bill's advisers convinced him not to use Morris for his presidential campaign. I phoned him in October of 1994.

"Dick," I said, "this election doesn't seem right to me." I told him I didn't believe the positive polls and wanted to know what he thought. "If I can get Bill to call you, will you help?"

Morris was working for four Republican candidates, but that wasn't the source of his reluctance.

"I don't like the way I was treated, Hillary," said Morris in his rapid-fire New York accent. "People were so mean to me."

"I know, I know, Dick. But people find you difficult." I assured him that he would just be talking to Bill and me and that we were trying to understand the mood of the voters and what Democrats wanted to do. Morris couldn't resist the challenge. He quietly designed a set of questions to measure the national mood and shared the results of his polling, which were discouraging. Despite the giant economic strides Bill had made—the deficit was finally coming back under control, hundreds of thousands of jobs had been created and the economy was starting to grow—the recovery hadn't fully taken hold and most people just didn't believe it yet. Many who did wouldn't give Democrats any credit for the turnaround. The party, Morris told us, was in deep trouble, and the best hope for turning things around would be for Democratic candidates to emphasize the concrete victories that people could acknowledge and applaud, such as the Brady bill, Family Leave and AmeriCorps. He argued that doing this might encourage Democratic turnout. Instead of running against the Contract, which was what most Democratic candidates were doing, we needed to be more assertive about Democratic accomplishments. Bill agreed and tried to persuade congressional leaders to claim credit for what they had done and to defend themselves against the GOP onslaught.

Two weeks before Election Day, Bill and I took a brief break from our concerns about the midterm election and traveled to the Middle East, where Bill witnessed the signing of the Israeli-Jordanian peace agreement. And I celebrated my forty-seventh birthday in three different countries—Egypt, Jordan and Israel. On October 26, I saw the Pyramids at Giza in the morning light, and while Bill met with President Mubarak and Yasir Arafat to discuss the Middle East peace process, President Mubarak's wife, Suzanne, hosted a birthday breakfast, complete with cake, in a dining room overlooking the Sphinx.

Hosni and Suzanne Mubarak are an impressive couple. Suzanne has a master's degree in sociology and has been an energetic advocate for improved opportunities and education for women and children in Egypt, despite some opposition to these efforts from Islamic fundamentalists. President Mubarak has the manner and visage of an ancient Pharaoh—and is occasionally compared to one today. He has held power since the 1981 assassination of Anwar Sadat. In those decades, he has tried to govern Egypt while controlling Muslim extremists who have made several attempts to assassinate him. Like other Arab leaders whom I have met, Mubarak recognizes the dilemma he faces in governing a country beset by tensions between a Western-oriented educated minority that wants to pursue modernization and the more conservative majority, whose fear over the demise of its values and traditional ways of life can be politicized. Walking that tightrope—and staying alive—is a daunting challenge, and Mubarak's tactics occasionally have led to criticisms that he is too autocratic.

We flew from Cairo to the Great Rift Valley in Jordan for the signing of the peace treaty between Jordan and Israel, which ended an official state of war between the two countries. The desert setting at the Arava crossing on the border reminded me of the scenery in *The Ten Commandments*. But the pageantry and grandeur of the event made for a story more dramatic than any out of Hollywood. Two visionary leaders were taking personal and political risks for peace. Battle-hardened soldiers, Prime Minister Yitzhak Rabin and King Hussein bin Talal never gave up on their hopes for a better future for their people.

One did not need to know that Hussein was descended from the Prophet Muhammad to be struck immediately by his arresting presence and innate nobility. Though small in stature, he had a commanding air. He conveyed a unique combination of gentleness and power. His speech was deferential, marked by the liberal use of "sir" and "ma'am." Yet his ready smile and modest manner underscored his dignity and strength. He was a survivor who intended to carve out a place for his nation in a dangerous neighborhood.

His partner in life, Queen Noor, the former Lisa Najeeb Halaby, is an American-born Princeton graduate. Her father, the former Chairman of Pan American Airlines, was of Syrian-Lebanese descent, and her mother was Swedish. Noor, who has a degree in architecture and urban planning, was working as Director of Planning for Royal Jordanian Airlines when she met the King, fell in love and married him. She glowed with pride and affection in his presence and that of their children, laughing easily and often with them. She became deeply involved in the educational and economic development of her adopted country and represented its positions and aspirations in America and around the world. With her intelligence and charm and the backing of her husband, she nudged her nation toward a more modern approach to women's and children's issues. Bill and I looked forward to any private time we could schedule with the King and Queen.

On that blistering hot afternoon in the Rift Valley, Noor, dressed in turquoise, as beautiful as any model, visibly delighted in her soldier King's commitment to peace. I coincidentally also wore turquoise, which prompted a remark from a woman in the crowd: "Now we know the color of peace is turquoise."

After the ceremony, Bill and I drove with the King and Queen to their vacation home in Aqaba on the Red Sea. Noor surprised me with my second birthday cake of the day, topped with trick candles that I could not blow out. The King, in on the joke, jumped up and offered to help. He was no more successful than I. With a twinkle in his eye, the King proclaimed: "Sometimes even a King's commands are not fol-lowed." I think often of that perfect afternoon when hope for peace was so high.

Later that day, Bill became the first American President to address a joint session of the Jordanian Parliament in the capital, Amman. Jet lag had begun to take its toll, and the traveling party was exhausted. I sat in the gallery watching Bill speak while all around me the heads of White House staff and cabinet officials began snapping back as one after another lost the battle to stay awake. I persevered by digging my nails into my palms and pinching my arms—a trick my Secret Service agents had taught me. I got my second wind in time for a private dinner with the King and Queen at their official residence. Rather than a for-mal palace, they lived in a large comfortable home, tastefully but modestly furnished. The four of us ate at a small round table in the cor-ner of a warm and inviting room. We spent the night in al-Hashimiya Palace, a modern royal guest home on a hill northwest of town with a splendid view of the sun-bleached hills and minarets of the Hashemite desert kingdom.

From Jordan we went to Israel, where Leah Rabin had a third birthday cake waiting for me and Bill delivered another historic ad-dress—this time before the Israeli Knesset in Jerusalem. Heading back home, I believed I was leaving Israel another step closer to peace and security.

This trip highlighted Bill's milestones in foreign affairs. In addition to his pivotal role in easing the tensions in the Middle East, he was now focusing on the decades-long Troubles in Northern Ireland. And, after a harrowing year of diplomacy and the landing of American troops in

Haiti, the junta had finally agreed to step down and return the elected President, Jean-Bertrand Aristide, to power. Out of sight of the public and press, a nuclear crisis in North Korea had been defused for the time being, as the result of a 1994 accord in which North Korea agreed to freeze and ultimately to dismantle its dangerous nuclear weapons program in exchange for aid from the United States, Japan and South Korea. Although we later learned that the North Koreans breached the spirit, if not the letter, of that agreement, at the time it averted a potential military conflict. Had the agreement not been reached, North Korea could have produced enough plutonium by the year 2002 to make dozens of nuclear weapons, or become a plutonium factory, selling the world's most lethal substance to the highest bidder.

Bill's actions on the world's stage gave him a bump in the opinion polls in the last week of October, and he was urged to get out on the campaign trail to support Democratic candidates. As always, he solicited opinions from a variety of friends and confidants, formal and informal advisers.

I felt it might be better for Bill not to campaign so much if the American people preferred seeing him as a statesman, not a politician. In the end, Bill couldn't resist the lure of the campaign trail and became campaigner-in-chief for his party.

It had been an uneasy season, both out on the hustings and back at the White House, where two unsettling incidents had occurred. In September, a man crashed a small plane into the Executive Mansion, just west of the South Portico entrance. Fortuitously, we were sleeping in Blair House that night because the renovations of the heating and air-conditioning system in the residence forced us out of our private quarters. The pilot was killed in the wreck, and no one knows exactly why he staged his stunt. Apparently, he was depressed and looking for attention but may not have meant to kill himself. In retrospect, the fact that he could so easily breach security should have made everyone more aware of the dangers even a small plane could pose.

Then, on October 29, I was at a campaign event with Senator Dianne Feinstein at the Palace of Fine Arts Theatre in San Francisco when the Secret Service ushered me into a small side room. The head of my detail, George Rogers, told me the President was on the phone and wanted to talk to me. "I don't want you to worry," Bill said, "but you're going to hear that someone just shot at the White House." A man in a raincoat had been lingering at the fence along Pennsylvania

Avenue when he suddenly pulled a semi-automatic rifle from under his coat and opened fire. Several passersby tackled him before he could reload and, miraculously, nobody was injured. It was a Saturday, and Chelsea was at a friend's house while Bill was upstairs watching a football game. They were never in physical danger, but it was disconcerting to learn that just before he started shooting, the gunman had seen a tall, white-haired visitor on the grounds who looked from a distance like the President. The shooter was an unbalanced gun advocate who had made threatening calls to a Senator's office because he was angry about the Brady bill and the assault weapons ban. The new law had prevented him from buying a pistol a month earlier. By the time I red-eyed back to the White House, everything looked normal, except for a few bullet holes in the West Wing facade.

Later that day, Bill and I spoke to Dick Morris on the speakerphone in my little study next to the master bedroom in the White House. He had analyzed the polling data he'd amassed and told us we were going to lose both the House and the Senate decisively.

I absorbed the bad news that confirmed my gut instincts. Bill, too, believed Morris's assessment. He did the only thing he thought would help, heading out to campaign even harder. That week he barnstormed Detroit, Duluth and points west and east. It didn't make much difference.

I began my schedule on Election Day much as I would any other. I greeted Eeva Ahtisaari, First Lady of Finland, and Tipper Gore and I met with Marike de Klerk, the former First Lady of South Africa, who was visiting Washington. Toward the end of the afternoon, the mood in the White House corridors was funereal.

Bill and I had dinner with Chelsea in the little kitchen on the second floor. We wanted to be alone as we absorbed the election returns, which forecast a full-blown disaster. Although Senator Feinstein narrowly won reelection, the Democrats lost eight Senate seats and an astounding fifty-four seats in the House—ushering in the first Republican majority since the Eisenhower Administration. Democratic incumbents were routed everywhere. Party giants like Speaker Tom Foley of Washington and Governor Mario Cuomo of New York lost their reelection bids. My friend Ann Richards lost the Governorship of Texas to a man with a famous name: George W. Bush.

Chelsea eventually retreated to her bedroom to prepare for another school day. Bill and I sat alone at the kitchen table, monitoring the tallies on the television screen and trying to make sense of the results. The American people had sent us a powerful message. The election turnout was pitifully low, with less than half of registered voters coming to the polls and significantly more Democrats than Republicans staying home. The only flicker of light for us in this dismal landscape was that the Republicans' "huge mandate" reflected the votes of less than a quarter of the electorate.

This fact, however, did nothing to moderate Newt Gingrich's glee as he faced the cameras that night to claim credit for the Republican sweep. He already knew that he would become the next Speaker of the House, the first Republican to hold that position since 1954. He magnanimously offered to work with Democrats to push the Contract with America through Congress in record time. It was disheartening to imagine the next two years with a Republican-controlled House and Senate. The political battles would be even harder, and the Administration would be on the defensive to keep intact the gains already made for the country. With Republican leadership calling the shots, the Congress would likely demonstrate the accuracy of Lyndon Johnson's aphorism: "Democrats legislate; Republicans investigate."

Deflated and disappointed, I wondered how much I was to blame for the debacle: whether we had lost the election over health care; whether I had gambled on the country's acceptance of my active role and lost. And I struggled to understand how I had become such a lightning rod for people's anger.

Bill was miserable, and it was painful to watch someone I loved so much hurting so deeply. He had tried to do what he thought was right for America, and he knew that both his successes and failures had helped to defeat his friends and allies. I remembered how he felt when he'd lost in 1974 and 1980; this was worse. The stakes were higher, and he felt he'd let his party down.

It would take time, but Bill was determined to understand what went wrong with this election and to figure out how to articulate and reassert his agenda. As always, we started a conversation that would continue for months. We held meetings with friends and advisers to focus on what Bill should do next. More than anything, I wanted Bill's Presidency to succeed. I believed in him and his hopes for the nation's future. I also knew I wanted to be a helpful partner for him and an effective advocate for the issues I had cared about throughout my life. I just didn't know how I was going to get there from here.

CONVERSATIONS
WITH ELEANOR

There's an old chinese curse, "may you live in interesting times," that became a running joke in our family. Bill and I would ask each other, "Well, are you having an interesting time yet?" Interesting didn't describe the experience. The weeks following the disastrous midterm elections were among the most difficult of my White House years. On my better days, I tried to view the defeat as part of the ebb and flow of the electoral cycle, akin to a political market correction. On bad days, I faulted myself for botching health care, coming on too strong and galvanizing our opponents. There were plenty of people—inside and outside the White House—who were ready to point fingers. It was hard to ignore the grumbling, but Bill and I focused on what we could do to rally our forces. We had to develop a new strategy for a new environment.

One dreary November morning, I stopped by my office after a meeting with Bill in the Oval Office and glanced at the framed photograph of Eleanor Roosevelt displayed on a table. I am a huge fan of Mrs. Roosevelt, and I have long collected portraits and mementos from her career. Seeing her calm, determined visage brought to mind some of her wise words: "A woman is like a teabag," Mrs. Roosevelt said. "You never know how strong she is until she's in hot water." It was time for another talk with Eleanor.

I often joked in my speeches that I had imaginary conversations with Mrs. Roosevelt to solicit her advice on a range of subjects. It's actually a useful mental exercise to help analyze problems, provided you choose the right person to visualize. Eleanor Roosevelt was ideal. I had been tracking her career as one of America's most controversial First Ladies, sometimes quite literally. Wherever I ventured, Mrs. Roosevelt seemed to have been there before me. I have visited dust bowl towns, poor neighborhoods in New York City and outposts as remote as Uzbekistan where Eleanor already had blazed a trail. She championed many causes that are important to me: civil rights, child labor laws, refugees and human rights. She drew harsh criticism from the media and some in government for daring to define the role of First Lady in her own terms. Eleanor was called everything from a Communist agitator to a homely old meddler. She rankled members of her husband's administration—Interior Secretary Harold Ickes, Sr. (father of Bill's Deputy Chief of Staff), complained that she should stop interfering and "stick to her knitting"—and she drove FBI Director J. Edgar Hoover crazy. But her spirit and commitment were indomitable, and she never let her critics slow her down.

So, what would Mrs. Roosevelt have to say about my present predicament? Not much, I thought. In her view, there was no point in agonizing over day-to-day setbacks. You simply had to press on and do the best you could under the circumstances.

Controversy can be terribly isolating, but Eleanor Roosevelt had good friends she relied on for support when she felt unsure or besieged in the world of politics. FDR's trusted adviser Louis Howe had been her confidant, as were Associated Press reporter Lorena Hickok and her personal secretary, Malvina "Tommy" Thompson.

I was fortunate to have a wonderful, loyal staff and a large circle of friends. Although I have trouble imagining Mrs. Roosevelt blowing off steam with her confidants, that's what I did. Arkansas friends Diane Blair and Ann Henry, who visited the White House during those post-election weeks, knew me well, and they offered me personal support as well as helpful perspectives on politics and history.

Friends from around the country and overseas called to see how I was holding up. Queen Noor, something of a news junkie, followed American politics from Amman. She phoned me shortly after the midterm elections to boost my spirits. When her family faced tough times, she told me, they told one another to "soldier on." I liked that phrase and began using it to encourage my staff. Sometimes, though, I was the one who needed the pep talk.

One morning near the end of November, Maggie Williams called a meeting of ten women whose opinions I especially valued: Patti, my scheduler; Ann, the White House social secretary; Lisa, my press secretary; Lissa, my speechwriter; Melanne, my Deputy Chief of Staff; Mandy Grunwald; Susan Thomases; Ann Lewis, a longtime Democratic activist and shrewd political analyst who appeared often on television defending my agenda and the Administration's; and Evelyn Lieberman, a formidable presence in Hillaryland where she ran interference on operations and logistics. She later became the first woman to serve as Deputy Chief of Staff at the White House and was subsequently appointed Undersecretary of State for Public Diplomacy and Public Affairs under Madeleine Albright. These women had been getting together once a week to discuss policy ideas and political strategies. Evelyn, in her usual brassy way, had coined a name for the all-female gatherings: "the Chix meetings." Because they were lively, broadranging and completely off-the-record, I participated whenever I could.

The Chix had assembled for this meeting in the historic Map Room on the first floor of the Residence. This is where President Franklin D. Roosevelt, along with Winston Churchill and other Allied leaders, plotted troop movements during World War II on military maps displayed on the walls. Thirty years later, during the Vietnam War, then–Secretary of State Henry Kissinger and the Soviet Ambassador to the United States met in the Map Room after President Nixon ordered the mining of Haiphong Harbor. Early in the Ford Administration, the room was converted into a storage area.

When I discovered its history, I decided to refurbish the Map Room and restore its grandeur. I located one of FDR's original strategy maps showing the Allied positions in Europe in 1945. The map had been rolled up and saved by the President's young military aide, George Elsey, who donated it to the White House when he learned that I wanted to restore the room. I hung it over the fireplace.

The map evoked emotional reactions from visitors who had lived through World War II. When Professor Uwe Reinhardt, a German-born economist who advised me about health care, saw it in the Map Room, his eyes filled with tears. He told me that, as a young boy, he and his mother were trapped in Germany while his father had been sent to the Russian front. Uwe used the map to show me where he and his mother hid to avoid the fighting and bombing, and how the American soldiers had rescued them. Another time, Bill and I had dinner in front of the fireplace in the Map Room with Hilary Jones, an old friend from Arkansas who had served in the European Theater. Hilary used the map to trace the path his unit had taken as they fought their way north from Italy.

Given the history of the room, it seemed appropriate that a meeting to map my strategy should take place there. Maggie convened these meetings because she understood that in the pressure cooker of the White House it was important for me to have a place where I could say whatever was on my mind without worrying about misinterpretation, or leaks to the press. She thought these meetings would help all of us—especially me—refocus on the issues that mattered and reaffirm our commitment to the Administration's agenda.

The women were already seated around a large square table when I walked in. Until that moment, I had been able to conceal my distress and discouragement from everyone on my staff except Maggie, who seemed to know exactly how I felt, whether I showed it or not. Now it all came out. Fighting back tears, my voice cracking, I poured out apologies. I was sorry if I had let everyone down and contributed to our losses. It wouldn't happen again. I told them I was considering withdrawing from active political and policy work, mainly because I didn't want to be a hindrance to my husband's Administration. And I was canceling my appearance at a forum on First Ladies that evening, an event sponsored by George Washington University and moderated by a friend of mine, historian Carl Sferrazza Anthony. I didn't see the point in going. Everyone listened calmly, in total silence. Then, one by one, each woman told me why I couldn't give up or back down. Too many other people, especially women, were counting on me.

Lissa Muscatine described a talk she had given recently to a class at American University, where she explained her job as a White House speechwriter. She told the students that the President and I did more than pay lip service to women's rights in the workplace. The White House had hired Lissa even though she was pregnant with twins when she applied for the job. She told the students that when she came back to work for me full-time after her maternity leave, I had encouraged her to structure her hours and to work from home if necessary so that she could spend time with her children. After the class, a dozen young women gathered around her to ask questions and say how encouraging it was to hear about working mothers in the White House.

"Young people look to you for guidance in their own lives. You're a role model," Lissa said. "What kind of message would you be sending if you stopped being actively involved?"

Buoyed by my friends' support, I dutifully trooped to the Mayflower Hotel that evening for the First Ladies forum. The audience was enthusiastic and clearly in my corner, which was heartening. I felt energized and hopeful for the first time since the election and ready to get back into the fray, particularly now that Bill would have to deal with a Republican-controlled Congress and its outspoken leaders. Eleanor Roosevelt once said, "If I feel depressed, I go to work." That sounded like good advice to me.

Newt Gingrich handed me the perfect opportunity. The soon-to-be Republican Speaker of the House was eager to flex his political muscle. Almost immediately, his impulsiveness and right-wing bombast raised red flags for him and his party, when a minor controversy erupted over remarks he made about welfare reform and orphanages. Some Republicans had suggested that the nation could reduce welfare rolls by placing the children of welfare mothers in orphanages. The idea was to prohibit states from paying welfare benefits for two groups of children: those whose paternity was not established and those born out of wedlock to women under eighteen. The savings, according to this proposal, would be used to establish and operate orphanages and group homes for unwed mothers.

I thought this was a horrible idea. All the work I have done on behalf of children convinced me that they are almost always best off with their families, that poverty is not a disqualification from good parenting, that financial and social support for families with special problems, including poverty, should be a first step before we give up on them and take away their children. Only when children are endangered by abuse and neglect should the government intervene on their behalf and move them into alternative settings outside their homes.

In a speech before the New York Women's Agenda on November 30, 1994, I criticized Gingrich and his Republican team for promoting legislation that punished children for circumstances over which they had no control. I said his remarks about orphanages were absurd and unbelievable. How ironic, I thought: In the 1992 campaign, Republicans had labeled me as "anti-family" because I supported removing abused and neglected children from parents who couldn't or wouldn't take care of them. Now Republicans were proposing that kids be removed from their parents simply because they were born out of wedlock or to poor mothers.

A few days later, Gingrich appeared on NBC's *Meet the Press* and swung back: "I'd ask her to go to Blockbuster and rent the Mickey Rooney movie about Boys Town [an orphanage]. . . . I don't understand liberals who live in enclaves of safety who say, 'Oh, this would be a terrible thing. Look at the Norman Rockwell family that would break up. . . .' " I answered Gingrich with a long article in *Newsweek*. My conclusion: "This is big-government interference into the lives of citizens at its worst."

The *Newsweek* article curbed the orphanages debate, but the atmosphere grew stranger after Gingrich's mother, thinking she was speaking off-the-record, told Connie Chung in a televised interview that her son regularly referred to me as a "bitch."

I decided to ignore the latest round of bluster and to try a different tack with Gingrich: I sent him a handwritten note inviting him and his family to a tour of the White House. A few weeks later Gingrich; his then wife, Marianne; his sister, Susan, and his mother joined me for their tour. Apart from the fact that it happened at all, the visit wasn't memorable, save for one brief exchange while we were having tea in the Red Room. Looking around at the period furniture, Gingrich began pontificating about American history. His wife soon interrupted him.

"You know, he will go on and on whether he knows what he's talking about or not," said Marianne.

Gingrich's mother quickly jumped to his defense. "Newty is a historian," she said. "Newty *always* knows what he's talking about."

In a way, the post-election fracas was helpful to me, because it sharpened my focus on positive ways to respond to right-wing diatribes. I realized I needed to tell my own story and define my own values in a format that could be evaluated directly by people without being distorted or mischaracterized. Writing the *Newsweek* article had alerted me to the potential of my own voice. I began to ponder more ambitious writing projects that would lay out my views about the need for self-reliance and social support systems in improving people's lives. I wanted to write a book about raising children in today's world and to galvanize people around the idea that, to quote an African proverb, "it takes a village to raise a child." I had never written a book, but I soon made the acquaintance of people who had, and they offered guidance.

Bill and I had met Marianne Williamson, a best-selling author, at one of our Renaissance Weekends, and she had suggested we get together with a group of people outside the political world to discuss Bill's goals for the remaining two years of his term. That struck a chord with me, and we invited her to convene a gathering at Camp David on December 30 and 31.

Williamson's guest list included Tony Robbins, whose book *Awaken the Giant Within* was a national best-seller, and Stephen R. Covey, who wrote the hugely popular 7 *Habits of Highly Effective People*. If millions of Americans were listening to their advice, I figured it might help to hear what they had to say. Williamson also invited Mary Catherine Bateson and Jean Houston. A professor, author, anthropologist and daughter of the seminal anthropologists Gregory Bateson and Margaret Mead, Bateson specializes in cultural anthropology and gender issues. I was already a fan of her 1989 book, *Composing a Life*, which describes how women construct their lives by combining the ingredients of day-to-day living that work best for them. Choices are no longer governed by the kinds of conventions that traditionally determined women's roles. We not only can, but must imagine and improvise as we go along, taking advantage of unique talents and opportunities and responding to unforeseen twists and turns along the way.

I found myself engrossed in hours of conversation with Mary Catherine and Jean Houston, a writer and lecturer on women's history, indigenous cultures and mythology. While Mary Catherine is a soft-spoken academic who favors cardigans and sensible shoes, Jean wraps herself in brightly colored capes and caftans and dominates the room with her larger-than-life presence and crackling wit. She is a walking encyclopedia, reciting poems, passages from great works of literature, historical facts and scientific data all in the same breath. She is also a trove of great jokes and puns and is ready to share her cache with anyone in need of a good laugh.

Jean and Mary Catherine were experts in two subjects of immediate importance to me. Both had written numerous books, and I needed help and advice from experienced authors. I also had been asked by the State Department to represent the United States on a trip to five countries in South Asia. This trip would be a watershed event for me, and I was eager to throw myself into preparations. Jean and Mary Catherine had traveled extensively in the region, so I invited them to share their impressions with me and my staff before I left for South Asia in March and again after our return.

I had resisted the idea of exploiting the First Lady title, preferring to concentrate on specific policies and actions. I distrust the way symbols can be manipulated and misused, and I've always believed that people should be judged on the basis of actions and consequences, not just what they say and claim to stand for. A First Lady occupies a vicarious position; her power is derivative, not independent, of the President's. This partly explained my sometimes awkward fit in the role of First Lady. Ever since I was a little girl, I had worked to be my own person and maintain my independence. As much as I loved my husband and my country, adjusting to being a full-time surrogate was difficult for me. Mary Catherine and Jean helped me better understand that the role of First Lady is deeply symbolic and that I had better figure out how to make the best of it at home and on the world stage.

Mary Catherine argued that symbolic actions were legitimate and that "symbolism can be efficacious." She believed, for example, that merely by traveling to South Asia as First Lady with Chelsea would send a message about the importance of daughters. Visiting poor rural women would underscore their significance. I understood her point, and I soon became a convert to the view that I could advance the Clinton agenda through symbolic action.

My friendship with Jean came to light a year later in a book by Bob Woodward, *The Choice*, about the 1996 political campaign. Woodward referred melodramatically to Jean as my "spiritual adviser" and described some verbal exercises she had introduced to me and my staff to help us find new ways of thinking about our work. He was particularly keen to talk about the time Jean asked me to imagine a conversation with Eleanor Roosevelt. As I often invoked Eleanor in my speeches and even referred to imaginary conversations with her to make a point, I had no trouble responding to Jean's suggestion, and never expected it to generate any interest. But a passage from Woodward's book about the exercise was excerpted on the front page of *The Washington Post* as an exposé.

That night, Jim and Diane Blair were having supper with us on the Truman Balcony, and Jim, deadpan as always, said: "Well, Hill, after this Eleanor business I guess you don't have to worry about Whitewater anymore."

"What do you mean?"

"Well, if they come after you now, you can always plead insanity."

The day after the *Post* piece, I appeared at an annual family conference hosted by Al and Tipper Gore in Tennessee. "Shortly before I arrived, I had one of my conversations with Eleanor Roosevelt," I said to gales of laughter and applause. "And she thinks this is a terrific idea as well!"

Laughing at myself was an essential survival tool, and preferable to the alternative of climbing back into the bunker—though that, too, was occasionally a temptation during the months after the Democrats lost control of the House and Senate.

Bill and I knew that a Republican Congress would guarantee at least two more years of Whitewater investigations and Kenneth Starr seemed to be invigorated by the election results. In late November, Webb Hubbell fell into Starr's net.

Webb had resigned from his job at the Justice Department the previous March, to avoid any controversy, he said, while he fought allegations that he had cheated on his billing of clients at the Rose Law Firm. Webb never let on that there was a shred of evidence to support any charges against him. Even when he came to Camp David the previous summer to play golf with Bill, he had assured us that he was innocent.

But on Thanksgiving Day in 1994, we were at Camp David when I heard a radio report that Webb Hubbell and Jim Guy Tucker, the Arkansas Governor who succeeded Bill, were going to be indicted. By now, I was used to inaccurate press reports. Although I was upset at the news, I assumed it was wrong. I also knew that, unsubstantiated or not, this story would spread like wildfire, and that Webb or his lawyer had to respond immediately. Bill and I telephoned Webb at home, where he was busy roasting turkey. After wishing Webb a happy Thanksgiving, Bill handed the phone to me.

I told Webb what I'd heard about the impending indictments. "You've got to refute this right away," I said. "You can't let this misinformation stay out there. It's terrible."

Webb said he hadn't gotten a letter from the prosecutors informing him he was the potential target of a criminal indictment. Then he promptly changed the subject, telling me who was coming for dinner and what he and his wife, Suzy, were cooking. I was annoyed that he seemed so nonchalant. Either he did not take the news report seriously, I thought, or he just was not going to let it bother him. That Thanksgiving phone call was the last time Bill and I spoke to Webb. In his own memoir, *Friends in High Places*, Webb explains that his lawyer had received a target letter the day before our phone conversation but had decided to wait until after Thanksgiving to tell Webb. He also admits that the charges against him were true and that he had stolen from the law firm in a futile attempt to get out from under a crippling debt that he had hidden from his family and friends.

On December 6, 1994, Starr's office announced that Hubbell would plead guilty to mail fraud and tax evasion. He confessed that between 1989 and 1992, he submitted more than four hundred doctored bills to cover personal expenses, cheating his clients and partners at the Rose Law Firm of at least $394,000.

I was shocked. Webb had been a trusted colleague and was widely admired as a civic leader in Arkansas. He was a dear friend. I had spent more hours in his company than I could count. The idea that he had cheated and misled those closest to him was upsetting beyond words. His plea bargain signaled a new escalation on the Whitewater battlefield, and it was hard to take.

During the Christmas season, I received two identical gifts. Anne Bartley, a friend and philanthropist from Arkansas who volunteered in the White House, and Eileen Bakke, whom I knew from Renaissance Weekends and my prayer group, each gave me a copy of *The Return of the Prodigal Son*, by Henri Nouwen, a Dutch priest. Nouwen explores the parable Jesus told about the younger of two sons who had left his father and brother to lead a dissolute life. When he finally returned home, he was welcomed by his father and resented by his dutiful older brother. During the stresses of 1993 and 1994, I had read my Bible and other books about religion and spirituality. As a family, we regularly attended Foundry Methodist Church in downtown Washington, and I drew great sustenance from the sermons and personal support offered by the congregation and its senior minister, Rev. Dr. Phil Wogaman. My prayer group continued to pray for me, as did countless other people around the world. It all helped so much. But one simple phrase in Nouwen's book struck like an epiphany: "the discipline of gratitude." I had so much to be grateful for, even in the midst of lost elections, failed health care reform efforts, partisan and prosecutorial attacks, and the deaths of those I loved. I just had to discipline myself to remember how blessed I was.

SILENCE
IS NOT SPOKEN HERE

O N A COLD AFTERNOON LATE IN MARCH 1995, I TOOK
my first extended trip overseas without the President. Forty-one
passengers filled a vintage government jet and took off from Andrews
Air Force Base for a twelve-day official visit to five countries in South
Asia. My companions included White House staff, State Department
aides, members of the media, Secret Service agents, Jan Piercy, my friend
from Wellesley and U.S. Executive Director of the World Bank, and best
of all, Chelsea. The trip happily coincided with her spring break from
school. She had just turned fifteen and was blossoming into a poised,
thoughtful young woman. I wanted to share some of the last adventures
of her childhood, and I wanted to watch her react to the extraordinary
world we were about to enter, to see it through her eyes as well as
my own.

After a seventeen-hour flight, we landed in Islamabad, Pakistan, in
the late evening in a pounding rainstorm. The State Department had
asked me to visit the subcontinent to highlight the administration's
commitment to the region, because neither the President nor the Vice
President could make a trip soon. My visit was meant to demonstrate
that this strategic and volatile part of the world was important to the
United States and to assure leaders throughout South Asia that Bill
supported their efforts to strengthen democracy, expand free markets
and promote tolerance and human rights, including the rights of
women. My physical presence in the region was considered a sign of
concern and commitment.

Although we had only a short time in each country, I wanted to meet with as many women as possible to stress the correlation between women's progress and a country's social and economic status. Development issues had interested me since my years of working with Bill on behalf of poor, rural communities in Arkansas, but this was my first serious exposure to the developing world. I had gotten some preparation earlier in March when I traveled to Copenhagen, Denmark, to represent the United States at the United Nations World Summit for Social Development. That conference underscored my conviction that individuals and communities around the world are already more connected and interdependent than at any time in human history, and that Americans will be affected by the poverty, disease and development of people halfway around the globe.

The Chinese have an ancient saying, that women hold up half the sky, but in most of the world, it's really more than half. Women handle a large share of the responsibility for the welfare of their families. Yet their work often goes unrecognized and unrewarded inside the family or by the formal economy. These inequities are starkly visible in South Asia, where more than half a billion people live in grinding poverty— the majority of them women and children. Poor women and girls are oppressed and discriminated against, denied education and medical care and victimized by culturally sanctioned violence. Law enforcement often turns a blind eye to the crimes of wife beating, bride burning and female infanticide, and in certain communities, women who are raped can be jailed for adultery. Despite such traditions of prejudice, there were signs of change across the Indian subcontinent, in schools that educate girls and in micro-lending programs that give women access to credit, enabling them to earn their own incomes.

The U.S. government had supported many successful projects, but the new Republican majorities in the Senate and House were targeting foreign aid, which amounted to less than 1 percent of the federal budget, for large cuts. I had long supported the U.S. Agency for International Development—USAID—and hoped to use the media spotlight that follows a First Lady to demonstrate the tangible impact of U.S.-funded programs in the developing world. Cutting off this aid would both harm individual women in dire straits and contradict strategies that have been shown to benefit poor countries as well as the United States. When women suffer, their children suffer and their economies stagnate, ultimately weakening potential markets for U.S. products. And when women are victimized, the stability of families, communities and nations is eroded, jeopardizing the prospects for democracy and prosperity globally.

Violence and instability plagued every country I was scheduled to visit. Just three weeks before our arrival in Pakistan, Muslim extremists had ambushed a van carrying U.S. consulate workers in Karachi. Two of them were killed. And Ramzi Yousef, one of the main plotters in the 1993 World Trade Center bombing, had recently been arrested in Pakistan and extradited to the United States for trial.

The Secret Service was nervous about the trip and would have preferred that I restrict my travels to government compounds and isolated resorts. They were amusingly at odds with the State Department, which wanted to send me to hot spots around the world—places where ongoing conflict made security too difficult for visits by the President or Vice President. The point of my mission was to meet rural as well as urban women, to jettison the predictable itineraries and get into the villages where most people lived. Advance teams and security experts planned each stop carefully, and I was painfully aware of how difficult and disruptive it was for our host countries and our embassies to accommodate such an unorthodox trip. Their extra efforts on my behalf made me feel even more obligated to make my presence as productive as possible.

When the sun rose over the Margalla Hills, I saw Islamabad for the first time. A planned city of wide avenues rimmed by low green mountains, it is a showcase of midcentury modern architecture and reforestation projects, typical of many of the capital cities that sprang up after national independence, built on neutral soil with good intentions and foreign aid. At first I didn't feel I was in South Asia at all. But that notion evaporated as soon as I made a courtesy call on Begum Nasreen Leghari, the wife of Pakistan's President, Farooq Ahmad Khan Leghari.

An elegantly dressed woman, Mrs. Leghari spoke excellent English with a lilting British accent. She lived in conditions of strict isolation, known as "purdah," never seen by men outside her immediate family. She had to be fully veiled on the rare occasions she left her house. She did not attend her husband's inauguration but watched the ceremony on television. When she invited me to her living quarters on the second floor of the presidential residence, I could be accompanied only by female aides and Secret Service agents.

Mrs. Leghari peppered me with questions about America. I was equally curious about her life and asked whether she wanted change for the next generation of women in her family. I learned that her recently married daughter was on the guest list of a large dinner I was attending the next night in Lahore, and I asked Mrs. Leghari about the contradiction. "That is her husband's choice," she said. "She's no longer of our home. So she does whatever he chooses." She accepted her daughter's status and mobility because her son-in-law had chosen them on her behalf. The wife of Mrs. Leghari's son, however, lived with her in purdah, because her son chose the traditional path of his father.

The contradictions within Pakistan became still more apparent at my next event, a luncheon hosted in my honor by Prime Minister Benazir Bhutto and attended by several dozen accomplished women in Pakistan. It was like being rocketed forward several centuries in time. Among these women were academics and activists, as well as a pilot, a singer, a banker and a police deputy superintendent. They had their own ambitions and careers, and, of course, we were all guests of Pakistan's elected female leader.

Benazir Bhutto, a brilliant and striking woman then in her mid-forties, was born into a prominent family and educated at Harvard and Oxford. Her father, Zulfikar Ali Bhutto, Pakistan's Populist Prime Minister during the 1970s, was deposed in a military coup and later hanged. After his death, Benazir spent years under house arrest. In the late 1980s, she emerged as head of his old political party. Bhutto was the only celebrity I had ever stood behind a rope line to see. Chelsea and I were strolling around London during a holiday trip in the summer of 1989. We noticed a large crowd gathered outside the Ritz Hotel, and I asked people what they were waiting for. They said Benazir Bhutto was staying at the hotel and was soon expected to arrive. Chelsea and I waited until the motorcade drove up. We watched Bhutto, swathed in yellow chiffon, emerge from her limousine and glide into the lobby. She seemed graceful, composed and intent.

In 1990, her government was dissolved over charges of corruption, but her party won again in new elections in 1993. Pakistan was increasingly troubled by rising violence and general lawlessness, particularly in Karachi. Law and order had deteriorated as the rate of ethnic and sectarian murders rose. There were also rampant rumors of corruption involving Asif Zardari, Bhutto's husband, and supporters.

At the luncheon she hosted for me, Benazir led a discussion about the changing roles of women in her country and told a joke about her husband's status as a political spouse. "According to newspapers in Pakistan," she said, "Mr. Asif Zardari is de facto Prime Minister of the country. My husband tells me, 'Only the First Lady can appreciate it's not true.' "

Bhutto acknowledged the difficulties faced by women who were breaking with tradition and taking leading roles in public life. She deftly managed to refer both to the challenges I had encountered during my White House tenure and to her own situation. "Women who take on tough issues and stake out new territory are often on the receiving end of ignorance," she concluded.

In a private meeting with the Prime Minister, we talked about her upcoming visit to Washington in April, and I spent time with her husband and their children. Because I had heard that their marriage was arranged, I found their interaction particularly interesting. They bantered easily together, and seemed genuinely smitten with each other. Only months after my trip, accusations of corruption against them grew more harsh, and in August 1996, Bhutto elevated her husband to a cabinet post. By November 5, 1996, she was ousted amid allegations that Zardari had used his position for personal enrichment. He was convicted of corruption and imprisoned; she left her country with her children, under threat of arrest and unable to return.

I have no way of knowing whether the accusations against Bhutto and her husband are well-founded or baseless. I do know that during the short time I was there, I was drawn into a world of unfathomable contrasts. Nasreen Leghari and Benazir Bhutto came from the same culture. President Leghari put his wife in purdah while Ali Bhutto sent his daughter to Harvard. An arranged marriage seemed to produce genuine delight. Pakistan, India, Bangladesh and Sri Lanka have all been governed by women elected as Presidents or Prime Ministers in a region where women are so devalued that some newborn girls may be killed or abandoned.

I wanted to know what would become of the future generation of educated Pakistani women, some of whom Chelsea and I met the next day at the Islamabad College for Girls, Benazir Bhutto's high school. Many of their concerns were familiar to the mother of a curious and enterprising young woman. They worried aloud about how they could change their society and where they might fit into it as highly educated women. "You're never going to find the ideal man," said one girl. "You have to be a lot more realistic." Her voice would stay with me. She was of a culture where choice in marriage was rarely the woman's. Yet she knew enough of the realities of modern life to contemplate the uncertain options of women everywhere.

I continued that conversation about women's choices when I visited Lahore University of Management Science, where women were studying business. The program was supported in part by Pakistani Americans who understood that Pakistan's economy and standard of living would never advance unless women were educated and played an active role. No one could doubt the success of South Asian immigrants in America, where they flourished in business and the professions.

Their successes in our country illustrated the importance of a well-functioning non-corrupt government, a free market, a society that values individuals, including girls and women, a culture that tolerates all religious traditions and an environment free of violence and war.

No country in South Asia has yet achieved all these conditions. Men and women who could have contributed to their own country's advancement are instead contributing to ours. Sri Lanka, for example, where I ended my trip, had a high rate of literacy for both men and women, but the country had lived in terror for years because of a guerrilla insurgence by the Hindu Tamil Tigers against the majority Buddhist Sinhalese population and government. The relentless campaign of terror undermined its potential for economic growth and foreign investment.

Before we left Islamabad, Chelsea and I paid a visit of respect to the Saudi-built Faisal Mosque, named for the former Saudi King and one of the largest mosques in the world. With its nearly three-hundred-foot-tall minarets and magnificent canopy, this modern mosque was one of more than fifteen hundred the Saudi government and private citizens were building on six continents. We removed our shoes and padded around the vast prayer halls and courtyards designed to accommodate up to one hundred thousand believers. Chelsea, who had been studying Islamic history and culture in her school, asked our guide well-informed questions. Like the Judeo-Christian Bible, the Quran is open to different interpretations, most of which promote peaceful coexistence with people of other religions; some, like Wahhabism, do not. Wahhabism is an ultraconservative Saudi brand of Islam that is gaining adherents around the world. While I deeply respect the basic tenets of Islam, Wahhabism troubles me because it is a fast-spreading form of Islamic fundamentalism that excludes women from full participation in their societies, promotes religious intolerance and, in its most extreme version, as we learned with Osama bin Laden, advocates terror and violence.

The next day I visited the embassy to talk to the American and Pakistani staff, who were terribly shaken by the recent murders of their colleagues in Karachi. I wanted to acknowledge their courage in serving our country and reassure them that, despite isolationist voices in Congress, their services were invaluable and appreciated by the President and by millions of American citizens. This was a not so thinly veiled reference to some Republican House members who boasted that they didn't have passports, never traveled outside our country and planned to slash the State Department budget. I also wanted to thank the embassy staff for all the extra work my trip had required of them. From their perspective, the best part of a VIP visit was the moment the diplomatic plane took off—and they could hold a "wheels up" party to recover. I joked that maybe I would only pretend to leave, then sneak back to celebrate with them.

Under extraordinary security, we flew to Lahore, the capital of Punjab. The Pakistanis were so afraid of an incident that they positioned hundreds of soldiers along the route from the airport. Unlike modern Islamabad, Lahore is an ancient site with glorious Moghul architecture. The roads had been cleared of all normal traffic, and the ordinarily teeming city seemed depopulated. On parts of our route, colorful printed cloth had been hung on clotheslines to hide the slums alongside the highway. But where the material had fallen down, I could see children and emaciated dogs scrambling around piles of garbage.

We drove out to a rural village that, despite its lack of electricity, was considered advantaged because it had a health clinic and a school that educated girls. The clinic was a concrete-block building staffed by a handful of doctors and technicians who were responsible for an area with a population of one hundred fifty thousand people. The staff was heroic in its efforts but lacked many crucial resources. We brought donations of medical supplies and necessities, as we tried to do wherever we visited. Patients, mostly mothers with their children, sat quietly on benches against the wall. They seemed astonished to see so many Americans in their little village but graciously allowed Chelsea and me to hold their babies and ask them questions through an interpreter.

Another concrete building a hundred yards away housed the primary school for girls. That was as far as their education was likely to go, because the nearest secondary school—high school—was for boys only. I spoke to a woman who had ten children, five boys and five girls. She sent her five boys to the secondary school, but her girls had nowhere to go because they couldn't travel to or attend the nearest girls' school. She wanted a secondary school nearby for her girls. She talked very openly about birth control and said that if she had known then what she knew now, she wouldn't have had so many children. We visited a multigenerational, crowded family compound just behind the school, with children and animals roaming around the courtyard. The oldest family members sat in hammocks watching the commotion created by my visit, while the male head of the family greeted me warmly and showed me several of the compound's one-room homes, which contained sleeping and eating areas for individual families. Communal activity took place outdoors, where the women gathered to prepare and cook food. Two young girls showed Chelsea how to use black kohl coloring on her eyes. Fashion is a universal feminine touchstone.

I had given a lot of thought to how Chelsea and I should dress on the trip. We wanted to be comfortable, and under the sun's heat, I was glad for the hats and cotton clothes I had packed. I didn't want to offend people in the communities I was visiting, but I was also wary of appearing to embrace customs reflecting a culture that restricted women's lives and rights. On Jackie Kennedy's historic tour of India and Pakistan in 1962, she was photographed wearing sleeveless shifts and knee-length skirts—not to mention a midriff-baring sari that caused an international sensation. Public opinion seemed to have grown more conservative in South Asia since then. We consulted State Department experts, who offered tips on how to behave in foreign countries without embarrassing ourselves or offending our hosts. The South Asia briefing papers warned against crossing legs, pointing fingers, eating with the "unclean" left hand or initiating physical contact with the opposite sex, including a handshake.

I made sure to pack several long scarves that I could throw around my shoulders or put over my head if I entered a mosque. I had noticed the way Benazir Bhutto covered her hair with a light scarf. She wore a local form of dress called *shalwar kameez*, a long, flowing tunic over loose pants that was both practical and attractive. Chelsea and I decided to try out this style. For the extravaganza at the Lahore Fort that night, I wore a red silk *shalwar kameez*, and Chelsea donned one in a turquoise green that complemented her eyes. The Governor of Punjab had invited five hundred guests to the red sandstone fortress, once headquarters of the medieval Moghul empire, that loomed on a hill overlooking the city. We arrived on a clear, starry evening and stepped out of our cars into a scene from the *Arabian Nights*. Beneath a fireworks display, troupes of musicians and dancers greeted us on either side of a long red carpet. Camels and horses draped in jeweled robes and headdresses shuffled and spun to flute music. Chelsea and I were entranced and squeezed each other's hands in wonder. Two huge wind-carved turrets guarded the entrance to the inner fort, where thousands of flickering oil lamps lit the courtyards and passageways, and the air was fragrant with rose petals. I looked at my enchanting, suddenly grown-up daughter wrapped in brilliant silk, and wished Bill were there to see her too.

The evening ended in a dash to the airport and a flight to New Delhi. I had wanted to visit India ever since I was a freshman in college and Margaret Clapp, the President of Wellesley College, left to head a women's college in Madurai, India. Before she went, she made the rounds to our dormitories, describing what she would be doing. I was intrigued. Before I decided on law school, I had considered going to India to study or teach. A quarter-century later, I was making my first trip there, representing my country. Bill had asked me to go because he wanted to oversee the development of good relations with India after forty years of the Indian policy of nonalignment and its ties with the Soviet Union during the Cold War. I wanted to see for myself the world's largest democracy and learn more about grassroots efforts to spur development and women's rights. I was excited about what I'd be seeing, even though I knew my time and exposure would be limited.

My first day, I had a crowded schedule that included a visit to one of Mother Teresa's orphanages, where girls far outnumbered boys because daughters were not as valued as sons by their families. Mother Teresa was traveling outside India, but Sister Priscilla gave us a tour. Well-cared-for babies reached out their arms, and Chelsea and I picked them up while Sister Priscilla told us about each one. Some infant girls had been abandoned in the streets; more often they were left at the orphanage by mothers who couldn't care for them or said that their fathers didn't want them. Some babies had club feet or cleft lips or other physical disabilities and were abandoned by families too poor to pay for medical treatment. Many of the children would be adopted by Westerners, although adoption within India was becoming more common. Sister Priscilla told me my visit had caused the local government to pave the dirt road, which she laughingly deemed a minor miracle.

I lunched with a group of Indian women at Roosevelt House, the Ambassador's residence, and dined with President Shanker Dayal

Sharma. The next day, I was scheduled to meet with Prime Minister P. V. Narasimha Rao. It was important to duplicate whatever I had done in Pakistan, lest I offend either country since I knew that both kept score.

I had agreed to make a major speech on women's rights at the Rajiv Gandhi Foundation, but I was having trouble writing it. I was looking for one clear image that would express what I wanted to say. At the women's luncheon, Meenakshi Gopinath, the principal of Lady Sri Ram College, a secondary school, presented me with my inspiration— a hand-printed poem written by one of her students, Anasuya Sengupta. It was called "Silence," and it began:

> *Too many women*
> *In too many countries*
> *Speak the same language.*
> *Of silence . . .*

I couldn't get the poem out of my head. As I worked on my speech late into the night, I realized that I could use the poem to convey my belief that issues affecting women and girls should not be dismissed as "soft" or marginal but should be integrated fully into domestic and foreign policy decisions. Denying or curtailing education and basic health care for women is a human rights issue. Restricting women's economic, political and social participation is a human rights issue. For too long, the voices of half the world's citizens have not been heard by their governments. The voices of women became my theme, and I decided to end my speech by quoting the poem.

The Rajiv Gandhi Foundation, named for the assassinated Prime Minister, was established by his widow, Sonia, who had invited me to speak. A soft-spoken, Italian-born woman, Sonia Gandhi had fallen in love with Rajiv, the handsome son of Prime Minister Indira Gandhi, when they were students at Cambridge University in England. They married and moved to India. From all accounts, Sonia was happily raising two children when catastrophe struck her family. First, her brother-in-law, Sanjay—whom many believed would follow his mother and grandfather, Jawaharlal Nehru, into politics—was killed in a plane crash. Then, in 1984, Indira Gandhi was assassinated by her own security guards. Rajiv, the presumptive heir to Congress Party leadership, became Prime Minister. But while campaigning for election in 1991,

Rajiv was murdered by a suicide bomber from the Tamil Tiger guerrillas, who were waging war against the Sri Lankan government and against the Indian government that supported it. Sonia Gandhi was thrust into public life as the symbol of continuity in the Congress Party. She had found her own public voice in the wake of devastating personal tragedy.

By the time I was to deliver my speech, jet lag and sleeplessness had taken their toll. I could barely see the pages, but I concluded with these lines from Anasuya's poem:

> *We seek only to give words*
> *to those who cannot speak*
> *(too many women*
> *in too many countries)*
> *I seek only to forget*
> *The sorrows of my grandmother's*
> *Silence.*

The poem struck a chord with the audience members, many of whom were touched that I would draw on the thoughts of a schoolgirl to evoke the condition of women everywhere. Anasuya, lovely, humble and shy in the face of all the publicity her poem generated, was astounded that women all over the globe were requesting copies of it.

Her words also affected my traveling companions in the Washington press corps, who responded personally to what I was saying about women's lives and rights. Reporters asked me after my speech why I hadn't addressed these issues sooner. I understood the question, though I had been working for twenty-five years on improving the status and dignity of women and children in America. In this region, where purdah and abandoned baby girls coexisted with women prime ministers, I could see the issue in higher relief—and so could the press. Health care reform, family leave, the Earned Income Tax Credit or lifting the global gag rule on abortion were all part of the same theme: empowering people to make the choices they decide are right for them and their families. Traveling halfway around the world helped make that clear. Part of the reason was simple: The reporters assigned to cover my trip were a captive audience. But it was also true that my message abroad carried few of the political overtones of my proposals for specific policies at home.

The transformation that took place in my relationship with the press was one of the pleasant surprises of the trip. Like veterans of different armies from an old war, we began our journey wary of each other. But as the days wore on, we began to see each other in a different light. For me, the ground rules helped: Everything that happened on the plane or in the hotels was strictly off-the-record, as was everything that Chelsea said or did on her own. Once I was confident that the reporters were respecting the "code of the road," I felt more comfortable opening up around them. It also helped that the press and I were sharing the same experiences, from our immersion in foreign cultures to moments of levity at informal group dinners.

The press corps, which had never interacted with Chelsea before, now observed her poise and her grit. One day she would help weigh malnourished children so fragile that they winced at the gentlest touch; a few hours later she would dine with a Prime Minister. She asked good questions and made insightful comments and, naturally, many of the journalists started pressuring me to allow them to quote her. I finally gave in after we visited the Taj Mahal and she said: "When I was little, this was sort of the embodiment of the fairy-tale palace for me. I would see pictures of it and would dream I was a princess or whatever. Now that I'm here it's spectacular."

It was a lovely and harmless comment, but I immediately wished we hadn't opened that door. It was hard to close again. Once the print reporters had the quote, Lisa Caputo, my press secretary, was deluged by television journalists desperate to have Chelsea repeat it on tape. I had to remind everybody what the ground rules were, and I made a mental note to consider putting Chelsea in "purdah" when we returned to Washington!

My most vivid memories of India were not of the Taj Mahal, breathtaking as it was, but of two visits I made in the city of Ahmadabad in the state of Gujarat. The first was to Mahatma Gandhi's simple ashram, where he sought a meditative retreat from the roiling struggle to create an independent India. The deprivation I had seen and the simplicity of his life reminded me of the excesses of mine. Gandhi's beliefs in non-violent resistance to oppression and the need to organize large opposition groups to a government's policies influenced the American civil rights movement and was critical to Martin Luther King's campaign to end racial segregation. In his own country, Gandhi's life and principles of self-reliance and rejection of the caste system inspired a remarkable woman, Ela Bhatt. Following Gandhi's example, she founded the Self-Employed Women's Association (SEWA) in 1971. Liz Moynihan, Senator Moynihan's extraordinary wife, had introduced me to Bhatt and encouraged me to make a trip to SEWA and see for myself what one determined woman could create.

Both a trade union and a women's movement, SEWA claimed more than one hundred forty thousand members, including some of the poorest, least educated and most shunned women in India. These women entered into arranged marriages and then lived in their husbands' households under the watchful eyes of their mothers-in-law. Some had lived in purdah until their husbands died, were disabled or left, and they had to support their families; all struggled day-to-day to survive. SEWA offered small loans to enable them to earn their own income and also provided basic literacy and business education training. Ela Bhatt showed me the large books kept in SEWA's one-room office that recorded the loans and repayments. Through this system of "microfinance," SEWA was providing employment for thousands of individual women and changing deeply held attitudes about women's roles.

Word of my visit had spread through the villages of Gujarat, and nearly one thousand women flocked to the meeting, some of them walking nine or ten hours along hot, dusty paths through the countryside. Tears filled my eyes when I saw them waiting for me under a large tent. Fanning themselves in their sapphire-, emerald- and ruby-colored saris, they looked like an undulating human rainbow. They were Muslim and Hindu, including untouchables, the lowest Hindu caste. There were kite makers, scrap pickers and vegetable vendors, and Chelsea sat down among them.

One by one, women stood up to tell me how SEWA had changed their lives, not only because of the small loans they received and the help SEWA gave them in their businesses, but also because of the solidarity they felt with other struggling women. One woman struck a common chord when she explained that she was no longer afraid of her mother-in-law. In their culture, the mother-in-law typically exerts rigid control over her son's wife as soon as the couple marry and move in with his family. Having her own market stall and her own income gave this woman welcome independence. She added that she was no longer afraid of the police either because a group of SEWA-sponsored vendors now protected her from harassment by overbearing officers in the market. The dignified bearing, chiseled faces and kohl-rimmed eyes of the speakers belied their difficult lives.

Finally, I was asked to make closing remarks. As I finished, Ela Bhatt took the microphone and announced that the women wanted to express their gratitude for my visit from America. In a stunning flash of moving color they all sprang to their feet and began singing "We Shall Overcome" in Gujarati. I was overwhelmed and uplifted to be in the midst of women who were working to overcome their own hardships as well as centuries of oppression. For me, they were a living affirmation of the importance of human rights.

I was still thinking of their faces and words the next day as we flew from sea level to Nepal's capital, Kathmandu, which sits in the middle of the Himalayan mountains, in a low valley at an altitude of just over 4,200 feet, the same as that of Salt Lake City. On a clear day, you can see a panorama of snow-capped peaks ringing the city.

The landscapes of Nepal are among the most beautiful in the world, but the inhabited regions of the country are overcrowded. Human waste is used for fertilizer and clean water is a rarity. The Americans I met all had stories of getting sick after spending time in Nepal, making it sound like an inevitable rite of passage. Peace Corps members showed up to see me wearing T-shirts that listed all the diseases they had survived.

We took extraordinary precautions, since we were only halfway through our trip and even one sick day would throw off the rest of our schedule. Our hosts went out of their way to accommodate our concerns. "Mom, you won't believe what the Secret Service agents told me," said a startled Chelsea our first day. "They said the hotel pool was drained before we arrived, and they refilled it with bottled water!" I never learned if this was true, but it would not have surprised me.

During a courtesy visit to the royal palace, I was received by King Birendra Bir Bikram Shah Dev and Queen Aishwarya in a room with a huge tiger pelt on the floor. The Queen had met me upon my arrival at the airport and told me she looked forward to talking with me. I hoped I would have a chance to discuss health care and girls' education with her, but the King did all the talking. Until recently, he had reigned over a kingdom essentially sealed from the outside world. Now the country was undergoing a transition to representative government, and he wanted to discuss potential American aid and investment. Nepal was also facing violence and unrest from Maoist guerrillas in the country-side. That, however, turned out to be less of a threat to the royal family than a pathology within the palace. It is still difficult to accept the fate of the King and Queen and eight family members, shot dead in that very palace a few years later. Their assassin, according to official reports, was the Crown Prince, who was enraged because he was not allowed to marry for love.

Early the next morning, Chelsea and I went for a long walk in the hills above the city. People stood on the roadside to watch us pass by, and one bright-eyed girl, about ten or eleven, joined us. She spoke a smattering of English, mostly names of places, like "New York City" or "California," which she would punctuate with an adjective like "big" or "happy." Then she nodded or laughed as though we were friends having a long conversation. She completely won me over. The higher we walked, the more I saw how every square inch of land was used for something—houses, terraced farming, roads or Buddhist monasteries that dotted the hillsides. I heard the tinkling of bells from the monastery nearest to us and saw white prayer banners waving from its ramparts. When we walked back down to our cars, the girl's father was waiting. By then, I had learned that she didn't attend school but had picked up her bits of English by attaching herself to tourists and trekkers. I complimented the father on his daughter's intelligence and curiosity, but I doubt I communicated effectively. Though I knew that money was an inadequate token of gratitude and concern, I wanted her father to recognize that I valued his daughter. I hoped that her work ethic and resourcefulness might raise her stature in her family, and encourage them to consider different life choices for her. I have often wondered what became of her.

Later that morning, we visited a women's health clinic founded by American women living in Nepal. Nepal had one of the world's highest maternal and infant death rates—a staggering 830 maternal deaths for every 100,000 births, compared with the world average of 400 and the American average of less than 7. The clinics, a partnership among USAID, Save the Children and the Nepalese government, employed a commonsense, low-tech approach to preventive care and had established a program to provide pregnant women and midwives with "safe home delivery kits." The kits contained a plastic sheet, a bar of soap, a piece of twine, wax and a razor blade. In Nepal, a plastic sheet for a woman in labor to lie on, soap for the midwife to clean her hands and utensils, string to tie off the umbilical cord and a clean razor blade to cut it can make the difference between life and death to a mother and her newborn.

On a stopover in the Royal Chitwan National Park in southern Nepal, Chelsea and I rode an elephant. To be honest, if I hadn't known I was going to be photographed for posterity, I would have just put on a pair of jeans. Instead, I was garbed in a kind of *Out of Africa* look, with a khaki shirt and skirt and straw hat. The picture of Chelsea and me that flashed around the world showed a happy mother-daughter team perched on our pachyderm and watching a rare Asian rhino. Later, when we got back to Washington, James Carville remarked: "Don't you just love it? You spent two years trying to get people better health care and they tried to kill you. You and Chelsea rode an elephant, and they loved you!"

Bangladesh, the most densely populated country on earth, presented the starkest contrast of wealth and poverty I saw in South Asia. Looking out the window from our hotel room in Dhaka, I could see a wooden fence that ran between shanties and garbage heaps on one side and the swimming pool and cabanas where visitors like me could enjoy a drink and a swim on the other. It was like looking at a stereopticon of the global economy. Here, the authorities made no effort to hide the destitute behind brightly colored cloth. The city was wall-to-wall people, more people per square foot than I had ever seen anywhere, all moving in small cars that clogged the roads or in huge crowds that spilled into those roads. More than once, I gasped as a car narrowly skimmed a group of people. Walking outside in the heat and humidity was like stepping into a steam sauna. But this was another country I had long wanted to visit, because it was home to two internationally recognized projects—the International Center for Diarrheal Disease Research (ICDDR/B) in Dhaka, Bangladesh, and the Grameen Bank, a pioneer of microcredit. The ICDDR/B is an important example of the positive results that come from foreign aid. Dysentery is a leading cause of death, particularly among children, in parts of the world where there are limited sources of clean drinking water. The ICDDR/B developed "oral rehydration therapy" (ORT), a solution composed mostly of salt, sugar and water, that is easy to administer and responsible for saving the lives of millions of children. This simple, inexpensive solution has been called one of the most important medical advances of the century, and the hospital that pioneered it depends on American aid. The success of

ORT is also a model for the type of low-tech, low-cost treatment developed abroad that can be replicated in the United States.

I had first learned about the Grameen Bank more than a decade earlier, when Bill and I invited the bank's founder, Dr. Muhammad Yunus, to Little Rock to discuss how microcredit lending programs might help some of the poorest rural communities in Arkansas. The Grameen Bank provides loans to very poor women who have no other access to credit. With loans averaging about $50, women have started small businesses—like dressmaking, weaving and farming—that help lift them and their families out of poverty. These women have not only proven to be excellent credit risks—the Grameen Bank has a loan repayment rate of 98 percent—but dedicated savers as well, who tend to reinvest their profits in their business and their families. I helped set up a development bank and micro-lending groups in Arkansas, and I wanted to promote micro-lending throughout the United States, modeled on the success of Yunus and the Grameen Bank. They have provided or facilitated assistance to similar programs around the world, distributing $3.7 billion in collateral-free loans to 2.4 million members with borrowers in more than forty-one thousand villages in Bangladesh and elsewhere.

But its triumphs in helping landless women gain self-sufficiency had made the Grameen Bank (and other similar programs) a target for Islamic fundamentalists. Two days before we arrived in Dhaka, some two thousand extremists marched on the capital to denounce secular aid organizations, which they accused of tempting women to defy a strict interpretation of the Quran. In the months before our visit, village banks and girls' schools had been torched, and one of Bangladesh's leading woman writers had received death threats.

One of the most disconcerting aspects of security is that you never know how to identify a truly dangerous moment. The Secret Service had received intelligence suggesting that an extremist group might try to disrupt my visit. When I traveled outside the capital to visit two villages in southwestern Bangladesh, flying in a U.S. Air Force C-130 transport plane, we were again on high alert. In the village of Jessore, we visited a primary school where the government was testing a program that rewarded families with money and food if they allowed their daughters to attend. This seemed like a novel inducement to persuade families to send their girls to school in the first place—and then let them stay there. We showed up at the school, which was in the middle of open fields, and I went into the classrooms to talk to the girls and their teachers. While talking to students, I noticed a commotion outside and saw Secret Service agents running around. Thousands of villagers had materialized out of thin air, pouring over a little rise, ten to twenty people deep as far as I could see. We had no idea where they came from or what message they might have wanted to deliver. We never found out because my agents swept us out of there, afraid of a crowd they might not be able to control.

Our visit to the Grameen Bank in the village of Mashihata was worth battling the crowds and the long, bumpy drive. I had been invited to visit two villages—one Hindu and one Muslim—but I could not manage both because of my schedule. Remarkably, the Muslim women decided to come to the Hindu village for our meeting.

"*Swagatam*, Hillary, *swagatam*, Chelsea," the children sang in Bengali, "Welcome, Hillary, welcome, Chelsea!" My old friend Muhammad Yunus was there to greet me, bearing samples of clothing that some of Grameen's women borrowers had made for sale. Both Chelsea and I were wearing similar outfits, which he sent to the hotel for us, and he was delighted. He said a few words echoing the theme I had been developing in my own speeches.

"Women have potential," he said. "And access to credit is not only an effective way to fight poverty, it is also a fundamental human right."

I sat under a thatched pavilion surrounded by Hindu and Muslim women, and they told me how they had all come together, defying the fundamentalists. I told them I was there to listen to them, and to learn.

A Muslim woman stood up and said, "We are sick of the mullahs, they are always trying to keep women down."

I asked what sorts of problems they faced, and she said: "They threaten to ban us if we take loans from the bank. They tell us the bank people will steal our children. I tell them to leave us alone. We are trying to help our children have better lives."

The women asked me questions to try to relate my experiences to theirs. "Do you have cattle in your home?" said one.

"No," I replied, grinning at the traveling press corps, who by that time were like members of a large extended family, "unless you count the press room."

The Americans laughed out loud, while the Bangladeshis pondered the meaning of my quip.

"Do you earn your own income?" asked a woman with a decorative red dot, or *teep*, on her forehead between her eyes, traditionally signifying that she was married.

"I am not earning my own income now that my husband is President," I said, wondering how to explain what I was doing. I told them I used to earn more than my husband, and I planned to earn my own income again.

The children of the village put on a play for us, and a few women approached Chelsea and me to show us how to wear our own decorative *teeps* and how to wrap a sari. I was struck by the positive spirit of the people I met in this poor, isolated village who lived without electricity or running water, but with hope, thanks, in part, to the work of the Grameen Bank.

I wasn't the only one moved by the village women. One of the American journalists who stood near me, listening to our discussion, leaned in and whispered, "Silence is not spoken here."

OKLAHOMA CITY

"THE FIRST LADY IS SORRY SHE CAN'T BE WITH you tonight," Bill Clinton told the crowd of Washington journalists and politicians in March 1995. "If you believe that," he went on, "I've got some land in Arkansas I'd like to sell you." It was another Gridiron dinner, but this time I couldn't be there because I was traveling in South Asia, so I prerecorded a five-minute parody of the hit movie *Forrest Gump* to play at the end of the show.

As the tape rolled, a white feather drifted out of a blue sky and landed in front of the White House near a park bench, where I, Hillary Gump, sat with a box of candy on my lap.

"My mama always told me the White House is like a box of chocolates," I said in my best Tom Hanks imitation. "It's pretty on the outside, but inside there's lots of nuts."

The skit, written and directed by author and comic Al Franken of *Saturday Night Live* fame, was a send-up of both the movie and my life, featuring scenes from my childhood, college days and political career. Mandy Grunwald, Paul Begala and *Tonight Show* host Jay Leno contributed ideas. Each time the camera returned to me on the bench, I was wearing a different wig, poking fun at my ever changing hairstyles. At the end of the spoof, Bill did a walk-on cameo. He sat next to me on the bench and took my box of chocolates, offering me one piece in return, then asking if he could have some french fries.

When Chelsea and I called Bill to check in from the trip, he told me the performance had gotten a standing ovation. Few other things we tried to do in Washington went as smoothly.

By the time I returned from South Asia, the President and his administration were preparing to square off with the Republican Congress over the Contract with America. Newt Gingrich pushed most of his Contract through the Republican-dominated House in the first hundred days of the 104th Congress, but only two measures had been signed into law. The legislative action moved to the Senate, where there were still enough Democrats to filibuster or sustain a presidential veto. Bill had to decide whether to try to reshape the Republican legislation through the veto threat or to offer his own alternatives. He ended up doing both. He also regained the momentum by confronting an opponent who had bluntly declared his Presidency "irrelevant."

The White House had been stuck in a holding pattern since the midterm election, and it was time to set a new course. Bill is famously more patient than I am, and when anyone urged him to be more confrontational and even aggressive in taking on Gingrich, he'd explain that first people had to understand exactly where he and the Republicans differed on the issues. That way the fight would not be about Bill Clinton and Newt Gingrich, but about their disagreements over cuts in Medicare, Medicaid, education and environmental protection.

Bill has an uncanny ability to see down the road in politics, to gauge the consequences of each actor's move and to plan for the long run. He knew the real battle would be over the budget later in the year and that, for him and his Presidency, 1996 was the target for success. At first, Bill counseled patience because he assumed—rightly, as it turned out—that voters would tire of the Republicans' overreaching and begin to fear the radical changes they proposed. But when Gingrich announced his intention to celebrate the achievements of the Republican Congress with an unprecedented prime-time speech to the nation, Bill decided it was time to reclaim the initiative.

In Dallas on April 7, 1995, Bill transformed what was slated as a speech on education issues into a manifesto for his administration. He outlined what he had achieved in deficit reduction and job creation and where he wanted to go: a minimum-wage increase, incremental improvements in health care coverage and tax breaks for the middle class. He attacked the worst aspects of the Republican Contract, such as the welfare bill, as "weak on work and tough on kids." He assailed cuts in education and programs such as school lunches and childhood immunizations. And he laid the groundwork for compromises that would avoid government gridlock. If the Republicans didn't cooperate, responsibility for failing the American public would shift to them and to

Gingrich. It was a great speech, laying out his vision but putting the opposition on notice.

Throughout the spring of 1995, Bill consulted endlessly with friends and allies, gathering and sifting opinions to formulate and develop his strategy. I encouraged Bill to include Dick Morris in his consultations about a new strategy, partly because Morris advised Republicans, and his insights into what the Republicans were thinking could be helpful as Bill tried to move forward. Morris also could be a useful back channel to the opposition when Bill wanted to plant an idea.

At first, Morris's involvement was a closely held secret, but after the Dallas speech, Bill decided to introduce Morris to the staff. Bill's West Wing aides were unpleasantly surprised when they found out that Dick Morris had been advising the President for more than six months. Harold Ickes was appalled, since he and Morris nursed an ideological and personal enmity that dated back twenty-five years to their days in the fractious Democratic politics of Manhattan's Upper West Side. George Stephanopoulos was distraught that Bill would listen to a political turncoat like Morris and unhappy about having to compete with a rival adviser. Leon Panetta didn't like Morris's personality or the way he circumvented the West Wing hierarchy. Every one of their concerns was justified, but Morris's presence helped in unexpected ways.

After the loss of Congress, many of Bill's advisers were walking around the West Wing like shell-shocked soldiers. But nothing is more unifying than a common enemy. Not only did they now have the Republican Congress to motivate them, they had Dick Morris.

One of Bill's greatest strengths is his willingness to invite disparate opinions and then sort them out to reach his own conclusion. He challenged himself and his staff by bringing together people whose experiences were varied and whose perspectives often clashed. It was a way to keep everyone, especially him, fresh and alert. In a rarefied environment like the White House, I don't think you can afford to surround yourself with people whose temperaments and views are always in sync. The meetings might run on schedule, but easy consensus can lead, over time, to poor decisions. Throwing Dick Morris into the mix of egos, attitudes and ambitions in the West Wing ratcheted up everyone's performance.

For numbers and analysis, Morris depended on Mark Penn, a brilliant and intense pollster hired by the Democratic National Committee. Penn and his business partner, Doug Schoen, another veteran political strategist, provided the research used to help shape White House communications. They, along with Morris, began attending weekly Wednesday night meetings in the Yellow Oval Room. Bill and I had learned to take Morris's opinions with a pound of salt and overlook his histrionics and self-aggrandizing. He was a good antidote to conventional wisdom and a spur to Washington bureaucratic inertia. His influence on the Clinton Administration has frequently been exaggerated, sometimes by liberal critics, most often by Morris himself. But he did help Bill develop a strategy to break through the wall of obstructionist Republicans who were blocking his legislative agenda and promoting their own.

When opposing camps are in two polar positions and neither believes it can afford to be seen as moving toward the other, they can decide to move toward a third position—like the apex of the triangle—what came to be called "triangulation." This was essentially a restatement of the philosophy Bill had developed as Governor and as Chairman of the Democratic Leadership Council. In the 1992 campaign, he championed moving beyond the "brain-dead" politics of both parties to craft a "dynamic center." More than old-fashioned political compromise of splitting the difference, triangulation reflected the approach Bill had promised to bring to Washington.

When, for example, the Republicans tried to claim ownership of welfare reform, an issue Bill had been working on since 1980 and one he was committed to act on before his first term was up, Bill would avoid saying no. Instead, he would support the objectives of reform but insist on changes that would improve the legislation and attract enough political support from more moderate Republicans and Democrats to defeat the extreme Republican position. Of course, in politics, as in life, the devil is in the details. The details of welfare reform or budget negotiations were hard fought and difficult and sometimes resembled a Rubik's Cube more than an isosceles triangle.

Though Morris brought energy and ideas to Bill's initiatives, he was not responsible for implementing them. That fell to Leon Panetta and the rest of the Administration. Leon had become Chief of Staff in June of 1994, replacing Mack McLarty, who had done an excellent job under very difficult circumstances in the first year and a half. Panetta, a deficit hawk when he served in Congress from California, had been Bill's choice to head the Office of Management and Budget, and he had played a leading role in devising the deficit reduction plan and then shepherding it through Congress. As Chief of Staff, he ran a tight ship, imposing greater control over the President's schedule and preventing aides from dropping by the Oval Office whenever they felt like it. His expertise in Congress and with the budget would prove to be of crucial importance in the budget battle ahead.

The new Republican majority was looking for ways to legislate their radical agenda. They started with the annual budget bill, trying to gut programs by denying funding. They wanted to dismantle the regulatory functions of government, such as consumer and environmental protections, support for the working poor, tax enforcement and corporate regulations. President Lyndon Johnson's Great Society program— which resulted in Medicare, Medicaid and historic civil rights legislation—was denounced by Newt Gingrich as a "counterculture value system" and "a long experiment in professional government that has failed."

Bill and I were increasingly disturbed by the fervor with which the GOP leaders spouted rhetoric that attacked government, community and even conventional notions of society. They seemed to believe that old-fashioned rugged individualism was all that mattered in late-twentieth-century America, except when, of course, their supporters wanted special legislative favors. I consider myself very much an individualist and somewhat rugged—perhaps a little ragged as well—but I also believe that as an American citizen I am part of a mutually beneficial network of rights, privileges and responsibilities.

It was in the context of this extreme Republican rhetoric that I pushed forward with my book *It Takes a Village*. Gingrich's advocacy of orphanages for poor children born out of wedlock had energized me. After spending years worrying about how to protect and nurture children, now I feared that political extremism could sentence the poor and vulnerable to a Dickensian future. Although it wasn't political in a partisan sense, I wanted my book to describe a vision different from the uncompassionate, elitist and unrealistic views emanating from Capitol Hill.

Despite the right-wing mantra denouncing "liberal media bias," the reality was that the loudest and most effective voices in the media were anything but liberal. Instead, public discourse was increasingly dominated by reactionary pundits and TV and radio personalities. I decided to convey my thoughts and opinions directly to the public by writing them myself. In late July, I began a syndicated weekly newspaper col-

umn called "Talking It Over," following once again the footsteps of
Eleanor Roosevelt, who had written a column six days a week called "My
Day" from 1935 to 1962. My first columns covered topics ranging from
the seventy-fifth anniversary of women's suffrage to a celebration of
family vacations. The exercise of putting my ideas on paper gave me a
clearer sense of how to recast my role as an advocate within the Administration as I began to focus on discrete domestic projects that were more
achievable than massive undertakings such as health care reform. On my
agenda now were children's health issues, breast cancer prevention, and
protecting funding for public television, legal services and the arts.

I learned more about the prevalence and impact of breast cancer, as
well as obstacles to its prevention and treatment, from talking with doctors, patients and survivors at "listening sessions" I convened in senior
centers and hospitals across the country. Starting at a meeting of the
National Breast Cancer Coalition (NBCC) in Williamsburg, Virginia,
during the 1992 campaign, I was struck by the resilience of breast cancer survivors. When the bus carrying attendees broke down en route,
the women simply got off and hitchhiked the rest of the way. I worked
with the NBCC, founded by a determined survivor and advocate, Fran
Visco, over the course of the Administration to obtain more funding for
research and expanded treatment for uninsured women.

I met frequently with breast cancer survivors at the White House.
Through the experiences of my mother-in-law and so many others, I
understood the fear and uncertainty that accompanies a cancer diagno-
sis. One of the most faithful volunteers in my office at the White
House, Miriam Leverage, battled breast cancer for six years before succumbing to the disease in 1996 after a valiant fight. A retired school-
teacher and proud grandmother, Miriam underwent two surgeries,
radiation treatment and five rounds of chemotherapy. She always reminded me and my staffers to perform self-examinations and get regular mammograms, something I had done every year since turning forty.

I launched the Medicare Mammography Awareness Campaign in
conjunction with Mother's Day in 1995 to raise awareness about the importance of early detection and to make sure that women eligible under
Medicare took advantage of mammography. Only 40 percent of older
women, whose mammograms were paid for by Medicare, actually had
the screening. Because one in eight women in our country is expected to
develop breast cancer, early detection is essential. I worked with corporate sponsors, public relations professionals and representatives of con-

sumer groups on the "Mama-gram" campaign to encourage older women to get mammograms and to educate them about the benefits of early detection. The national campaign included inserts in Mother's Day greeting and floral cards, reminding mothers of the importance of regular mammograms, along with promotional store displays, printed grocery bags and public service announcements. Over the next few years, I worked to expand Medicare coverage so that more women would be eligible for annual mammograms without having to make a co-payment, and I was pleased when Bill announced new regulations to ensure the safety and quality of mammography. These efforts dovetailed with my work to support increased funding for research on breast cancer detection, prevention, treatment and potential cures, and to launch a breast cancer stamp with the U.S. Postal Service that channels a portion of its revenues to research.

One of the most vexing and heartbreaking issues that came to my attention as I crisscrossed the U.S. was Gulf War syndrome. Thousands of men and women who served our nation in the military in the Persian Gulf during Operation Desert Storm in 1991 suffered from a variety of ailments, among them chronic fatigue, gastrointestinal disorders, rashes and respiratory problems. I received haunting letters from vets who had risked their lives on behalf of our country abroad and couldn't keep jobs or support their families at home because of these illnesses. One veteran I met, Colonel Herbert Smith, had led a healthy and productive life before his tour in the Persian Gulf. While serving in Operation Desert Storm, he developed swollen lymph nodes, rashes, fatigue, joint pain and fever. After six months in the Gulf, he was forced to return home. Yet doctors were unable to diagnose his illness or offer treatment.

It was heartbreaking to hear Col. Smith describe the agony of living day after day, year after year, not knowing why he had become sick. Even worse for Col. Smith was the skepticism about his illness he encountered from some military doctors. One military doctor accused him of "bleeding" himself to fake anemia in order to receive disability benefits. Col. Smith developed nerve damage to his brain and vestibular system, leaving him severely disabled and unable to continue working. And yet his pleas and those of other veterans were not being heard.

I called for a comprehensive study of Gulf War syndrome, including efforts to determine whether our troops could have been exposed to chemical or biological agents or been affected by oil fires, radiation or other toxins. I met with officials from the Departments of Defense, Veterans Affairs and Health and Human Services to determine what the government should do both to respond to the needs of these veterans and to prevent similar problems in the future. I recommended a Presidential Advisory Committee that Bill appointed to review the issue. He later signed legislation to cover disability benefits for eligible Gulf War veterans with undiagnosed illnesses and directed the Veterans Administration to set up better systems to screen and monitor our troops in the future.

Domestic issues like these dominated my White House agenda during the spring of 1995. Then, the attention of the entire nation turned to an unfathomable tragedy.

For me, April 19 began as an ordinary day of meetings and interviews. Around 11 A.M., I was sitting in my favorite chair in the West Sitting Hall, going over scheduling requests with Maggie and Patti when Bill called urgently from the Oval Office with the news that there had been an explosion at the Alfred P. Murrah Federal Office Building in Oklahoma City. The three of us immediately went into the kitchen and turned on the small television to see the screen filled with the first horrifying pictures broadcast from the scene.

We learned over the next few hours that the damage had been caused by a truck bomb, but no one had solid information about who was responsible. Bill immediately dispatched teams from FEMA, the FBI and other government agencies to Oklahoma City to handle the emergency and to lead the investigation. Because the federal offices were destroyed by the bombing, many essential personnel were dead or injured. A Secret Service agent who had left the White House just seven months earlier for assignment to Oklahoma was one of five agents killed that day. Among the 168 innocent people who died in the bombing were nineteen children, most of whom attended the day care center on the second floor of the building.

The images from Oklahoma City were disturbingly intimate: a little girl, limp as a rag doll, carried out of the smoking rubble by a heartbroken fireman; a terrified office worker being lifted onto the stretcher. The familiarity of the setting and the number of casualties brought the tragedy home to America in ways that other atrocities up until then could not. That was the point of the attack.

We were also reminded that the "bureaucrats" who were always under attack by anti-government zealots could be our neighbors, friends or relatives—that they have real lives and could lose them.

The first thing people needed was information about the bombing and then the reassurance that everything possible was being done to protect them from further attacks. I was particularly concerned about children who were aware of the explosion at the child care center and might fear that their own schools weren't safe. We talked with Chelsea and asked for her advice about how to reassure young children.

On Saturday after the bombing, in a television and radio broadcast, Bill and I talked to a group of children whose parents were federal employees working for the same federal agencies as those attacked in Oklahoma. We thought it was important that as a mother and a father we both speak to the anxieties about such a terrible tragedy.

"It's okay to be frightened by something as bad as this," Bill told the children sitting on the floor of the Oval Office as their parents stood nearby.

"I want you to know that your parents . . . love you and are going to do everything they can to take care of you and to protect you," I said. "There are many more good people in the world than bad and evil people."

Bill told the children that we would catch and punish whoever caused the bombing. And then he asked them to express their own thoughts about it.

"It was mean," said one child.

"I feel sorry for the people that died," said another.

One question broke my heart, and I couldn't answer it. "Who would want to do that to kids who had never done anything to them?"

The rest of the country was seeing Bill as I knew him, a man with an unparalleled empathy and ability to bring people together in difficult times. Before we left the next day to visit families of the victims and to take part in a prayer service, we planted a dogwood tree on the South Lawn in memory of the victims. Bill and I met with a number of victims and their families in private before attending the large memorial service where Bill and the Rev. Billy Graham spoke, helping to heal a hurting nation. Whenever I watched Bill embrace sobbing family members, talk with heartbroken friends or comfort the terminally ill, I fell in love with him all over again. His sympathy draws from a deep well of caring and emotion that enables him to reach out to people in pain.

By the time we got to Oklahoma City, a suspect had been arrested who had ties to militant anti-government groups. It appeared that Timothy McVeigh had chosen April 19 to attack the country he had come to despise because it was the anniversary of the terrible Waco fire, which killed more than eighty members of the Branch Davidian cult, including children. McVeigh and his ilk represented the most alienated and violent elements of the extreme right wing, whose actions sickened every sensible American. Right-wing radio talk shows and websites intensified the atmosphere of hostility with their rhetoric of intolerance, anger and anti-government paranoia, but the Oklahoma City bombing seemed to deflate the militia movement and marginalize the worst haters on the airwaves.

Bill spoke forcefully against the hate-mongers and anti-government zealots in a commencement speech at Michigan State University in early May. "There is nothing patriotic about hating your country, or pretending that you can love your country but despise your government."

While the country coped with the Oklahoma City tragedy, the Office of the Independent Counsel did not rest. On Saturday, April 22, after the children's meeting in the Oval Office, Kenneth Starr and his deputies arrived at the White House to take sworn statements from me and the President. I had been interviewed by Robert Fiske the previous year, before he was replaced, but this would be my first encounter with Starr and his staff. Preparing for the interview was not something that David Kendall or I took lightly. Knowing that every word I uttered would be dissected by the OIC, David insisted that I cram in prep time no matter how busy I was. Often that meant meeting late at night or spending hours digesting information that he delivered to me in large black binders. I came to dread the sight of those binders because they were tangible reminders of the trivialities and minutiae I would be subjected to under oath, all of which could be used to trip me up legally.

Bill went in for his interview in the Treaty Room, the President's study on the second floor of the residence. Representing the White House were Abner Mikva, a former Congressman and federal judge, now White House counsel, and Jane Sherburne, an experienced litigator who had left her private law firm to handle legal issues attached to the investigation. They were joined by our private attorneys, David Kendall and his partner Nicole Seligman, two of the smartest and most caring people I've ever known. Starr and three other lawyers sat on one side of the long conference table we had brought in for the interviews. We sat on the other.

As he came out of his interview, Bill told me his encounter with

Starr had been amiable, and, to my amazement, Bill had asked Jane Sherburne to give Starr and his assistants a tour of the Lincoln Bedroom next door. Somewhat characteristically, I was not prepared to be as charitable as my husband, and this was only the first illustration of the differences between Bill's way of dealing with Starr and mine. We were both in the eye of the storm, but I seemed to be buffeted by every gust of wind, while Bill just sailed along. The idea of hard-core Republican partisans rummaging through our lives, looking at every check we had written in twenty years, and harassing our friends on the flimsiest of excuses infuriated me.

The Republicans opened up a new front when Al D'Amato, the Republican Senator from New York and Chairman of the Senate Banking Committee, convened hearings on Whitewater. I have since made my peace with Senator D'Amato, now one of my most prominent constituents, but the hearings he and his fellow Republican Senators and their staffs conducted inflicted great emotional and monetary damage on innocent people.

Despite Fiske's finding that Vince Foster's death was a suicide unrelated to Whitewater, D'Amato seemed to be fixated on Vince's death, and he paraded past and present White House aides in front of the cameras to grill them about the sad event. Maggie Williams, normally centered and strong, was brought to tears by relentless questioning about events surrounding Vince Foster's death. It was unbearable to watch Maggie raked over the coals again and again and to know that her legal bills were mounting daily.

D'Amato called my friend Susan Thomases a liar as she tried to answer his questions. Her decades-long struggle with multiple sclerosis had impaired her memory, and she tried as hard as she could to respond to the bullying interrogation. I couldn't console her or anyone caught up in this nightmare, because any discussion I might have with someone about any matter the investigators chose to ask about could suggest collusion or coaching. I had to avoid any discussion that could cause someone to answer "Yes" if asked whether he or she had talked to me.

Standing on the sidelines, unable to speak out to defend my friends and colleagues, or even to speak to them about the injustices they were enduring, was one of the hardest things I've ever done. And it would get worse before it got better.

WOMEN'S RIGHTS
ARE HUMAN RIGHTS

THE ARREST OF A DISSIDENT IS NOT UNUSUAL IN China, and Harry Wu's imprisonment might have received scant attention in the American media. But China had been chosen to host the upcoming United Nations Fourth World Conference on Women, and I was scheduled to attend as honorary Chair of the U.S. delegation. Wu, a human rights activist who had spent nineteen years as a political prisoner in Chinese labor camps before emigrating to the United States, was arrested by Chinese authorities on June 19, 1995, as he entered Xinjiang Province from neighboring Kazakhstan.

Although he had a valid visa to visit China, he was charged with espionage and thrown in jail to await trial. Overnight, Harry Wu became widely known, and U.S. participation in the women's conference was cast into doubt as human rights groups, Chinese American activists and some members of Congress urged our nation to boycott. I sympathized with their cause, but it disappointed me that, once again, the crucial concerns of women might be sacrificed.

Typically, governments (including that of the United States) limit their foreign policies to diplomatic, military and trade issues, the staple of most treaties, pacts and negotiations. Seldom are issues such as women's health, the education of girls, the absence of women's legal and political rights or their economic isolation injected into the foreign policy debate. Yet it was clear to me that in the new global economy, individual countries and regions would find it difficult to make economic or social progress if a disproportionate percentage of their female population remained poor, uneducated, unhealthy and disenfranchised.

The U.N. women's conference was expected to provide an important forum for nations to address issues such as maternal and child health care, microfinance, domestic violence, girls' education, family planning, women's suffrage, property and legal rights. It would also offer a rare opportunity for women from around the world to share stories, information and strategies for future action in their own countries. The conference is held roughly every five years, and I hoped my presence would signal the U.S. commitment to the needs and rights of women in international policy.

I had been working on women's and children's issues in the United States for twenty-five years, and, although women in our own country had made gains economically and politically, the same could not be said for the vast majority of women in the world. Yet virtually no one who could attract media attention was speaking out on their behalf.

At the time of Harry Wu's arrest, my staff and I were deeply involved in planning for the conference. But there were already grumblings from the usual suspects in Congress who felt the United States should not participate. Among them were Senators Jesse Helms and Phil Gramm, who announced that the conference was "shaping up as an unsanctioned festival of anti-family, anti-American sentiment." Some members of Congress were skeptical of any event sponsored by the United Nations and were equally dismissive of a gathering focused on women's issues. The Vatican, vociferous on the subject of abortion, joined forces with some Islamic countries concerned that the conference would become an international platform to promote the women's rights they opposed. And some on the American political left were unhappy about the prospect of U.S. participation because the Chinese government was indicating that non-governmental organizations (NGOs) advocating maternal health, property rights for women, microfinance and many other issues might be excluded from the official gathering. Chinese authorities made it difficult for Tibetan activists and others to get visas to enter China. Furthermore, there was widespread discomfort, which I shared, about the host nation's dismal record on human rights and its barbaric policy of condoning forced abortions as a means of imposing its "one child policy."

Sensitive to concerns across the political spectrum, I worked with Melanne Verveer and the President's staff to assemble a delegation for Beijing. Bill named people from varied backgrounds to represent our nation, including Republican Tom Kean, the former Governor of New

Jersey; Sister Dorothy Ann Kelly, President of the College of New Rochelle; and Dr. Laila Al-Marayati, Vice-Chair of the Muslim Women's League. Madeleine Albright, then U.S. Ambassador to the United Nations, was the official head of the delegation.

Months of meetings and strategy sessions with representatives from the United Nations and other countries were thrown into limbo after Wu's imprisonment. Over the next six weeks, there was no shortage of opinions about whether the United States should send a delegation to the conference and whether I should be part of it. I was particularly troubled by a personal letter from Mrs. Wu, who was understandably worried about her husband's fate and felt that my participation in the conference "would be sending a confused signal to the leaders in Beijing about the resolve of the U.S. to press for Harry's release."

It was a legitimate concern for me and for others in the White House and State Department. I knew the Chinese government wanted to use the conference as a public relations tool to improve its image around the world. If I went, I helped China look good. If I boycotted, I triggered bad publicity for the Chinese leadership. We were in a diplomatic bind in which Harry Wu's imprisonment and my attendance at the conference were linked. Our government continued to state privately and publicly that I would not attend if Mr. Wu remained under arrest. When the disagreements became more vehement and resolution seemed unlikely, I considered going anyway, as a private citizen.

Complicating the decision were equally serious concerns about the overall status of U.S.-China relations. Tensions were running high over disagreements about Taiwan, nuclear proliferation, China's sale of M-11 missiles to Pakistan and ongoing human rights abuses. Relations deteriorated even further in mid-August when the Chinese engaged in the bravado of military exercises in the Taiwan Straits.

Less than a month before the start of the conference, the Chinese government evidently decided that it couldn't afford to generate more bad publicity. In a sham trial in Wuhan on August 24, a Chinese court convicted Harry Wu of spying and expelled him from the country. Some media commentators, and Wu himself, were convinced that the United States had made a political deal with the Chinese: Wu would be released, but only if I agreed to come to the conference and refrain from critical remarks about the host government. Clearly it was a delicate diplomatic moment, but there was never a quid pro quo between our government and China. Once the Wu case was resolved, the White House and State Department determined that I should make the trip.

Back home in California, Mr. Wu criticized my decision, reiterating that my attendance might be construed as a tacit approval of China's record on human rights. His Congresswoman, Nancy Pelosi, called to tell me that my presence would be a public relations coup for the Chinese. Bill and I were vacationing in Jackson Hole, Wyoming, and we discussed at length the pros and cons. He supported my view that once Wu had been released, the best way to confront the Chinese about human rights was directly, on their turf. At an event in Wyoming celebrating the seventy-fifth anniversary of America's constitutional amendment extending to women the right to vote, Bill defused the issue and defended U.S. participation as important for women's rights. His message was: "The conference presents a significant chance to chart further gains in the status of women."

By the end of August, our family vacation in the Tetons was winding down. We stayed at the comfortable Western-style home of Senator Jay Rockefeller and his wife, Sharon, where I spent much of my time working on my book, watching enviously as Bill and Chelsea went hiking and horseback riding in one of our nation's most majestic settings. Chelsea, who had spent five weeks at a rigorous camp in southern Colorado, shooting rapids, climbing mountains, building shelters above the tree line and developing other outdoor skills, persuaded us to go camping. I hadn't camped out since college, and Bill never had, unless you count the one night we spent sleeping in his car in Yosemite Park while driving across the country. We were game, but clueless. When we told the Secret Service we wanted to hike and camp in a secluded spot in the Grand Teton National Park, they went into overdrive. By the time we arrived at our campsite, they had staked out the perimeter and had agents patrolling with nightvision goggles. Chelsea laughed at our idea of "roughing it"—a tent with a wooden floor and air mattresses!

We left Wyoming for Hawaii, where Bill spoke at the observance of the fiftieth anniversary of V-J Day at Pearl Harbor and at the National Memorial Cemetery of the Pacific on September 2, 1995. The cemetery, better known as the Punchbowl for its location in the middle of a crater of an extinct volcano, is the site of more than thirty-three thousand graves of those who lost their lives in the Pacific Theater during World

War II, including those killed at Pearl Harbor and later in Korea and Vietnam. The sight of those graves and the thousands of World War II veterans and their families who attended the service was a solemn reminder of the extraordinary sacrifices made for our freedoms.

I stayed up all night in the little cottage we occupied at Kaneohe Marine Base, working on my book and the latest draft of my speech for Beijing. One happy by-product of the Harry Wu incident was that it generated huge publicity for the UN conference. All eyes were now on Beijing, and I knew that all eyes would be on me too. My staff and I had been working on remarks that would forcefully defend the U.S. position on human rights and expand conventional notions of women's rights. I would criticize Chinese government abuses, including coerced abortions and the routine squelching of free speech and free assembly. Soon enough I was on an Air Force jet for the nearly fourteen-hour flight to Beijing, but without my favorite traveling companion. Chelsea had to go back to Washington with her father to start school.

After we ate dinner on the plane, the cabin lights were turned off and most of the passengers bundled themselves in blankets and curled up to sleep as we crossed the Pacific. But the speech team still had work to do. We were on our fifth or sixth draft, and we needed to show the text to our resident foreign policy experts, who had joined us in Honolulu along with other administration officials and support staff. Winston Lord, the gentlemanly former Ambassador to China whom Bill appointed Assistant Secretary of State for East Asian and Pacific Affairs; Eric Schwartz, a human rights specialist on the National Security Council; and Madeleine Albright huddled at a dimly lit worktable and pored over the text. Their job was to catch any inaccuracies or inadvertent diplomatic gaffes. Given all that had preceded it, one wrong word in this speech might lead to a diplomatic brouhaha. Their review was critical, I knew, but I was always wary whenever the experts weighed in. Often they were so intent on leaving their carefully nuanced, diplomatic imprint on a draft that they turned a good speech into mush. Not so in this case.

"What do you want to accomplish?" Madeleine had asked me earlier.

"I want to push the envelope as far as I can on behalf of women and girls," I said.

Madeleine, Win and Eric recommended that I strengthen a section defining human rights and refer to a recent affirmation of those rights at the World Conference on Human Rights in Vienna. They suggested beefing up passages about the effects of war on women, particularly the devastating proliferation of rape as a tactic of war and the increasing number of women refugees resulting from violent conflict. Most important, they understood that the power of the speech lay in its simplicity and emotion. They kept me out of trouble but were careful not to intrude with a heavy hand.

Brady Williamson, a Wisconsin lawyer who led my advance team, received daily inquiries from Chinese officials as to what I was going to say in my speech. They made it clear that while they welcomed my physical presence at the conference, they didn't want to be embarrassed by my words and hoped that I "appreciated China's hospitality."

On trips such as these, sleep is a precious commodity. We rarely got enough and became accustomed to attending meetings, dinners and other events with eyelids drooping and heads nodding. When we finally arrived at the China World Hotel, one of Beijing's luxury establishments for foreign visitors, it was after midnight. I had time for only a few hours of sleep before heading off to my first official event on Tuesday morning, a colloquium on women's health sponsored by the World Health Organization, where I spoke about the gap in health care between women in rich countries like ours and those in poor countries.

Finally, it was time to enter the Plenary Hall, which looked like a mini United Nations. Although I had delivered thousands of speeches, I was nervous. I felt passionately about the subject, and I was speaking as a representative of my country. The stakes were high—for the United States, for the conference, for women around the world and for me. If nothing came out of the conference, it would be viewed as another missed opportunity to galvanize global opinion on behalf of improving conditions and increasing opportunities for women and girls. I didn't want to embarrass or let down my country, my husband or myself. And I didn't want to squander a rare opportunity to advance the cause of women's rights.

Our delegation had been busy negotiating with other delegations over the language in the conference's plan of action. Some delegates clearly disagreed with the American agenda for women. The fact that women's rights was an emotional issue made the delivery of my speech harder for me. I had learned during health care reform that my own strong feelings rarely help me in my delivery of a public address. Now I had to make sure that the tone or pitch of my voice would not confuse the message. Like it or not, women are always subject to criticism if they show too much feeling in public.

Looking out into the audience, I saw women and men of all complexions and races, some in Western garb and many dressed in their nation's traditional clothing. The majority wore headphones to listen to simultaneous translations of the speeches. That was a curveball that I hadn't anticipated: as I spoke, there was no response to my words, and I found it difficult to get into a rhythm or gauge the crowd's reaction because the pauses in my English sentences and paragraphs didn't coincide with those in the dozens of other languages the delegates were hearing.

After thanking Gertrude Mongella, the Secretary-General of the conference, I began by saying that I appreciated being a part of this great global gathering of women:

> This is truly a celebration—a celebration of the contributions women make in every aspect of life: in the home, on the job, in the community, as mothers, wives, sisters, daughters, learners, workers, citizens and leaders. . . . However different we may appear, there is far more that unites us than divides us. We share a common future. And we are here to find common ground so that we may help bring new dignity and respect to women and girls all over the world—and in so doing, bring new strength and stability to families as well.

I wanted the speech to be simple, accessible and unambiguous in its message that women's rights are not separate from, or a subsidiary of, human rights and to convey how important it is for women to make choices for themselves in their lives. I drew on my own experiences and described women and girls I had met all over the world who were working to promote education, health care, economic independence, legal rights and political participation, and to end the inequities and injustices that fall disproportionately on women in most countries.

Pushing the envelope in this speech meant being clear about the injustice of the Chinese government's behavior. The Chinese leadership had blocked non-governmental organizations from holding their NGO forum at the main conference in Beijing. They forced NGOs devoted to causes ranging from prenatal care to microlending to convene at a makeshift site in the small city of Huairou, forty miles north, where there were few accommodations or facilities. Although I didn't mention China or any other country by name, there was little doubt about the egregious human rights violators to whom I was referring.

I believe that on the eve of a new millennium, it is time to break our silence. It is time for us to say here in Beijing, and the world to hear, that it is no longer acceptable to discuss women's rights as separate from human rights. . . . For too long, the history of women has been a history of silence. Even today, there are those who are trying to silence our words.

The voices of this conference and of the women at Huairou must be heard loud and clear: It is a violation of human rights when babies are denied food, or drowned, or suffocated, or their spines broken, simply because they are born girls.

It is a violation of human rights when women and girls are sold into the slavery of prostitution.

It is a violation of human rights when women are doused with gasoline, set on fire and burned to death because their marriage dowries are deemed too small.

It is a violation of human rights when individual women are raped in their own communities and when thousands of women are subjected to rape as a tactic or prize of war.

It is a violation of human rights when a leading cause of death worldwide among women ages fourteen to forty-four is the violence they are subjected to in their own homes by their own relatives.

It is a violation of human rights when young girls are brutalized by the painful and degrading practice of genital mutilation.

It is a violation of human rights when women are denied the right to plan their own families, and that includes being forced to have abortions or being sterilized against their will.

If there is one message that echoes forth from this conference, let it be that human rights are women's rights . . . and women's rights are human rights, once and for all.

I ended the speech with a call to action to return to our countries and renew our efforts to improve educational, health, legal and political opportunities for women. When the last words left my lips—"Thank you very much. God's blessings on you, your work and all who will benefit from it"—the serious and stony-faced delegates suddenly leaped from their seats to give me a standing ovation. Delegates rushed to touch me, shout words of appreciation and thank me for coming. Even the delegate from the Vatican commended me for the speech. Outside the hall, women hung over banisters and rushed down escalators to grab my hand. I was thrilled that my message had resonated, and it was a relief that the press reports, too, were good. *The New York Times* editorial page wrote that the speech "may have been her finest moment in public life." What I didn't know at the time was that my twenty-one-minute speech would become a manifesto for women all over the world. To this day, whenever I travel overseas, women come up to me quoting words from the Beijing speech or clutching copies they want me to autograph.

The reaction of the Chinese government was not so positive. I learned later that the government had blacked out my speech from closed-circuit TV in the conference hall, which had been broadcasting highlights of the conference.

While the Chinese officials would try to control what their citizens heard, they kept themselves surprisingly well-informed, as I learned when we retreated to the hotel to relax for a few hours after the speech. I hadn't seen a newspaper since leaving Hawaii and casually mentioned to my aides that it would be nice to get a copy of the *International Herald Tribune*. Within minutes, we heard a thump against the door to my room. The *Tribune* had arrived, as if on cue. But we had no idea who had heard that I wanted it or who had delivered it.

Before leaving for China, I had received briefings from the State Department and Secret Service that included intelligence information as well as protocol and diplomatic issues. I had been cautioned to assume that everything I said or did would be tape-recorded, particularly in the hotel room.

Whether the newspaper's arrival was a coincidence or an example of the Chinese government's internal security, it led to some good laughs, and we realized that we'd all been unusually tense about being watched and recorded. From that point on, my staff regularly winked at the television screen and spoke into lamps, making loud requests for pizza, steak and milkshakes and hoping that our security handlers would deliver again. But after three days, only the newspaper had arrived at the door.

The day after the Beijing speech, I went to Huairou to speak to the NGO representatives whose forum had been exiled from the main conference. Accompanying me was another member of the U.S. delegation, the Administration's dedicated Secretary of Health and Human Services, Donna Shalala, who served in Bill's cabinet for eight years. She was known for her unwavering commitment to improving the health and welfare of Americans—and her mettle, which would be tested in Huairou. It was a gloomy day. Rain poured down; the air was raw. We drove north in a small caravan past flat fields and rows of rice paddies to the site of what was now billed as the NGO Forum. Though they had taken the precaution of moving the forum to a location an hour's drive from the main UN gathering, Chinese officials still worried about the thousands of activist women in Huairou. My presence, in their view, only escalated the stakes. They were unhappy that I had criticized their government in my speech the day before and must have been even more concerned about what I would say to the women whom they had banished from Beijing.

Due to the rain, the forum had to be moved inside a converted movie house, and it was packed with three thousand people, double the capacity, by the time we arrived. Hundreds more were trying to get in. Standing outside for hours in the driving rain, with muddy puddles underfoot, these activists were blocked by the Chinese police. As my car approached the hall, the police, bandying nightsticks, pushed the crowd back from the entrance. This was not a polite confrontation. As the police pushed harder and harder, many in the crowd struggled to stay on their feet. Some fell into a slippery sea of mud.

Melanne had arrived ahead of me with Neel Lattimore, my first-rate deputy press secretary, who was famous for his pithy one-liners and artful handling of my relations with the media. Neel brought professionalism and humor to one of the most delicate jobs in the White House. As Melanne was pushed back and forth by the surging crowd, a Secret Service agent recognized her and extended his long arm, which she held on to like a life preserver while he literally pulled her inside. The intrepid Kelly Craighead went into the crowd with Secret Service agents to find Donna and other missing members of my group and pulled them to safety. By the time they caught up with us, they were sopping wet but otherwise none the worse for wear. Neel was taking care of our press contingent, and he shepherded the press out of their bus, lagging behind to make sure everyone was accounted for. By the time he started through the rain-drenched crowd, he couldn't make it. When he asked for help from one of the Chinese officials monitoring the crowd, he was pushed and yelled at and forced to leave the area al-together. He couldn't get inside to find us, and they wouldn't let him wait near our cars. He eventually found his own way back to Beijing.

The Chinese police, through their harsh tactics outside the hall, had done an extraordinary job of energizing the NGO representatives, who sang, yelled, clapped and cheered as I walked on stage.

I loved the feeling of the crowd and told them how much I admired and championed the work these groups did, often in dangerous situa-tions, to build and sustain civil society and democracy. NGOs are miti-gating forces that help keep the private sector and the government in check. I talked about NGOs I had seen in action around the world, and then I read "Silence," the poem written for me by the student in New Delhi. It seemed to be the perfect antidote to the Chinese government's suppression of the NGO Forum and its attempts to silence the words and ideas of so many women. I was buoyed by the courage and passion of women who had traveled thousands of miles, at great personal ex-pense, to break the silence and raise their voices on behalf of their causes. For years afterwards, the scenes I witnessed at Huairou re-mained etched in my mind. Seldom does one see so tangibly, in one set-ting, the differences between living in a free society and living under government control.

Once it became clear I would make the controversial trip to China, the Administration requested that I stop for an overnight visit in Mongolia, a former Soviet satellite that in 1990 had chosen the path of democracy rather than follow the Communist lead of neighboring China. The fledgling democracy was struggling because the spigot of Soviet aid had been turned off, and the country faced difficult economic times. It was important for the United States to show support for the Mongolian people and their elected leadership, and a visit from the First Lady to one of the most remote capitals of the world was one way to do it.

Ulan Bator is the world's coldest capital, and even in early Septem-ber, snow is not unusual. But we arrived on a crystal-clear day with bright sunshine. We drove about forty-five minutes into the high plains to visit one of Mongolia's thousands of nomadic families. Three gener-ations of this family lived in two large tents, known as *gers*, made out of heavy felt stretched over a wooden frame. I had brought a handmade saddle as a gift, and in presenting it to the grandfather patriarch, I explained that my husband came from a region with horses and cattle. Asking questions through an interpreter, I learned that this was the site of their summer home and that they were preparing to leave soon for their winter home near the Gobi desert, where the weather is milder. They traveled with their livestock by horse and cart and subsisted on meat, mare's milk and other dairy products made from it, just as their ancestors had done hundreds of years before.

The backdrop of their life on the steppes was stunning in its vastness, serenity and natural beauty. The family's young children raced on horseback, and their beautiful young mother showed me how to milk a horse. Inside the family's ger, every square inch served a purpose. The only sign of modern technology was an old, rusty transistor radio. As is the custom of hospitality in Mongolia, I was offered a bowl of fermented mare's milk.

I thought it tasted like warm, day-old plain yogurt, not something I'd seek out, but not so horrible that I couldn't sip it politely. I generously offered some to the American press, all of whom declined. The next day, when one of the White House physicians who traveled with us on overseas trips—we called him Dr. Doom—found out about my culinary adventure, he ordered me to take a course of strong antibiotics to prevent a horrible livestock disease.

"Don't you know you can get brucellosis from raw milk?" he scolded.

I was mesmerized by this place and these lives, but I was scheduled to have lunch with President Ochirbat, followed by tea with a group of women and then an address to students at the National University. We had to go.

In Ulan Bator, there were no traces of indigenous Mongolian culture, as the Soviets had destroyed most of the buildings and monuments that were uniquely Mongolian and replaced them with sterile, Stalinist-era structures. The people had been forbidden even to speak the name of Genghis Khan, the leader who ruled the vast thirteenth-century Mongolian empire. As we drove into Ulan Bator, people stood ten deep on the sidewalk to watch with curiosity as our cars went by. They didn't wave or call out, as crowds do in many countries; respect was offered quietly. I appreciated the extraordinary turnout generated for an American dignitary, although I later learned that our convoy of cars was as much an attraction as I was.

After every paragraph of my speech at the university, I had to pause while my words were translated into Mongolian. I spoke of the courage of the Mongolian people and their leadership, urging them to continue their struggle toward democracy. Winston Lord had come up with the idea that Mongolia should be held as an example for anyone doubting democracy's ability to take root in unlikely places. And Lissa introduced a refrain: "Let them come to Mongolia!" From then on, whenever we visited a country that was struggling to become democratic, we would break into a chorus of: "Let them come to Mongolia!" And so they should.

Flying home, I thought about how many of the women I had met seemed to identify with my challenges and with each other's, giving me a deep sense of connection and solidarity with women the world over. I may have gotten the headlines on this trip, but it was the women I had met whose lives and achievements against great odds deserved the world's respect. They sure had mine.

SHUTDOWN

I RETURNED FROM ASIA IN TIME TO GET CHELSEA settled into school. Although she still indulged my maternal impulse to help her, she was a fifteen-year-old and eager to test her independence. I gave in when she pleaded to be allowed to ride with her friends, instead of always trailing behind in a car driven by the Secret Service. I wanted her to live like a typical teenager, though we both knew her situation was anything but typical. Despite the obvious differences that living in the White House presented, her life revolved around friends, school, church and ballet. Five days a week, after school, she took a couple of hours of lessons at the Washington School of Ballet, then returned to the White House to face the mountain of homework assigned to juniors as they ramped up for the college applications process ahead. Chelsea no longer needed nor always welcomed my hovering presence, so I had time to immerse myself in finishing my book *It Takes a Village*. I had to put in long hours writing and enlist help to make my deadline of Thanksgiving.

I was planning to go to Latin America in October for the first time to attend the annual meeting of the First Ladies of the Western Hemisphere. Bill and I had hosted a Summit of the Americas in Miami in December 1994, which had given us the opportunity to meet all the Hemisphere's leaders and their spouses. Bill was determined that the U.S. play a positive role in promoting democratic values in the area, since every country—with the exception of Cuba—was now a democracy.

This was good news for the people of the region and for the United States, but our government needed to help our neighbors make progress in improving their economies, alleviating poverty, decreasing illiteracy and improving health care. The end of internal conflicts and the promise of expanded trade and investment opportunities could raise the standard of living and might someday lead to a Hemispheric alliance from the Canadian arctic to the southern tip of Argentina. But a tremendous amount of work had to be done to create the possibility of such prosperity.

On this trip, however, I was heading south to visit U.S. development programs that were assisting women and children, whose status directly reflects a nation's economic and political progress. I was eager for the opportunity to work with my counterparts to develop and implement a common agenda to eradicate measles and reduce maternal mortality rates throughout the Hemisphere. In the past, American policy in the region led to the funneling of foreign aid to military juntas that opposed communism and socialism but sometimes repressed their own citizens. Successive American governments supported regimes that committed human rights violations against people from El Salvador to Chile. The Clinton Administration hoped to make it clear that the days of the U.S. ignoring such abuses were over.

I first stopped in Nicaragua, a country of over four million people ravaged by years of civil war and a massive earthquake that had almost flattened the capital, Managua, in 1972. Violeta Chamorro, Nicaragua's first woman President, headed an ambitious but fragile government in a country that had known only dictatorship and war in past decades. In 1990, in one of the first legitimately democratic elections in Nicaragua's history, President Chamorro won a surprise victory as leader of an opposition movement. An elegant, striking woman, she welcomed me to her hacienda-like house in Managua. She had turned it into a shrine to her late husband, a crusading newspaper editor who was assassinated by the forces loyal to dictator Anastasio Somoza in 1978. Displayed in the yard was her husband's bullet-riddled car—a memento mori of the dangerous environment in which she governed. Once again, I was struck by the courage of a woman whose personal tragedy led her to fight for democracy and against unaccountable power.

In one of Managua's poorest barrios, I visited women who had formed a microcredit borrowing group called "Mothers United." Supported by USAID and run by the Foundation for International Community Assistance (FINCA), these women were an excellent example of successful American foreign aid at work. They showed me the products they made or purchased to re-sell—mosquito netting, baked goods, automobile parts. One of the women surprised me when she said she had seen me on television, visiting the site of the SEWA project in Ahmadabad, India. "Are Indian women like us?" she asked. I told her that the Indian women I met also wanted to improve their lives by earning money that would enable them to send their children to school, fix up their homes and reinvest profits in their businesses. The encounter made me more determined in my efforts to increase the amount of money our government invested in microcredit projects around the world and to establish microcredit projects in our country. In 1994, I had advocated the creation of the Community Development Financial Institutions Fund (CDFI) to support community-based banks across the United States dedicated to providing grants, loans and equity financing to people in distressed areas that had been deserted by traditional banks. I was convinced that microcredit could help individuals, but most countries needed good national economic policies like those that were working in Chile, where I went next.

Chile had suffered for years under the brutal dictatorship of General Augusto Pinochet, who left office in 1989. Under its democratically elected President, Eduardo Frei, Chile was becoming a global model of economic and political success. Frei's wife, Marta Larrachea de Frei, was a First Lady after my own heart. Assisted by a professional staff, she tackled issues ranging from microfinance to education reform. At a microcredit project in Chile's capital, Santiago, Marta and I met a woman who used her loan to buy a new sewing machine for her dressmaking business. When she told us that she felt "like a caged bird who had been set free," I hoped that all women would eventually be free and prepared to make their own choices in life—just like Marta's four daughters and mine.

Fernando Henrique Cardoso, President of Brazil since 1994, had also come to office determined to revitalize the economy after a period of instability. His wife, Ruth Cardoso, a sociologist, assumed a formal position in her husband's government working to improve the living conditions for poor Brazilians in crowded cities and vast rural areas. I met with the Cardosos at the presidential residence in Brasilia, a modernistic complex of glass, steel and marble. At the gathering Ruth had convened, we discussed the status of women in Brazil. It was a mixed assessment. For educated, affluent women, choices were wide open, in sharp contrast to the vast majority of Brazilian women, who lacked education and opportunities. The Cardosos told me they were focused on changing the education system, in which disparities were intensified because public primary education in many parts of the country was available only a few hours a day, limiting the opportunity for a good education to those who could afford private schools or tutors. Access to higher education was largely free to the students who qualified, but most of them were upper class.

This disparity between rich and poor was made vivid in a stop in Salvador de Bahia on Brazil's coast. Well-known for its exciting mix of cultural influences, Salvador is a city pulsating with the influences of the Afro-Brazilians whose ancestors had been brought there as slaves. In a square overflowing with jubilant revelers, I watched a performance by the band Olodum, a local sensation that had become world renowned as Paul Simon's backup band. Comprised of dozens of young men pounding drums of all shapes and sizes, Olodum made music that was electric and deafening, leaving the crowd dancing on the cobblestones.

If Olodum evoked the positive expression of people's lives in Salvador, a maternity hospital I visited the next morning bespoke the hardships of everyday living. Half the patients were mothers with their newborns; the other half were gynecological patients, many admitted because of botched back-alley abortions. The Minister of Health, who served as my guide for the hospital visit, bluntly told me that despite laws against abortion, "Rich women have access to contraception if they choose; poor women do not."

By the time I arrived in Asunción, capital of landlocked Paraguay, for the meeting of the Western Hemisphere's First Ladies, I had seen evidence of the myriad problems confronting Latin America, as well as grassroots solutions. At the conference, we worked together on a plan to immunize all children against measles and to expand opportunities for girls to attend school. On the way to a reception hosted by President Juan Carlos Wasmosy and his wife, Maria Teresa Carrasco de Wasmosy, at the presidential palace, I climbed aboard the bus and spotted an empty seat next to an amiable-looking lady with white hair. She looked familiar, but I couldn't remember who she was. Probing for clues, I asked her how long it had taken her to reach Paraguay (which would give me an idea of her country's geographical location) and how things were going in her homeland. "Fine," she said stone-faced. "Except for the embargo."

I had managed to seat myself next to Vilma Espin, Fidel Castro's sister-in-law, who was representing him at the conference. Thankfully, no one misinterpreted my seating arrangement as a rapprochement to Cuba.

Although this trip lasted only five days, it became a blueprint for my future travels to Central and South America and the Caribbean, and the personal interactions reinforced the value of building relationships that can smooth the path toward cooperation on important projects.

I had already seen the importance of such relationships in the context of the Middle East. A few weeks before my trip to Latin America, Queen Noor of Jordan, Leah Rabin of Israel and Suzanne Mubarak of Egypt had come to Washington with their husbands for the signing of a historic peace accord ending Israel's military occupation of certain West Bank cities. Before the formal signing ceremony in the East Room on September 28, 1995, I hosted a tea for the spouses of attending Middle Eastern leaders.

In the Yellow Oval Room on the second floor, Leah, Suzanne, Noor and I greeted one another like old friends. We did our best to welcome a new member of the group, Suha Arafat, wife of the Palestinian leader. I was curious about her. I knew that she came from a prominent Palestinian family and that her mother, Raymonda Tawil, was a famous poet and essayist, an unconventional woman in her culture. Suha, who had worked for the PLO before her surprise marriage, was much younger than Arafat. She had recently given birth to a daughter, and that gave us common ground for conversation. Each of us tried to make her feel comfortable, but Suha seemed ill at ease.

Leah, Suzanne, Noor and I often discussed the ongoing negotiations. No state secrets were exchanged, but we could provide an informal conduit of information and feedback, and Noor or Leah sometimes called me with a message that the King or Prime Minister wanted to convey to the President through informal channels.

I now look back on that tranquil afternoon in the fall of 1995 as a period of calm before a terrible storm.

In his remarks at the treaty signing in the East Room later that day, King Hussein kidded me about the no-smoking rule I had introduced to the White House. "At least Prime Minister Rabin and I did not smoke while we are here. . . . Thank you so much for your good influence in that regard." I had offered to waive the rule for him and Prime Minister Rabin, but he declined any "special privilege." "Besides," he added, "it will guarantee short meetings!"

The reception that evening at the nearby Corcoran Gallery turned into an oratory marathon. As Yitzhak Rabin, who followed Yasir Arafat's epic-length speech, finally took the podium, he looked directly at Arafat and said, "You know, . . . in Israel there is a saying: What is a Jewish sport? . . . Speechmaking." He paused for a beat. "I start to believe, Chairman Arafat, that you are close to being Jewish." Arafat joined in as the audience roared with good-natured laughter.

After he returned home, Rabin escalated his efforts to ensure a future in which Israel would be secure from violence and terrorism. Tragically, he did not live to realize his dream.

On Saturday, November 4, 1995, I was upstairs working on my book when Bill called to tell me that Rabin had been shot as he left a peace rally in Tel Aviv. His assassin was not a Palestinian or an Arab, but a fanatic right-wing Israeli who condemned Rabin for negotiating with the Palestinians and agreeing to trade land for peace. I ran downstairs and found Bill surrounded by advisers. I threw my arms around him and just held on. This was a deeply personal loss. We admired Rabin as a leader, and Bill regarded him as a friend—even as something of a father figure. Bill and I retreated to our bedroom, to be alone with our grief. Two hours later in the Rose Garden, Bill made one of the most eloquent and heartfelt statements of his Presidency, bidding farewell to a great leader and friend: "Tonight, the land for which he gave his life is in mourning. But I want the world to remember what Prime Minister Rabin said here at the White House barely one month ago: 'We should not let the land flowing with milk and honey become a land flowing with blood and tears. Don't let it happen.'"

"Now it falls to us, all those in Israel, throughout the Middle East and around the world who yearn for and love peace to make sure it doesn't happen. Yitzhak Rabin was my partner and my friend. I admired him, and I loved him very much. Because words cannot express my true feelings, let me just say *shalom, chaver*—good-bye, friend."

Those last words in Hebrew became a validating and rallying cry. When we arrived in Israel for Rabin's funeral, we saw billboards and bumper stickers quoting Bill.

Bill invited a distinguished delegation, including former Presidents Jimmy Carter and George H. W. Bush, the Chairman of the Joint Chiefs of Staff and forty members of Congress, to travel with us to attend the funeral in Jerusalem on November 6. Upon our arrival, Bill and I went immediately to see Leah at her residence. My heart was breaking for her. Like Jackie Kennedy, she had been with her husband when he was shot down. She looked drawn and older than she had just weeks earlier in Washington. We found few words adequate to convey our desolation. At the funeral service at Har Herzl Cemetery, Arab Kings, Prime Ministers and Presidents paid their respects to a warrior who died for peace. After Bill delivered his eulogy, Leah gave him a long, loving hug. The most poignant tribute was the most personal. Rabin's granddaughter Noa Ben Artzi-Pelossof spoke to her beloved grandfather: "Grandpa, you were the pillar of fire before the camp, and now we're just a camp left alone in the dark, and we're so cold."

For security reasons, Arafat did not attend the funeral, but Bill met with Mubarak, Hussein and Shimon Peres, the acting Prime Minister, who had negotiated the Oslo Accords and shared the Nobel Peace Prize with Arafat and Rabin in 1994. As Rabin's granddaughter eloquently reminded us, peace is like a fragile hearth fire that has to be constantly tended or it will die.

On the long flight back to Washington, Bill invited Presidents Carter and Bush to join him in the Air Force One conference room to reminisce about Rabin and to discuss the status of the Middle East peace process. Carter had successfully overseen the Camp David Agreement between Israel and Egypt, and Bush had convened the Madrid Conference, which brought all the parties in the Middle East together for peace talks for the first time. When we finally decided to get some rest, Bill and I headed to the private presidential quarters at the front of the plane, which include an office, a bathroom and a compartment with two sofa beds. Bill and I weren't sure how to accommodate two ex-Presidents, so we offered them the pull-down beds in the comfortable and relatively spacious doctors' and nurses' room. The rest of our invited guests stretched out on couches or in their seats in the VIP cabins at the back of the plane. A few days later we learned that Newt Gingrich was resentful over his accommodations and what he viewed as the unceremonious backstair exit offered him and other guests when the plane arrived at Andrews Air Force Base.

A showdown had been brewing on the federal budget since the prior spring, when the Republicans who controlled Congress started drafting funding bills to reflect the principles of their Contract with America. They called for both a huge tax cut and a balanced budget in seven years, a combination that defied the laws of arithmetic and could be achieved only with deep reductions in education, environmental protection and health care programs such as Medicare and Medicaid. They proposed a welfare reform package that included draconian social-engineering ideas such as denying welfare payments—for life—to single mothers under eighteen. They vowed to cancel a scheduled decrease in Medicare premiums, effectively raising rates for seniors.

Bill was always willing to work with the Republicans, but their budget was unacceptable. He signaled that he would veto any bill that weakened Medicare, hurt children and left the poor without a safety net. And he announced that he would offer his own balanced budget, without the cruel cuts and phony numbers of the Gingrich plan. By the end of the summer recess, the Republicans still didn't have a budget agreement, and at the close of the federal fiscal year on September 30, the government ran out of operating funds. Congress and the President agreed on a "continuing resolution" or CR—a temporary budget extension—that authorized the Treasury to issue checks while negotiations continued. But this stopgap resolution was due to expire at midnight, November 13, and there was neither a new budget nor an agreement on extending the CR.

As the budget deadline approached, I was trying to meet my own publishing deadline for my unfinished book, madly drafting and redrafting chapters in longhand. But I weighed in directly and through my staff about how crucial I thought it was for Bill to stand against the budget priorities articulated by Gingrich.

Despite Republican threats to shut down the government, Bill rejected the new resolution sent to him after Rabin's funeral, which was even harsher. Gingrich seemed to be playing a game of political "chicken," but he had misjudged his adversary. Bill vetoed this resolution too.

While Bill was engaged in round-the-clock negotiations in the West Wing, he checked in often to ask what I thought about a particular issue. He knew I was concerned about the Republican proposals on Medicare and Medicaid, and I asked him if one of my staff members, Jennifer Klein, could participate in the negotiations and help analyze and document exactly how the Republican proposals would endanger Medicare and dismantle Medicaid. On these sensitive topics I wanted a direct channel to Bill's staff. He agreed, and for the duration of the budget battles, Jen helped Chris Jennings—the President's top health care adviser and someone I relied on for his expertise throughout my time at the White House—lead the Administration's effort to protect these and other health care programs.

On November 13, the government ran out of money to spend, and the President under the law had to shut it down. This was an excruciating decision for Bill, and it showed. He worried about the effects of closing the government's doors and furloughing eight hundred thousand federal workers. Only employees deemed "essential" could legally remain on the job, working without pay. A program like Meals on Wheels was not funded, putting at risk about six hundred thousand of the elderly who depended on it. The Federal Housing Administration couldn't process thousands of home sales. The Department of Veterans Affairs stopped paying widows and other beneficiaries their due proceeds from veterans' life insurance policies. The national monuments on the Mall closed their doors. Yellowstone National Park and the Grand Canyon turned away visitors. Two truckloads of Christmas trees destined for the annual Pageant of Peace in Washington were stranded somewhere east of Ohio because the National Park Service couldn't unload them or plant them for the ceremony.

A peculiar quiet settled over the White House. Most of the employees in the residence and East Wing were sent home. The Secret Service was considered essential; clerks and florists were not. The West Wing staff was reduced from 430 to about 90; my official staff was cut to 4. Volunteers filled in to try to manage the work that didn't stop under any circumstances. But these were small inconveniences. If there were no resolution, the real problems would begin at the end of the month, when government paychecks were due to go out. And I worried about what we would do if another national emergency or international crisis occurred.

Each side of the aisle blamed the other for the government shutdown, but Gingrich tipped his hand at a breakfast meeting with reporters on November 15. Gingrich suggested that he had sent a tougher version of the budget resolution to the White House because he felt that Bill had snubbed him on Air Force One during the return trip from Prime Minister Rabin's funeral.

"It's petty, but I think it's human," Gingrich said. "You've been on the plane for twenty-five hours and nobody has talked to you and they ask you to get off the plane by the back ramp. . . . You just wonder, where is their sense of manners? Where is their sense of courtesy?"

The next day, the front page of the *New York Daily News* featured the enormous headline CRY BABY over a cartoon image of Gingrich in diapers. That afternoon, the White House released a photograph taken by White House photographer Bob McNeely. There was Gingrich on the flight, talking with the President and Majority Leader Dole, looking perfectly content. Gingrich's quote—and the photograph—were all over the media. With one self-indulgent remark, he punctured his credibility and ensured that the American people knew to blame Congress, not the Administration, for the government shutdown. The fight was not over, but the field was shifting.

The government was closed for six days, the longest shutdown in history. Both sides finally agreed to another CR that would finance the government until December 15. Many people had suffered enormous anxiety and hardship, but for the long-term sake of the country, it was essential for Bill to stand his ground.

When I look at our schedules from the last three months of 1995, it's hard to believe how many events and issues we were tackling. I finally put the finishing touches on *It Takes a Village* during another Thanksgiving at Camp David surrounded by our families and good friends. Then it was time to kick off the Christmas season with the Pageant of Peace and National Tree Lighting Ceremony, which included those Ohio Scotch pines that had finally been delivered when the government reopened.

On November 28, Bill and I embarked on an official trip to England, Ireland, Germany and Spain. I first went to England in 1973 with Bill when we skipped our Yale Law School commencement. As cash-starved students, we flew on student standby fares for less than one hundred dollars apiece, stayed in cheap bed-and-breakfasts or on friends' couches and kept whatever schedule we chose. In 1995, however, we were returning to England on Air Force One, driving the streets in an armored limousine and scheduled to the minute.

Bill's relations with Prime Minister Major had gotten off to a rocky start when we learned that Major's government cooperated with the first Bush Administration by attempting to unearth records of Bill's activities in England during the student protests against the Vietnam War. No such records existed, but overt meddling in American politics by the Tories was disconcerting. Relations were further strained in 1994 when Bill granted a visa to Gerry Adams, the head of Sinn Fein, the political wing of the Irish Republican Army.

No American President had ever become involved in mediating the Irish Troubles, but Bill was determined to help work toward a solution. There was no doubt that Adams had been somehow involved in IRA activities in the past, and the U.S. State Department agreed with the British government's arguments against granting the visa. But the Irish government had decided that dealing with Adams and Sinn Fein made sense. They argued that Bill could play a role in creating an environment conducive to peace negotiations. In this case and others, Bill was willing to take political risks to demonstrate that you don't make peace with your friends and you can't make peace with your enemies unless you're willing to talk to them. He decided to grant the visa, and his bet paid off. Northern Ireland was enjoying a cease-fire, and we would soon be on our way to Belfast to celebrate.

Of all the trips we took during the eight years of Bill's Presidency, this one was among the most special. Bill was proud of his Irish ancestry through his mother, a Cassidy. Chelsea fell in love with Irish folk tales when she was a little girl. She first saw Ireland in 1994 in the middle of the night at Shannon Airport during a refueling stop on our flight to Russia. She asked if she could go out into the field and touch Irish soil. I watched as she picked up some sod and put it in a bottle to take home. One of Bill and Chelsea's favorite books was Thomas Cahill's *How the Irish Saved Civilization*, which Bill gave to friends and colleagues. Yet except for the stopovers at Shannon Airport, none of us had been to Ireland, north or south.

Now we felt the emotional resonance of the beautiful traditional Gaelic greeting: *Céad míle fáilte*—"One hundred thousand welcomes."

Our first stop in Belfast was the Mackie plant, a factory that assembled textile machinery and one of the few in Northern Ireland that successfully integrated Catholic and Protestant employees in its workforce. Two children, a Catholic schoolgirl whose father had been murdered in 1987 and a Protestant boy, joined hands to introduce Bill. Because of the history of sectarian separatism, most people in Belfast lived in religiously segregated neighborhoods and went to church-run schools. This joint appearance by the children was meant to symbolize a new vision for the future.

While Bill met with the various factions, I split off to meet with women leaders of the peace movement. Because they were willing to work across the religious divide, they had found common ground. At the Lamplighter Traditional Fish and Chips restaurant, I met sixty-five-year-old Joyce McCartan, a remarkable woman who had founded the Women's Information Drop-in Center in 1987 after her seventeen-year-old son was shot dead by Protestant gunmen. She had lost more than a dozen family members to violence. Joyce and other women had set up the center as a safe house: a place for women of both religions to convene and talk over their needs and fears. Unemployment was high, and both Catholic and Protestant women worried about young people in the community who had nothing to do. The nine women sitting around the table described how frightened and worried they were when their sons and husbands left the house and how relieved they were when they arrived safely back home. "It takes women to bring men to their senses," Joyce said.

These women hoped that the cease-fire would continue and that the violence would end once and for all. They poured tea from ordinary stainless steel teapots, and when I remarked how well they kept the tea warm, Joyce insisted I take a pot to remember them by. I used that dented teapot every day in our small family kitchen at the White House. When Joyce died shortly after our visit, I was honored to be asked to return to Belfast in 1997 to deliver the first Joyce McCartan Memorial Lecture at the University of Ulster. I brought the teapot with me and put it on the podium as I spoke of the courage of Irish women like Joyce who, at kitchen tables and over pots of tea, had helped chart a path to peace.

From Belfast, we helicoptered on Marine One to Derry along the coast of Northern Ireland. Derry is the home of John Hume, one of the architects of the peace process who shared the Nobel Peace Prize with David Trimble, the leader of the largest Protestant party, the Ulster Unionist Party. A large rumpled man with a kind face and silver tongue, Hume was the leader of the SDLP, the Social Democratic and Labour Party, founded in 1970 to push for a peaceful resolution to the Troubles. He had been on the front lines of non-violence and reconciliation for decades, and Bill wanted to acknowledge, in Hume's community, the personal risk he had taken for peace. Chanting, "We want Bill, we want Bill," tens of thousands thronged the streets in the freezing cold to roar their approval of Bill and America, and I was filled with pride and respect for my husband.

Another huge crowd awaited us at the City Hall when we returned to Belfast for the Christmas tree-lighting ceremony. A young naval steward accompanying the President surveyed the sea of faces. "These people all look the same," he said. "Why have they been killing each other?"

I stood before the crowd and read excerpts from letters written by children expressing their hopes for a lasting peace. Then Bill, with two young letter writers at his side, threw the switch that illuminated the lights on the Christmas tree. He, too, spoke of hope and peace, and he told everyone assembled at this festive gathering that our day in Belfast and in Derry and Londonderry County would long be with us as one of the most remarkable of our lives. I wholeheartedly agreed.

We ended the evening at a reception at Queens University sponsored by the English Secretary for Northern Ireland, Sir Patrick Mayhew, and attended by representatives of the various factions. Many had been in the same room together only once before, when they came to the White House to celebrate St. Patrick's Day the previous March. At the Belfast gathering, the Catholic leadership stood near the band, while the Protestants clung to the opposite side of the room. Ian Paisley, the hard-core Protestant leader of the Democratic Unionist Party, made an appearance but wouldn't shake hands with the "papists." Like fundamentalists everywhere, he seemed stuck in a time warp, unwilling to concede a new reality.

The next morning we flew to Ireland's capital, Dublin. Since the early 1990s, Ireland had been referred to by economists as the "Celtic Tiger" because of explosive economic growth and a new prosperity that was actually bringing Irish immigrants back home. Bill had appointed Jean Kennedy Smith, President Kennedy's sister, as Ambassador to Ireland in 1993, and she was doing a terrific job. In Dublin, we paid an official courtesy call on Mary Robinson, the first female President of Ireland, at her official residence, Áras an Uachtaráin. President Robinson and her husband, Nick, down-to-earth and easy to talk to, were committed to the Irish peace process and eager to hear about Belfast and Derry. She showed us a light that is kept burning in the front window to welcome anyone Irish who, having left Ireland, finds the way home.

From there I went to the National Gallery to address the women of the north and south of Ireland. In a speech carried live on national Irish television, I praised the bravery of Irish women who had stood up for peace. I joked about the Irish television personality who had recently welcomed a group of women lawmakers to his show by asking, "Who's minding the children?" I smiled and said, "I long for the day when men are asked the same question." Debate raged in Ireland about what choices women should be "allowed" to make, especially in the realm of family life. A week earlier, the Irish had narrowly passed a referendum legalizing divorce over vigorous opposition from the Roman Catholic

Church. The women attending the event knew very well that despite the progress women had made economically, politically and socially, many obstacles remained.

I met up with Bill at the Bank of Ireland next to the College Green of Trinity University, where we spent time with Bono and other members of the band U2, who have since become friends. Bill and I have worked with Bono on the global issues he champions, debt relief for poor countries and more resources to fight HIV/AIDS. When we walked onto the stage constructed for Bill's speech, I gasped. There were probably one hundred thousand people jammed into the narrow streets and across the green to hear the American President speak. Bill exhorted the immense crowd to work for peace, saying that no conflict is too intractable to remain forever unresolved and that the Troubles, too, could yield to a peaceful future.

After another address, before the Irish Parliament, known as the Dáil, we hit the streets for some shopping and a visit to Cassidy's Pub. Our advance teams used genealogical information to track down any Cassidy who might be related to Bill, and they joined us inside for a pint of Guinness. I soon concluded that all the Irish are related in some way or another.

At Ambassador Smith's residence early that evening, we were thrilled to meet Seamus Heaney, the Nobel Prize–winning poet, and his wife, Marie. Heaney's poem "The Cure at Troy" had inspired Bill's theme that this was a time in Ireland "where hope and history rhyme."

Ireland invigorated and inspired me, and I wished we could bottle up the good feelings and take them back home.

A TIME TO SPEAK

B ILL'S PARTING WORDS IN BELFAST—"MAY THE CHRIST-mas spirit of peace and goodwill flourish and grow in you"—hadn't penetrated Washington, where partisan battles continued into the holiday season. The annual Congressional Ball, hosted by the White House on December 5, was attended by the same people who were fighting Bill over the budget and decking our halls with subpoenas. Yet they were eager to wait in a long receiving line in the Diplomatic Reception Room to be photographed with us. Bill of course welcomed everyone warmly. It wasn't until the next day that he showed the Republican leaders his steel when he vetoed the seven-year budget reconciliation bill for fiscal year 1996.

The Republicans had incorporated brutal cuts in environmental protections, education funding and programs that help poor women, children and seniors, including Medicaid and Medicare. Bill signed the veto with the same pen that Lyndon Johnson had used thirty years earlier when he signed Medicare into law. At stake, Bill pointed out, were "two very different futures for America." He knew the Republicans didn't have the necessary votes to override a presidential veto, and he urged them to soften their positions and negotiate with the White House to break the impasse. But Gingrich's revolutionary freshmen refused to budge from their ideological crusade to dismantle the power of the federal government.

The government's authority to spend money expired again at midnight on December 16. This time there was a "partial" shutdown—some federal workers were furloughed, working without a paycheck until the government reopened. It was a truly terrible hardship to impose on people, especially during the holidays. And before Congress recessed for its Christmas break on December 22, Gingrich Republicans added to the callousness by passing a radical welfare reform act that, if left to stand, would imperil millions of vulnerable women and children.

Welfare reform had been debated by Bill's staff since the presidential campaign, when Bill promised to "end welfare as we know it." I agreed that the system was broken and needed to be fixed, but I was adamant that whatever reform we advocated would ensure an adequate safety net that provided incentives for individuals to move from welfare to work. I expressed my opinions vigorously and often to my husband as well as to his staff members charged with shaping reform. I argued that any reform package must preserve Medicaid and provide child care for working mothers. Although I stayed out of the public debate, I actively participated in the internal one. I made clear to Bill and his policy advisers in the West Wing that if I thought they were caving in to a mean-spirited Republican bill that was harmful to women and children, I would publicly oppose it. I understood Bill's dilemma, and I wanted to influence his decision. Bill's staff worked with mine and we made some real progress in framing a rebuttal to the Republicans. The President vetoed the Republican welfare bill as promised.

The Republicans finally were being held accountable for both the budget impasse and the shutdowns, and the drop in their approval ratings led to a fracturing of the party's united front. By January, Senator Bob Dole, likely looking ahead to the launch of his presidential campaign in New Hampshire, started talking compromise. Gingrich's strategy of "playing chicken" with Bill had failed, and I felt great relief that we could reopen the government and get workers back on the payroll now that Bill had prevailed.

As the second session of the 104th Congress opened on January 3, 1996, only three minor pieces of the Gingrich Contract had been signed into law. Bill had sustained eleven vetoes. He had managed to stave off disastrous cuts to Medicare and Medicaid and to save programs like AmeriCorps and Legal Aid services, which had been destined for the chopping block. By the end of the month, both sides reached a compromise funding agreement and reopened the government.

One institution unaffected by the shutdown was the Senate Banking Committee, whose work was deemed "essential." Without pause, it continued to haul our friends, lawyers and associates up to the Hill to fish for evidence of wrongdoing, while VA hospitals were prohibited from treating most patients, and other government employees were furloughed without pay.

On November 29, while we were in Europe, the Republicans' key witness, L. Jean Lewis, had been cross-examined by Senator Paul Sarbanes of Maryland and the Democratic counsel on the D'Amato committee, Richard Ben-Veniste. Lewis was the RTC official who had filed a criminal referral in August 1992 with the FBI and the U.S. Attorney in Little Rock, naming as felony suspects not only the McDougals but everyone who contributed to a fund-raiser McDougal held for Bill at Madison Guaranty in 1985. She listed Bill and me as possible witnesses. Ben-Veniste charged that Lewis was politically biased against us and had submitted this referral just before the 1992 election to affect the outcome. According to the final Whitewater Report published in 2002, this pre-election effort to implicate us in a criminal probe was encouraged by people in the Bush White House and Justice Department.

To rebut her testimony before the Banking Committee, Ben-Veniste cross-examined Lewis intensely, suggesting that she was lying when she said she had accidentally made a lengthy tape recording of a conversation she had with an RTC official who visited Lewis at her Kansas City office. Ben-Veniste got Lewis to state that, while she was a conservative Republican, she had no political bias against Bill and had never called him a liar. He then presented a letter she'd written in 1992 that made exactly that charge. Democrats also introduced evidence that Lewis had sought to market a line of T-shirts and mugs carrying messages that were critical of both Bill and me. Before the questioning concluded, Lewis collapsed and had to be helped from the hearing room.

The general public heard little about this development in the ongoing Whitewater drama. Among the television networks, only C-SPAN covered the details of the Lewis appearance. Days after her memorable and self-destructing testimony, *The New York Times* continued to give credence to Lewis's unsubstantiated accusations and to refer to her as a "star witness." Undaunted by the facts, the D'Amato committee continued to probe my association with McDougal's savings and loan. Ken Starr's investigation was supposedly confidential, but his team was displaying a remarkable talent for calculated leaks to the media.

In late 1995, Dick Morris came to see me to deliver a bizarre message: I was going to be indicted for something as yet undefined, and "people close to Starr" suggested I accept the indictment and ask Bill to pardon me before trial. I assumed Morris was carrying water for his Republican clients or contacts, so I chose my words very carefully. "Tell your sources to report to Starr's people that even though I have done nothing wrong, I'm well aware that, in the immortal words of Edward Bennett Williams, 'a prosecutor can indict a ham sandwich if he chooses.' And if Starr does, I would never ask for a pardon. I will go to trial and show Starr up for the fraud he is."

"Are you sure you want me to say that?" Morris asked me.

"Word for word," I replied.

In the ruckus over budgets and shutdowns, an important development in the Whitewater investigation passed almost unnoticed: Findings of the RTC report on Whitewater were finally made public just before Christmas. This independent report corroborated our contention that Bill and I had minimal involvement with the Whitewater investment and no liability in the collapse of Madison Guaranty. After examining forty-seven witnesses, compiling two hundred thousand documents and spending $3.6 million, the RTC investigators found no evidence of misconduct on our part and no factual basis for any aspect of the Whitewater "scandal."

Like Jean Lewis's discredited testimony, the report was minimally covered in the news media. *USA Today* didn't acknowledge it at all; *The Washington Post* buried the news in paragraph 11 of a front-page story about Whitewater subpoenas and *The New York Times* ran a few paragraphs on the report. Republicans dismissed the RTC investigation as too narrow and continued their hearings.

I was encouraged by this news when I met with David Kendall at the White House early on January 4, 1996, for one of our periodic catch-up sessions. David always tried to keep things light at our briefings by photocopying his favorite political cartoons for me or clipping the most outrageous tabloid stories, such as "Hillary Gives Birth to Alien Baby" or whatever they dreamed up that week.

We met in the Family Room, between the large master bedroom and the Yellow Oval Room on the second floor of the residence. The Bushes and Reagans relaxed and watched television there, and Harry Truman and Franklin Roosevelt had each used it as a bedroom. Bill and I furnished it with a television and card table along with a comfortable couch and armchair. Midway through the meeting, an usher knocked on the door and handed David a note, which he folded up and put in his pocket. When we finished our conversation, David left.

The next morning David called and asked if he could come see me. "Something has come up," he said.

David explained that the note he'd been given the day before was from Carolyn Huber, asking him to stop by her East Wing office on his way out. Carolyn, our longtime assistant in Arkansas, came to Washington to handle our personal correspondence and to organize, catalog and archive personal papers—everything from old school report cards to vacation photos to major speeches—that were now stored in hundreds of boxes throughout the residence and at a special White House storage facility in Maryland. David often asked Carolyn to help locate documents requested by the independent counsel, and, throughout the previous months, she had turned over thousands of pages of records from our boxes and her files.

When he arrived at her office, she handed him a sheaf of papers. David quickly realized what they were: a 1992 computer printout detailing the legal work I and others had done at the Rose Law Firm for Madison Guaranty back in 1985–86. Although Madison Guaranty billing records were included in the Special Counsel's subpoenas, the logical place to find them was in the records of the Rose Firm and Madison Guaranty. Their absence in our records did not surprise David or me, although we were anxious for them to appear, since I was certain they would support my recollection about what little legal work I had done. I was relieved that they had finally been found.

"Where on earth have they been?" I asked him.

"I don't know," said David. "Carolyn was going through a box of papers in her office and came across them. As soon as she realized what they were, she sent me the note."

"What does this mean?" I asked David.

"Well, the good news is we found them. The bad news is this gives the press and prosecutors the chance to go wild again."

And they did. William Safire, a former Nixon speechwriter, called me a "congenital liar" in his New York Times column. My picture appeared on the cover of Newsweek under the headline SAINT OR SINNER? And there was renewed talk of a grand jury subpoena and a possible indictment in the Whitewater investigation.

The copy of the billing records, we later concluded, was probably made during the 1992 campaign so that Bill's campaign staff and the Rose Law Firm could respond to the media questions about Madison Guaranty, Jim McDougal and Whitewater. Vince Foster, who handled the queries at the time, had scribbled notes on the documents. I believed they would corroborate what I had been saying all along: that my work for McDougal's savings and loan so many years ago had been minimal, in time and compensation.

On January 9, 1996, with the careful help of White House ushers, the Green Room was transformed into a temporary television studio for my interview with Barbara Walters. Technicians snaked cables along the floor and set up equipment that bathed the room in a golden light so gentle and flattering that even the powdered-wig portrait of Benjamin Franklin above the fireplace seemed to glow with youth. Barbara and I made pleasant small talk while the crew adjusted the sound levels.

This interview had been scheduled for January 9, 1996, long in advance, to promote *It Takes a Village* on the eve of its publication. Now I expected Barbara, whom I admired and liked, had other topics on her mind. It was not the best way to kick off an eleven-city book tour, but I welcomed the chance to respond to the latest volley of allegations. When the cameras began to roll, she got straight to the point.

"Mrs. Clinton, instead of your new book being the issue, you have become the issue. How did you get into this mess, where your whole credibility is being questioned?"

"Oh, I ask myself that every day, Barbara," I said, "because it's very surprising and confusing to me. But we've had questions raised for the last four years, and eventually they're answered and they go away and more questions come up and we'll just keep doing our best to answer them."

"Are you distressed?"

"Occasionally I get a little distressed, a little sad, a little angry, irritated. I think that's only natural. But I know that that's part of the territory and we'll just keep plowing through and trying to get to the end of this."

When Barbara Walters asked me about the missing records, I said: "You know, a month ago, people were jumping up and down because the billing records were lost and they thought somebody might have destroyed them. Now the records are found and they're jumping up and down. But I'm glad the records were found. I wish they had been found a year or two ago, because they verify what I've been saying from the very beginning. I worked about an hour a week for fifteen months. That was not a lot of work for me, certainly."

Barbara had trouble visualizing why the documents were so hard to find.

"What does it look like up there with your records?"

"It's a mess. . . ."

"That's hard to understand."

"But I think people do need to understand that there are millions of pieces of paper in the White House, and for more than two years now, people have been diligently searching."

It was difficult to convey the disarray we had lived with ever since moving into the White House. We had arrived in 1993 with all of our worldly possessions haphazardly packed in boxes, largely because we didn't own a home where we could store things. Shortly after we moved into the residence, we found ourselves in the midst of a major renovation of the heating and air-conditioning systems to bring the White House up to environmental energy standards. We had to stuff boxes into closets and spare rooms while workers put new ducts into the ceilings and walls. It seemed that each week we had to move around boxes again, just to stay one step ahead of the construction.

During the summer of 1995, duct work was being done on the roof and on the third floor, an informal area with extra guest rooms, the Solarium, an office, an exercise room, a laundry room and several storage areas. One of these, which we called the "book room," was a storage area where we had built shelves to handle our overflow of books. With several doors leading from it to the laundry room, exercise room and a small hallway used by the residence staff, it was one of the busiest spots in the residence, with people marching through at all hours of the day and night. We had set up tables in the book room for the boxes of papers and personal effects that were regularly shuttled from an off-site warehouse to the White House and back again so that they could be examined and cataloged. Carolyn Huber also had several file cabinets in the room for papers she was organizing. And complicating matters, the tables were often covered with dropcloths to protect them from plaster and dust raining down from the ceiling during construction work.

The ongoing search for documents in response to subpoenas added to the mess. David Kendall asked us to set up a copying machine in the book room so that he and his assistants could copy documents before turning them over to the Office of the Independent Counsel. And that was where, in the summer of 1995, Carolyn later testified that she found a sheaf of folded papers on one of the tables. Carolyn thought they were old records that had been left for her to file. Unaware of their significance, she tossed them into a box of other records that was taken to her office, already jammed with boxes she planned to sort through when she had more time. Months later, when she started sifting through all of these items, she unfolded the papers and recognized them as the long-lost billing records.

Carolyn did the honorable thing by calling David immediately to tell him about her discovery. She had been doing her best to stay ahead of an avalanche of paperwork and subpoena requests, and by her own admission, it sometimes took her a while to get through it all. I have not talked to Carolyn about the billing records or the investigation because I never wanted to be accused of influencing her testimony. But I trust her completely and know that her oversight was an innocent and understandable mistake.

Senator D'Amato's committee immediately proceeded to look for evidence—never found—of obstruction and perjury in the discovery of the billing records. The committee immediately requested additional funding for a two- or three-month extension to complete its hearings, which had already cost taxpayers nearly $900,000. A few months later, the RTC filed a supplemental report confirming that the billing records supported my account of my legal activities. I certainly had no reason to conceal them and regretted that they had not been found earlier.

And so it went. The hearings and the media coverage continued, and every time I sat down for an interview with another radio host or morning talk show personality to discuss It Takes a Village, I was asked about the billing records. The only bright moments that month were my appearances in bookstores, schools, children's hospitals and other programs supporting children and families around the country. The crowds were huge and the audiences warm and supportive, further evidence of the disconnect between Washington and the rest of the nation.

This disconnect is one of the reasons I wanted to write *It Takes a Village*. When I thought about the growing pressures on children in America, it struck me how ineffectual the increasingly partisan rhetoric in Washington was in solving the problems that these children face.

Many of my beliefs about what is best for children and families don't fall easily into any category of politics or ideology, and a lot of the people I met on my book tour said that they felt the same way. The people who stood in line for hours didn't want to talk about the most recent episode of mudslinging in the nation's capital. They wanted to talk about how hard it is to find quality, affordable child care; the challenges of raising children without the support of extended families; the pressures of raising children in a mass culture that too often celebrates risky behaviors and distorts values; the importance of good schools and affordable college tuitions; and a range of issues weighing on the minds of parents and other adults in today's fast-changing world. I was heartened by these conversations, and hoped that my book would help promote a national conversation about what is best for America's children.

It Takes a Village offered information about ideas and programs developed at the community level that were making a difference in the lives of children and families. Often, a model program in one community isn't replicated elsewhere because there are few channels for communication. A concerned group of parents in Atlanta, for example, might benefit from learning about an innovative afterschool program for at-risk teens in Los Angeles. I wanted to give visibility to successful grassroots efforts that would resonate in communities around the country. I also hoped I could generate royalties for children's charities since I was giving all the author's proceeds away. In the end, I was able to contribute nearly one million dollars.

My book tour also offered moments that were personally comforting. In Ann Arbor, Michigan, on January 17, dozens of people showed up at the bookstore wearing "Hillary Fan Club" T-shirts. Ruth and Gene Love, a retired couple from Silver Spring, Maryland, had started the club in their kitchen in 1992. There were hundreds of members around the country and a few international chapters. The Loves, aptly named, became wonderful friends who invariably seemed to know when I needed a boost. They would send out their "fans" to greet me with smiles, T-shirts and homemade signs when I traveled.

In San Francisco, James Carville hosted a dinner for me at a restaurant he had just bought and invited some of my closest friends to come, mostly to cheer me up. My free-spirited friend Susie Buell said she didn't follow all of the dramas going on back in Washington, but she did have something to say to me: "Bless your heart." That was all I needed to hear.

During my book tour, I spoke at my alma mater, Wellesley College, on January 19, 1996, and spent the night at the gracious home of its superb President, Diana Chapman Walsh. The President's house sits on the shores of Lake Waban, and I got up early and went for a long walk along the trail that encircles the lake. I had just returned when David phoned to tell me that Kenneth Starr had issued a subpoena to call me before the grand jury to testify about the missing billing records. This time there would be no quiet deposition in the White House. I would have to testify before the full grand jury the following week. I was upset, yet I knew I couldn't express my feelings to anyone other than Bill or my lawyers.

Melanne had insisted on traveling with me because she knew how difficult the book tour would be with the daily pressure of press questioning. This act of personal friendship cost her emotionally and financially, since she had to ride out the tough times with me and pay her own way too. That day at Wellesley was especially hard because I could not tell Melanne what was happening. Ever acute, she picked up on my agitation and ran interference for me. I will never forget her kindness and loyalty.

I returned to the White House discouraged and embarrassed, worried that this latest turn of events might destroy whatever credibility I retained, and I worried about what it would mean for Bill's Presidency. Bill was upset and concerned for me. He kept telling me how sorry he was that he couldn't protect me from all this.

Chelsea was worried for me too. She followed closely the developments in the investigation, more so than I sometimes wished. Just as I wanted to shield her, she wanted to protect and comfort me. At first I tried to avoid burdening her with what I was experiencing, but eventually I realized that, as she grew older, she felt better when she knew what I was feeling.

Bill had outmaneuvered the Republicans over the government shutdowns, but his political success could not protect either of us from the misuse of the criminal process. He felt powerless in the face of Starr and his allies. Anger is not the best state of mind in which to prepare for a grand jury appearance. Being a lawyer helped me somewhat because I understood the process. But I couldn't eat or sleep for a week before my appearance, and I lost ten pounds—not a diet I would recommend. Although I worked on my testimony, which was simple and straightforward, I was more focused on how to control my anger at the whole process. The grand jurors were performing their duty as citizens. They deserved my respect, even if the lawyers working for Starr did not.

David argued strongly to the Starr prosecutors that calling me before the grand jury was unjustified and a misuse of the process. I could be questioned privately under oath as I had been before, even on videotape. But Starr insisted on summoning me to the courthouse. One of his goals may have been to humiliate me publicly, but I was determined not to let him break my spirit. I might be the first wife of a President to testify before a grand jury, but I'd do it on my own terms. David told me we could avoid the photographers and TV crews outside the courthouse by driving the Secret Service limousine into the basement parking lot and taking an elevator to the third floor. I rejected the suggestion. Sneaking into the building would make me look as though I had something to hide.

When my car pulled up in front of the United States District Court for the District of Columbia at 1:45 on that brisk afternoon, January 26, 1996, I got out, smiled and waved at the crowd, and walked into the federal courthouse. I knew I had to conceal my true feelings about Starr and his absurd proceedings. All week I had prepared myself mentally and spiritually for this moment. Breathe deeply, I kept telling myself, and pray for God's help.

As I prepared to enter the grand jury room, I waved at my hardworking lawyers and said, "Cheerio! Off to the firing squad!"

The grand jury met in the large courtroom on the third floor. Under the federal procedures governing grand juries, witnesses cannot take a lawyer into the grand jury room. I was on my own. All but two of the twenty-three grand jurors were in attendance—ten were women, and most were African American. They seemed entirely representative of the district where they served. Each of Ken Starr's eight male deputies looked just like him.

Starr left the questions to one of his deputies while he sat at the prosecutor's table and stared at me. I answered all of the questions, many of them over and over again. I was out in the hallway during one of three breaks when a juror walked over and asked if I would sign his copy of *It Takes a Village*. I looked at David, who was grinning, and then I signed the book. I later learned that after an investigation into this "incident," the juror was dismissed from the panel.

After four hours, it was over. In a side room, I quickly debriefed my lawyers, David and Nicole Seligman and Jack Quinn, the new White House counsel, and Jane Sherburne. We talked about what I would tell the reporters who were anxiously awaiting me. As I walked to the exit, I passed by offices and noticed that no one seemed to have gone home. Many people were hanging around so they could wave to me or say something supportive.

It was already dark when I stepped outside and agreed to take a few brief questions from the media. They wanted to know how I was feeling.

"It's been a long day," I said.

"Would you rather have been somewhere else today?"

"Oh, about a million other places."

When I was asked about the missing billing records, I told them, "I, like everyone else, would like to know the answer about how those documents showed up after all these years. I tried to be as helpful as I could in their investigation efforts."

I waved as I climbed into the limousine for the ride back to the White House. When I walked into the Diplomatic Receiving Room, Bill and Chelsea were waiting for me with big hugs and eager questions about how it went. I told them I was just glad it was over.

In the ensuing press coverage, much was made of the flowing, embroidered black wool coat I wore that day. One reporter noted that the garment was "emblazoned on the back with a gold dragon," which prompted the Beltway commentators to ponder its symbolic meaning: Was it a totem? Was I the dragon lady? The White House was obliged to issue a statement that the appliquéd swirls on the coat made by Connie Fails, my designer friend in Little Rock, meant nothing: it was just an abstract pattern that one fashion columnist wrote looked like an "art deco rendering of seashells." My press office reminded reporters that I had worn the coat during the 1993 inaugural events—when no one had commented on the design—but this did not end the chatter. The coat had "turned into a Washington political Rorschach test," one reporter observed. True enough.

The following night, I forced myself to show up at yet another of Washington's rituals, the Alfalfa Club Dinner. This is a club with only one purpose: to hold a mock presidential nomination during an annual white-tie dinner. I was seated at the dais with my husband and a covey of cabinet Secretaries and Supreme Court Justices in the ballroom of the Capital Hilton Hotel. The mock nominee that year was Colin Powell. He got up to speak and greeted the dignitaries present: "Ladies and gentlemen, Republican extremists, Democrats and other nonessentials, subpoened guests." That was, I assumed, a category of one—me. I raised my arm up in the air and laughed as Powell turned and smiled mischievously at me. After Powell finished speaking, one of Bill's top advisers walked over to me and whispered, "Until you've testified at least five times before a grand jury like I have, you're just small potatoes."

WAR ZONES

KNOWING THE IMPORTANCE OF AMERICA'S LONG AND complex relationship with France, Bill and I were anxious about our first State Dinner for French President Jacques Chirac and his wife, Bernadette, in February 1996. Chirac, a conservative politician from the party of de Gaulle had been the mayor of Paris for eighteen years. And though Chirac is fluent in English and had traveled extensively in America as a young man, his personal affection for the U.S. did not always translate into his government's support for our policies. Bill worked hard to win French cooperation, however, most notably in 1999 when he persuaded France to go along with NATO air strikes to reverse ethnic cleansing in Kosovo despite the lack of a specific U.N. resolution.

Diplomacy is a tricky business, even when it comes to relations with our allies. The close affiliation and mutual respect between our countries stems back to their help with our Revolution, but there are times when French and American policies diverge and relations are strained, as we've seen with the U.S.-led war in Iraq, which the French government vehemently and vocally opposed.

The first hurdle for the dinner was the menu. The French are legendary for their cuisine, so I fretted about the perfect meal to serve them at the White House. Our American-born and -trained chef, Walter Scheib, was not intimidated in the least and assured me that he would combine the best of both culinary traditions.

The round tables in the State Dining Room were draped in damask and awash with crystal, silver and roses. As a midwinter snow fell on Washington, diplomats, business leaders, artists and movie stars chattered over lemon-thyme lobster and roasted eggplant soup, rack of lamb and sweet potato puree served with the finest American wines. From this first meal to our subsequent encounters with the Chiracs, Bill and I discovered that, if the world of diplomacy is tricky, it is also filled with surprises.

"Of course, I love many things American, including the food," said President Chirac, seated to my right. "You know, I used to work in a Howard Johnson's restaurant."

Despite the occasional serious political differences between the United States and France, Bill and I maintained a comfortable dialogue with the Chiracs during our years in the White House, and I enjoyed a visit I made with Bernadette Chirac to central France. The niece of General de Gaulle's aide-de-camp, Bernadette is an elegant, cultured woman who since 1971 had been a local elected official from a constituency in the Correze region. She was the only presidential spouse I knew who had been elected on her own. I was fascinated by the independent role she had carved out for herself and her stories of walking and driving herself from house to house, asking for votes. She later invited me to accompany her to visit her constituency, and in May 1998 I spent a wonderful day touring Correze with her, meeting the people she represented.

Soon it was time to celebrate another family milestone: Chelsea's sixteenth birthday. I could hardly believe how quickly our daughter was growing up. It seemed like yesterday that she was taking her first dance lessons and crawling into my lap to read a book. Now she was my height, and she wanted to get a driver's license. That was scary enough, but even more frightening: her father was teaching her how to drive.

Outside of golf carts, the Secret Service never let Bill drive himself around, which was a good thing. It's not that my husband isn't mechanically inclined, it's just that he has so much information running through his head at any given moment that he doesn't always notice where he's going. But he insisted on performing his fatherly duty, borrowing a car from the Secret Service fleet at Camp David.

After the first lesson on backing up and parallel parking, I met Chelsea as she returned to Aspen Lodge. "So! How'd it go?"

She said, "Well, I think Dad learned a lot."

Being the child of a President is never easy, from the loss of anonymity to the round-the-clock security. Even as she got older, Bill and I were determined that she lead as normal a life as possible. We worked hard to keep our schedules free to have dinner in the family kitchen with her so that we could catch up with one another, talk over weekend plans or family trips. No matter what else was going on, I tried to hang around the second floor when she came from ballet in case she felt like talking. At the very least, I wanted a sighting of her before she disappeared into her room.

We also did our best to shield her from the investigations and harsh media coverage, but I'm sure those added pressures made life in the White House even more challenging for Chelsea. It forced her to mature early and to become a quick judge of character, identifying and discarding fawners and false friends and building relationships with true friends who remain close to her today.

We celebrated her sixteenth birthday on February 27, 1996, with an evening at the National Theatre for a performance of *Les Misérables.* Then Bill and I invited a busload of her friends for a weekend at Camp David. Chelsea planned the activities, which included an afternoon game of paintball. The Marines stationed at the camp were only a few years older than the guests, so they organized opposing bands of camo-clad teenagers who ran through the woods and tagged one another with paintballs. Bill kept shouting directions and battle strategies for whichever team seemed to be lagging. After the birthday dinner in Laurel Lodge, complete with a gigantic carrot cake prepared by the incomparable White House pastry chef Roland Mesnier, we regrouped in Hickory Lodge for movies and bowling in the alley installed by President Eisenhower. Sometime after midnight, Bill and I finally admitted to ourselves that we were no longer sixteen.

Chelsea and her friends already were looking beyond high school, and although it made me heartsick that we wouldn't have her at home much longer, I tried not to burden her with my feelings about it. I just crossed my fingers that she would choose a campus close to Washington.

Every year, Sidwell Friends School hosts a "college night" for juniors and their parents. Bill and I went along with Chelsea to hear representatives from different colleges talk about what you have to do to qualify and how to apply. Chelsea was quiet during the short drive back to the White House. Then, out of the blue, she said, "You know, I think I might be interested in visiting Stanford."

Forgetting everything I know about reverse psychology and mother-daughter dynamics, I blurted out, "What! Stanford is too far away! You can't go that far away. That's all the way over on the West Coast—three time zones away. We'd never get to see you."

Bill squeezed my arm and said to Chelsea, "Honey, you can go wherever you want." And, of course, I knew that if she wanted to go to Stanford and was accepted, I'd be thrilled for her. I well remembered my father ruling out choices, and Bill and I vowed never to do that. I did fervently hope, however, that she'd stay in the Washington time zone. But the conversation forced me to face reality: regardless of where she went, in a year and a half she'd be leaving us. She might have been ready, but I wasn't, and I was determined to spend even more time with her, or at least as much as she'd let me!

The State Department had asked me to go as an emissary to Bosnia-Herzegovina to reinforce the importance of the Dayton Peace Accords, which had been signed in November. Gains on the ground by the Croat-Muslim coalition that the United States had helped support, coupled with the NATO airstrikes that Bill had advocated, finally forced the Serbs to negotiate a settlement. I was also scheduled to make stops at U.S. military bases in Germany and Italy, and spend a week in Turkey and Greece, two important U.S. and NATO allies that had a difficult, tense relationship over Cyprus and other unresolved issues.

Bill and I discussed whether Chelsea should skip the Bosnia leg of the trip. We weighed the security risks and decided that if we took appropriate precautions, she and I would be fine. She was mature enough to grow from the experience. Besides, we'd be traveling with a USO troupe that included singer Sheryl Crow and comedian Sinbad, all of whom were willing to take the risks associated with the trip.

I thought Bill, Secretary of State Warren Christopher and his special envoy, Ambassador Richard Holbrooke had pulled off a miracle in Dayton convincing Serbs, Croats and Muslims to end the fighting and agree to a new governing framework. In order to isolate the warring groups and establish basic security, the United States had sent over eighteen thousand peacekeeping troops, who would join forty thousand from other countries. The administration wanted to send a strong signal that the peace accords were to be honored and would be enforced. My staff used to tease me, suggesting that the State Department had a directive: If the place was too small, too dangerous or too poor—

send Hillary. That was fine with me, because the out-of-the-way and dicey venues were often the most compelling. I was honored to go to Bosnia.

On Sunday, March 24, our converted 707 arrived at Ramstein Air Base in Germany, near Baumholder, home to the First Armored Division, which provided most of the U.S. forces in Bosnia.

The German people had warmly welcomed Bill and me to a celebration of German unity in Berlin two years earlier, when we walked through the Brandenburg Gate with Chancellor and Mrs. Kohl and stood on ground that, until 1989, had been part of Communist East Germany. An engaging, emotional and even playful man, Helmut Kohl became Bill's friend and political partner. Kohl was dedicated to transcending forty years of division in his country and merging East and West into one German nation. He was also instrumental in building the European Union, adopting a common currency and supporting U.S. efforts to end conflict in the Balkans. Cooperation between our countries was a vivid example of the post-war alliance working to achieve peace and security in Europe.

After arriving at Baumholder, Chelsea and I attended church services, met with the families of our troops, and enjoyed a brief performance in the mess hall by Sheryl and Sinbad. Around 6:30 the next morning, our entourage boarded a C-17 transport plane and took off for Tuzla Air Base, Bosnia-Herzegovina. In addition to the entertainers, we brought pallets of mail and gifts for the troops, including donations from American companies of 2,200 long-distance calling cards and 300 movies on video. The White House contributed six cases of M&M's with the presidential seal on every box. For the children in Bosnia, who had lost years of schooling because of the fighting, American companies donated school supplies and toys.

I spent the hour-and-forty-minute flight wandering around the cavernous metal belly of the huge transport plane, chatting with the crew and members of the press corps, who were strapped into benchlike jump seats. It was like touring the inside of a blimp, but louder. The pilot, then one of just four female C-17 pilots in the Air Force, kept the plane cruising high over the devastated countryside, above the reach of surface-to-air missiles and sniper fire. As a reminder of the dangers that remained despite the official cease-fire, each of us was required to wear a flak jacket on the plane, and the Secret Service moved Chelsea and me up to the armored cockpit for the landing. Above the airstrip, the captain dipped a wing and made a near-perpendicular landing to evade possible ground fire.

Security conditions were constantly changing in the former Yugoslavia, and they had recently deteriorated again. Due to reports of snipers in the hills around the airstrip, we were forced to cut short an event on the tarmac with local children, though we did have time to meet them and their teachers and to learn how hard they had worked during the war to continue classes in any safe spot they could find. One eight-year-old girl gave me a copy of a poem she had written entitled "Peace." Chelsea and I presented the school supplies we had brought, along with letters from seventh-grade children at Baumholder whose parents and teachers had initiated a pen pal program. We were then hustled off to the fortified American base at Tuzla, where more than two thousand American, Russian, Canadian, British and Polish soldiers were encamped in a large tent city.

Sheryl Crow, Sinbad and Chelsea and I flew in Black Hawk helicopters to visit soldiers in forward positions. We were flanked by gunships, an indication of what a dangerous job peacekeeping could be. We touched down at Camp Bedrock and Camp Alicia, Army outposts in northeastern Bosnia. We watched our troops demonstrate how they were clearing mines from the fields and roads—a grim mission and another reminder of the precarious life our soldiers led. Many voices back home were raising questions about America's role in Bosnia. Some argued that soldiers should not be involved in "peacekeeping," even though it has been part of our military's historic mission in places and times as disparate as the Sinai desert after the peace agreement between Israel and Egypt and the DMZ after the Korean War. Others argued that European, not American, troops should bear responsibility for maintaining secure borders in the region. Because of these concerns, I spent time talking with the soldiers and their officers, asking for their opinions and listening to their assessments of their mission. One lieutenant told me he hadn't understood the role the United States could play until he saw Bosnia for himself.

"Before we came," he said, "it was hard to fathom what was going on here." He described ethnic groups who had lived peacefully together and suddenly were killing each other over their religions. "You go out in the villages and see all the damage," he told me. "You see roofs blown off of houses. You see whole neighborhoods that were completely bombed out. You see people who had to survive for years with hardly any food to eat or water to drink. But now, wherever we go, the kids wave at us and smile," he told me. "To me, that's reason enough to be here."

I got my own look at the desolation of war from the window of our chopper. From a distance, the rolling countryside seemed beautiful and green, typical of pastoral Europe. But as I flew lower I could see that there were few farmhouses with an intact roof, and it was the rare building that had not been pocked by bullets. The fields weren't tilled; they were torn up by shelling. It was springtime, but nobody was planting because of the dangers posed by land mines and snipers. The forests and the roads were not safe either. It was awful to see the extent of the suffering and to recognize how much work remained before the people of Bosnia could resume a semblance of normal life.

I had planned a stop in Sarajevo to meet with a multiethnic delegation to hear their ideas about what the United States government and private organizations could do to help heal a society ripped apart by war. The security situation forced me to cancel my trip to Sarajevo, but the people I was to meet were so disappointed that they insisted on braving the journey along fifty miles of treacherous roads to meet me in Tuzla.

We gathered in the conference room at U.S. Army headquarters. My visitors, including the first Bosnian Cardinal of the Roman Catholic Church and the leader of the Orthodox Church in the Serb Republic, looked exhausted and beaten down by their ordeals, but they were anxious to talk. They described what they had tried to do to maintain a sense of normalcy in a world turned upside down by war. They described the shock of discovering that their long-time friends and colleagues would no longer talk to them and sometimes became actively hostile. When the violence started, bombs and snipers became a way of life. The Bosnian chief of Kosovo Hospital's trauma ward told me the hospital had been kept open even after running out of supplies and losing power. A Croat kindergarten teacher, who lost her own twelve-year-old son in the siege of Sarajevo, reported that her class shrank in size as children fled with their families, stopped coming to school or became casualties of the chaotic and arbitrary violence. A Serbian journalist who had been beaten and imprisoned by his fellow Serbs for attempting to protect Bosnian Muslims confirmed that psychological wounds are often more damaging than physical devastation. In many places I visited, the scarring effect of war on the hearts and minds of citizens was still evident decades and even centuries later. Rebuilding infrastructure in the aftermath of war is one thing; rebuilding trust among people is quite another.

After the meeting, I toured the camp, examining the soldiers' living conditions and dropping into the infirmary, mess and recreation hall. When Sheryl and Sinbad returned to Tuzla, they put on a great USO show. Chelsea had been a big hit with the soldiers and their families throughout the trip, shaking hands and signing autographs with her usual warmth and grace. She was even drafted into the entertainment when the sergeant major emcee called her to the stage from her seat in the audience. Without a hint of self-consciousness, she hopped up to the mike for some silly banter.

"Your name's Chelsea?" the sergeant major joked.

"Something like that," she replied, laughing.

He then urged her to demonstrate the Army cheer she'd been hearing from the crowd.

"*Hoooo*-hah!"

"That was good," he said. "Try again."

"*HOOOO*-hah!" she bellowed. The crowd broke into applause and returned some raucous cheers of their own.

Although the usual media rules applied—no interviews with Chelsea, no unauthorized photos—she was obviously more self-assured and playful on this trip than ever. Like her father, she was naturally friendly and curious and at ease in a crowd. When we visited U.S. troops stationed in Aviano, Italy, later that day, Chelsea demonstrated more of her élan. She joined me in posing for pictures with a group of Air Force pilots and mechanics. As we walked away, a voice hollered from behind us:

"Hey, Chelsea! How's your driving going?"

She wheeled around to answer the young man in combat fatigues who obviously had been following her recent press coverage.

"It's all right," she said, smiling. She walked a bit farther, then turned again and shouted: "Beware if you come to D.C.!"

This trip left lasting impressions on Chelsea and me. We were so proud of our men and women in uniform, who exemplified the best of America's values and diversity. If the people of the Balkans needed further evidence of the benefits of pluralism, all they had to do was sit at a table in the mess at Tuzla or Camp Bedrock or Camp Alicia surrounded by an array of skin colors, religions, accents and attitudes. This diversity is one of America's strengths, and it could be theirs as well.

Before wrapping up the trip in Istanbul and Athens, we flew from Turkey's capital, Ankara, to Ephesus, an ancient Greek city on Turkey's southern coast that has been beautifully restored. It was a flawless day, sunny and clear, with breathtaking views of the coastline and the blue-green Aegean Sea below. I remember thinking what a perfect day it was for flying and what a perfect moment to be alive.

I arrived back in Washington on the last day of March, physically tired but filled with information and impressions to share with Bill. The problems I saw in Bosnia made the ongoing sagas in Washington seem small and inconsequential. And the sagas continued. But, for a change, Ken Starr was under scrutiny.

In an editorial critical of the Office of the Independent Counsel, *The New York Times* chastised Starr for continuing in his million-dollar-a-year private law practice while investigating the White House. The case, said the editorial, "demands a prosecutor who is evenhanded and unencumbered," but it stopped short of calling for Starr's resignation as independent counsel, arguing—nonsensically, I thought—that his possibly tainted investigation was "too far along to start over." Nonetheless, it was refreshing that the press was alerting the public to Starr's ongoing legal representations of businesses such as tobacco companies, whose interests were in transparent conflict with those of the Clinton Administration. When Kenneth Starr was appointed independent counsel, he was not required or pressured to resign his senior partnership in the Kirkland & Ellis law firm; nor did he feel obliged to drop his profit participation in lawsuits that were directly affected by Clinton Administration policy.

A few intrepid journalists—Gene Lyons of the *Arkansas Democrat-Gazette* and Joe Conason of the *New York Observer*—had been reporting about Starr's conflicts of interest in limited-circulation publications, but now the story began to build in the mainstream Washington press corps.

As a veteran of the Reagan and first Bush Administrations, Starr's partisan Republican credentials were already well-known. So, to a lesser extent, were his connections to the religious Right and to Paula Jones. But Starr's continuing business relationships with our political opponents had until recently been overlooked.

On March 11, 1996, *USA Today* reported that Starr was earning $390 an hour to represent the state of Wisconsin in an effort to uphold its school voucher program, an educational policy that the Clinton Administration opposed. His fees were paid by the archconservative Bradley Foundation. The list went on: An article in *The Nation* magazine laid out the facts proving that Starr had an actual conflict of interest when he, in his part-time capacity as prosecutor, was investigating the RTC at the same time the RTC was investigating his law firm, Kirkland & Ellis. The RTC had sued Kirkland & Ellis for negligence in a Denver S&L case. Starr's own pecuniary interest in his law firm partnership was directly at stake, and at the very least, there was an appearance of a conflict of interest, which the media ignored. Starr should have recused himself from the RTC investigation. And while the settlement between the RTC and his law firm, in which the firm paid $325,000, was kept secret under a confidentiality agreement, every aspect of the Rose Firm's legal work for Madison Guaranty was thoroughly investigated by the RTC, Congress and the press. There was no investigation of the settlement and Starr's actions.

The sudden burst of unfavorable press in March had no noticeable effect on Starr. He ignored *The New York Times*'s admonition to "take a leave from his firm and all its cases until his Whitewater duties are over." On the contrary: On April 2, the independent counsel argued an important case on behalf of four major tobacco companies in the Fifth Circuit Court of Appeals in New Orleans.

I was dismayed by the double standard that protected Starr and his patrons from accountability, while the conservative faction openly played the "conflict of interest" card to eliminate nonpartisan jurists and investigators. Robert Fiske, the original special prosecutor, had been removed from his post in August 1994 to make way for Starr. Fiske was removed on a conflict-of-interest charge far more tenuous than the many political and financial conflicts that should have prevented Starr's appointment in the first place and should have required Starr's resignation at several points along the way.

Starr used a trumped-up conflict-of-interest complaint to remove from a separate case one of the most prestigious jurists on the federal bench in Arkansas because the judge had ruled against him. This case was unrelated to Bill and me; it didn't even involve Madison Guaranty, the McDougals or anyone associated with the Whitewater investment. Starr had used his power as independent counsel to indict Jim Guy

Tucker, the Democratic Governor of Arkansas who succeeded Bill, on fraud and conspiracy charges involving Tucker's purchase of cable television stations in Texas and Florida. In June 1995, Starr was using threats and indictments as a tool of intimidation, threatening everyone he could and offering to cut them deals if they would say something—anything!—to incriminate Bill or me. U.S. District Judge Henry Woods was assigned the Tucker case and, after examining the facts, threw out Starr's indictment of Tucker because it had nothing to do with the Whitewater investigation. Based on Woods's reading of the independent counsel law, Starr had exceeded his authority. Starr appealed the decision and asked that Judge Woods be thrown off the case.

Judge Woods, a former FBI agent and distinguished lawyer, had been appointed to the bench by President Jimmy Carter. At seventy-seven, he was wrapping up a stellar career as a jurist and a champion of civil rights in the South. In more than fifteen years on the bench, Judge Woods had earned a reputation for fair, nearly airtight decisions that were rarely overturned—until he got in Starr's way.

The three judges sitting on the federal court panel that heard Starr's appeal were conservative Republicans appointed to the Eighth Circuit Court of Appeals by Presidents Reagan and Bush. The three judges granted both of Starr's requests, reinstating the indictment and agreeing to remove Woods, not because they believed he would be biased, but because critical newspaper and magazine articles about him might cause the "appearance" of prejudice.

This unusual and unprecedented ruling offended me as a lawyer. A prosecutor should not be allowed to throw a judge off a case because he doesn't like a ruling. And, in this case, Starr did not first make an application to Judge Woods to recuse himself. If he had, the judge could have defended himself, responded to Starr's contentions, set the matter for a hearing and made a record. Since Starr made the motion first in the Court of Appeals, Judge Woods did not have any opportunity to reply.

The disparaging news reports that the appellate judges used to disqualify Judge Woods could be traced back to Justice Jim Johnson, an old segregationist politician in Arkansas who had once earned the endorsement of the Ku Klux Klan in his race for governor and who despised Bill and Judge Woods because of their liberal New South views on race. Johnson's op-ed piece attacking Woods and nearly everyone else in Arkansas politics ran in the right-wing *Washington Times*. The op-ed was full of false information that most other media accepted as fact. After his removal, Judge Woods told the *Los Angeles Times:* "I have the distinction of being the only judge in Anglo-American history, as far as I can determine, who was removed from a case on the basis of newspaper accounts, magazine articles and television transcripts."

I felt terrible that Jim Guy Tucker and his wife, Betty, had been caught up in Starr's fishing expedition. Despite Starr's effort, Jim Guy, who had lost the primary election for Governor in 1982 to Bill, wouldn't lie about us. This didn't prevent Starr from pushing ahead with another indictment that put Tucker on trial with Jim and Susan McDougal in Little Rock, Arkansas, in March 1996.

This time Tucker and the McDougals were charged with conspiracy, wire fraud, mail fraud, misapplication of S&L funds and making false entries in S&L records. Most of the accusations against them could be traced to David Hale, a shady Arkansas Republican businessman. The indictment alleged that Hale had connived with Jim McDougal to get loans from Madison Guaranty and from the Small Business Administration for various projects, including for land deals or for companies of Hale, the McDougals and Jim Guy Tucker; that these loans were not repaid; and that the uses of and justifications for the loans were falsely described. The twenty-one-count indictment made no mention of Whitewater Development Co., Inc., the President or me.

Hale was an accomplished thief and a con artist—and he was motivated. He was cooperating with Starr in the hopes of avoiding a long prison sentence for his previous crimes. The Small Business Administration, which had lent Hale's company millions of dollars intended to benefit small businesses and low-income people, reported that it had lost $3.4 million due to Hale's improper activities, self-dealing and prohibited transactions. The SBA finally placed his company in receivership, and in 1994, Hale pleaded guilty to conspiring to defraud the SBA of $900,000, but his sentencing was postponed until just before the McDougal/Tucker trial two years later. His story had changed greatly over time, and he was eager to provide whatever testimony the prosecutors wanted. The defense lawyers argued hard to convince the judge to admit testimony about Hale's connections with right-wing activists, financial payments from the OIC, his more than forty phone calls with Justice Jim Johnson before and since his deal with Starr, and the free legal counsel he received from attorney Ted Olson, an old friend of Kenneth Starr and a lawyer for the Arkansas Project and for the *Amer-*

ican Spectator, the right-wing propaganda publication. Olson would later mislead the Senate Judiciary Committee about his involvement in these activities during the consideration of his nomination to become Solicitor General under President George W. Bush. Despite his evasiveness, he was confirmed.

Although the presiding judge at the McDougal-Tucker trial wouldn't admit evidence of most of Hale's lucrative connections into court records and the full story would not come out for years, details of the secret Arkansas Project began to be aired in public for the first time. Hale was a well-paid pawn in a furtive campaign designed to discredit Bill and bring down his administration. Not only was Hale paid at least $56,000 in cash by the OIC after he agreed to testify, Hale was also secretly paid by the Arkansas Project. Journalist David Brock later disclosed that Hale was paid from the "educational" slush fund at the *American Spectator* financed by Richard Mellon Scaife. Brock later wrote, "At its inception . . . the Arkansas Project was a means of providing covert support for Hale to implicate Clinton in a crime."

When Judge Henry Woods was shown evidence of the group's complicity in the smear campaign against him, he demanded a federal investigation of the Arkansas Project. The federal judges of his district—who had been appointed by both Democrats and Republicans—unanimously joined in this demand. But no investigation of Judge Woods's charges ever took place. Judge Woods took senior status in 1995 and died in 2002. He was one among many good people tarred by Starr's partisan brush.

After the OIC had finished presenting its case, which relied heavily on Hale's testimony, Jim McDougal, increasingly erratic, insisted on testifying in his own defense. Many observers felt that his testimony seriously damaged the defense case for all three defendants. The prosecutors were able to convict the three on several felony counts. Tucker resigned as Governor while pursuing his appeals. And Kenneth Starr turned up the pressure on Jim and Susan McDougal to produce incriminating evidence that didn't exist.

As the convoluted facts of Whitewater finally started coming out in court, I could feel a subtle change in the atmospheric pressure in Washington. On Capitol Hill, Senator D'Amato stopped his Whitewater hearings when the Democrats threatened a filibuster to block his funding. For the first time in years, I was beginning to hope that we could put Whitewater behind us.

Yet despite these hopeful moments, the spring of 1996 was not destined to be a time of celebration. On April 3, an Air Force T-43 jet carrying the Secretary of Commerce Ron Brown, his staff and a delegation of American business leaders crashed into a hillside along the coast of Croatia in a violent rainstorm. Ron had gone to the Balkans to promote investment and trade as part of the administration's long-term strategy for peace in that troubled region. This was typical of Ron's approach in the Cabinet. He instinctively understood that promoting global economic opportunity was good for America's strategic interests and good for American business. Ron and thirty-two other Americans and two Croatians died in the crash.

I was devastated. Ron and his wife, Alma, were dear friends. They had been among our staunchest allies since the 1992 campaign, when Ron served effectively as Chairman of the Democratic National Committee. Ron had guided the party through the ups and downs of that campaign with aplomb and good humor. Even when Bill's prospects dimmed in the face of relentless attacks, Ron never faltered. He believed Bill could and would win if Democrats persevered. And he was right. Ron was also great fun. With a smile on his face and a perpetual twinkle in his eyes, he could cheer up anyone, and I was his beneficiary time and again. "Don't let the whiners get you down," he'd remind me.

Upon hearing the news, Bill and I went to see Alma and Ron's children, Michael and Tracey. Their house, full of family and friends, felt like the site of a revival meeting as we all laughed and cried and told stories about Ron. I later learned that Ron's plane was the same aircraft—and had been staffed by some of the same crew—that had flown Chelsea and me only a week earlier, on that resplendent clear afternoon over Turkey.

Bill and I met the U.S. Air Force plane carrying thirty-three flag-draped caskets at Dover Air Base in Dover, Delaware. Among the victims was Lawry Payne, a smart and enterprising man who advanced some of my trips, and Adam Darling, a twenty-nine-year-old Commerce Department staffer who had become a favorite of Bill's and mine after he volunteered to ride his bicycle across the country in support of Bill's 1992 campaign.

In his brief remarks on the tarmac, Bill reminded us that the crash victims who died in the service of their country represented the best America had to offer.

"The sun is going down on this day," he said as I blinked back tears.

"The next time it rises it will be Easter morning, a day that marks the passage from loss and despair to hope and redemption, a day that more than any other reminds us that life is more than what we know . . . sometimes even more than what we can bear. But life is also eternal . . . What they did while the sun was out will last with us forever."

PRAGUE SUMMER

WHEN I VENTÚRED FOR THE FIRST TIME TO CENtral and Eastern Europe over the Fourth of July in the summer of 1996, infant democracies had replaced communism in the former Soviet-bloc countries. Hundreds of millions of people had been liberated from lives of tyranny behind the Iron Curtain, but as I was to see for myself, embracing democratic values is just the first step. Building functioning democratic governments, creating free markets and establishing civil societies after decades of dictatorship requires time, effort and patience as well as financial aid and investment, technical training and moral support from countries like ours.

As part of his foreign policy agenda, Bill supported the expansion of NATO eastward from the Atlantic to include countries of the former Warsaw Pact. He believed this was essential to strengthening America's long-term relationships with Europe and to further European integration. There was significant opposition to NATO expansion from within the United States and Russia, which did not want to see NATO at its own borders. The challenge for Bill and his team was to determine which countries were already eligible for NATO membership and to keep the door open for other Central and Eastern European nations that aspired to future NATO status by reassuring them of America's continuing support. I was asked to represent Bill in a region he thought needed U.S. encouragement and a show of solidarity.

For part of the trip I teamed up with our United Nations Ambassador and later Secretary of State, Madeleine Albright, whose family had first fled Nazism in her native Czechoslovakia only to return after the war and flee again when communism took over. They eventually settled in the United States. Madeleine was herself an emblem of the opportunities and promise that democracy represents.

My trip began in Bucharest, Romania, once among the most beautiful capitals in Europe. Bucharest had been compared to Paris at the turn of the twentieth century but had lost much of its elegance and luster during forty years of Communist rule. I could see remnants of an earlier cosmopolitan era in the neglected fin de siècle buildings along broad boulevards once lively with cafés. Now the dominant architecture was Soviet-style Socialist realism, visible even in the empty carcasses of giant buildings that were never completed.

No one could possibly quantify the horrors suffered in Romania before the violent downfall of Nicolae Ceaușescu, the Communist dictator who, along with his wife, terrorized the nation for years until he was ousted and executed on December 25, 1989. My first stop was the Square of the Revolution, where I placed flowers at the monument honoring victims of the uprising that finally toppled the Ceaușescus. I met with representatives of the December 21 Association, named for the first day of the uprising, who described the history of their revolution. A crowd of three thousand Romanians had gathered to greet me in the city's main square, a lovely setting marred by the bullet holes in the walls of adjacent buildings. I was surprised by the packs of wild dogs roaming the streets—something I hadn't seen in any other city—and I asked our guide about them. "They're everywhere," he told me. "People can't afford to keep them as pets, and there's no system for rounding them up." The dogs proved to be an omen of far greater neglect in Romania.

Among the horrific legacies of the Communist regime was a swelling population of children with AIDS. Ceaușescu had banned birth control and abortion, insisting that women bear children for the sake of the state. Women told me how they had been carted from their workplaces once a month to be examined by government doctors whose task was to make sure that they weren't using contraceptives or aborting pregnancies. A woman identified as pregnant was watched until she delivered her baby. I could not imagine a more humiliating experience: lines of women undressing as they waited for medical bureaucrats to examine them under the watchful eyes of police. When I defend my pro-choice position in the debate over abortion in our country, I frequently refer to Romania, where pregnancy could be monitored on behalf of the state, and to China, where it could be forcibly terminated. One reason I continue to oppose efforts to criminalize abortion is that I do not believe any government should have the power to dictate, through law or police action, a woman's most personal decisions. In Romania, as elsewhere, many children were born unwanted or into families that could not afford to care for them. They became wards of the state, warehoused in orphanages. Often sick or malnourished, they were treated with blood transfusions, which Ceauşescu promoted as government policy. When the Romanian blood supply became tainted with the AIDS virus, the country had a pediatric AIDS catastrophe. At an orphanage in Bucharest, my staffers and I witnessed children, some covered with tumors, others visibly perishing, as AIDS ravaged their small frames. While some of my staff retreated to a corner of the building, sobbing, I steeled myself against tears, knowing that if I lost my composure, it would only confirm the hopeless situation borne by these children and by the adults who cared for them.

The new Romanian government worked tirelessly with the help of foreign assistance to improve the children's care and to permit more adoptions by families outside the country. Yet the adoption system was plagued with corruption. Charges that children were being sold to the highest bidder resulted in a ban on international adoption in 2001 after the European Union criticized Romania's practices. Work is still needed to clean up the corruption and modernize the child welfare system, but since my visit, Romania, which has made impressive progress against heavy odds, has become a member-elect of both NATO and the European Union.

Poland had already made impressive economic and political progress by 1996. President Aleksander Kwaśniewski spoke excellent English and had traveled throughout the United States before entering politics as a member of the Polish Communist Party. Taking office in 1995 at the age of forty-one, he represented a generational contrast to Poland's first democratically elected President, Lech Wałęsa, the heroic leader of the Solidarity labor union strikes at the Lenin Shipyard in Gdańsk in 1980. Solidarity was instrumental in toppling communism in Poland, and Wałęsa, who won the Nobel Peace Prize in 1983, had been President during the first visit Bill and I made to Warsaw in 1994. At the state dinner he hosted for us with his wife, Danuta, a lively argument broke out between the Wałęsas, who defended the fast pace of economic changes, and a representative of farmers, who argued for slower change and greater economic protection. Many of Poland's hard economic decisions, inevitable in a shift from a state-run economy to a free market, were made on Wałęsa's watch. His party lost the next election in 1995, and he was replaced by Kwaśniewski, who successfully broadened his party's post-Communist base to include young people.

Jolanta Kwaśniewska, the new president's wife, joined me in Kraków, where Gothic towers and gray spires grace one of Europe's best-preserved medieval cities. She and I are mothers of only daughters, and that made for animated discussions about the perils and pleasures of raising them. Together we visited two intellectuals the Communists had labeled "dissidents"—Jerzy Turowicz and Czeslaw Miłosz. Turowicz had published a Catholic weekly for fifty years despite constant pressure from the Communist Polish authorities to shut it down. Miłosz, who won the Nobel Prize for literature in 1980 for a body of work that included *The Seizure of Power* and *The Captive Mind*, had advocated for free thought and free speech throughout the Communist era. These two extraordinary men, whose courage and conviction sustained like-minded dissidents around the world for decades, seemed almost wistful for the moral clarity of their fight against communism.

I encountered similar sentiments among others who survived years of Nazism and communism, when good and evil were so easily defined. There cannot be a more chilling testimony to evil than the Nazi concentration camps at Auschwitz and Birkenau. Documentary and movie footage of the surprisingly mundane brick buildings of Auschwitz and the long, silent railroad track of Birkenau cannot convey the horror of these places where Jews, dissident Poles, Gypsies and others were delivered to their deaths. I visited rooms filled with children's clothing, eyeglasses, shoes, dentures and human hair—mute but damning testaments to the Nazi atrocities. I felt numb and sick when I thought of the millions whose futures were so brutally stolen. As we stood along the railroad tracks leading to the gas chambers, my guide told me that when the Allied troops were liberating Poland, the Nazis dynamited the crematoria to destroy the evidence of what they had done.

When I was about ten, I remember going with my dad to a roadhouse bar and restaurant on the Susquehanna River near the Rodham cottage at Lake Winola. As the bartender talked to my dad, I noticed the tattooed numbers on his wrist. When I later asked my dad about them, he explained that the man had been an American prisoner of war captured by the Nazis. I asked more questions, and my dad told me that the Nazis also tattooed numbers on the arms of millions of Jews and killed them in gas chambers or used them as slaves in concentration camps. I knew that my grandmother Della's husband, Max Rosenberg, was Jewish, and I was horrified that someone like him could have been murdered just because of his religion. Coming to terms with the existence of such evil at a distance is difficult, but at my next stop in Warsaw, I met people for whom that challenge had become profoundly personal.

Waiting in a meeting room of the Ronald S. Lauder Foundation Jewish Community Center were twenty people who had learned in recent years that they were Jewish. A man in his fifties had been told by the woman he knew as his mother that his biological parents had given him to her, to spare him from the Holocaust. A teenager had learned from her parents that her maternal grandparents pretended not to be Jewish in order to avoid being sent to concentration camps. Now this young woman would have to decide who she was. On a return trip to Poland in October 1999, I visited the Foundation to recognize the reestablishment of Judaism in Poland. After the Polish press reported on my speech, the Foundation received calls and letters from Polish Jews living in the countryside who said that until they read about my visit, they had thought they were the only Jews left. Just as societies were facing their histories, so, too, were countless individuals.

In fact, Madeleine Albright, whom I met in the Czech Republic, would share a similar experience. Growing up, Madeleine had no idea that her parents were Jewish. She had been raised Catholic but would soon learn—through a journalist working on her biography—that three of her grandparents had died in Nazi concentration camps. Her family emigrated from Czechoslovakia to England and ultimately to Denver, where Madeleine finished high school before enrolling at Wellesley. Although she was surprised by the news of her Jewish heritage, Madeleine told me that she understood her parents' anguished efforts to protect their children.

Madeleine and I met with President Václav Havel, the playwright and human rights activist who had spent years in prison for his dissident activities. After the Velvet Revolution in 1989 that peacefully transformed Communist Czechoslovakia into a democracy, Havel became the nation's first President. Three years later, when Czechoslovakia split into two separate countries—Slovakia and the Czech Republic—he was elected President of the new Czech Republic.

I first met Havel in Washington at the dedication of the Holocaust Museum in 1993. He was a great friend of Madeleine, who spent her early childhood in Prague and spoke fluent Czech. By then an international icon, Havel was shy, yet eloquent, funny and utterly charming. I found him enormously compelling, and he and Bill bonded over their mutual love of music. Havel gave Bill a saxophone on Bill's first trip to Prague in 1994, when they visited a jazz club that had been at the center of the Velvet Revolution. Havel insisted that Bill play with the performers and then accompanied him on the tambourine! Bill's renditions of "Summertime" and "My Funny Valentine" and other songs they played together were made into a CD that earned cult status in Prague.

Recently widowed, Havel invited Madeleine and me to his private home for dinner, rather than dining at the official presidential quarters in the Prague Castle. When my car pulled up, he was waiting on the sidewalk with a bouquet of flowers and a small gift, a sculpted headband made out of aluminum by one of his artist friends.

After a lively dinner, Havel led us on a walk through the old city and across the famous Charles Bridge, a popular destination for musicians, teenagers and tourists. During his years as a dissident, the bridge had been a gathering point where people could play music or swap records and tapes acquired through the black market—and where they could exchange messages undetected by the authorities. Music, particularly American rock music, was instrumental in keeping hope alive after the 1968 Soviet crackdown. In 1977, Havel led protests following the arrest and trial of a Czechoslovakian rock band called the Plastic People of the Universe, named for Frank Zappa lyrics. Having signed a human rights manifesto known as Charter 77, and been sentenced to hard labor for being a "subversive," he drew on his literary and intellectual ideas to sustain him. A collection of letters he wrote from prison to his late wife, Olga, is now a classic of dissident literature.

Havel, a political philosopher as much as a playwright, believed that globalization often exacerbated nationalistic and ethnic rivalries. Rather than uniting people in a common global culture, a mass culture in which everyone wears the same jeans, eats the same fast-food and listens to the same music doesn't inevitably bring people closer. Rather, he argued, it can make them less secure about who they are, and, as a result, lead to extreme efforts—including religious fundamentalism, violence, terrorism, ethnic cleansing and even genocide—to validate and retain distinct identities. Havel's theory had particular relevance to the new democracies of Central and Eastern Europe, where intolerance and nationalistic tensions had begun to flare up, particularly in places like the former Yugoslavia and Soviet Union.

Havel successfully lobbied Bill and other American leaders to move the headquarters of Radio Free Europe from Berlin to Prague. During the Cold War, the U.S. government had sponsored Radio Free Europe to challenge Communist propaganda throughout the Soviet empire. In a post–Cold War Europe no longer divided by an Iron Curtain, Havel reasoned that Radio Free Europe should take on a new role—promoting democracy. Both Bill and the U.S. Congress agreed with Havel's logic, and in 1994 approved the move of the RFE headquarters to Prague, where it was housed in the old Soviet-style Parliament at one corner of historic Wenceslas Square. This is where Soviet tanks had parked after rolling into the city to squelch a budding democracy movement in the summer of 1968. Havel understood political symbolism.

I spoke at Radio Free Europe headquarters on July 4—an Independence Day message broadcast to twenty-five million listeners in Central and Eastern Europe and the New Independent States. I applauded the role Radio Free Europe had played before the revolution, when many Czechs held their radios toward the window so they could pick up the RFE signal and tune in to Western broadcasts. Inspired by Havel's warnings about the downsides of globalization and cultural homogenization, I called for "an alliance of democratic values" that would help people confront "the unavoidable questions of the twenty-first century," like balancing individual and community rights, raising families amidst the pressures of the mass media and consumer culture, and retaining our ethnic pride and national identity while cooperating regionally and globally.

I said that democracy is a work-in-progress, one that our own nation, after more than two centuries, was still trying to perfect. Building and sustaining a free society is like a three-legged stool: one leg is a democratic government, the second is a free market economy and the third is a civil society—the civic associations, religious institutions, voluntary efforts, NGOs and individual acts of citizenship that together weave the fabric of democratic life. In the newly free countries, civil society is as important as free elections and free markets to internalize democratic values in citizens' hearts, minds and everyday lives.

I closed with a story Madeleine had told me about a tour she had made through the western Czech Republic in 1995 to celebrate the fiftieth anniversary of the end of World War II. In every town she visited, the Czech people waved American flags with forty-eight stars. American troops had passed out the flags a half century earlier, and the Czechs had preserved them through years of Soviet domination, just as they had kept faith that freedom would eventually come.

I was delighted to spend time with Madeleine after our trip in 1995 to the U.N. women's conference in China. She and I were determined to build on Beijing and continue to advocate for the importance of women's issues and social development in U.S. foreign policy. After she became Secretary of State, we had regular lunches in her private dining room on the seventh floor of the State Department, joined by her Chief of Staff, Elaine Shocas, and Melanne. Over time, we changed some minds and helped shift the foreign policy agenda so that it more aptly reflected our nation's democratic values of equality and inclusion.

Madeleine and I became allies because of our shared vision and experience, which included Wellesley College. We also became friends, and in the three days we spent in Prague, we talked nonstop during a splendid boat trip on the Vltava River past Prague Castle while July Fourth fireworks were set off in our honor. We walked around Prague, and she pointed out local sights and greeted well-wishers in her native Czech.

One moment from the trip epitomized Madeleine's resourcefulness and pragmatism. Before a meeting with Prime Minister Václav Klaus, she and I had to review some confidential diplomatic information, but there was no private place to meet. Suddenly, Madeleine grabbed my arm and tugged me toward a door.

"Follow me," she said. The next thing I knew, we were huddled in the ladies' rest room—the perfect, and only, spot available for two women to have a private conversation.

Madeleine and I left Prague for Bratislava, the capital of Slovakia and the seat of a government then headed by Prime Minister Vladimír Mečiar, a throwback to the era of authoritarian regimes. He wanted to outlaw nongovernmental organizations, seeing them as threats to his rule. Before our trip, NGO representatives asked if I would attend a gathering of NGOs scheduled during my visit to draw greater attention to Mečiar's repressive treatment of these organizations and to highlight his unwillingness to embrace democracy. My presence at the meeting, held in the Concert Hall, home of the Slovak Philharmonic Orchestra, emboldened the participants to speak frankly about issues such as minority rights, environmental damage and flawed election procedures and to criticize the government's attempts to terminate and criminalize their work.

Of all the world leaders with whom I have met privately, only two have acted in ways that I found personally disturbing: Robert Mugabe in Zimbabwe, who giggled incessantly and inappropriately while his young wife carried on the conversation, and Mečiar, whom I met later that afternoon at the Government Offices. A former boxer, he sat on one end of a small couch; I sat on the other. I told Mečiar that I had been impressed with the NGOs at the Concert Hall, and the important work the groups were doing. He leaned toward me and, in a menacing tone, constantly clenching and unclenching his fists, ranted on about their duplicity and traitorous challenges to the state. By the end of our meeting, I was wedged tightly into the corner of the couch, appalled at his bullying attitude and barely controlled rage. The Slovak people voted him out of office in September 1998, with considerable help from the NGOs, which mobilized the electorate to vote in favor of change.

All of the countries I visited wanted to discuss their potential membership in NATO, and in Hungary I discussed its prospects in a private meeting with Prime Minister Gyula Horn. I favored NATO expansion so I tried to be encouraging. I also met with Hungary's President Árpád Göncz, a heroic figure with the distinction of having been on the wrong side of both the Nazis and the Communists. A playwright like Havel, he was the first President elected by Hungarians as they made the transition to democracy. As Göncz welcomed me to the large house that served as a presidential residence, he confessed that he didn't know what to do with all the rooms. "It is just my wife and me," he said. "We only use one bedroom. Maybe we should invite lots of people to live here!" Göncz, white haired and humorous, looked like a fit St. Nicholas. His demeanor became serious when we discussed the Balkans, and he voiced the fear that Europe, and indeed the West, was in for a long struggle with ethnic conflict. In what turned out to be a prophetic comment, he warned about Islamic extremists and argued that the same expansionist impulses that had led the Ottoman Empire to the gates of Budapest in the sixteenth century were again thriving among Muslim fundamentalists, who rejected the secular pluralism of modern democracies and the freedom of others for religious belief and women's choices.

People often wonder how much freedom I had to tour the cities I visited and whether I could go anywhere without my Secret Service escort. For the most part, I traveled in motorcades and was surrounded by agents. But in Budapest, I had the rare treat of going to the famous Gundel's Restaurant where I ate in the garden, lit by hanging lanterns, serenaded by a violinist. And then, on a gorgeous afternoon, I had a couple of hours free to see the old city on foot. Melanne, Lissa, Kelly and Roshann Parris, a top-notch advance woman from Kansas City, did their best to disguise themselves as tourists. My lead agent, Bob McDonough, the only agent to accompany me, did the same. I wore a straw hat, sunglasses and a casual shirt and slacks, and we took off down the city's narrow streets, past shops, public baths and into the neo-Gothic cathedral. The only giveaway was that the host government insisted on "protecting" me while I was in their country, so two Hungarian security agents—wearing dark suits and thick-soled shoes and carrying weapons—walked several steps ahead. We had been out for more than an hour before an American tourist yelled from across the street, "Hillary! Hi!" My cover blown, people started gawking, waving and yelling greetings. I shook hands and said hello and resumed walking for several more hours.

Later, we were greeted by a young American couple who asked if they could be photographed with me. The man was in the Army and stationed in Bosnia. He knew I had visited months before and was eager to tell me his experiences. "So far, so good," he said in a classic American understatement. Meeting this earnest young man and his wife brought to mind President Göncz's fears about a future filled with conflicts, and I wondered what lay ahead for them and all of us.

KITCHEN TABLE

I'M A PUSHOVER FOR BIG, STIRRING CEREMONIES, AND the opening moments of the 1996 Summer Olympics in Atlanta on July 19 were as good as it gets. Bill declared the games open to a fanfare of horns and cymbals, followed by a soaring operatic chorale that enveloped the tens of thousands of athletes and spectators packed into Olympic Stadium. Muhammad Ali, shaking from Parkinson's disease, steadied his right arm and held up a blazing torch to light the Olympic flame. It was an unforgettable moment for the world and for the ailing champ.

The celebrations turned to horror a week later when a pipe bomb detonated in Centennial Olympic Park, near the games, killing one woman and injuring 111 people. Bill condemned the bombing as "an evil act of terror." I laid flowers in the park, near the site of the attack.

Within days of the bombing, the FBI named a part-time security guard, Richard Jewell, as the likely suspect. Jewell, who had first been called a hero for discovering the pipe bomb, struggled to defend himself against the full weight of the accusation. For months, the media staked out his home and broadcast twenty-four-hour coverage. Finally, in late October, Jewell was exonerated, and the bombing was ultimately linked to Eric Rudolph, a fanatic anti-abortion activist believed to have escaped into the Appalachian wilderness, and never caught.

The Olympic bombing brought an unsettling end to a summer marked by tragic events, including the crash of Flight 800, a passenger jet that went down in the Atlantic after taking off from New York's Kennedy Airport, and the terrorist bombing of Khobar Towers, a U.S. military installation in Saudi Arabia, that killed nineteen Americans.

Since his first State of the Union, Bill had sounded the alarm on global terrorism. In the 1980s, terrorism was not regarded as a pressing national security threat, though more than five hundred Americans were killed by terrorists in that decade. The 1993 World Trade Center and 1995 Oklahoma City bombings escalated Bill's concern. He frequently talked publicly and privately about how easy travel, open borders and technology gave terrorists new opportunities and means to wreak violence and fear. He immersed himself in the literature on the subject and he met regularly with experts on chemical and biological warfare. He would often return to the residence anxious to tell me about these meetings. What he learned dismayed him. In 1995, he sent comprehensive anti-terrorism legislation to Congress to toughen laws for prosecuting terrorists, to ban fund-raising that channeled money to terrorist causes or organizations and to increase controls over biological and chemical weapon materials. The legislation that finally passed in 1996 omitted key elements that he had requested, so he went back to Congress for increased funding and authority, including provisions for wiretapping and chemical identification. It was difficult, however, to focus public attention or muster congressional support for the actions he thought necessary.

Domestic issues dominated both the Democratic and Republican agendas in the months before the summer's political conventions. The Republicans were hammering on their usual issues: bashing big-spending liberals and "social engineering" programs: welfare, abortion rights, gun control and environmental protection. Bill's reelection campaign centered on government policies that he argued would build community, expand opportunity, demand responsibility and reward enterprise.

I thought about how to present the issues I championed and better relate them to the public's concerns. Countless families, including my own, tend to congregate after school or work to discuss the issues of the day, often sitting around the kitchen table. I began describing Democratic Party issues as "kitchen table issues," which became a catch-phrase in the campaign. The discussion of kitchen table issues led some Washington pundits to talk derisively about "the feminization of politics," an attempt to marginalize, even trivialize, policies such as family leave or extended mammogram coverage for older women or adequate hospital stays for mothers after delivering their babies. With that in mind, I coined my own term—"the humanization of politics"—to publicly advance the idea that kitchen table issues mattered to everybody, not just to women.

By 1996, as he had promised in the 1992 campaign, Bill had reduced the nation's deficit by more than half, presided over a booming economy that had created 10 million jobs, cut taxes through the Earned Income Tax Credit for 15 million low-wage workers, protected workers from forfeiting their health care coverage when they lost their jobs and raised the minimum wage. And we were successful in passing initial reform in our nation's adoption laws: a nonrefundable tax credit of up to $5,000 per child for all parents who adopt and $6,000 for parents who adopt children with special needs; and a prohibition on denying or delaying adoptions on the basis of race, color or national origin. Ever since I had worked on behalf of foster children as a law student, I had hoped to improve the chances that foster children would find permanent, loving families. These new provisions helped, but I knew that more needed to be done. I convened adoption experts in a series of White House meetings in 1996 and outlined a blueprint that led to the passage of the Adoption and Safe Families Act of 1997, which for the first time provided financial incentives for states to move children from foster care to permanent adoptive homes.

Time was also running out for the sixty-year-old welfare system, which had helped to create generations of welfare-dependent Americans. Bill had promised it would be reformed, and the White House had been engaged in months of difficult negotiations and bare-knuckled political conflict. The Republicans knew the public strongly favored welfare reform, and they hoped either to railroad Bill into passing a bill that was far too hard on women and children, denying essential services to millions of needy recipients, or to use his vetoes of their punitive proposals against him in the upcoming election. Instead, welfare reform became a success for Bill. I strongly argued that we had to change the system, although my endorsement of welfare reform came at some personal cost.

America's first welfare program was introduced in the 1930s to help widows with children at a time when there were few opportunities for women to enter the workplace. By the mid-1970s, the percentage of births to unwed mothers was rising, and by the mid-1980s, unmarried mothers were the overwhelming majority of welfare recipients. By and large, they were women with little education and few job skills. Even if they could find work, they could not earn enough to escape poverty or get jobs with health insurance for their children; therefore there was little incentive for them to leave welfare for work. Staying home became a rational choice for some in the short run, but it led to the development of a permanent welfare class, and it fed taxpayer resentment, especially among low-income working parents. I didn't think it was fair that one single mother improvised to find child care and got up early every day to get to work while another stayed home and relied on welfare. I shared Bill's belief that we should provide incentives and support like child care and health insurance to help people work instead of rely on welfare.

During Bill's first term as Governor, Arkansas participated in a Carter Administration "demonstration" project designed to provide more support and encouragement to move people from welfare to work. Seven years later in 1987 and again in 1988, Bill was the lead Democratic governor working with Congress and the Reagan White House on welfare reform. He chaired the National Governors Association hearings, where he presented testimonials from women who had moved off welfare under his plan in Arkansas, and they described how much better they felt about themselves and about their children's futures. Bill was invited to the ceremony in October 1988 when President Reagan signed into law a welfare reform bill that included many provisions he and the Governors had sought.

By 1991, when Bill launched his campaign for President, it was clear that the reforms weren't producing much change because the Bush Administration didn't fund the new programs or aggressively implement them in the states. Bill promised to "end welfare as we know it" and to make the program pro-work and pro-family.

At the time Bill took office, America's welfare program, Aid to Families with Dependent Children, or AFDC, received more than half of its funds from the federal government but was administered by the states, which contributed between 17 and 50 percent of the payments. Federal law required coverage of poor mothers and children, but the states set the monthly benefits. As a result, there were fifty different systems that provided benefits ranging from a high of $821 for a family with two children in Alaska to a low of $137 in Alabama. AFDC recipients were also eligible for food stamps and Medicaid.

On the legislative agenda of 1993 and 1994, the economic plan, NAFTA, the crime bill and health care took precedence over welfare reform. And when the Republicans gained control of Congress, they had their own ideas about how to reform the system. They advocated strict limits on how long people could be on welfare; block grants of

1. Ryan Moore, a seven-year-old from South Sioux City, Nebraska, so inspired me and my staff that we hung a giant photo of him on the wall in the Hillaryland offices. We wanted a plan that would guarantee all children the health care they needed regardless of their parents' economic or insurance status.

2. For the first time, on September 28, 1993, a First Lady was the lead witness on a major Administration legislative proposal. I wanted my words to convey the human dimension of the health care problem. I didn't realize that the laudatory responses to my testimony might just be the latest example of "the talking dog syndrome."

3. Both to educate myself further and to gain public attention for health care reform, I traveled around the country listening to personal stories about rising medical costs, inequitable treatment and bureaucratic quagmires. Having the support of Dr. Koop, appointed Surgeon General by President Reagan, was a great boon. He delivered the hard truth about the need for health care reform.

4. James Carville, our friend and adviser, has one of the most brilliant tactical minds in American politics, and h can really make me laugh.

5. At the 1994 Gridiron Dinner, we decided to parody the insurance lobby's anti-reform TV spot, with Bill playing "Harry" and me "Louise." Al Franken and Mandy Grunwald helped us expose our opponents' scare tactics and have some fun doing it.

6. Inspired by the Freedom Riders who traveled by bus across the South in the early sixties to spread the message of desegregation, health reform advocates organized a nationwide bus tour in the summer of 1994. In Seattle, my Secret Service agents feared I was in real physical danger.

7. Reform riders from the Health Security Express told their personal stories during an event on the White House South Lawn. Whenever I watched Bill identify with someone's pain, as he did that afternoon, I fell in love with him all over again.

8, 9 and 10. The Hillary-land gang arranged a surprise forty-sixth birthday party at the White House. I put on a black wig and hoopskirt to transform myself into one of my First Lady heroines, Dolley Madison. I impersonated another Dolly—Parton—at a later party and wore a ponytail at a fifties-theme bash.

8   9   10

Anyone who ever had the pleasure of spending time with Virginia Cassidy Blythe Clinton Dwire Kelley knew her as an American original—big-hearted, good-humored, fun-loving and totally without prejudice or pretense. She and I grew to respect each other's differences, and we developed a warm, loving relationship. But it did take time.

12, 13, 14 and 15. Camp David was one of the few places where we could totally relax, just as we had once done in the kitchen of the Arkansas Governor's Mansion with Liza Ashley and Dick Kelley. Bill's brother, Roger, visited the presidential retreat over the holidays, along with his son Tyler and my brother Tony's son Zachary, who were great pals. Hugh and his wife, Maria, often joined the family get-togethers.

11

12

13

15

14

16   17

18   19

16 and 17. Harold Ickes, an old friend and political pro, joined the administration as Deputy Chief of Staff. Within days, he was diverted to organize a "Whitewater Response Team." Later, he counseled me about whether to run for Senate. Once I decided, Mark Penn became pollster for my Senate campaign and provided me the same good advice and friendship he had offered my husband.

18, 19 and 20. Whitewater became a limitless investigation of our lives. It cost the taxpayers over $70 million in Independent Counsel expenses alone and disrupted the lives of many innocent people. David Kendall, our personal attorney, was a godsend, along with attorneys Cheryl Mills and Nicole Seligman.

21. Bob Barnett, a lawyer and close friend, counseled us through good times and bad.

22. Sid Blumenthal introduced me to future British Prime Minister Tony Blair, knowing that we and the Blairs would be political and personal allies.

23

24

23. By the end of April 1994, the media had questions about Whitewater and commodities trading. I felt it was time to offer them what they wanted: me. Although I selected my outfit on a whim that morning, my sixty-eight-minute encounter with the Fourth Estate would go down in history as the "Pink Press Conference."

24. The needlepoint pillow of the cover of my book *It Takes a Village* was a gift from Hillaryland volunteer Phyllis Fineshriber. I donated all the book's proceeds—nearly one million dollars—to children's charities.

25. Israeli Prime Minister Rabin created an aura of strength. Bill thought of him as a friend and even a father figure. His wife, Leah, exuded energy and intelligence.

26. Emperor Akihito and Empress Michiko arrive at the White House. The Empress was one of the most fascinating women I have met.

27. Six of the seven living First Ladies assembled for the opening of the U.S. Botanic Garden. Jackie's absence cast a deep shadow on the event for me. She died the following month.

28. I first met Russia's President Yeltsin at a state dinner. He kept up a running conversation about the food, informing me that red wine protected Russian sailors on nuclear submarines from the ill-effects of strontium 90.

29. Nelson Mandela developed a special bond with Chelsea, who'd read about his life. When we visited Mandela in South Africa in 1997, he showed us his former prison cell on Robben Island and spoke of forgiving his captors. I had been preoccupied with the hostility in Washington; this was a reminder to count my blessings.

30. As the office of the Presidency was being undermined by endless investigations, Bill went on with the business of running the government. German Chancellor Helmut Kohl predicted to me in 1994 that Bill would be reelected in 1996. That was a minority opinion in America at that time, and Kohl's conviction surprised me—as did the Chancellor's sense of humor.

30

31. The U.N.'s Fourth World Conference on Women was held in Beijing in 1995, and I was honorary Chair of the American delegation. The speech I made there established that "women's rights are human rights." The stakes were huge—for the United States, for the conference, for women around the world and for me.

31

32. Gingrich complained that Bill had snubbed him on Air Force One, returning from Prime Minister Rabin's funeral. This photo of Bill, Gingrich and then Senate Majority Leader Bob Dole proved otherwise.

32

33. The weeks following the disastrous midterm election were among the most difficult of my eight years in the White House. I knew people were saying, "This is Hillary's fault. She blew it with health care and lost us the election." Long a fan of Eleanor Roosevelt's, I turned to her for inspiration again, with help from an image concocted by a close friend.

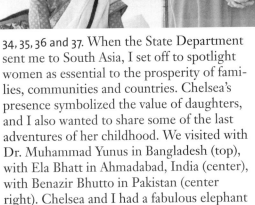

34, 35, 36 and 37. When the State Department sent me to South Asia, I set off to spotlight women as essential to the prosperity of families, communities and countries. Chelsea's presence symbolized the value of daughters, and I also wanted to share some of the last adventures of her childhood. We visited with Dr. Muhammad Yunus in Bangladesh (top), with Ela Bhatt in Ahmadabad, India (center), with Benazir Bhutto in Pakistan (center right). Chelsea and I had a fabulous elephant ride in Nepal.

38. Of all the places we visited during the eight years of Bill's Presidency, none was more invigorating and inspiring than Ireland. I met with peace activist Joyce McCartan (right) over cups of tea at the Lamplighter Traditional Fish and Chips restaurant in Belfast. She told me, "It takes women to bring men to their senses."

39   38

40. I might go down in history as the first wife of a president to testify before a grand jury, but I did it on my own terms.

40

39. Bill and I worked well with Jacques and Bernadette Chirac, despite some significant political differences. Bernadette was the only presidential spouse I knew who had actually been elected on her own, and I was fascinated by this separate role she had carved out.

41. I traveled to Bosnia-Herze-govina in 1996 to promote the Dayton Peace Accords. I became the second First Lady to visit a combat zone without the Presi-dent—following, as usual, in the footsteps of Eleanor Roosevelt. Chelsea was a hit with the American troops, who personi-fied the diversity of America.

41

42. After the second election, I felt I was entering this new chapter of my life like steel tempered in fire: a bit harder at the edges, but more durable. Bill had grown into his Presidency, and it endowed him with a gravitas that showed on his face and in his eyes.

43. On inaugura- tion day, Chelsea's miniskirt took me by surprise. It was too late for her to change—and I doubt she would have. I was getting used to being the mother of a teenager.

43

45

46

44, 45 and 46. Chelsea had attended public school in Arkansas, but in Washington, we chose Sidwell Friends, a Quaker school, because private schools were off limits to the news media. At the school's "Mother-Daughter Show," we moth- ers played our daughters in comic sketches. Chelsea's passion for pirouetting had me hamming it up and Bill putting.

47. The kitchen has been the heart of every house I've lived in, and the second floor of the White House was no different. The tiny table became the center of our family life—it was where we ate, did homework, celebrated our birthdays, laughed together, wept together and talked into the night.

47

49

48. Every cliché about the empty nest syndrome applied to me. It was time to get a dog. We forgot to consult Socks, who despised Buddy instantly and forever.

48

49. After our experience in Washington, I understood why Chelsea might choose a college 3,000 miles away. I went into overdrive as soon as we got to her dorm at Stanford. Bill seemed to go into a slow-motion trance until it was time for us to leave. "Can't we come back after dinner?" he asked.

50. After the Lewinsky story broke, I kept my commitment to appear on the *Today* show. I might have phrased my point more artfully, but I stand by what I told host Matt Lauer, that there was a "right-wing conspiracy," an interlocking network of groups and individuals who wanted to turn the clock back on many of the advances our country had made.

50

51   52   53

51, 52 and 53. I have never been the sort of person who routinely pours out her deepest feelings, but I felt better with my closest friends around me. Diane Blair (left) and her husband, Jim, were among the first friends I made in Arkansas when I followed Bill there in 1974. Diane taught with me at the University of Arkansas. Ann Henry hosted our wedding reception in Fayetteville. Vernon and Ann Jordan have been loving, wise counselors.

54

54. Our common experiences with Tony and Cherie Blair created not only a special kinship, but also an important philosophical and political alliance. When Bill and I met them at 10 Downing Street, we started a non-stop discussion about our common concerns.

55   56   57

55, 56 and 57. Betsy Johnson Ebeling (center) was the sixth-grade friend who led me around town like a Seeing Eye dog when I refused to wear the thick glasses I'd needed since I was nine. Ricky Ricketts pulled off my fake ponytail in ninth grade. Susan Thomases (left), our longtime friend, helped Bill run for President.

58. There were many unforgettable trips to Latin America. In Antigua, Guatemala, I was greeted by three young women, one of whom—I hope—might be able to be President of her country one day.

58

59. Having heard me talk endlessly and enthusiastically about my trip to Africa, Bill went in 1998, the first sitting President to make an extended trip to that continent. In Accra, Ghana, we were welcomed by President Jerry Rawlings, his wife, Nana Konadu, and the largest crowd I ever saw. We also visited Cape Town and saw Nelson Mandela, who once told us that "the greatest glory of living lies not in never falling, but in rising every time you fall."

59

60

60. Some days were better than others, like this one in Botswana. Bill and I caught the last rays of sun over the Chobe River, on a day I wanted never to end. A harsher light would shine on us in Washington.

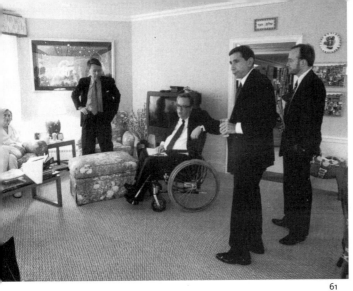

61. After Bill testified to the Grand Jury by closed-circuit television from the Map Room of the White House that there had been an inappropriate, intimate relationship with Monica Lewinsky, I met in the Solarium with David Kendall, Chuck Ruff, Mickey Kantor and Paul Begala, feeling dumbfounded, heartbroken and outraged that I'd believed him. Why he deceived me is his own story, and he needs to tell it in his own way.

61

62

62. The last thing I wanted to do was to go on vacation with Bill Clinton, but I was desperate to get out of Washington. I had to focus on what I needed to do for myself, my daughter, my family, my marriage and my country. I knew that the Presidency was in the balance. The touching concern of Walter and Betsy Cronkite lifted my spirits.

63

63. Stevie Wonder offered one of the kindest gestures anyone made during this difficult period, and his message, delivered through music, was overwhelming. He came to the White House and sang a song he'd written for me about the power of forgiveness. I kept moving my chair closer to him as he played.

64. After the impeachment vote, a delegation of Democrats, led by Dick Gephardt (center), came to the White House in a show of solidarity with the President. The White House staff, led by John Podesta, kept focused on the country's business.

65. Madeleine Albright and I slipped into the ladies' room in Prague so we could have a private talk away from the press. White House photographer Barbara Kinney, whose commitment to her work took her to many surprising locations, followed us in.

66. Susan McDougal served long months in jail for refusing to testify before the Whitewater Grand Jury, which she insisted was a trap to force her to falsely implicate Bill and me.

67. Forging good relationships with my fellow spouses provided back channels to heads of state. During some early rough patches, Queen Noor of Jordan called to check in on me. She told me that when members of her family faced hard times they would tell each other to "soldier on." I joined Queen Noor in Amman to mourn her soldier King.

68. After Senator Moynihan announced his retirement, Democratic party leaders in New York encouraged me to step into the race. I'm very happy I did. His death in March 2003 was a great loss to our nation.

69. Among the hardest decisions I've had to make in my life was to run for the U.S. Senate from New York. For years, I had given speeches about the importance of women participating in politics and government. As one young athlete told me, it was time for me to "dare to compete." Here I am with my biggest supporters, Bill, Chelsea and my mother.

70 and 71. As I was getting ready for the evening, Chelsea came in with the latest results. It was clear that I was going to win by a much bigger margin than expected. As pleased as I was by my campaign's success, our joy was tempered by the roller-coaster presidential race.

72

72. A seasoned campaigner and a rookie candidate talk politics at the New York State Fair. My journey had taken me from Illinois to the East and then to Arkansas, where I married a man who would become President. In 2000, the son of a former President would occupy the Oval Office, and a First Lady would serve in the Senate for the first time in history.

73. One of the first things I noticed about Bill Clinton was the shape of his hands. His wrists are narrow and elegant and his long fingers deft, like those of a pianist or a surgeon. When we first met in law school, I loved just watching him turn the pages of a book. Now his hands are showing signs of age, twisted by thousands of handshakes and golf swings and miles of signatures.

73

74

74. Bill and I are now embarked on a new chapter in our lives. We've moved to Chappaqua, New York, and though we can't predict where this latest path will lead us, I'm ready for the journey.

75

75. After I held the Bible for all of Bill's swearing-in ceremonies, he and Chelsea held the Bible for me while Al Gore swore me in during this mock ceremony. I was now Senator Clinton.

welfare funds to the states, including Medicaid, school lunches and food stamps; the cessation of all benefits to legal immigrants, even those who were working and paying taxes; and, as introduced by Newt Gingrich, a system of orphanages to house and raise children born out of wedlock to teen mothers. The Republican plan provided minimal support to help people make the transition to work.

Bill and I, along with members of Congress who wanted productive reform, believed that people able to work should work. But we recognized that assistance and incentives were necessary to help people move permanently from welfare to employment and that successful reform would require large investments in education and training, subsidies for child care and transportation, transitional health care, tax incentives to encourage employers to hire welfare recipients, and tougher child support collection efforts. We also opposed cutting off benefits to legal immigrants and shipping children of poor parents to orphanages.

In late 1995, the administration and Congress began serious efforts to pass legislation. Much political posturing ensued. I think many Republicans were hoping that if they kept enough "poison pills" in the bill, they would put the President in a lose-lose situation. If he signed the bill, he would disappoint key Democratic constituencies and leave millions of poor kids vulnerable. If he vetoed it, the Republicans would have a popular issue in the 1996 election with voters who wanted reform and didn't know the details of the legislation.

Some in the White House urged the President to sign whatever reform the Congress sent him. To do otherwise, they argued, would incur huge political costs for both the Administration and congressional Democrats in the upcoming election campaign. Many disagreed, arguing that the only solution was for Bill to outmaneuver the Republicans and convince the public that reform was his issue. My feelings about welfare ran deep and were probably more complicated than my husband's. I believed that the system desperately required reform, but I had spent time as an advocate for children and women caught up in the system, and I knew that welfare was often essential as a temporary support for poor families. Yes, I had seen it exploited; but I had also seen it rescue people who used it to weather a rough period. Although I had privately argued against Administration decisions before, I had never publicly opposed an Administration policy or any of Bill's decisions. Now, however, I told him and his top staff that I would speak out against any bill that did not provide heath care through Medicaid, a federal guarantee of food stamps, and child care assistance for people making the transition off welfare. I also believed that these kinds of supports should be available to the working poor to lift them above the poverty line too.

The Republicans passed a bill with strict time limits on welfare, no supports for the transition to work, no benefits for legal immigrants, an end to federal oversight and accountability in how states spent federal welfare money. In short, the states would be free to determine what to offer in monthly payments, child care, food stamps and medical care or whether to offer them at all. After a vigorous debate inside the White House, the President vetoed the bill. Then the Republicans passed another bill with only minimal changes. I didn't have to lobby hard with Bill, who knew he could not sign this one either. Bill vetoed it, insisting that all poor children were entitled to child care, nutrition and medical benefits.

The third bill passed by Congress had the support of the majority of the Democrats in the House and Senate. It contained more financial support for moving people to work, offered new money for child care and restored the federal guarantees of food stamps and medical benefits. But it cut off most benefits to legal immigrants, imposed a five-year lifetime limit on federal welfare benefits, and maintained the status quo on monthly benefit limits, leaving the states free to set benefit limits. The federal welfare grants to the states were set at the amount states received in the early 1990s, when welfare rolls were at an all-time high. That meant the states would have the financial resources to provide the safety net that true reform required, and incentives to allot significant funding to programs that supported and encouraged work and independence.

The President eventually signed this third bill into law. Even with its flaws, it was a critical first step to reforming our nation's welfare system. I agreed that he should sign it and worked hard to round up votes for its passage—though he and the legislation were roundly criticized by some liberals, advocacy groups for immigrants and most people who worked with the welfare system. Bill vowed to fight to restore immigrant benefits and, by 1998, had made some limited progress by working with Congress to reinstate Social Security and food stamp benefits for certain classes of legal immigrants, including children, the elderly and the disabled. Block granting welfare funds was acceptable to both of us, since states, which set the benefit levels anyway, would be receiving significantly more money to help move people from welfare to work. I was most concerned with the five-year lifetime limit, because it applied whether the economy was up or down, whether jobs were available or not, but I felt, on balance, that this was a historic opportunity to change a system oriented toward dependence to one that encouraged independence.

The legislation was far from perfect, which is where pragmatic politics entered in. It was preferable to sign the measure knowing that a Democratic administration was in place to implement it humanely. If he vetoed welfare reform a third time, Bill would be handing the Republicans a potential political windfall. In the wake of the disastrous 1994 elections, he was concerned about further Democratic electoral losses that would jeopardize his leverage to protect social policies in the future.

Bill's decision, and my endorsement of it, outraged some of our most loyal supporters, including longtime friends Marian Wright Edelman and her husband, Peter Edelman, an Assistant Secretary for Health and Human Services. Because of my history with the Children's Defense Fund, they hoped I would oppose the measure and couldn't understand my support. They genuinely believed the legislation was shameful, impractical and harmful to children, which Marian conveyed in "An Open Letter to the President" published in *The Washington Post*.

In the painful aftermath, I realized that I had crossed the line from advocate to policy maker. I hadn't altered my beliefs, but I respectfully disagreed with the convictions and passion of the Edelmans and others who objected to the legislation. As advocates, they were not bound to compromise, and unlike Bill, they didn't have to negotiate with Newt Gingrich and Bob Dole or worry about maintaining a political balance in Congress. I remembered all too well the defeat of our health care reform effort, which may have happened in part because of a lack of give-and-take. Principles and values in politics should not be compromised, but strategies and tactics must be flexible enough to make progress possible, especially under the difficult political conditions we faced. We wanted to pass a welfare plan that would motivate and equip women to obtain a better life for themselves and their children. We also hoped to persuade the American public, now that the old welfare system had been replaced, to address the greater problem of poverty and its consequences: one-parent and no-parent families, inadequate housing, poor schools and lack of health care. I hoped welfare reform would be the beginning, not the end, of our concern for the poor.

Weeks after Bill signed the law, Peter Edelman and Mary Jo Bane, another friend and Assistant Secretary at HHS who had worked on welfare reform, resigned in protest. These were principled decisions, which I accepted and even admired, despite my very different view of the merits and promise of the legislation. I still saw Marian and Peter socially from time to time, and I was thrilled when Bill awarded Marian the Medal of Freedom for her lifetime commitment to civil rights and children on August 9, 2000. She was an important mentor in my life, and our rift over welfare was sad and difficult.

By the time Bill and I left the White House, welfare rolls had dropped 60 percent from 14.1 million to 5.8 million, and millions of parents had gone to work. States had supported part-time and low-wage work by continuing to provide medical benefits and food stamps for these workers. By January 2001, child poverty had decreased by more than 25 percent and was at its lowest rate since 1979. Welfare reform, the increase in the minimum wage, the reduction in taxes on low-income workers and the booming economy had moved almost eight million people out of poverty—one hundred times the number of people who left the poverty rolls during the Reagan years.

A significant contributor to the success of reform was the Welfare to Work Partnership, which Bill had asked one of his longtime friends, Eli Segal, to launch as a means of encouraging employers to hire former welfare recipients. Eli, a successful businessman, had worked with Bill in the McGovern campaign and served as Chief of Staff in the 1992 campaign. As an assistant to the President, he was charged with creating the National Service Corporation and AmeriCorps. Eli worked closely with Shirley Sagawa, a policy aide on my staff, to draft the legislation that set up the program, and he became the corporation's first CEO. AmeriCorps provided community service opportunities and college scholarships to more than two hundred thousand young people between 1994 and 2000, working in partnerships with businesses and communities. Eli followed the same model for the Welfare to Work Partnership, which enlisted employers to hire and train former welfare recipients. Under his leadership, the Partnership flourished, with more than twenty thousand businesses providing 1.1 million welfare recipients with skills, jobs and independence.

Welfare reform was implemented during good economic times.

The real test will occur when the economy is down and welfare rolls rise again. The legislation is due to be reauthorized, and as a Senator, I intend to work to build on its successes and fix its deficiencies. Benefits for legal immigrants who work and pay more than $5 billion in taxes should be restored completely. The five-year limits for lifetime benefits should be waived for people who lose jobs in a jobless economy. More money should be spent on education and training, and some education hours should count toward work requirements. And the states should be held accountable for how they spend federal welfare dollars.

As Bill gained greater support from the American people in the months preceding the 1996 election, his adversaries desperately cast about for anything that could weaken his momentum. *Time* magazine recognized the trend in early July, when it ran an article with the headline "The Starr Factor." It reported, "For months Clinton has been waiting for the GOP contender who would turn the '96 race into a real battle. It looks as though he has found him at last—and it's not Bob Dole. Every serious matter bedeviling the President has Kenneth Starr connected to it somewhere. . . . With the Dole campaign still unable to gain traction on its own, Republican hopes are riding on a presidency worn to pieces by subpoenas and indictments."

The latest pseudoscandal appeared to be timed for the summer convention season and hinged on the actions of two midlevel White House employees, Craig Livingstone and Anthony Marceca, in the Office of Personnel Security. In 1993, they had requested FBI background files on White House pass holders to assemble a record of everyone with a legitimate White House security pass. The Office of Personnel Security, despite its imposing title, did not perform "security checks"—that was done by the FBI. Nor was it responsible for security—that was the job of the Secret Service. I never quite figured out what else it did, but it was responsible for keeping track of present White House employees, making sure their clearances were up to date, and giving security briefings to new White House personnel. When President Bush left the White House in January 1993, his people took all the files of the Office of Personnel Security—which they were allowed to do under the Presidential Records Act—for the Bush Library. The incoming Administration thus had none of its own records (as distinct from the Secret Service's records) of the permanent employees in the White House. Livingstone and Marceca were trying to rebuild these OPS records when they received from the FBI hundreds of files, including some from Reagan and Bush officials. They did not recognize the mistake. When another staffer finally did, she sent the files to the archives rather than returning them to the FBI. The White House acknowledged this bureaucratic snafu and apologized for it. Nonetheless, "Filegate" was added to Kenneth Starr's list of investigations.

Before the story was put to rest, an FBI agent told the Senate Judiciary Committee staff that his background check of Craig Livingstone suggested that Livingstone was given his job as head of White House personnel security because his mother and I had been friends. In fact, Mrs. Livingstone and I didn't know one another, but we had been photographed together once in a large group at a White House Christmas party. I was in Bucharest at a school whose curriculum our government was helping to revamp when a traveling American reporter asked me about my relationship with the Livingstone family. I told him that I didn't recall meeting Craig or his mother, but if I ever did encounter her, I'd say, "Mrs. Livingstone, I presume?"

During August, I took Chelsea on a college tour through New England. Though I was dreading the moment when she would leave home for college, I was excited about visiting colleges with her. I also secretly hoped she'd fall in love with my alma mater, Wellesley, or at least choose a college on the East Coast so I could easily visit and she could come home on a whim. I worked out a deal with the Secret Service to travel from campus to campus in a nondescript van with as few agents visible as possible. We visited six campuses with relatively little notice, and I would have been thrilled if she had attended any one of them.

Chelsea, however, was eager to see Stanford, so off we went to Palo Alto. The Provost at the time, Condoleezza Rice, graciously welcomed us at the start of a daylong visit that captivated Chelsea. She loved the setting of the University amidst the foothills, the temperate weather and the Mission-style architecture. When I called Bill that night, I told him I thought Stanford was clearly her first choice—the price, I guess, of raising an independent child.

For our summer vacation, we again chose Jackson Hole, Wyoming. I had been frantically trying to finish writing *It Takes a Village* the year before, and now I was free to hike with Bill and Chelsea through meadows of late summer wildflowers in the Grand Tetons and explore nearby Yellowstone National Park. The sweeping grasslands and geyser basins were preserved for future generations of Americans back in 1872 when the U.S. government designated Yellowstone as the country's—and the world's—first national park. Since then, America's national parks have provided a model and an inspiration for other nations to protect their natural heritage. Whenever I visit one of our national parks, I'm reminded of how our country has been blessed with such abundant natural resources. Our job goes beyond preserving the beautiful scenery; we have to be caretakers of a healthy, balanced environment. In Yellowstone, where gray wolves had been exterminated by trappers, government biologists reintroduced a small population to help restore the natural relationship between predator and prey in the park. During our visit to Yellowstone, Chelsea, Bill and I hiked up to the holding pens where a pack of wolves was being acclimated for release. There were no reporters around, just wildlife officials, us and a few astonished Secret Service agents who never expected to have to protect the First Family from a pack of *real* wolves.

Bill announced a historic agreement to stop a large, foreign-owned gold mine on the border of Yellowstone from threatening the pristine environment. The older I become, the more passionate I am about protecting our Earth from unnecessary and irreversible damage. A strong economy and a clean environment are not mutually exclusive goals—in fact, they go hand-in-hand, since all life and economic activity ultimately depend on our stewardship of our natural surroundings. During the White House years, I supported the "greening" of the White House, a project aimed at improving the environmental performance of the building complex through lower energy use, comprehensive recycling and other measures. Through a program I started, Save America's Treasures, I raised money for our parks and visited many. I supported Bill and Al's commitment to protecting more land, cleaning up the air and water, tackling global climate change and pursuing conservation and alternative energy sources. But my principal focus became the effects of environmental factors on our health. My study of the illnesses of Gulf War veterans and my work on the rising incidence of asthma among children and breast cancer among women persuaded me that environmental effects on health begged for long-term research.

The Republican Convention opened in San Diego on August 12. By tradition, the party holding its convention gets unfettered publicity while nominating its candidates and unveiling its campaign message.

The other party's candidate stays quietly on the sidelines, which was fine with me since I thought we all needed some time off. I didn't watch the speeches on television, but I quickly heard from friends about Elizabeth Dole's remarks to delegates on the second night of the convention. The former Reagan and Bush Cabinet Secretary had waded into the crowd, microphone in hand, and spoken lovingly about her husband, his career and his beliefs. Poised and intelligent, she was a lawyer by training and a political pro whose presence and eloquence strengthened her husband's campaign. And though Bob Dole was a tough opponent for us, I was glad to see a woman under pressure rise to the occasion and get the praise she deserved. It's a strange twist of fate that we now both serve in the Senate.

Mrs. Dole's speech inevitably provoked comparisons between us, and she had barely exited the stage before my staff was bombarded with questions about how I intended to handle my speech at the Democratic Convention. Reporters wondered whether I would stand at a podium or wander into the crowd, as she did. Tempting as it was to try something new, I felt that I was better off sticking to my own themes and style.

I arrived in Chicago on Sunday, August 25, three days ahead of Bill, who was coming on a train from West Virginia with Chelsea. Betsy Ebeling had organized a gathering of my family and friends at Riva's Restaurant, which sits on Navy Pier overlooking Lake Michigan. I quickly caught Chicago's excitement about hosting the convention. Mayor Richard M. Daley, namesake and son of Chicago's late political giant, had also done a terrific job getting the city ready: the streets were lined with newly planted trees, not with protesters demonstrating against an unpopular war, as they had been during the 1968 convention when his father was Mayor. This time everything went off without a glitch.

My scheduled speech to the delegates on Tuesday evening would mark the first time a First Lady had ever delivered a televised prime-time address at a national political convention. Eleanor Roosevelt was the first to address a convention, but that was in 1940, the pre-television era. The forty-eight hours before my speech were crammed with events. I addressed the Democratic Women's Caucus, met with various state delegations, celebrated the opening of a park in Jane Addams's honor and visited a community school. I also worked on the speech, which was still evolving on Monday evening, when I went to the United Center to practice on a TelePrompTer. The Center is the home of the world-champion Chicago Bulls basketball team, which became the inspiration for one of my all-time favorite political buttons. The 1996 Bulls included the incomparable Michael Jordan, Scottie Pippen, whom I knew from Arkansas, and the NBA's "bad boy," Dennis Rodman. A political button sold at the convention featured a photo of my face with Rodman's multicolored hair and this caption: "Hillary Rodman Clinton: As Bad as She Wants To Be."

By early Tuesday morning, I didn't feel satisfied with my speech. I was missing Bill, who was still on the train and out of reach for the kind of reassurance and help I counted on from him. In a little over twelve hours, I would address the biggest audience of my life, and I was struggling to find the right words to convey my themes and beliefs.

Bob Dole became my unwitting savior. All of a sudden it hit me. In his acceptance speech at the Republican Convention, he had attacked the premise of my book, *It Takes a Village*. He mistakenly used my notion of the village as a metaphor for "the state" and implied that I, and by extension Democrats, favor government intrusions into every aspect of American life. "And after the virtual devastation of the American family, the rock upon which this country was founded, we are told that it takes a village, that is collective, and thus the state, to raise a child," he said in his speech. ". . . And with all due respect, I am here to tell you it does not take a village to raise a child. It takes a family to raise a child."

Dole missed the point of the book, which is that families are the first line of responsibility for children, but that the village—a metaphor for society as a whole—shares responsibility for the culture, economy and environment in which our children grow up. The policeman walking the beat, the teacher in the classroom, the legislator passing laws and the corporate executive deciding what movies to make all have influence over America's children.

I seized upon the village theme, and we swiftly drafted the speech around it. Then I went to the tiny room in the basement of the United Center for one last rehearsal with Michael Sheehan, an extraordinary media coach who made Herculean efforts to teach me to use the TelePrompTer, which I had never worked with before and couldn't seem to master. Though I might finally have found the words I'd been searching for, I'd blow the speech if I delivered them looking like a robot, so I practiced until it felt right.

At last, it was time to go. Chelsea had spent two days with Bill on his train journey but had left him to be with me. She joined my mother and brothers, Dick Kelley, Diane Blair, Betsy Ebeling and a host of friends in a skybox suite where they had a great view of the podium.

About twenty thousand people were jammed into the convention hall, and the mood was high-pitched. Two of our party's greatest orators—former New York Governor Mario Cuomo and civil rights leader Jesse Jackson—spoke before me, revving up the Democratic faithful with old-fashioned fire-and-brimstone speeches touting the party's values.

As I walked out onto the stage, the crowd erupted into a frenzy of clapping, chanting and foot-stomping that touched me and helped to alleviate my nervousness. My motions to urge the crowd to sit down were futile, so I just waved and let the cheers wash over me.

Finally the roars faded, and I began to speak. My remarks were simple and direct. I asked people to imagine what the world would be like when Chelsea was my age, the year 2028. "One thing we know for sure is that change is certain," I said. "Progress is not. Progress depends on the choices we make today for tomorrow and on whether we meet our challenges and protect our values."

After mentioning issues such as expanding the Family Leave law, simplifying adoption laws and passing a bill to guarantee that mothers and babies are not sent home from the hospital less than forty-eight hours after childbirth, I got to the crescendo written in response to Bob Dole:

> For Bill and me, there has been no experience more challenging, more rewarding and more humbling than raising our daughter. And we have learned that to raise a happy, healthy, and hopeful child, it takes a family. It takes teachers. It takes clergy. It takes businesspeople. It takes community leaders. It takes those who protect our health and safety. It takes all of us.
> Yes, it takes a village.
> And it takes a President.
> It takes a President who believes not only in the potential of his own child, but of all children, who believes not only in the strength of his own family, but of the American family.
> It takes Bill Clinton.

Again the crowd erupted. They not only believed that Bill cared about children, they understood that I was directly confronting the Republicans' radical individualism and narrow and unrealistic view of what it took for most Americans to raise their children at the close of the twentieth century.

On Wednesday night, Chelsea and I went to meet Bill, who got off the train with upsetting news. A supermarket tabloid was about to publish a story claiming that Dick Morris had paid for frequent visits by a call girl to a hotel he stayed in when he was in Washington. The tabloid story that ran on Thursday quoted the call girl extensively. She said that Morris bragged about writing my convention speech, as well as the Vice President's—he hadn't written either. Morris resigned from the campaign, and Bill issued a statement thanking him for his work and calling him a "superb political strategist." After Morris left, the campaign went on seamlessly because Mark Penn continued to offer the thoughtful research and analysis.

Bill's appearance before the convention to accept his nomination triggered a wild demonstration from the delegates when he walked onstage on Thursday night. From the second he began speaking, he commanded the public spotlight and used it with perfect pitch and passion to make his case to continue leading America. He reviewed America's progress, beginning with where we had been as a nation in 1992 and where we had come during his Presidency. Up in the skybox, Chelsea and I watched with enormous pride as he delivered a virtuoso performance. About two-thirds of the way through, we went down to be ready to join him onstage for the finale of the convention. By the time we got backstage, he was nearing the conclusion. He ended by harking back to his 1992 campaign and affirming that "after these four good, hard years, I still believe in a place called Hope, a place called America." So did I.

SECOND TERM

BILL AND I SPENT THE FINAL DAY OF HIS LAST CAM-
paign flying around the country in a mad dash to get out the vote, living on the edge of exhaustion, taking nothing for granted until the bal-
loting was over or, as Bill would say, till the last dog dies. With each hour,
the mood on Air Force One grew lighter as we gained confidence that
Bill would become the first Democratic President since Franklin Roosevelt to serve two full terms. On election eve, Bill, Chelsea and I were
giddy with excitement and lack of sleep. America was in the throes of a
silly dance craze that season, and somewhere over Missouri, in the middle of the night, Chelsea led our entourage in an impromptu rendition of
the Macarena (all of us looking a little like campers slapping off a swarm
of mosquitoes). When Mike McCurry, the President's press secretary,
briefed the press on the activities up in the front of the plane, he was careful to report that the commander in chief danced "in a presidential manner." Sometime after 2 A.M., we began our descent into Little Rock.

There was no question that we would vote and then wait for the returns in Arkansas, where Bill's journey to the White House had begun.
We decamped in a suite of rooms at a downtown hotel, resting and visiting with friends and family. Tens of thousands of people were already
gathering in Little Rock, anticipating a victory celebration when the
polls closed. We kept out of sight except to go to our polling place and
attend a luncheon hosted by Senator David Pryor, who was retiring
that year.

I was thankful to be surrounded by familiar faces, caught up in an
outpouring of support by a hometown crowd, but there was already a
hint of nostalgia in the air, because everyone knew this was Bill's last run
for office. A President can serve only two terms. The man who lived to

campaign had finally reached the finish line in his last race. There was another sobering undercurrent running through the jubilant crowd. When he addressed the luncheon, Senator Pryor reminded us of the independent counsel who had set up shop across town in Little Rock two years earlier and still hadn't wrapped up his investigation. "I think the biggest round of applause you could get in Arkansas is to say, 'Let's get this election over with and let Ken Starr go home,' " he said. The investigation, he pointed out, had "ruined a lot of lives, broke a lot of people financially. . . . We feel it's time for them to let us go on."

When we learned that Bill had won the election by a solid eight percentage points, I felt it was more than a victory for the President: it was a vindication of the American people. They made sure that this election was about the things that mattered to them—work, home, family, the economy—not about old political grudges and phony scandals. Our message had cut through the toxic atmosphere in Washington to reach the voters. The campaign mantra of 1992—"It's the economy, stupid"—was still operative, but with a new emphasis on what the rebounding economy could do to improve the lives of all Americans. We recognized that people's personal concerns could become political if they used their voices and their votes to be heard.

Election days are torture because there's nothing to do but wait. To divert myself, I joined some of my friends for lunch at Doe's Eat Place, a steak restaurant that was a spin-off from the legendary Doe's in Greenville, Mississippi. After lunch, I decided to drive over to my mother's house in the Hillcrest section of Little Rock, and I cajoled my lead agent, Don Flynn, into sitting beside me. For some reason Don's knuckles were white as dice by the time we arrived. I haven't driven since.

Just after midnight, following Dole's concession speech, Bill and I joined hands and, with the Gores, walked out of the Old State House, Arkansas's first Capitol building, and the site of Bill's campaign launch on October 3, 1991.

I could see the faces of our friends and supporters in the large crowd, and I remembered the very first time I had visited the Old State House, in January of 1977, at a reception we held for everyone who had come to see Bill sworn in as the Arkansas Attorney General. I was grateful to the people of Arkansas, who had given me so much over the years, and I felt the depth of Bill's emotion: "I thank the people of my beloved native state," he said. "I would not be anywhere else in the world tonight. In front of this wonderful old Capitol that has seen so much of my own life and our state's history, I thank you for staying with me for so long, for never giving up, for always knowing that we could do better."

Bill would have his chance to "build a bridge to the twenty-first century," and I would do my best to help him. My on-the-job training during the first term had taught me to use my position more effectively, both behind the scenes and publicly. I had moved from a highly visible role as Bill's chief health care adviser, testifying before Congress, delivering speeches, traveling around the country and meeting with congressional leaders, to a more private—but equally active—role during the two years following the midterm elections in 1994.

I had begun working inside the White House and with other Administration officials to save vital services and programs targeted by Gingrich and the Republicans. I also spent two years helping the President's top advisers refine welfare reform and stave off cuts in legal services, the arts, education, Medicare and Medicaid. As part of our continuing effort on health care reform, I lobbied Democrats and Republicans on Capitol Hill to initiate a comprehensive program to make vaccines available at low or no cost for children.

Looking ahead to Bill's second term, I planned to speak out publicly to help shape White House policy on issues affecting women, children and families. Despite better material conditions among many in advanced economies such as ours, families were under great stress. The gap between rich and poor was growing wider. I wanted to guard the social safety net—health care, education, pensions, wages and jobs— that was in danger of fraying for citizens less able to absorb the changes resulting from the high-tech revolution and a global consumer culture. I had worked with Bill during the 1996 presidential campaign to elevate issues like family leave, student loans, health care for children and the elderly and raising the minimum wage. The public had ratified his leadership in the election, and we could concentrate on efforts to bring positive change to people's lives. The Republican rallying cry against big government was meant to undermine people's trust in the efficacy of widely accepted federal programs like Social Security, Medicare and public education. Through an initiative known as "Reinventing Government," headed by Vice President Gore, the federal government was smaller than it had been since the Kennedy Administration. I knew that any continuing federal role had to be demonstrably effective, putting more police on the streets, for example, or more teachers in the class-room. That meant listening to Americans.

In 1994, I had promoted the largest survey of working women ever conducted by the U.S. Department of Labor. Called "Working Women Count," the survey reflected the worries of millions of working women, who comprise nearly half of our nation's labor force. Regardless of income or background, the women had two dominant concerns: affordable quality child care and balancing work and family life. While raising Chelsea, I had relied on friends, family and a series of caregivers who came into our home when Bill and I were at work. Most parents are not so fortunate.

I met with women who had participated in the survey to learn more about their lives. One single mother from New York City described the key to her daily survival: "Everything is timed," she said. She outlined her schedule: rise at 6 A.M., get ready for work, make breakfast, feed the cat and wake up her nine-year-old son. Catch up on ironing while he gets ready for school. Walk her son to school, go to work until 5 P.M., and then pick him up from his after-school program. Make dinner, help with homework, pay the bills or straighten up the house and then fall into bed. She took pride in the fact that she could support her family and had managed to work her way up from part-time bookkeeper to full-time executive secretary, but it was a demanding and exhausting schedule. As one thirty-seven-year-old intensive care nurse from Sante Fe told me, "We have to be a wife, a mother and a professional, and to be ourselves, which usually takes last place."

The New York mother was grateful for the after-school program run by the Police Athletic League (PAL). Local police told me they supported such programs because they understood that if a working parent wants to keep a child out of trouble, there has to be a safe, productive environment in the after-school hours. Yet many parents did not have access to good after-school programs or quality care for pre-school children. Not enough workplaces provided or subsidized child care; day care centers often turned away sick kids; and most charged high fees for late pick-ups. A mother from Boston told me that she sometimes skipped her lunch break so that she could leave work in time to pick up her three-year-old from day care. Hers was a common predicament. An assistant bank vice president I met in Atlanta told me, "I nearly kill pedestrians trying to get to the day care center on time, trying to avoid the late fees after 6 P.M." A federal judge and mother explained: "When I was a lawyer, all of the partners had wives who didn't work. They didn't have to worry about picking up the dry cleaning or picking up the kids." That sounded like what Albert Jenner had said to me in 1974 when I suggested that I might want to be a trial lawyer and he told me I couldn't because I didn't have a wife.

In 1994, Dr. David Hamburg, President of the Carnegie Corporation, encouraged me to use my role as First Lady to highlight the deficiencies in American child care and encourage greater federal support for working parents. During the welfare reform debate in 1996, I had insisted that the administration retain access to child care as an essential ingredient in helping poor mothers move from welfare to work. I would later broaden my message as I studied the results of new research indicating the importance of stimulating children's brains in the early years. The idea was to learn how child care could reflect this research and enhance early childhood development in the early years. I supported the innovative program, Reach Out and Read, which encouraged doctors to "prescribe" that adults read to babies and toddlers. I met with numerous child care experts and key children's advocacy organizations and traveled around the country to see different approaches to improving the quality of child care and remedying the paucity of child care options available to working parents. In Miami, I met with business leaders to discuss corporate responsibility for child care, and followed up with a White House event highlighting the successful programs of different businesses. At the Marine base at Quantico, Virginia, I visited one of the U.S. military's impressive child care centers for military families, which I hoped would be seen as an example for the rest of society.

I convened two White House conferences, the first on Early Childhood Development and Learning and the second on Child Care. We assembled experts, advocates, business leaders and politicians to focus the nation's attention on critical areas of family life and outline federal initiatives to give working men and women the help they needed to be productive employees and responsible parents. My staff continued to work closely with the President's domestic policy advisers to develop the groundbreaking policies that Bill announced in his 1998 State of the Union Address. I was proud that the Administration put forward a $20 billion investment in improving child care over the next five years. The funds would be used to increase access to child care for low-income working families and after-school opportunities for older children, expand Head Start and provide tax incentives for businesses and institutions of higher education that invest in child care. An Early Learning Fund was established to provide financial assistance to states and communities in their efforts to improve the quality of child care providers, reduce child-to-staff ratios and increase the number of licensed providers. I worked hard to make after-school care more accessible, and in 1998, the Administration introduced the 21st Century Community Learning Centers program, which provides enriching after-school and summer school opportunities to approximately 1.3 million children. After-school care has been shown to increase achievement in reading and math; it also decreases youth violence and drug use and gives parents much needed peace of mind.

I continued to promote domestic initiatives through public appearances, speeches and in meetings and phone calls with members of Congress as well as outside organizations. Over the course of eight years, my talented domestic policy staff—Shirley Sagawa, Jennifer Klein, Nicole Rabner, Neera Tanden, Ann O'Leary, Heather Howard and Ruby Shamir—was invaluable. Bill and I also convened White House strategy sessions on how to curb media violence directed at children, improve education for Hispanic students who had a high dropout rate and expand work and learning opportunities for American teenagers.

The first piece of legislation Bill signed into law in 1993 was the Family and Medical Leave Act, sponsored by Democratic Senator Christopher Dodd of Connecticut, which allowed millions of working people to take up to twelve weeks of unpaid leave for family emergencies or to care for a family member who was sick, without fear of losing their jobs. Millions of Americans took advantage of the protections of the law and discovered the profound difference it made in their lives. A woman in Colorado wrote me that her husband had recently died of congestive heart failure after several years of illness. Under the Family and Medical Leave Act, she had been able to take time off from work to transport him to doctor appointments and hospital visits, and to comfort him at the end. She did not have to spend the critical last months of her husband's life worrying that she would not have a job after he died.

I urged my staff to come up with ideas to improve the law, and we worked with the Department of Labor, the Office of Personnel Management and the National Partnership for Women and Families to modify family and medical leave so that federal workers could use up to twelve weeks of accrued paid sick leave to care for an ill family member.

I hoped this federal system would become a model around the country, and I pushed for a regulation permitting states to use their unemployment insurance system to offer paid leave to new parents. At least sixteen state legislatures were considering such proposals when the Bush Administration eliminated the regulation, foreclosing an avenue of support for new parents.

Proposed bankruptcy reform moving through Congress threatened to undermine the spousal and child support many women depended on. The number of Americans filing for bankruptcy had risen 400 percent in twenty years, a staggering statistic with important implications for our nation's economic stability. Were a growing number of Americans simply using bankruptcy as a financial planning tool to escape mounting personal debts? Was the rise due to an irresponsible banking and credit card industry that solicited, and recklessly approved, unqualified cardholders? Or were responsible Americans facing mounting personal expenses that they simply could not manage on their own, such as health care bills that were not covered by insurance? How politicians answered these questions drove the policy solutions they favored. Those who believed that the credit card industry was largely to blame for the increased debt carried by Americans favored solutions that limited aggressive tactics to sign up cardholders who were known credit risks. Those who thought that people were using the system to avoid paying debts they rightly owed preferred solutions that would make it more difficult to declare bankruptcy or would limit the amount of debt forgiven in bankruptcy cases.

Missing from this debate, I discovered, was any discussion of what happens to women and children who depend on legally required child and spousal support that is not being paid. Hundreds of thousands of bankruptcy cases were bringing women into court because they were trying to collect child and spousal support withheld from them by deadbeat dads and ex-husbands who had declared bankruptcy. I recognized that changes in the bankruptcy law would have profound implications for women and families. In cases of bankruptcy, credit card companies wanted unpaid credit card bills to have the same priority as spousal and child support obligations. That meant that single women would have to compete with Visa and MasterCard to collect legally owed child support. I believed that child support obligations should come first and that bankruptcy reform must be balanced, expecting more responsibility from debtors and creditors alike. In 1998, I weighed in on the President's decision to veto one version of the bill that disproportionately favored the credit card industry over consumers, and later I worked with members of Congress to enhance the law's consumer protections and to add provisions to protect women and their families. In the Senate, one of the first measures I passed increased protections for women and children.

Women's economic empowerment also meant continuing the fight for equal pay and retirement security. Women are still not being paid equally to men, and many working women do not receive any or adequate income from pensions but rely on Social Security. The structure of Social Security is based on outdated notions of women as secondary breadwinners, or not as breadwinners at all. The payment that a person receives is determined by the contributions that he or she makes during his or her years of employment. Most women not only earn less than men and often do not receive private pensions, they are more likely to work part time, spend time outside of the labor force and live alone in their retirement years because, on average, they live longer than their husbands. For many elderly women, Social Security is all that stands between them and abject poverty. Determined to preserve the solvency of this essential safety net, I chaired a panel at the White House Conference on Social Security in 1998 to explore the system's structural discrimination against women.

Women and children also suffer from inequities in our health care system, one of my original motivations to work on reform. I led the Administration's efforts to end the practice of "drive-through deliveries," in which hospitals discharged new mothers twenty-four hours after giving birth. Now, women can stay for forty-eight hours after a normal delivery and ninety-six hours after a cesarean section.

Inspired by the life of AIDS activist Elizabeth Glaser, I also began working for better testing and labeling of pediatric drugs, including drugs to treat children with HIV/AIDS. I first met Elizabeth at the Democratic convention in 1992, where she spoke movingly about having contracted HIV through a blood transfusion while giving birth to her daughter, Ariel, in 1981. Unaware that she was infected, Elizabeth passed the disease on to her daughter through her breast milk and later to her son, Jake, in the womb. Elizabeth was outraged that medications available to her were denied to her daughter and son because they hadn't been tested for safety and efficacy for children. She and her husband, Paul Glaser, watched helplessly as their daughter succumbed to AIDS at age seven.

Elizabeth turned her personal loss into a mission on behalf of children with HIV/AIDS, founding the Pediatric AIDS Foundation to support and encourage research into the prevention and treatment of childhood AIDS. Until her death in 1994, I worked with Elizabeth to require that medications were being properly tested and administered to children, and then I continued the cause in her memory. Jake has benefited from the advances in treatment and is doing well.

While some drugs are not available for desperately ill children, others are routinely prescribed with little understanding of the proper dosages or potentially harmful side effects. Jen Klein, my staffer who headed the successful White House effort to improve pediatric labeling and testing, was keenly aware of the issue because her own son, Jacob, was taking medications for asthma. In 1998, the Food and Drug Administration introduced requirements that pharmaceutical companies test drugs for use in children, but some companies sued, and a federal court ruled that the FDA did not have the authority to require testing. As a Senator, I've been working to pass a law that gives the FDA the power it needs to do what Elizabeth advocated.

Because of my Beijing speech the year before, my visibility around the world had dramatically increased, and my office was bombarded with requests for me to make speeches and attend meetings on my own to discuss issues affecting women in the countries we visited. Prior to Beijing, when we traveled on official visits abroad, I accompanied Bill where appropriate and attended the spouses programs. In mid-November, when we made state visits to Australia, the Philippines and Thailand, I followed my own agenda as well as Bill's. We also scheduled some necessary R&R. We visited the Great Barrier Reef while we were in Australia after stops in Sydney and Canberra. At Port Douglas, Bill announced American support for the International Coral Reef Initiative, to stem the erosion of reefs around the world, and then we took a boat out to the reef in the Coral Sea. I was anxious to get in the water. "C'mon you guys!" I said to my staff. "Life is too short to worry about getting your hair wet!"

It's always a big production when a President goes swimming. Navy divers and Secret Service agents in flippers and masks circled us as Bill and I marveled at a giant clam and curtains of iridescent fish darting through turquoise waters.

There were other wonderful moments on that trip. Bill played golf with Australia's most famous "Great White Shark," the legendary Greg Norman, having prepared by putting up and down the aisles of Air Force One during the flight over. I visited the world famous Sydney Opera House where I spoke to an audience of distinguished women about the presidential election and the emphasis Bill and I had placed on matters concerning women and families, what some pundits called the "feminization of politics" but which I considered the "humanization."

At a wildlife preserve, Bill cuddled a koala named Chelsea. It's a small miracle—or an example of fortunate oversight—that he got anywhere near the animal. An overeager White House advance person had taken it upon himself to protect Bill against any possible allergy attack overseas. During a courtesy visit to the Governor-General's house in Canberra, Bill and I stood with Sir William and Lady Deane, admiring their vast green lawn. Lady Deane turned to Bill, "We're sorry about the kangaroos," she said, "We think they've caught them all."

Bill looked puzzled.

"What are you talking about?" I asked.

"Oh dear," she said. "We were told to get all the kangaroos off the lawn because if one of them came near the President, it would cause an allergic reaction."

As far as Bill knows, he isn't allergic to kangaroos, but someone said he was, so the urge to protect him prevailed. Our loyal and dedicated advance teams were eager to help, and I'm grateful for their diligent efforts to anticipate our every need, but I felt terrible when their solicitude became an imposition on others around us. At a state dinner hosted for us by President François Mitterrand and his wife, Danielle, at the Elysée Palace in Paris in 1994, Madame Mitterrand apologized to me because the tables would look so bare without flower arrangements. "What do you mean?" I asked.

"I was told that the President was allergic to flowers."

He isn't allergic to cut flowers either, as he told his staff for years, usually to no avail. We couldn't have accomplished anything without so many wonderful staff people, but on rare occasions we got more help than we needed!

By now it was understood that when I traveled with the President, I would emphasize issues relating to women, health care, education, human rights, the environment and grassroots efforts such as microcredit to jump-start economies. I usually branched off from Bill's official delegation to meet with women in their homes and workplaces, tour hospitals that used innovative approaches to expanding health care to children and families and visit schools, especially those educating girls. In these settings, I learned about the local culture and reinforced the message that a nation's prosperity is linked to the education and well-being of girls and women.

On our first visit to the Philippines in 1994, Bill and I had toured Corregidor, the American base that had fallen to the Japanese during World War II. There, General Douglas MacArthur was forced to abandon the islands, though promising, "I shall return." Filipino soldiers had fought valiantly alongside Americans, paving the way for MacArthur's eventual return in 1944. The Philippines had undergone wrenching political changes in the decades since World War II and people were still recovering from the effects of twenty-one years of autocratic rule under Ferdinand Marcos. Corazon Aquino, whose husband was assassinated as a result of his opposition to Marcos, had led the way in restoring democracy in her country. "Cory" Aquino ran against Marcos for President in 1986. Marcos was declared the winner, but his victory was attributed to suspected fraud and intimidation. Popular protests drove Marcos out of office, and Aquino became President, another woman thrust into politics as a result of personal loss.

President Aquino was succeeded by Fidel Ramos, a former general educated at West Point, who brought a quick smile and sense of humor to his daunting responsibilities. He and his wife, Amelita, were our hosts for both of the trips we made to Manila. At the state lunch in 1994, he insisted that Bill play a saxophone, and when Bill demurred, he arranged for the band to call Bill up to play, accompanied on the piano by Mrs. Ramos. She also gleefully showed me one of the many closets in the former presidential residence still filled with Imelda Marcos's shoes.

After speaking at a conference attended by thousands of women from all over the Philippines, I left Manila for the hill country of northern Thailand and was to meet Bill in Bangkok for a state visit hosted by King Bhumibol Adulyadej and Queen Sirikit that coincided with the King's fiftieth anniversary on the throne.

Flying into the town of Chiang Rai, near the Laotian and Burmese frontier, I savored the spectacular view of green rice paddies and meandering rivers spread out below me. I was greeted on the tarmac by musicians beating drums and cymbals and playing the *sah*, a stringed in-strument with a melancholy, piercing sound. Girls in traditional hill country tribal garb danced, while miraculously balancing the array of flowers and candles attached to their wrists. My arrival coincided with the Loy Krathong Festival, when the streets are filled with celebrants on their way to the Mae Ping River to launch floating clusters of flow-ers and candles into the water. The ancient custom, I was told, symbol-izes the end of the troubles of one year and the hopes for the next.

The hopefulness of this ritual stood in stark contrast with the dire lives of the young girls I later visited in a rehabilitation center for for-mer prostitutes. This region of northern Thailand was part of the "Golden Triangle," an epicenter of trafficking of all kinds: drugs, con-traband and women. I was told that 10 percent or more of the girls in the area were coerced into the sex industry. Many were sold into prosti-tution before they reached puberty, because clients preferred young girls, wrongly convinced that they did not carry AIDS, endemic among prostitutes. At the New Life Center in Chiang Mai, American mission-aries gave former prostitutes a safe haven and a chance to learn voca-tional skills they needed to support themselves. I met one girl at the Center who had been sold by her opium-addicted father when she was eight years old. After a few years, she escaped and returned home—only to be sold again to a whorehouse. Now only twelve, she was dying of AIDS at the Center. Her skin hung off her bones, and I watched helplessly as she summoned all her strength to draw her tiny hands to-gether in the traditional Thai greeting when I approached her. I knelt next to her chair and tried to speak to her through a translator. She did not have the strength to talk. All I could do was hold her hand. She died shortly after my visit.

On a tour of a local village, I witnessed disturbing evidence of local supply-and-demand economics that brought this girl to her death. My guides explained that every house with a TV antenna sticking out of its thatched roof represented a wealthier family—and that almost always meant one that had sold a daughter into the sex trade. Families in the poorer mud huts without televisions either refused or had no daughters to sell. This visit reinforced my resolve to bridge the disconnect be-tween global politics and local lives. In a meeting with representatives of the Thai government and women's groups, I discussed the govern-ment's plan to crack down on the trafficking of women, particularly young girls, into Bangkok's sex trade by toughening the enforcement of its anti-prostitution laws and imposing serious jail terms for brothel owners, clients and families that sell their children into prostitution. Trafficking in women is a human rights violation that enslaves girls and women and distorts and destabilizes economies of whole regions, just as drug smuggling does. Thailand was not unique. Over the course of my travels, I began to understand how vast the industry of trafficking human beings—particularly women—had become. Today, the State Department estimates that as many as four million people, often living in extreme poverty, are trafficked each year. I began speaking out about this horrific violation of human rights and pushing the Administration to assume global leadership in combating it. In Istanbul, Turkey, at the OSCE (Organization for Security and Cooperation in Europe) meeting in 1999, I participated on a panel to urge international action. I worked with the State Department and members of Congress already concerned with the issue. The Trafficking Victims Protection Act, passed in 2000, is now the law of the land, helping women trafficked to the United States and providing assistance and aid to governments and NGOs combating traffic abroad.

We flew back to Washington in time for Thanksgiving and headed off for a family gathering at Camp David. Our guests included Harry and Linda, and Harry's brother, Danny Thomason, who'd known Bill since 1968, when Danny taught school in Hot Springs. Best of all, we now had two nephews, Tony's son, Zachary, and Roger's son, Tyler. The men played golf despite the freezing weather, competing for what they called the Camp David trophy. We ate our meals and spent our time in Laurel, where I had a big-screen television brought in so that every play in every football game could be seen from every corner of the room. At dinner, we voted on which movie to watch that night in the camp's theater, and in the event of a tie, or strong dissent, we sometimes ran a double feature.

The Republicans had lost nine seats in the House and two in the Senate, but they still were in control of both chambers of Congress, and they gave more leadership positions to ideologues rather than to moderates or pragmatists. The new Chairman of the House Government Reform and Oversight Committee, Rep. Dan Burton from Indiana, was the Hill's leading conspiracy theorist. He had achieved minor celebrity for firing a .38-caliber pistol at a watermelon in his backyard as part of a bizarre attempt to prove that Vince Foster was murdered.

Several key Republicans, including Senate Majority Leader Trent Lott, had already vowed that it was their "responsibility" to continue investigating the Clinton Administration. But the Whitewater inquiry seemed to be losing momentum. Senator D'Amato had suspended his hearings in June. Despite prolonged questioning, Kenneth Starr had failed to wrest any damning tidbit from Webb Hubbell, who was serving eighteen months in federal prison for defrauding his clients and partners.

As Bill's second inauguration approached, there were a number of changes in the cabinet and the White House staff. Leon Panetta, Bill's Chief of Staff, decided to return to private life in California. Erskine Bowles, a North Carolina businessman and trusted friend who was then serving as Leon's deputy, would be taking his place. Erskine's wife, Crandall, a savvy and successful businesswoman, had been in my class at Wellesley. Harold Ickes, our longtime friend who started out with Bill in 1991 and did a superb job of organizing New York in the 1992 campaign, returned to his law firm and consulting business. Evelyn Lieberman took over as head of Voice of America. George Stephanopoulos left to teach and write his memoirs.

I lost my Chief of Staff too. Maggie wanted her life back. She had never intended to stay for more than one term, and I understood her decision. Maggie and her husband, Bill Barrett, were moving to Paris. I was so happy for her: Maggie had weathered the worst of abuses from the revolving investigations. Of course, she wasn't the only person who got sucked into the whirlwind, but I saw her every day and knew what a toll the last years had extracted.

Melanne Verveer became my new Chief of Staff. She had been by my side on nearly every overseas trip and was a galvanizing force behind the international movement we were championing to train and equip women for leadership positions. Great company, Melanne has an impressive command of legislative issues as well as many friendships in Congress.

Several cabinet positions had opened up after the election, including Secretary of State. Ever since Warren Christopher announced his impending retirement in early November, Washington had been consumed with the guessing game of who would replace him. There was a list of hopefuls, each with his own constituency.

I hoped Bill would consider appointing Madeleine Albright as the first woman Secretary of State. I thought she'd done a superb job at the United Nations, and I was impressed by her diplomatic skills, grasp of world affairs and personal courage. I also admired her fluency in French, Russian, Czech and Polish, not to mention English—four more languages than I spoke. She had advocated early U.S. military engagement in the Balkans, and in many ways, her life story was reflective of Europe and America's journey over the last half century. Madeleine identified in a visceral way with people's yearnings for freedom from oppression and desire for democracy.

Some in the Washington foreign policy establishment were pushing their own choices and the whispering campaign against Madeleine began immediately: She was too forward leaning, too aggressive, not ready, the leaders of certain countries wouldn't deal with a woman. Then an item appeared in *The Washington Post* in November 1996, claiming that the White House considered her only a "second tier" candidate. Likely planted by one of her opponents to sabotage her candidacy, the tactic backfired, drawing more attention to Madeleine's qualifications. Now her candidacy had to be taken seriously.

I never spoke about her candidacy with Madeleine, and even my closest staff didn't know that I was encouraging Bill to include her in his deliberations. Other than my husband, the only person with whom I discussed the appointment was Pamela Harriman, then Ambassador to France. Several days after *The Washington Post* piece ran, Pamela came to visit me at the White House. Despite four years in Paris as U.S. Ambassador, she was still in the thick of Washington society and gossip, and she was buzzing with curiosity about Madeleine Albright.

"I've been talking to *everyone*," she said in that wonderful smoky British accent. "You know, some people actually think Madeleine might be named Secretary of State."

"Really?"

"Yes, what do you think?" she said.

"Well, I wouldn't be surprised if it happened."

"You wouldn't?"

"No, I think she's done an excellent job, and I happen to think that all things being equal, it would be nice to have a woman in the position."

"Well, well, I don't know. I'm not sure. There are some other very qualified people who also want it," Pamela cautioned.

"I know there are, but I wouldn't bet against Madeleine if I were you."

I knew my opinion was one among many Bill solicited. When he made a decision, it was his alone. So I listened as he mulled, and occasionally I'd interject a comment or a question. When Bill asked me about Madeleine, I told him there was nobody who had been more supportive of his policies and was as articulate and persuasive on the issues. I also added that her appointment would make many girls and women proud. I still wasn't certain whom Bill would pick until he finally called Madeleine on December 5, 1996, and asked her to be his Secretary of State. I was delighted. After the announcement, Pamela Harriman sent me a note that said: "I'll never bet against you *or* Madeleine."

Madeleine became the first woman in history to hold the job, and, at least for her tenure, the rights and needs of women were integrated into America's foreign policy agenda. She made that clear when she hosted a celebration of International Women's Day at the State Department in 1997. I was honored to share the podium with her as we discussed the importance of women's rights to global progress. I spoke out strongly against the barbaric rule of the Taliban in Afghanistan. I believed that the United States should not recognize their government because of its oppression of women; nor should American business enter into contracts for pipeline construction or any other commercial enterprise.

I was much more relaxed for the second inaugural, and I enjoyed the events without worrying that I was about to fall asleep on my feet. At the same time, there was less of the excitement and awe that we had experienced in 1993. Of course, our world was very different now. I felt I was entering this new chapter of my life like steel tempered in fire: a bit harder at the edges but more durable, more flexible. Bill had grown into his Presidency, and it endowed him with a gravitas that showed on his face and in his eyes. He was only fifty, but his hair was almost completely white, and for the first time in his life he was looking his age. But he still had that boyish smile, sharp wit and infectious optimism that I'd fallen in love with twenty-five years before. I still lit up when he entered a room and I still found myself admiring his handsome face. We shared an abiding belief in the importance of public service, and we were each other's best friend. Even though we'd had our share of problems, we still made each other laugh. That, I was certain, would get us through another four years in the White House.

I was not the same person who had worn the violet blue gown in 1993. Nor could I fit into it after four years of White House fare. And I had grown not only older but blonder. The press still kept track of my changing hairstyles, but they were finally giving me a pass in the fashion department. I had become friends with the designer Oscar de la Renta and his glamorous wife, Annette, after we met at the first Kennedy Center Honors reception Bill and I hosted at the White House in 1993. I was wearing one of his dresses that I had bought off the rack, and when he and Annette went through the receiving line and saw it, he told me how flattered he was and offered his help. I loved his elegant designs, and he made me a fabulous embroidered gold tulle gown with a matching satin cape for the second round of Inaugural Balls. I also wore one of his coral-colored wool suits with a matching coat for the swearing-in ceremony. In a break with tradition, and with Oscar's strong advice, I ditched the hat. The only fashion censure I got that day was for wearing a brooch with the coat, which was strictly my decision. I like brooches!

But I had a complaint of my own. Our sixteen-going-on-seventeen-year-old Chelsea came downstairs covered up in a calf-length coat, and I didn't realize what was under it until we were ready to leave the White House. I caught a glimpse of her midthigh miniskirt and asked to see the outfit. She opened her coat, and photographer Diana Walker, who was doing a behind-the-scenes assignment for *Time*, caught my face. It was too late for Chelsea to change—and she might not have even if I had begged. She got a lot of attention when she walked in the parade without her coat, but she just waved and smiled and handled herself with confidence and aplomb. She had needed all of her poise—and sense of humor—earlier that day during lunch at the Capitol.

The Republicans controlled Congress, hence the Republicans determined the seating arrangements for the traditional congressional luncheon. Perhaps it was someone's idea of a joke to seat me next to Newt Gingrich and to put Chelsea between the House Republican Whip, Tom DeLay, and the frisky nonagenarian Senator from South Carolina, Strom Thurmond. DeLay, who had been saying all kinds of awful things about Chelsea's father, was amiable, and Chelsea reciprocated. He talked about how his own daughter worked in his office and how important it was to have your family involved in your public life. And he offered to give Chelsea a tour of the Capitol.

Strom Thurmond made small talk too. "You know how I got to live this long?" he asked Chelsea. Thurmond was ninety-five. He was the oldest serviceman to parachute behind the line in Normandy just before D-Day and had been married to two former beauty queens. The Senator had fathered four children in his sixties and seventies. "Push-ups! One-armed push-ups!" he advised Chelsea. "And never eat anything bigger than an egg. I eat six meals a day the size of an egg!"

Chelsea nodded politely and picked at her salad. Another course arrived.

"I think you're nearly as pretty as your mama," the Senator said with that silky Southern charm that had gained him quite a reputation.

By the middle of the meal, he mused, "You're as pretty as your mama. She's real pretty and you're pretty too. Yes, you are. You're as pretty as your mama."

By the time dessert arrived, Thurmond was saying, "I do believe you're prettier than your mama. Yes, you are, and if I was seventy years younger, I'd court you!"

My lunchtime conversation wasn't nearly as colorful as Chelsea's. Newt Gingrich seemed subdued. I persevered through the meal with him, talking about nothing in particular. *How's your mother? Fine, thanks. How's yours?* It had been a bad couple of years for Gingrich.

Although he had won reelection as Speaker of the House, he had lost his national popularity and lost ground in the House. He also had recently been grilled by the House Ethics Committee for ethical lapses. Accused of improperly using tax-exempt organizations to finance a series of political lectures and then misleading the committee about the funding, Gingrich claimed it was an innocent mistake and blamed his lawyer. The committee found he had given questionable and misleading statements on thirteen occasions during the course of the investigation. He was fined and reprimanded. I doubted that Gingrich's problems in the House would deter him from prolonging the Whitewater investigations as long as he could. In fact, I couldn't shake the apprehension I had been feeling since the noon swearing-in ceremony.

The day was somewhat overcast and cool, and the atmosphere in front of the Rotunda felt even frostier. By tradition, the Chief Justice of the Supreme Court administers the oath of office for each new

President, but neither Bill nor I relished the idea of sharing such an important moment with William Rehnquist, who despised us and our politics. Early in his career as a clerk to Supreme Court Justice Robert Jackson, Rehnquist wrote a memo that had strongly favored upholding the Court's key pro-segregation decision of 1896, a case called *Plessy* v. *Ferguson*, which enunciated the doctrine of "separate but equal." He endorsed a Texas law permitting white-only primary elections. "It is about time the Court faced the fact that the white people in the south don't like colored people," he wrote in 1952. And in 1964, according to sworn testimony, Rehnquist led efforts to challenge the qualifications of black voters at the polls in Arizona. In 1970, as Richard Nixon's Assistant Attorney General, he proposed a constitutional amendment to limit and disrupt implementation of the landmark *Brown* v. *Board of Education* school desegregation case of 1954. Since being named to the Court by Nixon in 1971, he consistently tried to turn back the Court's progress on race—and by extension the country's. His was the only vote, for example, favoring federal tax-exempt status for Bob Jones University, which banned interracial dating and had an expulsion policy on that basis. He made no effort to hide his friendships with many of the extreme conservatives who had been trying to undermine Bill's Presidency since the first inauguration. As the country would later learn in the election-deciding case of *Bush* v. *Gore*, his lifetime tenure as a Supreme Court Justice did not inhibit his ideological or partisan zeal.

I suggested that Bill ask either of his two appointees, Justice Ruth Bader Ginsburg or Justice Stephen Breyer, to administer the oath of office. But his regard for tradition prevailed. His inaugural address, after all, touched on the theme of reconciliation and healing and specifically referred to the "divide of race" as "America's constant curse." Bill called on Americans to "forge new ties that bind together."

When the time came, Chelsea and I held the Bible on which Bill laid his left hand, while he raised his right hand for the oath. When Rehnquist finished swearing him in, Bill reached over to shake the Chief Justice's hand.

"Good luck," Rehnquist said without smiling. Something about his tone made me think we would need it.

INTO AFRICA

THE SECOND TIME MY HUSBAND JOINED GREG NOR-
man to play golf, he ended up on crutches for two months. Bill
didn't fall into a sand trap, and it wasn't a wild swing that got him—he
simply took a false step on a dark stair in front of Norman's house in
Florida, and lurched backward, tearing 90 percent of his right quadriceps. It happened just after 1 A.M. on Friday, March 14, 1997, and he
called to tell me about it on his way to the hospital. He was in terrible
pain, but trying, as he said, "to put my best leg forward." I was relieved
that his sense of humor hadn't been injured, but my worry cells went into
overdrive. Bill's only concern was getting back to the White House and
then flying to Helsinki, Finland, for a long-scheduled meeting with Boris
Yeltsin the following Wednesday—no matter what the doctors said. I
called Dr. Connie Mariano, Director of the White House Medical Unit
and the President's physician, to ask her opinion. She told me that Bill
would need surgery, but he could safely fly back from Florida and have it
done in Washington.

I met Air Force One at Andrews AFB on Friday morning and
watched from the tarmac as a scrum of Secret Service agents carried my
normally indestructible husband out of the belly of the plane. They
placed him in a wheelchair atop a portable hydraulic lift and lowered
him to the ground. I rode in a van with Bill to Bethesda Naval Hospital,
where surgeons would operate on his leg. Bill was cheerful despite his
excruciating pain and still totally focused on going to Helsinki. I asked
him to wait until we knew how the surgery went, but he'd already decided it would be fine. Bill often reminds me of the boy who is digging
furiously in a barn filled with manure. When someone asks why, he says,
"With all this manure, there's got to be a pony in here somewhere."

He refused to have general anesthesia or to take narcotic pain-killers because, as President, he had to be alert and on call twenty-four hours a day. This presented a problem. The surgery he needed to re-attach his quadriceps tendon to the top of his kneecap was painful and painstaking. If he underwent general anesthesia, Bill would be required by the Twenty-fifth Amendment to the Constitution to temporarily cede presidential power to the Vice President, who was standing by. There had been no such turnover since 1985, when President Reagan underwent surgery for colon cancer. Bill was determined not to invoke the transfer of powers. The upcoming meeting with Yeltsin concerned the expansion of NATO, which the Russians vehemently opposed. Bill didn't want news reports that might signal his weakness or vulnerabil-ity. He opted for localized anesthesia and chatted with his doctors about the Lyle Lovett music piped into the operating room while the orthopedic surgeon and his team drilled holes in his kneecap, pulled the shredded quadriceps muscle through, then sutured the ends back onto the undamaged part of the muscle.

I waited anxiously during the operation in a special suite reserved for the President and his family, where Chelsea joined me after school. Our family has been blessed with good health. The only time I'd been admitted to a hospital was when I gave birth. Other than an outpatient procedure on Bill's sinuses in the early 1980s and Chelsea's tonsillec-tomy a few years later, none of us had undergone surgery. I did not take our good fortune for granted, because I knew that "there but for the grace of God go I"—or someone I love.

Finally, after three hours in surgery, Bill was wheeled into the suite at 4:43 P.M. He looked pale and exhausted, but he was in good spirits be-cause Dr. Mariano and the surgeon told us the operation had been a success and he had excellent prospects for a full recovery. Chelsea and I had been watching a Cary Grant movie, and Bill's first words were: "Where's the basketball tournament?" We quickly changed the channel to a March Madness game.

Other than the Razorbacks, all Bill wanted to talk about was his trip to Finland. Dr. Mariano and the surgeons explained the possible risks of long-distance air travel and asked me if I could talk him out of going. I said I'd try, as long as his health depended on it, but I doubted I'd be successful. I called Sandy Berger, Bill's National Security Adviser, who, with his wife, Susan, had been our friends since the 1970s. Sandy has a firm grasp of the issues and an uncanny ability to marshal facts and arguments when presenting options for the President to consider. He encouraged my overseas work and believed that development and human rights issues were critical pieces of any foreign policy agenda. Sandy explained the importance of the Helsinki trip and why he hoped Bill could go, but he acknowledged that if Bill's medical team said he shouldn't fly, then he shouldn't fly. I conveyed Sandy's message to Bill: Sandy would regretfully concede to the doctors.

"Well, *I* won't," said Bill. "I'm going."

I called Dr. Mariano from Bill's bedside.

"Look, he wants to go," I told her. "So we have to figure out how we're going to get him there and back safely."

"But he can't be on an airplane so long," she protested. "There could be blood clots."

I looked over at my fuming husband, and thought that he might throw a clot if they *didn't* let him go.

"What are they saying?" he demanded.

"Can't Yeltsin come here?" I asked him.

"No! I've gotta go."

"He's going to Helsinki," I told Dr. Mariano. "Just make sure he doesn't get a blood clot."

"We'll have to pack him in dry ice."

"Fine, pack him in dry ice."

Dr. Mariano finally relented and began assembling a flying medical team for the trip to Finland.

Chelsea and I left Bill's bedside later that evening so she could get ready to attend the Viennese Opera Ball sponsored by the Austrian Embassy. She had taken waltz lessons, and her dad insisted she go. On Saturday, I went back to the hospital after doing a tour of our living quarters, looking for all the obstacles someone in a wheelchair or on crutches would face. With the help of a Navy physical therapist, I made a list of the work that had to be done before Bill came home: rugs and cords had to be taped down, a shower guardrail had to be installed, furniture had to be moved. This exercise gave me insight into what life is like every day for people in wheelchairs, including a prior White House occupant, Franklin Delano Roosevelt.

On Sunday, Bill arrived at the White House in a wheelchair-compatible van, his leg stretched out in front of him. He went right to bed, but instead of falling asleep, he gulped down extra-strength Tylenol and watched the remaining college basketball finals on television.

I had been scheduled to leave with Chelsea on Saturday for Africa. I thought I should cancel the trip and accompany Bill to Helsinki or, at least, postpone our departure until he left on Tuesday. He wouldn't hear of it. If we changed our plans, he reasoned, some people might think his operation hadn't been a success. We arrived at a compromise: Bill would head to Helsinki on schedule, and Chelsea and I would leave for Africa on Sunday, only one day late.

In addition to the journalists and photographers who usually accompanied me, *Vogue* magazine sent acclaimed photographer Annie Leibovitz to chronicle our journey. Although she was famous for her portraits of celebrities, she threw herself into capturing the beauty and majesty of Africans and the landscape they inhabited. I had agreed to write the article that would accompany the Leibovitz photographs, and I wanted to shine a spotlight on self-help efforts supported by American foreign assistance and private charities, speak out about women's rights, support democracy and encourage Americans to learn more about Africa. The importance of this last objective was illustrated when a journalist asked me before the trip, "What is the capital of Africa?" Bringing Chelsea along was, as always, a special treat for me, and her presence sent a message in places where the needs and abilities of young girls were too often overlooked: The President of the United States has a daughter whom he considers valuable and worthy of the education and health care she needs to help her fulfill her own God-given potential.

Chelsea and I first stopped in Senegal, ancestral home of millions of Americans who had been sold into slavery through Goree Island off the coast of Dakar, the Senegalese capital. At the small fort where slaves were held, leg irons and chains were still attached to the walls of musty cells, stark reminders of the human capacity for evil. This was where innocent people, ripped from home and family and reduced to chattel, were herded through the Door of No Return at the back of the fort, dropped onto the beach and loaded into boats to be rowed out to the anchored slave ships. I shut my eyes and breathed in the humid, stale air, imagining my wild despair if I or my daughter had been kidnapped and sold into slavery.

I later learned about efforts to eliminate a cultural practice that I consider another form of enslavement, female genital mutilation. In the village of Saam Njaay, an hour and a half from Dakar, a revolution in women's lives and health was in the making. Molly Melching, a former Peace Corps volunteer, had stayed in Senegal to co-found Tostan, an innovative nongovernmental organization that set up small-scale village-based business and education projects. As a result of Tostan's work, women began speaking up about the pain and terrible health effects—including death—they had seen or experienced because of the ancient practice of cutting the genitalia of prepubescent girls. After Tostan organized a village-wide discussion, the village voted to end the practice. When male leaders from that village traveled to other villages to explain why the practice was bad for girls and women, other villages voted to prohibit it. The movement snowballed and its leaders petitioned President Abdou Diouf to outlaw the practice throughout the country. When I met with President Diouf, I praised the grassroots movement and endorsed the villagers' request that Senegal pass legislation banning the practice. I also sent a supportive letter to Tostan, which they used in their campaign. A law banning the practice was passed within the year, but enforcing it has been difficult. Deeply engrained cultural traditions die hard.

This example of popular action to improve people's lives gave me hope as we traveled on to South Africa, the paramount symbol of change on the continent. Nelson Mandela was one of the leaders of that change. Another was Archbishop Desmond Tutu, the vocal conscience of the anti-apartheid movement who inspired Mandela to establish the Truth and Reconciliation Commission. I met with Bishop Tutu and members of the Commission in Cape Town in an ordinary conference room where they were taking testimony from victims and perpetrators of violence as a means of exposing the truth and encouraging reconciliation among the races after generations of injustice and brutality. Mandela and Tutu understood the challenge and the importance of institutionalizing forgiveness. Under the process they established, those who had committed crimes could step forward and confess in return for amnesty. And victims could finally have answers. As one victim put it: "I want to forgive, but I need to know who and what to forgive."

Mandela set the example of forgiveness. When he gave Chelsea and me a tour of the prison on Robben Island where he was confined for eighteen years, Mandela explained that he had years to think about what he would do when and if he got out. He went through his own truth and reconciliation process, which led him to make the remarkable statement I had heard at his inauguration when he introduced three of his former jailers. Forgiveness is not an easy task anywhere, anytime. The loss of life or liberty is always painful, more so if it results from what Dr. Martin Luther King called "the stale bread of hatred." For most of us mere mortals, forgiveness is harder to summon than the desire to settle old scores. Mandela showed the world how to make the choice to forgive and move forward.

Like the rest of the continent, South Africa still has to contend with overwhelming poverty, crime and disease, but I was encouraged by the hope I saw in the faces of students—from the uniform-clad children learning English in a classroom in Soweto (thanks, in part, to a USAID project) to the budding scientists and poets at the University of Cape Town. And when I gave a speech on a dusty patch of land at the edge of Cape Town, I met women who were actually building a better future for themselves and their children. With ceremonial markings painted on their faces and voices raised in song, they pushed wheelbarrows, poured concrete and mixed paint for their new dwellings. Homeless squatters who had lived in deplorable conditions, they had formed their own housing and credit association, modeled on the Self-Employed Women's Association in India that I had visited. Pooling their savings, they bought shovels, paint and cement, learned how to lay foundations and put in a sewer line and started their own community. When Chelsea and I visited, they had built 18 homes; when I brought Bill there a year later, there were 104. I loved a line from one of their songs that translated roughly as "Strength, money and knowledge— we cannot do anything without them." Good advice for women everywhere.

I left South Africa well aware of the challenges its leaders faced, yet optimistic about its future. But in Zimbabwe, its landlocked northern neighbor, I found a country whose great promise was being stunted by disastrous leadership. Robert Mugabe, the head of state since the country's independence in 1980, had grown increasingly autocratic and hostile to his perceived enemies. President Mugabe said little during my courtesy visit with him in the presidential residence in the capital, Harare. He paid close attention to his young wife, Grace, while I made conversation with her, and he periodically broke into giggles for no apparent reason. I left believing that he was dangerously unstable and hoping he would relinquish power. My opinion has been borne out in recent years, as Mugabe has suppressed all political opposition and sanctioned a terror campaign to drive white farmers off their land and to intimidate blacks who challenge him. He has plunged his people into chaos and famine.

I later met with a group of women in politics, the professions and business at an art gallery in Harare. They described the tension that exists between the rights they hold on paper and the ancient customs and attitudes that still prevail. They recounted stories of women being beaten by their spouses for having "bad manners" or wearing pants. One woman summed up the problems they faced: "As long as you have a law that a man can have two wives, but a woman cannot have two husbands, you are not dealing with reality."

I left Harare feeling dispirited at the deterioration of services and facilities and the manifest failures of a leader who had stayed too long in power. But my spirits lifted at our next stop, Victoria Falls, where the Zambezi River cascades into a magnificent gorge. Chelsea and I walked through mist rising from the pounding waters, and watched it turn to shimmering rainbows in the morning sun. Africa's breathtaking beauty and natural resources must be protected while economic opportunities for people expand. But that is no simple challenge, as I learned during my visit to Tanzania, a sprawling East African country formed in 1964 from two former colonies whose names entranced me as a child: Tanganyika and Zanzibar. In the capital, Dar es Salaam, I met President Benjamin Mkapa, a cheerful former journalist who had worked hard to develop a national economy that benefited from the country's natural resources and strategic location on the Indian Ocean. With the vigorous assent of his wife, Anna Mkapa, and the women ministers in attendance at our meeting, I encouraged the president to eliminate laws that limited women from owning and inheriting property, restrictions that not only were unfair but hobbled the economic potential of half the country's population. In 1999, Tanzania passed the Land Law Act and the Village Act, repealing and replacing the laws that had previously discriminated against women.

Tanzania is also a crucial actor in bringing peace and stability to war-torn central Africa. In Arusha, I visited the International Criminal Tribunal for Rwanda, which was investigating genocide. The success of this tribunal, which has the power to try and punish war criminals, is vitally important for all Africans, but especially for women and children, who are often the first victims of civil strife. In Rwanda, rape and sexual

assault were committed on a mass scale, tactical weapons in the geno-
cidal violence that raged there in 1994. In Kampala, Uganda, I met with
a delegation of Rwandan women whose soft, musical voices belied the
horrors they had survived. One young woman described how, after
being attacked with a machete, she tried to reattach her partially sev-
ered arm with string while she futilely sought medical care. When infection inevitably set in, she hacked off the arm herself. The women
gave me a photo album filled with pictures of bones, skulls, dazed survivors, and orphaned children. I could barely force myself to look. I regret deeply the failure of the world, including my husband's Administration, to act to end the genocide.

Uganda was memorable for other reasons. In the face of the African
AIDS epidemic, Uganda's government made a commitment to prevent
the spread of the HIV virus through an intervention and education
campaign. The consequences of the global AIDS pandemic were and
still are most severely felt in sub-Saharan Africa, a region that accounts
for 70 percent of all the world's HIV/AIDS cases. Every segment of society has been affected by the crisis. In some of the worst hit countries,
such as Uganda, infant mortality was rising at alarming rates in the late
1990s and life expectancy was plunging. Economies were suffering
under the weight of shrinking workforces and overburdened health
care systems. During Bill's Administration, the U.S. tripled funding for
international AIDS programs in just two years for prevention, care and
treatment, and health infrastructure. USAID increased condom distribution, providing one billion around the world, and the U.S. worked
with other countries to create and fund a broad global partnership, the
Joint United Nations Program on AIDS, which has developed coordinated strategies for fighting the disease. Acknowledging Africa's urgent
needs, Bill signed an Executive Order to help make HIV/AIDS-related
drugs and medical technologies more affordable and accessible in beneficiary sub-Saharan African countries. The Peace Corps began training
all 2,400 volunteers in Africa as AIDS educators.

With USAID support, a pioneering anonymous testing and counseling center in sub-Saharan Africa was established in Kampala. As I
drove in from the airport at Entebbe, I saw billboards touting the ABCs
of AIDS prevention: Abstain, Be faithful or wear a Condom. The campaign was led by Uganda's charismatic President, Yoweri Museveni,
who believed in confronting head-on problems that traditionally had
been ignored and neglected in the rest of the continent. Equally in-

volved in the campaign against AIDS was Museveni's wife, Janet, who was an active participant in the National Prayer breakfast. When I helped dedicate the AIDS Information Center, I learned from an American doctor there that the policy of testing and providing results in the same day, pioneered at the clinic, was being put to use in the United States. Our foreign assistance was advancing the search for a vaccine and cure in Uganda, and the U.S. was also benefiting.

No issue is more critical in Africa than stopping the ongoing conflicts—tribal, religious and national—that destroy lives and impede progress on every front. Eritrea is Africa's newest nation, a democracy born out of a thirty-year civil war of independence from Ethiopia, in which women fought alongside men. As I stepped off the plane in Asmara, I saw a red, white and blue banner that said, YES, IT DOES TAKE A VILLAGE. Women in brilliantly colored dresses greeted me by throwing popcorn at me, a welcoming practice meant to protect visitors from evil forces and to assure good fortune. As we drove from the airport, another large banner proclaimed, WELCOME, SISTER.

The President of Eritrea, Isaias Afwerki, and his wife, Saba Haile, a former freedom fighter, lived in their own small house, but they received me at the Presidential Palace. As we watched folk dancers perform in a courtyard built by the Italians during their colonial occupation, I asked President Afwerki, who had given up his university studies to fight in the resistance, if he had ever found time to dance during their long war. "Of course," he replied. "We had to dance to remind ourselves of a world without war."

In late May 1998, conflict broke out again between Ethiopia and Eritrea over a disputed border. Thousands were killed and the promise of peace for both peoples was tragically delayed. Bill sent Tony Lake, his former National Security Adviser, and Susan Rice, Assistant Secretary of State for African Affairs, to the region. Eventually the Clinton Administration helped broker a peace agreement. I can only hope now that the potential I saw for a better future—complete with popcorn and dancing—can be realized in both nations.

When Chelsea and I returned from Africa, we regaled Bill with our adventures. His summit with Boris Yeltsin had been productive, but not nearly as illuminating or exotic as our trip. Bill's leg was healing, but he was still hobbling around the White House on crutches. The Republican opposition wasn't about to allow a time out for injury. A month earlier, in February 1997, Kenneth Starr's prosecutorial career took a bizarre turn when he announced that he was resigning as independent counsel to accept a position at Pepperdine University as Dean of the law school and head of its new school of public policy. But Starr's exit strategy backfired when right-wing pundits blasted him for quitting the investigation before finding something to implicate us. At the same time, some in the media picked up a thread that directly connected the supposedly impartial independent counsel to one of his decidedly partisan patrons. It turned out that Starr's Deanship was to be underwritten by a generous gift from Richard Mellon Scaife, a regent of Pepperdine University. Within days, Starr bowed to pressure from the right and changed his mind about taking the job. He apologetically announced that he would stay on as independent counsel until his work was done.

I don't know if we would have been better off with or without Starr. But one possible consequence of Starr's remaining at the OIC was an even more desperate effort to find anything to justify the continued investigations. David Kendall, who constantly monitored the media coverage of Whitewater, noted an increase in stories emanating from Starr's office. Newspaper reports indicated that OIC investigators were revisiting "sources" in Arkansas, such as the trooper bodyguards, to probe the President's personal life. Meanwhile, Jim McDougal had made a deal with prosecutors for a reduced sentence. He was eager to grant interviews, and changed his story, once again trying to implicate Bill and me in his schemes. His ex-wife, Susan, was suffering in jail for refusing to testify before the Whitewater Grand Jury, which she insisted was a trap to charge her with perjury for telling the truth. Anyone who believes that prosecutors can't abuse the American criminal justice system should read Susan's book, *The Woman Who Wouldn't Talk: Why I Refused to Testify Against the Clintons and What I Learned in Jail*. It's a chilling account of the abuse she suffered from Starr's crowd and a sobering reminder that protecting our freedom depends on guaranteeing the rule of law for everyone.

Members of Starr's team, and Starr himself, appeared to be leaking secret grand jury testimony, which was against the law. In a *New York Times Magazine* article on June 1, 1997, Starr questioned my truthfulness and alluded to possible obstruction charges. For David Kendall that was the last straw, and he suggested it was time for a counteroffensive. He wrote a letter, which Bill and I approved, accusing Starr of a "leak and smear" campaign in the media. Three former special prosecutors, including a conservative Republican former U.S. Attorney, publicly agreed with Kendall that the OIC's behavior was outrageous. But the public relations war continued.

Meanwhile, the Paula Jones sexual harassment case got a second wind. Back in January, Bob Bennett, Bill's lawyer in the Jones case, argued before the U.S. Supreme Court that a President should not be burdened by defending civil lawsuits while in office. Bennett's point was that if this was allowed, any President could be tied up in litigation brought by his political enemies or by publicity seekers, and it would erode the ability of the Chief Executive to perform his duties. But on May 27, 1997, all nine justices concurred that the President's privilege did not extend to civil suits, and *Jones* v. *Clinton* could go forward. I thought it was a terrible decision and an open invitation for political opponents to sue any President.

Chelsea chose to go to Stanford, three thousand miles away, and I looked ahead to her high school graduation and departure for college with a knot in my stomach. I tried not to reveal my looming sense of loss to her, fearing I might spoil this special moment in her life. I comforted myself by spending as much time with her as I could, and I commiserated with other mothers suffering from impending separation anxiety during a month of intensive preparation for a hallowed Sidwell Friends tradition: the Mother-Daughter Show. Mothers of Sidwell daughters are encouraged to take part in an evening of comic sketches that poke gentle fun at their graduating seniors. I teamed up with several moms of Chelsea's friends for skits in which each of us played the part of our daughters. My role involved a lot of pirouetting like a ballerina and chatting on the telephone about plans to go out. The opening scene required us to drape ourselves in sheets like togas and sing "I Believe I Can Fly." I was able to get in touch with my inner ham, but fortunately for Chelsea, my voice was drowned out by the other mothers during this opening musical number.

The graduation ceremony of the Sidwell Friends Class of 1997 was much like any other, except that the President of the United States gave the commencement address. He brought me to tears when he asked the graduates to recognize that their parents might "seem a little sad or act a little weird. You see, today we are remembering your first day in school and all the triumphs and travails between then and now. Though we have raised you for this moment of departure and we are very proud of you, a part of us longs to hold you once more as we did when you could barely walk, to read to you just one more time, *Good Night, Moon* or *Curious George* or *The Little Engine That Could.*" When we returned from the ceremony, the entire White House staff had gathered in the East Room to congratulate Chelsea. Everyone got a piece of Roland Mesnier's fabulous graduation cake that was, fittingly, shaped like an open book. These men and women had first met Chelsea as a child wearing braces and had watched and helped her blossom into a wonderful young woman.

VITAL VOICES

As SUMMER APPROACHED, THE ADMINISTRATION WAS gearing up for three big jobs: negotiating a balanced budget with Congress, holding an economic summit in Denver, Colorado, and organizing a high-level meeting in Madrid on the controversial expansion of NATO.

One of the most important lessons I learned during my years as First Lady was how dependent the affairs of state and the policies of nations are on the personal relationships among leaders. Even ideologically opposed countries can reach agreements and forge alliances if their leaders know and trust one another. But this sort of diplomacy requires constant nurturing and informal dialogue among the principals, which is one reason why the President, Vice President and I took frequent trips overseas.

The G-7 summit, an annual meeting of the world's major industrial nations—the United States, Great Britain, France, Germany, Japan, Italy and Canada—had increasingly become a political as well as an economic forum. Russia had been invited as a guest at previous G-7 summits, but by 1997, when the United States was scheduled to host the meeting in Denver, Boris Yeltsin was pushing for his country's full inclusion. The Finance Ministers of several member states opposed the change on the ground that Russia was still economically weak, dependent on the G-7 and the international financial institutions for support and often resistant to reforms necessary for long-term prosperity. But Bill and his fellow leaders thought it was important to support Yeltsin and felt that it would send an important message to the Russian people about the positive benefits of cooperation with the United States, Europe and Japan. So Russia was invited, and the June gathering in Den-

ver was hastily renamed the "Summit of Eight," later to officially become the G-8.

Bill was determined to bring Yeltsin into the inner circle of world
leaders. The strategy was to enhance Yeltsin's status in Russia, since he
was perceived to be his country's best hope for democracy, and to entice
the Russians into accepting the expansion of NATO in Eastern Europe.
Madeleine Albright and Strobe Talbott, Deputy Secretary of State and
Russia expert, were the main architects of this approach within the Administration. Madeleine worked tirelessly to cajole and sometimes
push Moscow into the Western orbit, which I'm told earned her the
Russian nickname "Madame Steel."

In the early days of Bill's Presidency, I questioned the value of state
visits in which the men sequestered themselves for meetings and the
wives were treated to stage-managed tours of cultural landmarks. Now
I realized that forging good relationships with my fellow spouses provided convenient low-key communication among the heads of states. I
also found many of my counterparts to be fascinating companions, and
some became good friends.

In Denver, I invited the visiting First Ladies on a scenic train ride
up to Winter Park ski resort for lunch with a mountaintop view of the
Colorado Rockies. I was just getting to know Cherie Blair, wife of
Britain's newly elected Prime Minister, Tony Blair, but I already liked
her enormously. I knew most of the other women from previous summits, and was excited to see Naina Yeltsin evolve in her role since we'd
first met in Tokyo in 1993. She had been a civil engineer who had
worked on water systems and then was thrust into the treacherous waters of Russian politics. From the beginning, she was personable and articulate about children and their health care needs. In 1995, I had
helped her secure a donation of nutritional formula Russia needed to
treat children suffering from phenylketonuria (PKU), an inherited disease that affects the central nervous system.

Aline Chrétien, whose husband, Jean, had been elected Prime Minister of Canada in 1993, was intelligent, sharply observant and elegant.
I was impressed by her self-discipline and willingness to take on new
challenges. During the eight years we saw each other, she studied and
faithfully practiced piano. She also knew how to have fun. We had a
great time skating together on the frozen canals around Ottawa in
1995. Kamiko Hashimoto of Japan, lively and curious, made a wonderful impression. Flavia Prodi of Italy, a serious and thoughtful academic,

tried to explain Italian politics, which seemed to change constantly while Italian society and culture persisted no matter who was governing.

As the train rolled through the spectacular scenery, some folks came out along the track to wave, and a few held signs welcoming our visitors. Then, while I was standing outside on the platform of the last car, two young men appeared out of nowhere, bent over, dropped their pants, and mooned us. I was momentarily horrified, but then I had to laugh at such an irreverent and unforgettable addition to my carefully planned spousal itinerary.

Although the Denver meetings were serious and often tense, we tried to put everyone at ease at the evening social events. In deference to the once wild West, the main dinner party had a frontier theme, complete with rattlesnake and buffalo, a mini rodeo and a country and western band. Bill gave his guests cowboy boots as gifts. Prime Ministers Ryutaro Hashimoto of Japan and Jean Chrétien of Canada happily donned their boots, pulling up their pant legs to show them off when they arrived for dinner.

Sharing meals is an important element of diplomacy and sometimes a tricky one. The night before the meeting convened in Denver, Madeleine Albright invited her Russian counterpart, Yevgeny Primakov, to dinner at a local restaurant. She treated him to a regional delicacy called "mountain oysters," a polite term for deep-fried cow testicles. I assured the spouses that they were not on my menu.

Whenever we traveled abroad, the State Department always gave us fact sheets about the countries we visited, along with helpful protocol hints. Sometimes I was warned about unusual foods I might be served and how I could avoid eating them without insulting my hosts. One veteran Foreign Service officer suggested I should "push the food around" on my plate to simulate consumption, a trick well-known to every five-year-old. But no diplomatic manual could possibly have prepared me for my dining experiences with Boris Yeltsin.

I like and respect Yeltsin and I consider him a true hero who saved democracy twice in Russia: first when he climbed onto a tank in Red Square in 1991 and spoke out in defiance of the military coup attempt and again in 1993, when a military cabal tried to take over the Russian White House and Yeltsin stood firmly for democracy, aided by strong support from Bill and other world leaders. He is also, in his own way, delightful company. He has a great heart and can always make me laugh. Of course, he has a reputation for being unpredictable, and as is often apparent, he enjoys a drink or two.

I was usually seated next to Yeltsin at official dinners, with Bill on his other side and Naina next to Bill. He did not speak English, but a simultaneous translator sitting behind us conveyed his words to Bill and me in the same deep, raspy voice and with all of Boris's inflections. Boris rarely touched his food. As each course was set before us, he'd push it away or ignore it while continuing to tell us stories. Sometimes the food itself became a story.

When the Yeltsins hosted us at the brand-new Russian Embassy in Washington in September 1994, Bill and I were seated with them on a dais before dozens of tables filled with luminaries from Washington society as well as Russian and U.S. officials. Suddenly Yeltsin motioned Bill and me to lean toward him. "Heel-lary," he said. "Beel! Look at those people out there. You know what they are thinking? They all are thinking, 'How could Boris and Bill be up there and not us?' " This was a telling comment. Yeltsin was smarter than some of his adversaries understood, and he was well aware of the whispering campaign from the Kremlin to the State Department that he was not acceptable or polished enough. He also knew that some of the same people disapproved of Bill's exuberance and looked down upon his Arkansas roots. We smiled and picked up our forks, but Yeltsin kept going. "Hahhh!" he laughed and turned to the President. "I have a treat for you, Bill!"

A whole stuffed piglet was laid out on the table in front of us. With one swipe of his knife, Yeltsin sliced off an ear and handed it to my husband. He cut the other ear for himself, raised it to his mouth and bit off a piece, gesturing for Bill to do the same.

"To us!" he said, holding up the remainder of the ear as though it were a glass of fine champagne.

It's a good thing Bill Clinton has an iron stomach. His ability to eat anything put in front of him is one of his many political talents. I do not share his intestinal fortitude, and Yeltsin knew it. He loved to tease me, and this was one moment when I was glad that a sow has only two ears.

Years later, toward the end of Yeltsin's and Bill's terms in office, we had one final dinner together in the Kremlin. It was held in the domed St. Catherine Hall, one of the loveliest of the ornate dining halls in the old palace. Toward the middle of the meal, Yeltsin said to me in his rumbling, conspiratorial voice, "Heel-lary! I will miss seeing you. I have a picture of you in my office, I look at it every day." There was a mischievous gleam in his eye.

"Well, thank you, Boris," I said. "I hope we will still see each other from time to time."

"Yes, you must come to see me, you must promise to see me."

"I hope I'll get to see you, Boris."

"Good!" he said. "Now, Hillary, I have a very special treat for you tonight."

"What is it?"

"I'm not going to tell you! You must wait until it comes!"

We sat through course after course and toast after toast and finally, just before dessert, a waiter set bowls of hot soup in front of us.

"This is it, Hillary, your special treat!" said Boris, grinning as he sniffed the pungent steam. "Mmm! Delicious!"

"What is it?" I asked as I picked up my spoon.

He paused dramatically. "Moose lips!"

Sure enough, floating in the murky broth was my own set of moose lips. The gelatinous shapes looked like rubber bands that had lost their stretch, and I pushed them around the bowl until the waiter took them away. I tasted a lot of unusual food for my country, but I drew the line at moose lips.

The Denver meeting was a success, but building good relations with the Russians was a long-term project that carried over to the NATO summit in Madrid in July. Bill and I traveled to Europe a few days ahead of the conference for a visit to the Mediterranean island of Majorca as guests of King Juan Carlos I and Queen Sofia of Spain. Once there, we met up with Chelsea and Nickie Davison, her best friend from high school, who were traveling together.

I always looked forward to spending time with Juan Carlos and Sofia, who were great company, warm, witty, down-to-earth and always fascinating. In 1993, we met the King and Queen and their son, Felipe, who attended Georgetown University in Washington. I particularly admired the King's courage in resisting Fascism in his country. He became head of state at age thirty-seven, after Franco's death in 1975, and immediately declared his intention to reestablish democracy in Spain. In 1981, he single-handedly thwarted a military takeover of Parliament by appearing on television to denounce the coup leader and to order his troops back to the barracks. Sofia, a Princess of Greece when she married Juan Carlos, is a trained pediatric nurse and as charming and accomplished as her husband. A great philanthropist, she championed microcredit programs years before most people had heard about the concept.

We continued on to Madrid, for the summit of NATO members. Spain's Prime Minister José María Aznar and his wife, Ana Botella, hosted a private dinner in the garden of the Moncloa Palace, their official residence, for the NATO leaders and spouses. Bill's commitment to expanding NATO finally came to fruition when Poland, Hungary and the Czech Republic were asked to join. The next night, the King and Queen hosted a large dinner at the neoclassical palace in central Madrid to celebrate this historic expansion. We first saw the palace in 1995, when the King and Queen hosted a small dinner. The real fun started after we'd eaten, when the King gave us a tour. He confessed that he had no idea what was in most of the rooms, so he would make up stories as he opened doors. Pretty soon we were all telling tales about imaginary events that might have happened. Both the King and Queen have a marvelous sense of humor, and my favorite sight was Bill and the King eyeing the longest dining table I'd ever seen (it looked as though it could seat a hundred guests) and discussing the merits of running and sliding down its length. Now two years later that same long table accommodated heads of state and government from all over Europe at a formal dinner.

After our official duties were over, Sofia and Juan Carlos took Bill, Chelsea and me to the Alhambra Palace in Granada. When Bill and I had first started dating, he told me that the most beautiful natural sight he had ever seen was the sun setting over the Grand Canyon, and the most beautiful man-made one, the Alhambra Palace lit by the rays of the setting sun as it sank over the plains of Granada. When I shared the story with the King, he insisted that I must see it for myself. We toured the castle and then ate dinner at a restaurant in a centuries-old house with a stunning view of the palace. We watched the sun go down, painting the walls a rusty pink. As we lingered into the night, we saw the palace's own lights come up, equally stunning.

After such an evening, I felt I could levitate to my next destination: Vienna, where I was keynote speaker at a forum entitled " Vital Voices: Women in Democracy." Conceived and organized by Swanee Hunt, our Ambassador to Austria, and nurtured by Melanne Verveer, this meeting of one thousand prominent European women was the official launch of the U.S. government's Vital Voices Democracy Initiative.

The project was close to my heart, a prime example of the Administration's efforts to incorporate woman's issues into foreign policy. An outgrowth of Beijing, the Vital Voices initiative brought together representatives of our government, NGOs and international corporations to promote progress for women in three areas: building democracy, strengthening economies and working to achieve peace. In too many countries, women were still denied the right to participate in the political arena, derive an independent income, own property or enjoy legal protections from abuse and violence. With help from the United Nations, the World Bank, the European Union, the Inter-American Bank and other organizations, Vital Voices provides technical assistance, skills seminars and networking opportunities that give women the tools and resources they need to advance civil society, free market economies and political participation in their own countries.

I thought personal attention to political and individual development was missing in our own diplomatic rhetoric about democracy and free markets. Women and children suffered disproportionately during the difficult transition from communism to capitalism and democracy because they no longer could rely on fixed incomes common to centralized economies or on free education and health care provided by the state. Vital Voices encourages women's entrepreneurship in places as diverse as South Africa and the Baltic states, supports efforts to involve women in the political sphere in Kuwait and Northern Ireland and galvanizes women to combat trafficking of women and children in Ukraine and Russia. Through an effective, nonprofit global partnership, the organization continues to educate and train women around the world, many of whom have become political leaders in their own countries.

Our hectic schedule finally slowed down enough for us to return to Martha's Vineyard in August for summer vacation. It was a place where we felt comfortable and relaxed. One day, I was persuaded to try a round of golf with Bill, whose leg had healed enough to permit a return to his favorite pastime. Frankly, I don't like golf. And I'm a terrible player. I side with Mark Twain: "Golf is a good walk spoiled."

I can trace my aversion to the sport back to an incident that took place the summer before ninth grade, when the only way I could convince my mother to allow me to date a certain high school boy was to let him take me golfing in the middle of the afternoon. I was blind as a bat, and of course I was too vain to wear my glasses. I couldn't see the golf ball, but I decided to hit anything white. So I took a mighty swing and the ball exploded into powder. I'd hit a big white mushroom. Two rounds of professional lessons and corrective contact lenses didn't improve my game. I preferred reading and swimming in the surf while Bill perfected his swing with Vernon Jordan and his other golfing buddies.

On the last weekend in August, Bill and I were attending an evening beach party when a staff member murmured something in his ear. I watched from a distance and saw the shock register on Bill's face. Then I heard the news too. Princess Diana had been in a terrible car crash in Paris. Like everyone else in the world, we were in a state of disbelief.

We left the party and immediately called our new Ambassador to France, Felix Rohatyn, who replaced Pamela Harriman after her untimely death earlier that year. We stayed up most of the night calling London and Paris to find out what had happened. It was still hard to accept that such a beautiful and vibrant young woman as Diana could die so suddenly.

I had last seen Diana two months earlier. We'd met at the White House, where she talked passionately and intelligently about two of her chief causes: banning land mines and educating people about HIV/AIDS. She seemed much more self-assured since her separation from Charles, and I sensed that she was finally coming into her own. We talked about her upcoming trip to Thailand for AIDS awareness and to Africa for land mine eradication. She told me that she hoped her boys might study in America someday, and I offered to be a resource for her and them. She was clearly looking forward to the future, which made her death all the more tragic.

Early the next morning, I received a call from a representative of Diana's family, asking if I would attend the funeral in London. I was honored. During the service in Westminster Abbey, where I was seated with the Blairs and members of the royal family, my heart went out to Diana's sons, whom she had cherished. The venerable cathedral where Diana's mother-in-law had been crowned Queen forty-four years earlier was packed, and more than one million people gathered in the streets outside, listening to the service over a public address system. Hundreds of millions of others around the world watched on television. When Diana's brother, Charles, delivered his eulogy, he took some famous swipes at the royals for their treatment of his sister, and I could hear the applause from the audience outside the church. It sounded like a thunderclap miles away that rolled over the crowd and gained intensity as it rumbled through the streets, through the Abbey's doors and down the stone center aisle to the front of the cathedral. Everybody in our section seemed to freeze as the applause echoed. Elton John played "A Candle in the Wind," with new lyrics that captured the poignancy of the Princess's fragile, fleeting life.

The day before Diana's funeral, the world lost another of its most compelling personalities when Mother Teresa died in Calcutta. Aside from the obvious differences, each of these women had a talent for spotlighting the most vulnerable and neglected people and using her celebrity in calculated ways to help others. Poignant photographs of Diana and Mother Teresa together convey the sweetness of their relationship, and both had spoken to me of their affection for one another.

I flew back to Martha's Vineyard from Diana's funeral, then turned around a few days later to fly to Calcutta for Mother Teresa's. The White House had asked a distinguished delegation of Americans who knew or supported Mother Teresa to accompany me. Among them was Eunice Shriver, who had recently been ill. She overrode her doctor's objections and came along, sitting up the whole way, which she said was more comfortable than the couch I urged her to use in the front of the plane. She said her rosary and prayed with the Missionaries of Charity who were representing Mother Teresa's flock in America. I was grateful I could represent my husband and country in honoring a woman who had touched the world with her unshakable faith and down-to-earth pragmatism.

Mother Teresa's open casket was carried through the crowded streets of Calcutta into an indoor arena packed with people. The service went on for hours because the leaders of each national and religious delegation were called, one at a time, to lay a wreath of white flowers on the funeral bier. I had lots of time to reflect on my brief but enriching relationship with Mother Teresa.

We first met in February 1994 at the National Prayer Breakfast in a Washington hotel ballroom. I remember being struck by how tiny she was and I noticed that she was wearing only socks and sandals in the bitter winter cold. She had just delivered a speech against abortion, and she wanted to talk to me. Mother Teresa was unerringly direct. She disagreed with my views on a woman's right to choose and told me so. Over the years, she sent me dozens of notes and messages with the same gentle entreaty. Mother Teresa never lectured or scolded me; her admonitions were always loving and heartfelt. I had the greatest respect for her opposition to abortion, but I believe that it is dangerous to give any state the power to enforce criminal penalties against women and doctors. I consider that a slippery slope to state control of reproduction, and I'd witnessed the consequences of such control in China and Communist Romania. I also disagreed with her opposition—and that of the Catholic Church—to birth control. However, I support the right of people of faith to speak out against abortion and try to dissuade women, without coercion or criminalization, from choosing abortion instead of adoption.

While we never agreed about abortion and birth control, Mother Teresa and I found much common ground in many other areas including the importance of adoption. We shared the conviction that adoption was a vastly better choice than abortion for unplanned or unwanted babies. At our first meeting, she told me about her homes for orphans in India and enlisted my help in setting up a similar facility in Washington, D.C., where babies could be cared for until adoption.

When I agreed to assist with the project, Mother Teresa revealed her skills as a relentless lobbyist. If she felt the job was lagging, she wrote letters asking me what progress we had made. She sent emissaries to spur me on. She called me from Vietnam, she called me from India, always with the same message: When do I get my center for babies?

It turned out to be harder than I could have imagined to move the D.C. bureaucracy to set up a home for infants who were given up by their mothers for adoption. Not even the White House had an easy time cutting red tape with the housing authorities and human services officials. Finally, in June 1995, the Mother Teresa Home for Infant Children opened in a safe, pleasant neighborhood in Washington, D.C. Mother Teresa flew in from Calcutta, and I met her for the opening ceremonies. Like a happy child, she gripped my arm in her small, strong hand and dragged me upstairs to see the freshly painted nursery and rows of bassinets waiting to be filled with infants. Her enthusiasm was irresistible. By then I fully understood how this humble nun could move nations to her will.

The extent of her influence was in full display at the arena in Calcutta as Presidents and Prime Ministers knelt before her open casket. I could imagine her looking down at the scene and wondering how she might harness all those assembled to help the poor in all the countries represented that day.

Mother Teresa left a powerful legacy and a well-equipped successor in Sister Nirmala, a fellow Missionary of Charity who had worked with Mother Teresa for years. After the memorial service, Sister Nirmala invited me to visit their Calcutta orphanage and asked me to a private meeting at the Mother House, headquarters of their order. When I arrived, Sister Nirmala led me into a simple whitewashed room, lit only by tiers of flickering devotional candles arranged against the walls. When my eyes adjusted, I saw that Mother Teresa's closed casket had been brought here to her home, where she would remain forever. The nuns formed a circle around the coffin and stood in quiet prayer, then Sister Nirmala asked me to offer a prayer. I was taken aback and hesitated, feeling inadequate to the occasion. Then I bowed my head and thanked God for the privilege of having known this tiny, forceful, saintly woman during her time here on earth. I had no doubt she would be watching from heaven as each of us in our own way tried to fulfill her admonition to love God and one another.

By mid-September, the occasion I had dreaded for years finally arrived: Chelsea was moving to California to start her freshman year at Stanford. To minimize my own anxiety about this bittersweet life passage, I spent weeks beforehand making lists of all the things she needed to take to school. She and I made shopping trips to Linens 'n Things and Bed Bath & Beyond, where I bought a DustBuster, a clothes steamer, contact paper for drawers and an array of items that only a mother would think essential to dormitory life.

Our hope was that Chelsea's arrival on campus in mid-September 1997 would be as low-key as possible. Stanford's administration was receptive to our concerns for her privacy and had worked out security issues with the Secret Service that would allow Chelsea as normal a college experience as feasible. Although she would have twenty-four-hour protection, it was to be unobtrusive, both for Chelsea's sake and the university's. The young agents assigned to her detail would look and dress like students, and they would quietly set up residence in a dorm room near Chelsea's. Stanford, in turn, was happy to limit media access to the campus so that journalists without credentials for specific events could not camp out near Chelsea's dorm or follow her from class to class.

Chelsea, Bill and I arrived in Palo Alto on a gorgeous autumn day.

At Stanford's request, we had agreed to one photo opportunity our first day on campus to satisfy nearly two hundred journalists from around the world seeking pictures and comments about Chelsea's arrival. Other than that, she was left alone by the media and began her college career much like the other 1,659 students in the Stanford Class of '01.

We made our way to a three-story concrete dormitory that would be Chelsea's home away from home. The last-minute shopping and packing had left me exhausted, and as is typical of many mothers, I went into overdrive as soon as we got inside the dorm. Chelsea's room, which she shared with another young woman, was barely big enough to accommodate bunk beds, two desks and a couple of dressers. I was on a mission, rushing around in a vain attempt to organize Chelsea's belongings, arranging closet space, putting away linens and towels, measuring and cutting up contact paper to fit the drawers, while keeping up a nervous banter with my daughter. "What about storing your cleaning supplies under the bed? Here's a good place to keep your toiletries. I don't think you should arrange your desk like that."

Bill, meanwhile, resembled most of the other fathers, who seemed to go into a slow-motion trance the moment they set foot on campus. Bill had insisted on carrying Chelsea's luggage himself, and then, armed with a minuscule wrench, he tackled the bunk bed, which Chelsea and her roommate wanted to take apart. After deducing that the bunk first needed to be turned upside down, Bill completed the task and then retreated to the window, where he stood and stared out morosely, looking like a dazed boxer who had just been pummeled in the ring.

My own frantic method of coping with the impending separation from my daughter nearly drove Chelsea crazy, and I was relieved to be reminded that our experience was not unique. At the convocation for students and parents, Blake Harris, the student speaker, hilariously described his own mother a few years earlier:

"Parents, you have done your best. And you will miss your child when you leave here tonight. And, they will miss you also in about a month and for about fifteen minutes. Take my parents, for example. My mom cried when I went to visit colleges. When we arrived . . . my mom was just dying to get in that last little bit of mothering. She decided it was absolutely crucial that she line my dresser drawers with contact paper. And I let her. I just didn't have the heart to tell her that if my clothes were ever clean, it was unlikely they would ever find their way into a drawer." Chelsea and I looked at each other and doubled over with laughter. At least, I felt like I wasn't alone.

By late afternoon, it was time for all the parents to leave, freeing the students to arrange and rearrange their possessions without parental interference. Most of the other mothers and I gathered up our belongings, including unused contact paper, and began to make our way to the exits. After weeks of planning, shopping, packing, unpacking and organizing, we had steeled ourselves for this moment. At some level, we were actually ready to say good-bye and let our children begin their new lives.

Watching the fathers, however, I realized that they had no such preparation. Just as it was time to leave, they seemed to awaken from their collective fog, suddenly anxious over the prospect of parting from their offspring.

"What do you mean, it's time to leave?" Bill said. "Do we really have to go now?" He looked bereft. "Can't we come back after dinner?"

THIRD WAY

I VISITED CHEQUERS, THE OFFICIAL COUNTRY RESI-
dence of Britain's Prime Minister, in late 1997, invited by Prime Minister and Mrs. Blair to a small meeting of American and British political thinkers. Our hosts gave me a marvelous tour. Queen Elizabeth I's ring. The table Napoleon used at St. Helena. Cromwell's secret passage. The prison room, so called because Lady Mary Grey spent two years locked up there in the mid-1500s for marrying without permission from the throne. These were among the relics of history that a British Prime Minister lived with amidst the narrow hallways, spiral staircases and nooks and crannies of the stately sixteenth-century estate.

Tony Blair had been elected six months earlier on a platform of progressive ideas that refashioned traditional Labour Party thinking about social and economic issues. In the aftermath of his election, he had credited Bill for inspiring him and his party to chart a different direction as the United Kingdom and Europe confronted the challenges of globalization and economic and political security.

Tony and Cherie Blair had been focusing on many of the same issues that Bill and I had been thinking about for years. I first discovered this political symbiosis when Tony was still the Labour Party leader. Our mutual friend, Sid Blumenthal, an American journalist and author who had written extensively about American and British politics, insisted that we get together. Sid had been a good friend of Bill's and mine for years, and I valued his political analysis and sharp wit. He began working at the White House in 1997, and his wife, Jackie, an experienced organizer and advocate, joined the Administration in 1996.

"You and the Blairs are political soul mates," Sid told me. "You have to meet each other."

When Sid and Jackie hosted a reception for Tony at their home in 1996, they invited me to come. I found Blair at the hors d'oeuvres table, where for thirty minutes we remained locked in conversation about politics and public policy in our respective countries. I instantly felt a connection. He, too, was trying to devise alternatives to traditional liberal rhetoric, assumptions and positions in the hope of finding ways to advance economic growth, individual empowerment and social justice in the global information age.

Whether you call it New Democrats, New Labour, the Third Way or the Vital Center, Tony Blair and Bill Clinton clearly shared a political vision. But the question confronting each of them was how to invigorate a progressive movement that had lost steam through much of the 1970s and 1980s, giving rise to Reaganism in the United States and Thatcherism in Britain.

The Republican Party in the United States had been masterful at creating a groundswell for conservative ideas after Senator Barry Goldwater's resounding defeat by Lyndon B. Johnson in the 1964 Presidential election. Shocked by the margin of their party's losses, several Republican multimillionaires embarked on a strategy to seed conservative, even right-wing political philosophy, and to develop and advance specific policies to further it. They funded think tanks, endowed professorships and seminars and developed media channels for communicating ideas and opinions. By 1980, they had also begun financing political advertising campaigns through the National Conservative Political Action Committee, one of the first political organizations to use the mass media as a vehicle for negative campaigning. Through direct mail and television ads, NCPAC broke an accepted taboo in national and local elections, attacking opponents' records and positions more harshly and going after Democratic candidates personally and relentlessly. This was the dark underbelly of the Republican Right, which rose to power with a very different public face: sunny, self-confident Ronald Reagan. Reagan won the Presidency twice in the 1980s, and the Republicans made significant gains in Congress.

I was skeptical about the effectiveness of negative advertising when I first saw it up close during Bill's 1980 gubernatorial reelection campaign. But I was wrong. Negative campaigning, which everyone professes to abhor, has proven to be so effective that both parties have adopted it, though Republicans and their allied interest groups use it more effectively than Democrats. Most candidates believe they have no choice but to respond and counterpunch, but the distortions and false-hoods created by negative ads have undermined faith not only in candidates but in the political system.

We and the British have different political systems and methods of campaigning, but Bill and I shared with the Blairs the same struggle to advance more progressive ideas in the public arena. Bill's electoral success was due to a combination of his political skills, his understanding of how stale the Democratic Party had become and the remedies he proposed. The party had led the country through the Depression, World War II, the Cold War and the civil rights revolution. Now its leaders needed to rethink how our core values could be translated into modern solutions for the global security challenges we face at the beginning of the twenty-first century and the changing patterns of work and family in American life. Bill tried to move Democrats beyond what he called the "brain-dead politics of the past"—right versus left, liberal versus conservative, business versus labor, growth versus environment, pro-government versus anti-government—to craft a "dynamic center." Working with the Democratic Leadership Council and its founder and leader, Al From, among others, Bill became one of the first Democrats in the 1980s to offer a new Democratic philosophy and to organize the party around a modern vision of how government should work. They advocated a partnership with the private sector and citizens to promote economic opportunity, individual responsibility and a greater sense of shared community.

In his effort to reform the Labour Party, Blair was outlining similar themes on the other side of the Atlantic. I remember being in London in the late 1980s and watching the annual Labour Party Convention on television. I was struck by how many speakers referred to one another as "comrades," a linguistic throwback to a discredited past. After nearly two decades of Conservative Party dominance, Blair emerged in the 1990s as an energetic, charismatic new face of the Labour Party. After his election as Prime Minister in May 1997, Blair invited Bill to London for an official visit, where we found ourselves in nonstop conversation.

Tony and Cherie, both barristers, the English term for trial lawyers, had met as clerks at one of the Inns of Court. A mother of three in 1997 when her husband became Prime Minister, Cherie continued her legal work, taking on difficult criminal cases as well as representing clients in the European Court of Human Rights. In 1995, she was named a QC (Queen's Counsel)—a great honor—and served from time to time as a judge. I admired the way she pursued her profession, even taking on cases where she had to argue against the government. She specialized in employment litigation, and several of her clients were notable, even controversial. In 1998, she represented a gay worker employed by the national railroad in his claim to equal rights with his non-gay peers. I could not imagine a First Lady suing the government of the United States under comparable circumstances!

As the spouse of a new Prime Minister, Cherie suddenly faced an onslaught of public demands and responsibilities, and she had no extra staff help, except two part-time aides to handle scheduling and correspondence. The wife of a Prime Minister has a less symbolic role than a First Lady because the Queen or other members of the Royal Family perform many of those duties. When Cherie and I met, she was eager to discuss with me any ideas about how she could manage her responsibilities. I encouraged her to be herself, a difficult undertaking, I'd discovered, and tried to reinforce her instincts to shield her children, keeping them as far out of the tabloid spotlight as possible. Cherie had already been baptized by fire when, early the morning after the election, she opened the door of her private home to collect a flower delivery, only to be photographed in her nightclothes.

When she, Tony, Bill and I met over a long dinner at Le Pont de la Tour, a restaurant near the Tower of London on the Thames River, the conversation never stalled. We shared ideas about problems in education and welfare and our concerns about the pervasive influence of the media. Over the course of dinner, we decided to initiate a discussion among our advisers to explore common ideas and strategies.

Organizing the first meeting took months, because of resistance from officials in each of our countries. The National Security Council and British Foreign Office worried that we would offend other friendly nations and governments by holding meetings that included only the United States and Britain. I countered that if the so-called special relationship between our countries meant anything, surely bilateral, informal meetings should not offend our other allies. Bill and I persevered because we knew that each of our countries could learn from the other and create a constructive political environment. We did make concessions, however. In order to limit attention, Bill would not attend the first meeting that Tony wanted to host at Chequers. We also decided to focus on domestic issues, skirting the possible foreign policy implications of bilateral meetings and recognizing that in an era of globalization, domestic policy now has significant international consequences.

The final list of participating Americans included Melanne; Al From; Sid Blumenthal, by then an Assistant to the President; Andrew Cuomo, Secretary of Housing and Urban Development; Larry Summers, then Deputy Secretary of the Treasury; Frank Raines, Director of the Office of Management and Budget; speechwriter and consultant Don Baer and Professor Joseph Nye from the Kennedy School of Government at Harvard University. Blair invited Anthony Giddens, Director of the London School of Economics, and members of his government, including Gordon Brown, Chancellor of the Exchequer; Peter Mandelson, Minister without Portfolio; Baroness Margaret Jay, Deputy Leader of the House of Lords; and David Miliband, Director of Policy.

I left Washington on October 30, stopping first in Dublin and Belfast. The new Irish Taoiseach, Bertie Ahern, hosted a large reception in St. Patrick's Hall at Dublin Castle. Ahern, a savvy and affable politician, was proving to be an effective Prime Minister and strong supporter of the peace process. He had been separated from his wife for a number of years and maintained a long-term relationship with a lovely and lively woman, Celia Larkin. Their involvement was one of those public secrets that everyone knew but no one publicly acknowledged. Bertie chose the occasion of my visit to go public. As Ambassador Jean Kennedy Smith accompanied me onto the stage to address the crowd, Bertie and Celia walked up the stairs. The Irish press was electrified. As soon as Bertie and I finished speaking, they rushed for their phones and computers. The reporter for the *Irish Independent*, Susan Garrity, who was based in Washington and had flown over with me to cover the trip, told me later that she overheard one reporter yelling into the phone, "I'm telling you, he put his mistress on the stage with the First Lady. Can you believe it? The First Lady!" This earth-shaking news had no impact on the political fortunes of Ahern, who was reelected in 2002, and it certainly wasn't a topic of conversation at the private dinner Bertie, Celia and I later attended with some of my favorite Irish, Seamus and Marie Heaney and Frank McCourt, author of *Angela's Ashes*.

The next morning, I flew to Belfast to deliver the first Joyce McCartan Memorial Lecture at the University of Ulster. I spoke of Joyce's relentless commitment to peace and recognized the women like her who, despite their own personal losses, had contributed to greater understanding between the traditions during the Troubles and who were now playing a role in the peace process. I especially admired Monica McWilliams and Pearl Sager, who were representing the Women's Coalition at the talks taking place under former Senator George Mitchell, whom Bill had appointed to chair the negotiations.

On this trip, I witnessed firsthand the importance of ongoing contacts between Catholics and Protestants at a roundtable discussion of young people from both communities held in the new Waterfront Hall, a monument to Belfast's optimism about the future. Conferences such as this supported the peace process and brought together students who would not likely have met under any other circumstances. They lived in segregated neighborhoods and went to rigidly sectarian schools. I'll long remember what one young man said to me when I asked what he thought it would take to establish lasting peace. "We need to go to school together like you do in America," he replied.

One reason I support improving our public school system through higher standards and greater accountability and oppose weakening it through vouchers is that it brings together children of all races, religions and backgrounds, and has shaped and sustained our pluralistic democracy. Very few countries in the world benefit from such diversity in education. As our society grows ever more diverse, it will become even more important for children to study together and learn to tolerate and respect their differences as they affirm their common humanity.

Also attending the Belfast conference was Marjorie "Mo" Mowlam, Tony Blair's Secretary of State for Northern Ireland. Mo had recently completed debilitating treatments for a nonmalignant brain tumor, which had caused her hair to fall out. She wore a wig and later asked if I'd mind if she took it off. I learned that she did this at official meetings, exposing her bald head with its few wisps of blond hair. I wondered whether removing her wig was a subtle way of suggesting that she had nothing to hide in her work on behalf of the peace process—or a not so subtle reminder that she was a woman more interested in substance than show. Mo became a delightful new friend.

I flew from Belfast to London and then drove forty miles north to Buckinghamshire, where Chequers sits on one thousand acres of rolling English countryside, its grounds lined with stone paths and manicured gardens. An immense front door signals the entrance to the redbrick manor house that has served as a weekend getaway for Prime

Ministers since 1921, after the estate was bequeathed to the British government. Tony met me at the door wearing blue jeans and his trademark boyish grin.

That evening, the Blairs, Melanne and I enjoyed a private dinner and stayed up late into the night, sitting in front of the large stone fireplace in the Great Hall, talking about a broad array of subjects ranging from Yeltsin and his inner circle to French perfidy vis-à-vis Iran and Iraq to U.S. involvement in Bosnia. We also discussed what Tony called the "cellular fatigue" that seems to come with public life these days and the connection between our religious faith and public service. Both of us rooted our political beliefs in our faith, which molded our commitment to social action. I talked about John Wesley's invocation, which I had taken to heart when I was confirmed in the Methodist faith—Live every day doing as much good as you can, in every way that you can—and about what theologians have described as "the push of duty and the pull of grace."

The next morning, the other American and British participants arrived. Over coffee in the Great Parlor on the second floor, we discussed policies that could support families in their primary functions of raising children, as well as education and employment policies. After our discussions, we walked through the gardens, looking out over the lush green meadow that seemed to stretch to the horizon. England can be gray and wet in late autumn, but on this day the sky was deep blue and the sun was bright, making the surroundings vivid with color. As I looked beyond the lawns and rosebushes, I realized that although Chequers was guarded and secure, there was no visible fence or any indication that it was a secluded government facility.

At dinner, I sat next to Tony Giddens, a brilliant and prolific scholar who has written extensively about the Third Way. Giddens told me that when the history of the bloody twentieth century is written, the advancing status of women will be seen as a historic change, as profound as the extraordinary march of technology and the successful defense and proliferation of Western democracy.

As soon as we got back to the United States, Sid and I briefed Bill and recommended that he continue the Third Way meetings, which he did. He hosted one at the White House in the Blue Room during the Blairs' official visit in 1998, and convened follow-up meetings that included other like-minded leaders, including Italian President Romano Prodi and Swedish Prime Minister Goran Persson at New York University in September 1998, and German Chancellor Gerhard Schroeder, Italian Premier Massimo D'Alema and Brazilian President Fernando Henrique Cardoso in Florence in November 1999.

These Third Way meetings introduced a new way for the Administration to work with America's traditional allies. And we had few allies better than Italy. Bill and I had visited Tuscany and Venice in 1987 with a group of Governors, and I looked for any excuse to return. In 1994, we traveled to Naples for the G-7 Summit, hosted by Prime Minister Silvio Berlusconi. I fulfilled a lifelong desire to explore Neapolitan art and culture, and to visit Pompeii, Ravello and the Amalfi Coast. I wished I could have lingered there, or at least returned by now. Similarly, when we made our state visit to Rome, I enjoyed every moment, and I was delighted when Florence was chosen for the Third Way Conference co-hosted by New York University under the leadership of John Sexton, then Dean of the law school, now President of the university. These visits to Italy gave me the chance to spend time with a succession of Prime Ministers—Berlusconi, Prodi, D'Alema and Carlo Ciampi, all of whom were good allies, particularly on Bosnia, Kosovo and NATO expansion.

In Palermo, Sicily, I attended a Vital Voices leadership training program and spoke in the restored Opera House at a conference sponsored by Leoluca Orlando, the Mayor of Palermo. Orlando believed in the power of culture to change lives and societies. He had led a grassroots campaign to take back Palermo from the grip of the Mafia. He organized schoolchildren to "adopt" a monument that they would care for as a way to instill values of civic responsibility and caring. He spoke often to clergy and business leaders to encourage them to assist him in ending the reign of terror the people were living under. Finally, after a series of cold-blooded assassinations of public officials, the women of Palermo had had enough. They hung bedsheets from their windows, proclaiming in bold letters: BASTA—Enough. This collective show of power combined with popular demonstrations turned the tide in Sicily's long struggle with the Mafia.

Orlando's creative governing was a living example of a Third Way approach to problem-solving that brought his people a respite from fear and violence. Openness to ideas for improving people's lives is the hallmark of good leadership, but sometimes leaders need encouragement, especially if they are new democracies trying to implement principles of equality and self-government for the first time. The Administration thought that high-level visits were important in our efforts to forge diplomatic ties with nascent democracies. And that's how I came to be sitting on an airplane about to take off to Kazakhstan, Kyrgyzstan, Uzbekistan, Ukraine and Russia—Siberia, to be exact—some of the most remote locales I ever visited. But first we had to get there, which proved more nerve-racking than expected.

Again, I was traveling with Kelly and Melanne, and with Karen Finney, my deputy press secretary, a tall young woman with great stamina and humor. We took off from Andrews Air Force Base on Sunday night, November 9, aboard a Boeing 707 that had been used in the past as Air Force One. We had been in the air about ten minutes and I had settled down with my briefing book about Kazakhstan, our first stop, when a crew member calmly told me that we had to return to Andrews because of problems with one of the engines. I wasn't particularly worried. I knew a plane that size could easily fly on three of its four engines. And I had total confidence in Air Force pilots, the best in the world. I went back to my book.

We landed smoothly at Andrews with only three engines in operation and immediately were met by fire trucks with lights flashing. While mechanics investigated, I called Bill to tell him about the delay, hopeful that we would be able to take off again when the engine was fixed.

We finally got word a few hours later that we couldn't leave until the next afternoon, so at midnight we all went home. When I arrived at the White House, I found Bill talking on the phone to Chelsea, who was in her dorm and had seen a "Breaking News" report on CNN.com: "First Lady's plane turns back . . . fuel dumped . . . everyone on board safe." I got a call from my mother, who just wanted to hear my voice. Other friends phoned after seeing the headline in *The Washington Post*: FIRST LADY'S JET ABORTS; CENTRAL ASIA TRIP DELAYED. All of the fuss made it seem as if I had ejected from the plane and parachuted to earth.

We left the next day when the repairs were complete. The journey was not for the weak or meek. We landed on dirt runways with no lights, watched men with shovels try to de-ice our plane and were expected to sample a wide array of vodkas at every stop and at all hours of the day and night. It was one of the most exotic and evocative trips I took during my tenure at the White House. Mountainous, stark and eerily beautiful, the so-called "Stans" were home to the old Silk Road traveled by Marco Polo. Many of the Kazakhs, Kyrgyz and Uzbeks, some of whom still dressed in traditional indigenous costumes, were descendants of the Golden Horde, the soldiers of Genghis and Kublai Khan. In the post-Soviet era, they were trying to create a modern equivalent of the Silk Road so that their nations and economies could flourish into the twenty-first century. Although Russified during the Soviet era, each country had retained a distinct ethnic character and a surprisingly diverse population.

Kazakhstan is an oil- and gas-rich country with the potential to improve the standard of living for its citizens, assuming, of course, that public and private corruption doesn't siphon off all the revenue. I visited a small women's-wellness center funded through U.S. foreign aid. Because of the unavailability of contraception, abortion had become a common form of family planning under communism. The Clinton Administration's policy was to make abortion "safe, legal and rare." We worked to discourage abortion and minimize the spread of sexually transmitted diseases by providing aid for family planning and improved maternal health. This policy contradicted the global gag rule that had been imposed by President Reagan, continued by President Bush and rescinded by Bill on the second day of his Presidency (later reinstated by George W. Bush). The resumption of American aid was beginning to show results. The doctors at the Almaty clinic told me that the rates of both abortion and maternal deaths were decreasing, further proof that our practical policy was more effective at making abortion rare than the Republicans' more visceral anticontraception approach.

I knew that Kyrgyzstan, Kazakhstan's mountainous neighbor to the southeast, needed medical supplies. Working with Richard Morningstar, the President's Special Adviser on Assistance to the New Independent States of the former Soviet Union, I arranged to bring several pallets of humanitarian assistance—$2 million in medicines, medical supplies and clothing.

Arriving in the Uzbekistan capital, Tashkent, I went directly to see President Islam Karimov, a former Soviet Communist with a reputation for authoritarianism who, it turned out, was fascinated by my husband. He asked how Bill remained in touch with people without losing the authority of the Presidency. Karimov, like counterparts throughout the newly independent states, had no experience with democracy. There was no organized curriculum for such leaders to learn the formal and informal "habits of the heart" that underlie the theory and practice of democracy.

And there was a struggle going on for the hearts and minds of the Muslims throughout Central Asia. Karimov was criticized in the West for cracking down on Islamic fundamentalists, but he viewed them as political agitators. He was willing to foster religious tolerance for others, as I learned when I visited a newly reopened synagogue down an alley off a side street in Bukhara, one of the Ancient Market towns on the old Silk Road caravan route. I met the rabbi, who also served as an OB-GYN. He explained how the remnants of a once thriving Jewish community, dating back to the Diaspora following the destruction of the Temple in Jerusalem in A.D. 70, had survived the Mongols and the Soviets and were now enjoying the tolerance and protection of the Karimov government.

In Registan Square, in Samarkand, Karimov proudly told me that the Shir Dor Madrassa, a historic Islamic school for educating boys, was again accepting students and would teach them the traditional interpretations of Islam that had taken root in Central Asia, as opposed to the interpretations imported from some Arabic countries that had radicalized and militarized some Uzbeks. He described forces who wanted to destabilize his government and establish an Islamic state like that of the Taliban, then ruling neighboring Afghanistan. While he encouraged the resumption of religious activity, he would not tolerate foreign-sponsored political opposition camouflaged in religious claims.

As an American viewing the Shir Dor Madrassa, I was conflicted. After years of oppression by the Soviets, these religious schools were open and flourishing, but I was concerned about the lack of educational opportunities for girls and by the fact that madrassas elsewhere had become exporters of radical fundamentalism. In the days following September 11, 2001, I remembered Shir Dor and other madrassas I saw. The term is now linked in America with brainwashing training camps for extremists and potential terrorists.

In developing nations, the educational infrastructure for both boys and girls must be a priority, and understanding the role that madrassas play in the Islamic world is crucial. In countries like Pakistan where the public schools are often unaffordable, they might be the only option for the sons of ambitious poor parents, though education there may be limited strictly to the memorization in Arabic of the Quran. The new fundamentalism in Asia could be traced to Arab-led movements and madrassas. Karimov, who feared this foreign influence, was trying to nurture the religious tolerance that had marked Central Asia in the past. If the U.S. gave more aid to help countries fund public nonradical schools, it might save money and lives in avoided conflicts and terrorist acts down the road.

Word of our visit apparently had spread throughout Samarkand. As Karimov and I were leaving a USAID-sponsored project that promoted the export of crafts produced by local women, we saw a large crowd gathered, held back by the ever present police, who had formed a human rope line to keep the people away. I said to Karimov: "You know, Mr. President, if my husband were here, he'd walk across the street and shake hands with those people."

"He would?"

"Yes, because in a democracy, those people are the boss. Bill would cross the rope line not just because he's friendly, but because he knows who he works for."

"Okay, let's go."

To the amazement of his aides, the police and the crowd, the President walked over and stuck out his hand, where it was grasped by some very eager Uzbeks.

I came home to celebrate a key legislative victory, the signing of the Adoption and Safe Families Act on November 19. Reforming adoption and foster care had been important to me since my days at Yale Law School when I first represented the foster mother who wanted to adopt her foster child.

During Bill's first term, I had worked with Dave Thomas, the founder of the Wendy's fast-food chain and a staunch Republican, and other corporate and foundation leaders to spearhead adoption reform. Dave was adopted and had devoted considerable energy and resources to streamlining the foster care system. At the time, five hundred thousand American children remained trapped in the limbo of foster care. Returning home was not an option for one hundred thousand of them, and only twenty thousand found permanent placements with families each year. My hope was that, through new legislation, we could speed up the process and remove arbitrary barriers that prevented many caring families from being able to adopt.

Deanna Mopin, a teenager from Kansas who was placed in foster care at age five after being abused in her own home, was one of the lead speakers at a White House celebration of National Adoption Month in 1995. Shy and ill-at-ease, she described what it was like to live with nine other foster children under one roof, unable to go to the movies or buy school clothes without permission from her "house parents" and two social workers. The next time I saw Deanna, she had been adopted and had blossomed into a confident, happy young woman.

My domestic policy staff had worked tirelessly with Administration officials and Congressional staffers to craft the new legislation, which included financial incentives to states, efforts to keep families together in appropriate circumstances and faster time frames for making permanent placement decisions and for terminating parental rights in cases of abuse and neglect. Passing this important legislation was instructive. We were learning that in working with a recalcitrant Congress, we could often move more expeditiously on a targeted issue, rather than on a broad initiative such as health care or welfare reform.

The sweeping changes in federal adoption law would speed up the placement of thousands of foster children like Deanna into safe and permanent homes. "The legislation represents a fundamental shift in the philosophy of child welfare, from a presumption that the chief consideration ought to be returning a child to his biological parents, to one in which the health and safety of the child is paramount," *The Washington Post* said. One of the most surprising and satisfying aspects of this legislative success was the opportunity to work with Tom DeLay, perhaps the most partisan and effective leader of the extreme conservatives in the House. But on this issue, he was steadfast in his support. He and his wife have cared for foster children, and after I became a Senator, we continued to work together.

Within five years of the signing of the Adoption and Safe Families Act, the number of children adopted more than doubled, exceeding the goals of the legislation. I realized, however, that approximately twenty thousand young people "age out" of the foster care system when they turn eighteen, without ever having been placed in a family home. Just as they confront the critical transition to independence, they become ineligible for federal financial support, and a disproportionate number of them become homeless, living without health insurance or other crucial assistance. On a trip to Berkeley, I met with a remarkable group of young people from the California Youth Connection, a support and advocacy organization for older children in foster care and those who had recently aged out. They stressed the difficulty of entering adulthood without any of the emotional, social and financial support that families often provide. Joy Warren, a beautiful blond college graduate, spent most of her teen years in temporary foster homes, but managed to focus on her studies and was admitted to U.C. Berkeley and then Yale Law School. Joy had two younger sisters, one of whom was still in foster care, which intensified the pressure she felt to assume adult responsibilities at an early age. She became an intern in my White House office, assisting my staff in developing new legislation to address the needs of young people aging out of the foster care system. I worked with Republican Senator John Chafee of Rhode Island and Democratic Senator Jay Rockefeller of West Virginia on what became the Foster Care Independence Act of 1999, which provides young people aging out of foster care with access to health care, educational opportunities, job training, housing assistance, counseling and other support and services.

I turned fifty in October, and though the rule books say that this is a difficult passage, it felt insignificant compared to living without Chelsea. My days and nights were crammed with meetings and events leading up to the holidays, but I was surprised by how barren the White House seemed without the sound of Chelsea's music coming from her bedroom or the giggles of her friends as they gossiped and ate pizza in the Solarium. I missed watching her pirouette down the long center hallway. Sometimes I'd catch Bill just sitting in Chelsea's bedroom, looking around wistfully. I had to admit that my husband and I were caught up in a generational cliché, a milestone in life that only members of our self-conscious age group would define as a syndrome. We were now empty nesters. While we felt more freedom to go out at night and socialize with friends, coming home to a quiet house was jarring. Our nest needed refilling: it was time to get a dog.

We hadn't had a canine companion since our cocker spaniel, Zeke, died in 1990. We had loved that dog, and it was hard to imagine finding another to take his place. Shortly after we buried Zeke, Chelsea brought home a black-and-white kitten she named Socks, who moved with us to the White House, where he clearly preferred to be an only cat.

But after Bill was elected to a second term and we knew Chelsea would be leaving for college, we started thinking about getting another dog. We got a book about dogs, and Bill, Chelsea and I spent a lot of time looking at all the different pictures and reading about different breeds. Chelsea wanted a teeny-tiny dog she could carry around with her, and Bill wanted a big dog he could run with. We worked through that and finally decided that a Labrador would be just the right size and temperament for our family and the White House.

I wanted to give the dog to Bill as a Christmas present, so I set out to locate the perfect puppy. In early December, a bouncing three-month-old chocolate Lab met the President for the first time. The puppy scampered straight into Bill's arms, and they fell in love on the spot. All we had to do was figure out a name for the dog. We vacillated and made lists. People wrote letters with suggestions and devised dog-naming contests. Two of my favorite candidates were Arkanpaws and Clin Tin Tin.

The process was getting out of hand, and we realized we'd better hurry up and name the poor little thing. We finally decided on a simple and, to our minds, noble name: Buddy.

Buddy was the nickname of my husband's favorite uncle, Oren Grisham, a devoted dog owner and trainer who had died the previous spring. When Bill was growing up in Hope, Uncle Buddy let him play with his hunting dogs. The more Bill talked about the new puppy, the more he remembered his uncle Buddy and the clearer it became that we should name the dog after him. The only glitch, I thought, was that one of the butlers on the White House staff was named Buddy Carter. We didn't want him to take offense at our naming a dog Buddy. But we asked him, and he loved the idea. In fact, I believe he started to identify with that dog. "Buddy got in trouble again," he'd joke with us when the dog had chewed up the newspaper. "Not me, the other Buddy."

Months later, when our new canine pal was sent off to be neutered, Buddy Carter came into the residence shaking his head and muttering, "Not a good day for Buddy today. Not a good day at all."

The little Lab settled swiftly into my husband's routine. He slept by his feet in the Oval Office and stayed up late into the night. They were perfect for each other, since Buddy had, or developed, many of Bill's traits. Buddy loved people, possessed a sunny, optimistic disposition, and had the ability to focus and concentrate with singular intensity. Buddy was obsessed with two things: food and tennis balls. He was an absolute maniac when it came to chasing balls. He retrieved the ball, if you let him, until he fell down exhausted. Then he'd get up and look for his dinner.

Buddy quickly became the center of our family life, which was hard for Socks to deal with. Socks had been showered with all the attention

for years. One of my favorite photos showed Socks surrounded by photographers outside the Arkansas Governor's Mansion before our move
to Washington. Unfortunately, Socks despised Buddy. We tried so hard
to convince them to get along. But if we left them in the same room, we
inevitably came back to find Socks with his back arched, hissing at
Buddy, who was intent on chasing the cat under the couch. Socks had
blunt-clipped claws, but he never passed up an opportunity to take a
swipe at Buddy and once landed a direct hit on the puppy's nose. Both
of them had their fans and each received thousands of letters, mostly
from children who expressed their affection—and preference—for one
or the other. In fact, I had to set up a separate correspondence unit at
the U.S. Soldiers' and Airmen's Home to answer their mail. In 1998, I
published some of the letters in *Dear Socks, Dear Buddy*, giving the proceeds to the National Park Foundation, the charity that raises funds to
support our national park system.

Before we knew it, Christmas had come and gone, and we were off for
our trip to Hilton Head, South Carolina, for Renaissance Weekend and
a gathering of fifteen hundred friends and acquaintances.

I looked forward to seeing our friends and loved the long, serious
conversations at Renaissance. But I needed some rest, and I was eager
for the four days we had planned on St. Thomas in the U.S. Virgin Islands after New Year's. We had visited this beautiful Caribbean island
the year before, staying in a house overlooking Magens Bay. This year,
we were returning to the same location, taking Buddy along with us.

We landed at the little airport in Charlotte Amalie, the capital, and
drove along the curvy mountain road lined with coconut and mango
trees to our secluded spot on the north side of the island. The warm air
and tropical breezes were so welcoming, as was the house, set on a hill
with winding steps leading down to a tiny beach below. The Secret Service was headquartered next door, and the Coast Guard had cleared
boats out of the little bay to enhance security—and privacy. As we
looked out across the water, there was virtually no sign of life. It was an
idyllic setting.

Bill, Chelsea and I did what we usually do on vacations: We played
cards and word games and put together a one-thousand-piece jigsaw
puzzle. We brought plenty of books that we read, swapped and discussed over informal meals. Otherwise, we swam, walked, jogged,

hiked and cycled together. Normally, Bill plays golf every chance he can, and since our vacations usually coincide with football and basketball seasons, our accommodations must have adequate television reception. We were not, however, ever truly alone. The Secret Service was on duty nearby, and the Navy stewards who travel with a President were ready to cook or clean whenever needed. And, of course, essential staff was with us: the doctor, nurse, military aide, press staff and security adviser. But we got used to the entourage, and they respected our privacy. The paparazzi did not.

One afternoon midway through the trip, Bill and I put on our bathing suits and ventured down to the beach for a swim. Unbeknownst to us, a photographer from Agence France-Presse, the French wire service, was hiding in the bushes on a public beach across the bay. He must have had a powerful telephoto lens, because the next day a photo of us slow-dancing on the beach appeared in newspapers around the world. Mike McCurry, the White House press secretary, was angry about the invasion of privacy and the fact that the photographer was, as he told the press corps, "sneaking around in bushes and taking pictures surreptitiously." Obviously, the incident raised questions about security as well as privacy. If you're close enough to take a picture with a telephoto lens, you're close enough to shoot a gun with a scope. Bill wasn't upset. He liked the photo.

A debate ensued in the press over whether the photographer had violated journalistic ethics and invaded our privacy for prurient interests. That led to speculation by some journalists that we had "posed" for the photo in hopes that our embrace would be captured on film.

Hello? As I told a radio interviewer a few weeks later, "Just name me any fifty-year-old woman who would knowingly pose in her bathing suit—with her back pointed toward the camera."

Well, maybe people who look good from any angle, like Cher or Jane Fonda or Tina Turner.

But not me.

SOLDIERING ON

"THANK YOU, MRS. CLINTON," SAID ONE OF KEN-neth Starr's deputies. "That's all we'll need for now."

David Kendall sat next to me in the Treaty Room during an inter-view with the independent counsel to clear up some final matters in the investigation of the mishandled FBI files. "They've got to ask these questions, just so they can say they asked," David assured me. He was right: the questions were brief and perfunctory. Kenneth Starr was in attendance but said nothing during the ten-minute Q and A.

David later remarked that the prosecutors had seemed more smug than usual—"like the cats who swallowed the canary," in the words of one lawyer in the room—but I didn't pick up any unusual frequencies that morning. I was just grateful that the case was closed on one more of the non-scandals being probed by the OIC. It was January 14, 1998, and Starr's inquiry was in its fourth year. Like every other investigation in the independent counsel's portfolio, Filegate was a dry hole. A midlevel White House employee in the Office of Personnel Security had blun-dered by using an outdated list to order FBI file summaries for current staff, and had inadvertently been sent files on some security pass holders from the Reagan and first Bush Administrations. But it was neither a conspiracy nor a crime. The previous fall, Starr had finally conceded that Vince Foster really had committed suicide. (Robert Fiske had reached that conclusion three years earlier, but it took four more official investigations, including Starr's, to confirm it.) Starr had also run into a dead end in his original probe of the Whitewater land deal. The culture of investigation followed us out the door of the White House when cler-ical errors in the recording of gifts mushroomed into a full-blown flap, generating hundreds of news stories over several months.

The most active litigation we were contending with was a civil case unrelated to the OIC investigation. Paula Jones's legal team was being paid for and guided by the Rutherford Institute, a legal aid organization with a fundamentalist right-wing agenda. Bill's lawyers had fully expected the case to be thrown out of court on a motion for summary judgment before it got to trial, but the Supreme Court had decided to let the case proceed. Jones therefore was entitled to depose witnesses, including the President. Bill was scheduled to be interviewed under oath on Saturday, January 17, 1998.

Although there had been opportunities to settle with Jones out of court, I had opposed the idea in principle, believing that it would set a terrible precedent for a President to pay money to rid himself of a nuisance suit. The lawsuits would never end. With the wisdom of hindsight, of course, not settling the Jones suit early on was the second biggest tactical mistake made in handling the barrage of investigations and lawsuits. The first was requesting an independent counsel at all.

Bill had been up late the night before, preparing for his testimony. When he left, I wished him luck and gave him a big hug. I waited for him in the residence, and when he came back, he looked agitated and exhausted. I asked him how he thought it went, and he told me it was a farce and that he resented the whole process. Although we had planned to go out with friends to a Washington restaurant, he wanted to cancel in favor of a quiet dinner at home.

As usual, there was a lot on everyone's plate at the beginning of the new year. The White House was rolling out new initiatives every week in anticipation of the upcoming State of the Union Address. While moving toward a balanced budget, the President planned significant expansions in Medicare and education, as well as the major increase in child care benefits that my staff had advocated to double the number of eligible children.

Then on Wednesday morning, January 21, Bill woke me up early. He sat on the edge of the bed and said, "There's something in today's papers you should know about."

"What are you talking about?"

He told me there were news reports that he'd had an affair with a former White House intern and that he had asked her to lie about it to Paula Jones's lawyers. Starr had requested and obtained permission from Attorney General Janet Reno to expand his investigation to look into possible criminal charges against the President.

Bill told me that Monica Lewinsky was an intern he had befriended two years earlier when she was volunteering in the West Wing during the government shutdown. He had talked to her a few times, and she had asked him for some job-hunting help. This was completely in character for Bill. He said that she had misinterpreted his attention, which was something I had seen happen dozens of times before. It was such a familiar scenario that I had little trouble believing the accusations were groundless. By then, I also had endured more than six years of baseless claims fomented by some of the same people and groups associated with the Jones case and the Starr investigation.

I questioned Bill over and over about the story. He continued to deny any improper behavior but to acknowledge that his attention could have been misread.

I will never truly understand what was going through my husband's mind that day. All I know is that Bill told his staff and our friends the same story he told me: that nothing improper went on. Why he felt he had to deceive me and others is his own story, and he needs to tell it in his own way. In a better world, this sort of conversation between a husband and wife would be no one's business but our own. Though I had long tried to protect what was left of our privacy, I could do nothing now.

For me, the Lewinsky imbroglio seemed like just another vicious scandal manufactured by political opponents. After all, since he had started running for public office, Bill had been accused of everything from drug-running to fathering a child with a Little Rock prostitute, and I had been called a thief and a murderer. I expected that, ultimately, the intern story would be a footnote in tabloid history.

I believed my husband when he told me there was no truth to the charges, but I realized that we faced the prospect of another horrible and invasive investigation just at the point when I thought our legal troubles were over. I knew, too, that the political danger was real. A nuisance civil action had metastasized into a criminal investigation by Starr, who would undoubtedly take it as far as he could. Leaks to the media from the Jones camp and the Office of the Independent Counsel implied that Bill's testimony in his sworn deposition may have conflicted with other witness descriptions of his relationship with Lewinsky. It appeared that the questions in the Jones deposition were designed solely to trap the President into charges of perjury, which might then justify a demand for his resignation or impeachment.

This was a lot of bad news to absorb in one morning. But I knew that both Bill and I had to carry on with our daily routines. Aides in the West Wing were walking around in a daze, muttering into their cell phones and whispering behind closed doors. It was important to reassure the White House staff that we would deal with this crisis and be prepared to fight back, just as we had in the past. I knew that everyone would be looking to me for their cues. The best thing I could do for myself and those around me was to forge ahead. I could have used more time to prepare for my first public appearance, but that was not to be. That afternoon, I was scheduled to give a speech on civil rights to a large gathering at Goucher College at the invitation of our old friend Taylor Branch, author of a Pulitzer Prize–winning book on Martin Luther King, *Parting the Waters.* Since I was not about to let down the college or Taylor, whose wife, Christy Macy, worked for me, I headed to Union Station and caught a train to Baltimore.

David Kendall telephoned me during the train ride, and it was good to hear his voice. Other than my husband, he was the only person with whom I felt I could talk freely. The year before, Starr had subpoenaed notes from conversations I'd had with White House lawyers about Whitewater, and a court had ruled that attorney-client privilege did not apply to government-paid lawyers. According to David, the OIC was likely planning to subpoena every employee, friend and family member who might have information about the Lewinsky case.

As the Amtrak train lumbered through the Maryland suburbs, David told me he had been hearing snippets of rumors since the day before the Jones deposition. Journalists had called him with questions about another woman's involvement in the case. He thought it might be a troublesome development, but not serious enough to set off any alarms. Now he confirmed that on January 16, Attorney General Reno wrote a letter to the three-judge oversight panel recommending that Starr be allowed to expand his investigation to the Lewinsky matter and possible obstruction of justice. We later learned that Reno's recommendation was based on incomplete and false information provided to her by the OIC. Bill had been blindsided, and the unfairness of it all made me more determined to stand with him to combat the charges.

I chose to keep going and fight back, but it wasn't pleasant to listen to what was being said about my husband. I knew that people were wondering, "How can she get up in the morning, let alone go out in public? Even if she doesn't believe the charges, it has to be devastating just to hear them." Well, it was. Eleanor Roosevelt's observance that every woman in political life must "develop skin as tough as rhinoceros hide" had become a mantra for me as I faced one crisis after another. No doubt my armor had thickened over the years. That may have made things endurable, but it didn't make them easy. You don't just wake up one day and say, "Well, I'm not going to let anything bother me, no matter how vicious or mean-spirited." It was, for me, an isolating and lonely experience.

I also worried that the armor I had acquired might distance me from my true emotions, that I might turn into the brittle caricature some critics accused me of being. I had to be open to my feelings so that I could act on them and determine what was right for me, no matter what anyone else thought or said. It's hard enough to maintain one's sense of self in the public eye, but it was twice as difficult now. I constantly examined myself for traces of denial or hardening of emotional arteries.

I made my speech at Goucher's winter convocation, then returned to the Baltimore train station, where a mob of reporters and camera crews was waiting for me. I hadn't been so swarmed in years. The journalists were yelling questions, and someone shouted above the rest, "Do you think the charges are false?" I stopped and turned to the microphones.

"Certainly I believe they are false—absolutely," I said. "It's difficult and painful any time someone you care about, you love, you admire, is attacked and is subjected to such relentless accusations as my husband has been."

Why is Bill Clinton being attacked?

"There has been a concerted effort to undermine his legitimacy as President, to undo much of what he has been able to accomplish, to attack him personally when he could not be defeated politically."

It was not the first time I had said this, nor would it be the last. With any luck, people might start to understand what I was saying. In my view, the prosecutors were undermining the office of the Presidency by using and abusing their authority in an effort to win back the political power they had lost at the ballot box. At that point, their actions became everyone's concern. I felt as if I had the dual responsibility of defending my husband and my country. They couldn't beat his positions or the successes of his policies, and they couldn't undermine his popularity. So they vilified him—and, by extension, me. The stakes were as high as they could get.

Like me, Bill did not back out of any prior commitments. He went ahead with previously scheduled interviews for National Public Radio, Roll Call and PBS television. He discussed foreign policy and the upcoming State of the Union Address scheduled for Tuesday, January 27. Then he patiently responded to each question about his personal life with essentially the same answer: The allegations weren't true. He didn't ask anybody to lie. He would cooperate with the investigation, but it would be inappropriate to say more at this time.

Our old friend Harry Thomason flew in to offer help and moral support. Ever the television producer, Harry thought that Bill's public statements were coming off as too tentative and legalistic and urged Bill to show how outraged he felt about the allegations. And so he did. At a January 26 press event designed to focus on funding children's after-school care, as Al Gore and Education Secretary Richard Riley and I stood by his side, the President issued a forceful denial that he'd had sexual relations with Lewinsky. I thought his show of anger was justified under the circumstances, as I understood them.

Washington was obsessed with the scandal to the point of hysteria. New facts were emerging daily about the mechanics of what was essentially a sting operation to entrap the President, including secret, illegal tape recordings. The Administration made a pitiful yet valiant attempt to preview initiatives in the upcoming State of the Union address, but the airwaves were saturated with speculation and predictions about Bill's ability to remain in office.

The next day was the State of the Union address, and I kept a long-scheduled commitment to go to New York to appear on the *Today* show that morning. I would rather have had a root canal, but a cancellation would have created its own avalanche of speculation. So off I went, confident that I knew the truth but dreading the prospect of discussing such matters on national television. Bill's advisers and mine weighed in with advice. Some worried that I would antagonize Starr if I talked about the partisan nature of his investigation. David Kendall felt no need for such constraints.

Matt Lauer was hosting the show that morning without Katie Couric, whose husband, Jay Monahan, had tragically lost his battle with colon cancer three days earlier. Everyone was in a somber mood on the set in New York's Rockefeller Center. I took a seat across from Matt, and immediately following the seven o'clock news, he began the interview.

"There has been one question on the minds of people in this country, Mrs. Clinton, lately. And that is, what is the exact nature of the relationship between your husband and Monica Lewinsky? Has he described the relationship in detail to you?"

I answered: "Well, we've talked at great length. And I think as this matter unfolds, the entire country will have more information. But we're right in the middle of a rather vigorous feeding frenzy right now, and people are saying all kinds of things and putting out rumor and innuendo. And I have learned over the last many years being involved in politics, and especially since my husband first started running for President, that the best thing to do in these cases is just to be patient, take a deep breath and the truth will come out."

Lauer mentioned how our friend James Carville had described the situation as a war between the President and Kenneth Starr. "You have said, I understand, to some close friends, that this is the last great battle. And that one side or the other is going down here."

"Well, I don't know if I've been that dramatic," I said. "That would sound like a good line from a movie. But I do believe that this is a battle. I mean, look at the very people who are involved in this. They have popped up in other settings. This is—the great story here for anybody willing to find it and write about it and explain it is this vast right-wing conspiracy that has been conspiring against my husband since the day he announced for President. A few journalists have kind of caught on to it and explained it. But it has not yet been fully revealed to the American public. And, actually, you know, in a bizarre sort of way, this may do it."

Later, when David Kendall called to discuss my appearance, I told him I had thought about him as I was going in to the interview.

"I heard your words of wisdom ringing in my ear," I said.

"And which words of incredible wisdom were you hearing?" said David, going for the bait.

"Screw 'em!" I laughed.

David, who was raised as a Quaker, chuckled and said sheepishly, "It's an old Quaker expression."

"Oh, like 'Screw thee'?"

We were both laughing hard now, letting off steam.

Sure enough, the "vast conspiracy" line got Starr's attention. He took the unusual step of firing off a statement complaining that I had cast aspersions on his motives. He called the notion of a conspiracy "nonsense." As they say in Arkansas, "It's the hit dog that howls." My comment seemed to have touched a nerve.

Looking back, I see that I might have phrased my point more artfully, but I stand by the characterization of Starr's investigation. At that point, I didn't know the truth about the charges against Bill, but I knew about Starr and his connection to my husband's political opponents. I do believe there was, and still is, an interlocking network of groups and individuals who want to turn the clock back on many of the advances our country has made, from civil rights and women's rights to consumer and environmental regulation, and they use all the tools at their disposal—money, power, influence, media and politics—to achieve their ends. In recent years, they have also mastered the politics of personal destruction. Fueled by extremists who have been fighting progressive politicians and ideas for decades, they are funded by corporations, foundations and individuals like Richard Mellon Scaife. Many of their names were already in the public record for any enterprising journalist who went looking for them. A few in the media began searching.

Meanwhile, there was speculation in the news about the State of the Union address that night. Would the President mention the scandal? (He would not.) Would members of Congress boycott the speech? (Only a few did, although some Republicans sat on their hands all night.) Would the First Lady show up to support her husband? You bet I did.

Of course, we were all nervous about Bill's reception, but I knew it would be all right as soon as I walked in to take my seat in the House Gallery. I was greeted by a cascade of sympathetic applause and the whoops of more than a few women in the audience. Bill looked relaxed and confident as he strode in to an even louder ovation. I thought his speech was electrifying, truly one of the best of his career. He recapped the progress the country had made in the past five years and outlined the steps he would take to solidify the gains made during his Presidency. To the surprise of some in our own party and to the consternation of the opposition, he promised to submit a balanced federal budget, three years ahead of schedule, and to "save Social Security first" to prepare for the impending tidal wave of baby boomer retirements. The economy was booming, and he proposed an increase in the minimum wage. He also advocated substantial increases in education, health and child care programs. "We have moved past the sterile debate between those who say government is the enemy and those who say government is the answer," he said. "[W]e have found a third way. We have the smallest government in thirty-five years, but a more progressive one. We have a smaller government, but a stronger nation."

Months earlier, I had accepted an invitation to speak at the annual World Economic Forum that takes place most years in Davos, Switzerland, a beautiful little ski village in the Alps. Every February about two thousand business moguls, politicians, civic leaders and intellectuals from all over the world assemble to talk about global affairs and forge new alliances or cement old ones. It was the first time I would attend the forum, and again, canceling was out of the question.

I was relieved that some of the American attendees at Davos were old friends, including Vernon Jordan and Mayor Richard Daley. Elie and Marion Wiesel were particularly kind. His experience as a Holocaust survivor has given Elie a kind of genius for empathy. He never flinches from anyone else's suffering, and his heart is big enough to absorb a friend's pain without a second thought. He greeted me with a long hug and asked, "What is wrong with America? Why are they doing this?"

"I don't know, Elie," I said.

"Well, I just want you to know that Marion and I are your friends, and we want to help you." Their understanding was the greatest gift they could give.

None of the other people I knew at Davos mentioned the uproar in Washington, although they did go out of their way to be supportive. "Please come to dinner with us," they offered. Or: "Oh, come sit by me. How are you doing?"

I was always doing just fine. There was nothing more I could say.

My speech went well, despite the less-than-scintillating title the conference organizers suggested: "Individual and Collective Priorities for the 21st Century." I described the three essential components of any modern society: an effective functioning government, a free market economy and a vibrant civil society. It is in this third area, outside the marketplace and the government, where everything exists that makes life worth living: family, faith, voluntary association, art, culture. And I spoke about the expectations and realities of the human experience. "There isn't any perfect human institution," I said. "There is no perfect market except in the abstract theories of economists. There is no perfect government except in the dreams of political leaders. And there is no perfect society. We have to work with human beings as we find them." A lesson I was learning every day.

The morning after my speech, I seized the chance to hit the nearby slopes. I have never been a good skier, but I love the sport. It was wonderful to lose myself in sheer physical sensation—the cold, clear air rushing by as I glided down the mountain, wishing I could ski for hours. Even with my Secret Service detail trailing behind me, for a few moments I was delivered from gravity.

IMAGINE THE FUTURE

POLITICAL FOES SOMETIMES SHOW UP IN UNEX-
pected places. As the temporary keepers of the White House, Bill
and I opened its doors for holiday gatherings and important celebrations—and we didn't blacklist anyone who disagreed with our politics.
This made for the occasional awkward moment on the receiving line. On
January 21, 1998, just after the Lewinsky story broke, Bill and I were
hosting a black-tie dinner to celebrate the completion of fund-raising for
the White House Endowment Fund, a nonprofit organization that raises
private money to pay for restoration projects at the White House. The
fund, initiated by Rosalynn Carter and continued by Barbara Bush, set a
fund-raising goal of $25 million. About half that amount had been raised
when I became First Lady, and I was pleased that we were able to meet
and then exceed the original goal. This for me was a labor of love for the
White House, and the dinner was an opportunity to thank all the donors
who had contributed.

Bill and I were greeting our guests in the Blue Room when a moon-
faced man reached out to shake hands. As the military aide announced
his name and a White House photographer prepared to snap his picture, I realized it was Richard Mellon Scaife, the reactionary billionaire
who had bankrolled the long-term campaign to destroy Bill's Presidency. I had never met Scaife, but I greeted him as I would any guest in
a receiving line. The moment passed unnoticed, but later, when the
guest list was released, some journalists were shocked to learn that I had
approved him. When asked why he had been invited, I said that Scaife
had every right to attend the event because of his financial contribution
to White House preservation during the Bush Administration. But I
was astonished that he chose to stand in line to meet the enemy.

Our next gala event was the official dinner in honor of Tony Blair on February 5, 1998. Given the friendship Bill and I had developed with Tony and Cherie, as well as the historic ties and special relationship between our nations, I wanted to pull out all the stops for the Blairs. And we did, with the largest dinner we ever hosted inside the White House, held in the East Room because the State Dining Room was too small. For the after-dinner entertainment, I lined up Sir Elton John and Stevie Wonder to perform together, a truly great Anglo-American musical alliance.

When Speaker of the House Newt Gingrich accepted our dinner invitation, I decided to seat him on my left, while Blair, as expected by protocol, would sit on my right. Gingrich admired Blair as a transformational political leader, a term he had once used to describe himself. I was curious about what they might say to each other and also hoped to glean Gingrich's thoughts on the latest Starr charges. A spate of commentators had introduced the specter of impeachment, and although there was no legitimate constitutional basis for such a move, I knew that might not deter the Republicans from trying. Gingrich was the key: If he gave the go-ahead, the country was in for a rough ride.

After a long discussion at our dinner table about NATO expansion, Bosnia and Iraq, Gingrich leaned in my direction. "These accusations against your husband are ludicrous," he said. "And I think it's terribly unfair the way some people are trying to make something out of it. Even if it were true, it's meaningless. It's not going anywhere." That was what I had hoped to hear, but I was surprised. I later reported to Bill and David Kendall that Gingrich seemed to believe that the allegations against Bill were not serious. He completely changed his tune when he led the Republican charge for Bill's impeachment. For the moment, though, I took this conversation as evidence that Gingrich was more complicated and unpredictable than I had thought. (Months later, when his own marital infidelities were exposed, I better understood why Gingrich may have wanted to dismiss the issue.)

In February, Starr decided to subpoena members of the Secret Service to compel them to testify before the grand jury. Starr was looking for something that would contradict Bill's deposition in the Jones case, and wanted the agents to report on conversations they might have overheard or activities they might have witnessed in the course of protecting the President. It was unprecedented to force Secret Service agents to testify, and Starr's subpoena put them in an untenable position. The agents are nonpolitical professionals whose job involves long hours, difficult conditions and tremendous pressures. Inevitably, they are privy to the confidences of those under their watch, confidences they know they must not compromise. If the agents aren't trusted by the President, they won't be allowed the proximity necessary to do their job, which is to keep the President and his family out of harm's way— not to eavesdrop on behalf of the independent counsel or other investigative bodies.

I respect and admire the agents I've met over the years. The protector and the protected make an extraordinary effort to maintain a professional distance, but when you spend nearly every waking hour in each other's company, you develop relationships of trust and caring. My family and I have also come to know the agents as warm, funny and thoughtful human beings. George Rogers, Don Flynn, A. T. Smith and Steven Ricciardi, who successively served as my lead agent, invariably struck the right balance of informality and professionalism. I will never forget Steve Ricciardi's calm presence after the September 11 attack when he got on the phone with Chelsea, who was with her friend Nickie Davison in lower Manhattan, to make sure she was safe.

Lew Merletti, a Vietnam veteran who had led the Presidential Protective Division (PPD) and then became the director of the Secret Service, met with Starr's operatives and warned them that forcing agents to testify would compromise the necessary trust between agents and Presidents, undermining presidential safety now and in the future. Having guarded Presidents Reagan, Bush and Clinton, Merletti based his assessment on long experience in the field. Previous heads of the Secret Service concurred. The Treasury Department, which oversees the Service, asked the court to deny Starr's request, and former President Bush wrote letters opposing Starr's attempt to force agents to testify. But Starr pressed with his subpoenas. The conditions under which the agents worked and the unique role of the Secret Service counted for little in his calculus. In July, he compelled testimony from Larry Cockell, the head of PPD, and filed motions to compel others to testify. Ultimately, the courts sided with Starr on the legal grounds that agents and protectees, unlike lawyers and clients or doctors and patients, could not assert "privilege" within a confidential relationship. Before the end of the year, Starr had forced more than two dozen agents on the White House detail to testify.

By early spring of 1998, the public seemed to be tiring of Starr's investigation. Many Americans took offense at the prurient, sensational disclosures from the Office of the Independent Counsel and recognized that even if Bill had made mistakes in his personal life, his transgressions hadn't interfered with his ability to carry out his presidential responsibilities.

The media began to pursue the possibility that there was some organized effort against us. On February 9, *Newsweek* magazine published a two-page chart entitled "Conspiracy or Coincidence?" It traced the connections linking twenty-three conservative politicians, contributors, media executives, authors, lawyers, organizations and others who fueled and funded the various scandals investigated by Starr.

Then, in the April issue of *Esquire* magazine, David Brock wrote an open letter to the President, apologizing for his Troopergate story, which had been published in the *American Spectator* in 1994 and which led to the Paula Jones lawsuit. It was the beginning of Brock's crisis of conscience. His book *Blinded by the Right* fully documents his own complicity in the organized efforts to destroy Bill and his administration and the determination, tactics and objectives of the right-wing movement in America.

We took the offensive on the legal front. The Office of the Independent Counsel was prohibited by federal law from disclosing secret grand jury information. Yet grand jury information routinely leaked from Starr's office, usually to a select group of reporters whose stories were favorable to the independent counsel. David Kendall filed a contempt order and held a press conference to announce that he was asking that the judge supervising the Whitewater grand jury, Norma Holloway Johnson, prohibit the disclosure of such information. This action had the desired effect. For a while, the leaks stopped.

On April 1, while Bill and I were overseas on the final leg of his presidential trip to Africa, Bob Bennett phoned with an important message for the President: Judge Susan Webber Wright had decided to throw out the Paula Jones lawsuit, finding that it lacked factual or legal merit.

During the spring, Starr hired Charles Bakaly, a public relations guru, to improve his image. Perhaps guided by Bakaly, Starr gave a speech to a bar association in North Carolina in June in which he compared himself to Atticus Finch, the courageous white Southern lawyer in Harper Lee's *To Kill a Mockingbird*. In the novel, Finch takes on the case of a black man accused of raping a white woman in his small Alabama town. Finch, in an act of moral courage and heroism, opposed the unfettered power of a prosecutor who twisted evidence to serve his own purposes. I had always seen a lot of Atticus Finch in Vince Foster, and the character's appropriation by Starr, a man whose sense of moral superiority justified overlooking rules, procedures and decency, was more than David or I could bear. David fired off an op-ed piece that ran in *The New York Times* on June 3. "Like Atticus," Kendall wrote, "public officials need to be skeptical—about their own motives, about their opponents' motives and even about their version of the 'truth.' "

By mid-June, Judge Johnson ruled that there was "probable cause" to believe the OIC was leaking information illegally and that David could subpoena Starr and his deputies to find the source of the leaks. Grand jury secrecy is vitally important because a federal grand jury has, quite properly, broad powers to investigate. The law is strict that grand jury proceedings must be kept secret out of fairness to those people who are investigated but never charged. Judge Johnson found that the leaks to the media about the OIC's investigation had been "serious and repetitive" and that the OIC's definition of "confidentiality" was too narrow. It was ironic that her decision, which was in our favor but delivered "under seal" because it related to grand jury proceedings, was one of the few facts about Starr's investigation at the time that did not leak to the press.

Against this backdrop, Bill forged ahead with his agenda throughout the first half of 1998, battling with the "gang of three"—Gingrich, DeLay and Dick Armey. I marshaled opposition to their plan to kill the Administration's budget for the National Endowment for the Humanities and to sap federal support for cultural activities throughout the country. I had written an op-ed in *The New York Times* in 1995 about the importance of federal support for the arts. I also championed public television and brought Big Bird and other Sesame Street characters to the White House for a press conference. The puppets were saved, but we continued to fight to preserve the limited but vital support the federal government provided to all the arts.

Bill had a new nominee for Ambassador to the United Nations, Richard Holbrooke, whom Senate Republicans were in no mood to confirm. Holbrooke had negotiated the Dayton Peace Accords and served as Bill's Ambassador to Germany and Assistant Secretary of State for European and Canadian Affairs in the Administration's first term. Dick had also acquired fervent enemies, generally for reasons to

his credit. He was ferociously intelligent, strong, often blunt and fearless. During his negotiations to end the war in Bosnia, Dick occasionally called me to discuss an idea or ask me to convey information to Bill.
When Bill nominated Dick to be Ambassador in June of 1998, Dick's
detractors tried to torpedo his appointment. Melanne and I worked
hard to get him confirmed and urged him to persevere through the
process that increasingly deters qualified people from accepting nominations for important posts. After fourteen months, Dick prevailed and
went to the U.N. in August of 1999, where he shepherded through
Congress the long delayed payment of our U.N. dues and worked with
Secretary-General Kofi Annan to make the HIV/AIDS pandemic a
United Nations priority.

The highlight of spring was Bill's long-anticipated trip to Africa,
his first to the continent and the first extended visit to sub-Saharan
Africa made by a sitting President. Since we had first met, Bill had
opened my horizons to the world beyond our country, but now it was
my turn to show him what I had discovered.

We arrived in Accra, the capital of Ghana, on March 23, 1998, to a
welcome by the largest crowd I had ever seen. More than half a million
people gathered in the searing heat in Independence Square to hear Bill
speak. I had loved traveling with Bill ever since he took me to England
and France in 1973. He rose to every public occasion, delighted in
meeting strangers, and had a vast appetite for new experiences.

Standing on the stage and facing the immense crowd, he told me to
look behind us at the rows of tribal kings who were decked out in vibrant robes and festooned with gold jewelry. He squeezed my hand.
"We're a long way from Arkansas, little Hi'ry."

And indeed we were. Ghana's President, Jerry Rawlings, and his
wife, Nana Konadu, hosted a luncheon for us at Osu Castle, the President's official residence. Slaves and convicts had once been kept in its
dungeon. Rawlings, who first came to power in a military coup in 1979,
confounded his critics by bringing stability to his country. Elected
President in 1992 and reelected in 1996, he peacefully relinquished his
office in a free election in 2000. His wife, Nana, a graceful woman who
wore her own striking designs made of Kente cloth, shared with me an
intimate connection: Hagar Sam, a Ghanaian midwife who helped deliver Chelsea in Little Rock, had also delivered the four Rawlings
children. Like many enterprising people all over the world, Hagar

continued her education in America, studying at Baptist Hospital in Little Rock and working for my obstetrician.

Every day was an eye-opener for Bill. In Uganda, President and Mrs. Museveni traveled with us to the Wanyange village near the source of the Nile. I had asked the two Presidents to highlight the positive results of microcredit loans. From house to house, we saw the evidence of success: borrowers who used their loans to build a rabbit hutch or buy a bigger cooking pot to make extra food to sell or purchase goods to take to the market. Outside one of the houses, my husband came face-to-face with another Bill Clinton—a two-day-old boy whose mother had named him in honor of the American President.

Bill wanted to go to Rwanda to meet with survivors of the genocide. The best estimates were that in less than four months, between five hundred thousand and one million people were killed. The Secret Service insisted that meetings occur at the airport because of ongoing security problems. Sitting in an airport lounge with survivors of one of the worst genocides in human history reminded me again what human beings are capable of doing to one another. For two hours, victim after victim calmly recited the circumstances of his or her encounter with evil. No country or international force, including the United States, had intervened to halt the killings. It would have been difficult for the United States to send troops so soon after the loss of American soldiers in Somalia and when the Administration was trying to end ethnic cleansing in Bosnia. But Bill publicly expressed regret that our country and the international community had not done more to stop the horror.

In Cape Town, Bill and I were greeted by President Mandela, who ushered Bill into a speech before the South African Parliament. We lunched afterwards with a racially diverse group of parliamentarians who before independence would never have met one another socially. Bill also visited Victoria Mxenge to see the more than one hundred new houses built since Chelsea and I had visited a year earlier. The women had named a street after me, and they gave me a souvenir street sign with my name on it.

South Africa's summer was ending, and there was a chill in the air as Bill walked through the cell blocks on Robben Island with Mandela. Black prisoners had been required to wear shorts when working in the limestone quarry on the island, even in cool weather. The coloreds, or mixed-race prisoners, wore long pants. During monotonous hours of rock breaking, Mandela drew letters in the limestone powder, trying to teach his fellow prisoners how to read when the guards weren't looking. Years of exposure to the caustic dust damaged Mandela's tear ducts, and caused his eyes to water and itch. But they lit up whenever he was around his new love, Graça Machel, the widow of Samora Machel, the President of Mozambique, who died in a suspicious plane crash in 1986. She was a guiding light in her own war-torn country and had championed the causes of women and children across Africa. Mandela's marriage to Winnie, which had included decades of separation, prison and exile, did not survive. He was at ease around Graça and clearly smitten. Under the prodding of his old friend Archbishop Tutu, they married in July 1998.

Mandela insisted that Bill and I call him by his colloquial tribal name, Madiba. We were more comfortable addressing him as "Mr. President." We simply honored and admired him so much. Mandela repeatedly asked why we hadn't taken Chelsea out of school to come with us. "You tell her that when I come to the United States she has to see me," he said. "No matter where I am."

Bill and I wished Chelsea were with us too. We were on our way to Botswana, a landlocked arid nation with the contrasting distinction of having one of the highest per capita incomes in sub-Saharan Africa and the highest AIDS infection rate in the world. The government was attempting to marshal its resources to combat the spread of the disease and trying to provide treatment, but the costs were prohibitive without international assistance. This visit convinced Bill to push hard to triple U.S. funding for international AIDS programs in just two years and to make a substantial financial commitment to fund efforts to develop a vaccine.

Although our trip thus far had been exhilarating, it had not yet included any chance for Bill to see the wildlife that Chelsea and I had marveled at the year before. During a brief visit to the Chobe National Park, Bill and I woke up before dawn for a morning game drive. After sighting elephants, hippos, eagles, crocodiles and a mother lion and four cubs, we spent the late afternoon floating down the Chobe River. We sat alone in the back of a boat as the sun went down on a day I'll never forget.

At our final stop in Senegal, Bill went to Gorée Island, as I had. He saw the Door of No Return and delivered a moving apology for

America's role in slavery. The statement was controversial among some Americans, but I believed it was appropriate. Words matter, and words from an American President carry great weight around the world. Expressing regret for genocide in Rwanda and our legacy of slavery sent a message of concern and respect to Africans who confront the intertwined challenges of poverty, disease, repression, starvation, illiteracy and war. But Africa needs more than words; it needs investment and trade if its economies are ever going to develop. That requires both significant changes in most governments and a partnership with the United States. That's why the African Growth and Opportunity Act, which Bill proposed and Congress passed, is so critical. It creates incentives for American companies to do business in Africa.

Within a month, still talking and thinking about Africa, Bill and I were off to China for a state visit. I was delighted that we could take Chelsea and my mother along and excited about returning for a longer stay that would allow me to see more than I had during my 1995 visit.

China was already modernizing its economy, and its future direction would have a direct impact on American interests. Bill favored engagement with China, but as I had learned in 1995, that was easier said than done. We embarked on a long-planned state visit that spring, hoping to confront China's violations of human rights while opening up its huge market to American business and reaching some understanding about Taiwan. A difficult balancing act.

Because it was a state visit, the Chinese government insisted on a formal arrival ceremony in Beijing. We usually conduct these ceremonies on the White House South Lawn, and the Chinese usually conduct theirs in Tiananmen Square. Bill and I debated whether we should attend a ceremony in Tiananmen Square, where Chinese authorities had used tanks to forcibly suppress pro-democracy demonstrations in June of 1989. Bill didn't want to appear to endorse China's repressive tactics and violations of human rights, but he understood the square's importance over centuries of Chinese history and agreed to respect the Chinese request. I was haunted by the events at Tiananmen, remembering the square as we had seen it in television footage in 1989—students constructing a makeshift "Goddess of Democracy" resembling our Statue of Liberty, in defiance of soldiers like the ones in the honor guard lined up in formation, waiting to be reviewed by the President of the United States.

I had met President Jiang Zemin in October of 1997 when he and his wife, Madame Wang Yeping, came to the United States for a state visit. Jiang spoke English and conversed easily. Before the visit, many of my friends had asked me to raise with him the issue of China's suppression of Tibet. I had met with the Dalai Lama to discuss the Tibetans' plight, and so I asked President Jiang to explain China's repression of the Tibetans and their religion.

"What do you mean?" he said. "Tibet has historically been a part of China. The Chinese are the liberators of the Tibetan people. I have read the histories in our libraries, and I know Tibetans are better off now than they were before."

"But what about their traditions and the right to practice their religion as they choose?"

He became passionate, even banging the table once. "They were victims of religion. They are now freed from feudalism."

Despite a developing global culture, the same facts can be and often are viewed through starkly different historical and cultural prisms and the word "freedom" is defined to fit one's political perspective. Still, I didn't think Jiang, who is quite sophisticated and had succeeded in opening up and modernizing the Chinese economy, was being quite straight with me on Tibet. The Chinese, for historical and psychological reasons, were obsessed with avoiding internal disintegration. In the case of Tibet, that led to overreaction and oppression, as obsessions often do.

During our visit to China, Bill and I again raised our concerns about Tibet and the general state of human rights in China. Predictably, the Chinese leaders were adamant and dismissive. When I'm asked why a U.S. President should visit any country with whom we have such serious differences, my answer is always the same: America, the most diverse nation in human history, now wields unparalleled power. But we can be quite insular and uninformed about other countries and their perspectives. Our leaders and our people benefit from learning more about the world in which we live, compete and try to cooperate. Regardless of how much we have in common with people everywhere, deep differences are created by history, geography and culture and those can be bridged only—if at all—through direct experience and relationships. A high-profile presidential visit, with the attention it generates in the country visited and back in America, at least can lay the basis for greater understanding and trust. Because

China is so important, the argument for an official visit was particularly compelling.

The Center for the Women's Law Studies and Legal Services of Beijing University is a small legal aid office surprisingly similar to the one I had run as a young law professor at the University of Arkansas. The Center was aggressively using the law to advance women's rights, a first step in enforcing a 1992 law protecting women's rights. The Center had tried to put teeth in the law, bringing a class-action suit on behalf of factory workers who had not been paid in months, suing an employer who forced women engineers to retire earlier than their male colleagues and helping to prosecute a rapist. I met several of the Center's clients, including one woman who was fired when she had her first child without the approval of her company's family planning unit. Set up in 1995 with financing from the Ford Foundation, the Center had already given advice to nearly four thousand people and provided free legal services in more than one hundred cases. I was encouraged to see advocacy like this as well as the experiment in village democracy China had undertaken. Change in China is a certainty; progress toward greater freedom is not. I think the United States has a big stake in fostering closer ties and understanding.

The Chinese government surprised us by permitting the uncensored broadcast of the news conference Bill and Jiang held—during which they had an extended exchange on the subject of human rights, including Tibet—and of Bill's address to students at Beijing University, in which he stressed that "true freedom includes more than economic freedom."

Bill, Chelsea, my mother and I toured the Forbidden City and the Great Wall. We attended Sunday services at the state-sanctioned Protestant Chongwenmen Church—a right forbidden to many—to demonstrate our public support for greater religious freedom in China. Early one morning we visited the "dirt market," a flea market where vendors unable to get space in the large permanent tent displayed their wares on blankets on the dirt outside. And President Jiang hosted Bill and me at a magnificent state dinner in the Great Hall of the People, which featured traditional Chinese and Western music. Before the performance concluded, both leaders had taken turns conducting the People's Liberation Army Band. The next night, Jiang invited us, along with Chelsea and my mother, to a small private dinner at the compound, where he and the other highest-ranking officials lived with their families. After dining in an old tea house, we walked outside into the soft summer night to sit on the bank of a small lake. The lights of Beijing were faint in the distance.

If Beijing is China's Washington, D.C., Shanghai is its New York. Bill's schedule was filled with meetings with businessmen and a visit to the Shanghai Stock Exchange. I encountered another funny but telling instance of control by the Chinese government. We had scheduled an informal luncheon at a restaurant as a break in the relentless official schedule. When we arrived, Bob Barnett, who was doing advance for the site, told me that a few hours earlier the police had showed up and told everyone working in the nearby stores to leave. They were replaced by attractive young people wearing Western clothes.

At the modern Shanghai Library, which would be an architectural treasure in any city, I spoke about the status of women, constructing my remarks around the old Chinese aphorism that women hold up half the sky. But in most places, I added, when you combine both unpaid domestic work and income-producing work, we end up holding more than half.

Intent on emphasizing religious freedom, Secretary Albright and I toured the newly restored Ohel Rachel Synagogue, one of several synagogues built by the large Jewish community that had flourished in the nineteenth and twentieth centuries as Jews fled to Shanghai from Europe and Russia. Most of the Jews left China after the Communists seized power because the government did not officially recognize Judaism and the synagogues. Ohel Rachel had been used as a warehouse for decades. Rabbi Arthur Schneier from the Park East Synagogue in New York City, who along with Cardinal Theodore McCarrick and Dr. Donald Argue had reported to Bill on the status of religious freedom in China, presented a new Torah for the restored Ark.

From the frenzied pace of Shanghai we flew to Guilin, a place favored by artists over the centuries. The gently winding Li River flows between tall formations of spirelike limestone mountains. Many of China's most stunning vertical landscape paintings depict this beautiful place.

As soon as we returned from China, I focused on our own cultural and artistic history and a celebration of the millennium that I had been thinking about for months. Democracy requires large reservoirs of intellectual capital to continue the extraordinary enterprise of our nation's founders, intellectual giants whose imaginations and philosophical principles enabled them to envision, and then devise, our enduring system of government. Sustaining our democracy for more than 225 years assumes American citizens who understand our nation's rich past, including its productive alliances abroad, and can imagine the future we should create for our children. Over the last several years, I had become concerned about a cavalier anti-intellectualism in our public discourse. Some members of Congress had proudly announced that they had never traveled outside of our country.

The arrival of a new millennium offered an opportunity to showcase the history, culture and ideas that have made America the longest-living democracy in human history and are crucial to the preparation of our citizens for the future. I wanted to focus attention on America's cultural and artistic history. I enlisted my creative deputy chief of staff, Ellen McCulloch-Lovell, to head our millennium effort, and together, we adopted a theme that summed up my hopes for our endeavor: "Honor the Past, Imagine the Future."

I organized a series of White House lectures and performances in the East Room in which scholars, historians, scientists and artists explored issues from the cultural roots of American jazz to genetics to women's history. The brilliant scientist Stephen Hawking explored the latest breakthroughs in cosmology. Dr. Vinton Cerf and Dr. Eric Lander discussed the Human Genome Project, which is unlocking the secrets of our genetic makeup. Already we know that all human beings are 99.9 percent genetically the same, which has important implications for our peaceful co-existence in an all-too violent world. The great trumpeter Wynton Marsalis illustrated why jazz is the music of democracy. Our poets laureate joined with teenagers to recite their own works. These forums became the first cybercasts from the White House, allowing people all over the world to enjoy them and participate in the question-and-answer sessions afterwards.

As part of our two-year commemoration, I initiated Save America's Treasures, a program to restore and recognize cultural and historic landmarks and artifacts around our country. In every community, there is something—a monument, a building, a work of art—that tells a story about who we Americans are. Yet we too often neglect that history and fail to learn from it. The Star-Spangled Banner, which inspired our national anthem, hung in tatters in the National Museum of American History. Its painstaking repair would cost millions; its loss would be incalculable.

At a kickoff for Save America's Treasures, Bill and I announced a donation of $10 million from Ralph Lauren and the Polo Company for the restoration of the flag that inspired our national anthem. Over the next two years, Save America's Treasures matched $60 million from the federal government with $50 million in private donations and used the funds to restore old films, renovate pueblos, refurbish theaters and save many other examples of America's heritage.

In July, I embarked on a four-day bus trip from Washington to Seneca Falls, New York, stopping along the way at places of significance: Baltimore's Fort McHenry; Thomas Edison's factory in New Jersey; George Washington's military headquarters in Newburgh, New York; a park in Victor, New York, dedicated to Iroquois culture and Harriet Tubman's house in Auburn, New York.

Harriet Tubman is one of my heroines. A former slave, she escaped to freedom on the Underground Railroad and then courageously returned to the South time and again to lead other slaves to freedom. While not formally educated, this extraordinary woman was a nurse and scout in the United States Army during the Civil War and became a grassroots activist who raised money to school, clothe and house newly freed black children during Reconstruction. She was a force unto herself and an inspiration to Americans of all races. "If you are tired, keep going," she said to the slaves she led on treacherous paths from slavery to freedom. "If you are scared, keep going. If you are hungry, keep going. If you want a taste of freedom, keep going."

The emotional capstone of the tour was an event at the Women's Rights National Historical Park in Seneca Falls, attended by sixteen thousand people. This marked the 150th anniversary of the campaign for women's suffrage led by Elizabeth Cady Stanton and Susan B. Anthony.

Inspired by the history that this small town represented for women and for America, I opened my remarks with the story of Charlotte Woodward, a nineteen-year-old glove maker living in nearby Waterloo 150 years ago. I asked the audience to imagine her life, working for low wages, knowing that if she married, her pay, her children and even the clothes on her body would belong to her husband. Imagine Charlotte's curiosity and growing excitement on July 19, 1848, when she traveled by horse-drawn carriage to Seneca Falls to attend the first Women's Rights Convention in America. She saw the roads filled with others like herself, forming one long procession on the path to equality.

I spoke of Frederick Douglass, the black abolitionist, who came to Seneca Falls to continue his lifelong struggle for freedom. I wondered what the brave men and women who signed this declaration "would say if they learned how many women fail to vote in elections? They would be amazed and outraged. . . . One hundred and fifty years ago, the women at Seneca Falls were silenced by someone else. Today, women—we silence ourselves. We have a choice. We have a voice."

Finally, I urged women to be guided into the future by the vision and wisdom of those who had gathered in Seneca Falls.

"The future, like the past and present, will not and cannot be perfect. Our daughters and granddaughters will face new challenges, which we today cannot even imagine. But each of us can help prepare for that future by doing what we can to speak out for justice and equality, for women's rights and human rights, to be on the right side of history, no matter the risk or cost."

It was fitting that my spring and summer of discovery should end on this historic ground. I had witnessed the fragile bloom of democracy taking root in China, Africa, Eastern Europe and Latin America. The drive for freedom in those countries was the same drive that made America. The link between Harriet Tubman and Nelson Mandela was a part of the same human journey, and I was looking for the best way to honor it. Because so much blood has been shed for the right to vote, here and all over the world, I have come to think of it as a secular sacrament. Choosing to run for elected office is a tribute to those who sacrificed for our equal right to vote for our leaders. I returned home with a renewed reverence for our flawed but vigorous system of government and new ideas about how to put it to work for all citizens. And when I thought about the obstacles Bill and I still faced in Washington, I dipped deep into the well of inspiration that Harriet Tubman had handed down to us all and vowed to just keep on going.

AUGUST 1998

AUGUST 1998 WAS A BLOODY MONTH, AND ITS EVENTS seemed to signal a turning point at the end of a hopeful decade. In much of the world, the mid-1990s had been a time of reconciliation and growing stability. The Soviet empire had dissolved without causing another world war, and Russia was working with the United States and Europe to construct a safer future. South Africa had held free elections. Virtually all of Latin America had embraced democracy. Ethnic cleansing in Bosnia had ceased and rebuilding had begun. The peace talks and cease-fire in Northern Ireland were successful. Despite terrible setbacks, leaders in the Middle East seemed to be edging toward peace. As always, there were pockets of conflict and suffering in all parts of the globe, but many hostilities had eased.

This period of relative calm was shattered on August 7 when the American Embassies in Kenya and Tanzania were simultaneously bombed by Islamic terrorists, injuring more than 5,000 people and killing 264, among them 12 Americans. Most of the victims were African office workers and pedestrians. It was the most devastating of a series of attacks on American targets overseas and an omen of things to come. Bill was more focused than ever on finding the causes of the terror campaign and isolating its leaders. It was increasingly evident to the intelligence community that a diabolical Saudi exile named Osama bin Laden was organizing and bankrolling much of the terrorism in the Muslim world, and his attacks were getting bigger and bolder.

In Iraq, Saddam Hussein had again defied U.N. demands requiring that weapons inspectors be granted full access to his facilities without notice. Bill conferred at length with U.N. officials and U.S. allies to weigh the proper response to Hussein. It was remarkable to everyone except those who knew him that Bill was able to shut out the political distractions around him in Washington and concentrate on the international crises. But Bill and his national security team were having a hard time directing Congressional attention and government resources to the growing threats at home and abroad. Perhaps that was because so much energy in the news media, Congress and the FBI was directed to an investigation of the President's private life.

In late July, I learned from David Kendall that Starr had negotiated an immunity deal with Monica Lewinsky. She testified before the Whitewater Grand Jury—which no longer had anything to do with Whitewater—on August 6. Starr was determined to subpoena the President to testify, and Bill had to decide whether or not to cooperate. Bill's legal team opposed the idea, asserting that the target of an investigation should never testify before a grand jury. If it came to a trial, anything he said could be used against him. But the political pressure to testify was intense. Another midterm election was coming up, and Bill did not want this issue to cloud it. I agreed that Bill had to testify, and I didn't think there was any reason to worry if he did. It was just another hurdle. David Kendall was briefing Bill and me regularly on developments in the Starr investigation, and I knew the prosecution had requested a blood sample from the President without specifying its significance. David thought it was possible the OIC was bluffing, trying to spook Bill right before his testimony.

I knew from my own experience that a grand jury appearance is nerve-racking. On Friday night, August 14, Bob Barnett met with me in the Yellow Oval Room to talk over some unrelated business and, as a friend, to see how I was holding up. After we'd finished, Bob asked me if I was worried. "No," I said, "I'm just sorry all of us have to endure this."

Then Bob said, "What if there's more to this than you know?"

"I don't believe there is. I've asked Bill over and over again."

Bob persisted. "What if Starr springs something on him?"

"I wouldn't believe anything Starr said or did based on my own experience."

"But," Bob continued, "you have to face the fact that something about this might be true."

"Look, Bob," I said. "My husband may have his faults, but he has never lied to me."

Early the next morning, Saturday, August 15, Bill woke me up just as he had done months before. This time he didn't sit by the bed, but paced back and forth. He told me for the first time that the situation was much more serious than he had previously acknowledged. He now realized he would have to testify that there had been an inappropriate intimacy. He told me that what happened between them had been brief and sporadic. He couldn't tell me seven months ago, he said, because he was too ashamed to admit it and he knew how angry and hurt I would be.

I could hardly breathe. Gulping for air, I started crying and yelling at him, "What do you mean? What are you saying? Why did you lie to me?"

I was furious and getting more so by the second. He just stood there saying over and over again, "I'm sorry. I'm so sorry. I was trying to protect you and Chelsea." I couldn't believe what I was hearing. Up until now I only thought that he'd been foolish for paying attention to the young woman and was convinced that he was being railroaded. I couldn't believe he would do anything to endanger our marriage and our family. I was dumbfounded, heartbroken and outraged that I'd believed him at all.

Then I realized that Bill and I had to tell Chelsea. When I told him he had to do this, his eyes filled with tears. He had betrayed the trust in our marriage, and we both knew it might be an irreparable breach. And we had to tell Chelsea that he had lied to her too. These were terrible moments for all of us. I didn't know whether our marriage could—or should—survive such a stinging betrayal, but I knew I had to work through my feelings carefully, on my own timetable. I desperately needed someone to talk to so I called a friend who was also a counselor to seek guidance. This was the most devastating, shocking and hurtful experience of my life. I could not figure out what to do, but I knew I had to find a calm place in my heart and mind to sort out my feelings.

Thankfully there were no public appearances on my schedule that weekend. We were supposed to be on vacation, but we had delayed our departure for Martha's Vineyard until after Bill's grand jury appearance. Despite the emotional wreckage all around him, Bill had to prepare his testimony and work on a statement to make to the nation.

As we struggled with this personal and public crisis, the world provided another cruel reality check: In Omagh, Northern Ireland, a renegade Irish Republican gang detonated a car bomb in a crowded market, killing twenty-eight, wounding more than two hundred and badly damaging the peace process that Bill had worked so long and hard to nurture with Irish leaders. As reports of the casualties came in that Saturday afternoon, I remembered the times I'd sat with women in all parts of Ireland to talk about the Troubles and to look for a way to achieve peace and reconciliation. Now that's what I had to try to do in the midst of my own heartrending troubles.

Bill gave his four-hour testimony on Monday afternoon in the Map Room. Starr had agreed to withdraw the subpoena, and the voluntary session was videotaped and relayed on closed circuit to the grand jury chamber. This spared Bill the indignity of appearing in court as the first sitting President summoned before a grand jury, but it was the only humiliation dispensed with that day. When it was over, at 6:25 P.M., Bill emerged from the room composed but deeply angry. I had not been present for his testimony, and I was not ready to talk to him, but I could tell from his body language that he had been through an ordeal.

David Kendall had alerted the TV networks that Bill would briefly address the nation at 10 P.M. eastern standard time. Some of Bill's most trusted advisers—White House Counsel Chuck Ruff, Paul Begala, Mickey Kantor, James Carville, Rahm Emanuel, Harry and Linda Thomason—gathered in the Solarium to help him work on his statement. David Kendall was there, as was Chelsea, who was trying to make sense of what was happening. I stayed away, at first. I didn't much want to help Bill compose his public statement on a matter that violated my sense of decency and privacy. Finally, though, out of habit, maybe curiosity, perhaps love, I went upstairs. When I walked into the room at about 8 P.M., someone quickly switched off the sound on the television set. They knew I couldn't stand to hear whatever was being said. When I asked how things were going, it was clear that Bill still hadn't decided what to say.

He wanted people to know that he deeply regretted misleading his family, his friends and his country. He also wanted them to know that he did not believe he had lied during the Jones deposition because the questions had been so clumsy—but that sounded like legalistic hair-splitting. He had made a terrible mistake, then tried to keep it a secret, and he needed to apologize. At the same time, he didn't think he could afford to appear vulnerable to his political enemies or to those of the nation. In the days before his confession to me, we had discussed the dangerous standoff looming in Iraq, precipitated on August 5 by Saddam Hussein's announcement of a ban on continued weapons inspections. And only Bill and I, along with his foreign policy team, knew that within hours of his statement about his personal transgression, the United States would launch a missile strike against one of Osama bin Laden's training camps in Afghanistan, at a time when our intelligence indicated bin Laden and his top lieutenants would be there, to retaliate for the embassy bombings in Kenya and Tanzania. With the whole world watching—much of it wondering what the fuss was about—Bill felt that the President of the United States couldn't afford to appear on television looking weak.

As the hour for his statement approached, everyone was putting in his or her two cents, and this was not helping Bill. He wanted to use this opportunity to point out the unfairness and excesses of Starr's investigation, but there was a vigorous argument over whether he should take a shot at the independent counsel. Even though I was furious with him, I could see how upset he was, and it was awful to watch. So I finally said, "Well, Bill, this is your speech. You're the one who got yourself into this mess, and only you can decide what to say about it." Then Chelsea and I left the room.

Eventually everyone else left Bill alone, and he finished writing the statement by himself. Immediately after his speech, Bill was criticized for not apologizing enough (or, rather, for appearing less than sincere in his apology because he also criticized Starr). I was still too upset to have an opinion. James Carville, who may be the most contentious, in-your-face, don't-give-'em-an-inch friend we have, thought it was probably a mistake to attack Starr. This was a moment to admit wrongdoing and leave it at that. I still don't know who was right. The press hated the statement, but over the next days, reactions from most Americans indicated that they considered a consensual relationship between adults a private matter, and they did not believe that it affected a person's ability to do a good job, whether in the courtroom, the operating room, the Congress or the Oval Office. Bill's standing in public opinion polls remained high. His standing with me had hit rock bottom.

The last thing in the world I wanted to do was go away on vacation, but I was desperate to get out of Washington. Chelsea had wanted to go back to Martha's Vineyard, where good friends were waiting. So Bill, Chelsea and I left for the island the following afternoon. Buddy, the dog, came along to keep Bill company. He was the only member of our family who was still willing to.

Just before we left, Marsha Berry, my imperturbable press secretary, made a statement on my behalf: "Clearly, this is not the best day in Mrs. Clinton's life. This is a time when she relies on her strong religious faith."

By the time we settled into our borrowed house, the adrenaline of the crisis had worn off, and I was left with nothing but profound sadness, disappointment and unresolved anger. I could barely speak to Bill, and when I did, it was a tirade. I read. I walked on the beach. He slept downstairs. I slept upstairs. Days were easier than nights. Where do you turn when your best friend, the one who always helps you through hard times, is the one who wounded you? I felt unbearably lonely, and I could tell Bill did too. He kept trying to explain and apologize. But I wasn't ready to be in the same room with him, let alone forgive him. I would have to go deep inside myself and my faith to discover any remaining belief in our marriage, to find some path to understanding. At this point, I really didn't know what I was going to do.

Shortly after we arrived, Bill returned briefly to the White House to oversee the Cruise missile strikes against one of Osama bin Laden's training camps in Afghanistan. The United States had waited to launch until there was confirmation from intelligence sources that bin Laden and his top aides were at the target sites. The missiles missed him, apparently just by a matter of hours. In the annals of damned-if-you-do-or-don't situations, this was a classic. In spite of clear evidence that bin Laden was responsible for the embassy bombings, Bill was criticized for ordering the attack. He was accused of doing it to divert attention from his own troubles and the growing talk of impeachment by both Republicans and commentators, who still didn't understand the dangers presented by terrorism in general and bin Laden and al Qaeda in particular.

Bill returned to a house thick with silence. Chelsea spent most of her time with our friends Jill and Ken Iscol and their son, Zack. They offered their home and hearts for my confused and hurting daughter. It was excruciating for Bill and me to be locked up together, but it was hard to get out. The media had staked out the island and were ready to descend as soon as we appeared in public. I was in no mood for socializing, but I was touched by how our friends rallied around us. Vernon and Ann Jordan were sympathetic, of course. Katharine Graham, who had had her own experience with the agony of infidelity, made a point of inviting me to lunch. And then Walter Cronkite called and coaxed the three of us to come out on his boat for a sail.

We didn't want to go at first. But Walter and his wife, Betsy, had a comforting attitude about the people who were calling for Bill's head and criticizing me for putting up with him. "This is just unbelievable," Walter said. "Why don't these people get a life? You know, I've lived long enough to know that good marriages go through tough times. None of us is perfect. Let's go sailing!"

We took him up on his offer. Although I was too numb at that point to say I relaxed, it was refreshing to be out on the open water. And the Cronkites' kind concern lifted my spirits.

Maurice Templesman, who came to Martha's Vineyard every summer, was also wonderful to me. I had gotten to know him even better since Jackie's death, and he visited us in the White House. He called and asked if I would come by. We met on his yacht one evening and watched the lights of boats coming into the harbor at Menemsha. He talked for a while about Jackie, whom he missed terribly, and told me he understood how hard her life had been at times.

"I know that your husband really loves you," he said. "And I hope you can forgive him."

Maurice didn't want to infringe on my privacy, and he offered his advice gently. I accepted it with gratitude. After we talked, it was an immense relief just to sit quietly by the water in the company of a good friend.

I looked up at the night sky and its bright wash of stars, just as I had as a child in Park Ridge, while lying on a blanket with my mother. I thought about how the constellations hadn't changed since the first sailors set out to explore the world, using the positions of the stars to find their way back home. I have found my way through a lifetime of uncharted territory with good fortune and abiding faith to keep me on course. This time I needed all the help I could get.

I was thankful for the support and counsel I received during this time, particularly from Don Jones, my youth minister, who had become a lifelong friend. Don reminded me of a classic sermon by the theologian Paul Tillich, "You Are Accepted," which Don had once read to our youth group in Park Ridge. Its premise is how sin and grace exist through life in constant interplay; neither is possible without the other. The mystery of grace is that you cannot look for it. "Grace strikes us when we are in great pain and restlessness," Tillich wrote. "It happens; or it does not happen."

Grace happens. Until it did, my main job was to put one foot in front of the other and get through another day.

IMPEACHMENT

B Y THE END OF AUGUST, THERE WAS DÉTENTE, IF NOT peace, in our household. Although I was heartbroken and disappointed with Bill, my long hours alone made me admit to myself that I loved him. What I still didn't know was whether our marriage could or should last. The day-to-day was easier to forecast than the future. We were returning to Washington and a new phase in a never-ending political war. I hadn't decided whether to fight for my husband and my marriage, but I was resolved to fight for my President.

I had to get a grip on my feelings and focus on what I needed to do for myself. Fulfilling my personal and public obligations drew on a reservoir of different emotions—requiring different thinking and different judgments. For more than twenty years, Bill had been my husband, my best friend, my partner in all of life's trials and joys. He was a loving father to our daughter. Now, for reasons he will have to explain, he had violated my trust, hurt me deeply and given his enemies something real to exploit after years of enduring their false charges, partisan investigations and lawsuits.

My personal feelings and political beliefs were on a collision course. As his wife, I wanted to wring Bill's neck. But he was not only my husband, he was also my President, and I thought that, in spite of everything, Bill led America and the world in a way that I continued to support. No matter what he had done, I did not think any person deserved the abusive treatment he had received. His privacy, my privacy, Monica Lewinsky's privacy and the privacy of our families had been invaded in a cruel and gratuitous manner. I believe what my husband did was morally wrong. So was lying to me and misleading the American people about it. I also knew his failing was not a betrayal of his country.

Everything I had learned from the Watergate investigation convinced me that there were no grounds to impeach Bill. If men like Starr and his allies could ignore the Constitution and abuse power for ideological and malicious ends to topple a President, I feared for my country.

Bill's Presidency, the institutional Presidency and the integrity of the Constitution hung in the balance. I knew what I did and said in the next days and weeks would influence not just Bill's future and mine, but also America's. As for my marriage, it hung in the balance, too, and I wasn't at all sure which way the scale would, or should, tip.

Life moved on, and I moved with it. I accompanied Bill to Moscow for another state visit on September 1 and then on to Ireland to meet Tony and Cherie Blair and to walk the streets of Omagh where the bombing occurred. The detonation of five hundred pounds of explosives in a busy shopping area did not succeed in shattering the cease-fire, as the bombers had hoped. It simply inspired people to work even harder for peace. Shocked hard-liners on both sides of the conflict softened their positions in response.

Gerry Adams, the leader of Sinn Fein, the political arm of the IRA, announced publicly that violence in its seventy-seven-year-old war to end British rule was "a thing of the past." Following Adams's public statement, David Trimble, the Ulster Unionist leader, agreed to meet with Sinn Fein for the first time. All sides concurred that such hopeful developments would not have been possible without the direct diplomacy of Bill Clinton and his envoy, former Senate Majority Leader George Mitchell.

The agony of Omagh was a reminder of the worthy risks Bill was willing to take for peace around the world, of all the good he had accomplished. Bill spent innumerable hours trying to persuade the Irish, Bosnians, Serbs, Croats, Kosovars, Israelis, Palestinians, Greeks, Turks, Burundians and others to give up past grievances and overcome barriers to peace. His efforts were sometimes successful, sometimes not. Many of the successes were fragile, as we later learned in the collapse of the Middle East peace process. But even the failures forced people to come to grips with the pain and humanity of the other side. I was always proud and grateful that Bill persevered in the search for peace and reconciliation.

The huge contingent of reporters who followed the President to Russia and Ireland was looking for more than a peace mission story. They were watching both of us closely for clues to the state of our marriage. Did we stand close together or apart? Was I frowning or crying behind dark glasses? And what was the significance of the knitted sweater I bought for Bill in Dublin, which he wore to Limerick for his first golf game in more than a month? I desperately wanted to restore a zone of privacy for myself and my family, but I wondered if that would ever be possible again.

While Bill was negotiating with foreign leaders abroad, Joe Lieberman, Senator from Connecticut, admonished him publicly. Lieberman, who had been a friend since Bill had worked on his first campaign for the Connecticut state senate in the early seventies, took to the Senate floor to denounce the President's conduct as immoral and harmful because "it sends a message of what is acceptable behavior to the larger American family."

When Bill was asked by reporters in Ireland to respond to Lieberman's speech, he replied: "Basically I agree with what he said. I've already said that I made a bad mistake. It was indefensible, and I'm sorry about it. I'm very sorry about it." It was the first of many unconditional public apologies my husband would make on his long journey of atonement. But I realized that apologies would never be enough for hardcore Republicans and might not be enough to avert a meltdown within the Democratic Party. Other Democratic leaders, including Congressman Richard Gephardt of Missouri, Senator Daniel Patrick Moynihan of New York and Senator Bob Kerrey of Nebraska, condemned the President's personal actions and said he should in some way be held accountable. None, however, advocated impeachment.

By the time we returned to the White House, there were several challenges on my mind, personal and political. Bill and I had agreed to participate in regular marital counseling to determine whether or not we were going to salvage our marriage. On one level, I was emotionally shell-shocked and trying to deal with the raw wound I had suffered. On another level, I believed Bill was a good person and a great President. I viewed the independent counsel's assault on the Presidency as an ever escalating political war, and I was on Bill's side.

When people ask me how I kept going during such a wrenching time, I tell them that there is nothing remarkable about getting up and going to work every day, even when there is a family crisis at home. Every one of us has had to do it at some time in our lives, and the skills required to cope are the same for a First Lady or a forklift operator. I just had to do it all in the public eye.

Even if I was undecided about my personal future, I was absolutely convinced that Bill's private behavior and his misguided effort to conceal it did not constitute a legal or historical basis for impeachment under the Constitution. I believed he ought to be held accountable for his behavior—by me and by Chelsea—not by a misuse of the impeachment process. But I also knew that the opposition could use the press to create an atmosphere in which political pressure would grow for impeachment or resignation, regardless of the law. I worried about the Democrats who might be stampeded into calling for Bill's resignation, and tried to concentrate on what I could do to help get them reelected in November. In spite of polls showing large majorities against impeachment, many Democrats up for reelection believed that, unless they were tough on the President, they would lose their seats. It was a legitimate concern in some districts. In much of the country, however, impeachment and Starr's investigation could tarnish Republican candidates who sought to exploit the process.

In early September, David Kendall discovered that the OIC was ready to send a referral on impeachment to the House Judiciary Committee, which would then decide whether the matter should go to the full House of Representatives for a vote. I had studied this area of the law in 1974, when my duties for the House Judiciary Committee's impeachment staff had included writing a memo outlining the procedures for impeaching a President and another on the standards of evidence required to trigger an impeachment. According to the Constitution, the House must approve by majority vote the articles of impeachment, which are similar to a criminal indictment of a federal official. The articles are then sent to the Senate for trial. Although a jury in a criminal trial must be unanimous for a guilty verdict, only a two-thirds majority of the Senate is required for conviction and removal from office. The Constitution reserves impeachment as a remedy for only the most serious of offenses: "Treason, Bribery or other high Crimes and Misdemeanors." The Founding Fathers who wrote the Constitution designed impeachment to be a slow, painstaking process because they believed that it should not be easy to remove a federal official, particularly the President, from office.

In 1868, the House of Representatives impeached President Andrew Johnson for defying Congress's wish that a harsh post–Civil War reconstruction policy be imposed on the South. I thought the House was wrong, but at least they acted against Johnson on grounds of his official actions as President. Johnson was tried and acquitted in the Senate by one vote. Richard Nixon was the second American President to face impeachment proceedings, and I knew firsthand how carefully that process safeguarded the use of grand jury evidence, following the letter and the spirit of the Constitution. That investigation was carried out under tight security and confidentiality for eight months before articles of impeachment having to do with President Nixon's actions as President were presented to the Judiciary Committee. Chairman Peter Rodino and Special Counsel John Doar set examples of discreet nonpartisan professionalism.

David Kendall asked for an advance copy of the OIC's referral to the House Judiciary Committee so that he could draft a response—a request grounded in simple fairness and precedent from the Nixon impeachment. Starr refused. On September 9, Starr's deputies drove two vans to the Capitol steps and delivered copies of the more than 110,000-word "Starr report," complete with thirty-six boxes of supporting documents, to the sergeant-at-arms. Starr's piece of grandstanding was appalling; the quick decision by the House Rules Committee to make the entire report available on the Internet, even more so.

Federal law requires that grand jury evidence be kept confidential so that testimony elicited by a prosecutor from a witness without the clarifying effect of cross-examination cannot prejudice a case or harm an innocent person. This is one of the basic tenets of our judicial system. The Starr report was a compilation of raw grand jury testimony obtained from witnesses who were never cross-examined, and it was released to the public without regard to fairness or balance.

I have not read the Starr report, but I've been told that the word *sex* (or some variation of it) appears 581 times in the 445-page report. *Whitewater*, the putative subject of Starr's probe, reportedly appears four times, to identify a figure, like the "Whitewater Independent Counsel." Starr's distribution of his report was gratuitously graphic and degrading to the Presidency and the Constitution. Its public release was a low moment in American history.

Starr recommended that the House Judiciary Committee consider eleven possible grounds of impeachment. I was convinced that he had overstepped his legal authority. The Constitution requires the legislative branch of government—not the independent counsel, which is a creation of the executive and judicial branches—to investigate evidence of impeachable offenses. Starr's duty was to deliver an unbiased summary of the known facts to the committee, which would then deploy its own staff to assemble evidence. But Starr appointed himself prosecutor, judge and jury in his zeal to impeach Bill Clinton. And the more I believed Starr was abusing his power, the more I sympathized with Bill— at least politically.

Starr's list of impeachable offenses included charges that the President lied under oath about his personal behavior, obstructed justice and abused his office. Bill never obstructed justice or abused his office. He maintained that he did not lie under oath. Whether or not he did, a lie under oath about a private matter in a civil suit was not grounds for impeachment, according to the vast majority of constitutional experts and historians.

The day after Starr delivered his report to Congress, Bill and I attended a Democratic Business Council reception, where I introduced him as "my husband and our President." Privately, I was still working on forgiving Bill, but my fury at those who had deliberately sabotaged him helped me on that score. My schedule was loaded with events, and I showed up for every one of them. That day, there was a speechwriting meeting, a colon cancer prevention event, an AmeriCorps reception and several other appearances. If the White House staff saw me carrying on as usual, I hoped it would encourage them to do the same. If I could get through the day, they could too.

For weeks, Bill had apologized to me, to Chelsea and to the friends, Cabinet members, staffers and colleagues he had misled and disappointed. At a White House prayer breakfast with religious leaders in early September, Bill offered an emotional admission of his sins and a plea for forgiveness from the American people. But he would not give up his office. "I will instruct my lawyers to mount a vigorous defense using all available appropriate arguments," he said. "But legal language must not obscure the fact that I have done wrong. If my repentance is genuine and sustained . . . then good can come of this for our country as well as for me and my family. The children of this country can learn in a profound way that integrity is important and selfishness is wrong, but God can change us and make us strong at the broken places."

Bill cast his political fate with the American people. He asked for their compassion and then went back to work for them with the same commitment that he had brought to his Presidency from his first day in the White House. And we continued with our regular counseling sessions, which forced us to ask and answer hard questions that years of nonstop campaigning had allowed us to postpone. By now, I wanted to save our marriage, if we could.

The public response to Bill's forthright apologies raised my spirits. The President's job approval was holding steady through the crisis. A solid majority of about 60 percent of Americans also said that Congress should not begin impeachment proceedings, that Bill should not resign and that the explicit details in the Starr report were "inappropriate." My own approval rating was nearing an all-time high and would eventually peak somewhere around 70 percent, proving that the American people are fundamentally fair and sympathetic.

Although the case for impeachment was both unpopular and unjustified under the constitutional standard, I assumed that the House Republicans would pursue it if they thought they could. The only way to avoid impeachment was through a strong showing in the November elections. But the party in the White House traditionally loses congressional seats in midterm elections, as we had in 1994, and especially in a President's second term. Democratic candidates everywhere were feeling justifiably nervous about the President's political health.

On September 15, a delegation of about two dozen Democratic Congresswomen met with me in the Yellow Oval Room. The representatives sat on couches and chairs, while butlers served coffee and pastries. The women had come to urge me to take a public role in the upcoming election, but I think they also wanted to see and hear for themselves how I was holding up and what I was planning to do next. Once they realized that I was serious about standing up for the Constitution, the President and the Democratic Party, they asked me to get out and campaign for them.

We talked about how to direct the voters' attention away from impeachment and back to the issues that mattered to voters—federal help to reduce class size and to help with school construction, Social Security and health insurance reforms, better foster care and adoption practices and protection of the environment.

"I'll help you in any way I can," I said. "But I also need you to help hold the party together, and to keep the Democratic Caucus members where they belong—behind the Constitution and the President."

"We are not here to talk about the President's behavior," Representative Lynn Woolsey told reporters after the meeting. "We are here to talk about what's important, more important to the people of this country." Woolsey later explained: "We told her that as women, we know that women can do more than one thing at a time in an emergency. . . . So we asked her to get on a plane and stop at places where her voice so desperately needs to be heard."

And so I did. Campaigning in dozens of congressional races, I was kept occupied all day by my frenetic schedule. But the nights were difficult, especially after Chelsea returned to Stanford. Bill and I had only ourselves, and it was still awkward. I didn't avoid him as I had before, but there was still tension between us and not as many shared laughs as I was used to on a daily basis with my husband.

I am not the sort of person who routinely pours out her deepest feelings, even to my closest friends. My mother is the same way. We have a tendency to keep our own counsel and that trait only deepened when I began living my life in the public eye. It was a welcome distraction when my good friends Diane Blair and Betsy Ebeling came to stay with me for a few days in mid-September. I was blessed with close friends, but once the relentless investigating started, I felt compelled to protect them from being dragged into any probe. After August 1998, I felt even more cut off and alone because I did not want to talk to Bill as I always had before. I spent a lot of time alone, praying and reading. But it made me feel better to have friends around who had known me forever, who had seen me pregnant and sick and happy and sad and could understand what I was going through now.

On September 17, during Diane and Betsy's visit, Stevie Wonder called and asked if he could come over to see me at the White House. He had attended the state dinner for another of his fans, Czech President Václav Havel, and his new wife, Dagmar, the night before, and he wanted to return privately to play a song he had written for me.

Capricia escorted Stevie, his assistant and one of his sons into the second-floor corridor of the residence, where a grand piano stood under a large painting by Willem de Kooning. Diane and Betsy sat on a settee, and I sat in a small chair near the piano as Stevie began to sing a haunting, lilting melody. He hadn't finished all the words, but the song was about the power of forgiveness, with the refrain, "You don't have to walk on water . . ." As he played, I kept moving my chair closer to the piano until I was sitting right next to him. When Stevie finished, tears filled my eyes and, when I looked around, tears were running down Betsy's face and Diane's. This was one of the kindest gestures anyone made during this incredibly difficult period.

I was also touched when *Vogue* Editor in Chief Anna Wintour called to propose an article and photo shoot for the December issue of the magazine. It was gutsy of her to offer and counterintuitive for me to accept. In fact, the experience did wonders for my spirits. I wore a glorious burgundy velvet Oscar de la Renta creation for the cover shoot. For a day, I escaped into a world of makeup artists and haute couture. The Annie Leibovitz photographs were great, giving me the chance to look good when I had been feeling so low.

September 21, the day Bill addressed the opening session of the United Nations in New York, played out like an absurdist farce. When the Starr report didn't force Bill to resign, the Republican leadership upped the ante and released the President's videotaped grand jury testimony. As Bill entered the enormous General Assembly Hall to an enthusiastic and unusual standing ovation, all of the major television networks were simultaneously broadcasting a tape of his August interrogation by Starr's deputies. As the hours of agonizing testimony droned on over the airwaves, Bill gave a forceful speech to the U.N. about the growing threat of international terrorism and the urgent need for a united response from all civilized people. I'm sure few Americans heard Bill's warning about the dangers terrorists posed to us. When he finished speaking, the Presidents, Prime Ministers and delegates gave him another warm and prolonged ovation. The reception from his international peers affirmed Bill's leadership, a timely recognition of the good work he had done as President.

Bill also met with Pakistani Prime Minister Nawaz Sharif to discuss curbing Pakistan's nuclear program and the overall threat posed by nuclear proliferation on the subcontinent, and with Secretary-General Kofi Annan about how to respond to Iraq's continued defiance of U.N. resolutions. Later, he joined me at a forum on the global economy at New York University with Italian President Romano Prodi, Swedish Prime Minister Goran Persson, Bulgarian President Petar Stoyanov and our friend, British Prime Minister Tony Blair.

By the time we returned to the White House the next day, it looked as if the Republicans' publicity stunt had failed. The spectacle of the President keeping his composure while being barraged with prurient questions that no one would want to answer seemed to create more sympathy among the American people for Bill's predicament.

The following evening, Nelson Mandela, who had also attended the U.N. session, visited us at the White House with his wife, Graça Machel. At a reception for African American religious leaders in the

East Room, Mandela spoke about his genuine love and respect for Bill. After praising the relationship Bill had forged with South Africa and the rest of the continent, Mandela noted gently, "We have often said that our morality does not allow us to desert our friends." He turned to Bill and addressed him directly. "And we have got to say tonight, we are thinking of you in this difficult and uncertain time in your life." Mandela drew laughter and applause when he pledged not to "interfere in the domestic affairs of this country." But he was clearly making a plea to Americans to demand an end to the impeachment spectacle. Mandela, who had mastered his anger and forgiven his own jailers, was, as always, philosophical.

"But if our expectations, if our fondest prayers and dreams are not realized," he said, "then we should all bear in mind that the greatest glory of living lies not in never falling, but in rising every time you fall."

I was still trying to rise. By seeing each hour through to the end, and starting over every morning, I was rebuilding my life imperceptibly, one day at a time. It was a challenge to forgive Bill; the prospect of forgiving the hired guns of the right wing seemed beyond me. If Mandela could forgive, I would try. But it was hard, even with the help of many friends and role models.

Some weeks after Mandela's visit, the Dalai Lama called on me at the White House. At our meeting in the Map Room, he presented me with a white prayer scarf and told me he thought often of me and my struggle. He encouraged me to be strong and not give in to bitterness and anger in the face of pain and injustice. His message dovetailed with the support I was receiving from my prayer group, especially Holly Leachman and Susan Baker, who came to visit and pray with me, Secret Service agent Brian Stafford, then head of the President's Protective Division, and Mike McCurry, the President's press secretary through the hardest days. Each went out of his way to check in on me and see how I was faring under the pressure. Democratic members of Congress called to ask what I wanted them to do. One Congressman said, "Hillary, if you were my sister, I'd punch Bill Clinton right in the nose!" I assured him that I appreciated his concern, but I really didn't need that kind of help. Some Republicans confided that they disagreed with their party's decision to pursue impeachment.

On October 7, a delegation of freshmen House members came to see me in the White House. Once again, we met in the Yellow Oval Room as sunlight streamed through the windows. They were worried that the Republicans would force an impeachment vote before the midterm election. I gave the best pep talk I could. "We can't let them hound the President out of office," I said. "Not like this. You're members of Congress. Your job is to protect the Constitution and do what's right for the country. So let's walk through this." Then drawing on my experience twenty-five years earlier, I explained what the Constitution said about impeachment, how the framers envisioned the impeachment power would be used and how it had been interpreted in the more than two hundred years since. As we closed the meeting, I also assured the members that if it came down to a vote, both the President and I wanted them to heed their consciences and their constituents; we would understand, whatever they decided.

The consensus among Democrats and the few remaining moderate Republicans on the Hill was that censure—a vote of reprimand—would be the most appropriate response to Bill's behavior. But powerful Republicans were adamantly opposed to the compromise. Henry Hyde, chairman of the House Judiciary Committee, derided the notion of censure as "impeachment lite." Hyde was particularly intransigent. He blamed the White House for a September 16 piece in *Salon*, an Internet magazine, that reported that he had carried on a lengthy love affair during the 1960s, while he was married to his late wife. Hyde called his infidelity, which took place when he was in his forties, a "youthful indiscretion." He was outraged and indignant that the media had exposed such a personal transgression, and Republicans called for an investigation of the magazine. Despite my many political and ideological differences with Hyde, I was sympathetic to his distress, although mystified that he didn't see the double standard in his reaction.

I spent the fall crisscrossing the country on a campaign marathon. I urged people to vote as if their lives depended on it. I concentrated on areas where the races were tight and my own popularity high. As I had six years earlier, I campaigned hard for Barbara Boxer, who was defending her Senate seat against a strong challenger in California, and for Patty Murray, the effective "mom in tennis shoes" Senator from Washington. I also tried to help Senator Carol Mosley Braun in Illinois. Before the end, I made stops in Ohio, Nevada and back in Arkansas on behalf of a dynamic young Senate candidate, Blanche Lincoln. "We have to send a very clear signal to the Republican leadership in Congress that Americans care about the real issues," I told a crowd in Janesville, Wisconsin. "They care about education, health care and Social Security. And they want a Congress that cares about what they care about."

I poured my heart into Representative Charles Schumer's campaign to defeat New York Senator Al D'Amato. An intelligent and doggedly progressive Democrat, Chuck Schumer was one of Bill's most steadfast supporters. D'Amato had chaired the Whitewater hearings in the Senate, where he had paraded blameless White House secretaries, ushers and a baby-sitter in front of the committee, finding nothing but saddling them with legal bills. D'Amato was vulnerable to Schumer's vigorous challenge.

I was in New York attending a fund-raiser for Schumer when I realized my right foot was so swollen that I could barely put my shoe on. When I got back to the White House, I called Dr. Connie Mariano, who, after a cursory look at my foot, whisked me off to Bethesda Naval Hospital to determine if I had developed a blood clot from my nonstop flying around the country. Sure enough, I had a big clot behind my right knee that required immediate treatment. Dr. Mariano told me to stay in bed taking blood thinners for at least a week. Although I wanted to take care of myself, I was determined not to cancel any of my campaign stops. So we compromised. She sent along a nurse to administer the medicine I needed and to monitor my condition.

As voting day approached, the GOP launched a massive ad campaign that focused on the scandal. The scheme was unsuccessful. Voters seemed to be more disgusted with Republican political tactics than with the President's personal life. I believe we would have picked up additional seats if more Democrats had called the Republicans on their fervor for impeachment. But going against Washington's conventional wisdom was too big a gamble for most candidates to take. The pundits were still predicting a Republican surge.

On Election Day, the exit polls started coming in, and Bill was in an upbeat mood. He sat with staff members in John Podesta's West Wing office, monitoring the results. John, a smart, no-nonsense political adviser, who had served in Bill's first Administration as staff secretary, recently had returned as chief of staff after Erskine Bowles ended his tenure. An aide had shown Bill how to follow the returns on the Internet, and he sat at John's computer eagerly surfing political websites. As always, I was too nervous to watch the returns. So I invited Maggie and Cheryl Mills, an accomplished lawyer in the counsel's office, to join me in the movie theater for a screening of Oprah Winfrey's new film of the

Toni Morrison novel *Beloved*. When we emerged later that night there was good news: The vote was historic. Democrats gained 5 seats in the House and narrowed the Republican margin: It was now 223 to 211. The Senate held steady at 55 Republicans to 45 Democrats. Barbara Boxer won reelection to the Senate, and the best news of the night was that Chuck Schumer beat Al D'Amato in New York. Republicans and the media pundits thought Democrats would lose up to 30 House seats and 4 to 6 Senate seats. Instead, Democrats won seats in the House, the first time since 1822 that a President's party had done so in his second term.

Another surprise soon followed. Three days later, Friday, November 6, Senator Moynihan taped an interview with New York television legend Gabe Pressman announcing that he would not run for a fifth term. The interview was to be aired on Sunday morning, but the news leaked early.

Late on Friday night, the White House operator patched through a call from Representative Charlie Rangel, the veteran Congressman from Harlem and a good friend.

"I just heard that Senator Moynihan announced he is going to retire. I sure hope you'll consider running because I think you could win," he said.

"Oh, Charlie," I said. "I'm honored you would think of me, but I'm not interested, and besides, we have a few other outstanding matters to resolve right now."

"I know," he said. "But I'm really serious. I want you to think about it."

He may have been serious, but I thought the idea of running for Senator Moynihan's seat was absurd, although this wasn't the first time it had come up. A year earlier, at a Christmas reception at the White House, my friend Judith Hope, the chair of the New York Democratic Party, mentioned that she didn't think Moynihan would run again. "If he doesn't," she said, "I wish you would run." I had thought Judith's comment was farfetched then and I still thought so.

I had other things on my mind.

WAITING FOR GRACE

THE 1998 MIDTERM ELECTION PRODUCED YET AN-
other surprise when Newt Gingrich stepped down as Speaker of
the House and announced that he would resign from Congress. At first,
this seemed like a victory for our side and the likely derailment of impeachment. Bob Livingston of Louisiana was set to succeed Gingrich as
Speaker, but Tom DeLay, the Majority Whip and the real power in the
Republican Caucus, pressured the Republicans into opposing any reasonable compromise such as a censure vote. When Erskine Bowles asked
Gingrich why the Republicans would pursue a course that was neither
right nor constitutional, Gingrich replied, "Because we can."

The Whitewater inquiry and the Paula Jones lawsuit that had
touched off this constitutional showdown were all but forgotten.
Jones's lawyers had appealed Judge Wright's dismissal of the case and
for the past month had been sending out signals that she was ready to
settle for $1 million. The law was clearly in Bill's favor, but the three-
judge panel on the Eighth Circuit Court of Appeals was dominated by
two of the same conservative Republicans who had issued the legally indefensible ruling that earlier had removed Judge Henry Woods from a
Whitewater-related case on the basis of newspaper articles. Given that
history, Bill worried that there was a good chance that partisan politics
again would trump law and precedent, and the judges would rule that
the case could proceed to trial. On November 13, Bill's attorney, Bob
Bennett, told Bill that Jones had agreed to drop her suit for a payment
of $850,000. Although he hated to settle a case he'd already won and
that Judge Wright had found to be without legal or factual merit, Bill
decided that there was no other sure way to put this episode to rest. He
did not apologize and made no concessions of wrongdoing. Bennett

simply said, "The President has decided he is not prepared to spend one more hour on this matter." And then it was over.

For weeks I had been expecting the House Judiciary Committee to issue a raft of subpoenas, which is what was done during the 1974 Nixon impeachment inquiry. The committee's responsibility is to conduct its own investigation, not rubber-stamp the independent counsel's allegations. I was disgusted when Hyde announced that the committee would be calling Kenneth Starr as its main witness. Starr spoke uninterrupted for two hours and then answered questions from committee members for the rest of the afternoon. It was almost nine o'clock at night when David Kendall finally was given a chance to cross-examine Starr. Working under a ridiculously unrealistic time limit imposed by the committee's Republican majority, David began his remarks with a summary of the process.

"My task is to respond to the two hours of uninterrupted testimony from the independent counsel, as well as to his four-year, $45 million investigation, which has included at least twenty-eight attorneys, seventy-eight FBI agents and an undisclosed number of private investigators; an investigation which has generated by computer count 114,532 news stories in print and 2,513 minutes of network television time, not to mention twenty-four-hour scandal coverage on cable; a 445-page referral; 50,000 pages of documents from secret grand jury testimony; four hours of videotape testimony; twenty-two hours of audiotape, some of which was gathered in violation of state law, and the testimony of scores of witnesses, not one of whom has been cross-examined.

"And I have thirty minutes to do this."

During the Soviet-style show trial procedure, Starr had to admit that he had not himself examined a single witness before the grand jury. He had nothing to add to his referral. But he did announce that the OIC finally had cleared the President of any impeachable offenses in the so-called Travelgate and Filegate investigations.

Barney Frank, the sharp and skillful Democratic Congressman from Massachusetts, asked Starr when he had reached that conclusion.

"Some months ago," said Starr.

"Why did you withhold that before the election when you were sending a referral with a lot of negative stuff about the President and only now . . . give us this exoneration of the President several weeks after the election?"

The independent counsel had no response.

The next day, Sam Dash, the OIC's ethical adviser who had appeared oblivious to previous lapses by Starr and his subordinates, resigned in protest over Starr's testimony. Dash, who had been chief counsel for the Senate Watergate Committee in 1973 and 1974, wrote a letter accusing Starr of abusing his position by "unlawfully" injecting himself into the impeachment process. His resignation had no apparent effect on the proceedings. Nor did an open letter issued by four hundred historians—including co-sponsors Arthur M. Schlesinger, Jr., of City University of New York; Sean Wilentz of Princeton University and C. Vann Woodward of Yale University—that openly urged Congress to reject impeachment because the constitutional standards for it had not been met. Their statement should be required reading in civics classes:

> As historians as well as citizens, we deplore the present drive to impeach the President. We believe that this drive, if successful, will have the most serious implications for our constitutional order.
>
> Under our Constitution, impeachment of the President is a grave and momentous step. The Framers explicitly reserved that step for high crimes and misdemeanors in the exercise of executive power. Impeachment for anything else would, according to James Madison, leave the President to serve "during the pleasure of the Senate," thereby mangling the system of checks and balances that is our chief safeguard against abuses of public power.
>
> Although we do not condone President Clinton's private behavior or his subsequent attempts to deceive, the current charges against him depart from what the Framers saw as grounds for impeachment. The vote of the House of Representatives to conduct an open-ended inquiry creates a novel, all-purpose search for any offense by which to remove a President from office.
>
> The theory of impeachment underlying these efforts is unprecedented in our history. The new processes are extremely ominous for the future of our political institutions. If carried forward, they will leave the Presidency permanently disfigured and diminished, at the mercy as never before of the caprices of any Congress. The Presidency, historically the center of lead-

ership during our great national ordeals, will be crippled in meeting the inevitable challenges of the future.

We face a choice between preserving or undermining our Constitution. Do we want to establish a precedent for the future harassment of presidents and to tie up our government with a protracted national agony of search and accusation? Or do we want to protect the Constitution and get back to the public business?

We urge you, whether you are a Republican, a Democrat or an Independent, to oppose the dangerous new theory of impeachment, and to demand the restoration of the normal operations of our federal government.

In early December, the Vice President's father, Albert Gore, Sr., died at age ninety-one at his home in Carthage, Tennessee. On December 8, Bill and I flew down to Nashville for a service in the War Memorial Auditorium. Al Gore stood next to the flag-draped casket and delivered a beautiful eulogy for his father, the once powerful and courageous U.S. Senator who lost his seat in 1970 because he opposed the Vietnam War. Al spoke directly from his heart with humor and empathy. It was the best speech I'd ever heard him give.

There has been immense speculation about how our relationship with the Gores was affected by the impeachment scandal. Al and Tipper were as shocked and hurt as everybody else in August when Bill admitted his wrongdoing, but both were supportive throughout the ordeal, personally and politically. They were there whenever we needed them, sometimes when we asked for their help, sometimes when they sensed we could use it.

Starting on December 11 and finishing early on the twelfth, the Judiciary Committee voted along party lines to refer four articles of impeachment to the full House for a vote. This was no surprise, though we still had held out hope that we could gain enough support for a compromise on censure.

While Congress pursued impeachment, Bill focused on his official duties and I on mine. I felt strongly that I had a duty as First Lady to continue my public responsibilities, including a trip I was determined to make with members of Congress to Puerto Rico, the Dominican Republic and Haiti to bring aid and comfort to citizens there who were recovering from Hurricane Georges. Keeping my regular schedule often got me up and going. I never believed that I had the luxury of climbing into bed and pulling the covers over my head.

From December 12 to 15, Bill and I visited the Middle East. We went with Prime Minister Benjamin "Bibi" Netanyahu and his wife, Sara, to Masada, a symbol of Jewish resistance and martyrdom that Bill and I had first visited seventeen years before when we were part of a Holy Land tour led by Bill's Southern Baptist pastor, Dr. W. O. Vaught. He had since died, and I wished often that he had been around as a pastor to counsel, and confront, Bill. I was deeply appreciative that three ministers did offer guidance—Rev. Phil Wogaman, Rev. Tony Campolo and Rev. Gordon MacDonald met and prayed with him regularly as he sought understanding and forgiveness.

On that earlier visit, we had also gone to Bethlehem; now we returned there with Yasir Arafat to visit the Church of the Nativity, where we sang Christmas carols with Christian Palestinians, still holding out hope for the peace process. Bill was scheduled to make a groundbreaking address to the Palestinian National Council and hold other meetings with the Palestinians, and we landed at the brand new Gaza International Airport. This was a momentous event because the opening of the airport had been one of the tenets of the recent Wye Peace Accords that Bill had brokered between Arafat and Netanyahu to help advance economic opportunity for the Palestinians.

Although the Middle East provided a positive picture at that time, Bill continued to monitor closely the defiance of Saddam Hussein, who refused to agree to a resumption of U.N. arms inspections in Iraq. From a political point of view, this was the worst possible time for a military response to Hussein. With the impeachment vote looming, any action by the President could be challenged as an attempt to distract or delay Congress. On the other hand, if Bill put off air strikes on Iraq, he could be accused of sacrificing national security to avoid the political heat. The Islamic holy month of Ramadan was imminent, and the window of opportunity for an attack was closing. On December 16, Bill's defense and intelligence advisers informed him that the time was right. Bill ordered air strikes to knock out Iraq's known and suspected weapons of mass destruction sites and other military targets.

An openly skeptical Republican leadership postponed the impeachment debate when the bombing started. "Clinton's decision to bomb Iraq is a blatant and disgraceful use of military force for his own personal gain," said Republican Congressman Joel Hefley. Trent Lott, the Senate Republican Majority Leader, publicly disputed the President's judgment. "Both the timing and the policy are subject to question," he said of the military action. Lott backpedaled when his statement was interpreted as an indication that partisan politics came before national security in this Congress.

The House leadership was determined to force a vote on impeachment in the lame duck session, before the Republican majority was reduced to eleven members in January. On December 18, as bombs fell on Iraq, the impeachment debate began. I had refrained from making any direct public statement for several months, but that morning I spoke to a group of reporters outside the White House. "I think the vast majority of Americans share my approval and pride in the job that the President's been doing for our country," I said. "And I think in this holiday season, as we celebrate Christmas and Chanukah and Ramadan—and at the time for reflection and reconciliation among people—we ought to end divisiveness because we can do so much more together."

Dick Gephardt asked me to meet with the House Democratic Caucus on Capitol Hill, right before the scheduled votes on the articles of impeachment. Standing before the Democrats the next morning, I thanked everyone for supporting the Constitution, the Presidency and the leader of their party, my husband.

"You all may be mad at Bill Clinton," I said. "Certainly, I'm not happy about what my husband did. But impeachment is not the answer. Too much is at stake here for us to be distracted from what really matters." I reminded them that we were all American citizens living under the rule of law and that we owed it to our system of government to follow the Constitution. The case for impeachment was part of a political war waged by people determined to sabotage the President's agenda on the economy, education, Social Security, health care, the environment and the search for peace in Northern Ireland, the Balkans and the Middle East—everything we, as Democrats, stood for. We couldn't let it happen. And no matter how the vote went that day, Bill Clinton would not resign.

We all knew last-ditch efforts to avoid impeachment would fail. Walking out through the marble corridors that had seen so much of American history, I was saddened for my country as our cherished system of laws was abused in what amounted to an attempted Congressional coup d'état. As a freshly minted law school graduate, I had studied the politically motivated impeachment of President Andrew Johnson. As a member of the congressional staff that had investigated Richard Nixon, I knew how hard we worked to ensure that the impeachment process was fair and conducted according to the Constitution.

This grave event was nearly upstaged by a bizarre drama on the floor of the House. The night before the voting began, Bob Livingston, the designated Speaker, was exposed as an adulterer. By Saturday morning, as Livingston stood before his colleagues in the grand House chamber of the Capitol, everyone knew he admitted that he had "strayed" in his marriage. Moments after he demanded the President's resignation, amid heckles and angry shouts from the floor, he stunned everyone by resigning his position as Speaker, another unintended victim of his own party's campaign of personal destruction. Like Gingrich, he left the House.

Two articles were defeated, two were adopted. Bill was impeached for perjury in the grand jury and obstruction of justice. He would now be put on trial in the U.S. Senate.

After the impeachment vote, a delegation of Democrats rode buses from the Capitol to the White House in a show of solidarity with the President. I linked arms with Bill as we walked out of the Oval Office to meet them in the Rose Garden. Al Gore gave a moving statement of support, calling the House vote on impeachment "a great disservice to a man I believe will be regarded in the history books as one of our greatest Presidents." Al's approval rating, like mine, soared. The American people had figured out what was going on.

Bill thanked everyone who had stuck by him and promised not to give up. He would serve, he said, "until the last hour of the last day of my term." It was a peculiarly upbeat gathering, given the terrible event that had just occurred, and I was grateful for the public testimonial to Bill. But I was working hard to contain the pain I felt gathering in my back. By the time the event ended and I walked back to the residence, I could hardly stand.

The timing was very bad, because it was Christmas season, and impeachment or no impeachment, the White House was hosting receptions day and night, and that meant standing in receiving lines for hours. I survived a few of them, but soon I was flat on my back and unable to move, the casualty of accumulated tension and, as it turned out, footwear.

One of the White House physicians who examined me called in a physical therapist from the Navy. After the Navy therapist examined me, he asked, "Ma'am, have you been wearing high heels a lot lately?"

"Yes."

"Ma'am," he said, "you shouldn't wear high heels again."

"Never?"

"Well, yes, never." He looked at me curiously, and asked, "With all due respect, ma'am, why would you want to?"

It was both comforting and odd to spend the holidays doing the same things we always did, despite the specter of an impending Senate trial hovering in the room like an uninvited and unwanted guest. I received hundreds of letters of support. Among the most thoughtful was a message from Lady Bird Johnson, who had been following events from her home in Texas:

> Dear Hillary,
>
> You made my day! When I saw you with the President on television with you by his side (was it the South Lawn?), reminding us of the country's progress in many areas such as education and health and how far we have yet to go, I sent a prayer your way. Then I learned that you went to Capitol Hill to speak to Democrats and rally their support.
>
> It made me feel good, and I think that is a gauge for what a great many of our nation's citizens think.
>
> Cheers to you and Admiration,
> Lady Bird Johnson

Lady Bird's words of experience and kindness warmed my heart. It was reassuring that someone who understood the pressures I was under recognized why I was so determined to support my husband.

Once again we spent New Year's Eve at the annual Renaissance Weekend at Hilton Head, South Carolina. So many friends and colleagues went out of their way to encourage us and to thank Bill for his leadership as President. The most moving tribute came from retired Admiral Elmo Zumwalt, Jr., former Chief of Naval Operations during the Vietnam War. Admiral Zumwalt gave a short speech addressed to Chelsea titled "If These Were My Last Words." He wanted her never to lose sight of her father's accomplishments, even as the events in Congress threatened to overshadow them.

"Your father, my commander in chief," he said, "will be remembered as the President: Who reversed fifteen years of decline in our military strength, thus ensuring the continuing viability of our armed forces. . . . Who stopped the killings in Haiti, Bosnia, Ireland and Kosovo. . . . Who moved the peace process forward in the Middle East. . . . Who initiated debate and action to improve social security, our education systems and health care coverage. . . ."

Admiral Zumwalt also told Chelsea that her mother would be remembered "for opening the eyes of the world" to the rights of women and children and for my efforts to improve their lives, as well as for my support of my family in crisis. His words were an invaluable gift to Chelsea—and to me.

Sadly, those were the last words Chelsea would hear from Admiral Zumwalt, who died a year later. He will be remembered by his country as one of the great patriots and humanitarians of his generation, and by me and my family as a true and steadfast friend.

The Senate trial began on January 7, 1999, soon after the 106th Congress was sworn in. Chief Justice William Rehnquist arrived in the Senate Chamber dressed for the occasion. Instead of the usual plain black judicial robes, he wore an outfit he had designed, down to the chevrons of gold braid on its sleeves. In response to questions from the press, he said he got the idea from the costumes in a production of Gilbert & Sullivan's comic opera *Iolanthe*. How fitting that he should wear a theatrical costume to preside over a political farce.

I studiously avoided watching the trial on television, in part because I viewed the entire process as a colossal miscarriage of the Constitution and partly because there was nothing I could do to affect the outcome. Bill's case was in the hands of a superb legal team—the White House lawyers, who included Counsel Chuck Ruff, Deputy Counsel Cheryl Mills, Lanny Breuer, Bruce Lindsey and Greg Craig, who had left a top job at the State Department to join the White House staff, and his personal lawyers, David Kendall and his partner, Nicole Seligman.

I had met with the legal team to offer suggestions about strategy and presentation, but there wasn't much I could contribute other than my support. Because the vote to impeach in the House was considered similar to an indictment, Republican members of the House were sent to the Senate as managers or "prosecutors." They were supposed to present "evidence" of the impeachable offenses while Bill's lawyers would defend him. No live witnesses were introduced. Instead, the House managers relied on grand jury testimony and depositions they conducted of Sid Blumenthal, Vernon Jordan and Monica Lewinsky. Sid Blumenthal has written a fascinating behind-the-scenes account of his experience during the impeachment in his book, *The Clinton Wars*.

The Constitution requires that two-thirds of the Senate vote to convict the President before he can be removed from office. It hadn't yet happened in American history, and I did not expect it would happen now. No one involved seriously thought that sixty-seven Senators would vote to convict, so perhaps the House managers saw no reason to conduct even the semblance of a professional prosecution. There were few rules governing procedures or the evidence presented in the managers' case. As a result, the proceedings bore little resemblance to a real trial—it was more like a group tirade denouncing my husband.

Throughout the five weeks of the spectacle, the President's lawyers made a presentation on the law and the facts that I believe historians and legal scholars will turn to when trying to understand this regrettable moment in American history. In a stirring argument, Cheryl Mills decisively repudiated the House managers' position that acquitting the President would not only undermine the rule of law but also the nation's civil rights laws. Mills, an African American, proclaimed: "I'm not worried about civil rights, because this President's record on civil rights, on women's rights, on all of our rights is unimpeachable. . . . I stand here before you today because President Bill Clinton believed I could stand here for him."

Dale Bumpers, the former Senator from Arkansas, delivered a powerful argument on Bill's behalf. Bumpers, a master orator and Bill's close friend, wove together American history and Arkansas stories to deliver a compelling case in favor of acquittal. He forcefully reminded us that the Constitution was on trial. In his marvelous autobiography, *The Best Lawyer in a One-Lawyer Town*, Bumpers relates how Bill had called to ask him to speak on his behalf. After thinking it over, Bumpers realized that "Every family in America could relate, to one degree or another, to the trials and tribulations, so much a part of the human drama, that the Clintons had experienced." And then he asked, "Where were the elements of forgiveness and redemption, the very foundation of Christianity?"

Throughout the trial, I never doubted that we would prevail in the end. I was relying more on my faith every day. It reminded me of an old saying from Sunday school: Faith is like stepping off a cliff and expecting one of two outcomes—you will either land on solid ground or you will be taught to fly.

DARE TO COMPETE

THE CONSTITUTIONAL SHOWDOWN ON CAPITOL Hill provided an odd backdrop for the growing speculation about my entry into the New York Senate race. I still had no interest in running for Senator Moynihan's seat, but by the beginning of 1999, the Democratic leadership was in a full-court press to change my mind. Tom Daschle, the Senate Minority leader whom I greatly respected, called to encourage me. So did many Democrats from New York and around the country. As flattering as the attention was, I felt that other seasoned New York Democrats would be better suited to enter the race. Congresswoman Nita Lowey, New York State Comptroller H. Carl McCall and Andrew Cuomo, Secretary of Housing and Urban Development in the Clinton Administration, were at the top of the list.

The likely GOP nominee, New York City's mayor, Rudolph Giuliani, would be a formidable opponent for any Democratic candidate. Party leaders, worried about losing a long-time Democratic seat, were intent on fielding a similarly high-profile candidate who could raise the staggering amounts of money that such a race requires. In a sense, I was a desperation choice—a well-known public figure who might be able to offset Giuliani's national profile and his party's deep pockets. In that context, it wasn't surprising that the idea of my candidacy was resuscitated a few days into the new year during the taping of NBC's *Meet the Press.*

The guest on Sunday, January 3, was Senator Robert Torricelli of New Jersey, who, as head of the Democratic Senatorial Campaign Committee, was responsible for recruiting candidates and raising money for Democratic campaigns. The host, Tim Russert, had asked

Torricelli about the race before the show and announced on the air that Torricelli believed I would run.

When I heard about Torricelli's remarks, I called him. "Bob, you're out there talking about my life," I said. "You know I'm not running. Why are you saying this?" Torricelli sidestepped the question, knowing full well that he had opened the floodgates. Andrew Cuomo and Carl McCall took themselves out of the race, choosing to focus instead on the 2002 gubernatorial contest, and Nita Lowey said she would wait to decide whether to wage a campaign of her own.

With each of these developments, public speculation about my entry into the race intensified. But privately, I was being counseled against it. The few friends I spoke to consistently urged me not to run. My top White House staff were also opposed. They worried about the stresses I would be subjected to as a candidate and the emotional costs of a lengthy campaign.

When King Hussein of Jordan died on February 7 after a brave struggle with cancer, Bill and I put everything else aside for a few days to make another long, mournful journey to the Middle East to the Jordanian capital of Amman. Former Presidents Ford, Carter and Bush traveled on Air Force One. The prospects for peace in the Middle East suffered irreparable losses with the deaths of two great men, Rabin and now Hussein. The streets of Amman were crowded with mourners from all over the world. Queen Noor, dressed in black and wearing a white head scarf, graciously greeted the dignitaries who came to pay their respects to her remarkable husband. Shortly before his death, the King had designated his eldest son, Abdullah, as his successor. King Abdullah and his gifted Queen, Rania, have more than fulfilled expectations, bringing great energy and grace to their difficult responsibilities.

When we returned home from the King's funeral, the impeachment trial was a dark cloud hanging over our family. Bill and I were still struggling to repair our relationship and trying to protect Chelsea from the fallout on Capitol Hill. Thrown into this mix was the public pressure I felt to make a decision about the Senate race, a decision that would have immediate and long-term consequences in my life and my family's.

A conversation with Harold Ickes, an expert on New York politics, persuaded me that I had to acknowledge the growing public pressure to run and take the question of a campaign seriously. Harold's greatest asset as a friend is his candor, even bluntness. Although he is a truly sweet and lovely man, he has a bark that can scare you to death. Every other word is an expletive, even when he's dishing out a compliment. In his typically colorful way, he offered some advice.

"If you think you're not gonna run, then go out and issue a Shermanesque statement," Harold said. "But if you're still mulling it over, don't say anything yet. With impeachment going on, nobody is going to press you on it right now anyway."

Harold and I agreed to meet on February 12, the day, it turned out, that the Senate was due to vote on impeachment. I was confident that a majority of the Senate would be guided by the Constitution and vote to acquit. As we awaited the outcome, I listened intently as Harold assessed the New York political landscape and explained the vicissitudes of a New York Senate campaign. He spread out a large map of the state, and we pored over it for hours as he offered a running commentary about the obstacles I would face. He pointed to towns from Montauk to Plattsburgh to Niagara Falls, and it became clear that to take a campaign to New York's 19 million citizens, I would have to physically cover a state of 54,000 square miles. On top of that I would have to master the intricacies of local politics, of dramatic differences in the personalities, cultures and economies of upstate New York and the suburbs. New York City was its own universe: a cauldron of competing politicians and interest groups. The five boroughs were like individual mini-states, each presenting needs and challenges different from counties and cities upstate and also from the suburbs of neighboring Long Island and Westchester.

As our meeting stretched over hours, Harold zeroed in on all of the negatives of entering the race. I was not a New York native, had never run for office and would face Giuliani, an intimidating opponent. No woman had ever won statewide in New York on her own. The national Republican Party would do everything in its power to demonize me and my politics. A campaign would be nasty and emotionally draining. And how would I campaign in New York while I was First Lady? The list went on.

"I don't even know if you'd be a good candidate, Hillary," he said.

I didn't know either.

That afternoon, the U.S. Senate voted to acquit Bill of the impeachment charges by a wide margin. Neither charge against him received a majority of votes, let alone the required two-thirds. The outcome itself was anticlimactic, causing no elation, only relief. Most important, the Constitution and the Presidency remained intact.

I still hadn't decided whether to run, but, thanks to Harold, I now had a more realistic view of what a campaign would require. With the impeachment trial behind us, it was time to address the issue. On February 16, my office released a statement acknowledging that I would give careful thought to a potential candidacy and would decide later in the year.

Harold gave me a list of 100 New Yorkers to contact, and, in late February, I began calling and meeting with each of them—beginning with Senator Moynihan and his wife, Liz, who had run her husband's campaigns and was extraordinarily knowledgeable about New York politics. Senator Moynihan offered generous public support, telling NBC's Tim Russert, who had once worked for him, that my "magnificent, young, bright, able Illinois-Arkansas enthusiasm" would suit New York and New Yorkers. "She'd be welcome and she'd win," he said. That took my breath away—especially the adjective "young." I also consulted with former New York City Mayors Ed Koch and David Dinkins, who were supportive and encouraging. Senator Schumer was helpful and practical, having just survived his own brutal statewide campaign. Democratic Speaker Sheldon Silver, party Chair Judith Hope and members of Congress, mayors, state legislators, county chairmen, labor leaders, activists and friends all weighed in with their views. So did Robert F. Kennedy, Jr., an environmental activist whose father had held the seat before Senator Moynihan. He, too, was enthusiastic and promised to tutor me on pressing environmental issues in the state.

Yet, as encouraging as many people were, plenty of others worked feverishly to discourage me. Close friends, in particular, couldn't fathom why I would consider a grueling Senate campaign after the emotional upheaval of the past few years. Life on the campaign trail would be a far cry from the comfort and security of the White House. Each day would begin at dawn and seldom be finished before the wee hours of the morning. This peripatetic existence would mean eating meals on the fly, living out of a suitcase for months on end and relying on friends around the state to let me stay in their homes when I was on the road. Worst of all, it would mean little time during our last year in the White House with my family and even less time with friends.

There were also doubts about whether Congress was where I could be most effective. For months, I had been mulling over my options for life after the White House. Some friends argued that I would have more influence promoting change in the international arena than in the one hundred–member Senate. After nearly three decades as an advocate and eight years as First Lady, I had accumulated broad experience working on behalf of women, children and families. Even if I managed to win, I wasn't sure it was worth giving up a visible platform for an intense political campaign and the daily demands of life as a politician. And there were more opportunities to consider: I had been approached about running foundations, hosting a television show, assuming a college presidency or becoming a corporate CEO. These were appealing choices and far more comfortable than the prospect of a tough Senate race.

Mandy Grunwald, a skilled media consultant who grew up in New York and was a veteran of Senator Moynihan's recent campaigns, echoed Harold's warnings. She cautioned that I would have to learn to deal with an aggressive New York press corps (not one of my specialties). Mandy bluntly explained that I would not receive any free passes just because I was the new kid on the block: Mistakes were not overlooked by the New York press. They are often blown up in the tabloids, broadcast on the local news at 6, 7, 12, 4, 5, 6, 10 and 11 o'clock, and dissected by newspaper columnists. Then the radio talk show hosts get their turn. And that wouldn't be all. Given the historic nature of a First Lady running for the Senate, I could also expect more than the usual New York press contingent scrutinizing my campaign. Just the prospect of my running prompted national and international media outlets to flood my White House press office with interview requests.

The treacherous waters of New York politics also caused me some concern. Knowledgeable New Yorkers frankly advised that I could never win because I wasn't Irish, Italian, Catholic or Jewish, and an ethnic identity was imperative in such a diverse state. Another constituency that would pose an unusual challenge was Democratic women, particularly professional women my age who normally would be my natural base but were skeptical of my motives and my decision to stay married to Bill.

One day in the spring, I was running down the list of hurdles I would face when Patti Solis Doyle, my scheduler and an astute political adviser, interrupted my monologue and blurted out: "Hillary, I just don't think you can win this race." She was so sure that I shouldn't— and wouldn't—run that she and her husband, Jim, made tentative plans to move home to Chicago.

My White House staff had other reasons to worry about what it would mean if the First Lady suddenly turned into a candidate for the U.S. Senate. My staff was going full steam ahead with my domestic policy agenda. They wanted to be sure I would continue to support these efforts if I ran. I told them that, Senate race or not, I would continue advocating for all of our initiatives—from Save America's Treasures to after-school care. The prospect of a campaign also raised the question of whether I could continue to serve as a representative of American interests abroad. Throughout Bill's tenure, I had traveled the world on behalf of women's rights, human rights, religious tolerance and democracy. Thinking and acting globally might be exactly the opposite of what I would need to do if I were running a New York campaign. In the midst of my deliberations, I had to keep commitments for official visits to Egypt, Tunisia and Morocco and a trip to a Kosovar refugee camp along the Macedonian border. I had spoken out strongly in favor of Bill's leadership of NATO in the bombing campaign to force Slobodan Milošević's troops out of Kosovo. I helped the Macedonians reopen textile factories to put people back to work in order to avoid economic instability that could have undermined NATO's goal of returning the Kosovars to their homes.

As the spring progressed, I hashed over all of the campaign scenarios with advisers and friends, and each discussion turned into a spirited debate about my future. One thing we talked about is euphemistically referred to as "the spouse problem." In my case, that was an understatement. It's always difficult to figure out the appropriate role for the wife or husband of a political candidate. My dilemma was unique. Some worried that Bill was still so popular in New York and such a towering political figure in America that I would never be able to establish an independent political voice. Others thought the controversy attached to him would overwhelm my message. Logistical considerations relating to "my spouse" were tricky. If I were to announce my candidacy at a kick-off event, would the President of the United States sit quietly behind me on the stage, or would he speak too? Over the course of the race, would he campaign on my behalf, as he would for other Democratic candidates across the country, or would that consign me to being his surrogate again? A fine line would have to be drawn between asserting myself as a candidate in my own right and taking advantage of the President's support and advice.

One benefit of my decision-making process was that Bill and I were talking again about matters other than the future of our relationship. Over time, we both began to relax. He was anxious to be helpful, and I welcomed his expertise. Bill patiently talked over each of my concerns and carefully evaluated the odds I faced. The tables were now turned, as he played for me the role I had always performed for him. Once he had given his advice, it was my decision to make. We both knew that if I ran, I would be on my own as I had never been before. With each conversation, I found myself swinging back and forth. One minute it seemed like a great idea to run. The next minute, I thought it was crazy. So I kept pondering what to do, waiting for lightning to strike.

I needed a push. Finally, I got one, but it didn't come from a political adviser or Democratic leader. In March, I went to New York City to join tennis legend Billie Jean King at an event promoting an HBO special about women in sports. We gathered at the Lab School in the Chelsea neighborhood of Manhattan, joined by dozens of young women athletes who were assembled on a stage adorned with a giant banner that said "Dare to Compete," the title of the HBO film. Sofia Totti, the captain of the girls' basketball team, introduced me. As I went to shake her hand, she leaned toward me and whispered in my ear.

"Dare to compete, Mrs. Clinton," she said. "Dare to compete."

Her comment caught me off guard, so much so that I left the event and began to think: Could I be afraid to do something I had urged countless other women to do? Why am I vacillating about taking on this race? Why aren't I thinking more seriously about it? Maybe I should "dare to compete."

The encouragement from Sofia Totti and so many others reminded me of a scene in one of my favorite movies, *A League of Their Own*. The star of a women's professional baseball team, played by Geena Davis, wants to leave the team before its season ends to return home with her husband. When the team's coach, played by Tom Hanks, challenges her decision, she says, "It just got too hard." Hanks replies, "It's supposed to be hard. If it wasn't hard, everyone would do it—the hard is what makes it great." After years as a political spouse, I had no idea whether I could step from the sidelines into the arena, but I began to think that I might enjoy an independent role in politics. All over the United States and in scores of countries, I had spoken out about the importance of women participating in politics and government, seeking elective office and using the power of their own voices to shape public policy and chart their nations' futures. How could I pass up an opportunity to do the same?

Many of my friends weren't persuaded. One afternoon in the spring, Maggie Williams and I went for a long walk. One of my closest friends and advisers, Maggie is a woman of great political acumen. She knew time was running out on making a decision, and for more than an hour she listened to me talk about whether I should enter the race.

"I just don't know what to do," I told her.

"I think it's kooky," she said. "And anyone who cares about you will tell you the same thing."

"Well, I think I might do it," I said.

I wasn't surprised by Maggie's reaction. She was protective and didn't want me to be hurt. But by trying to talk me out of it, Maggie helped me think through and face the reasons to go forward.

Some people said that serving in the Senate might be a letdown after the White House. But all the issues I care about are affected by the U.S. Senate. And if I wasn't a Senator, I certainly would be trying to influence those who were. "The U.S. Senate is the most important democratic body in the world," Bob Rubin told me. "It would be an honor to be elected and to serve." I agreed.

The mechanics of a campaign began to seem more manageable too. I thought I could win if I could raise the $25 million needed for a statewide race in New York. Our good friend Terry McAuliffe, a native of Syracuse and an experienced and effective fundraiser, told me that if I were willing to work harder than I ever had in my life, I could win. That was encouraging. I also thought that I could make inroads in traditional Republican bastions. Parts of upstate New York reminded me of neighboring Pennsylvania, where my father had his roots. And many of rural New York's problems were similar to those that had plagued Arkansas: hard-pressed farmers, disappearing manufacturing jobs and young people leaving for better opportunities. Besides, Mayor Giuliani didn't seem eager to spend time outside New York City, which was still predominantly Democratic. If I proved to New York voters that I understood the issues their families faced and was determined to work hard for them, I just might be able to do it.

If electoral politics sometimes seemed to be a universe of its own, I

still had plenty of doses of reality to keep things in perspective throughout the late spring and early summer of 1999. Susan McDougal was finally acquitted of obstruction of justice in the Whitewater case on April
12, 1999, having served eighteen months in jail for refusing to testify
before the Whitewater grand jury. Over the course of her trial, other
witnesses had stepped forward to say they, too, had been pressured by
Starr. It was another repudiation of Starr's legal tactics, but I hated the
inordinate price Susan McDougal had paid. She steadfastly maintained
that Starr had pressured her to falsely implicate Bill and me, and when
she refused, she was held in contempt and imprisoned, doing some of
her time in solitary confinement. In Jung Chang's *Wild Swans*, the story
of three women's ordeals in China from before the Communist
takeover to the Cultural Revolution, I ran across another Chinese saying that summed up my opinion of Starr's investigations: "Where there
is a will to condemn, there is evidence."

Then on April 20, two students at Columbine High School in Colorado opened fire on their classmates and held their school under siege
for hours before turning their guns on themselves. Twelve students and
one teacher died in the massacre. The teenage killers reportedly felt
alienated at their school and had meticulously planned the attack as a
demonstration of their own power and desire for revenge. They were
able to obtain a small arsenal of pistols, shotguns and other weapons,
some of which were concealed in their trench coats when they went
into the school.

A month after the shootings, Bill and I went to Littleton, Colorado,
to visit with the families of victims and survivors. It was gut wrenching
to see the faces of parents who were living through their worst nightmare, dealing with the loss of their own children in such a senseless,
disturbing act of violence. Parents and teenagers alike asked Bill and me
to make sure these horrible losses were not in vain. "You can give us a
culture of values instead of a culture of violence," Bill told a gathering
of Columbine students in the gymnasium of a neighboring high school.
"You can help us to keep guns out of the wrong hands. You can help us
to make sure kids who are in trouble—and there will always be some—
are identified early and reached and helped."

The Columbine tragedy was not the first, nor the last, episode involving gun violence at an American high school. But it ignited a call
for more federal action to keep guns out of the hands of the violent,
troubled and young—a lethal combination. Bill and I convened an

event attended by forty members of Congress from both parties to announce a White House proposal to raise the legal age of handgun ownership to twenty-one and limit purchases of handguns to one per month. And I spoke out again about the pervasiveness of violence on television, in movies and in video games. Despite the public outcry, Congress failed to act on two simple measures regarding guns: to close the so-called gun-show loophole that allows people to buy guns without background checks and to require child safety locks on guns.

This Congressional lack of will to buck the all-powerful gun lobby and pass sensible gun safety measures made me think about what I might be able to do, as a Senator, to pass common sense legislation. In an interview in May, I told CBS anchor Dan Rather that, if I ran for the Senate, it would be because of what I had learned in places like Littleton—and in spite of what I had lived through in Washington.

The Senate race began to take shape. Giuliani met in Texas with Governor George W. Bush, who had just announced the formation of his presidential exploratory committee. The Mayor also labeled me a carpetbagger and announced that he would go to Arkansas to raise money for his campaign. A clever ploy, I thought—one that raised him both attention and money and gave me a taste of the campaign to come. Rep. Lowey, one of the most effective and popular members of Congress, announced that she would not run. In June, I took the first concrete steps necessary for a Senate campaign, announcing that I would form an exploratory committee. I enlisted the help of media consultant Mandy Grunwald and Mark Penn, the shrewd and insightful pollster who worked with Bill, and I began interviewing potential campaign staff.

During the White House years, I had often escaped to New York City with my mother or Chelsea to take in Broadway shows, museum exhibits or just to visit friends. Even before I contemplated a run for the Senate, the state had been on the top of our short list of places to live after Bill's term ended. This desire grew over the years and had now hardened into a firm decision. While Bill intended to build his presidential library in Arkansas and to spend time there, he also loved New York. From a purely practical standpoint, it was a perfect base of operations for him, given the amount of time he would be traveling and speaking at home and overseas, and continuing his public service through his foundation.

We had already talked about buying a house, and before long, we were house hunting. But this ordinarily routine process was complicated by the security concerns of the Secret Service. We couldn't live on certain kinds of streets, and any house we bought had to have space for security personnel. Nevertheless, the search was fun for me. We had lived in the Arkansas Governor's Mansion and the White House, but we hadn't owned our own home for almost twenty years. Eventually we found the perfect place, an old farm house and barn in Chappaqua, north of New York City in Westchester County.

I also started reaching out to potential contributors for the first time on my own behalf. At a major fundraiser for the Democratic Party in Washington on June 7, 1999, Bill and I were welcomed on stage by former Texas Governor Ann Richards, whose sharp wit and homespun humor were legendary on the political circuit.

"Hillary Clinton, the next junior senator from New York, and, of course, her lovely husband, Bill," she said in her deep Texas drawl. "Man, I bet he's really going to shake up that Senate spouses club."

Bill accepted the good-natured teasing and delighted in the public support I was receiving. He understood the sacrifices I had made over the years so that he could serve in government. Now, recognizing that I had a chance to move beyond the derivative role of political spouse and test my political wings, he encouraged me to forge ahead. It would be awkward for him to watch from the sidelines, but he gave me unconditional and enthusiastic support as his wife—and as a candidate.

I received a boost in late June from another unexpected source: Father George Tribou, the priest who had run the Catholic boys' high school in Little Rock for many years. He had become a friend of mine even though he disagreed with my pro-choice position. He had stayed overnight in the White House, and I had arranged for him to meet His Holiness Pope John Paul II during the papal visit to St. Louis in 1999. Father Tribou wrote me a letter dated June 24, 1999:

> Dear Hillary,
>
> I want to tell you what I have been telling students for 50 years:
> It is my opinion that on Judgment Day the first question God asks is not about the Ten Commandments (although He gets to them later!) but what He asks each of us is this:
> WHAT DID YOU DO WITH THE TIME AND THE TALENTS I GAVE YOU?. . .

Those who feel you are not up to handling the hostile
New York press and the taunts of your opponents fail to realize
that, having been tried in the fire, you can handle anything.
. . . Bottom line: run, Hillary, run! My prayers will be with you
all the way.

The most difficult decisions I have made in my life were to stay married to Bill and to run for the Senate from New York. By now I knew I wanted our marriage to last if it could because I loved Bill and I realized how much I cherished the years we had spent together. I knew that I could not have parented Chelsea alone as well as we had together. I had no doubt that I could construct a satisfying life by myself and make a good living, but I hoped Bill and I could grow old together. We were both committed to rebuilding our marriage with the tools of our faith, love and shared past. With my mind clearer about where I wanted to go with Bill, I felt freer to take the first steps toward a race for the Senate.

I knew that any campaign would be a baptism by fire. Although by now I was a seasoned campaigner, going from one end of the country to another—and everywhere in between—on behalf of candidates for Governor, Congress and President, I had never been out on the stump campaigning for myself. I would have to learn to address crowds in the first person—I was accustomed to referring to "he," "she" or "we," not "I." And there was a real possibility I would have to speak out against Clinton Administration policies if they weren't beneficial to New York. But for the moment, I focused on getting to know my prospective constituents. I planned a "listening tour" that would take me around New York in July and August and allow me to hear from citizens and local leaders about their concerns and aspirations for their families and communities. The tour began in the most appropriate place to launch a campaign for the seat held by Senator Daniel Patrick Moynihan—his beautiful 900-acre farm in Pindars Corners. When I arrived there on July 7, I found the Senator, his wife, Liz, and more than two hundred reporters waiting to hear my announcement. My veteran advance man, Rick Jasculca, was astonished. "There's even a reporter here from Japan!" he said.

With the Senator by my side, I announced that I was forming an official campaign committee in anticipation of running for the U.S. Senate. "I suppose the questions on everyone's mind are: Why the Senate?

Why New York? And why me?" I said to the assembled press. Then I spoke briefly about issues that mattered to me and to New York and acknowledged the legitimacy of questions about my running from a state where I had never lived.

"I think that's a very fair question, and I fully understand people raising it. And I think I have some real work to do to get out and listen and learn from the people of New York and demonstrate that what I'm for is maybe as important, if not more important, than where I'm from."

A few minutes later, Senator Moynihan and I walked back to his farm house for a brunch of ham and biscuits. Soon I was on my way.

NEW YORK

I HAD EXPECTED HURDLES AS A ROOKIE CANDIDATE, and I certainly encountered some, but I never imagined how much I would enjoy the campaign. From the moment I left Senator Moynihan's farm to begin my listening tour in July 1999, I was captivated by the places I visited and the people I met throughout New York.

New Yorkers, with their resilience, diversity and passion for the future, represented everything I treasure about America. I came to know the small towns and farms set in the rolling countryside "Upstate" and the cities like Buffalo, Rochester, Syracuse, Binghamton and Albany that were once centers of the American Industrial Revolution and were now retooling themselves for the Information Age. I explored the Adirondacks and the Catskills and vacationed on the shores of Skaneateles Lake and Lake Placid. I visited the campuses of New York's great public and private colleges and universities. I met with groups of business owners and farmers from Long Island to the Canadian border who explained to me all the challenges they faced. And I settled into my new home, part of the downstate suburbs whose fine public schools and parks reminded me of the neighborhood where I grew up.

I loved New York City's raw energy, its mix of ethnic neighborhoods and its big-hearted, straight-talking people. I made new friends in every corner of the city, visiting diners, union halls, schools, churches, synagogues, shelters and penthouses. New York's diverse communities are living reminders that the city symbolizes America's unique promise to the rest of the world, a fact that would be tragically underscored on September 11, 2001, when Manhattan was attacked by terrorists who hated and feared the freedom, diversity and choices that America represents.

My campaign was a total immersion in the state's history: The Native Americans of the Iroquois Confederacy, whose commitment to democratic principles influenced the thinking of our Founders, lived throughout New York before it was a state; the Revolutionary War was fought and won in the Champlain, Mohawk and Hudson Valleys; barge traffic along the Erie Canal opened up the rest of the nation to economic growth; the world's arts, letters and culture were shaped in New York City; the movements for the abolition of slavery, women's suffrage, labor unions, civil rights, progressive politics and gay rights all sprang from New York soil. I came to love the rhythm of events across the huge, sprawling state. I did the salsa down Fifth Avenue in the Puerto Rican Day Parade, ate a sausage sandwich at the State Fair and attempted the polka at the Polish festival in Cheektowaga.

Balancing the requirements of the campaign with my obligations as First Lady presented a unique challenge. Doing two jobs at once tested both the White House staff, who had stuck with me through thick and thin for nearly eight years, and the dedicated team of campaign aides working on the Senate race in New York. Occasionally, the White House requested that I take a trip or do an event based on the President's priorities or my interests as First Lady, causing my campaign advisers to blanch at the thought of my involvement in anything that wasn't related to New York or its issues. Despite these inevitable tensions, everyone performed superbly.

Not that the campaign was idyllic. Especially at the start, I made my share of mistakes. And mistakes in New York politics aren't easily brushed aside. When the Yankees came to the White House to celebrate their World Series win in 1999, manager Joe Torre gave me a cap, which I promptly donned. Bad move. Nobody believed what *The Washington Post* and *San Francisco Examiner* had reported years earlier, that I was a die-hard Mickey Mantle fan. They just thought I was pretending to be what I obviously was not: a lifelong New Yorker. Over the next few days, my prospective constituents saw a lot of pictures of me in that Yankees cap, with less-than-flattering captions to go along with the photos.

The worst instance came during an official visit to Israel in the fall of 1999, when I attended an event as First Lady with Suha Arafat, wife of the Palestinian leader. Mrs. Arafat spoke before me in Arabic. Listening to an Arabic-to-English translation through headphones, neither I nor other members of our delegation—including U.S. Embassy

staff, Middle East experts and respected American Jewish leaders—
heard her outrageous remark suggesting that Israel had used poison gas
to control Palestinians. When I went to the podium moments later to
deliver my remarks, Mrs. Arafat greeted me with an embrace, a traditional greeting. Had I been aware of her hateful words, I would have
denounced them on the spot. The New York tabloids ran photos of me
receiving a kiss on the cheek from Suha Arafat, with accompanying stories about her remarks. Many Jewish voters were understandably upset
with Mrs. Arafat's comments and disappointed that I had not taken the
opportunity to disavow her remarks. My campaign eventually overcame the fallout, but I had learned a hard lesson about the hazards of
merging my role in the international diplomatic arena with the complexities of local New York politics.

Throughout the campaign, there was a humorous disconnect between the national view of the race and the way it was covered in New
York. National columnists and cable pundits routinely predicted that
the "carpetbagger" issue would kill me, and I would drop out of the
race. In their frequent commentaries, they also admonished me for refusing to speak to the press. This was a source of great amusement for
my staff, because I routinely granted interviews to the New York reporters covering the race. My relations with the press improved with
time under the tutelage of my communications director, Howard Wolfson. Howard had worked for Nita Lowey and Chuck Schumer and understood the rough and tumble of dealing with the New York media.
He became a familiar and eloquent presence on television, speaking for
the campaign. With his help, I eventually learned to relax and let down
my guard with the press, and I came to enjoy the daily interactions with
reporters assigned to cover my campaign.

As unnerving as it was to find my footing in the shifting sands
of New York politics, I had no plans to drop out of the race. I simply
tried to stay focused on getting to know the people of New York and
letting them get a sense of me. Despite the state's size, I was determined
to run a grassroots campaign rather than communicate to prospective
constituents solely through paid media. While radio and television
publicity is important and necessary, nothing substitutes for face-to-
face conversations in which the candidate often learns more than the
voters do.

My goal was to visit all sixty-two counties, and for more than a year

I traveled the state in a Ford conversion van—nicknamed the HRC Speedwagon by the press—with my longtime aide Kelly Craighead and Allison Stein, an energetic campaign staffer. I stopped at diners and cafés along the road, just as Bill and I had done during his campaigns. Even if only a handful of people were inside, I'd sit down, have a cup of coffee and talk about whatever topics were on their minds. Campaign professionals call this "retail politics," but to me, it was the best way to stay in touch with people's everyday concerns.

This hectic existence was a far cry from life in the White House. Bill and I had moved some of our belongings into the house we had purchased on the end of a cul de sac in Chappaqua, less than an hour north of New York City, but I did not have much free time to spend there. The place was usually empty except for the required contingent of Secret Service agents, who set up their command post in an old renovated barn in the backyard. I rarely got to sleep before midnight, and I usually hit the road by 7 A.M. If there was time, I would stop for muffins, egg sandwiches and coffee at Lange's, a great family delicatessen down the road from my house.

But instead of feeling tired, I found that I drew energy from the campaign itself. Not only was I getting a nonstop crash course in New York and its issues, I was discovering my capacities and limits for life as a political candidate. And I was finally moving beyond my role as a surrogate campaigner and allowing myself to operate on my own. It's a slow process with a steep learning curve. With so many advisers, friends and supporters offering constant—and often conflicting—advice, I was learning how to listen carefully, weigh the options and then go with my instincts.

I finally felt that I was starting to connect to voters. Gradually, I could sense the mood of the electorate shifting my way. When I first began campaigning, no matter what part of the state I visited, people came out to see me in large numbers. This was not necessarily a groundswell of support. Rather, the crowd viewed me as a curiosity. After two or three visits to many towns and cities, I became a more familiar presence, and my prospective constituents seemed genuinely comfortable sharing their stories and worries with me. We had real conversations about the issues that mattered to them, and people began to care less about where I was from than what I was for. Upstate voters, even Republicans, listened carefully to my proposals for revitalizing the region's economy. They asked tough questions, laughed at some of my inept jokes and often had a kind comment about my hair. I felt increasingly welcomed wherever I stopped.

Learning about the variety and complexity of the state's political terrain was important to me. And so was reaching out to women, some of whom were disappointed or offended that I had stayed married to Bill. I respected their questions and hoped they would understand that I had to make a decision that was right for me and my family.

I didn't want to give speeches to explain such a private part of myself. I attended small gatherings at the homes of women supporters in different parts of the state. The host invited about twenty friends and neighbors to have coffee with me. We talked informally, away from the camera lights and political reporters. I answered questions about my marriage, why I moved to New York, health care, child care and whatever else was on their minds. Gradually, many women who were otherwise inclined to support me seemed willing to accept my decision to stay with Bill, even if they would have chosen differently.

My campaign also benefited from what is called a "bump"—a surge of support—after my appearance in January 2000 on *The Late Show with David Letterman*. One television appearance on a late-night talk show generated as much or more attention than days' worth of speeches about the issues. I hadn't even planned to go on the show, at least not so far in advance of the election. But Letterman regularly called Howard, pleading for me to appear. Each time, Howard put him off, which became a running joke and a nightly staple of Letterman's opening monologue. After a month of Letterman's ribbing, I agreed to come on as a guest on January 12.

I hoped it would be fun, but I also knew that late-night comics sometimes skewer their guests, so I was a little nervous. Letterman, who lives near Chappaqua, asked me about our new house and warned me that "every idiot in the area is going to drive by honking now."

"Oh, was that you?" I said. Letterman and the audience roared, and, after that, I relaxed and had a great time. Some months later, I branched out into other comedic venues, performing a deadpan routine as a "carpetbagger" at the annual press dinner in Albany, and later appearing on Jay Leno's *Tonight Show*.

In February 2000, I formally declared my candidacy at the State University of New York in Purchase, near our home in Chappaqua.

The crowd was filled with jubilant supporters and political leaders from all over the state. Bill, Chelsea and my mother were all there. Senator Moynihan introduced me and told of his visits with Eleanor Roosevelt at her home in Hyde Park. He paid me the ultimate compliment, saying, "Hillary, Eleanor Roosevelt would love you."

Patti Solis Doyle, the first person I had hired in 1992, coordinated my White House and campaign schedules, and she later took a leave of absence from the government to work full-time in New York, overseeing logistics and helping to run campaign strategy. Patti also worked with the fast-growing and influential Latino community, whose enthusiastic support of my campaign delighted me. I was so proud of Patti and the exceptional job she did for me. I often thought back to our first day in the White House, when her Mexican immigrant parents, who had dreamed of a better life for their six children, came to the Inauguration and cried with joy that their daughter was on the staff of the First Lady of the United States.

On the campaign, Patti joined an experienced and talented team led by my campaign manager, Bill de Blasio, who proved to be an outstanding strategist and trusted emissary among the many communities of New York; communications director Howard Wolfson, who ran an extraordinary rapid response operation; political director Ramon Martinez, who shared his sharp political instincts and encouraged me to reach out to new constituencies and "show them some love"; Gigi Georges, who coordinated my campaign with other Democratic candidates in New York and mobilized a genuine grassroots effort; deputy campaign manager for policy Neera Tanden, who had mastered every detail and nuance of the issues facing the state; research director Glen Weiner, who knew more about my opponents than their own staffs probably did; and finance director Gabrielle Fialkoff, who gracefully handled the thankless but critical job of raising the money to make the campaign possible. All of them worked night and day with dozens of other campaign staffers and thousands of volunteers on what became one of the most effective campaigns I have ever seen.

More good news was that Chelsea had taken enough extra courses at Stanford to be able to come home for the first half of her senior year to help her father in the White House and me in New York. She joined our Speedwagon crew to campaign for me whenever she could, which always boosted my spirits. She was a natural on the campaign trail. I was so proud of the young woman she had become and grateful that she had emerged from eight trying years as a kind, caring person with her head on straight. I am very lucky to be her mother.

For the first months of the campaign, I'd taken most of the heat from the media. Now it was the Mayor's turn. New Yorkers and the press took note that Giuliani was making little effort, other than fundraising, to win the Senate seat. He ran a campaign that was primarily New York City oriented. He rarely traveled outside his home base, and, when he did, he gave the impression that he would rather be home. He had offered no ideas for dealing with the faltering upstate economy or with racial tensions simmering beneath the surface in New York City. And he began to make mistakes.

A fatal police shooting in New York City in March of a black man named Patrick Dorismond underscored the Mayor's political vulnerabilities. Giuliani's handling of this tragic case inflamed old hostilities between his office and the city's minority populations. In this situation, the Mayor exacerbated a crisis when a calm and reassuring tone was needed. Citizens in many neighborhoods, especially minority ones, felt that the police under the Mayor's leadership could not be trusted. Their wariness was fed by well-known cases like the shooting of Amadou Diallo in the Bronx the year before. Police officers, in turn, were legitimately frustrated that they were being misunderstood while trying to do their jobs effectively because of a city leadership at war with the communities they were trying to protect. When Giuliani released Dorismond's sealed juvenile records, casting aspersions on a man who was dead, he merely drove the wedge deeper and intensified the distrust.

The more Giuliani continued with his divisive rhetoric, the more determined I was to offer a different approach. In a speech at Riverside Church in Manhattan, I laid out a plan for improving relations between the police and minorities, including better recruitment, training and compensation for the NYPD. Then I went to Harlem to speak at the Bethel A.M.E. Church.

Giuliani's handling of the Dorismond case was wrong, and I intended to call him on it. Instead of easing the tensions and uniting the city, he had poured salt in the wound.

"New York has a real problem, and we all know it," I said. "All of us, it seems, except for the Mayor." The packed sanctuary erupted in cheers and hallelujahs.

My appearance in Harlem was a turning point in the campaign. After trailing Giuliani for months, I had finally gained traction, and I was even doing well upstate. Sustained attention to the voters and their local issues was paying off in growing support. I felt like I was beginning to get the hang of campaigning, and I was finding my political voice.

In mid-May, I was formally nominated as the U.S. Senate candidate from New York at the state Democratic convention in Albany. It was an enthusiastic gathering that brought together more than ten thousand urban, rural and suburban party activists and political leaders, including Senators Moynihan and Schumer and many others whose generous advice and support carried me to the campaign finish line. At the last minute, the President of the United States appeared—much to the delight of the crowd—and of the Democratic nominee.

Shortly after my nomination, a seismic shift rattled the New York political landscape. On May 19, Mayor Giuliani announced his withdrawal from the Senate race after being diagnosed with prostate cancer and following news reports about his long-running extramarital affair. Suddenly, he was the one thrashing out his personal life in public. In spite of our political differences, I took no pleasure in this ironic twist, knowing all too well the private pain for everyone involved, especially the Giuliani children.

Mayor Giuliani ended his term with strength and compassion, reassuring and comforting the nation after the attacks on September 11, 2001. Because of our work together on behalf of the city and the victims of terrorism, we developed a productive and friendly relationship, which, I think, came as a surprise to both of us.

The Mayor's departure from the race was not the welcome relief that some anticipated. For months, I had planned a campaign against him. He may have been my toughest opponent, but I felt that my candidacy presented a clear choice to New York voters, and voters were responding. By the time his campaign ended, I was eight or ten points ahead, according to public opinion polls. Now I had to start over with a brand new opponent, Congressman Rick Lazio.

My campaign left little time for anything else in my life. When I did break away, it was either for official White House events I could not miss or, sadly, for what seemed to be a never-ending procession of memorial services for friends and colleagues. Casey Shearer, the twenty-one-year-old son of our dear friends Derek Shearer and Ruth Goldway suffered fatal heart failure while playing basketball one week before his graduation from Brown University. King Hassan II of Morroco died in July, and the United States lost a valued friend and ally. His son and successor, King Mohammed VI invited Bill, Chelsea and me to the funeral where Bill, in a sign of respect, joined thousands of male mourners in walking behind the coffin for three miles through the streets of Rabat, lined with more than one million Morrocans.

The previous summer, John F. Kennedy, Jr., his wife, Carolyn, and her sister Lauren died tragically in a private plane crash off Martha's Vineyard. Bill and I felt great affection for John, whom we had gotten to know in private gatherings at his mother's home on the Vineyard and at public events. We wanted John, his sister, Caroline, and her children to feel free to visit the White House at any time. After he was married, John brought his bride for a personal tour. When he saw that Bill was using his father's desk in the Oval Office, it stirred a faint memory in him of playing beneath it and peeking through its small inset door while President Kennedy made phone calls. I remember John standing silently in front of the official portrait of his father, painted by Aaron Shikler, which we had hung in a prominent place of honor on the State Floor. It was heartbreaking to attend yet another funeral for someone with so much life and promise, surrounded by members of a family who had given so much to our country.

I also received terrible news about my friend Diane Blair. I frequently consulted with Diane during my campaign. She had graduated from Cornell University and knew New York well. She encouraged me to relax and enjoy myself, and she always laughed at tales of my missteps. Diane, an avid tennis player, seemed very fit at age sixty-one. In early March 2000, just a few weeks after she received a clean bill of health during a routine check-up, she noticed suspicious lumps on her leg. Within a week, she was diagnosed with metastatic lung cancer. She called to give me the news, and I was beyond devastated. The prognosis was grim. I simply could not imagine going through the ups and downs of the coming years without Diane. Over the next few months, no matter how busy I was on the campaign, I tried to call her every day. Bill and I flew to Fayetteville, Arkansas, several times to be with Diane and with Jim, who took such good care of her. Although she underwent highly toxic chemotherapy treatments that left her weak and caused her hair to fall out, Diane was a valiant fighter who never lost her smile or her loving spirit. Even in her last months, she and Bill competed to see who could do the *New York Times Sunday Magazine* crossword puzzle faster.

When Jim called in June to tell me the end was near, I left the campaign behind and flew to see Diane for the last time. By then, hospice nurses—living saints in my view—were tending her around the clock. Surrounded by her family and a legion of devoted friends, she slipped in and out of sleep as I stood next to her bed, holding her hand and leaning close to hear whatever she labored to say. As I got ready to leave, I bent down to kiss her good-bye. She pressed my hand tightly and whispered to me, "Don't ever give up on yourself and what you believe in. Take care of Bill and Chelsea. They need you. And win this election for me. I wish I could be there when you do. I love you." Then Bill and Chelsea joined me at her bedside. She looked intently at us. "Remember," she said.

"Remember what?" Bill asked.

"Just remember."

Five days later she died.

Bill, Chelsea and I later flew to Fayetteville for a memorial service to celebrate Diane's extraordinary life. Just as Diane would have wanted it, the service was upbeat, lively and filled with music and stories of her personal and public passion to better her world. Presiding at the celebration, I said that Diane squeezed more out of her too-brief life than any of us could have done in three or four hundred years. I don't know anyone who tried harder or had more success at living. Bill summed up Diane in a moving eulogy, saying: "She was beautiful and good. She was serious and funny. She was completely ambitious to do good and be good, but fundamentally selfless." She certainly made my life happier. I never had a better friend, and I miss her every day.

On July 11, Bill began a two-week meeting at Camp David with Prime Minister Ehud Barak and Yasir Arafat in an effort to resolve outstanding issues in the ongoing peace negotiations between Israel and the Palestinians under the Oslo Accords. Barak, a former general and Israel's most decorated soldier, was anxious for a final agreement that would fulfill the vision of Yitzhak Rabin, under whom he had served. Barak and his vivacious wife, Nava, quickly became friends whose company I enjoyed and whose commitment to peace I admired. Unfortunately, while Barak came to Camp David to make peace, Arafat did not.

Although he told Bill repeatedly that peace had to be achieved while Bill was in office, Arafat was never ready to make the hard choices necessary to reach an agreement.

While campaigning, I kept in close touch with Bill, who expressed his growing frustration. One night, Barak even called me asking for any ideas I might have to convince Arafat to negotiate in good faith. At Bill's request, Chelsea had accompanied him to Camp David and joined the group for informal lunches, dinners and casual conversations. Bill had also asked my assistant, Huma Abedin, to help with hosting the delegations. An American Muslim who grew up in Saudi Arabia and speaks Arabic, Huma displayed the skill and grace of a seasoned diplomat as she interacted with the Palestinian and Israeli representatives during breaks in the meetings and over games of darts and pool.

Finally, at noon on July 25, Bill announced the close of the unsuccessful Camp David summit, acknowledging the deep disappointment he felt and urging both sides to continue working to find "a just, lasting and comprehensive peace." Their efforts continued during Bill's remaining six months in the White House and nearly succeeded in talks in Washington and the Middle East in December 2000 and January 2001, when Bill put forward his last, best offer of a compromise peace proposal. In the end, Barak accepted Bill's offer, but Arafat refused. The tragic events of the last few years show what a terrible mistake Arafat made.

By August 2000, it was time for the Democratic National Convention in Los Angeles. Bill and I were scheduled to address the delegates on the first night, August 14, and then leave the city, making room for Vice President Gore and his vice presidential pick, Senator Joe Lieberman, to accept the nomination and take center stage.

I was greeted on stage by Democratic women Senators Barbara Mikulski, Dianne Feinstein, Barbara Boxer, Patty Murray, Blanche Lincoln and Mary Landrieu, who herself had been through a wrenching Senate race in 1996. With all the attention focused on what I was going to do next, I wanted to make sure that, when I took the podium, the American people knew how much I appreciated the privilege of serving for eight years as their First Lady. "Bill and I are closing one chapter of our lives—and soon, we'll be starting a new one . . . Thank you for giving me the most extraordinary opportunity to work here at home and around the world on the issues that matter most to children, women and families. . . . [and] for your support and faith in good times—and in bad. Thank you . . . for the honor and blessing of a lifetime."

Bill's speech followed mine, and his mere presence evoked a rush of nostalgia throughout the Staples Center, with people chanting "four more years" and enveloping him in a thunderous and warm reception. He gave a powerful accounting of his Presidency and a rousing endorsement of Al Gore. Then our role in the convention was over, and we were gone.

Within days, I began to prepare for three upcoming debates against Lazio. A young, telegenic Republican from Long Island, Lazio enjoyed strong support in the suburbs. Unlike Giuliani, he was not divisive or hard-edged, nor was he well-known outside his district. With support and encouragement from Republican leaders across the country, he presented himself as the anti-Hillary candidate, running a negative campaign for most of the summer. It was not very effective. One of the odd advantages I had was that everyone already thought they knew everything about me, good or bad. Lazio's attacks were old news. My campaign ignored the personal tone of Lazio's campaign and lasered in on his voting record, as well as his work in Congress as one of Gingrich's top lieutenants. People knew little about him, and our information about his positions was all they needed to fill in the blanks.

Our first debate was in Buffalo on September 13 and was moderated by a Buffalo native, Tim Russert of NBC's *Meet the Press*. After a series of questions about health care, the upstate economy and education, Russert showed a news clip of my appearance on the *Today* show when I went out on a limb defending Bill after the Lewinsky story broke. Then Russert asked if I "regret[ted] misleading the American people" and whether I wanted to apologize for "branding people as part of a vast right-wing conspiracy."

Although I was taken aback by the question, I had to respond, so I did: "You know, Tim, that was a very painful time for me, for my family and for our country. It is something I regret deeply that anyone had to go through. And I wish we all could look at it from the perspective of history, but we can't yet. We're going to have to wait until those books are written. . . . I've tried to be as forthcoming as I could, given the circumstances that I've faced. Obviously, I didn't mislead anyone. I didn't know the truth. And there's a great deal of pain associated with that, and my husband has certainly acknowledged . . . that he did mislead the country as well as his family."

The questions also covered school vouchers, the environment and other local issues, and that's when Lazio made a critical mistake: He said that the upstate economy had "turned the corner." But to anyone who lived upstate or who had spent time there, Lazio sounded out of touch. By then, I had visited the region frequently and had held extensive discussions with residents about the problems of job loss and young people leaving the area. I had also developed an economic plan for the region that voters were taking seriously.

When the focus of the debate turned to campaign commercials and the use of so-called soft money—funds spent by outside political committees on behalf of a candidate or an issue—Russert showed clips of a Lazio commercial featuring the Congressman in a photo juxtaposed with Senator Daniel Patrick Moynihan, a coupling that had never taken place. The ad distorted the truth and exploited the popularity of a venerable New York public servant. It was paid for with soft money, large contributions that could be used by political parties or outside groups to support a candidate or attack his opponent. In the spring, I had called for a ban on all soft money, but I wasn't going to commit to it unilaterally. The Republicans had refused to forswear the use of soft money from outside groups, some of whom were busily raising $32 million in support of Lazio's Senate bid.

Near the end of the debate, from behind his podium, Lazio began hectoring me about soft money and challenging me to ban large Democratic Party contributions in my campaign. I could barely get a word in when he marched over to me, waving a piece of paper-called the "New York Freedom from Soft Money Pact"—and demanding my signature. I declined. He pressed in closer, shouting, "Right here, sign it right now!"

I offered to shake hands, but he kept badgering me. I only had time to utter one sentence in response before Russert ended the debate. I don't know whether Lazio and his advisers thought they could fluster me or provoke me into anger.

Throughout the campaign, I had steeled myself for the possibility of personal attacks and was determined to stay focused on the issues— not on Lazio as a person. Like an internal mantra, I repeated to myself: "the issues, the issues." Besides being more helpful to voters, it seemed a more civilized way to run a campaign.

The debate was another turning point in the race that helped push some voters into my corner, although I didn't realize it right away. When I got off the stage, I had no idea how I had done and wasn't sure how Lazio's confrontational ploy would be received. His campaign immediately declared victory—and the press was buying it. Many of the first stories highlighted Lazio's stunt and all but declared him the winner.

Nonetheless, my team was upbeat. Ann Lewis and Mandy Grunwald sensed that Lazio had come across as a bully rather than the nice guy he was trying to project. Public opinion polls and focus groups soon made it clear that a lot of voters, especially women, were offended by Lazio's tactics. As Gail Collins wrote in *The New York Times*, Lazio had "invaded" my space. And many voters didn't like it.

The public reaction didn't stop Lazio from continuing a campaign that was largely negative—and personal. He sent out a fundraising letter stating that his message could be summed up in six words: "I'm running against Hillary Rodham Clinton." His campaign was not about the people of New York; it was about me. So I began to tell audiences around the state: "New Yorkers deserve more than that. How about seven words: jobs, education, health, Social Security, environment, choice?"

Lazio also dredged up health care reform in a series of ads designed to touch a nerve with voters. But, as I had learned from months on the road, New Yorkers generally seemed to appreciate my effort to reform health care, even if it had not succeeded in revamping the whole system. In the intervening years, health care costs had soared, and HMOs and insurance companies were more restrictive in their coverage. On the campaign trail, I frequently talked about specific incremental reforms that I had helped push through and ways the Senate could address rising health care costs through legislation.

Late in the campaign, on October 12, the USS *Cole* was attacked by terrorists in Yemen. The powerful explosion killed seventeen American sailors and ripped a hole in the destroyer's hull. This attack, like the embassy bombings, was later traced to al-Qaeda, the shadowy network of Islamic extremists led by Osama bin Laden that had declared war on the "infidels and crusaders." That label applied to all Americans and many others across the world, including Muslims who denounced violent tactics and extremism. I cancelled my campaign events to go with Bill and Chelsea to Norfolk Naval Station in Virginia for the memorial service. I had met with the families of the American Embassy bombing victims in August of 1998; now I offered condolences to the families of our murdered sailors, young men and women who were serving their country and providing security in a critical region of the world.

I despise terrorism and the nihilism it represents, and I was incredulous when the New York Republican Party and Lazio campaign insinuated that I was somehow involved with the terrorists who blew up the *Cole*. They made this despicable charge in a television ad and an automatic telephone message directed to hundreds of thousands of New York voters twelve days before the election. The story they concocted was that I had received a donation from somebody who belonged to a group that they said supported terrorists—"the same kind of terrorism that killed our sailors on the USS *Cole.*" The phone script told people to call me and tell me to "stop supporting terrorism." It was sickening. This last-minute desperation tactic blew up, however, thanks to a vigorous response by my campaign and with help from former New York City Mayor Ed Koch, who cut a television commercial scolding Lazio: "Rick, stop with the sleaze already."

By the final weeks of the campaign, I began to feel confident that I would win. But we had one last campaign scare the week before the election, when the race suddenly began to tighten. Lazio had been running an ad with two actresses playing suburban women who wondered how I had the nerve to show up in New York and think I deserved to be Senator. We didn't know whether voters were responding to Lazio's ad or were influenced by the terrorism phone calls, or whether the shift in the race was simply a momentary fluke.

I hashed it over with Mark and Mandy until two in the morning and decided to make one last effort to reach out to women who might still be ambivalent about my candidacy. Lazio was particularly vulnerable, I thought, on breast cancer research, an issue that I had worked on for eight years. After he entered the Senate race, the House leadership allowed him to hijack an important breast cancer funding bill that had been the brainchild of California Rep. Anna Eshoo and enjoyed broad bipartisan support. House leaders listed him as the lone sponsor of that bill, so that he could point to it in the campaign as a sign of his commitment to women's issues. That was bad enough. Worse, when the bill finally passed, he supported cutting funding for the program. I cared passionately about breast cancer treatment and research and was disgusted when I learned that Lazio had played politics with such an important and emotional issue.

Marie Kaplan, a breast cancer survivor and advocate from Lazio's own district on Long Island, had become one of my most faithful campaign volunteers. "Why not ask Marie to make an ad?" I suggested. And we did. In many ways, it was the best ad of the campaign. Marie explained what Lazio had done to the breast cancer funding bill and then said: "I have friends with questions about Hillary. I tell them, 'Get over it. I know her.' On breast cancer and health care and education and a woman's right to choose, Hillary would never walk away. She'll be there for us.'" She summed up everything I wanted people to think about as they cast their ballots.

I worked up until the last minute, campaigning in Westchester County with Representative Nita Lowey early on Election Day, November 7. Bill and Chelsea voted with me at our local polling station, Douglas Grafflin Elementary School in Chappaqua. After seeing Bill's name on ballots for years, I was thrilled and honored to see my own.

As the results came in during the evening, it was clear that I was going to win by a much bigger margin than expected. I was getting dressed in my hotel room when Chelsea burst in to deliver the news: The final tally was 55 percent to 43 percent. Hard work had paid off, and I was grateful for the chance to represent New York and to contribute to our nation in a new role.

The presidential race, meanwhile, was a roller coaster. Little did we know at the time that thirty-six days would elapse before the country learned who the new President would be. Nor could we imagine the demonstrations, lawsuits, appeals and challenges that would arise over the disputed votes in Florida or the addition to our political lexicon of terms like "butterfly ballot" and "dimpled chad."

The uncertainty in the presidential race tempered my elation on election night, but it did nothing to subdue the joyful victory party at the Grand Hyatt Hotel near Grand Central Terminal in New York City. The ballroom was packed with campaign staffers, friends, supporters and loyal Hillaryland aides who had taken leaves of absence from the White House during the last week of the campaign to help with "GOTV" (get-out-the-vote) activities. I was overwhelmed by the generosity and openness of New Yorkers, who listened to what I had to say, got to know me and took a chance on me. I was determined not to let them down. I joined Bill, Chelsea, my mother, and scores of supporters in a deluge of confetti and balloons.

Dozens of hugs and handshakes later, I stood at the podium to thank my supporters. I told them: "Sixty-two counties, sixteen months, three debates, two opponents and six black pantsuits later, because of you, we are here!"

After eight years with a title but no portfolio, I was now "Senator-elect."

Two days after the election, with the outcome of the presidential race between Al Gore and George W. Bush still in dispute, I returned to Washington to host a celebration of the White House's two-hundredth anniversary. It could have been an awkward evening, given the political tension in the air. All the living former Presidents and First Ladies were there (except President and Mrs. Reagan, who stayed at home in California because of President Reagan's Alzheimer's disease) as well as descendants and relatives of other Presidents. The magnificent black-tie gala sponsored by the White House Historical Association turned into a testament to American democracy as each former President spoke eloquently about our nation's endurance in the face of controversy and upheaval.

"Once again," said President Gerald Ford, "the world's oldest republic has demonstrated the youthful vitality of its institutions and the ability and the necessity to come together . . . after a hard-fought campaign. The clash of partisan political ideas does remain just that—to be quickly followed by a peaceful transfer of authority."

Here was living proof that America's foundation was stronger than individuals and politics, and that while Presidents, Senators and House members come and go, the continuity of the government remains unbroken.

In the end, Al Gore won the popular vote by over five hundred thousand ballots but lost the presidency in the Electoral College. The Supreme Court voted 5–4 on December 12 to stop a recount of votes in Florida, effectively sealing the victory for Bush. Seldom if ever in our history has the people's right to choose their elected officials been thwarted by such a blatant abuse of judicial power.

Even before the merits of the appeal were heard, Justice Antonin Scalia telegraphed the irrationality of the partisan decision to come by granting a stay that abruptly stopped the counting of ballots in Florida on December 9, 2000. Continuing the recount, according to Scalia, might cause "irreparable harm" to Governor Bush. Scalia wrote that counting the ballots might "cast a cloud upon what [Bush] claims to be the legitimacy of his election." His logic seemed to be: Counting the ballots must be stopped, because the ballots might show that Bush did not win after all. The decision in *Bush* v. *Gore* turned the normally conservative Supreme Court on its head. Instead of deferring to the highest court of Florida on pure matters of Florida state law, the Court reached out to find federal issues on which to overrule it. And rather than continuing its narrow view of equal protection claims, the majority went out of its way to find a violation of equal protection.

The majority said Florida's recount standard, requiring any ballot to be counted if it reflected the clear intent of the voter, was not specific enough because it could be interpreted differently by different vote counters. Their solution was to deny the right to vote to all citizens subject to the recount, no matter how clearly their ballots were marked. Amazingly, the Court carefully warned that "[o]ur consideration is limited to the present circumstances, for the problem of equal protection in election processes generally presents many complexities." They knew the decision was indefensible and had no intention of letting its reasoning be applied to other cases. It was just the best argument they could come up with on short notice to achieve the result they had already decided to impose. I have no doubt that if Bush, rather than Gore, had been behind in the incomplete count, the five conservative justices would have joined in a decision to recount all the ballots.

Americans have now moved beyond that controversial election and accepted the rule of law, but as we look to the next elections, we must ensure that every citizen is free to vote without fear, coercion or confusion at polling places with modern equipment and trained poll workers. We can only hope that the Supreme Court exercises greater restraint and objectivity if it ever handles a disputed presidential election again.

Bill and I were dismayed by the outcome of the election and concerned about what a return to the failed Republican policies of the past might mean for our nation. My only comfort was that I would soon begin my new job and have the opportunity to use my voice and vote on behalf of the values and policies I thought best for New York and America. Finally, the day arrived. Since only members of Congress and their staff are allowed on the Senate floor—with no exceptions for Presidents—Bill had to witness my swearing-in from the visitor's gallery, along with Chelsea and other family members. For the past eight years, I had watched from above as Bill shared his vision for our country in this same building. On January 3, 2001, I stepped onto the floor of the Senate to swear to "support and defend the Constitution of the United States against all enemies foreign and domestic . . . and faithfully discharge the duties of the office on which I am about to enter." When I turned and looked to the gallery above me, I saw my mother, my daughter and my husband smiling at the newest Senator from New York.

Three days later, on a rainy Saturday afternoon, we held a farewell party under a big tent on the South Lawn for everyone who had worked or volunteered in the White House over the previous eight years. People showed up from all over the country to see friends and reminisce about their work in the Administration. It was a spirited reunion that gave Bill and me the opportunity to say one final "thank you" to hundreds of men and women who had endured long hours and made personal sacrifices to join Bill's Administration in service to our country. From the twenty-three-year-old office assistant to the sixty-something cabinet secretary, these were the men and women who helped advance Bill's agenda and his vision of America.

As our staffers toasted each other, Al and Tipper Gore joined Bill and me several hours into the party.

"Here is the candidate who won the most votes in the presidential election," I said, introducing Al to a cheering ovation. Al asked for a show of hands for everyone who had found spouses or had babies during their time in the Administration. Hands shot up throughout the crowd. And then, in a surprise that Capricia had arranged, the curtain on stage rose and Fleetwood Mac emerged from the wings. When the band broke into the opening chords of "Don't Stop Thinking About Tomorrow," the anthem of Bill's 1992 campaign, the crowd erupted in a loud, joyous and off-key chorus wailing the refrain.

I had taken those lyrics to heart. It may have been a cliché, but the phrase that best summed up my political philosophy was: "It's always about the future," about what must be done to make America safer, smarter, richer, stronger and better, and how Americans can prepare to compete and cooperate in a global community. As I thought about my own tomorrows, I was excited about serving in the Senate but also overcome by nostalgia for the people who had been part of our journey, especially those who were no longer with us.

For the next two weeks, I wandered from room to room taking mental snapshots of all my favorite things in the White House, marveling at the architectural details, gazing at the pictures on the walls, trying to recapture the wonder I felt when I first arrived. I lingered in Chelsea's rooms and tried to hear in my mind the laughter of her friends and the sound of her music. She had grown from a child to a young woman in this place. Many of her memories growing up in the White House as the daughter of a President were happy. I was sure of that.

Every morning and every evening I found myself sinking into my favorite chair in the West Sitting Hall, a comfortable retreat where for eight years I had welcomed Chelsea home after school, met with staff, gossiped with friends, read books and collected my thoughts. Now, I reveled in this extraordinary time and this extraordinary place, watching the sunlight stream through the glorious fan-shaped window.

Many times over the last few weeks I thought back to Bill's first inauguration in 1993, an event that seemed as vivid as yesterday and as remote as a lifetime ago. Chelsea and I took one last walk down to the Children's Garden, hidden by the tennis court, where the grandchildren of Presidents left their handprints in the cement. Outside on the South Lawn, Bill and I looked out over the fence to the Washington Monument as we had countless times before. Bill threw tennis balls for Buddy to chase, while Socks kept his distance.

The White House staff busily prepared for the arrival of the new First Family, who would join us for coffee and pastries on January 20 before we all drove together to Capitol Hill for the swearing in. For the forty-third time in our nation's history, Americans would witness the peaceful transfer of power, as one Presidency came to a close and another began. When we entered the Grand Foyer for the last time as occupants of the People's House, the permanent residence staff had gathered to say farewell. I thanked the florist for the flowers she artfully placed in every room, the kitchen staff for the special meals they faithfully prepared, the housekeepers for their daily attention to detail, the grounds crew for their careful tending of the gardens, and all the other dedicated staff whose hard work graced the White House every day.

Buddy Carter, the veteran White House butler, received my last good-bye embrace and turned it into a joyous dance. We skipped and twirled across the marble floor. My husband cut in, taking me in his arms as we waltzed together down the long hall.

Then I said good-bye to the house where I had spent eight years living history.

AFTERWORD

Writing a book is a leap of faith, and there's no way to know whether you'll land on solid ground. After months of remembering, reliving, drafting, editing, rewriting and distilling thousands of anecdotes and ideas, I finally had to let go of this book, still unsure about who would read it or what they might think of it.

When *Living History* hit the bookstores in June 2003, the response was immediate and immensely gratifying. Following the book's release, I traveled across America and to four foreign countries, held dozens of book signings and gave hundreds of interviews. My right hand occasionally swelled from signing my name so many times, and I developed a newfound appreciation for ice packs and hand braces. By the end of the book tour, my signature resembled the tracks of a confused chicken.

I signed my book in small shops and supersize chains, on street corners, in the aisles of trains and planes, under tents and even in a few powder rooms. Sometimes book signings felt like festivals, as people sang songs, recited poems, or shouted chants. At one, a young girl with a violin serenaded the waiting crowd until it was her turn to meet me.

Late one summer night, hundreds of excited children stormed into the store where I was signing books—not to see me, but to camp out until midnight to snatch up the first copies of the new Harry Potter. Two copiously long-haired, bearded men, looking like characters from *Lord of the Rings*, lobbied me to join their quasi-religious campaign to "let men look as God intended." A middle-aged man handed me his business card with the handwritten message "If you're ever single, give me a call." An elderly woman confided that *Living History* was the first book she had ever bought. Countless readers, quoting from the book, told me to "soldier on" or "dare to compete." One time I looked up to see my daughter, Chelsea, standing in line grinning at me.

I'm often asked why this book has generated such intense interest, and I've been a bit mystified about that too. I knew that some readers just wanted to see how I would explain the personal challenges I had faced. Apparently, a few wanted a signed copy to sell on eBay. Others were eager to see me in the flesh and decide for themselves whether or not I was a normal human being.

At first, I was just happy that so many people wanted to come see me and to buy the book. Then I was delighted that they were actually reading it. Now I'm thrilled whenever readers mention how my story relates to their own experiences. Thousands of mothers, fathers, grandparents, students, assembly-line workers and CEOs—Americans of all ages, races and walks of life—who yearned to talk about their personal dreams and their concerns for our nation, came prepared with questions, speeches and sometimes requests for help. It seemed that my life, though lived in the spotlight and blessed with great opportunities, echoed the experiences of millions of other Americans. Even in foreign countries, the story of an American woman coming of age in the latter half of the twentieth century resonated.

Some readers told me they had no-nonsense, tough-love fathers like mine. Others commented that reading about my mother's difficult childhood helped them understand why I became an advocate for children. A mother from Southern California introduced me to her two foster children, telling them about my work in the White House to reform and streamline our nation's foster care and adoption system. Book buyers from around the world thanked me for writing about my overseas trips and highlighting conditions and issues in their native lands. At many events, customers in wheelchairs or guided by Seeing Eye dogs talked about the importance of laws protecting the rights of the disabled. And in early fall, a blind college student proudly presented me with a copy of the book she had written.

Many people described their own childhoods in the 1950s or how the 1960s—the civil rights movement, the struggle for women's rights and the nation's anguished debate over the Vietnam War—had led to their own political awakenings as well. There were even a few converts to the Democratic Party who said that before reading the book, they had no idea that I had once been a Goldwater girl and president of my college Republican Club. Doctors and nurses offered their own prescriptions for guaranteeing high-quality, affordable health care coverage for all Americans. And women of all ages had ideas and questions about the struggles we face every day trying to balance the demands of work and family.

Meeting tens of thousands of positive people lifted my spirits and renewed my faith in the future. They cared about their families, faith and friendships; their health and safety; the quality of their schools, workplaces and neighborhoods; the direction and leadership of our nation; and the world awaiting their children.

As I jot down these thoughts at my home in Chappaqua, New York, at the beginning of a new year—2004—I remain confident about our future. But, in a way, my feelings are divided. I am thankful for my personal blessings but worried about my country. I believe in the promise of America because I am a product of America's steady progress toward realizing its ideals of equality and justice, freedom and opportunity. I was born at a time in our country's history when the dreams of parents were achievable for their sons and daughters. I was given a superb public education. I had the benefit of other public resources, such as libraries and parks. Most of my generation had parents like mine who worked hard and sacrificed so that their children and grandchildren would have better lives. That intergenerational contract, which has worked for more than two hundred years, is now at risk.

When I first arrived in the Senate, I was dismayed to find the Bush administration and its congressional allies using every lever of power available to undo the economic, social and global progress achieved during my husband's presidency. I admit I viewed that prospect dimly because I believe my husband was a very good President who left our nation well prepared for the future. Soon, though, I realized that the agenda wasn't about undermining Bill's work over eight years, it was about dismantling decades of policies, protections and opportunities that had built the great American middle class at home and enduring alliances abroad.

In the Senate, I've tried to bridge the partisan divide by bringing Republicans and Democrats together whenever I could on issues ranging from homeland security to defense to education. I've reached out to political opponents, including a few who led the charge for my husband's impeachment.

But too often, ideology and partisanship, not evidence or values, dictate policy choices that have allowed little room for bipartisan cooperation. Much of the administration's agenda turns out to be neither compassionate nor conservative. I know what my compassionate mother thinks about a budget that gives her daughter and son-in-law tax cuts while kicking three hundred thousand poor kids out of after-school programs. I know what my conservative father would think about the huge deficits and debt we have accumulated in the last three years. A real conservative who understood the importance of conserving today to prepare for an uncertain future, he would be shocked at the fiscal irresponsibility of his government living for the moment with little apparent concern for what happens next. As my dad said about the deficits Bill inherited when he became President in 1993, this is no way to run a great country.

I have been fortunate to be part of this extraordinary human experiment known as America. As I say throughout my book, I have tried, in my own way, to fulfill my responsibility as a citizen by working to extend to others the unique opportunities and freedoms that should come to every American. These should be the values by which our nation is known throughout the world.

I represent the most diverse, exciting, dynamic state in the most diverse, exciting, dynamic nation in the world. And every day that I go to the floor of the United States Senate, I'm profoundly moved by that privilege and humbled by the responsibility I have been given by the people of New York. I want our government and our leaders to expand, not undermine, the hope and opportunities that made a life like mine possible. And as a Senator, I will do everything I can to ensure the same choices, opportunities, and dreams for all of America's children, now and for the future.

I am personally grateful for the many kindnesses *Living History* readers have shown me. One of the most thrilling aspects of books is their endurance, and I hope this one continues to be a source of information and inspiration to future readers.

JANUARY 2004
CHAPPAQUA, N.Y.

ACKNOWLEDGMENTS

THIS BOOK MAY NOT HAVE TAKEN A VILLAGE TO write, but it certainly took a superb team, and I am grateful to everyone who helped.

Before I thank those who were involved in helping me, I want to acknowledge the loss of a great American, Senator Daniel Patrick Moynihan of New York. As I was finishing this book, Senator Moynihan died on March 26, 2003. I now hold the Senate seat that was his for twenty-four years, and I also occupy his former Senate office. He came to see me there in the fall of 2002, and we talked about the new security issues facing our country. I looked forward to continuing that conversation. Our conversations were always lively, and he was unfailingly kind, even if we disagreed. When he learned that I had done my Wellesley thesis on Saul Alinsky, he asked to read it. I sent it to him with considerable trepidation. He, ever the professor, returned it with comments and an "A" grade. Even though I was at the time First Lady, and the thesis had been turned in twenty-five years before, I was delighted and relieved. With the passing of Daniel Patrick Moynihan, America's public and intellectual life lost one of its brightest lights. We will miss his wisdom and brilliance, always challenging our assumptions, constantly setting the bar higher.

The smartest decision I made was to ask Lissa Muscatine, Maryanne Vollers and Ruby Shamir to spend two years of their lives working with me. To their credit, they made sense of the mountains of information about my life and guided my efforts to explain and express my feelings about my time in the White House. I have relied on Lissa's strength, intelligence and integrity for ten years. Responsible for many of the words in my speeches as First Lady and in this book, she brought her knowledge of Washington politics and policy to this task, and I couldn't have done it without her. Maryanne helped me conceive this book and shepherded it—and me—over its ups and downs; she was a joy to work with and has the rare gift of understanding how to help another's voice emerge. Every word I could use to describe Ruby and her role would be inadequate. She held the process together from start to finish—amassing, reviewing and synthesizing millions of words written about me and scrutinizing every one I wrote. Her attention to detail and sweet spirit are rare to find in a single soul. Liz Bowyer once again came to the rescue with skill and insight to help me finalize the text—and save my sanity. Toward the end of this intense process Courtney Weiner, Huma Abedin and Carolyn Huber provided invaluable assistance in helping me meet my impending deadline.

Thanks to Simon & Schuster and Scribner, especially Carolyn Reidy, Simon & Schuster Publisher, and Nan Graham, Vice President and Editor in Chief at Scribner. This is my fourth book produced on Carolyn's watch, and she has been a pleasure to work with once again. Nan is a caring and savvy professional who wields her Paper Mate Sharpwriter mechanical pencil with precision, asks all the right questions and has a great sense of humor. Thanks also to David Rosenthal, Jackie Seow, Gypsy da Silva, Victoria Meyer, Aileen Boyle, Alexis Gargagliano and Irene Kheradi, who made the impossible happen. Vincent Virga's eye for the telling photo was invaluable. As always, my attorneys, Bob Barnett and David Kendall, of Williams and Connolly, were there whenever needed, providing wise and practical counsel. David Alsobrook, Emily Robison, Deborah Bush and John Keller of the Clinton Presidential Materials Project tracked down many of the documents and photographs for the book.

A host of friends and colleagues volunteered their precious time to be interviewed, check facts, review drafts and share their memories. I greatly appreciate each of them: Madeleine Albright, Beryl Anthony, Loretta Avent, Bill Barrett, W. W. "Bill" Bassett, Sandy Berger, Jim Blair, Tony Blinken, Linda Bloodworth-Thomason, Sid Blumenthal, Susie Buell, Katy Button, Lisa Caputo, Patty Criner, Patti Solis Doyle, Winslow Drummond, Karen Dunn, Betsy Ebeling, Sara Ehrman, Rahm Emanuel, Tom Freedman, Mandy Grunwald, Ann Henry, Kaki Hockersmith, Eric Hothem, Harold Ickes, Chris Jennings, Reverend Don Jones, Andrea Kane, Jim Kennedy, Jennifer Klein, Ann Lewis,

Bruce Lindsey, Joe Lockhart, Tamera Luzzatto, Ira Magaziner, Capricia Penavic Marshall, Garry Mauro, Ellen McCulloch-Lovell, Mack McLarty, Cheryl Mills, Kelly Craighead Mullen, Kevin O'Keefe, Ann O'Leary, Mark Penn, Jan Piercy, John Podesta, Nicole Rabner, Carol Rasco, Bruce Reed, Steve Ricchetti, Cynthia Rice, Ernest "Ricky" Ricketts, Robert Rubin, Evan Ryan, Shirley Sagawa, Donna Shalala, June Shih, Craig Smith, Doug Sosnik, Roy Spence, Gene Sperling, Ann Stock, Susan Thomases, Harry Thomason, Melanne Verveer, Maggie Williams, Bill Wilson.

The extended Hillaryland family helped me do the work I describe in these pages and kept me going through every challenge. Not already mentioned: Milli Alston, Ralph Alswang, Wendy Arends, Jennifer Ballen, Katie Barry, Anne Bartley, Erika Batcheller, Melinda Bates, Carol Beach, Marsha Berry, Joyce Bonnett, Ron Books, Debby Both, Sarah Brau, Joan Brierton, Stacey Roth Brumbaugh, Molly Buford, Kelly Carnes, Kathy Casey, Ginger Cearley, Sara Grote Cerrell, Pam Cicetti, Steve "Scoop" Cohen, Sabrina Corlette, Brenda Costello, Michelle Crisci, Caroline Croft, Gayleen Dalsimer, Sherri Daniels, Tracy LaBrecque Davis, Leela DeSouza, Diane Dewhirst, Helen Dickey, Robyn Dickey, Anne Donovan, Tom Driggers, Karen Fahle, Tutty Fairbanks, Sharon Farmer, Sarah Farnsworth, Emily Feingold, Karen Finney, Bronson Frick, John Funderburk, Key German, Isabelle Goetz, Toby Graff, Bradley Graham, Bobbie Greene, Jessica Greene, Melodie Greene, Carrie Greenstein, Sanjay Gupta, Ken Haskins, Jennifer Heater, Kim Henry, Amy Hickox, Julie Hopper, Michelle Houston, Heather Howard, Sarah Howes, Julie Huffman, Tom Hufford, Jody Kaplan, Sharon Kennedy, Missy Kincaid, Barbara Kinney, Ben Kirby, Neel Lattimore, Jack Lew, Peggy Lewis, Evelyn Lieberman, Diane Limo, Hillary Lucas, Bari Lurie, Christy Macy, Stephanie Madden, Mickie Mailey, Dr. Connie Mariano, Julie Mason, Eric Massey, Lisa McCann, Ann McCoy, Debby McGinn, Mary Ellen McGuire, Bob McNeely, Noa Meyer, Dino Milanese, Beth Mohsinger, Eric Morse, Daniela Nanau, Matthew Nelson, Holly Nichols, Michael O'Mary, Janna Paschal, Ron Petersen, Glenn Powell, Jaycee Pribulsky, Alice Pushkar, Jeannine Ragland, Malcolm Richardson, Becky Saletan, Laura Schiller, Mary Schuneman, Jamie Schwartz, Laura Schwartz, David Scull, Nicole Sheig, Janet Shimberg, David Shipley, Jake Simmons, Jennifer Smith, Shereen Soghier, Aprill Springfield, Jane

Swensen, Neera Tanden, Isabelle Tapia, Marge Tarmey, Theresa Thibadeau, Sandra Tijerina, Kim Tilley, Wendy Towber, Dr. Richard Tubb, Tibbie Turner, William Vasta, Jamie Vavonese, Josephine Velasco, Lisa Villareal, Joseph Voeller, Sue Vogelsinger, Esther Watkins, Margaret Whillock, Kim Widdess, Pam Williams, Whitney Williams, Laura Wills, Eric Woodard, Cindy Wright.

The logistics of the trips I took during the 1992, 1996 and 2000 campaigns and as First Lady were the responsibility of an advance staff that took good care of me and kept me (mostly) out of trouble thanks to: Ian Alberg, Brian Alcorn, Jeannie Arens, Ben Austin, Stephanie Baker, Douglas Band, David Beaubaire, Ashley Bell, Anthony Bernal, Bonnie Berry, Terry Bish, Katie Broeren, Karen Burchard, Regan Burke, Cathy Calhoun, Joe Carey, Jay Carson, George Caudill, Joe Cerrell, Nancy Chestnut, Jim Clancy, Resi Cooper, Connie Coopersmith, Catherine Cornelius, Jim Cullinan, Donna Daniels, Heather Davis, Amanda Deaver, Alexandra Dell, Kristina Dell, Tyler Denton, Michael Duga, Pat Edington, Jeff Eller, Ed Emerson, Mort Engelberg, Steve Feder, David Fried, Andrew Friendly, Nicola Frost, Cindy Gire, Grace Gracia, Todd Glass, Steve Graham, Barb Grochala, Catherine Grunden, Shanan Guinn, Greg Hale, Pat Halley (who wrote a humorous account of life as an advance person in *On the Road with Hillary*), Natalie Hartman, Alan Hoffman, Kim Hopper, Rob Houseman, Melissa Howard, Stefanie Hurst, Rick Jasculca, Lynn Johnson, Kathy Jurado, Ron Keohane, Mike King, Carolyn Kramer, Michele Kreiss, Justin Kronholm, Stephen Lamb, Reta Lewis, Jamie Lindsay, Bill Livermore, Jim Loftus, Mike Lufrano, Marisa Luzzatto, Tamar Magarik, Bridger McGaw, Kara McGuire Minar, Rebecca McKenzie, Brian McPartlin, Sue Merrell, Craig Minassian, Megan Moloney, David Morehouse, Patrick Morris, Lisa Mortman, Jack Murray, Sam Myers, Jr., Sam Myers, Sr., Lucie Naphin, Kathy Nealy, David Neslen, Ray Ocasio, Jack O'Donnell, Nancy Ozeas, Lisa Panasiti, Kevin Parker, Roshann Parris, Lawry Payne, Denver Peacock, Mike Perrin, Ed Prewitt, Kim Putens, Mary Raguso, Paige Reefe, Julie Renehan, Paul Rivera, Erica Rose, Rob Rosen, Aviva Rosenthal, Dan Rosenthal, Matt Ruesch, John Schnur, Pete Selfridge, Geri Shapiro, Kim Simon, Basil Smikle, Douglas Smith, Tom Smith, Max Stiles, Cheri Stockham, Mary Streett, Michael Sussman, Paula Thomason, Dan Toolan, Dave Van Note, Setti Warren, Chris Wayne, Todd Weiler, Brady Williamson.

This White House memoir could not do justice to my 2000 campaign for the Senate and the thousands of elected officials, Democratic activists, labor union members, contributors and concerned citizens who supported me. I could not have succeeded without the talent and dedication of a core group of professional and volunteer leaders who devoted themselves and have not already been acknowledged: Karen Adler, Josh Albert, Katie Allison, Carl Andrews, Jessica Ashenberg, David Axelrod, Nina Blackwell, Bill de Blasio, Amy Block, Dan Burstein, Raysa Castillo, Tony Chang, Ellen Chesler, Elizabeth Condon, Bill Cunningham, Ed Draves, Senta Driver, Janice Enright, Christine Falvo, Gabrielle Fialkoff, Chris Fickes, Kevin Finnegan, Deirdre Frawley, Scott Freda, Geoff Garin, Gigi Georges, Toya Gordan, Richard Graham, Katrina Hagagos, Beth Harkavy, Matthew Hiltzik, Ben Holzer, Kara Hughes, Gene Ingoglia, Tiffany JeanBaptiste, Russ Joseph, Wendy Katz, Peter Kauffmann, Heather King, Sarah Kovner, Victor Kovner, Justin Krebs, Jennifer Kritz, Jim Lamb, Mark Lapidus, Marsha Laufer, Cathie Levine, Jano Lieber, Bill Lynch, Ramon Martinez, Christopher McGinness, Sally Minard, Luis Miranda, Chris Monte, Libby Moroff, Shelly Moskwa, Frank Nemeth, Nick Noe, Ademola Oyefaso, Tom Perron, Jonathan Prince, Jeff Ratner, Samara Rifkin, Liz Robbins, Melissa Rochester, Charles Roos, David Rosen, Barry Sample, Vivian Santora, Eric Schultz, Chung Seto, Bridget Siegel, Emily Slater, Socrates Solano, Allison Stein, Susie Stern, Sean Sweeney, Jane Thompson, Megan Thompson, Melissa Thornton, Lyn Utrecht, Susana Valdez, Kevin Wardally, Glen Weiner, Amy Wills, Howard Wolfson; John Catsimatidis, Margo Catsimatidis, Alan Cohn, Betsy Cohn, Jill Iscol, Ken Iscol, Alan Patricof, Susan Patricof, and all the dedicated members of my finance committee and volunteers.

Any memoir reflects the family and personal relationships that define one's life. My dear friend Diane Blair helped me conceive of this book long before I began writing it, and her spirit shaped its message. I could not have lived my life without the love and support of my mother Dorothy Rodham; my late father, Hugh E. Rodham; my brothers, Hugh E. Rodham, Jr., and Tony Rodham; and a host of relatives and friends who kept me going and believing through challenges large and small, public and private.

A dear friend, Dr. Estelle Ramey, once summed up her distinguished life as a physician and researcher by saying: "I have loved and been loved; all the rest is background music." Bill and Chelsea, whose love has given me courage and comfort, and forced me to grow beyond comfortable boundaries, served as my chief critics and cheerleaders for this first attempt to explain the time we shared in the White House. They lived this history with me, for which I am deeply grateful.

Finally, I am responsible for the opinions and interpretations expressed in this memoir. These pages reflect how I experienced the events I describe. I'm sure there are many other—even competing—views of the events and people I describe. That's someone else's story to tell.

KEY TO PHOTOGRAPHS

Section 1

7: (l to r) Rawls Williams, Hillary Rodham Clinton, Kris Dernehl, United Way representative, Gordon Williams, Suzy O'Callaghan Lorenz, Hugh Rodham.

11: (l to r) Hillary Rodham Clinton, Matt Bunyan, Ellen Press.

12: (l to r) Joseph Madonia, Hillary Rodham Clinton, Larry Cass, Lois Brooks, Hardy Simonds, John Kirchoff, Darlain Stiles.

17: (l to r) first row: D. Golub, Mike Conway, Bob Alsdorf, Hillary Rodham Clinton, Jack Fuller; second row: Tony Rood, Rufus Cormier, Jeff Rogers, Paul Helmke, Dan Johnson, Bill Clinton.

46: (l to r) Capricia Penavic Marshall, Kelly Craighead Mullen, Marsha Berry, Patti Solis Doyle, Melanne Verveer, Missy Kincaid, Shirley Sagawa, Anne Donovan, Ellen McCulloch-Lovell.

50: (l to r) Linda Lader (in hat), Holly Leachman, Susan Baker, Hillary Rodham Clinton, Janet Hall, Eileen Bakke, Linda Slattery.

51: (l to r) first row, seated on the floor: Ann Stock, Liz Bowyer, Sara Farnsworth, Julie Hopper; second row: Loretta Avent, Evelyn Lieberman, Melanne Verveer, Lissa Muscatine, Alice Pushkar; third row: Marge Tarmey (on arm-chair), Evan Ryan, Katy Button, Carolyn Huber (on couch), Helen Dickey (in front of Hillary Rodham Clinton), Hillary Rodham Clinton, Ann McCoy, Diane Limo (in front of Ann), Sara Grote Cerrell, Jen Klein, Robin Dickey, Maggie Williams, Lisa Caputo, Nicole Rabner, Tracy LaBrecque Davis; fourth row (standing): Karen Finney, Pam Cicetti, Patti Solis Doyle, Capricia Penavic Marshall, Neel Lattimore, Sharon Kennedy, Eric Hothem.

INDEX

Cass, Larry, A11
Castro, Fidel, 88–89, 235, 314–15
Ceauşescu, Nicolae, 354
Cerf, Vinton, 461
Cerrell, Sara Grote, A51
Chafee, John, 247, 435
Chamber of Commerce, U.S., 145, 231
Chamorro, Violeta, 312
Chang, Jung, 503
Channing, Carol, 139
Chappaqua, N.Y., 29, 505, 511, 523
Charles, Prince of Wales, 237, 239, 416
Chavez, Cesar, 48
Cheney, Dick, 195
Chicago, Ill., 2, 3, 4, 6, 8, 22, 25, 37, 63,
    108–9
  1960 election and, 16–17
  1968 election and, 37
  1996 Democratic Convention in,
    397
Child, Julia, 139
child abuse and neglect, 49–51
child advocacy, 140
  in abuse and neglect cases, 49–50
  in Arkansas, 80–81
  Wright as HRC's example in, 46, 370
child care, 85, 326, 333, 367, 368, 381–83, 444,
    447, 500
  White House conference on, 382–83
child development, 49, 81, 93, 382
child labor laws, 259
child poverty, 370
children, children's issues, 10–11, 49–50, 64,
    132, 262, 269, 276, 278, 283–84, 333,
    356–57, 373, 429, 530–31
  adoption of, 49–50, 276, 355
  after-school programs for, 381, 383
  with AIDS, 354, 355
  Chernobyl-related cancer in, 218
  as fans of Buddy and Socks, 437
  in foster care, 49–50, 80–81, 365,
    433–35
  health care for, 148, 292, 380, 385
  with HIV/AIDS, 354–55, 385–86
  infant mortality and, 98–99
  Irish peace hopes of, 322–23
  of migrant farmworkers, 48–49
  in 1992 presidential campaign, 105
  Oklahoma City bombing and, 294–95
  in orphanages, 262–63, 276, 291, 355, 418,
    419
  PKU treatment for, 410
  prescription drugs for, 386
  prostitution of, 389–90
  vaccines for, 380
  war's effect on, 356–57, 403–4

welfare reform and, 262–63, 291, 326,
    365–69
  in White House, 127, 136, 137
  see also education
Children's Defense Fund (CDF), 64, 66, 83,
    103, 111, 369
Children's Health Insurance Program (CHIP),
    248
"Children Under the Law" (H. R. Clinton),
    50–51
child support, 367, 384–85
China, 298, 418, 457–60
  coerced abortion in, 299, 302, 305,
    354
  human rights in, 298–308, 360
Chirac, Bernadette, B39, 338–39
Chirac, Jacques, B39, 338–39
"Chix meetings," 259–62
Choice, The (Woodward), 265
Chrétien, Aline, 410
Chrétien, Jean, 411
Christopher, Warren, 112, 117, 182, 341,
    391
Chung, Connie, 263
Churchill, Winston, 238, 260
Ciampi, Carlo, 429
Cicetti, Pam, A51, 132
Citizens for a Sound Economy (CSE),
    246
civil rights, 22, 23, 24, 31, 40, 41, 46, 54, 57, 58,
    65, 259, 291, 369, 396, 424, 493
civil rights movement, 23, 44, 47, 195, 214,
    234, 279–80
Clapp, Margaret, 28, 276
Clarke, Nancy, 134
Clinton, Bill:
  as Arkansas Attorney General, 76, 78, 79, 91,
    92, 134, 379
  as Arkansas Governor, 82–83, 85, 88–90,
    91, 93–95, 98, 193, 199, 206–9, 224,
    365
  Blair and, 422–26, 427–29, 450
  Buddy acquired by, 435–37
  Chelsea's relationship with, 84–85, 91, 97,
    124, 135–56, 170, 339–41, 419–21,
    435
  "Contract" legislation and, 288–89,
    326
  disparate opinions invited by, 289–90
  and election of 2000, 525
  father-in-law's death and, 157–59,
    163–64
  in Finland meeting with Yeltsin, 397,
    398–400, 405
  first inaugural address of, 122–23, 124
  Foster's suicide and, 176, 177

Elizabeth II, Queen of England, 237, 238
Elliot, Gayle, 15
Elsey, George, 260
Emanuel, Rahm, 103, 121, 467
embassy bombings, 464, 468, 469, 522
Emerson, Thomas, 52
environment, environmentalism, 13, 111, 236,
    249, 288, 325, 364, 372–73, 387
Equal Rights Amendment, 31, 72
Eritrea, 405
Eshoo, Anna, 522
Eskew, Carter, 229
Espin, Vilma, 314, 314–15
Ethiopia, 405
ethnic cleansing, 169, 338, 358, 455, 464
Ethos, 33–34
Eugene Field School, 9, 14
European Court of Human Rights, 424
European Union, 342, 355, 415

Fahlstrom, Karin, 25, 31
Fails, Connie, 336
Faircloth, Lauch, 243, 244
Faisal, King of Saudi Arabia, 273
Faisal Mosque, 273
families, 132, 269, 323–24, 359, 375, 380,
    428
Family and Medical Leave Act, 85, 115, 203,
    252, 376, 383–84
family leave, 278, 364, 376, 380
family planning, 115, 275, 299, 305, 314, 354,
    418, 431, 451
"family values," 119
Farley, Carol, 15
Farnsworth, Sara, A51
Faubus, Orval, 97
Fayetteville, Ark., 63–64, 65, 70–72, 74, 76, 78,
    93, 517
Federal Bureau of Investigation (FBI), 44,
    45, 68, 173, 175, 177, 243, 294, 327,
    465
    and 1996 Summer Olympics, 363
    security checks conducted by, 371, 372
    Travelgate and, 173
    Whitewater documents and, 206
Federal Employees Health Benefit Plan, 150,
    232
Feinstein, Dianne, 255, 256, 519
Fekkai, Frederic, 171
feminism, 31, 108–10, 162
    see also women, women's issues
Ferraro, Geraldine, 195
Fialkoff, Gabrielle, 513
Filegate, 371–72, 439, 485
Fineshriber, Phyllis, B24
Finney, Karen, A51, 430

First Ladies, 111, 187, 262
    congressional testimony of, 188–89
    of Latin America, 311–15
    at National Garden Gala, 236
    role and responsibilities of, 118–19, 131, 134,
        139–41, 153–54, 259, 264–65
    in Smithsonian Exhibit (1992), 119
    see also specific First Ladies
First Ladies of the Western Hemisphere, 311,
    314–15
First Lady, Office of, see Office of the First
    Lady
Fiske, Robert, 219, 220–21, 222, 245, 296, 297,
    439
    Republican criticism of, 243–44
    Starr as replacement of, 244–45, 347
Flowers, Gennifer, 106–7
Flynn, Don, 131, 379, 451
Foley, Tom, 256
Food and Drug Administration, 386
food stamps, 366, 367, 368, 370
"Fooly Scare" (Grosch), 29
Ford, Betty, B27, 236
Ford, Gerald R., A14, 34–35, 219, 260, 496,
    524
    health care reform and, 146
    in 1976 presidential election, 76–78
    Nixon pardoned by, 76
Ford Foundation, 459
foreign aid, 269, 270, 283, 312, 431, 433
Forrest Gump, 287
Fort Chaffee, Ark., 88–89
Foster, Lisa, 174, 176, 219
Foster, Vince, A32, 141–42, 163, 235, 243,
    390–91, 439, 453
    depression and suicide of, 173–79, 219, 297,
        439
    HRC's friendship with, 81–82
    legal aid reform and, 78–79
    Travelgate and, 173–74
    in Whitewater conspiracy theories, 178, 297,
        390
    Whitewater files and, 178, 195, 201, 206,
        330
    WSJ editorial attack on, 174, 176–77, 178
foster care, 49–50, 80–81, 365, 433–35, 477,
    530
Foster Care Independence Act of 1999, 435
Foundation for International Community
    Assistance (FINCA), 312
Fowles, Jinnet, 28
France, 338–39, 409, 428
Franco, Francisco, 36–37, 77, 413
Frank, Barney, 485
Franken, Al, B5, 229, 287
Franklin, Aretha, 243

PERMISSIONS
ACKNOWLEDGMENTS

Letter from John F. Kennedy, Jr., reprinted with permission.

Letter from Mrs. Lyndon Johnson reprinted with permission.

Photo Credits: Unless otherwise credited, all photos are from the author's collection, the White House, and the Clinton Presidential Materials Project. Every effort has been made to identify copyright holders; in case of oversight, and on notification to the publisher, corrections will be made in the next edition. Insert I: *12, 13, 15,* Wellesley; *21,* David P. Garland; *26,* Donald R. Broyles/Office of Governor Clinton; *38,* Steven D. Desmond/Desmond's Prime Focus; *47,* courtesy Lissa Muscatine; *49,* Eugenie Bisulco. Insert II: *37,* India's Park Service; *60,* Diana Walker; *66,* AP/Wide World Photos © 2002; *73,* Alfred Eisenstaedt/TimeLife Pictures/Getty Images.

Photo inserts researched, edited, and designed by Vincent Virga, with the assistance of Carolyn Huber and John Keller.

Cover design by Jackie Seow.

Front cover photograph © by Michael Thompson.

Back cover photographs courtesy of The Clinton Presidential Materials Project and the author's private collection. Clockwise from top left: Bill and Hillary on their wedding day in 1975; at Yale in 1970; with Chelsea in the kitchen of the Governor's Mansion in 1983; in the Oval Office in 2001; at Stanford University's orientation ceremonies in 1997; swearing-in January 2001; speaking at the U.N. Fourth Wolrd Conference on Women in 1995; New Year's Eve in 1999. Center: Hillary as a toddler.

LIVING HISTORY

1. Hillary Rodham Clinton's father was a staunch Republican, her mother a Democrat who believed in a social safety net. Talk about the way both ideologies have shaped her personal and political life, and her ability to work with people whose views she does not share.

2. Who were Clinton's early role models? What are some of the early experiences that shaped her life? What made her leave the Republican party to become a Democrat? Do you think that she is a product of her times? If so, how?

3. Identity is a central theme of *Living History*. How does Clinton identify herself? How has she been identified by others? How has this affected her political career? Her personal life?

4. Hillary Rodham Clinton has had a long and complex relationship with the media. Discuss. How much power does the press wield? How do you think the press affects politics?

5. Discuss the media's focus on what the First Lady wears, how she cuts her hair and what she says and does. How important is the First Lady's appearance to you and why?

6. In "East Wing, West Wing," the chapter on the early months in the White House, Hillary Rodham Clinton refers to a "double bind" experienced by many women. What is the "double bind"? Have you ever perceived her, or any other woman, this way? If you have, how has this affected you, and how have you dealt with it?

7. During the first Bill Clinton presidential campaign, one remark in particular was used to undermine support for the Clintons among women. What did you make of the "tea and cookies" remark? If you are a working mother, did you discuss it with friends who are stay-at-home moms? Did you understand the comment differently after reading this book and seeing the context of the remark?

8. Discuss how politicians' personal lives enter the political arena. To what extent should the press report on the personal lives of public figures? Do you believe that knowing about a candidate's personal life helps you decide whether he or she will be an effective politician? Why or why not?

9. Explore what Hillary Rodham Clinton refers to as "the politics of personal destruction."

10. What are some of Clinton's key policy interests? Discuss the highlights of her early career and the influence she's had on some of the many issues she champions.

11. Discuss Clinton's work in the international arena. What issues was she dealing with? Do you agree with her that "women's rights are human rights"?

How do her efforts abroad relate to her domestic initiatives? What effect did her work abroad have on her image at home?

12. What impact might Hillary Rodham Clinton's story have on future First Ladies? For women running for office? For women in leadership positions in the spotlight?

13. Share your thoughts on the resistance to the President and Mrs. Clinton's health care reform efforts. Were you surprised by the political dimensions of the process or by the intensity of opposition to reform by some groups in the health care industry? What does Hillary Rodham Clinton mean when she says that her biggest mistake while pushing for health care reform was to "try to do too much, too fast"? What does Mrs. Clinton's perspective tell you about why the health care reforms were never passed?

14. In her discussion about welfare reform, Clinton says, "I realized that I had crossed the line from advocate to policy maker." What does it mean to make that transition? Is there an inherent conflict between people in those roles?

15. Reading "Conversations with Eleanor," discuss why Hillary apologizes to her staff and considers dropping out of active political and policy work. What is your reaction? What was the cause of Hillary's biggest credibility gap (in the public's view)? Was it legitimate? Why?

16. When did Hillary Rodham Clinton find her own voice in the Washington political scene? To what does she refer when she says, "The power of the First Lady is derivative, not independent, of the President"? How did she advance the Clinton agenda through symbolic action?

17. What are your impressions of the effect Hillary Rodham Clinton had on her husband's Presidency?

18. There are not supposed to be any second acts in American politics. Yet Hillary Rodham Clinton has surprised both Republicans and Democrats with her hard work and bipartisan efforts in the Senate. Talk about how she overcame extreme criticism as First Lady to become a respected Senator from New York.